U.S. Foreign Relations

AMERICAN GOVERNMENT AND HISTORY INFORMATION GUIDE SERIES

Series Editor: Harold Shill, Chief Circulation Librarian, Adjunct Assistant Professor of Political Science, West Virginia University, Morgantown

Also in this series:

AMERICAN EDUCATIONAL HISTORY—*Edited by Timothy Walch and Michael W. Sedlak**

AMERICA'S MILITARY PAST—*Edited by Jack C. Lane*

IMMIGRATION AND ETHNICITY—*Edited by John D. Buenker and Nicholas C. Burckel*

PROGRESSIVE REFORM—*Edited by John D. Buenker and Nicholas C. Burckel*

PUBLIC ADMINISTRATION IN AMERICAN SOCIETY—*Edited by John E. Rouse, Jr.*

PUBLIC POLICY—*Edited by William J. Murin, Gerald Michael Greenfield, and John D. Buenker**

SOCIAL HISTORY OF THE UNITED STATES—*Edited by Donald F. Tingley*

U.S. CONSTITUTION—*Edited by Earlean McCarrick*

U.S. CULTURAL HISTORY—*Edited by Philip I. Mitterling*

U.S. POLITICS AND ELECTIONS—*Edited by David J. Maurer*

URBAN HISTORY—*Edited by John D. Buenker, Gerald Michael Greenfield, and William J. Murin**

WOMEN AND FEMINISM IN AMERICAN HISTORY—*Edited by Donald F. Tingley and Elizabeth Tingley**

*in preparation

The above series is part of the

GALE INFORMATION GUIDE LIBRARY

The Library consists of a number of separate series of guides covering major areas in the social sciences, humanities, and current affairs.

General Editor: Paul Wasserman, Professor and former Dean, School of Library and Information Services, University of Maryland

Managing Editor: Denise Allard Adzigian, Gale Research Company

U.S. Foreign Relations

A GUIDE TO INFORMATION SOURCES

Volume 6 in the American Government and History Information Guide Series

Elmer Plischke

Professor Emeritus of Government and Politics
University of Maryland
College Park

and

Adjunct Professor of Political Science
Gettysburg College
Gettysburg, Pennsylvania

and

Adjunct Scholar
American Enterprise Institute for Public Policy Research
Washington, D.C.

Gale Research Company
Book Tower, Detroit, Michigan 48226

Library of Congress Cataloging in Publication Data

Plischke, Elmer, 1914-
   U. S. foreign relations.

   (American Government and history information guide
series ; v. 6)   (Gale information guide library)
   Includes index.
   1. United States—Foreign relations—Bibliography.
2. United States—Foreign relations administration—
Bibliography.   I. Title.   II. Series.
Z6465.U5P52   [JX1417]   026'.32773   74-11516
ISBN 0-8103-1204-2

VITA

Elmer Plischke is adjunct professor of political science at Gettysburg College, Pennsylvania; professor emeritus of government and politics at the University of Maryland; and adjunct scholar at the American Enterprise Institute for Public Policy Research, Washington, D.C. He received his Ph.B. cum laude from Marquette University, Milwaukee; his M.A. from the American University, Washington, D.C.; and his Ph.D. from Clark University, Worcester, Massachusetts.

Plischke is the author of CONDUCT OF AMERICAN DIPLOMACY; AMERICAN FOREIGN RELATIONS: A BIBLIOGRAPHY OF OFFICIAL SOURCES; AMERICAN DIPLOMACY: A BIBLIOGRAPHY OF BIOGRAPHIES, AUTOBIOGRAPHIES, AND COMMENTARIES; SUMMIT DIPLOMACY; PERSONAL DIPLOMACY OF THE PRESIDENT OF THE UNITED STATES; FOREIGN RELATIONS DECISION-MAKING: OPTIONS ANALYSIS; UNITED STATES DIPLOMATS AND THEIR MISSIONS: A PROFILE OF AMERICAN DIPLOMATIC EMISSARIES SINCE 1778; and MODERN DIPLOMACY: THE ART AND ARTISANS. He has also written numerous articles for various journals and encyclopedias, and has lectured at universities and colleges on U.S. foreign relations. Plischke has been a charter member of the Committee for the Study of Diplomacy since 1969 and a member, 1967-72, and chairman, 1969-70, of the Department of State Advisory Committee on "Foreign Relations of the United States."

CONTENTS

Contents

Contents

Contents

Contents

Contents

Contents

PREFACE

This compilation of analytical, descriptive, and documentary sources and resources on the conduct of U.S. foreign relations is designed to assist the serious student of American diplomacy. It includes a variety of both historical
and contemporary bibliographical guides, monographs, textbooks, essays, and
documentary materials. It is concerned with the foreign affairs process, not
with diplomatic history, current events, world politics, or substantive foreign
policy development and analysis.

There are five major segments. The introductory chapter fixes the parameters
of treatment and inclusion. It also notes problems of focus and the structuring
of research, describes planes of research design, and provides some basic resource commentary.

Part I presents materials that deal with "diplomacy" in general--that is, literature that is not restricted specifically to U.S. foreign relations practice. Broad
perspective and more specialized sources and resources are grouped separately.
The former listing encompasses various types of broad-gauged analyses of the
diplomatic process in both English and other languages, as well as a few histories of diplomacy. The more particularized literature focuses upon such matters as protocol, specialized attaches, diplomatic asylum, negotiation, international conferencing, functions and activities of diplomats, and the like. In
addition, separate chapters are devoted to the treatment and mistreatment of
diplomats and to "the new diplomacy." The latter distinguishes contemporary
practice from that which is generally known as traditional or classical diplomacy.

The central core of this compilation, embodied in part II, provides guidance
to a broad spectrum of sources and resources--largely unofficial--that may be
useful in the study specifically of the American diplomatic process. In addition to bibliographical guides, materials are arranged to afford separate listings
on the principal government agencies that are concerned with foreign affairs,
including the president, Congress, the Department of State, the National Security Council, the military, and others. Separate chapters supply published
references on decision making, crisis diplomacy and peace making, and systematic and theoretical foreign relations analysis, as well as selected volumes of

fiction. Part II also contains a menu of general surveys and specialized studies on the conduct of American foreign relations. The more particularized subjects range from policy formulation, diplomatic communication, overseas representation and field missions, treaty making, and secrecy, to the roles of public opinion and information programs, protection of nationals and their interests abroad, and consular, cultural, trade, and other affairs.

Part III, which is devoted to official sources, consists of two chapters--an essay on the publication and availability of U.S. documentation and a comprehensive compilation of citations to documentary resources. The latter canvasses the foreign relations documentation of the president, Congress, the Department of State, and the diplomatic service, but it also includes bibliographical listings of official materials on treaties and agreements, international conferences and organizations, and other government agencies and subjects. This compendium is intended to be illustrative rather than exhaustive, suggesting to the user the various categories and the massive aggregate of official documentation available to the student of American diplomacy.

The last major section, part IV, furnishes a list of published autobiographies, biographies, commentaries, diaries, and memoirs by and about presidents, Secretaries of State, diplomats, consuls, and other public officials involved in the conduct of U.S. foreign relations.

To facilitate utilization of this bibliography, items within major segments are grouped according to secondary and subsidiary subtopics, each of which is introduced with general commentary. Arrangement is primarily topical and alphabetical thereunder. In a few instances, however--as in the case of the series of proposals to reform the Department of State and the Foreign Service--entries are listed chronologically. Whereas citations are primarily to books and monographic literature, selected articles and essays are included in many sections. In some cases these are presented within separate subsections following the book-length materials. In others, where the quantity of entries is small, the books and articles are enjoined in a combined listing. By and large, items are cited only in those chapter sections where they are most directly applicable, although some that are equally pertinent to more than one subject category are cited additionally as warranted.

General bibliographical references are presented in the first chapter of part II. More specialized bibliographies are incorporated in topical sections and subsections where they are most relevant. Additional bibliographical compendia available in published volumes are noted in individual entries. An inclusive author and issuing agency index is included to assist the user. The detailed table of contents gives the user access to the subject areas covered in the text.

As with other guides to literary and documentary resources, it would be presumptuous to assume that this compilation is definitive. It does contain many materials that appear to be timeworthy, some that are continuing, and still others that suggest considerable potential for the future. Nevertheless, past experience indicates that, in addition to those basic analytical, descriptive, and other materials that enjoy notable longevity and continuing pertinence, a good many others are produced in quantity from time to time in response to waves of research fashion and specialized interest. In the post-World War II years, for example, these would include studies and anthologies on such subjects as systematic foreign relations analysis, bureaucratic and rational decision making, policy science, crisis management, and international terrorism. These mushrooming foci of attention supplement but scarcely supplant older concerns with such matters as foreign policy formulation, institutional and personnel organization and reform, interagency coordination, the commissioning of specialized diplomatic emissaries, treaty making, and international cooperation.

Additional topical areas of interest warrant greater attention and more intensive research. These embrace certain longtime features of diplomatic relations, such as privileges and immunities, protocol, language and translation, asylum, and the servicing of the interests of private Americans abroad. They also involve issues and practices that have increased in importance in recent decades. These include ministerial and technical negotiations, interrelationships of complementary and competing diplomatic forums, shuttle diplomacy, the application of technological developments to the diplomatic process, foreign relations documents management, the diplomatic problems of microstates, and others. Some of these are likely to arouse growing literary attention in the future.

It is hoped, therefore, that supplements to this compilation will emerge to provide continuing and systematic guidance to the voluminous and proliferating library of sources and resources on these and other aspects of the conduct of American foreign relations in the years to come. Moreover, in view of the endless flood of documents, analyses, and other materials that continue to be produced, this compilation is largely a selected nucleus of references to existing sources and resources and will need to be constantly updated and augmented.

U.S. FOREIGN RELATIONS

Chapter 1
INTRODUCTION

Despite the oft-repeated cliches concerning the American people's right to know and alleged secrecy enshrouding American foreign relations, the quantity of literary and documentary materials published or otherwise made publicly available is impressive. Their accessibility varies with the depth of penetration desired. As with other areas of study, the limited supply of published accounts and the degree of unencumbered access to sources are most constraining for definitive research on minute or sensitive subjects and contemporary events. These shortcomings are much less of a hindrance for investigating broader and less penetrating topics and issues and are least inhibiting for a general survey of the field.

Often, more attention is paid by the researcher, the author, the teacher, and the casual reader to substantive foreign policy than to the conduct of external relations, and gaps exist in the spectrum of diplomatic chronicling. Nevertheless, sweeping literary and editorial complaints of serious impediments to effective and basic understanding of the American foreign relations process can scarcely be attributed directly to an acute shortage of published or otherwise available resources. This compilation is designed to provide ready reference to selected historical and current sources on the conduct of American diplomacy. It is not intended to duplicate the more detailed specialized listings of certain particularized categories of sources and resources, nor does it presume systematic comprehensiveness for all facets of the subject. Some of the items cited, particularly certain official documentary materials, may serve primarily as research resources, while others focus rather on the needs of the classroom and general reading in the field.

Because of the very nature of the society of nations and its constant change, foreign relations by definition constitute a continuum. Because the objectives and policies of national states are inherently competitive, foreign relations are challenging and exciting. Because individuals often harbor their own views on the subject, and because democratic governance involves popular participation, foreign relations are believed to be everybody's business. Because the interests and responsibilities of governments frequently are global in extent, their foreign relations are a vital concern of the collective polity.

Introduction

Reflecting some of the consequences of these considerations, intensified research has been launched since World War II, and a considerable literature has emerged regarding a number of aspects of the changing American foreign relations role, such as the functioning of the presidency, the secretaryship of state, the Foreign Service, top-level and interdepartmental coordination within the National Security Council system, the policy process, and decision making. On the other hand, as might be anticipated, the greatest research and literary attention center, not upon the management of foreign affairs, but on matters of substantive policy and U.S. relations with specific countries, areas, institutions, developments, issues, and crises. While many of these are worthy ventures, diplomacy as a process for conducting intergovernmental relations appears to be less attractive to both the researcher and the publicist--at times even to the professional diplomat.

Nevertheless, in the search for truth, it is as important to know how foreign policy is made and implemented, and how diplomacy is administered, as it is to understand the nature of the foreign policy itself. "Diplomacy" is herein equated generally with the "conduct of foreign relations," and it reflects the national rather than either the subnational or the international perspective. It excludes simple descriptive analysis of foreign policy essence but encompasses policy making both centrally and in the field respecting both substantive and procedural policy, and it comprehends more, therefore, than merely international intercourse (communications) or intergovernmental negotiation.

It may be taken for granted that it is useful to understand the past in order to manage the present and prepare for the future intelligently. Where relevant, the practitioner, researcher, and student must be familiar with certain landmarks of historical development and analysis. Background and historically-oriented resources, therefore, are not deliberately excluded from this compilation.

FOCUS AND STRUCTURING OF RESEARCH

It is self-evident that, to be of value, the serious study or research venture needs to possess a fixed focus and defined parameters. These may be chronologically or functionally delimited, and they need to be determined with care on the basis of the purposes of the study, the resources obtainable, the amount of time available, and the end product desired. Choices are virtually unlimited, and there clearly is room for contributions reflecting a diversity of approaches. Often, fashions pertain in matters of research method and analytical treatment. Among the more prominent in recent decades are organization and management theory, decision making, systems analysis, gaming, policy science, opinion surveying, factual quantification, data banking, automation of information retrieval and documents control, cybernetics, and team research methods and projects. Some of these, like a substantial number of other aspects of the field, are inadequately probed in contemporary inquiry and literature. A review of published accounts reveals a dearth of organized studies of many aspects of the conduct of U.S. foreign relations, so there is ample room for a broad variety of fruitful investigation.

Like all fashions, both substantive and methodological usages, irrespective of their intrinsic importance, tend to be ephemeral. Treatment in published literature, official in-house studies, and other reports is fragmentary, often for good reasons. Comprehensive reviews of the overall conduct of foreign relations are scarce, and serious research gaps and subject biases exist. Much-needed fundamental, mundane, bread-and-butter studies usually are regarded as too prosaic and pedestrian to be appealing or gratifying, and the time-consuming, costly work of compendious compilations frequently is deferred or shunned. As a result, judgments may be rendered without adequate informational foundation, conceptualizations may be ventured by the novitiate, and reformative panaceas may be projected by the uninformed.

As with most studies of public affairs, the management of U.S. foreign relations--as a field of investigation and research--may be structured in differing ways. The historian generally elects to use the chronological route, hinging his study on identifiable sequential periods. Others may prefer a topical approach, organizing their analyses in a series of separable but parallel topics arranged in an ordered fashion. Depending on varying criteria, the latter may stratify the components of the subject on the basis of organizational factors, functions, or issues. Still others seek to reduce aspects of diplomatic problems and practice to systematic, if not scientific, analysis. Such primary and secondary patterns are not necessarily mutually exclusive and may be combined in order to supplement or reinforce each other. The framework employed by the researcher tends to reflect his particular perception, focus, and emphasis. He may commence, a priori, with some contrived preconception or hypothesis which he seeks to prove or disprove, and, consequently, the elements or phases of the subject which he incorporates will be selective.

PLANES OF RESEARCH DESIGN

Rewarding study and research require several obvious essentials. Most basic--in addition to motivation, need, time, and ideas is the availability of information resources and, for purposes of research, their fabrication into an effective research design. Study of the process of U.S. foreign relations juxtaposes the active concern of three primary components: the government itself, the academic community, and the information media. The first two have a good many parallel and complementary interests, while the concerns of journalism are often unique--the story of the moment generally outranking the complete chronicling or the analysis in depth. Yet, though not surprising, more immediate attention seems to be devoted to satisfying the informational demands of the news media than the needs of either the government historian or the academician.

As in any field of human knowledge, the analyst or researcher concentrating on the conduct of foreign relations may vary both his breadth and depth of treatment. On the most elementary plane, his projected inquiry may be broad but shallow, so that he might limit himself to a few basic and readily available sources of information. For certain restricted and rudimentary purposes, these may suffice. If he penetrates to a more comprehensive level, however, he needs to rely on additional resources--consisting largely of systematic or at least thoughtful and penetrating secondary accounts and a quantity of end product documentation. These may provide a general understanding of what has transpired, been said, or been decided. A third level of research design delves deeper still, embracing raw material resources and public records, which contribute directly to the formulation of end product documentation. Much official, government-supported and private academic research aspires to achieve this goal.

The final plane--even more fundamental--penetrates to the all-encompassing library of published accounts, both official and unofficial, and the mass of written and other basic materials, documentary drafts, interunit preliminary records, and individual views of participants as inscribed in memoranda, commentaries, reports, diaries, memoirs, and personal papers, or which may only be elicited by interview. Investigation which plumbs the recesses of these resource reservoirs is likely to be the most original, the most sagacious, and often the most enlightening. . The depth of treatment by the researcher, naturally, is directly related to both his objective and the availability of resources, and, just as research design and intent to circumscribe treatment may obviate the need for the more basic resources, so their unavailability may delimit the research experience and its consequences.

RESEARCH RESOURCE COMMENTARY

General guidance and commentary respecting resources and research on the conduct of U.S. foreign relations may be found in such publications as:

Gustafson, Milton O[dell]., ed. THE NATIONAL ARCHIVES AND FOREIGN RELATIONS RESEARCH. Athens: Ohio University Press for the National Archives, 1974. 292 p.

> Contains 23 essays by individual authors, on invitation, with summary discussion, respecting National Archives records and research on the Department of State and other agencies, the administrative history of the Department of State, domestic influences on foreign policy, diplomacy of war and peace, and U.S. relations with Europe, Latin America, East Asia, the Middle East, and Africa. Product of National Archives-sponsored symposium held in June 1969.

Humphrey, Richard A. "Procurement of Foreign Research Materials." DEPARTMENT OF STATE BULLETIN 14 (6 and 13 January 1946): 22-25, 34.

> Concerns procurement of documents and other materials from foreign countries for research purposes, and trends respecting availability following World War II.

O'Flaherty, J. Daniel. "Problems in the Conduct of United States Foreign Policy: A Compilation of Recent Critiques." In COMMISSION ON THE ORGANIZATION OF THE GOVERNMENT FOR THE CONDUCT OF FOREIGN POLICY, JUNE 1975 [Report], appendix X, vol. 7, pp. 327-35. Washington, D.C.: Government Printing Office, 1976.

One of three introductory papers prepared for Murphy Commission. Summarizes substantial number of criticisms of U.S. foreign policy process.

Platig, E. Raymond. "Foreign Affairs Analysis: Some Thoughts on Expanding Competence." INTERNATIONAL STUDIES QUARTERLY 13 (Spring 1969): 19-30.

Plischke, Elmer. "Research on the Conduct of United States Foreign. Relations." INTERNATIONAL STUDIES QUARTERLY 15 (June 1971): 221-50.

> Analyzes various approaches to perspective and treatment (i.e., historical, topical, functional, issues-oriented) and relates these to available literature, discusses planes of research design, and comments on research resource availability.

Rosenau, James N.; Burgess, Philip M.; and Hermann, Charles F. "The Adaptation of Foreign Policy Research: A Case Study of an Anti-Case Study Project." INTERNATIONAL STUDIES QUARTERLY 17 (March 1973): 119-44.

> Progress and expectations report of team research venture of Inter-University Comparative Foreign Policy Project (ICFP), intended to provide collaborative study of eight genotypic societies and offset the noncumulative, atheoretical, case-oriented study of individual scholars. Notes both potentialities and problems of collective research. List of prepared papers appended.

Simpson, Smith, ed. "Resources and Needs of American Diplomacy." ANNALS OF THE AMERICAN ACADEMY OF POLITICAL AND SOCIAL SCIENCE 380 (November 1968): 1-144.

> Compilation of essays concerned largely with the resources of American diplomacy, rather than resources for the study of the subject. Includes one particularly relevant essay on "Research and Analysis" by E. Raymond Platig.

Of related value are similar studies in the general field of international relations, including:

Fox, William T.R. "Interwar International Relations Research: The American Experience." WORLD POLITICS 2 (October 1949): 67-79.

> A cursory, historical account of international research between World Wars I and II, including institutional and individual components and contributions.

Palmer, Norman D., ed. A DESIGN FOR INTERNATIONAL RELATIONS RESEARCH: SCOPE, THEORY, METHODS, AND RELEVANCE. American Academy of Political and Social Science Monograph 10. Philadelphia: American Academy of Political and Social Science, 1970. 254 p.

Symposium of essays, prepared commentaries, and verbatim discussions of small group of experts on trends, theories, methodolo-
gies, and relevancy of international relations research. Essay
by E. Raymond Platig on "Research and Foreign Policy/Diplomacy"
is especially pertinent.

Platig, E. Raymond. INTERNATIONAL RELATIONS RESEARCH: PROBLEMS
OF EVALUATION AND ADVANCEMENT. Santa Barbara, Calif.: Clio Press,
1967. 211 p.

Assessment of research in international relations, growing out of
author's participation on the Committee on Research Evaluation
of the Carnegie Endowment. Covers international relations as a
field of learning, functions of systematic inquiry, research infra-
structure, and an overall evaluation.

Vayrynen, Raimo. "Notes on Foreign Policy Research." COOPERATION AND
CONFLICT 7 (1972): 87-96.

Analysis of the distinction between the traditional, scientific, and
radical or critical approaches to foreign policy research, with
some emphasis on comparative orientations and selected critical
problems, including the distinction between external behavior and
foreign policy, the role of subjective and objective factors, and
the need to analyze policy outcomes as well as the policy processes.

Part I

DIPLOMACY AND DIPLOMATS—GENERAL

English-language literature dealing with diplomacy per se--as distinguished, on the one hand, from that of a particular country or region and, on the other hand, from that pertaining to specialized aspects of foreign relations--is sparse. Aside from a substantial library of memoirs and personal commentaries, dealt with separately in part IV, much of the general literature on diplomacy--regarded as a process, an institution, and a function--has in earlier times been published in Latin, French, German, Spanish, and other languages.

Some of the basic writings of more recent times, appearing in English, are the products of British professional diplomatists, while American writers often are relatively unconcerned with the general nature and problems of diplomatic practice. This has been especially the case with the writings of professional diplomats and other officials dealing with external affairs who, if they publish at all, tend to devote their attention either to personal memoirs or to policy description, analysis, and commentary. While many of these efforts constitute useful additions to the literature, an increasing number of authors are turning rather to certain of the more specific aspects of the conduct of foreign relations and are noted elsewhere in this compilation.

A recent analysis of the treatment of diplomacy in basic, general English-language textbooks, cited below, indicates that of ninety such volumes in the field of U.S. foreign relations, published largely since World War II, and seventy-five similar volumes on general international relations and politics, more than half devote some attention to diplomacy as a significant component of the subject; but, while nearly three-fourths of the international relations textbooks accord such treatment, more than half of the U.S. foreign relations volumes ignore the subject completely. One reason for this, as noted in the introduction, is that much American foreign relations literature focuses principally on the essence of substantive policy or some phase of policy analysis and either avoids concern with the conduct of foreign relations entirely or touches upon it only minimally. On the other hand, of the international relations textbooks, the volumes using the traditional largely functional or topical treatment usually include a separate chapter or section on diplomacy; but those primarily focusing upon the chronicling of historical evolution and international political development, with national policy analysis and interaction, with international relations theory, with the behavior of participants, or with academic

methodology, are less inclined to recognize diplomacy as a distinguishable
component warranting individualized attention.

It also is worthy of note that of the 165 basic textbooks examined, only one
in ten concerned with U.S. foreign relations defines the meaning of diplomacy,
whereas nearly forty percent of the international relations and politics texts do
so. Even more surprising, examination of a series of broad-scale textbooks
presuming to deal with diplomacy in general reveals that less than half address
themselves to defining the subject. Looking to the matter of space allocation,
only some sixteen percent of the chapters in the ninety volumes on U.S. foreign
relations and merely five percent of the chapters in international relations textbooks deal with the conduct of diplomatic relations. By and large, space allocation in terms of pages is even more modest. Such restriction of interest
and emphasis is understandable for international relations textbooks, because
diplomacy must compete for attention with other important components of the
field, but it is revealing that only approximately fifteen percent of the pages
contained in the U.S. foreign relations texts may be deemed to deal with
diplomacy. Moreover, much of the analysis comprising even this fraction of
space fails to provide a balanced treatment of the topic and usually concentrates on certain popular subjects, such as the roles of political principals,
policy making, negotiation, secrecy, or diplomatic personnel.

For a more comprehensive analysis, with statistical tables, see:

Plischke, Elmer. "Treatment of 'Diplomacy' in International Relations Textbooks." WORLD AFFAIRS 135 (Spring 1973): 328–44.

> Statistical information with percentages given in table 1. Trends
> in textbook treatment of diplomacy depicted in table 2.

An earlier analysis of this subject is provided in:

Plischke, Elmer. "The Optimum Scope of Instruction in Diplomacy." In INSTRUC-
TION IN DIPLOMACY: THE LIBERAL ARTS APPROACH, edited by Smith Simpson,
pp. 15–21. American Academy of Political and Social Science Monograph 13.
Philadelphia: American Academy of Political and Social Science, 1972.

In both sets of textbooks studied, those on international relations and politics
and those on U.S. foreign relations, the treatment of diplomacy tends to be
superficial, fragmentary, and unsystematic. This condition doubtless flows from
the lack of both a universally acknowledged definition and a common design
and agreed parameters of the field.

It needs to be added, however, that certain aspects of diplomacy are given
individualized treatment in their own, more highly circumscribed but quantitatively substantial, literature. Even though brief consideration of diplomacy
may be found in a number of general texts, many of which are readily available, the most penetrating and systematic exposition needs to be sought in the
more specialized literature confined specifically to the conduct of foreign relations.

Chapter 2
BROAD PERSPECTIVE LITERATURE

English-language literature dealing with diplomacy, exclusive of memoirs, may be considered as falling into two categories. The first consists of those broad-scale historical, descriptive, and analytical volumes which are not functionally or topically restricted and which deal with the subject as a primary technique in the conduct of foreign affairs. Illustrative materials are provided in this chapter. The second main category consists of more functionally oriented or restricted materials, which are listed in the following chapter. Resources dealing specifically with U.S. practice are contained in part II of this compilation.

HISTORIES OF DIPLOMACY

Histories of the diplomatic process, surprisingly, are rare. They are not to be confused with "diplomatic histories," which constitute a substantial library of historical chronicling and are largely recountings of international politics or the gamut of foreign relations, of the overall interrelations of given geographic areas (such as inter-American relations or European diplomatic relations), or of developments respecting specific functional subjects (such as imperial expansion, cold war confrontation, disarmament, transnational conflict resolution, alliances and alignments, crisis diplomacy, treaty negotiation, and a host of others). The following are histories of the diplomatic process.

Adcock, F., and Mosley, D. DIPLOMACY IN ANCIENT GREECE. New York: St. Martin's, 1975. 287 p.

Lachs, P.S. THE DIPLOMATIC CORPS UNDER CHARLES II AND JAMES II. New Brunswick, N.J.: Rutgers University Press, 1965. 269 p.

Mattingly, Garrett. RENAISSANCE DIPLOMACY. Baltimore: Penguin, 1955. 284 p. Bibliog.

Nicolson, Harold. THE EVOLUTION OF DIPLOMATIC METHOD. New York: Macmillan, 1954. 93 p.

11

Numelin, Ragnar J. THE BEGINNINGS OF DIPLOMACY. New York: Philosophical Library, 1950. 372 p. Bibliog.

Queller, Donald E. EARLY VENETIAN LEGISLATION ON AMBASSADORS. Geneva: Droz, 1966. 151 p.

_____. THE OFFICE OF AMBASSADOR IN THE MIDDLE AGES. Princeton, N.J.: Princeton University Press, 1967. 251 p. Bibliog.

A number of foreign-language histories of diplomacy, principally in French and German, have also been published in the nineteenth and twentieth centuries, represented by:

Blaga, Corneliu S. L'EVOLUTION DE LA DIPLOMATIE: IDEOLOGIE MOEURS ET TECHNIQUE. Paris: Pedone, 1938. 483 p. Bibliog.

Borel, Francois. DE L'ORIGINE ET DES FONCTIONS DES CONSULS. Leipzig: Voss, 1831. 278 p.

Krauske, Otto. DIE ENTWICKLUNG DER STAENDIGEN DIPLOMATIE VOM FUENFZEHNTEN JAHRHUNDERT BIS 1818. Leipzig: Duncker and Humbolt, 1885. 245 p.

Potemkin, Vladimir Petrovich, ed. HISTOIRE DE LA DIPLOMATIE. Translated from Russian by Xenia Pamphilova and Michel Emistor. 2 vols. Paris: Librarie de Medicis, 1946. Bibliog.

For commentary on diplomatic history revisionism, see the following:

Siracusa, Joseph M. NEW LEFT DIPLOMATIC HISTORIES AND HISTORIANS: THE AMERICAN REVISIONISTS. Port Washington, N.Y.: Kennikat, 1973. 138 p. Bibliog.

BASIC CONCEPTS AND TERMINOLOGY

A number of studies define and analyze fundamental concepts and theoretical considerations in the foreign relations field, or provide glossaries of terminology, including:

Bailey, Thomas A. "Glossary of Diplomatic Terms." In his A DIPLOMATIC HISTORY OF THE AMERICAN PEOPLE, pp. 957-61. 9th ed. Englewood Cliffs, N.J.: Prentice-Hall, 1974.

Defines 165 expressions used in American diplomatic history.

Gamboa, Melquiades J. ELEMENTS OF DIPLOMATIC AND CONSULAR PRAC-
TICE: A GLOSSARY. Quezon City, Philippines: Central Lawbook, 1966.
489 p.

A dictionary of some 950 terms and acronyms used in diplomatic
practice.

Gross, Feliks. FOREIGN POLICY ANALYSIS. New York: Philosophical
Library, 1954. 179 p.

Deals at length with such concepts as foreign policy, national
interest, ideology, strategy and tactics, power factors, and scien-
tism.

Harmon, Robert B. "A Glossary of Diplomatic Terms." In his THE ART AND
PRACTICE OF DIPLOMACY: A SELECTED AND ANNOTATED GUIDE, pp.
160-74. Metuchen, N.J.: Scarecrow, 1971.

Defines some 135 concepts and terms.

Lerche, Charles O., Jr., and Said, Abdul A. CONCEPTS OF INTERNA-
TIONAL POLITICS. 3d ed. Englewood Cliffs, N.J.: Prentice-Hall, 1979.
336 p.

See especially chapters 2-6, on the policy process, capability,
diplomatic techniques, and institutions of the modern state system.

Lovell, John P. FOREIGN POLICY IN PERSPECTIVE: STRATEGY, ADAPTA-
TION, DECISION MAKING. New York: Holt, Rinehart, and Winston, 1970.
370 p.

See especially chapters 1, 5, 7-11, on foreign policy analysis,
state system, decision making, and values.

Plano, Jack C., and Olton, Roy, eds. THE INTERNATIONAL RELATIONS
DICTIONARY. 2d ed. Kalamazoo, Mich.: New Issues Press, 1979. 337 p.

Especially chapters 9 (on diplomacy), 6 and 7 (on foreign policy),
and 4 (on ideology and communications).

Plischke, Elmer. "Glossary." In his CONDUCT OF AMERICAN DIPLOMACY,
pp. 643-51. 3d ed. Princeton, N.J.: Van Nostrand, 1967.

Defines more than one hundred concepts and terms employed in
the conduct of diplomatic relations.

Reitzel, William; Kaplan, Morton A.; and Coblenz, Constance G. "Definition
of Terms." In their UNITED STATES FOREIGN POLICY, 1945-1955, pp. 471-
74. Washington, D.C.: Brookings Institution, 1956.

Treats such basic concepts as national interests, objectives, policies,
commitments, and principles.

U.S. Department of State. Library. INTERNATIONAL RELATIONS DICTIO-
NARY. Washington, D.C.: Government Printing Office, 1978. 48 p.

> Dictionary of terms, phrases, acronyms, catchwords, and abbre-
> viations used in conduct of foreign relations, arranged alphabeti-
> cally, with reference notes and cross-references.

An earlier, French glossary of diplomatic terminology is to be found in:

De Cussy, Ferdinand. DICTIONNAIRE OU MANUEL-LEXIQUE DU DIPLO-
MATE ET DU CONSUL. Leipzig: Brockhaus, 1846. 799 p.

GENERAL ANALYSES

A few studies address themselves directly to diplomacy and treat the subject
from a broad perspective and in some depth. The following are among the
most highly recognized.

Feltham, R.G. DIPLOMATIC HANDBOOK. 2d ed. New York: Longman,
1977. 144 p.

Gore-Booth, Lord, ed. SATOW'S GUIDE TO DIPLOMATIC PRACTICE. 5th
ed. New York: Longman, 1978. 544 p.

> Also see Satow below.

Nicolson, Harold. DIPLOMACY. London: Butterworth, 1939. 255 p. Bibliog.

Satow, Ernest M. A GUIDE TO DIPLOMATIC PRACTICE. London: Longmans,
Green, 1917. 4th ed., edited by Nevile Bland, 1957. 510 p.

Thayer, Charles W. DIPLOMAT. New York: Harper, 1959. 299 p. Bibliog.

Webster, Charles K. THE ART AND PRACTICE OF DIPLOMACY. London:
London School of Economics, 1952. Reprints. London: Chatto and Windus,
1961; New York: Barnes and Noble, 1962. 245 p.

BROAD PERSPECTIVE BUT SPECIALIZED TREATMENT

Some volumes, while concerned with diplomacy, address themselves to various
circumscribed or particularized aspects of, or treatments about, the subject,
of which the following are illustrative. Some of these emphasize the role of
the diplomat (Cambon, Jusserand, Strang, and Wicquefort); a few analyze

diplomacy in relation to other fields (Fisher) or address themselves to particular types of diplomacy (Graham); and some relate diplomacy to international law and organization (Best, Hardy, Ostrower, and Sen). Because they are so closely related to diplomatic practice, studies of consular affairs are also included (Feller and Hudson, Puente, Ravndal, Stowell, and Warden); also see listing on "Consular Affairs" in chapter 17.

Bernard, Montague. FOUR LECTURES ON SUBJECTS CONNECTED WITH DIPLOMACY. London: Macmillan, 1868. 205 p.

Best, Gary L. "Diplomacy in the United Nations." Ph.D. dissertation, Northwestern University, 1960. 269 p.

Briggs, Ellis O. ANATOMY OF DIPLOMACY: THE ORIGIN AND EXECUTION OF AMERICAN FOREIGN POLICY. New York: McKay, 1968. 248 p.

   Especially part 1, chapters 1-8.

Brown, N. Barker M., Jr. DIPLOMACY IN AN AGE OF NATIONALISM: ESSAYS IN HONOR OF LYNN MARSHALL CASE. The Hague: Nijhoff, 1971. 222 p.

Burton, John W. SYSTEMS, STATES, DIPLOMACY AND RULES. London: Cambridge University Press, 1968. 251 p.

Cambon, Jules M. THE DIPLOMATIST. Translated by C.R. Turner. London: Allan, 1931. 151 p.

Clark, Eric. DIPLOMAT: THE WORLD OF INTERNATIONAL DIPLOMACY. New York: Taplinger, 1974. 276 p.

Corbell, Percy E. LAW IN DIPLOMACY. Princeton, N.J.: Princeton University Press, 1959. 290 p.

Craig, Gordon A., and Gilbert, Felix, eds. THE DIPLOMATS: 1919-1939. 2 vols. Princeton, N.J.: Princeton University Press, 1953. 700 p.

d'Auvergne, Edmund, and Franck, Basil. ENVOYS EXTRAORDINARY. London: Harrap, 1937. 317 p.

Demiashkevich, Michael J. SHACKLED DIPLOMACY. New York: Barnes and Noble, 1934. 244 p.

Denza, Eileen. DIPLOMATIC LAW, COMMENTARY ON THE VIENNA CONVENTION ON DIPLOMATIC RELATIONS. Dobbs Ferry, N.Y.: Oceana, 1976. 348 p.

Broad Perspective Literature

"Diplomatic Method." INTERNATIONAL JOURNAL 30 (Winter 1974–75): 1–161.

Symposium of eleven articles by various authors, prepared for the Canadian Institute of International Affairs.

Do Nascimento e Silva, Geraldo E. DIPLOMACY IN INTERNATIONAL LAW. Leiden, The Netherlands: Sijthoff, 1972. 217 p.

Eayres, James. DIPLOMACY AND ITS DISCONTENTS. Toronto: University of Toronto Press, 1971. 198 p.

Feller, Abraham H., and Hudson, Manley O., eds. A COLLECTION OF THE DIPLOMATIC AND CONSULAR LAWS AND REGULATIONS OF VARIOUS COUNTRIES. 2 vols. Washington, D.C.: Carnegie Endowment, 1933.

Fisher, Glen H. PUBLIC DIPLOMACY AND THE BEHAVIORAL SCIENCES. Bloomington: Indiana University Press, 1972. 180 p.

Graham, Robert A. VATICAN DIPLOMACY. Princeton, N.J.: Princeton University Press, 1959. 442 p. Bibliog.

Hardy, Michael J. MODERN DIPLOMATIC LAW. Dobbs Ferry, N.Y.: Oceana, 1968. 150 p. Bibliog.

Hayter, William. THE DIPLOMACY OF THE GREAT POWERS. New York: Macmillan, 1961. 74 p.

Heatley, David P. DIPLOMACY AND THE STUDY OF INTERNATIONAL RE-LATIONS. Oxford: Clarendon Press, 1969. 292 p.

Hurwitz, Myron L., ed. THE DIPLOMATIC YEARBOOK. New York: Funk and Wagnalls in association with United Nations World, 1950. 836 p.

Jusserand, Jean A.A. Jules. THE SCHOOL FOR AMBASSADORS AND OTHER ESSAYS. New York: Putnam, 1925. 355 p.

Author was French ambassador to the United States.

Kelly, David Victor. THE RULING FEW: OR, THE HUMAN BACKGROUND TO DIPLOMACY. London: Hollis and Carter, 1952. 449 p.

Lauren, Paul Gordon, ed. DIPLOMACY: NEW APPROACHES IN HISTORY, THEORY AND POLICY. Riverside, N.J.: Free Press, 1979. 286 p.

Mendershausen, Horst. THE DIPLOMAT AS A NATIONAL AND TRANSNA-TIONAL AGENT: A PROBLEM IN MULTIPLE LOYALTY. Morristown, N.J.: General Learning Press, 1973. 19 p. Bibliog.

_____. THE DIPLOMAT AS A NATIONAL AND TRANSNATIONAL AGENT: DILEMMAS AND OPPORTUNITIES. Santa Monica, Calif.: Rand, 1969. 28 p.

Mowat, Robert Balmain. DIPLOMACY AND PEACE. London: Williams and Norgate, 1935. 295 p.

Ostrower, Alexander. LANGUAGE, LAW AND DIPLOMACY: A STUDY OF LINGUISTIC DIVERSITY IN OFFICIAL INTERNATIONAL RELATIONS AND INTERNATIONAL LAW. 2 vols. Philadelphia: University of Pennsylvania Press, 1965. Bibliog.

Pearson, Lester B. DIPLOMACY IN THE NUCLEAR AGE. Cambridge, Mass.: Harvard University Press, 1959. 114 p.

Plischke, Elmer, ed. MODERN DIPLOMACY: THE ART AND THE ARTISANS. Washington, D.C.: American Enterprise Institute, 1979. 456 p. Bibliog.

Puente, Julius I. THE FOREIGN CONSUL: HIS JURIDICAL STATUS IN THE UNITED STATES. Chicago: B.J. Smith, 1926. 157 p.

Ravndal, Gabriel Bie. THE ORIGIN OF THE CAPITULATIONS AND OF THE CONSULAR INSTITUTION. Washington, D.C.: Government Printing Office, 1921. 112 p.

Roetter, Charles. THE DIPLOMATIC ART: AN INFORMAL HISTORY OF WORLD DIPLOMACY. Philadelphia: Macrae Smith, 1963. 248 p.

Sen, Biswanath. A DIPLOMAT'S HANDBOOK OF INTERNATIONAL LAW AND PRACTICE. The Hague: Nijhoff, 1965. 522 p. Bibliog.

Stowell, Ellery C. CONSULAR CASES AND OPINIONS. Washington, D.C.: Byrne, 1909. 811 p.

Strang, William S. THE DIPLOMATIC CAREER. London: Deutsch, 1962. 160 p.

Torre, M., and Glaser, W. THE EFFECT OF ILLNESS ON DIPLOMATIC INTERCOURSE. New York: Research Institute for the Study of Man, 1963.

Trevelyan, Humphrey. DIPLOMATIC CHANNELS. Boston: Gambit, 1973. 157 p.

Warden, David Baillie. ON THE ORIGIN, NATURE, PROGRESS AND IN-FLUENCE OF CONSULAR ESTABLISHMENTS. Paris: Smith, 1813. 331 p.

Wellesley, Victor. DIPLOMACY IN FETTERS. London: Hutchinson, 1944. 224 p.

Wicquefort, Abraham van. THE AMBASSADOR AND HIS FUNCTIONS. Translated by Mr. Digby. 2 vols. The Hague: Steucker, 1681; Cologne: Marteau, 1690, 1715; and others.

The following provide political and legal analysis of the rights and duties of diplomats in U.S. practice:

Hackworth, Green H. DIGEST OF INTERNATIONAL LAW. Washington, D.C.: Government Printing Office, 1943. Vol. 4, pp. 459-512.

Moore, John Bassett. A DIGEST OF INTERNATIONAL LAW. Washington, D.C.: Government Printing Office, 1906. Vol. 4, pp. 553-622.

Whiteman, Marjorie M. DIGEST OF INTERNATIONAL LAW. Washington, D.C.: Government Printing Office, 1970. Vol. 7, pp. 126-74.

ESSAYS AND OTHER SHORT TREATMENTS

Quantitatively, book-length literature of this first broad-scale category is somewhat disappointing. However, it is augmented by shorter treatments of diplomacy contained in a good many basic texts in the fields of international relations and foreign affairs. The following subsections provide such representative literature.

International Relations Textbooks

Short treatments of diplomacy as a separately identifiable function in the relations of nations are given in a substantial segment of general international relations textbooks, including the following. Chapters that are especially relevant are identified in annotations. A substantial number of these deal with diplomacy in general, such as Crabb, Haas, Hartmann, Hill, Kulski, McClellan et al., Modelski, Organski, Padelford and Lincoln, Palmer and Perkins, Rienow, Schuman, Spiro, Stoessinger, Strausz-Hupe and Possony, and Wright. A few concern various aspects of the conduct of foreign relations, including Greene, Mills and McLaughlin, and Schleicher. Some treat such functions as negotiation, bargaining, and peaceful settlement, such as Atwater et al., Ball and Killough, Duchacek, Holsti, Kelmann, and Lanyi and McWilliams. Still others emphasize such matters as state interaction (Frankel), international intercourse (Hodges), the tools of statecraft (Lerche), controls of international behavior (Levi), conference diplomacy (Mowat), qualities of good diplomats (Regala), and peaceful change (Van Dyke).

Atwater, Elton, et al. WORLD AFFAIRS: PROBLEMS AND PROSPECTS.
New York: Appleton-Century-Crofts, 1958.

Chapter 11 on feasibility.

Ball, M. Margaret, and Killough, Hugh B. INTERNATIONAL RELATIONS.
New York: Ronald, 1956.

Chapters 9 and 10 on negotiation and settlement of disputes.

Boasson, Charles. APPROACHES TO THE STUDY OF INTERNATIONAL RELA-
TIONS. Assen, Netherlands: Van Gorcum, 1963.

Chapter 3 on historical reconnaissance.

Burton, John Wear. SYSTEMS, STATES, DIPLOMACY AND RULES. London:
Cambridge University Press, 1968.

Especially chapter 12.

Butterfield, Herbert, and Wight, Martin, eds. DIPLOMATIC INVESTIGATIONS:
ESSAYS IN THE THEORY OF INTERNATIONAL POLITICS. Cambridge, Mass.:
Harvard University Press, 1966.

Chapter 2 on histories of diplomacy.

Crabb, Cecil V., Jr. NATIONS IN A MULTIPOLAR WORLD. New York:
Harper and Row, 1968.

Chapter 4 on diplomacy in transition.

Deutsch, Karl W. THE ANALYSIS OF INTERNATIONAL RELATIONS. Englewood Cliffs, N.J.: Prentice-Hall, 1968.

Chapter 12 on diplomacy and coalitions.

Duchacek, Ivo D. NATIONS AND MEN: AN INTRODUCTION TO INTER-
NATIONAL POLITICS. 3d ed. Hinsdale, Ill.: Dryden, 1975.

Chapter 14 on coexistence and diplomacy.

Duchacek, Ivo D., with collaboration of Kenneth Thompson. CONFLICT AND
COOPERATION AMONG NATIONS. New York: Holt, Rinehart, and Winston,
1960.

Chapter 23 on principles and methods of negotiation.

Farnsworth, Lee W., and Gray, Richard B., eds. SECURITY IN A WORLD
OF CHANGE: READINGS AND NOTES ON INTERNATIONAL RELATIONS.
Belmont, Calif.: Wadsworth, 1969.

Chapter 2 on patterns of foreign affairs.

Frankel, Joseph. INTERNATIONAL RELATIONS. New York: Oxford University Press, 1964.

Chapters 2 and 5 on foreign policy making and instruments and techniques of state interaction.

Greene, Fred. DYNAMICS OF INTERNATIONAL RELATIONS: POWER, SECURITY, AND ORDER. New York: Holt, Rinehart, and Winston, 1964.

Chapters 12 and 13 on the conduct of foreign relations and the practice of diplomacy.

Haas, Ernst B., and Whiting, Allen S. DYNAMICS OF INTERNATIONAL RELATIONS. New York: McGraw-Hill, 1956.

Chapter 7 on diplomacy.

Hartmann, Frederick H. THE RELATIONS OF NATIONS. 5th ed. New York: Macmillan, 1978.

Chapter 5 on diplomacy.

_____, ed. WORLD IN CRISIS: READINGS IN INTERNATIONAL RELATIONS. 2d ed. New York: Macmillan, 1962.

Chapter 3 on diplomacy.

Hill, Norman L. CONTEMPORARY WORLD POLITICS. New York: Harper, 1954.

Chapter 3 on diplomacy.

_____. INTERNATIONAL POLITICS. New York: Harper and Row, 1963.

Chapter 2 on diplomacy.

_____, ed. INTERNATIONAL RELATIONS: DOCUMENTS AND READINGS. New York: Oxford University Press, 1950.

Chapter 6 on the conduct of international relations.

Hodges, Charles. THE BACKGROUND OF INTERNATIONAL RELATIONS. New York: Wiley, 1932.

Chapter 12 on international intercourse.

Holsti, Kalevi J. INTERNATIONAL POLITICS: A FRAMEWORK FOR ANALYSIS. 2d ed. Englewood Cliffs, N.J.: Prentice-Hall, 1972.

Chapter 8 on the instruments of policy, including diplomatic bargaining.

Jordan, David C. WORLD POLITICS IN OUR TIME. Lexington, Mass.: Heath, 1970.

Chapter 8 on foreign policy and diplomacy.

Kalijarvi, Thorsten V., et al. MODERN WORLD POLITICS. 3d ed. New York: Crowell, 1953.

Chapter 12 on diplomacy and power politics.

Kaplan, Morton A., ed. GREAT ISSUES OF INTERNATIONAL POLITICS: THE INTERNATIONAL SYSTEM AND NATIONAL POLICY. Chicago: Aldine, 1970.

Chapters 9 and 14 on U.S. foreign policy and Vietnam negotiations.

Kelmann, Herbert C., ed. INTERNATIONAL BEHAVIOR: A SOCIAL-PSYCHOLOGICAL ANALYSIS. New York: Holt, Rinehart, and Winston, 1965.

Chapters 13–15 on bargaining, negotiations, and personal contact in diplomatic forums and relations.

Kulski, Wladyslaw W. INTERNATIONAL POLITICS IN A REVOLUTIONARY AGE. 2d ed. New York: Lippincott, 1968.

Chapter 10 on diplomacy.

Lanyi, George A., and McWilliams, Wilson C., eds. CRISIS AND CONTINUITY IN WORLD POLITICS: READINGS IN INTERNATIONAL RELATIONS. New York: Random House, 1966.

Chapter 8 on negotiation and conciliation.

Lerche, Charles O., Jr. PRINCIPLES OF INTERNATIONAL POLITICS. New York: Oxford University Press, 1956.

Chapters 7 and 8 on informal and formal techniques.

Lerche, Charles O., Jr., and Said, Abdul A. CONCEPTS OF INTERNATIONAL POLITICS. 3d ed. Englewood Cliffs, N.J.: Prentice-Hall, 1979.

Chapters 2 and 4 on policy making and implementation of decisions.

Lerche, Charles O., Jr., and Lerche, Margaret E., eds. READINGS IN INTERNATIONAL POLITICS: CONCEPTS AND ISSUES. New York: Oxford University Press, 1958.

Chapter 3 on the tools of statecraft.

Levi, Werner. INTERNATIONAL POLITICS: FOUNDATIONS OF THE SYSTEM. St. Paul, Minn.: North Central, 1974.

Chapter 6 on controls of international behavior.

Lijphart, Arend, ed. WORLD POLITICS. Boston: Allyn and Bacon, 1966.

Especially pp. 116–44.

Macridis, Roy C., ed. FOREIGN POLICY IN WORLD POLITICS. 5th ed. Englewood Cliffs, N.J.: Prentice-Hall, 1976.

Chapter 1 on comparative study of foreign policy, including section on diplomacy.

Manning, Charles A.W. THE NATURE OF INTERNATIONAL SOCIETY. London: Bell, 1962.

Chapter 15 on influence and immunity.

Mills, Lennox A., and McLaughlin, Charles H. WORLD POLITICS IN TRANSITION. New York: Holt, 1956.

Chapters 11 and 13 on diplomacy and foreign affairs administration.

Modelski, George. PRINCIPLES OF WORLD POLITICS. New York: Free Press, 1972.

Chapter 9 on diplomacy.

Morgenthau, Hans J. POLITICS AMONG NATIONS: THE STRUGGLE FOR POWER AND PEACE. 5th ed. New York: Knopf, 1973.

Especially chapters 6, 31, and 32.

Mowat, Robert Balmain. INTERNATIONAL RELATIONS. New York: Macmillan, 1931. Reprint. Freeport, N.Y.: Books for Libraries Press, 1966.

Chapters 7–10 on initiative in diplomacy and diplomacy by conference.

Organski, A.F.K. WORLD POLITICS. 2d ed. New York: Knopf, 1968.

Chapter 13 on diplomacy.

Padelford, Norman J., and Lincoln, George A. THE DYNAMICS OF INTERNATIONAL POLITICS. 2d ed. New York: Macmillan, 1972.

Chapter 13 on diplomacy and the conduct of foreign affairs.

_____. INTERNATIONAL POLITICS: FOUNDATIONS OF INTERNATIONAL RELATIONS. New York: Macmillan, 1954.

Chapters 16 and 17 on the instruments of foreign policy and the conduct of foreign affairs.

Palmer, Norman D., and Perkins, Howard C. INTERNATIONAL RELATIONS: THE WORLD COMMUNITY IN TRANSITION. 3d ed. Boston: Houghton Mifflin, 1969.

Chapter 4 on diplomacy as an instrument of foreign policy.

Regala, Roberto. NEW DIMENSIONS IN INTERNATIONAL AFFAIRS. Manila, Philippines: Phoenix Press, 1967.

Chapter 2 on the qualities of good diplomats.

Rienow, Robert. CONTEMPORARY INTERNATIONAL POLITICS. New York: Crowell, 1961.

Chapter 11 on diplomacy.

Schleicher, Charles P. INTERNATIONAL RELATIONS: COOPERATION AND CONFLICT. Englewood Cliffs, N.J.: Prentice-Hall, 1962.

Chapter 7 on the conduct of foreign relations.

_____. INTRODUCTION TO INTERNATIONAL RELATIONS. New York: Prentice-Hall, 1954.

Chapters 11 and 12 on the conduct, machinery, and operations of foreign relations.

Schuman, Frederick L. INTERNATIONAL POLITICS: ANARCHY AND ORDER IN THE WORLD SOCIETY. 7th ed. New York: McGraw-Hill, 1969.

Chapter 6 on the art of diplomacy.

Schwarzenberger, Georg. POWER POLITICS: A STUDY OF WORLD SOCIETY. 3d ed. New York: Praeger, 1964.

Chapter 10 on instruments of International politics.

Sharp, Walter R., and Kirk, Grayson. CONTEMPORARY INTERNATIONAL POLITICS. New York: Farrar and Rinehart, 1944.

Chapter 20 on diplomacy and pacific settlement.

Sondermann, Fred A.; McLellan, David S.; and Olson, William C., eds. THE THEORY AND PRACTICE OF INTERNATIONAL RELATIONS. 5th ed. Englewood Cliffs, N.J.: Prentice-Hall, 1979.

Chapter 6 on diplomacy.

Spanier, John. GAMES NATIONS PLAY: ANALYZING INTERNATIONAL POLITICS. New York: Praeger, 1972.

Chapter 11 on foreign policy.

Spiro, Herbert J. WORLD POLITICS: THE GLOBAL SYSTEM. Homewood, Ill.: Dorsey, 1966.

Chapter 2 on the old and the new diplomacy.

Steiner, H. Arthur. PRINCIPLES AND PROBLEMS OF INTERNATIONAL RE-LATIONS. New York: Harper, 1940.

Chapter 6 on framework of foreign policy.

Stoessinger, John G. THE MIGHT OF NATIONS: WORLD POLITICS IN OUR TIME. 6th ed. New York: Random House, 1979.

Chapter 8 on diplomacy and political order.

Strausz-Hupé, Robert, and Possony, Stefan T. INTERNATIONAL RELATIONS IN THE AGE OF THE CONFLICT BETWEEN DEMOCRACY AND DICTATOR-SHIP. 2d ed. New York: McGraw-Hill, 1954.

Chapter 10 on diplomacy.

Van Dyke, Vernon. INTERNATIONAL POLITICS. 3d ed. New York: Appleton-Century-Crofts, 1972.

Chapter 15 on peaceful change.

Wright, Quincy. THE STUDY OF INTERNATIONAL RELATIONS. New York: Appleton-Century-Crofts, 1955.

Chapters 15 and 16 on the art of diplomacy and the conduct of foreign relations.

Ziegler, David W. WAR, PEACE, AND INTERNATIONAL POLITICS. Boston: Little, Brown, 1977.

Chapter 15 on diplomacy.

American Foreign Relations General Textbooks

Some volumes dealing with American foreign relations contain separate chapters concerned with some aspect of the diplomatic process. Few such volumes address themselves directly to the overall subject of diplomacy, however. Other volumes--including some textbooks--which cope more comprehensively with the subject, are listed below in part II. The following represent shorter treatments contained in American foreign relations literature:

Beloff, Max. FOREIGN POLICY AND THE DEMOCRATIC PROCESS. Baltimore: Johns Hopkins Press, 1955.

    Chapter 3 on institutions of democratic foreign policy.

Hickman, Martin B., ed. PROBLEMS OF AMERICAN FOREIGN POLICY. 2d ed. Beverly Hills, Calif.: Glencoe, 1975.

    Chapters 2-3 on men and institutions in foreign policy process, and chapter 4 on diplomacy and diplomats.

Hoffmann, Stanley. GULLIVER'S TROUBLES: OR THE SETTING OF AMERICAN FOREIGN POLICY. New York: McGraw-Hill, 1968.

    Chapter 8 on men and methods in the foreign relations process.

Irish, Marian, and Frank, Elke. U.S. FOREIGN POLICY: CONTEXT, CONDUCT, CONTENT. New York: Harcourt, Brace, Jovanovich, 1975.

    Chapter 9 on diplomatic and psychological instruments of foreign policy.

Johnson, E.A.J., ed. THE DIMENSIONS OF DIPLOMACY. Baltimore: Johns Hopkins Press, 1964.

    Chapter 6 on techniques in diplomacy.

Kennan, George F. AMERICAN DIPLOMACY: 1900-1950. New York: New American Library, 1952.

    Chapter 6 on diplomacy in the modern world.

Lerche, Charles O., Jr. AMERICA IN WORLD AFFAIRS. New York: McGraw-Hill, 1963.

    Chapter 4 on agencies in the conduct of foreign affairs.

Morley, Felix. THE FOREIGN POLICY OF THE UNITED STATES. New York: Knopf, 1951.

    Chapters 9-12.

Nathan, James A., and Oliver, James K. UNITED STATES FOREIGN POLICY AND WORLD ORDER. Boston: Little, Brown, 1976.

    Especially chapters 12-14.

Perkins, Dexter. THE AMERICAN APPROACH TO FOREIGN POLICY. Cambridge, Mass.: Harvard University Press, 1952.

Chapter 8 on the executive and foreign relations.

Seabury, Paul. POWER, FREEDOM, AND DIPLOMACY: THE FOREIGN POLICY OF THE UNITED STATES OF AMERICA. New York: Random House, 1963.

Chapter 10 on the faces of diplomacy.

Wannamaker, Temple. AMERICAN FOREIGN POLICY TODAY. New York: Bantam, 1964.

Chapter 2 on the foreign policy apparatus.

Essays, Articles, and Journal Literature

Supplementing such short treatments as a segment of a broader subject, the following are illustrative of the essay literature on diplomacy appearing in contemporary journals. Most such essays are commentaries either on the subject in general, or on particular aspects of the diplomatic process. Additional essay literature on the new diplomacy is provided in chapter 5.

Abramson, M. "Scofflaws in Striped Pants." CORONET 48 (August 1960): 122-28.

Acheson, Dean G. "Morality, Moralism, and Diplomacy." YALE REVIEW 47 (June 1958): 481-93.

Ball, George W. "The Practice of Foreign Policy." DEPARTMENT OF STATE BULLETIN 46 (28 May 1962): 872-77.

Blake, Nelson Manfred. "Ambassadors at the Court of Theodore Roosevelt." MISSISSIPPI VALLEY HISTORICAL REVIEW 42 (September 1955): 179-206.

Caccia, Harold. "What Is Diplomacy?" VITAL SPEECHES 28 (1 November 1961): 42-44.

Cahier, Philippe, and Lee, Luke T. "Vienna Conventions on Diplomatic and Consular Relations." INTERNATIONAL CONCILIATION, no. 571 (January 1969): 1-76.

Cooper, Duff. "The World Still Needs the Diplomat." NEW YORK TIMES MAGAZINE, 25 July 1948, pp. 5, 33, 35.

Gavrilovic, S. "On the Science of Professional Diplomacy." REVIEW OF INTERNATIONAL SCIENCE ADMINISTRATION 26, no. 4 (1960): 412-16.

Griswold, A. Whitney. "Wormwood and Gall: An Introspective Note on American Diplomacy." FOREIGN AFFAIRS 39 (October 1960): 27-39.

Hill, Norman. "Give Diplomacy a Chance." SOUTH ATLANTIC QUARTERLY 55 (October 1956): 405-15.

Hovet, Thomas, Jr. "United Nations Diplomacy." JOURNAL OF INTERNA-TIONAL AFFAIRS 17 (1963): 29-41.

Hurley, John J., Jr., ed. AN INTRODUCTION TO DIPLOMATIC PRACTICE. Washington, D.C.: Foreign Service Institute, U.S. Department of State, 1971. 91 p.

    Consists of four essays--two on diplomacy, one on the reporting function of diplomats, and a short essay on literature in the field.

Kennan, George F. "Diplomacy as a Profession." FOREIGN SERVICE JOUR-NAL 38 (May 1961): 23-26.

_____. "The Future of Our Professional Diplomacy." FOREIGN AFFAIRS 33 (July 1955): 566-86.

_____. "Training for Statesmanship." ATLANTIC MONTHLY, May 1953, pp. 40-43.

Kirkpatrick, Ivone. "As a Diplomat Sees the Art of Diplomacy." NEW YORK TIMES MAGAZINE, 22 March 1959, pp. 13, 84, 86.

Kissinger, Henry A. "The Limitations of Diplomacy." NEW REPUBLIC, 9 May 1955, pp. 7-8.

Lauren, Paul Gordon. "Ultimate and Coercive Diplomacy." INTERNATIONAL STUDIES QUARTERLY 16 (June 1972): 131-65.

McGhee, George C. "Bedrock Diplomacy." SATURDAY REVIEW WORLD, 27 July 1974, pp. 5, 41.

Middleton, Drew. "Notes on Diplomats and Diplomacy." NEW YORK TIMES MAGAZINE, 30 October 1955, pp. 14, 58, 60.

Neilson, Francis. "Labyrinths of Diplomacy." AMERICAN JOURNAL OF ECONOMICS AND SOCIOLOGY 18 (October 1958): 1-14.

Plischke, Elmer. "Treatment of 'Diplomacy' in International Relations Text-books." WORLD AFFAIRS 135 (Spring 1973): 328-44.

Roucek, Joseph S. "Some Sociological Aspects of Diplomacy." JOURNAL OF HUMAN RELATIONS 8 (Winter 1960): 209-42.

Rusk, Dean. "Methods of Diplomacy." DEPARTMENT OF STATE BULLETIN 45 (14 August 1961): 287-88.

Russell, Francis H. "The Principal Tasks of Diplomacy." DEPARTMENT OF STATE BULLETIN 30 (8 February 1954): 207-8.

Sears, Albert D., comp. "Diplomacy: The Art of International Parley Is Examined in an International Medley." NEW YORK TIMES MAGAZINE, 22 April 1956, p. 60.

    A column of witty quotations.

Singer, J. David. "Limitations of Diplomacy." NATION, 9 July 1960, pp. 26-28.

Whitaker, Jennifer Seymour. "Poker-Chip Diplomacy." NATION, 27 March 1976, pp. 371-72.

FOREIGN-LANGUAGE LITERATURE

English literature may also be supplemented by an extensive library of foreign-language publications on diplomacy, including such twentieth-century volumes as:

Cambon, Jules M. LE DIPLOMATE. Paris: Hachette, 1926. 120 p.

Clark, Eric. CORPS DIPLOMATIQUE. The Hague: Nijhoff, 1973. 276 p. Bibliog.

De Heyking, Alphonse. LA THEORIE ET LA PRATIQUE DES SERVICES CONSULAIRES. 4 vols. The Hague: Academie de Droit International, 1930.

De Szilassy, Julius (Gyula). TRAITE PRACTIQUE DE DIPLOMATIE MODERNE. Paris: Payot, 1928. 256 p.

Genet, Raoul. TRAITE DE DIPLOMATIE ET DE DROIT DIPLOMATIQUE. 3 vols. Paris: Pedone, 1931-32.

Gerbore, Pietro. FORMEN UND STILE DER DIPLOMATIE. Reinbek near Hamburg, Germany: Rowohlt, 1964. 299 p.

Krekeler, Heinz L. DIE DIPLOMATIE. Munich: Olzog, 1965. 254 p. Bibliog.

Moussa, Farag. MANUEL DE PRATIQUE DIPLOMATIQUE: L'AMBASSADE. Brussels: Bruylant, 1972. 411 p. Bibliog.

Numelin, Ragnar J. DIPLOMATI. Stockholm: Natur Och Kultur, 1954. 193 p.

Patau, Paul. DE LA SITUATION COMPAREE DES AGENTS DIPLOMATIQUES ET CONSULAIRES. Toulouse, France: Dirion, 1910. 215 p.

Peralta, Jaime Peralta. LA INSTITUCION DIPLOMATICA. Santiago: Editorial Jucidica de Chile, 1951. 546 p. Bibliog.

Sallet, Richard. DER DIPLOMATISCHE DIENST: SEINE GESCHICHTE UND ORGANISATION IN FRANKREICH, GROSSBRITANNIEN UND DEN VEREINIGTEN STAATEN. Stuttgart: Deutsche Verlags-Anstalt, 1953. 366 p.

Seelos, Gebhard. MODERNE DIPLOMATIE. Bonn: Athenaeum, 1953. 99 p.

Stowell, Ellery C. LE CONSUL: FONCTIONS, IMMUNITIES, ORGANISATION, EXEQUATOR. Paris: Pedone, 1909. 353 p.

van der Essen, Leon. LA DIPLOMATIE. Brussels: P.D.L., 1953. 205 p.

von Bluecher, Wipert. WEGE UND IRRWEGE DER DIPLOMATIE. Wiesbaden: Limes, 1953. 184 p.

von Kuehlmann, Richard. DIE DIPLOMATEN. Berlin: Hobbing, 1939. 171 p.

Wildner, Heinrich. DIE TECHNIK DER DIPLOMATIE: L'ART DE NEGOCIER. Vienna: Springer, 1959. 342 p. Bibliog.

Earlier foreign-language works of interest (aside from those whose English versions are cited in other sections of this compilation) include the following writings. Such literature, largely published in French, represents a broad spectrum of approaches and treatment, and supplemented with memoirs, which are referred to in part IV, provides an essential resource for the study of diplomatic trends and places the study of U.S. foreign relations in historical perspective.

Bousquet, Georges. AGENTS DIPLOMATIQUES ET CONSULAIRES. Paris: Dupont, 1883. 272 p.

Coulon, Henri. DES AGENTS DIPLOMATIQUES. Paris: Marchal and Billard, 1889. 162 p.

de Callieres, Francoise. DE LA MANIERE DE NEGOCIER AVEC LES SOVER-AINS. Paris, 1716. 200 p. Reprint. Notre Dame, Ind.: Notre Dame University Press, 1963. 145 p.

de Cussy, Ferdinand. DICTIONNAIRE OU MANUEL-LEXIQUE DU DIPLO-MATE ET DU CONSUL. Leipzig: Brockhaus, 1846. 799 p.

de Garden, Guillaume. TRAITE COMPLET DE DIPLOMATIE. 3 vols. Paris: Treuttel and Wuertz, 1833.

de Martens, Charles. LE GUIDE DIPLOMATIQUE. 5th ed. 2 vols. Leipzig: Brockhaus, 1866.

Dumont, Jean. CORPS UNIVERSEL DIPLOMATIQUE DU DROIT DES GENS. 8 vols. Amsterdam: 1721-31. Reprint. 5 vols. with supplement. Amsterdam: Chez les Janssons, 1739.

Lehr, Ernest. MANUEL THEORIQUE ET PRATIQUE DES AGENTS DIPLOMATI-QUES ET CONSULAIRES FRANCAIS ET ETRANGERS. Paris: Larose and Forcel, 1888. 425 p.

Leroy, Paul. DES CONSULATS, DES LEGATIONS ET DES AMBASSADES. 2d ed. Paris: Maresco Aine, 1876. 247 p.

Meisel, August Heinrich. COURS DE STYLE DIPLOMATIQUE. 2 vols. Dresden, Germany, 1823; Paris: Ailland, 1826.

Monnet, Raphael. MANUEL DIPLOMATIQUE ET CONSULAIRE. Rev. ed. Paris: Berger-Levrault, 1905. 472 p. Originally published in 1899.

Murray, Eustace C.G. DROITS ET DEVOIRS DES ENVOYES DIPLOMATIQUES. London: Bentley, 1853. 18 p.

Pecquet, Antoine. DISCOURS SUR L'ART DE NEGOCIER. Paris: Chez Nyon, 1737. 168 p.

Pradier-Fodere, Paul L.E. COURS DE DROIT DIPLOMATIQUE. 2 vols. Paris: Pedone-Lauriel, 1881. 711 p.

Chapter 3

SPECIALIZED ASPECTS OF DIPLOMATIC PRACTICE

The second main category of literature dealing with diplomacy per se--in addition to studies of foreign offices, traditional diplomatic and consular personnel systems, and policy formulation and decision making--embraces the broad span of literature pertaining to such aspects of the diplomatic process as negotiation, international conferencing, protocol, language, diplomatic functions, asylum, specialized attaches, the nature, organization, and operation of diplomatic and consular missions, the feminine perspective, and the like. The following illustrate this extensive literature:

GUIDING PRINCIPLES OF CONDUCT

Bailey, Thomas A. THE ART OF DIPLOMACY: THE AMERICAN EXPERIENCE. New York: Appleton-Century-Crofts, 1968. 303 p. Bibliog.

> Brief analyses of 267 fundamental maxims for conduct of U.S. foreign relations.

Machiavelli, Niccolo. THE PRINCE. Translated by Luigi Ricci and revised by E.R.P. Vincent. New York: New American Library, 1952. 127 p.

> Regarded as a classic study of statesmanship, conduct of interrelations, and power wielding.

FOREIGN OFFICES, DIPLOMATIC CORPS, AND EMISSARIES OF OTHER COUNTRIES

Comprehensive literature in the English language on the diplomatic leadership, foreign offices, and diplomatic and consular services--unlike that which concerns U.S. practice--is scarce. The following, including a few foreign-language titles, may be helpful, for comparative purposes, in understanding U.S. practice:

Ashton-Gwatkin, Frank T. THE BRITISH FOREIGN SERVICE. Syracuse, N.Y.: Syracuse University Press, 1950. 94 p.

Baillou, Jean, and Pelletier, Pierre. LES AFFAIRES ESTRANGERES. Paris: Presses Universitaires de France, 1962. 378 p.

Bishop, Donald G. THE ADMINISTRATION OF BRITISH FOREIGN RELATIONS. Syracuse, N.Y.: Syracuse University Press, 1961. 410 p. Bibliog.

Boyce, Peter J. "Foreign Offices of New States." INTERNATIONAL JOURNAL 30 (Winter 1974-75): 141-61.

Brecher, Michael. THE FOREIGN POLICY SYSTEM OF ISRAEL: SETTING, IMAGES, PROCESS. New Haven, Conn.: Yale University Press, 1972. 693 p.

Bruce, James B. THE POLITICS OF SOVIET DECISION-MAKING: POLICY PATTERNS IN SELECT CASES. University of Denver Monograph Series in World Affairs, no. 13. Denver: University of Denver, 1976. 183 p.

Buck, Philip W., and Travis, Martin B., Jr., eds. CONTROL OF FOREIGN RELATIONS IN MODERN NATIONS. New York: Norton, 1957. 856 p. Bibliog.

Busk, Douglas. THE CRAFT OF DIPLOMACY: HOW TO RUN A DIPLOMATIC SERVICE. New York: Praeger, 1967; London: Pall Mall, 1967. 293 p.

Cadieux, Marcel. THE CANADIAN DIPLOMAT. Toronto: University of Toronto Press, 1962. 113 p.

Carlisle, Douglas. VENEZUELAN FOREIGN POLICY: ITS ORGANIZATION AND BEGINNING. Washington, D.C.: University Press of America, 1978. 224 p.

Cecil, Lamar. THE GERMAN DIPLOMATIC SERVICE, 1871-1914. Princeton, N.J.: Princeton University Press, 1976. 352 p. Bibliog.

Colegrove, Kenneth W. "The Japanese Foreign Office." AMERICAN JOURNAL OF INTERNATIONAL LAW 30 (October 1936): 585-613.

End, Heinrich. ERNEUERUNG DER DIPLOMATIE: DER AUSWAERTIGE DIENST DER BUNDESREPUBLIK DEUTSCHLAND: FOSSIL ODER INSTRUMENT? Neuwied and Berlin: Lauchterhand, 1969. 185 p.

Farrell, R. Barry. "Foreign Policy Formation in the Communist Countries of Eastern Europe." EAST EUROPEAN QUARTERLY 1 (March 1967): 39-74.

Federal Republic of Germany. Foreign Office. 100 JAHRE AUSWAERTIGES AMT, 1870-1970. Bonn: Auswaertiges Amt, 1970. 215 p.

Frank, Paul. "Reorganization in the German Foreign Office." AUSSENPOLI-TIK (English ed.) 24 (2d quarter 1973): 147-53.

Gottheil, Diane Levitt. "National Capital Diplomacy: A Study of Diplomats and the Diplomatic Community in Israel." Ph.D. dissertation, University of Illinois, 1973. 492 p.

Hoffmann, Erik P., and Fleron, Frederick J., Jr., eds. THE CONDUCT OF SOVIET FOREIGN POLICY. 2d ed. Hawthorne, N.Y.: Aldine, 1980. 792 p.

Especially chapter 2 and parts of chapter 4.

Horn, David Bayne. THE BRITISH DIPLOMATIC SERVICE (1689-1789). Ox-ford: Clarendon, 1961. 324 p.

Jenks, Carl Major. "The Structure of Diplomacy: An Analysis of Brazilian Foreign Relations in the Twentieth Century." Ph.D. dissertation, Duke University, 1979. 317 p.

Kanet, Roger E. SOVIET AND EAST EUROPEAN FOREIGN POLICY: A BIB-LIOGRAPHY OF ENGLISH AND RUSSIAN-LANGUAGE PUBLICATIONS, 1967-1971. Santa Barbara, Calif.: ABC-Clio Press, 1974. 208 p.

Kux, Dennis, and Boerner, Michael. "The German and American Foreign Service: A Comparative Look." FOREIGN SERVICE JOURNAL 50 (January 1973): 15-16, 20.

Meissner, Boris. "The Foreign Ministry and Foreign Service of the USSR." AUSSENPOLITIK (English ed.) 28 (1st Quarter 1977): 49-64.

Norton, Henry K. "Foreign Office Organization: A Comparison of the British, French, German, and Italian Foreign Offices with That of the Department of State of the United States of America." ANNALS OF THE AMERICAN ACADE-MY OF POLITICAL AND SOCIAL SCIENCE 143 (May 1929): supplement.

Roudybush, Franklin. FOREIGN SERVICE TRAINING. Besancon, France: Presse Comptoise, 1955. 279 p.

Comparative study of foreign service training in Brazil, England, France, Germany, Japan, Russia, Uruguay, and other countries.

Strang, William. THE FOREIGN OFFICE. London: Oxford University Press, 1955. 226 p.

A treatment of the British Foreign Office.

Tamkoc, Metin. THE WARRIOR DIPLOMATS: GUARDIANS OF THE NATIONAL SECURITY AND MODERNIZATION OF TURKEY. Salt Lake City: University of

Utah Press, 1976. 394 p. Bibliog.

Thordarson, Bruce. TRUDEAU AND FOREIGN POLICY: A STUDY IN DECI-SION-MAKING. Toronto: Oxford University Press, 1972. 231 p.

Tilley, John, and Gaselee, Stephen. THE FOREIGN OFFICE. London: Put-nam, 1933. 335 p. Bibliog.

A treatment of the British Foreign Office.

U.S. Commission on the Organization of the Government for the Conduct of Foreign Policy. "Comparative Foreign Practices." In COMMISSION ON THE ORGANIZATION OF THE GOVERNMENT FOR THE CONDUCT OF FOREIGN POLICY, JUNE 1975, Appendix R, vol. 6, pp. 357–408. Washington, D.C.: Government Printing Office, 1976.

Wallace, William. THE FOREIGN POLICY PROCESS IN BRITAIN. Winchester, Mass.: Allen and Unwin, 1977. 336 p.

NEGOTIATION AND NEGOTIATING STYLE

After World War II, special research and attention was paid specifically to the matter of international negotiation, and studies were published regarding it as a process, on East-West negotiating differences, and respecting its systematiza-tion and limitation. In addition to the recountings of diplomatic memoirs and analyses noted in other chapters, such as those dealing with peaceful settle-ment of disputes, crisis management, and systematic policy analysis, the fol-lowing exemplify such recent literature:

Bartos, Otomar J. PROCESS AND OUTCOME OF NEGOTIATIONS. New York: Columbia University Press, 1974. 451 p.

Bell, Coral. NEGOTIATING FROM STRENGTH: A STUDY IN THE POLITICS OF POWER. New York: Knopf, 1963. 248 p. Bibliog.

Blaker, Michael. JAPANESE INTERNATIONAL NEGOTIATING STYLE. New York: Columbia University Press, 1977. 253 p.

Deals with Japanese attitude toward diplomacy and negotiations, and Japanese negotiation strategies and tactics.

Craig, Gordon A. "Totalitarian Approaches to Diplomatic Negotiations." In STUDIES IN DIPLOMATIC HISTORY IN HONOUR OF G.P. GOOCH, edited by Arshag O. Sarkissian, pp. 107-25. New York: Barnes and Noble, 1961.

Creaghe, John S. "Personal Qualities and Effective Diplomatic Negotiation." Ph.D. dissertation, University of Maryland, 1965. 314 p. Bibliog.

Dennett, Raymond, and Johnson, Joseph E., eds. NEGOTIATING WITH THE RUSSIANS. Boston: World Peace Foundation, 1951. 310 p.

Symposium of ten essays by negotiating Americans.

Druckman, Daniel, ed. NEGOTIATIONS: SOCIAL-PSYCHOLOGICAL PER-SPECTIVES. Beverly Hills, Calif.: Sage, 1977. 416 p.

Dulles, John Foster. "The Role of Negotiation." DEPARTMENT OF STATE BULLETIN 38 (3 February 1958): 159-68.

Fedder, Edwin H. "Communication and American-Soviet Negotiating Behavior." BACKGROUND 8 (1964): 105-20.

Fontaine, Roger W. ON NEGOTIATING WITH CUBA. Washington, D.C.: American Enterprise Institute, 1975. 99 p.

Halle, Louis J. "The Art of Negotiating with the Russians." NEW YORK TIMES MAGAZINE, 12 June 1955, pp. 9, 59-60, 62, 64.

Hayter, William. THE DIPLOMACY OF THE GREAT POWERS. London: Hamilton, 1960; New York: Macmillan, 1961. 74 p.

Holsti, K.J. INTERNATIONAL POLITICS: A FRAMEWORK FOR ANALYSIS. Englewood Cliffs, N.J.: Prentice-Hall, 1967. 505 p.

Chapter 8 on diplomatic bargaining.

Ikle, Fred Charles. HOW NATIONS NEGOTIATE. New York: Praeger, 1964. 272 p. Bibliog.

_____. "Negotiating Skill: East and West." In DYNAMICS OF WORLD POLITICS: STUDIES IN THE RESOLUTION OF CONFLICT, edited by Linda B. Miller, pp. 20-43. Englewood Cliffs, N.J.: Prentice-Hall, 1968.

Ilich, John. THE ART AND SKILL OF SUCCESSFUL NEGOTIATION. Englewood Cliffs, N.J.: Prentice Hall, 1973. 205 p.

Jensen, Lloyd. "Soviet-American Bargaining Behavior in the Postwar Disarmament Negotiations." JOURNAL OF CONFLICT RESOLUTION 7 (September 1964): 522-41.

Joy, Charles Turner. HOW COMMUNISTS NEGOTIATE. New York: Macmillan, 1955. 178 p.

Kertesz, Stephen D. "Reflections on Soviet and American Negotiating Behavior." REVIEW OF POLITICS 19 (January 1957): 3-36.

Kohler, Foy D. "Negotiation as an Effective Instrument of American Foreign Policy." DEPARTMENT OF STATE BULLETIN 38 (2 June 1958): 901–10.

Lacy, William S.B. "Patience a Necessity in Negotiation." DEPARTMENT OF STATE BULLETIN 38 (3 March 1958): 327–28.

Lall, Arthur S. HOW COMMUNIST CHINA NEGOTIATES. New York: Columbia University Press, 1968. 291 p.

_____. MODERN ·INTERNATIONAL NEGOTIATION: PRINCIPLES AND PRACTICES. New York: Columbia University Press, 1966. 404 p.

Miller, Clyde R. THE PROCESS OF PERSUASION. New York: Crown, 1946. 234 p.

Deals with psychology of persuasive communication.

Nogee, Joseph L. "Propaganda and Negotiation: The Case of the Ten-Nation Disarmament Committee." JOURNAL OF CONFLICT RESOLUTION 7 (September 1963): 510–21.

Potter, Pitman B. "Rigid Versus Adjustable Techniques in Diplomacy." AMERICAN JOURNAL OF INTERNATIONAL LAW 45 (October 1951): 721–23.

Reston, James B. "Negotiating with the Russians." HARPER'S MAGAZINE, August 1947, pp. 97–106.

Rogers, William P. "The Necessity for Strength in an Era of Negotiations." DEPARTMENT OF STATE BULLETIN 68 (14 May 1973): 589–92.

Rubin, Jeffrey Z., and Brown, Bert R. THE SOCIAL PSYCHOLOGY OF BARGAINING AND NEGOTIATION. New York: Academic Press, 1975. 359 p.

Scott, Andrew M. "Bargaining and Negotiation." In his THE FUNCTIONING OF THE INTERNATIONAL POLITICAL SYSTEM, pp. 172–82. New York: Macmillan, 1967.

Spector, Bertram I. "The Effects of Personality, Perception, and Power on the Bargaining Process and Outcome: A Field Theory and Political Analysis of a Negotiation Simulation." Ph.D. dissertation, New York University, 1972. 276 p.

U.S. Congress. Senate. Committee on Government Operations. Subcommittee on National Security and International Operations. INTERNATIONAL NEGOTIATION. 91st Cong., 1st and 2d sess. Washington, D.C.: Government Printing Office, 1969-70.

Series of studies, including PEKING'S APPROACH TO NEGOTIA-
TION: SELECTED WRITINGS (94 p.) and THE SOVIET APPROACH
TO NEGOTIATION: SELECTED WRITINGS (92 p.).

_____. INTERNATIONAL NEGOTIATION: AMERICAN SHORTCOMINGS
IN NEGOTIATION WITH COMMUNIST POWERS. 91st Cong., 2d sess.
Washington, D.C.: Government Printing Office, 1970. 17 p.

_____. NEGOTIATION AND STATECRAFT: A SELECTION OF READINGS.
91st Cong., 2d sess. Washington, D.C.: Government Printing Office, 1970.
59 p.

Compilation of 36 unofficial readings.

"When Diplomats Confer--The Art of Negotiation." NEWSWEEK, 10 April
1961, pp. 46-47.

Young, Kenneth Todd. NEGOTIATING WITH THE CHINESE COMMUNISTS:
THE UNITED STATES EXPERIENCE, 1953-1967. New York: McGraw-Hill,
1968. 461 p. Bibliog.

Zartman, I. William, ed. THE NEGOTIATION PROCESS: THEORIES AND
APPLICATIONS. Beverly Hills, Calif.: Sage, 1978. 244 p.

INTERNATIONAL CONFERENCES

Study of international conferences as a diplomatic process gained considerable
interest following World War I. Certain of the items listed below--especially
those of Dunn, Hankey, Hill, Pastuhov, and Satow, who produced basic analyses of multilateral conferences--illustrate the results of such concern. A few,
including those of Hester and Kaufmann, deal with developments since World
War II. Recent emphasis, however, is often directed at specific conferences--
represented by the studies of Davis and O'Connor, as well as a number of
doctoral dissertations. In addition, especially since World War II, studies of
conferences within the international organization--or "parliamentary diplomacy"
--have been published and are included in the last section of chapter 5.
Analyses of summit conferences, aside from a few listed here, are contained in
the section of chapter 7 that deals with presidential or summit diplomacy.
Official documents on conference management and participation are provided
in chapter 22, section on "International Conferences and Organizations." Biographical and memoir literature, listed in part IV, recount the roles played by
individual conference participants.

Baldwin, Simeon E. "The International Congresses and Conferences of the Last
Century as Forces Working Toward Solidarity of the World." AMERICAN JOUR-
NAL OF INTERNATIONAL LAW 1 (July, October 1907): 808-29.

Beitzell, Robert Egner. "Major Strategic Conferences of the Allies, 1941-1943: Quadrant, Moscow, Sextant and Eureka." Ph.D. dissertation, University of North Carolina (Chapel Hill), 1967. 518 p.

Burnett, Philip Mason. PREPARATION AT THE PARIS PEACE CONFERENCE FROM THE STANDPOINT OF THE AMERICAN DELEGATION. 2 vols. New York: Columbia University Press, 1940. 1,981 p.; abridged version, without documents, New York: Columbia University Press, 1940. 209 p.

   Concerns World War I peace conference.

Davis, Calvin DeArmond. THE UNITED STATES AND THE FIRST HAGUE PEACE CONFERENCE. Ithaca, N.Y.: Cornell University Press, 1962. 236 p.

Dunn, Frederick S. THE PRACTICE AND PROCEDURE OF INTERNATIONAL CONFERENCES. Baltimore: Johns Hopkins Press, 1929. 229 p.

Eckes, Alfred Edward, Jr. "Bretton Woods: America's New Deal for an Open World." Ph.D. dissertation, University of Texas (Austin), 1969.

Eubank, Keith. THE SUMMIT CONFERENCES, 1919-1960. Norman: University of Oklahoma Press, 1966. 225 p.

Galtung, Johan. "Summit Meetings and International Relations." JOURNAL OF PEACE RESEARCH 1, no. 1 (1964): 36-54.

Gordon, Lincoln. "Punta del Este Revisited." FOREIGN AFFAIRS 45 (July 1967): 624-38.

Hankey, Maurice. DIPLOMACY BY CONFERENCE. London: Smith, 1920. 179 p.

_____. DIPLOMACY BY CONFERENCE: STUDIES IN PUBLIC AFFAIRS, 1920-1946. London: Benn, 1946. 179 p.

Hester, Donald C. "Practice and Procedure in Preparing for International Conferences--With Special Emphasis on United States Techniques." Ph.D. dissertation, University of Maryland, 1959. 541 p. Bibliog.

Hill, Norman L. THE PUBLIC INTERNATIONAL CONFERENCE: ITS FUNCTION, ORGANIZATION AND PROCEDURE. Palo Alto, Calif.: Stanford University Press, 1929. 267 p. Bibliog.

Kaufmann, Johan. CONFERENCE DIPLOMACY: AN INTRODUCTORY ANALYSIS. Dobbs Ferry, N.Y.: Oceana, 1968. 222 p.

Middleton, Drew. "Backstage at a Global Conference." NEW YORK TIMES MAGAZINE, 18 March 1962, pp. 34, 130-33.

Moulton, Mildred. "A Structural View of the Conference as an Organ of International Cooperation: An Examination Emphasizing Post-War Practice as Shown in the Organization of Some Typical Conferences." Ph.D. dissertation, New York University, 1930. 126 p.

Mowat, Robert Balmain. INTERNATIONAL RELATIONS. Freeport, N.Y.: Books for Libraries Press, 1966.

    Chapters 8-10 on diplomacy by conference.

O'Connor, Raymond Gish. PERILOUS EQUILIBRIUM: THE UNITED STATES AND THE LONDON NAVAL CONFERENCE OF 1930. Lawrence: University of Kansas Press, 1962. 188 p.

O'Davoren, William. POST-WAR RECONSTRUCTION CONFERENCES: THE TECHNICAL ORGANIZATION OF INTERNATIONAL CONFERENCES. London: King and Staples, 1943. 166 p.

Pastuhov, Vladimir D. A GUIDE TO THE PRACTICE OF INTERNATIONAL CONFERENCES. Washington, D.C.: Carnegie Endowment, 1945. 275 p. Bibliog.

    Revision and enlargement of INTERNATIONAL CONFERENCES AND THEIR TECHNIQUE: A HANDBOOK (1944).

Pickering, Laurence Gene. "The United States and the Post-World War II International Trade Conferences." Ph.D. dissertation, University of Nebraska, 1954.

Plischke, Elmer. "The International Conference" and "International Conference Procedure." In his CONDUCT OF AMERICAN DIPLOMACY, pp. 469-95; 496-523. 3d ed. Princeton, N.J.: Van Nostrand, 1967.

_____. "International Conferences." In his INTERNATIONAL RELATIONS: BASIC DOCUMENTS, pp. 38-50. 2d ed. Princeton, N.J.: Van Nostrand, 1962.

    Contains documents illustrating conference procedure, including invitation, conference and delegation structure, flow chart, agenda, rules of procedure, voting, and final act.

_____. "International Conferencing and the Summit: Macro-Analysis of Presidential Participation. ORBIS 14 (Fall 1970): 673-713.

_____. "Summit Conferences." In his SUMMIT DIPLOMACY: PERSONAL DIPLOMACY OF THE PRESIDENT OF THE UNITED STATES, pp. 69-101. College Park: Bureau of Governmental Research, University of Maryland, 1958.

Ramberg, Bennett. "The Seabed Arms Control Negotiation: A Study of Multilateral Arms Control Conference Diplomacy." Ph.D. dissertation, Johns Hopkins University, 1975. 206 p.

Satow, Ernest M. A GUIDE TO DIPLOMATIC PRACTICE. London: Longmans, Green, 1917. 4th ed., edited by Nevile Bland, 1957. 510 p.

Chapters 25 and 26 on international conferences in 1917 edition. Also chapter 22 of fourth edition.

_____. INTERNATIONAL CONGRESSES. London: H.M. Stationery, 1920. 168 p.

Sharp, Walter R. "The Scientific Study of International Conferences." INTERNATIONAL SOCIAL SCIENCE BULLETIN 2 (Spring 1950): 104-16.

Sullivan, Mark. THE GREAT ADVENTURE AT WASHINGTON: THE STORY OF THE CONFERENCE. Garden City, N.Y.: Doubleday, Page, 1922. 290 p.

Account of the Washington naval arms limitation conference of 1921-22.

"The Technique of International Conferences" and "The United Nations, the Specialized Agencies and the Technique of Conferences." INTERNATIONAL SOCIAL SCIENCE BULLETIN 5, no. 2 (1953): 233-388.

U.S. Department of State. UNITED NATIONS CONFERENCE ON DIPLOMATIC INTERCOURSE AND IMMUNITIES, VIENNA, AUSTRIA, MARCH 2-APRIL 14, 1961. Washington, D.C.: Government Printing Office, 1962. 65 p.

PROTOCOL

Protocol, precedence, and diplomatic etiquette and procedure are included among the matters that have been given increased literary attention since World War II. Although most published commentary is in the nature of essays, appearing in either the DEPARTMENT OF STATE BULLETIN or popular magazines, a few more comprehensive analyses have been produced--see those of Buchanan, Miller, Radlovic, Symington, and Wood and Serres. A number of authors have served as chiefs of protocol since 1945, including Wiley T. Buchanan, Angier Biddle Duke (two appointments), John F. Simmons, James W. Symington, and Stanley Woodward. For comprehensive source material on the subject, the following books and articles need to be supplemented by chronicles of earlier diplomatists, the recountings of emissaries in their memoirs, and commentaries contained in general volumes on diplomacy included in other sections of this compilation.

Baker, Russell. "About Protocol." NEW YORK TIMES MAGAZINE, 22 September 1957, p. 76.

Buchanan, Wiley T., Jr. "An Old Hand at Protocol Recalls His White-Tie Years: It's the Most Fascinating Job in Washington." LIFE, 12 March 1965, pp. 74-75.

_____. "Protocol: The Fine Art of Pleasing the Nation's Guests." HOUSE AND GARDEN, July 1962, p. 86.

_____. RED CARPET AT THE WHITE HOUSE: FOUR YEARS AS CHIEF OF PROTOCOL IN THE EISENHOWER ADMINISTRATION. New York: Dutton, 1964. 256 p.

Cahn, Patricia. "Washington's Hostesses Serve Their National Specialties as Diplomatic Delicacies." SATURDAY EVENING POST, 26 May 1962, pp. 22-23.

"Dean's Diplomatic Dinner Party: Norway's Ambassador Continues a Tradition." LIFE, 11 March 1957, pp. 183-85.

Duke, Angier Biddle. "The Functions of Protocol in Today's World." DEPARTMENT OF STATE BULLETIN 50 (2 March 1964): 344-47.

_____. "Perspectives in Protocol." DEPARTMENT OF STATE BULLETIN 44 (20 March 1961): 414-18.

_____. "Protocol and Peacekeeping." DEPARTMENT OF STATE BULLETIN 51 (23 November 1964): 736-39.

_____. "Protocol and the Conduct of Foreign Affairs." DEPARTMENT OF STATE BULLETIN 49 (4 November 1963): 700-704.

"Greeter to the World." TIME, 6 December 1954, pp. 29-30.

Article about Protocol Officer John Farr Simmons.

Harkness, Richard, and Harkness, Gladys. "The Strange Business of Protocol." READER'S DIGEST, May 1956, pp. 41-44.

Higgins, Marjorie. "He Takes the Starch Out of Protocol." SATURDAY EVENING POST, 29 September 1962, pp. 24-25.

Article about Angier Biddle Duke.

Holzheimer, Hermann. "Protocol as a Function of Foreign Policy." AUSSEN-POLITIK (English ed.) 27 (3d quarter 1976): 349-60.

Kahn, E.T., Jr. "Profiles: Common Manners and Common Sense." NEW YORKER, 15 August 1964, p. 34 ff.

Article about Angier Biddle Duke.

Miller, Hope Ridings. EMBASSY ROW: THE LIFE AND TIMES OF DIPLO-MATIC WASHINGTON. New York: Holt, Rinehart, and Winston, 1969. 286 p.

Moreno, Salcedo Louis. A GUIDE TO PROTOCOL. Rev. ed. Manila: University Book Supply, 1959. 280 p. Bibliog.

Radlovic, I. Monte. ETIQUETTE AND PROTOCOL: A HANDBOOK OF CON-DUCT IN AMERICAN AND INTERNATIONAL CIRCLES. New York: Harcourt, Brace, 1957. 240 p.

"Rules of Precedence Relating to Foreign Service and Government Officers." DEPARTMENT OF STATE BULLETIN 19 (10 October 1948): 475.

Simmons, John F. "How We Work With Other Nations." DEPARTMENT OF STATE BULLETIN 33 (18 July 1955): 91-94.

Symington, James W. THE STATELY GAME. New York: Macmillan, 1971. 256 p.

Talmey, Allene. "Who Sits Where Now?" VOGUE, June 1961, pp. 64-65.

U.S. Department of State. Historical Office. "The Protocol Function in United States Foreign Relations: Its Administration and Development, 1776-1968." Research Project no. 767, October 1968. Washington, D.C.: De-partment of State, 1968. 85 p.

"Vodka Diplomacy: How U.S. Meets It." U.S. NEWS AND WORLD REPORT, 13 July 1956, pp. 61-63.

Wood, John Rhoden, and Serres, Jean. DIPLOMATIC CEREMONIAL AND PROTOCOL: PRINCIPLES, PROCEDURES AND PRACTICES. New York: Columbia University Press, 1970. 384 p. Bibliog.

Woodward, Stanley. "Protocol: What It Is and What It Does." DEPARTMENT OF STATE BULLETIN 21 (3 October 1949): 501-3.

Official commentary concerning U.S. practice over the years, with emphasis on legal rights and proprieties concerning diplomatic protocol and ceremonial, are provided in:

Hackworth, Green H. DIGEST OF INTERNATIONAL LAW. Washington, D.C.: Government Printing Office, 1943. Vol. 4, pp. 632-42.

Moore, John Bassett. A DIGEST OF INTERNATIONAL LAW. Washington, D.C.: Government Printing Office, 1906. Vol. 4, pp. 726-80.

Whiteman, Marjorie M. DIGEST OF INTERNATIONAL LAW. Washington, D.C.: Government Printing Office, 1970. Vol. 7, pp. 487-502.

For official purposes, matters of precedence and protocol are determined by the chief of protocol, a ranking Department of State official, and his staff. Since 1930, however, an unofficial social register and directory has been privately published, titled THE SOCIAL LIST OF WASHINGTON AND SOCIAL PRECE-DENCE IN WASHINGTON (Washington, D.C.: Carolyn Hagner Shaw and previously by her mother. Annual.) It is popularly called "The Green Book" because of its green suede-finished cover. It constitutes a current guide to approximately five thousand members of official and social Washington society, including the names of public officials, foreign diplomats and their staffs, and other prominent persons in the national capital. It also provides tables of un-official precedence, notes on matters of protocol, and advice on matters of oral and written address and social form.

DRESS AND ADDRESS

Although little has been published separately that systematically examines the language, dress, appearance, and manners of diplomats, some literature is emerging, the following of which is concerned primarily with diplomatic lan-guage. Except for Alexander Ostrower's comprehensive study and those of Ekvall and Roudybush, this literature generally is published in popular magazines. The statement by William S. Strang probably portends growing criticism of changing, if not retrograding, language employed in popular diplomatic forums. Additional commentary may be gleaned from references cited in chapter 5 on the new diplomacy.

Ekvall, Robert Brainerd. FAITHFUL ECHO: THE ROLE OF LANGUAGE IN DIPLOMACY. New York: Twayne, 1960. 125 p.

Ostrower, Alexander. LANGUAGE, LAW AND DIPLOMACY: A STUDY OF LINGUISTIC DIVERSITY IN OFFICIAL INTERNATIONAL RELATIONS AND

INTERNATIONAL LAW. 2 vols. Philadelphia: University of Pennsylvania Press, 1965. 963 p. Bibliog.

Phillips, Joseph B. "Diplomatic Shop Talk." NEWSWEEK, 10 January 1949, p. 37.

Plischke, Elmer. "From Satin and Lace to Tweeds," "Changes in the Language of Diplomacy," and "Changes in Style of Diplomatic Communications." In his CONDUCT OF AMERICAN DIPLOMACY, pp. 16-22. 3d ed. Princeton, N.J.: Van Nostrand, 1967.

Roudybush, Franklin. DIPLOMATIC LANGUAGE. Basel, Switzerland: Satz, 1972. 24 p.

Shenton, Herbert Newhard. COSMOPOLITAN CONVERSATION: THE LANGUAGE PROBLEMS OF INTERNATIONAL CONFERENCES. New York: Columbia University Press, 1933. 803 p.

Sorensen, Theodore C. "The Importance of Being Civil." SATURDAY REVIEW, 26 November 1966, p. 30.

Strang, William S. "New Harsh Language in Diplomacy." NEW YORK TIMES MAGAZINE, 15 April 1962, pp. 27, 118-20.

"Today's Diplomacy Needs Yesterday's Manners." SATURDAY EVENING POST, 18 December 1948, p. 112.

"Will Overalls Succeed Spats for Diplomats?" SATURDAY EVENING POST, 8 October 1955, p. 12.

ACTIVITIES AND FUNCTIONS OF DIPLOMATS

The following merely illustrate an extensive literature on the activities and functions of diplomats. Additional commentary, both generalized and particularized, is contained in most biographies and memoirs as well as in many other volumes and articles on diplomacy and on specific aspects of American foreign relations included in later sections of this compilation.

Akzin, Benjamin. PROPAGANDA BY DIPLOMATS. Washington, D.C.: Digest, 1936. 22 p.

Bonner, Paul H. AMBASSADOR EXTRAORDINARY. New York: Scribner, 1962. 306 p.

Cambon, Jules M. THE DIPLOMATIST. Translated by C.R. Turner. London: Allan, 1931. 151 p.

Craig, Gordon A., and Gilbert, Felix, eds. THE DIPLOMATS: 1919-1939. 2 vols. Princeton, N.J.: Princeton University Press, 1953. 700 p.

de Callieres, Francoise. ON THE MANNER OF NEGOTIATING WITH PRINCES. Translated by A.F. Whyte. Boston: Houghton Mifflin, 1919. Reprint. Notre Dame, Ind.: Notre Dame University Press, 1963. 145 p.

Dunham, Donald C. ENVOY UNEXTRAORDINARY. New York: Day, 1944. London: Hammond, Hammond, 1946. 162 p.

Harr, John Ensor. THE PROFESSIONAL DIPLOMAT. Princeton, N.J.: Princeton University Press, 1969. 404 p. Bibliog.

Jusserand, Jean A.A. Jules. THE SCHOOL FOR AMBASSADORS, AND OTHER ESSAYS. New York: Putnam, 1925. 355 p.

Spaulding, E. Wilder. AMBASSADORS ORDINARY AND EXTRAORDINARY. Washington, D.C.: Public Affairs, 1961. 302 p. Bibliog.

Strang, William S. THE DIPLOMATIC CAREER. London: Deutsch, 1962. 160 p.

Thayer, Charles W. DIPLOMAT. New York: Harper, 1959. 299 p. Bibliog.

Tully, Andrew M. WHITE TIE AND DAGGER. New York: Morrow, 1967. 277 p.

DIPLOMATIC ASYLUM

Two basic types of asylum need to be distinguished. On the one hand, there is "territorial asylum," or the affording of refuge within the territory of a foreign state. It is related to principles of immigration, expatriation, and naturalization. The extensive literature on these subjects, involving substantive policy and practice, is not included in this survey. On the other hand, "diplomatic and consular asylum," or "exterritorial asylum," is concerned with the granting of sanctuary in embassies, legations, and consular establishments, or in the residences or other property of foreign diplomats and consuls. More broadly speaking, this also may be identified as "extraterritorial asylum" when refuge aboard foreign public vessels and aircraft within territorial waters or the national airspace is included. The literature on this aspect of asylum is to be found primarily in international law textbooks, commentaries, and compilations of cases, which need to be consulted in addition to the following illustrative monographs and essays:

Briggs, Herbert W. "The Colombian-Peruvian Asylum Case and Proof of Customary International Law." AMERICAN JOURNAL OF INTERNATIONAL LAW 45 (October 1951): 728-31.

Evans, Alona E. "The Colombian-Peruvian Asylum Case: The Practice of Diplomatic Asylum." AMERICAN POLITICAL SCIENCE REVIEW 46 (March 1952): 142-57.

Garcia Mora, Manuel R. "The Colombian-Peruvian Asylum Case and the Doctrine of Human Rights." VIRGINIA LAW REVIEW 37 (November 1951): 927-65.

_____. INTERNATIONAL LAW AND ASYLUM AS A HUMAN RIGHT. Washington, D.C.: Public Affairs, 1956. 171 p.

Gilbert, Barry. "The Practice of Asylum in Legations and Consulates of the United States." AMERICAN JOURNAL OF INTERNATIONAL LAW 3 (July 1909): 562-95.

Greenburgh, R.B., and Duncan, Harold. "Recent Developments in the Law of Diplomatic Asylum." In GROTIUS SOCIETY TRANSACTIONS FOR THE YEAR 1955, pp. 103-22. London: Grotius Society, 1956.

Moore, John Bassett. ASYLUM IN LEGATIONS AND CONSULATES AND IN VESSELS. New York: Ginn, 1892. 94 p. Reprinted from POLITICAL SCIENCE QUARTERLY 7 (1892): 1-37, 197-231, 397-418.

Morgenstern, Felice. "Extra-Territorial Asylum." BRITISH YEAR BOOK OF INTERNATIONAL LAW 25 (1948): 236-61.

_____. "The Right of Asylum." BRITISH YEAR BOOK OF INTERNATIONAL LAW 26 (1949): 327-57.

Ronning, C. Neale. DIPLOMATIC ASYLUM: LEGAL NORMS AND POLITICAL REALITY IN LATIN AMERICAN RELATIONS. The Hague: Nijhoff, 1965. 242 p. Bibliog.

Although some materials, such as the articles on the Colombian-Peruvian asylum case, do not involve the United States as a direct participant, they analyze important diplomatic policy and legal principles which, in this particular case, entail Latin American as compared with U.S. practice, and which are important in inter-American relations. U.S. legal policy and practice concerning the various forms of asylum are discussed in some detail in:

Hackworth, Green H. DIGEST OF INTERNATIONAL LAW. Washington, D.C.: Government Printing Office, 1941. Vol. 2, pp. 621-49.

Moore, John Bassett. A DIGEST OF INTERNATIONAL LAW. Washington, D.C.: Government Printing Office, 1906. Vol. 2, pp. 755-883.

Whiteman, Marjorie M. DIGEST OF INTERNATIONAL LAW. Washington, D.C.: Government Printing Office, 1968. Vol. 6, pp. 428-502.

ATTACHES AND OTHER SPECIALIZED DIPLOMATIC OFFICIALS

Governments appoint a variety of specialized attaches to their diplomatic missions abroad. These may include specialists on such subjects as agricultural, commercial, cultural, educational, financial, labor, maritime, military (army, navy, and air), scientific, and other affairs. Little literature has been published on such diplomatic officers and their functions. A number of additional types of extraordinary diplomatic officers may be commissioned, such as ambassadors at large, political advisers to military commands (called POLADs by the United States), and executive agents or special representatives. Published literature on such appointees and their activities, though also scarce, is represented by a number of items contained in the following list. The studies of Boyes, Calhoun, and Erskine deal with special political advisers (POLADs), those by Nostrand and the U.S. Department of State concern the cultural attache, and those by Beauvais and Vagts review the nature and functions of military attaches. The studies of Waters and Wriston analyze the role of special presidential representatives generally, whereas those of Burke address themselves to the post-World War II office of ambassador at large. Additional materials on U.S. presidential special agents and missions is presented in chapter 7, section on summit diplomacy.

Beauvais, Armand Paul. ATTACHES MILITAIRES, ATTACHES NAVALS ET ATTACHES DE L'AIR. Paris: Presses Modernes, 1937. 214 p. Bibliog.

Berman, Maureen R., and Johnson, Joseph E. UNOFFICIAL DIPLOMATS. New York: Columbia University Press, 1977. 268 p.

　　Contains part 1, on unofficial conferences and meetings, and part 2, on the role of private persons in international affairs.

Boyes, Jon L. "The Political Adviser (POLAD): The Role of the Diplomatic Adviser to Selected United States and North Atlantic Alliance Military Commanders." Ph.D. dissertation, University of Maryland, 1971. 593 p. Bibliog.

Brady, James Reginald. "Problems of Implementing American Foreign Assistance Projects: Perceptions of the USAID Advisor." Ph.D. dissertation, University of Michigan, 1971. 294 p.

Burke, Lee H. "The Ambassador at Large: A Study in Diplomatic Method." Ph.D. dissertation, University of Maryland, 1971. 311 p. Bibliog.

_____. AMBASSADOR AT LARGE: DIPLOMAT EXTRAORDINARY. The Hague: Nijhoff, 1972. 176 p. Bibliog.

Calhoun, John A. "Diplomats and Commanders: A Study of Relations Between American Political Representatives and Military Commanders." U.S. Air War College, 1956. 74 p.

Erskine, John C. "The Role of the Political Adviser in the U.S. Armed Forces." Thesis, U.S. Army War College, 1960. 98 p.

Moore, John Bassett. A DIGEST OF INTERNATIONAL LAW. Washington, D.C.: Government Printing Office, 1906. Vol. 4, pp. 437-45.

Nichols, Roy F. ADVANCE AGENTS OF AMERICAN DESTINY. Philadelphia: University of Pennsylvania Press, 1956. 254 p.

   On diplomatic and consular agents other than those assigned to
   regular residential missions.

Nostrand, Howard Lee. THE CULTURAL ATTACHE. New Haven, Conn.: Hazen Foundation, n.d. 45 p.

Paullin, Charles O. DIPLOMATIC NEGOTIATIONS OF AMERICAN NAVAL OFFICERS, 1778-1883. Baltimore: Johns Hopkins Press, 1912. 380 p.

Sayre, Wallace S., and Thurber, Clarence E. TRAINING FOR SPECIALIZED MISSION PERSONNEL. Chicago: Public Administration Service, 1952. 85 p.

Smith, Cordell Audivell. "The Marshall Mission: Its Impact Upon American Foreign Policy Toward China, 1945-1949." Ph.D. dissertation, University of Oklahoma, 1963. 294 p.

U.S. Congress. Senate. Committee on Government Operations. Subcommittee on National Security and International Operations. POLITICAL ADVISERS TO U.S. MILITARY COMMANDERS: ANALYSIS AND ASSESSMENT. 91st Cong., 1st sess., committee print. Washington, D.C.: Government Printing Office, 1969. 18 p.

_____. STATE-DEFENSE OFFICER EXCHANGE PROGRAM: ANALYSIS AND ASSESSMENT. 91st Cong., 1st sess., committee print. Washington, D.C.: Government Printing Office, 1969. 16 p.

_____. STATE DEPARTMENT ADVISERS TO MILITARY TRAINING INSTITU-TIONS: ANALYSIS AND ASSESSMENT. 91st Cong., 1st sess., committee print. Washington, D.C.: Government Printing Office, 1969. 22 p.

U.S. Department of State. THE AMERICAN AGRICULTURAL ATTACHE. Washington, D.C.: Government Printing Office, 1957. 23 p.

_____. THE SCIENCE ADVISER OF THE DEPARTMENT OF STATE. Washington, D.C.: Government Printing Office, 1960. 27 p.

Includes section on science attaches.

"U.S. Scientists to Serve as Attaches in Overseas Posts." DEPARTMENT OF STATE BULLETIN 25 (6 August 1951): 234-35.

Vagts, Alfred. THE MILITARY ATTACHE. Princeton, N.J.: Princeton University Press, 1967. 408 p. Bibliog.

Waters, Maurice. THE AD HOC DIPLOMAT. The Hague: Nijhoff, 1963. 233 p. Bibliog.

_____. "The Ad Hoc Diplomat: A Legal and Historical Analysis." WAYNE LAW REVIEW 6 (Summer 1960): 380-92.

Wriston, Henry M. EXECUTIVE AGENTS IN AMERICAN FOREIGN RELATIONS. Baltimore: Johns Hopkins Press, 1929. 874 p.

_____. "The Special Envoy." FOREIGN AFFAIRS 38 (January 1960): 219-37.

FEMININE DIMENSION

A limited amount of literature has been published representing the feminine perspective on diplomatic life and practice. This material is often overlooked, but, with more women being appointed to the Foreign Service and as chiefs of diplomatic missions, it is likely to increase. Largely of the twentieth century, this literature consists primarily of individualized memoirs and reminiscences by and about women diplomats or the wives and other female members of the families of diplomats. The following selections do not include biographies of others written by women. For a more complete listing of memoirs, biographies, and commentaries, see part IV, "Memoirs and Biographical Literature."

Allen, Katharine M. FOREIGN SERVICE DIARY. Washington, D.C.: Potomac, 1967. 285 p.

Anderson, Isabel Weld [Perkins]. PRESIDENTS AND PIES: LIFE IN WASHINGTON, 1897-1919. Boston: Houghton Mifflin, 1920. 290 p.

Author was the wife of Ambassador Larz Anderson.

Baldridge, Letitia. OF DIAMONDS AND DIPLOMATS. Boston: Houghton Mifflin, 1968. 337 p.

Autobiography of private secretary to wife of Ambassador David K.
Bruce and secretary to Ambassador Clare Boothe Luce.

Bax, Emily. MISS BAX OF THE EMBASSY. Boston: Houghton Mifflin, 1939.
310 p.

Boyce, Richard Fyfe. THE DIPLOMAT'S WIFE. New York: Harper, 1956. 230 p.

Calkin, Homer L. WOMEN IN THE DEPARTMENT OF STATE: THEIR ROLE
IN AMERICAN FOREIGN AFFAIRS. 2d ed. Washington, D.C.: Government
Printing Office, 1978. 322 p.

A history of women in the Department of State and the Foreign
Service, with charts and tables.

Cerruti, Elizabeth P. AMBASSADOR'S WIFE. New York: Macmillan, 1952.
255 p.

Child, Maude Parker. THE SOCIAL SIDE OF DIPLOMATIC LIFE. Indianapolis:
Bobbs-Merrill, 1926. 305 p.

Also see works by Maude Parker cited below, p. 52.

d'Anethan, Baroness Elenora Mary [Haggard]. FOURTEEN YEARS OF DIPLO-
MATIC LIFE IN JAPAN. New York: McBride, Nast, 1912. 471 p.

de Bunsen, Madam Charles [Mary Isabella]. IN THREE LEGATIONS. New
York: Unwin, 1909. 375 p.

Dodd, Martha. MY YEARS IN GERMANY. London: Golancz, 1940. 319 p.

_____. THROUGH EMBASSY EYES. New York: Harcourt, Brace, 1939.
382 p.

Fraser, Mrs. Hugh [Mary C.]. A DIPLOMAT'S WIFE IN MANY LANDS.
2 vols. New York: Dodd, Mead, 1910.

_____. REMINISCENCES OF A DIPLOMAT'S WIFE. New York: Dodd,
Mead, 1912. 395 p.

Harper, Elizabeth J. THE ROLE OF WOMEN IN INTERNATIONAL DIPLO-
MACY. Washington, D.C.: U.S. Department of State, 1972. 8 p.

Survey of practice of some seventy countries, largely Third World
and non-European.

Harriman, Florence Jaffray. MISSION TO THE NORTH. Philadelphia: Lippincott, 1941. 331 p.

Hatch, Alden. AMBASSADOR EXTRAORDINARY: CLARE BOOTH LUCE. New York: Holt, 1956. 254 p.

Hoyt, Jo Wasson. FOR THE LOVE OF MIKE. New York: Random House, 1966. 210 p.

On diplomatic and consular service.

Imbrie, Katherine [Gillespie]. DATA RELATING TO THE ASSASSINATION OF UNITED STATES CONSULAR OFFICER ROBERT WHITNEY IMBRIE "BY THE MILITARY POLICE OF PERSIA" IN TEHRAN, PERSIA, JULY 18, 1924. Frederick, Md.: By the author, 1939. 45 p.

Johnson, Lady Bird [Claudia]. A WHITE HOUSE DIARY. New York: Holt, Rinehart, and Winston, 1970. 806 p.

Kelly, Hank [Henry Warren], and Kelly, Dot [Dorothy Smith]. DANCING DIPLOMATS. Albuquerque: University of New Mexico Press, 1950. 254 p.

Kirk, Lydia [Chapin]. POSTMARKED MOSCOW. New York: Scribner, 1952. 278 p.

Lawrence, May Viola [Tingley]. A DIPLOMAT'S HELPMATE. San Francisco: Crocker, 1918. 50 p.

MacDonnell, Lady [Anne]. REMINISCENCES OF DIPLOMATIC LIFE. London: Adam and Charles Black, 1913. 291 p.

McNair, Clare H. "Women in the Foreign Service." FOREIGN SERVICE JOURNAL 22 (June 1945): 30-31, 46.

Mesta, Perle S., with Robert Cahn. PERLE--MY STORY. New York: McGraw-Hill, 1960. 251 p.

Miller, Hope Ridings. EMBASSY ROW: THE LIFE AND TIMES OF DIPLOMATIC WASHINGTON. New York: Holt, Rinehart, and Winston, 1969. 286 p.

Mitchell, Eleanor Swann. POSTSCRIPT TO SEVEN HOMES. Francestown, N.H.: Jones, 1960. 217 p.

_____. SEVEN HOMES HAD I: EXPERIENCES OF A FOREIGN SERVICE WIFE. New York: Exposition, 1955. 172 p.

Morrow, Elizabeth Cutter. THE MEXICAN YEARS: LEAVES FROM THE DIARY OF ELIZABETH CUTTER MORROW. New York: Private printing by Spiral Press, 1953. 272 p.

O'Shaughnessy, Edith Louise. DIPLOMATIC DAYS. New York: Harper, 1917. 337 p.

_____. A DIPLOMAT'S WIFE IN MEXICO. New York: Harper, 1916. 355 p.

_____. VIENNESE MEDLEY. New York: Huebsch, 1924. 295 p.

Parker, Maude. IMPERSONATION OF A LADY. Boston: Houghton Mifflin, 1934. 270 p.

   Also see Maude Parker Child above, p. 50.

_____. SECRET ENVOY. Indianapolis: Bobbs-Merrill, 1930. 302 p.

Roosevelt, Eleanor. THE AUTOBIOGRAPHY OF ELEANOR ROOSEVELT. New York: Harper, 1961. 454 p.

Russell, Beatrice. LIVING IN STATE. New York: McKay, 1959. 272 p.

Spender, Lady Jean. AMBASSADOR'S WIFE. Sydney: Argus and Robertson, 1968. 207 p.

Vare, Daniele. THE LAUGHING DIPLOMAT. Garden City, N.Y.: Doubleday, Doran, 1938. 448 p.

Waddington, Mary King. LETTERS OF A DIPLOMAT'S WIFE, 1883-1900. London: Smith, Elder, 1903. 417 p.

Williams, Carman C. "The Wasted Resource: Foreign Service Wives." FOREIGN SERVICE JOURNAL 52 (May 1975): 6-7, 20-21.

Wilson, Edith [Bolling] Galt. MY MEMOIR. Indianapolis: Bobbs-Merrill, 1939. 386 p.

Winfield, Louise. LIVING OVERSEAS. Washington, D.C.: Public Affairs, 1962. 237 p.

For additional commentary on women in American foreign relations, emphasizing their role as ranking emissaries, see the following:

Plischke, Elmer. UNITED STATES DIPLOMATS AND THEIR MISSIONS: A

PROFILE OF AMERICAN DIPLOMATIC EMISSARIES SINCE 1778. Washington, D.C.: American Enterprise Institute, 1975. 201 p.

> Especially chapter 4, pages 77-79, and tables A-4, A-5, A-7, A-12, and A-16.

Spaulding, E. Wilder. AMBASSADORS ORDINARY AND EXTRAORDINARY. Washington, D.C.: Public Affairs, 1961. 302 p. Bibliog.

> Especially chapter 7.

OTHERS: PERSPECTIVES, FUNCTIONAL ROLES, COMMENTARIES, AND ANALYSES

Additional useful volumes and monographs on diplomacy, which are not readily accommodated by the topical sections of this or other chapters, include the following:

Acheson, Dean G. POWER AND DIPLOMACY. Cambridge, Mass.: Harvard University Press, 1958; New York: Atheneum, 1963. 137 p.

George, Alexander L.; Hall, David K.; and Simons, William E. THE LIMITS OF COERCIVE DIPLOMACY: LAOS, CUBA, VIETNAM. Boston: Little, Brown, 1971. 268 p.

Huddleston, Sisley. POPULAR DIPLOMACY AND WAR. Rindge, N.H.: Smith, 1954. 285 p.

Johnson, E.A.J., ed. THE DIMENSIONS OF DIPLOMACY. Baltimore: Johns Hopkins Press, 1964. 135 p.

Kertesz, Stephen D. THE QUEST FOR PEACE THROUGH DIPLOMACY. Englewood Cliffs, N.J.: Prentice-Hall, 1967. 182 p.

Kertesz, Stephen D., and Fitzsimons, M.A. DIPLOMACY IN A CHANGING WORLD. Notre Dame, Ind.: University of Notre Dame Press, 1959. 407 p.

McKenna, Joseph Charles. DIPLOMATIC PROTEST IN FOREIGN POLICY: ANALYSIS AND CASE STUDIES. Chicago: Loyola University Press, 1962. 222 p. Bibliog.

Mendershausen, Horst. THE DIPLOMAT AS A NATIONAL AND TRANSNATIONAL AGENT: A PROBLEM OF MULTIPLE LOYALTY. Morristown, N.J.: General Learning Corp., 1973. 19 p. Bibliog.

_____. THE DIPLOMAT AS A NATIONAL AND TRANSNATIONAL AGENT: DILEMMAS AND OPPORTUNITIES. Santa Monica, Calif.: Rand, 1969. 28 p.

Oudenijk, Willem Jacobus. WAYS AND BY-WAYS IN DIPLOMACY. London: Davies, 1939. 386 p.

Ponsonby, Arthur. DEMOCRACY AND DIPLOMACY: A PLEA FOR POPULAR CONTROL OF FOREIGN POLICY. London: Methuen, 1915. 198 p.

Poole, Dewitt C. THE CONDUCT OF FOREIGN RELATIONS UNDER MODERN DEMOCRATIC CONDITIONS. New Haven, Conn.: Yale University Press, 1924. 208 p.

Poullada, Leon B. "Diplomacy: The Missing Link in the Study of International Politics." Paper presented at annual meeting of American Political Science Association, September 1971. In AN INTRODUCTION TO DIPLOMATIC PRACTICE, edited by John J. Hurle, Jr., pp. 1-29. Washington, D.C.: Foreign Service Institute, U.S. Department of State, 1971.

Regala, Roberto. WORLD ORDER AND DIPLOMACY. Dobbs Ferry, N.Y.: Oceana, 1969. 205 p. Bibliog.

_____. WORLD PEACE THROUGH DIPLOMACY AND LAW. Dobbs Ferry, N.Y.: Oceana, 1964. 270 p.

Roucek, Joseph S. "Some Sociological Aspects of Diplomacy." JOURNAL OF HUMAN RELATIONS 8 (Winter 1960): 209-44.

Roudybush, Franklin. WORLD DIPLOMATIC LIST. Washington, D.C.: Government Printing Office, 1943. 350 p.

Simpson, Smith. "Diplomacy: Some Professional and Political Perspectives." FOREIGN SERVICE JOURNAL 53 (August 1976): 15-19.

Symcox, Geoffrey, ed. WAR, DIPLOMACY AND IMPERIALISM, 1618-1763. New York: Walker, 1974. 338 p.

Thompson, Kenneth W. AMERICAN DIPLOMACY AND EMERGENT PATTERNS. New York: New York University Press, 1962. 273 p. Bibliog.

Wriston, Henry M. DIPLOMACY IN A DEMOCRACY. New York: Harper, 1956. 115 p.

Young, George. DIPLOMACY OLD AND NEW. London: Swarthmore, 1921. 105 p.

Chapter 4
TREATMENT OF DIPLOMATS AND CONSULS

One of the earliest principles developed to facilitate diplomatic practice was the inviolability of the emissary, his chancellery and residence, and his communications and archives. This principle was originally founded on the presumption that the diplomat, serving as the personal overseas representative of his monarch or his state, must retain freedom of action, and that therefore he--like the sovereign or the sovereignty he represents--and his functioning, must be inviolable. In time, this rationalization was supported, if not superseded, by the simple need for reciprocal privileged treatment for both diplomats and consuls, from which flowed a "customary" and later a "conventional" schedule of positive and negative aspects of the official and unofficial treatment of these officials.

PRIVILEGES AND IMMUNITIES

Diplomats, consuls, and national representatives to and officials of international organizations are emancipated from many of the jurisdictional, legal, taxational, and other restrictions and obligations imposed on ordinary aliens residing in foreign lands. These prerogatives are known as "privileges and immunities." The privileges and immunities of diplomats and consuls need to be distinguished from those pertaining to representatives to and officials of international organizations and other agencies. The latter, which are somewhat more restricted, are called "international privileges and immunities" and are discussed in the publications of Ahluwalia, Crosswell, Fedder, Hill, Jenks, Jones, King, Michaels, and others. The principles and analyses expounded in these publications are applicable to international organizations that have their headquarters in the United States, such as the United Nations and the Organization of American States, to Americans serving as officials of such organizations throughout the world, and to other in-international agencies and agents.

Over the centuries, this subject, involving both national policy and international and municipal law, has engendered a highly developed and substantial quantity of literature. Aside from analysis and commentary contained in general international law texts and monographs, the following list emphasizes twentieth-century English-language materials:

Adair, E.R. THE EXTERRITORIALITY OF AMBASSADORS IN THE SIXTEENTH AND SEVENTEENTH CENTURIES. London: Longmans, Green, 1929. 282 p.

Ahluwalia, Kuljit. THE LEGAL STATUS, PRIVILEGES AND IMMUNITIES OF THE SPECIALIZED AGENCIES OF THE UNITED NATIONS AND CERTAIN OTHER INTERNATIONAL ORGANIZATIONS. The Hague: Nijhoff, 1964. 230 p. Bibliog.

Barnes, William. "Diplomatic Immunity from Local Jurisdiction: Its Historical Development from International Law and Application in United States Practice." DEPARTMENT OF STATE BULLETIN 43 (1 August 1960): 173-82.

Becker, Joseph D. "The State Department White List and Diplomatic Immunity." AMERICAN JOURNAL OF INTERNATIONAL LAW 47 (October 1953): 704-6.

Crosswell, Carol M. PROTECTION OF INTERNATIONAL PERSONNEL ABROAD. Dobbs Ferry, N.Y.: Oceana, 1952. 198 p.

Deak, Francis. "Immunity of Foreign Mission's Premises from Local Jurisdiction." AMERICAN JOURNAL OF INTERNATIONAL LAW 23 (July 1929): 582-94.

Eagleton, Clyde. "The Responsibility of the State for the Protection of Foreign Officials." AMERICAN JOURNAL OF INTERNATIONAL LAW 19 (April 1925): 293-314.

Fedder, Edwin H. "The Functional Basis of International Privileges and Immunities: A New Concept in International Law and Organization." AMERICAN UNIVERSITY LAW REVIEW 9 (January 1960): 60-69.

_____. "The Privileges and Immunities Granted by the United States to the United Nations and to the Specialized Agencies." Ph.D. dissertation, American University, 1957. 218 p.

Gordon, J.C. "Diplomatic Immunity." FOREIGN SERVICE JOURNAL 29 (January 1952): 23, 46-47.

Harvard Research in International Law. "Diplomatic Privileges and Immunities." AMERICAN JOURNAL OF INTERNATIONAL LAW, SUPPLEMENT 26 (April 1932): 15-187.

Hershey, Amos S. DIPLOMATIC AGENTS AND IMMUNITIES. Washington, D.C.: Government Printing Office, 1919. 218 p.

Hill, Martin. IMMUNITIES AND PRIVILEGES OF INTERNATIONAL OFFICIALS. Washington, D.C.: Carnegie Endowment, 1947. 281 p.

Jenks, C. Wilfred. INTERNATIONAL IMMUNITIES. Dobbs Ferry, N.Y.: Oceana, 1961. 178 p.

Jones, Helen Dudenbostel, comp. DIPLOMATIC PRIVILEGES AND IMMUNI-TIES--WITH PARTICULAR REFERENCE TO INTERNATIONAL ORGANIZATIONS: A SELECTED LIST OF MONOGRAPHS AND ARTICLES PUBLISHED SINCE 1931. Washington, D.C.: U.S. Library of Congress, General Reference and Bibliography Division, 1948. 9 p.

King, John Kerry. THE PRIVILEGES AND IMMUNITIES OF THE PERSONNEL OF INTERNATIONAL ORGANIZATIONS. Odense, Denmark: Strandberg, 1949. 282 p.

Kunz, Josef L. "Privileges and Immunities of International Organizations." AMERICAN JOURNAL OF INTERNATIONAL LAW 41 (October 1947): 828-62.

Lyons, A.B. "Personal Immunities of Diplomatic Agents." BRITISH YEAR BOOK OF INTERNATIONAL LAW 31 (1954): 299-340.

Michaels, David B. INTERNATIONAL PRIVILEGES AND IMMUNITIES: A CASE FOR A UNIVERSAL STATUTE. The Hague: Nijhoff, 1971. 249 p. Bibliog.

_____. "Privileges and Immunities of the International Civil Servant of Se-lected International Organizations: Survey of Treaty Law." Ph.D. disserta-tion, University of Maryland, 1970. 423 p. Bibliog.

Monroe, David Geeting. "Privileges and Immunities." JOURNAL OF CRIMI-NAL LAW AND CRIMINOLOGY 37 (March-April 1947): 480-83.

Ogdon, Montell. "The Growth of Purpose in the Law of Diplomatic Immunity." AMERICAN JOURNAL OF INTERNATIONAL LAW 32 (July 1937): 449-65.

_____. JUDICIAL BASES OF DIPLOMATIC IMMUNITY. Washington, D.C.: Byrne, 1936. 254 p.

Preuss, Lawrence. "Capacity for Legislation and the Theoretical Basis of Diplo-matic Immunity." NEW YORK UNIVERSITY LAW QUARTERLY REVIEW 10 (1932-33): 170-87.

_____. "Consular Immunities: The Kasenkina Case." AMERICAN JOURNAL OF INTERNATIONAL LAW 43 (January 1949): 37-56.

_____. "Diplomatic Privileges and Immunities of Agents Invested with Func-tions of an International Interest." AMERICAN JOURNAL OF INTERNATION-AL LAW 25 (October 1931): 694-710.

_____. "Immunity of Officers and Employees of the United Nations for Official Acts: The Ranallo Case." AMERICAN JOURNAL OF INTERNATIONAL LAW 41 (July 1947): 555-78.

_____. "The International Organizations Immunities Act." AMERICAN JOURNAL OF INTERNATIONAL LAW 40 (April 1946): 332-45.

_____. "Protection of Foreign Diplomatic and Consular Premises Against Picketing." AMERICAN JOURNAL OF INTERNATIONAL LAW 31 (October 1937): 705-13.

Reiff, Henry. DIPLOMATIC AND CONSULAR PRIVILEGES, IMMUNITIES AND PRACTICE. Cairo, Egypt: Ettemad Press, 1954. 290 p.

Stewart, Irvin. CONSULAR PRIVILEGES AND IMMUNITIES. New York: Columbia University Press, 1926. 216 p. Bibliog.

Sweeney, Joseph M. THE INTERNATIONAL LAW OF SOVEREIGN IMMUNITY. Washington, D.C.: U.S. Department of State, 1964. 59 p.

U.S. Department of Justice. "Legislation Proposed to Protect U.S. Officials and Foreign Diplomats." DEPARTMENT OF STATE BULLETIN 65 (6 September 1971): 268-70.

U.S. Department of State. UNITED NATIONS CONFERENCE ON DIPLOMATIC INTERCOURSE AND IMMUNITIES, VIENNA, AUSTRIA, MARCH 2-APRIL 14, 1961. Washington, D.C.: Government Printing Office, 1962. 65 p.

van Essen, Jan Louis Frederick. IMMUNITIES IN INTERNATIONAL LAW. Leiden, The Netherlands: Sijthoff, 1955. 56 p.

Van Vollenhoven, C. "Diplomatic Prerogatives of Non-Diplomats." AMERICAN JOURNAL OF INTERNATIONAL LAW 19 (July 1925): 469-74.

Wilson, Clifton E. DIPLOMATIC PRIVILEGES AND IMMUNITIES. Tucson: University of Arizona Press, 1967. 300 p. Bibliog.

_____. "Diplomatic Privileges and Immunities in Recent International Practice." Ph.D. dissertation, University of Minnesota, 1964. 582 p.

In addition, the following represent the foreign-language literature on the subject, which is also extensive. The principles treated are generally regarded as universally applicable.

Benezet, Jean Etienne. ETUDE THEORIQUE SUR LES IMMUNITES DIPLOMATIQUES. Toulouse, France: Lagarde and Sebille, 1901. 179 p.

Bodin, Albert. DES IMMUNITES CONSULAIRES DANS LES PAYS DE CHRE-TIENTE. Bordeaux, France: Cadoret, 1897. 144 p.

Dietrich, Victor. DE L'INVIOLABILITE ET DE L'EXEMPTION DE JURISDIC-TION DES AGENTS DIPLOMATIQUES ET CONSULAIRES EN PAYS DE CHRE-TIENTE. Paris: Marescq Jeune, 1896. 198 p.

Kauffmann, Siegmund. DIE IMMUNITAET DER NICHT-DIPLOMATEN: EIN BEITRAG ZUR KODIFICATION DES VOELKERRECHTS. Leipzig: Noske, 1932. 159 p. Bibliog.

Larrive, Georges. LES PRIVILEGES DES CONSULS DANS LES PAYS D'OCCI-DENT. Paris: Boyer, 1901. 125 p. Bibliog.

Miele, Mario. PRIVILEGES ET IMMUNITIES DES FONCTIONNAIRES INTER-NATIONAUX: AVEC LE TEXTE DES CONVENTIONS INTERNATIONALES EN VIGUER. Milan: Giuffre, 1958. 201 p.

Morton, Charles. LES PRIVILEGES ET IMMUNITES DIPLOMATIQUES. Lau-sanne, Switzerland: Imprimerie la Concorde, 1927. 176 p. Bibliog.

Odier, Pierre Gabriel. DES PRIVILEGES ET IMMUNITES DES AGENTS DIPLO-MATIQUES EN PAYS DE CHRETIENTE. Paris: Rousseau, 1890. 467 p.

Sadoul, Jacques. LA CONDITIONS DES AGENTS CONSULAIRES ET DIPLO-MATIQUES AU POINT DE VUE FISCAL. Paris: Pichou and Durand-Auzias, 1908. 143 p.

Secretan, Jacques. LES PRIVILEGES ET IMMUNITES DIPLOMATIQUES DES REPRESENTANTS DES ETATS MEMBRES ET DES AGENTS DE LA SOCIETE DES NATIONS. Lausanne, Switzerland: Payot, 1928. 120 p.

Stowell, Ellery C. LE CONSUL: FONCTIONS, IMMUNITES, ORGANISA-TION, EXEQUATOR. Paris: Pedone, 1909. 353 p.

Yeh, Sao-liang. LES PRIVILEGES ET IMMUNITES DES AGENTS DIPLOMA-TIQUES A L'EGARD DES ETATS TIERS. Paris: Jcl, 1938. 156 p. Bibliog.

Legal prescriptions in and commentary on U.S. practice concerning the princi-ple of extraterritoriality and diplomatic and consular privileges and immunities are contained in:

Hackworth, Green H. DIGEST OF INTERNATIONAL LAW. Washington, D.C.: Government Printing Office, 1943. Vol. 4, pp. 513-604.

Moore, John Bassett. A DIGEST OF INTERNATIONAL LAW. Washington, D.C.: Government Printing Office, 1906. Vol. 2, pp. 558-751; vol. 4, pp. 630-80; and vol. 5, pp. 32-61.

Whiteman, Marjorie M. DIGEST OF INTERNATIONAL LAW. Washington, D.C.: Government Printing Office. Vol. 7 (1970), pp. 253-447; and vol. 13 (1968), pp. 32-188.

MISTREATMENT OF DIPLOMATS AND CONSULS

Since World War II, the treatment of diplomatic and consular personnel has retrogressed in several ways, at times involving official restrictions and harassments--such as surveillance, isolation, economic and travel restraints, red tape, detention, arrest, and expulsion (as persona non grata) or forced recall. In other cases, mistreatment has been at the hands of rampant mobs and terrorists--involving not only demonstrations but also assaults, kidnappings, and even murder. The modes of maltreatment fall into three major groupings. Most actions of intentional mistreatment are directed less at individuals than against the governments they represent. The second type applies to specific individuals, such as the particular ambassador, military attache, or international mediator. The third category focuses upon groups of individuals--those representing a given country or ideology, bloc of states, international organization, or government policy position. Although this aspect of diplomatic relations has been given little serious literary attention, it is dealt with in the following:

Bennett, W. Tapley. "U.N. General Assembly Adopts Convention on Protection of Diplomats." DEPARTMENT OF STATE BULLETIN 70 (28 January 1974): 89-95.

Ford, Gerald R. "Senate Asked to Approve Convention on Protection of Diplomats." DEPARTMENT OF STATE BULLETIN 71 (9 December 1974): 803-4.

Green, Theodore F. "Soviet Harassment of Foreign Diplomats." DEPARTMENT OF STATE BULLETIN 27 (17 November 1952): 786-89.

Imbrie, Katherine [Gillespie]. DATA RELATING TO THE ASSASSINATION OF UNITED STATES CONSULAR OFFICER ROBERT WHITNEY IMBRIE "BY THE MILITARY POLICE OF PERSIA" IN TEHERAN, PERSIA, JULY 18, 1924. Frederick, Md.: By the author, 1939. 45 p.

Jones, Cecil B. "Mistreatment of Foreign Diplomats in the United States Since World War II." Master's thesis, University of Maryland, 1963. 221 p. Bibliog.

Kohlberg, A. "Let's Treat the Russians the Way They Treat Us." MERCURY 78 (February 1954): 77-81.

Macomber, William B., and Bush, George H. "Department [of State] Supports Bill Providing for Expanded Protection of Foreign Officials in the U.S." DEPARTMENT OF STATE BULLETIN 66 (24 April 1972): 609-14.

Spencer, Jean Elizabeth. "Soviet and European Satellite Treatment of Resident United States Diplomatic Personnel Since the Second World War." Master's thesis, University of Maryland, 1961. 341 p. Bibliog.

U.S. Congress. Senate. Committee on Foreign Relations. Special Subcommittee on Security Affairs. RESTRICTIONS ON DIPLOMATIC PERSONNEL BY AND FROM IRON CURTAIN COUNTRIES. 83d Cong., 1st sess. Washington, D.C.: Government Printing Office, 1953. 24 p.

Wilson, Clifton E. COLD WAR DIPLOMACY: THE IMPACT OF INTERNATIONAL CONFLICTS ON DIPLOMATIC COMMUNICATIONS AND TRAVEL. Tucson: University of Arizona Press, 1966. 67 p.

INTERNATIONAL TERRORISM, KIDNAPPING, AND SKYJACKING

International terrorism, kidnapping, and skyjacking transcend applicability solely to diplomatic and consular officials and members of their families, and their spread and intensification are evoking recent literary attention. A few studies are concerned specifically with the treatment of diplomats and other internationally protected persons, as follows:

Baumann, Carol Edler. THE DIPLOMATIC KIDNAPPINGS: A REVOLUTIONARY TACTIC OF URBAN TERRORISM. The Hague: Nijhoff, 1973. 182 p.

Bloomfield, Louis M., and Fitzgerald, Gerald F. CRIMES AGAINST INTERNATIONALLY PROTECTED PERSONS: AN ANALYSIS OF THE U.N. CONVENTION. New York: Praeger, 1975. 272 p. Bibliog.

Fitzhugh, David. "Terrorism and Diplomacy." FOREIGN SERVICE JOURNAL 54 (February 1977): 14-17.

The following studies concentrate on skyjacking, the diversion of aircraft in international flight, and aerial piracy:

Agrawala, S.K. AIRCRAFT HIJACKING AND INTERNATIONAL LAW. Dobbs Ferry, N.Y.: Oceana, 1973. 242 p. Bibliog.

Arey, James A. THE SKY PIRATES. New York: Scribner, 1972. 360 p.

Clyde, Peter. AN ANATOMY OF SKYJACKING. London: Abelard-Schuman, 1973.

Joyner, Nancy [Chutz] Douglas. AERIAL HIJACKING AS AN INTERNATION-
AL CRIME. Dobbs Ferry, N.Y.: Oceana, 1974. 344 p. Bibliog.

_____. "A Contemporary Concept of Piracy in International Law: The Status
of Aerial Hijacking as an International Crime." Ph.D. dissertation, Florida
State University, 1973. 351 p.

McWhinney, Edward. AERIAL PIRACY AND INTERNATIONAL LAW. Leiden,
The Netherlands: Sijthoff, 1971; Dobbs Ferry, N.Y.: Oceana, 1971. 213 p.

_____. THE ILLEGAL DIVERSION OF AIRCRAFT AND INTERNATIONAL LAW.
Leiden, The Netherlands: Sijthoff, 1975. 123 p. Bibliog.

Shelhoup, Kamal George. "Extradition and Political Asylum as Applied to
Aircraft Piracy." Ph.D. dissertation, Claremont Graduate School, 1979. 190 p.

U.S. Department of Transportation. Library Services Division. HIJACKING:
SELECTED READINGS, BIBLIOGRAPHIC LIST NO. 5 (JULY 1971). Washington, D.C.: Department of Commerce, 1971. 53 p.

A more substantial number of studies, as follows, deal with the growing problem of international terrorism, which some times affects diplomats as victims
and usually involves diplomatic negotiations.

Alexander, Yonah, ed. INTERNATIONAL TERRORISM: NATIONAL, REGION-
AL, AND GLOBAL PERSPECTIVES. New York: Praeger, 1976. 393 p. Bibliog.

Alexander, Yonah; Browne, Marjorie Ann; and Nanes, Allan S., eds. CON-
TROL OF TERRORISM: INTERNATIONAL DOCUMENTS. New York: Crane,
Russak, 1979. 215 p.
    Compilation of historical and contemporary documents on dealing
    with terrorists.

Alexander, Yonah; Carlton, David; and Wilkinson, Paul. TERRORISM: THEORY
AND PRACTICE. Boulder, Colo.: Westview, 1978. 200 p.

Alexander, Yonah, and Finger, Seymour M., eds. TERRORISM: INTERDISCI-
PLINARY PERSPECTIVES. New York: John Jay, 1977. 377 p.

Bassiouni, M. Cheriff, ed. INTERNATIONAL TERRORISM AND POLITICAL
CRIMES. Springfield, Ill.: Thomas, 1975. 594 p. Bibliog.
    Symposium on Conference on Terrorism and Political Crimes.

Bauman, Carol Edler. INTERNATIONAL TERRORISM. Milwaukee, Wis.: Institute of World Affairs, 1974.

Bell, J. Bowyer. A TIME FOR TERROR: HOW DEMOCRATIC SOCIETIES RESPOND TO REVOLUTIONARY VIOLENCE. New York: Basic Books, 1978. 304 p.

_____. TRANSNATIONAL TERROR. Washington, D.C.: American Enterprise Institute and Hoover Institution, 1975. 91 p.

Especially chapter 4 on "The American Response."

Carlton, D., and Schaerf, C., eds. INTERNATIONAL TERRORISM AND WORLD SECURITY. New York: Halstead, 1975. 332 p.

CIVIL VIOLENCE AND THE INTERNATIONAL SYSTEM. Adelphi Papers 82 and 83. London: International Institute for Strategic Studies, 1971.

Clutterbuck, Richard. GUERILLAS AND TERRORISTS. Salem, N.H.: Faber and Faber, 1977. 128 p.

Friedlander, Robert A. "The Origins of International Terrorism: A Micro Legal-Historical Perspective." ISRAEL YEARBOOK OF HUMAN RIGHTS 6 (1976): 49-61.

_____. "Terrorism and International Law: What is Being Done?" RUTGERS-CAMDEN LAW JOURNAL 8 (Spring 1977): 383-92.

_____, ed. TERRORISM: DOCUMENTS OF INTERNATIONAL AND LOCAL CONTROL. 2 vols. Dobbs Ferry, N.Y.: Oceana, 1978.

Gaucher, Roland. THE TERRORISTS: FROM TSARIST RUSSIA TO THE O.A.S. [Organization of American States]. London: Secker and Warburg, 1968. 325 p.

Hacker, Frederick J. CRUSADERS, CRIMINALS, CRAZIES: TERROR AND TERRORISM IN OUR TIME. New York: Norton, 1977. 355 p.

Halperin, Ernst. TERRORISM IN LATIN AMERICA. Beverly Hills, Calif.: Sage, 1976. 90 p. Bibliog.

Horowitz, Irving Louis. "Political Terrorism and State Power." JOURNAL OF POLITICAL AND MILITARY SOCIOLOGY 1 (Spring 1973): 147-57.

Hyams, Edward. TERRORISTS AND TERRORISM. London: Dent, 1975. 200 p.

Jack, Homer A. "Terrorism: Another U.N. Failure." AMERICA 129 (20 October 1973): 282-85.

Jacobs, Walter Darnell; Peterson, Carl A.; and Yarborough, William P. TER-
RORISM IN SOUTHERN AFRICA: PORTENTS AND PROSPECTS. New York:
American African Affairs Association, 1973. 35 p.

Jenkins, Brian Michael. COMBATTING INTERNATIONAL TERRORISM: THE
ROLE OF CONGRESS. Santa Monica, Calif.: Rand, 1977. 18 p.

_____. HIGH TECHNOLOGY TERRORISM AND SURROGATE WAR: THE IM-
PACT OF NEW TECHNOLOGY ON LOW-LEVEL VIOLENCE. Santa Monica,
Calif.: Rand, 1975. 26 p.

_____. HOSTAGE SURVIVAL: SOME PRELIMINARY OBSERVATIONS. San-
ta Monica, Calif.: Rand, 1976. 13 p.

_____. INTERNATIONAL TERRORISM: A NEW KIND OF WARFARE. Santa
Monica, Calif.: Rand, 1974. 13 p.

_____. THE POTENTIAL FOR NUCLEAR TERRORISM. Santa Monica, Calif.:
Rand, 1977. 11 p.

_____. SHOULD CORPORATIONS BE PREVENTED FROM PAYING RANSOM?
Santa Monica, Calif.: Rand, 1974. 13 p.

_____. WILL TERRORISTS GO NUCLEAR? Santa Monica, Calif.: Rand,
1975. 10 p.

Jenkins, Brian Michael, and Johnson, Janera A. INTERNATIONAL TERROR-
ISM: A CHRONOLOGY, 1968-1974. Santa Monica, Calif.: Rand, 1975.
58 p.

_____. INTERNATIONAL TERRORISM: A CHRONOLOGY (1974 SUPPLE-
MENT). Santa Monica, Calif.: Rand, 1976. 23 p.

Jenkins, Brian Michael; Johnson, Janera A.; and Ronfeldt, David. NUMBER-
ED LIVES: SOME STATISTICAL OBSERVATIONS FROM 77 INTERNATIONAL
HOSTAGE EPISODES. Santa Monica, Calif.: Rand, 1977. 47 p.

Kupperman, Robert, and Trent, Darrell. TERRORISM: THREAT, REALITY, RE-
SPONSE. Stanford, Calif.: Hoover Institution, 1979. 480 p.

Laqueur, Walter. GUERILLAS: A HISTORICAL AND CRITICAL STUDY. Boston: Little, Brown, 1976. 462 p.

_____. TERRORISM. Boston: Little, Brown, 1978. 277 p.

_____, ed. THE GUERILLA READER: A HISTORICAL ANTHOLOGY. Philadelphia: Temple University Press, 1977. 256 p.

_____. THE TERRORISM READER. Philadelphia: Temple University Press, 1978. 304 p.

Leonard, L. Larry. GLOBAL TERRORISM CONFRONTS THE NATIONS. New York: New York University Press, 1980. 186 p. Bibliog.

Livingston, Marius J., ed. INTERNATIONAL TERRORISM IN THE CONTEMPORARY WORLD. Westport, Conn.: Greenwood, 1978. 522 p.

Results of International Symposium on Terrorism, Glassboro State College, 1976.

Murphy, John F., and Evans, Alona E., eds. LEGAL ASPECTS OF INTERNATIONAL TERRORISM. Lexington, Mass.: Lexington, under the auspices of American Society of International Law, 1978. 690 p.

Parry, Albert. TERRORISM: FROM ROBESPIERRE TO ARAFAT. New York: Vanguard, 1976. 624 p.

Rapoport, David C. ASSASSINATION AND TERRORISM. Toronto: Canadian Broadcasting Co., 1971. 88 p.

Schreiber, Jan. THE ULTIMATE WEAPON: TERRORISTS AND WORLD ORDER. New York: Morrow--Quill Paperbacks, 1979. 192 p.

Stohl, Michael S. THE POLITICS OF TERRORISM. Basel, Switzerland: Marcel Dekker, 1979. 440 p.

TEN YEARS OF TERRORISM: COLLECTED VIEWS. New York: Crane, Russak, 1979. 196 p.

Symposium of nineteen authors, produced by Royal United Services Institute.

U.S. Congress. House of Representatives. Committee on Internal Security. TERRORISM. Hearings. 4 pts. 93d Cong., 2d sess. Washington, D.C.: Government Printing Office, 1974. 132 p., 236 p., 215 p., 346 p.

_____. TERRORISM: A STAFF STUDY. 93d Cong., 2d sess. Washington, D.C.: Government Printing Office, 1974. 246 p.

Wilkinson, Paul. POLITICAL TERRORISM. New York: Wiley, 1974. 160 p. Bibliog.

_____ . TERRORISM AND THE LIBERAL STATE. Somerset, N.J.: Wiley Interscience, 1978. 250 p.

Legal analysis respecting U.S. policy and practice concerning extraterritorial crime, mob violence, and terrorism is provided in:

Hackworth, Green H. DIGEST OF INTERNATIONAL LAW. Washington, D.C.: Government Printing Office, 1941. Vol. 2, pp. 179-206.

Moore, John Bassett. A DIGEST OF INTERNATIONAL LAW. Washington, D.C.: Government Printing Office, 1906. Vol. 6, pp. 787-883.

Terrorism has become so widespread in practice and as a subject of literary interest that a separate journal has been established to deal with it:

TERRORISM: AN INTERNATIONAL JOURNAL. New York: Crane, Russak, 1977-- . Quarterly.

Chapter 5

THE NEW DIPLOMACY

In both its conceptual and pragmatic versions, diplomacy is a dynamic process and changes with the times. In the twentieth century, especially during and after World War I, and again following World War II, the course of history engendered substantial modifications in diplomatic practice. These resulted in the emergence of the "new diplomacy," distinguishing it from the conventional or "classical" method of conducting foreign relations.

The literature is replete with allusions to particular brands of diplomatic practice that bear relationship to historical development. British diplomatist Sir Harold Nicolson, in THE EVOLUTION OF DIPLOMATIC METHOD (cited below, p. 69), for example, refers to the Greek, Roman, Italian (fifteenth and sixteenth centuries), French (seventeenth to nineteenth centuries), and the American (twentieth century) systems of diplomacy. A number of writers identify a new era of diplomacy, produced by the introduction of fundamental changes in diplomatic style at the time of World War I, which Nicolson brands "the American method." Others note even greater changes beginning in the 1940s.

More specifically, commencing with World War I, general conceptualization of the new diplomacy denoted fundamental changes in style, characterized at the time as consisting primarily of parliamentary diplomacy practiced in the international organization such as the League of Nations, the personal diplomacy of political leaders, and "open diplomacy." Some writers, such as Nicolson, regarded this new version as an emergent type of "democractic" or "democratized" diplomacy, portrayed by increased responsiveness to the people, less government confidentiality, a greater degree of legislative oversight or control, and popularization in the sense of placing less emphasis on formal protocol, together with intensified reliance on conference diplomacy.

Following many top-level meetings and conferences of the principal European leaders during the 1930s and the World War II conclaves of the president with the British prime minister, the Soviet premier, and other world leaders, some commentators began to emphasize summit diplomacy in the evolvement of the new diplomacy. All of these basic forms--democratic, conference, parliamentary, open, and personal diplomacy--contributed to the forging of the new diplomacy. After World War II, however, additional refinements and dimensions emerged, such as increased diplomacy at the ministerial and technical levels, multiforum diplomatic relations, and the like.

In view of these mutations, current perception of the new diplomacy differs substantially from that of the 1920s, when the expression first came into widespread use. Its most obvious distinction is from pre-World War I customary diplomatic practice, symbolized essentially by direct representation and largely bilateral negotiation by professional diplomats or appointees commissioned to serve specifically in a representational capacity. It goes without saying, however, that every age experiencing substantial innovation may conceive of its modification as constituting the "new diplomacy," and the version of today varies from that of the era of World War I, while that of the future is likely to differ just as materially from current practice.

Twentieth-century developments have resulted in three types of literary analysis--that which evaluates the new diplomacy in comparison to traditional nineteenth-century practice, that which describes and assesses recent and current changes, and that which discusses specific aspects of change. Additional, more delimited, literature concerned with particular aspects of change is presented in specific sections of other chapters, as noted below.

THE NEW VS. THE OLD DIPLOMACY

The following illustrate that literature which, often in a normative fashion, compares contemporary with classical diplomacy. The subjects dealt with in the following section tend to overlap with the subjects dealt with in other parts of this compilation, but the emphasis here is on the deviation between the principle or theory of diplomacy and the precise practice.

Bastert, Russell H. "The Two American Diplomacies." YALE REVIEW 49 (June 1960): 518-38.

Bell, Sidney. RIGHTEOUS CONQUEST: WOODROW WILSON AND THE EVOLUTION OF THE NEW DIPLOMACY. Port Washington, N.Y.: Kennikat, 1972. 209 p.

_____. "Woodrow Wilson and the Evolution of the New Diplomacy." Ph.D. dissertation, University of Wisconsin, 1969. 357 p.

Bliven, Bruce. "The New Techniques of Diplomacy." NEW REPUBLIC, 29 November 1943, pp. 782-84.

Butterfield, Herbert. "The New Diplomacy and Historical Diplomacy." In DIPLOMATIC INVESTIGATIONS: ESSAYS IN THE THEORY OF INTERNATIONAL POLITICS, edited by Herbert Butterfield and Martin Wight, pp. 181-205. Cambridge, Mass.: Harvard University Press, 1968.

Courtright, Margaret Anne Farris. "Times of Transition: Issues and Alternatives in Late Victorian and Contemporary American Foreign Policies." Ph.D. dissertation, Johns Hopkins University, 1975. 414 p.

"Diplomacy in Transition." JOURNAL OF INTERNATIONAL AFFAIRS 17, no. 1 (1963): 1–69.

> Symposium of six articles on various aspects of diplomacy, written by Andrew W. Cordier, Charles Burton Marshall, Quincy Wright, Thomas Hovet, Jr., Vernon V. Aspaturian, and Michael H. Cardozo.

Hughes, Charles Evans. "Some Observations of the Conduct of Our Foreign Relations." AMERICAN JOURNAL OF INTERNATIONAL LAW 16 (July 1922): 365–74.

Lacy, William S.B. "Usefulness of Classical Diplomacy." DEPARTMENT OF STATE BULLETIN 38 (3 March 1958): 326–27.

Mayer, Arno J. POLITICAL ORIGINS OF THE NEW DIPLOMACY, 1917–1918. New Haven, Conn.: Yale University Press, 1959. Reprint. New York: Fertig, 1969. 435 p. Bibliog.

_____. POLITICS AND DIPLOMACY OF PEACE-MAKING: CONTAINMENT AND COUNTERREVOLUTION AT VERSAILLES, 1918–1919. New York: Knopf, 1967. 918 p. Bibliog.

> Sequel to preceding item.

Mowrer, Paul Scott. OUR FOREIGN AFFAIRS: A STUDY OF NATIONAL INTEREST AND NEW DIPLOMACY. New York: Dutton, 1924. 348 p.

Nicolson, Harold. "Diplomacy Then and Now." FOREIGN AFFAIRS 40 (October 1961): 39–49.

_____. THE EVOLUTION OF DIPLOMATIC METHOD. New York: Macmillan, 1954. 93 p.

_____. "The Faults of American Diplomacy." HARPER'S MAGAZINE, January 1955, pp. 52–58.

O'Donnell, Charles P. "The New Diplomacy." COMMONWEAL 69 (10 October 1958): 43–45. "Reply" by Blair Bolles. COMMONWEAL 69 (14 November 1958): 177–78.

Plischke, Elmer. "The New New Diplomacy: A Changing Process." VIRGINIA QUARTERLY REVIEW 49 (Summer 1973): 321–45.

_____, ed. "Changing Diplomatic Practice." In his MODERN DIPLOMACY: THE ART AND THE ARTISANS, pp. 41-98. Washington, D.C.: American Enterprise Institute, 1979.

Price, Don K. THE NEW DIMENSION OF DIPLOMACY: THE ORGANIZA-TION OF THE U.S. GOVERNMENT FOR ITS NEW ROLE IN WORLD AFFAIRS. New York: Woodrow Wilson Foundation, 1951. 29 p.

Rossow, Robert. "The Professionalization of the New Diplomacy." WORLD POLITICS 14 (July 1962): 561-75.

Rusk, Dean. 'Old-Fashioned Diplomacy." DEPARTMENT OF STATE BULLE-TIN 44 (10 April 1961): 522.

Sohn, Louis B. "Multiple Representation in International Assemblies." AMERI-CAN JOURNAL OF INTERNATIONAL LAW 40 (January 1946): 71-99.

Spiro, Herbert J. WORLD POLITICS: THE GLOBAL SYSTEM. Homewood, Ill.: Dorsey, 1966. 345 p.

> Chapter 2, "The Old and the New," on the old and the new di-plomacy, pp. 12-40.

Taylor, A.J.P. "Case for a Return to the Old Diplomacy." NEW YORK TIMES MAGAZINE, 18 March 1951, pp. 9, 30, 31, 33, 35.

Vansittart, Lord. "The Decline of Diplomacy." FOREIGN AFFAIRS 28 (January 1950): 177-88.

Wilson, Philip W. "Open Methods in Modern Diplomacy." CURRENT HISTORY 35 (October 1931): 85-90.

Woodward, E.L. "The Old and the New Diplomacy." YALE REVIEW 36 (Spring 1947): 405-22.

Young, George. DIPLOMACY OLD AND NEW. London: Swarthmore, 1921. 105 p.

CHANGING DIPLOMATIC PRACTICE

Increasingly, literary analysis emphasizes the changing requirements and nature of diplomacy, addressing such matters as purposes, methods, levels and types of personnel, forums, styles, and procedures. It focuses especially on the ex-pansion of interrelations of governments and the diplomatic process--both quan-titative and qualitative--as it involves more countries, more emissaries of vary-ing types, more subjects dealt with by negotiation and in treaties, more multilateral diplomacy, more issues and problems, and more crises and conflicts. Much of the literature included in other chapters and sections of this bibliography touches on some aspect of such changing diplomatic practice. For example, see references to textbook chapters and essay literature listed in chapter 2, materials on negotiation, international conferencing, and the functions of diplomats included in chapter 3, analyses on secrecy and public opinion referred to in chapter 16, and some of the readings on crisis diplomacy given in chapter 18. The following represent the recent growth of more general monographic, essay, and article contributions on the subject:

Ball, George W. "The New Diplomacy." DEPARTMENT OF STATE BULLETIN 52 (21 June 1965): 1042-48.

Beaulac, Willard L. "Technical Cooperation as an Instrument of Foreign Policy--No Substitute for Traditional Diplomacy." DEPARTMENT OF STATE BULLETIN 32 (13 June 1955): 964-69.

_____. "U.S. Diplomacy In a Changing World." DEPARTMENT OF STATE BULLETIN 33 (29 August 1955): 335-38.

Bowles, Chester. "Total Diplomacy." DEPARTMENT OF STATE BULLETIN 46 (23 April 1962): 677-78.

_____. "Toward a New Diplomacy." FOREIGN AFFAIRS 40 (January 1962): 244-51.

Buchan, Alastair. CRISIS MANAGEMENT. THE NEW DIPLOMACY. Boulogne-sur-Seine, France: Atlantic Institute, 1966. 63 p.

Cable, John. GUNBOAT DIPLOMACY: POLITICAL APPLICATIONS OF LIMITED NAVAL FORCE. New York: Praeger, 1971. 251 p.

Callender, Harold. "Footnotes on Modern Diplomacy." NEW YORK TIMES MAGAZINE, 9 December 1956, pp. 15, 28, 30-32.

Cheever, Daniel, and Haviland, H. Field, Jr. "The New Diplomacy and World Order." In their ORGANIZING FOR PEACE: INTERNATIONAL ORGANIZATION IN WORLD AFFAIRS, pp. 815-22. Boston: Houghton Mifflin, 1954.

Cleveland, Harlan. "View From the Diplomatic Tightrope." DEPARTMENT OF STATE BULLETIN 46 (14 May 1962): 803-8.

Dayton, Katherine. "Peace Conference: New Diplomacy is Old Diplomacy." SATURDAY EVENING POST, 6 February 1932, pp. 31, 106.

Forgac, Albert T. NEW DIPLOMACY AND THE UNITED NATIONS. New York: Pageant, 1965. 173 p. Bibliog.

Gerard, Andre. "Diplomacy Old and New." FOREIGN AFFAIRS 23 (January 1945): 256-70.

Hammarskjold, Dag. "New Diplomatic Techniques in a New World." Address to Foreign Policy Association, October 21, 1953. VITAL SPEECHES 20 (1 December 1953): 107-9.

Harr, John Ensor. "The Profession: A New Diplomacy?" In his THE PROFESSIONAL DIPLOMAT, pp. 11-44. Princeton, N.J.: Princeton University Press, 1969.

_____. "The Professional Diplomat and the New Diplomacy." Ph.D. dissertation, University of California (Berkeley), 1967. 364 p.

Herter, Christian A. "New Dimensions in Diplomacy." DEPARTMENT OF STATE BULLETIN 37 (25 November 1957): 831-34.

Hoffman, Arthur S., ed. INTERNATIONAL COMMUNICATION AND THE NEW DIPLOMACY. Bloomington: Indiana University Press, 1968. 206 p.

Howe, Fisher. THE COMPUTER AND FOREIGN AFFAIRS: SOME FIRST THOUGHTS. Washington, D.C.: Government Printing Office, 1964. 88 p.

Ickes, Harold L. "Diplomacy With an Ax." NEW REPUBLIC, 3 December 1951, p. 17.

Juergensmeyer, John Eli. "Democracy's Diplomacy: The People-to-People Program--A Study of Attempts to Focus the Effects of Private Contacts in International Politics." Ph.D. dissertation, Princeton University, 1960. 637 p.

Kelen, Emery. "Push Button Diplomacy." UNITED NATIONS WORLD 3 (March 1949): 60-62.

Kennan, George F. "Training for Statesmanship." ATLANTIC MONTHLY, May 1953, pp. 40-43.

Kertesz, Stephen D. "Diplomacy in the Atomic Age." REVIEW OF POLITICS 21 (January, April 1959): 151-88, 357-88.

_____, ed. AMERICAN DIPLOMACY IN A NEW ERA. Notre Dame, Ind.: University of Notre Dame Press, 1961. 601 p.

Kirkpatrick, Ivone. "As a Diplomat Sees the Art of Diplomacy." NEW YORK TIMES MAGAZINE, 22 March 1959, pp. 13, 84, 86.

Kohler, Foy D. "Reflections of a Professional Diplomat." In THE NATIONAL ARCHIVES AND FOREIGN RELATIONS RESEARCH, edited by Milton O[dell]. Gustafson, pp. 277-92. Athens: Ohio University Press, 1974.

Krogh, Peter F. "New Directions in American Foreign Policy." FOREIGN SERVICE JOURNAL 50 (September 1973): 13-16.

Lasch, Christopher. "The Historian as Diplomat." NATION, 24 November 1962, pp. 348-53.

Lee, Robert E. "Education for the New Diplomacy." DEPARTMENT OF STATE BULLETIN 48 (25 March 1963): 423-27.

McCamy, James L. CONDUCT OF THE NEW DIPLOMACY. New York: Harper and Row, 1964. 303 p. Bibliog.

McGhee, George C. "The Changing Role of the American Ambassador." DEPARTMENT OF STATE BULLETIN 46 (25 June 1962): 1007-11.

Manning, Robert J. "Policy and People." DEPARTMENT OF STATE BULLE-TIN 49 (21 October 1963): 639-44.

Marshall, Charles Burton. "The Golden Age in Perspective." JOURNAL OF INTERNATIONAL AFFAIRS 17 (1963): 9-17.
    Entire issue on diplomacy in transition.

Marshall, James. "Citizen Diplomacy." AMERICAN POLITICAL SCIENCE REVIEW 43 (February 1949): 83-90.

Merchant, Livingston T. "Diplomacy and the Modern World." DEPARTMENT OF STATE BULLETIN 43 (7 November 1960): 707-13.

Morgenthau, Hans J. "The Permanent Values in the Old Diplomacy." In DI-PLOMACY IN A CHANGING WORLD, edited by Stephen D. Kertesz and M.A. Fitzsimons, pp. 10-20. Notre Dame, Ind.: University of Notre Dame Press, 1959.

Muller, Steve. "Revival of Diplomacy." WORLD POLICY 15 (July 1963): 647-54.

Murphy, Edmund. "Extra Curricular Diplomacy." FOREIGN SERVICE JOURNAL 33 (January 1956): 22-24, 48, 50.

Murphy, Robert D. "What Is Past Is Prologue." DEPARTMENT OF STATE BULLETIN 41 (21 December 1959): 898-902.

"New Breed of Part-Time Diplomats." BUSINESS WEEK, 28 April 1962, pp. 32-33.

"New Dimensions of Diplomacy." DEPARTMENT OF STATE BULLETIN 44 (6 February 1961): 192-93.

> An extract from the conclusion of the President's Committee on Information Activities Abroad.

Osborne, John. "The Importance of Ambassadors." FORTUNE, April 1957, pp. 146-51, 184-94.

Perkins, Dexter. THE DIPLOMACY OF THE NEW AGE: MAJOR ISSUES IN U.S. POLICY SINCE 1945. Bloomington: Indiana University Press, 1967. 190 p.

Pfaff, William. "Computerized Diplomacy." COMMONWEAL 82 (23 July 1965): 520-21.

Phelan, Edward J. "Diplomacy Old and New: Study of Its Gradual Evolution." CENTURY 120 (April 1930): 243-55.

Plischke, Elmer. "The New Diplomacy." In his CONDUCT OF AMERICAN DIPLOMACY, pp. 24-55. 3d ed. Princeton, N.J.: Van Nostrand, 1967.

Regala, Roberto. THE TRENDS IN MODERN DIPLOMATIC PRACTICE. Dobbs Ferry, N.Y.: Oceana, 1959. 209 p.

"Retreat to the Old Diplomacy." NATION, 18 July 1936, pp. 60-61.

Rogers, William P. "The New Foreign Service and the Job of Modern Diplomacy." DEPARTMENT OF STATE BULLETIN 65 (13 December 1971): 675-76.

Root, Elihu. "A Requisite for the Success of Popular Diplomacy." FOREIGN AFFAIRS 1 (September 1922): 3-10.

_____. "Requisite for the Success of Popular Diplomacy." FOREIGN AFFAIRS 15 (April 1937): 405-12.

Rossiter, Clinton L. "The Old Conservatism and the New Diplomacy." VIRGINIA QUARTERLY REVIEW 32 (Winter 1956): 28-49.

Rubin, Seymour J. "American Diplomacy: The Case for 'Amateurism.'" YALE REVIEW 45 (March 1956): 321-35.

Rusk, Dean. "Methods of Diplomacy." DEPARTMENT OF STATE BULLETIN 45 (14 August 1961): 287-88.

_____. "The Realities of Foreign Policy." DEPARTMENT OF STATE BULLE-TIN 46 (26 March 1962): 487-94.

Sands, Theodore. "Propaganda vs. Diplomacy." NATION, 30 May 1959, pp. 488-89.

Scheel, Walter. "Technology as an Element of Foreign Policy." AUSSEN-POLITIK (English ed.) 23 (3d Quarter 1972): 243-51.

Stearns, Monteagle. "Making American Diplomacy Relevant." FOREIGN AFFAIRS 52 (October 1973): 153-67.

Stevenson, Adlai E. "Science, Diplomacy, and Peace." DEPARTMENT OF STATE BULLETIN 45 (4 September 1961): 402-7.

Taylor, A.J.P. "The Judgment of the Diplomat." SATURDAY REVIEW, 11 December 1954, pp. 9-10, 54-56.

Thayer, Charles W. "Our Ambassadors: An Intimate Appraisal of the Men and the System." HARPER'S MAGAZINE, September 1959, pp. 29-35.

Thayer, Robert H. "Cultural Diplomacy and the Development of Mutual Under-standing." DEPARTMENT OF STATE BULLETIN 41 (31 August 1959): 310-16.

"Town Meeting Diplomacy." NORTH AMERICAN REVIEW 207 (February 1918): 181-83.

Warburg, James P. "Today's Challenges to Diplomacy." BULLETIN OF THE ATOMIC SCIENTISTS 19 (November 1963): 2-4.

Wright, Quincy. "The Decline of Classical Diplomacy." JOURNAL OF IN-TERNATIONAL AFFAIRS 17, no. 1 (1963): 18-28.

PARLIAMENTARY DIPLOMACY

Some analyses probe in greater depth specific aspects of changing diplomacy, which are categorized separately in this bibliography. For example, see the sections on negotiation and negotiating style, mistreatment of diplomats and consults, summit diplomacy, and crisis management. In addition, elements of the democratization of diplomatic practice and personnel are treated in some of the materials listed in sections devoted to the Foreign Service, public opinion, secrecy, and information and propaganda. Another component of change incorporated into a separate section is the matter of multilateral negotiation (see section on international conferences, pp. 37-40), a specialized aspect of which--conferences in permanent international organization forums, called parliamentary diplomacy--has become the subject of some individualized analysis, represented by the following:

Best, Gary L. "Diplomacy in the United Nations." Ph.D. dissertation, Northwestern University, 1960. 269 p.

Claude, Inis L., Jr. "Multilateralism: Diplomatic and Otherwise." INTERNATIONAL ORGANIZATION 12 (Winter 1958): 43-52.

Eban, Abba. "Multilateral Diplomacy in the Nuclear Age." UNIVERSITY OF PENNSYLVANIA LAW REVIEW 114 (May 1966): 984-96.

McLachlan, Donald. "The Death of Diplomacy." TWENTIETH CENTURY 149 (March 1951): 173-80.

Rusk, Dean. "Parliamentary Diplomacy: Debate vs. Negotiation." WORLD AFFAIRS INTERPRETER 26 (July 1955): 121-38.

Sanders, William. "Multilateral Diplomacy." DEPARTMENT OF STATE BULLETIN 21 (8 August 1949): 163-69, 199.

Singer, J. David. "The Return to Multilateral Diplomacy." YALE REVIEW 53 (October 1963): 36-48.

U.S. Commission on the Organization of the Government for the Conduct of Foreign Policy. "Multilateral Diplomacy." In COMMISSION OF THE ORGANIZATION OF THE GOVERNMENT FOR THE CONDUCT OF FOREIGN POLICY, JUNE 1975, vol. 1, appendix c, pp. 259-95. Washington, D.C.: Government Printing Office, 1976.

Part II

CONDUCT OF U.S. FOREIGN RELATIONS

The chapters contained in this part deal specifically with the conduct of American foreign relations, as compared with more general materials on diplomacy per se (part I), official U.S. sources and resources (part III), and diplomatic memoir literature (part IV). These chapters include materials in eight basic areas: bibliographical guides (chapter 6), the presidency and Congress (chapters 7-8), the Department of State and other executive agencies (chapters 9-13), decision making (chapter 14), general and a variety of specialized aspects of the conduct of foreign relations (chapters 15-17), crisis diplomacy (chapter 18), systematic and theoretical foreign relations analysis (chapter 19), and selected fiction (chapter 20). In the aggregate, these cover the gamut of the components of the foreign relations process, and the materials included testify to the widespread and changing interest in the subject.

Chapter 6

BIBLIOGRAPHICAL GUIDES

This chapter comprises selected bibliographies, catalogs, indexes, lists, and bibliographical essays that refer largely to unofficial published materials--books, monographs, articles--and unpublished dissertations, that may be useful for the study of the conduct of U.S. foreign relations. Some citations are to general sources (not restricted to foreign affairs), most are concerned with foreign relations directly, and a few deal with more restricted or tangential aspects of the subject. Bibliographical compilations that focus on certain specific topics or types of materials are incorporated in other chapters, as noted later. Guides to official documents and sources are included in a separate section of chapter 22. General encyclopedias, microfilm and microfiche materials, transparencies, oral histories, and related resources are not included, and guidance for these materials may be sought elsewhere.

GENERAL BIBLIOGRAPHIES AND OTHER GUIDES

Beers, Henry Putney, ed. BIBLIOGRAPHIES IN AMERICAN HISTORY: GUIDE TO MATERIALS FOR RESEARCH. 2d ed. New York: Wilson, 1942. 487 p.

> Arranged topically. Sections on U.S. documents, diplomatic history, political science, and territories and dependencies.

Bemis, Samuel Flagg, and Griffin, Grace Gardner, eds. GUIDE TO THE DIP-LOMATIC HISTORY OF THE UNITED STATES. Washington, D.C.: Government Printing Office, 1935. 979 p.

> For annotation, see chapter 23, p. 613.

Besterman, Theodore, ed. A WORLD BIBLIOGRAPHY OF BIBLIOGRAPHIES. 4th ed. 5 vols. Geneva: Societies Bibliographica, 1965-67.

> Arranged alphabetically by subject, and thereunder chronologically. Contains an author index. Includes sections on political science and international law.

BIBLIOGRAPHIC INDEX: A CUMULATIVE BIBLIOGRAPHY OF BIBLIOGRAPHIES. New York: Wilson, 1945, 1948, 1951. Annual.

Various compilers. Arranged alphabetically by subject and author, and alphabetically thereunder, with sections on history, international law, international organization, international relations, law, legislation, political science, world politics, and the like.

Boehm, Eric H., ed. BIBLIOGRAPHIES ON INTERNATIONAL RELATIONS AND WORLD AFFAIRS: AN ANNOTATED DIRECTORY. Santa Barbara, Calif.: Clio Press, 1965. 33 p.

Annotated listing of bibliographical sources and statistical and graphical description of world developments and geographical distribution of cited sources.

Brock, Clifton, ed. THE LITERATURE OF POLITICAL SCIENCE: A GUIDE FOR STUDENTS, LIBRARIANS AND TEACHERS. New York: Bowker, 1969. 232 p.

Useful guide for research in political science generally, but contains little guidance on diplomacy.

Brown, John Cudd, and Rieg, Michael B. ADMINISTRATION OF UNITED STATES FOREIGN AFFAIRS: A BIBLIOGRAPHY. 2d ed. University Park: Pennsylvania State University Library, 1972. 103 p.

Burchfield, Laverne, ed. STUDENT'S GUIDE TO MATERIALS IN POLITICAL SCIENCE. New York: Holt, 1935. 426 p.

Contains references to general works, periodicals, serials, newspapers, yearbooks, and similar materials. Contains sections on diplomacy, international law, international relations, international organization, territories and dependencies, and the like, with topical arrangement thereunder.

Burdette, Franklin L.; Willmore, Jerold N.; and Witherspoon, John V. POLITICAL SCIENCE: A SELECTED BIBLIOGRAPHY OF BOOKS IN PRINT: WITH ANNOTATIONS. College Park: Bureau of Governmental Research, University of Maryland, 1961. 97 p.

Especially chapters 4, 5, and 7.

Carnegie Endowment for International Peace. CURRENT RESEARCH IN INTERNATIONAL AFFAIRS: A SELECTED BIBLIOGRAPHY OF WORKS IN PROGRESS BY PRIVATE RESEARCH AGENCIES IN AUSTRALIA, CANADA, INDIA, PAKISTAN, UNION OF SOUTH AFRICA, UNITED KINGDOM, AND THE UNITED STATES. New York: 1952. 193 p.

Entries organized under the titles of organizations, schools, and universities, alphabetically arranged. Fifth in a series; the first four editions were published under the same title in INTERNATIONAL CONCILIATION as follows: no. 437 (January 1948), no. 446 (December 1948), no. 456 (December 1949), and no. 466 (December 1950).

Channing, Edward; Hart, Albert B.; and Turner, Frederick J., eds. GUIDE TO THE STUDY AND READING OF AMERICAN HISTORY. 2d ed. Boston: Ginn, 1912. 650 p.

> Topical arrangement with index arranged according to subject, author, and title.

Conover, Helen Field, comp. CURRENT NATIONAL BIBLIOGRAPHIES. Washington, D.C.: U.S. Library of Congress, 1955. 132 p.

_____, ed. A GUIDE TO BIBLIOGRAPHIC TOOLS FOR RESEARCH IN FOREIGN AFFAIRS. 2d ed. Washington, D.C.: U.S. Library of Congress, 1958. 160 p.

Coulter, Edith M. GUIDE TO HISTORICAL BIBLIOGRAPHIES: A CRITICAL AND SYSTEMATIC BIBLIOGRAPHY FOR ADVANCED STUDENTS. Berkeley: University of California Press, 1927. 104 p.

> Arrangement according to continent and country.

Coulter, Edith M., and Gerstenfeld, Melanie. HISTORICAL BIBLIOGRAPHIES: A SYSTEMATIC AND ANNOTATED GUIDE. Berkeley: University of California Press, 1935. 206 p.

> Main sections on Europe, Asia, Africa, Oceania, and America; arrangement thereunder by country, and then by author or title.

Council on Foreign Relations. FOREIGN AFFAIRS BIBLIOGRAPHY: A SELECTED AND ANNOTATED LIST OF BOOKS ON INTERNATIONAL RELATIONS, 1919-1932. Edited by William L. Langer and Hamilton Fish Armstrong. New York: Harper, 1933. 551 p.

> Lists books in various languages. Separate parts devoted to international relations, the world, geographic areas and similar categories. Parts vary with the times in subsequent compilations which follow.

_____. FOREIGN AFFAIRS BIBLIOGRAPHY: A SELECTED AND ANNOTATED LIST OF BOOKS ON INTERNATIONAL RELATIONS, 1932-1942. Edited by Robert Gale Woolbert. New York: Harper, 1945. 705 p.

_____. FOREIGN AFFAIRS BIBLIOGRAPHY: A SELECTED AND ANNOTATED LIST OF BOOKS ON INTERNATIONAL RELATIONS, 1942-1952. Edited by Henry L. Roberts, with Jean Gunther and Janis A. Kreslins. New York: Harper, 1955. 727 p.

_____. FOREIGN AFFAIRS BIBLIOGRAPHY: A SELECTED AND ANNOTATED LIST OF BOOKS ON INTERNATIONAL RELATIONS, 1952-1962. Edited by Henry L. Roberts with Jean Gunther and Janis A. Kreslins. New York: Bowker, 1964. 752 p.

_____. FOREIGN AFFAIRS BIBLIOGRAPHY: A SELECTED AND ANNOTATED LIST OF BOOKS ON INTERNATIONAL RELATIONS, 1962-1972. Edited by Janis A. Kreslins. New York: Bowker, 1976. 921 p.

Crawford, Elisabeth T., ed. THE SOCIAL SCIENCES IN INTERNATIONAL AND MILITARY POLICY: AN ANALYTIC BIBLIOGRAPHY. Washington, D.C.: Bureau of Social Science Research, 1965. 67 p.

Deutsch, Karl W., and Merritt, Richard L., eds. NATIONALISM AND NATIONAL DEVELOPMENT: AN INTERDISCIPLINARY BIBLIOGRAPHY. Cambridge: M.I.T. Press, 1970. 519 p.

Provides surveys and bibliographies, special works, and other materials, and deals with concepts, methods, the rise and fall of colonialism, and supranational integration.

Haas, Michael, ed. INTERNATIONAL ORGANIZATION: AN INTERDISCIPLINARY BIBLIOGRAPHY. Stanford, Calif.: Hoover Institute, 1971. 944 p.

Compilation of treatises on international organizations, including bibliographies, texts, documents, and other materials.

Harmon, Robert B., ed. THE ART AND PRACTICE OF DIPLOMACY: A SELECTED AND ANNOTATED GUIDE. Metuchen, N.J.: Scarecrow, 1971. 355 p.

Lists nearly nine hundred entries, topically arranged, on diplomacy and U.S. foreign relations, including English and foreign-language materials.

_____. POLITICAL SCIENCE: A BIBLIOGRAPHICAL GUIDE TO THE LITERATURE. New York: Scarecrow, 1965. 388 p.

Structured guide to resources, but less useful for diplomacy than the preceding item.

Hart, Albert Bushnell. THE FOUNDATIONS OF AMERICAN FOREIGN POLICY: WITH A WORKING BIBLIOGRAPHY. New York: Macmillan, 1901. 307 p.

Contains bibliography on American diplomacy, including general works, bibliographical aids, special articles, collections of documents, and other materials.

_____. "A Trial Bibliography of American Diplomacy." AMERICAN HISTORICAL REVIEW 6 (1901): 848-66.

Largely the same as the preceding entry.

Higham, Robin, ed. OFFICIAL HISTORIES: ESSAYS AND BIBLIOGRAPHIES FROM AROUND THE WORLD. Manhattan: Kansas State University Library, 1970. 644 p.

Bibliography of foreign and American literature on official histories, giving brief sketches and bibliographical references.

Holler, Frederick L. THE INFORMATION SOURCES OF POLITICAL SCIENCE. 2d ed. 5 vols. Santa Barbara, Calif.: ABC-Clio Press, 1975.

Annotated bibliography, with general reference sources in vol. 1, American government and international law in vol. 3, international- al relations in vol. 4, and public administration and a cumulative index in vol. 5.

Johnson, Harold S., and Singh, Baljit. INTERNATIONAL ORGANIZATION: A CLASSIFIED BIBLIOGRAPHY. East Lansing: Asian Studies Institute, Michi- gan State University, 1969. 261 p.

Provides bibliographical references arranged topically.

Macmahon, Arthur W. "The Administration of Foreign Affairs." AMERICAN POLITICAL SCIENCE REVIEW 45 (September 1951): 836–66.

Analytical review of contemporary publications on the conduct of American foreign relations.

Mason, John Brown. RESEARCH RESOURCES: ANNOTATED GUIDE TO THE SOCIAL SCIENCES. 2 vols. Santa Barbara, Calif.: ABC-Clio Press, 1968, 1971.

Guide to publications since 1776. Furnishes references to general, specialized, professional, and commercial studies, research re- sources, book reviews, indexes, and other materials. Vol. 1 sub- titled INTERNATIONAL RELATIONS AND RECENT HISTORY: IN- DEXES, ABSTRACTS, AND PERIODICALS, 243 p.; vol. 2 subtitled OFFICIAL PUBLICATIONS--U.S. GOVERNMENT, UNITED NA- TIONS, INTERNATIONAL ORGANIZATIONS, AND STATISTICAL SOURCES, 273 p.

Plischke, Elmer. "Research on the Conduct of United States Foreign Relations." INTERNATIONAL STUDIES QUARTERLY 15 (June 1971): 221–50.

Extensive bibliography provided in footnotes, pages 240–50.

Simpson, Smith. "Some Thoughts on Additional Reading." In AN INTRODUC- TION TO DIPLOMATIC PRACTICE, edited by John J. Hurley, Jr., pp. 90-91. Washington, D.C.: Foreign Service Institute, U.S. Department of State, 1971.

Trask, David F.; Meyer, Michael C.; and Trask, Roger R., eds. BIBLIOGRA- PHY OF UNITED STATES-LATIN AMERICAN RELATIONS SINCE 1810: A SE- LECTED LIST OF ELEVEN THOUSAND PUBLISHED REFERENCES. Lincoln: University of Nebraska Press, 1968. 441 p. SUPPLEMENT TO . . . . Edited by Michael C. Meyer. Lincoln: University of Nebraska Press, 1979. 193 p.

U.S. Congress. Senate. Committee on Foreign Relations. STRENGTHENING FREE WORLD SECURITY: A COLLECTION OF EXCERPTS AND BIBLIOGRA-PHIES. Prepared by Library of Congress. 86th Cong., 2d sess. Washington, D.C.: Government Printing Office, 1960. 91 p.

U.S. Congress. Senate. Committee on Government Operations. Subcommittee on National Policy Machinery. ORGANIZING FOR NATIONAL SECURITY: A BIBLIOGRAPHY. 86th Cong., 1st sess. Washington, D.C.: Government Printing Office, 1959. 77 p.

> Contains references to official and unofficial materials on such subjects as national security machinery, the presidency, State Department, Department of Defense, Congress, overseas activities, special problems and programs, and similar matters.

U.S. Congress. Senate. Committee on Government Operations. Subcommittee on National Security Staffing and Operations. ADMINISTRATION OF NATIONAL SECURITY: A BIBLIOGRAPHY. 87th Cong., 2d sess. Washington, D.C.: Government Printing Office, 1963. 89 p.

> Supplements the preceding item, with similar arrangement.

U.S. Department of State. EXECUTIVE-CONGRESSIONAL RELATIONS AND FOREIGN POLICY: A BIBLIOGRAPHICAL SURVEY. Washington, D.C.: 1949. 121 p.

U.S. Library of Congress. A DIRECTORY OF INFORMATION RESOURCES IN THE UNITED STATES: SOCIAL SCIENCES. 2d ed. Washington, D.C.: 1973. 700 p.

Vose, Clement E. A GUIDE TO LIBRARY SOURCES IN POLITICAL SCIENCE: AMERICAN GOVERNMENT. Washington, D.C.: American Political Science Association, 1975. 135 p.

> An instructional resource monograph, sponsored by the American Political Science Association.

Williams, Stillman P. TOWARD A GENUINE WORLD SECURITY SYSTEM: AN ANNOTATED BIBLIOGRAPHY FOR LAYMAN AND SCHOLAR. Washington, D.C.: United World Federalists, 1964. 65 p.

> Variety of materials on world law, world order, and world peace, arranged topically.

Zawodny, Janusz Kazimirez, ed. GUIDE TO THE STUDY OF INTERNATIONAL RELATIONS. San Francisco: Chandler, 1966. 151 p.

> Includes structured lists of bibliographies, journals, atlases, archives, collections of national libraries, and the like.

Additional, more restricted bibliographical guidance to materials on specific subjects is provided in other chapters. Aside from the separate section in Chapter 22 listing bibliographical guides to official United States publications and resources, the following may be consulted on such particular aspects of the conduct of American foreign relations (arranged by chapters).

Chapter	Subject	Author or Issuing Agency
4	Privileges and Immunities	Jones, Helen D., p. 57
	Terrorism	U.S. Department of Transportation, p. 62
7	Presidency	Greenstein, Fred I., et al., p. 109
		U.S. Library of Congress, p. 110
	Presidential Disability	Tomkins, Dorothy L., p. 119
	Executive Privilege	Smith, S.C., p. 150
	Vice-President	Tomkins, Dorothy L., p. 156
9	Foreign Service	Carlsen, Charles R., p. 208
		FOREIGN SERVICE JOURNAL, "Bibliography," p. 208
10	National Security Council System	U.S. Congress. Senate. Committee on Government Operations, p. 242
11	Intelligence Function	Blackstock, Paul W., and Schaf, Frank L., Jr., p. 249
		Devore, Ronald M., p. 249
		Harris, William Robert, p. 250
		U.S. Department of State, p. 250
12	Military	Albion, R.G., p. 259
		Burns, Richard Dean, p. 260
		Burt, Richard, and Kemp, Geoffrey, p. 260
		Gordon, Colin, p. 260
		Greenwood, John, et al., p. 260
		Lang, Kurt, p. 260
		Larson, Arthur D., p. 260
		Social Science Research Council, p. 260
		U.S. Congress. House. Committee on Foreign Affairs, p. 260
		U.S. Congress. Senate. Committee on Government Operations, p. 260-61
		U.S. Department of the Army, p. 261
		Wright, Christopher, p. 261
	Civil-Military Relations	Larson, Arthur D., p. 267
14	Decision Making	Gore, William J., and Silander, Fred S., p. 300
		Raser, John R., p. 300
		Wasserman, Paul, and Silander, Fred S., p. 300
16	Public Interest	Boston Public Library, p. 349
17	Information Program	U.S. Department of State, p. 383

Chapter	Subject	Author or Issuing Agency
17	Political Warfare	Smith, Chitra M., et al., p. 382
	Treaty Making	Hill, Sidney B., p. 391 Toscano, Mario, p. 395
	Trade and Aid	Amstutz, Mark R., p. 398 Hazelwood, Arthur, p. 398 U.S. Department of State, p. 398 U.S. Library of Congress, p. 398
	Science and Technology	Caldwell, Lynton K., p. 415 Knezo, Genevieve Johanna, p. 415 Rettig, Richard A., p. 415
	Human Rights	Veenhoven, Willem A., p. 415
18	Peace and War	Ziegler, Janet, p. 436
	Peace Keeping	Pikus, Robert, and Woito, Robert, p. 437 Smith, Gordon S., p. 437
	Peace Research	Cook, Blanche Wieser, p. 438 Durkee, Kinde, p. 438 Gray, Charles, et al., p. 439
	Peaceful Settlement	Almond, Nina, and Lutz, Ralph H., p. 453
20	Fiction	Boyce, Richard Fyfe, and Boyce, Katherine Randall, p. 502 Linebarger, Genevieve C., p. 502
22	Treaty Law	United Nations, Legal Department, p. 581
23	Memoirs	Boyce, Richard Fyfe, and Boyce, Katherine Randall, p. 614 Plischke, Elmer, p. 614

A good many studies in the field of American diplomacy contain handy, supplementary bibliographies and reading lists, of varying breadth and penetration. Some of the more comprehensive in scope and inclusion (each containing more than one hundred items) are to be found in:

Etzold, Thomas H. THE CONDUCT OF AMERICAN FOREIGN RELATIONS: THE OTHER SIDE OF DIPLOMACY. New York: New Viewpoints, 1977, pp. 133–54.

Harr, John Ensor. THE PROFESSIONAL DIPLOMAT. Princeton, N.J.: Princeton University Press, 1969, pp. 387–96.

McCamy, James L. CONDUCT OF THE NEW DIPLOMACY. New York: Harper and Row, 1964, pp. 287–95.

Plischke, Elmer. CONDUCT OF AMERICAN DIPLOMACY. 3d ed. Princeton, N.J.: Van Nostrand, 1967, pp. 625–42.

Stuart, Graham H. AMERICAN DIPLOMATIC AND CONSULAR PRACTICE. 2d ed. New York: Appleton-Century-Crofts, 1952, pp. 453–60.

Similarly, extensive bibliographies, incorporating some references on U.S. diplomacy, although concerned primarily with substantive foreign policy and external relations, are contained in such sources as:

Blake, Nelson M., and Barck, Oscar T., Jr. THE UNITED STATES IN ITS WORLD RELATIONS. New York: McGraw-Hill, 1960, pp. 789–812.

Carleton, William G. THE REVOLUTION IN AMERICAN FOREIGN POLICY: ITS GLOBAL RANGE. New York: Random House, 1963, pp. 481–516.

Crabb, Cecil V., Jr. AMERICAN FOREIGN POLICY IN THE NUCLEAR AGE. 3d ed. New York: Harper and Row, 1972, pp. 491–513.

Gordon, Morton, and Vines, Kenneth N., eds. THEORY AND PRACTICE OF AMERICAN FOREIGN POLICY. New York: Crowell, 1955, pp. 541–48.

Guerrant, Edward O., ed. MODERN AMERICAN DIPLOMACY. Albuquerque: University of New Mexico Press, 1954, pp. 293–307.

Irish, Marian, and Frank, Elke. U.S. FOREIGN POLICY: CONTEXT, CONDUCT, CONTENT. New York: Harcourt Brace Jovanovich, 1975, pp. 531–45.

Leonard, L. Larry. ELEMENTS OF AMERICAN FOREIGN POLICY. New York: McGraw-Hill, 1953, pp. 589–600.

Lovell, John P. FOREIGN POLICY IN PERSPECTIVE. New York: Holt, Rinehart, and Winston, 1970, pp. 355–62.

Vocke, William C., ed. AMERICAN FOREIGN POLICY: AN ANALYTICAL APPROACH. New York: Free Press, 1976, pp. 309–21.

Williams, Benjamin H. AMERICAN DIPLOMACY: POLICIES AND PRACTICE. New York: McGraw-Hill, 1936, pp. 479–92.

A few bibliographies, also inclusive but of a more specialized nature, are appended to various studies, including:

Barnes, William, and Morgan, John Heath. THE FOREIGN SERVICE OF THE UNITED STATES. Washington, D.C.: Government Printing Office, 1961, pp. 407–12.

Esterline, John H., and Black, Robert B. INSIDE FOREIGN POLICY: THE DEPARTMENT OF STATE POLITICAL SYSTEM AND ITS SUBSYSTEMS. Palo Alto, Calif.: Mayfield, 1975, pp. 253-59.

Ikle, Fred Charles. HOW NATIONS NEGOTIATE. New York: Praeger, 1964, pp. 256-64.

Kim, Young Hum. TWENTY YEARS OF CRISES: THE COLD WAR ERA. Englewood Cliffs, N.J.: Prentice-Hall, 1968, pp. 290-97.

Radway, Laurence I. FOREIGN POLICY AND NATIONAL DEFENSE. Glenview, Ill.: Scott, Foresman, 1969, pp. 191-202.

Schulzinger, Robert D. THE MAKING OF THE DIPLOMATIC MIND: THE TRAINING, OUTLOOK, AND STYLE OF UNITED STATES FOREIGN SERVICE OFFICERS, 1908-1931. Middletown, Conn.: Wesleyan University Press, 1975, pp. 199-231.

Warwick, Donald P. A THEORY OF PUBLIC BUREAUCRACY: POLITICS, PERSONALITY, AND ORGANIZATION IN THE STATE DEPARTMENT. Cambridge, Mass.: Harvard University Press, 1975, pp. 238-42.

Generally the citations incorporated into the above bibliographies and lists are restricted to unofficial monographs and some government documents, although a few listings also include references to article materials. A fairly comprehensive, though somewhat general, guide to unofficial bibliographies of official documentation is to be found in:

Plischke, Elmer, ed. AMERICAN FOREIGN RELATIONS: A BIBLIOGRAPHY OF OFFICIAL SOURCES. College Park: Bureau of Governmental Research, University of Maryland, 1955, pp. 47-53.

ADDITIONAL GUIDES AND INDEXES TO JOURNAL AND PERIODICAL RESOURCES

Most of the references included in this section provide research guidance to journal and periodical literature. General indexes include the INTERNATIONAL INDEX TO PERIODICALS and READER'S GUIDE TO PERIODICAL LITERATURE. Others are generally more specialized, such as the INDEX TO LEGAL PERIODICALS and those restricted to political science, public policy, and the social sciences. Some of the entries furnish guidance to abstracts and reviews of books and journal articles, and others constitute ready sources of factual information.

ABC POL SCI (ADVANCED BIBLIOGRAPHY OF CONTENTS: POLITICAL SCIENCE AND GOVERNMENT). Santa Barbara, Calif.: ABC-Clio Press, 1969-- . 8/year. Annual cumulation.

Affords access to the contents of some 250 periodicals in English and foreign languages. Indexes from each issue cumulated into an annual index constituting the ninth issue. Each issue contains a list of the serial publications covered, tables of contents of these serials, and subject and author indexes. Serials arranged alphabetically in each issue. Covers such functional fields as decision making, economics, foreign policy, international relations, law, political science, and public administration.

HUMANITIES INDEX. New York: Wilson, 1974-- . Quarterly.

Supersedes SOCIAL SCIENCES AND HUMANITIES INDEX (below). Contents arranged alphabetically by subject, giving standard bibliographical information concerning articles published in a variety of journals in the humanities, including the fields of history, political criticism, and related subjects. An author listing of citations to book reviews and an index appended.

INDEX TO LEGAL PERIODICALS. New York: Wilson, 1888-- . Monthly except September. Annual and triennial cumulation.

Provides a comprehensive, continuing index to law reviews and other legal periodicals. Citations indexed according to author and subject, with list of subject headings and cross-references employed for indexing provided in each annual and three-year cumulative volume. Each volume also contains an index of the periodicals covered and a table of legal cases.

INTERNATIONAL INDEX TO PERIODICALS. New York: Wilson, 1911-58. Quarterly.

Constitutes an author and subject index to periodical materials published on various topics in a variety of fields, including foreign affairs, international law and organization, international relations, and political science. Superseded by the SOCIAL SCIENCES AND HUMANITIES INDEX (below), which in turn split into the SOCIAL SCIENCES INDEX (below) and the HUMANITIES INDEX (above) in 1974.

NINETEENTH CENTURY READER'S GUIDE TO PERIODICAL LITERATURE, 1890-1899. 2 vols. New York: Wilson, 1944.

Superseded by READER'S GUIDE TO PERIODICAL LITERATURE (below).

PUBLIC INTERNATIONAL LAW: A CURRENT BIBLIOGRAPHY OF ARTICLES. Compiled by Max Planck Institute. Berlin, Heidelberg, and New York: Springer-Verlag, 1975-- . Semiannual.

Provides systematic bibliography of international legal literature. Especially sections 4 (on treaties), 14 (on diplomacy and consular matters), 23 (on peaceful settlement of disputes), 24 (on peace and security), and 26 (on war and armed conflict).

PUBLIC POLICY STUDIES DOCUMENTS. Pittsburgh: University Center for International Studies, University of Pittsburgh, 1940-- . Annual.

Reference compilation providing guidance to journal literature, covering more than 150 social science periodicals. Each annual volume consists of two parts. The first contains a series of five indexes--to authors, specific subjects (such as diplomatic relations), geographical areas, proper names, and journals. Also provides information concerning persons cited and key subjects and their interrelations. The second part furnishes short abstracts of the articles included in the indexes. The Center for International Studies also publishes similar guides in the fields of intercultural, Russian, and strategic studies.

READER'S GUIDE TO PERIODICAL LITERATURE. New York: Wilson, 1900-- . Quarterly.

Provides an author and subject index to periodical materials currently published on a broad range of topics in a variety of fields, including economics, foreign affairs, history, international law and organization, international relations, political science, and journal reviews.

SOCIAL SCIENCE CITATION INDEX. Philadelphia: Institute for Scientific Information, 1969-- . Annual.

Integrated, multidisciplinary, current reference and search system for newly published social science journal literature. Covers twenty-six hundred of the world's social science periodicals. Currently consists of four volumes per year. Provides four types of indexes and guidance material: a citation index (which identifies previously published items--books, articles, and similar publications--being referred to in current journal literature), author index, organization or institution index, and "permuterm" subject index (to assist the researcher when there are no earlier publications on a subject, to provide useful background study and guidance).

SOCIAL SCIENCES AND HUMANITIES INDEX. New York: Wilson, 1959-73. Quarterly.

Author and subject index to periodical literature, giving standard bibliographical information. Superseded the INTERNATIONAL INDEX TO PERIODICALS (above). Superseded by the HUMANITIES INDEX (above) and SOCIAL SCIENCES INDEX (below) in 1974.

SOCIAL SCIENCES INDEX. New York: Wilson, 1974-- . Quarterly.

Author and subject index to periodical literature published in more than 250 periodicals, giving standard bibliographical information for materials in the social sciences. An author listing of citations to book reviews and an index appended. Supersedes SOCIAL SCIENCES AND HUMANITIES INDEX.

UNITED STATES POLITICAL SCIENCE DOCUMENTS. Pittsburgh: University Center for International Studies, University of Pittsburgh, 1975-- . Annual.

Comprehensive guide to journal articles in political science. Constitutes a published version of the computer-based information system maintained by the center. Articles quickly identified and documents succinctly described. Contains five indexes--authors, subjects, geographic areas, proper names (such as organizations, institutions, laws, and the like), and journals. In-depth description scheme of cited entries in part 2, furnishing up to nine items of information. Each volume contains reference to several thousand articles from more than one hundred journals.

THE UNIVERSAL REFERENCE SYSTEM: POLITICAL SCIENCE, GOVERNMENT AND PUBLIC POLICY SERIES. 10 vols. New York: Plenum, 1968. Annual supplements.

Cumulative, basic guide to political science literature--books, monographs, and articles. Some two thousand to four thousand items cited in each volume. Volumes cover different subject fields, such as bibliography of bibliographies in political science, current events, international affairs, legislative process and decision making, and public policy. Annual supplements since 1967, each consisting of two or more volumes.

ABSTRACTS, DIGESTS, AND REVIEWS

BOOK REVIEW DIGEST. New York: Wilson, 1905-- . Annual.

Index to reviews of current literature--nonfiction and fiction--that are published in selected U.S. journals and periodicals. Author entries, alphabetically arranged, providing the title, publisher, year of publication, pages, and price, with review excerpts arranged alphabetically by the name of the journal in which the review appears. Includes subject index.

BOOK REVIEW INDEX. Detroit: Gale Research Co., 1965-- . Annual.

Index listing the works of authors for whom reviews appear in a substantial number of selected journals and periodicals. Entries listed alphabetically according to the last name of the author, including the title, date of publication, and name of periodical in which the review appears.

CURRENT BOOK REVIEW CITATIONS. New York: Wilson, 1976-- . Annual.

Index to book reviews published in more than one thousand journals and periodicals, including both U.S. and foreign books.
Consists of two parts. The first cites book reviews alphabetically
according to author's names, giving titles and dates of publication of the books reviewed. Part 2 consists of title entries and
serves as an index to the first part.

INTERNATIONAL POLITICAL SCIENCE ABSTRACTS. Paris: International
Political Science Association, 1951-- . Quarterly.

Provides short abstracts of journal literature in political science.
Annotations provided respecting organization, coverage, and inclusion or comprehensiveness. Items arranged in topical categories, such as international relations and organization, political
science, and public administration, and thereunder alphabetically
by names of authors. Supported by UNESCO.

PERSPECTIVE. Washington, D.C.: Heldref, 1972-- . Monthly (combined
issues for January-February, July-August).

Provides reviews, usually not exceeding four hundred to five hundred words, of books in such fields as government, international
affairs, and political science.

DATA AND FACTS

DEADLINE DATA ON WORLD AFFAIRS. Greenwich, Conn.: Educational
Division of DMS, 1955-- . Weekly.

Information service card file providing factual information for every
country and major international organization. Surveys world news
media in a cross-referenced manner. Supplemented weekly with a
chronology and a subject index covering more than five hundred
subject areas.

FACTS ON FILE. New York: Facts on File, 1940-- . Weekly. Annual
cumulation.

Looseleaf information resource on current events, providing a
factual record of the week's events in the United States and
abroad. Information abstracted daily from leading news sources,
edited, classified, and indexed. Semimonthly cumulative indexes,
bound yearbooks, and five-year master indexes also provided.

HUMAN RELATIONS AREA FILES. New Haven, Conn.: Human Relations
Area Files, 1949-- ; microfilm cards, 1958-- . Updated irregularly.

Systematic data filing and retrieval system, consisting of 5" by 8"
paper slips and 3" by 5" microfilm cards. Each item is a page of

an article, book or manuscript processed for the files, containing annotations according to more than seven hundred categories of cultural and related information. Multiple copies allow for cross-filing and grouping into convenient subject topics.

KEESING'S CONTEMPORARY ARCHIVES. Bath, Engl.: Keesing's Publications, 1931-- . Weekly.

Diary of world events, including maps, plates, and tables for illustrative purposes, with an index continually updated.

NEWS DICTIONARY. New York: Facts on File, 1964-- . Annual.

Summarizes facts covering the events of each year, based on U.S. and foreign news sources, with materials arranged alphabetically by subjects, such as foreign policy, regional areas, specific countries, and the like.

POLITICAL HANDBOOK OF THE WORLD. Binghamton, N.Y.: Center for Comparative Political Research of the State University of New York at Binghamton, 1928, 1930-- . Annual.

Contains essential political information concerning approximately 160 countries and 100 intergovernmental agencies, listed alphabetically. Also contains two appendices on the United Nations and statistical data for selected indices. For individual countries, supplies such material as an essay on the factual background and government, political parties, legislature and executive, news media, and diplomatic representation (listing the names of ambassadors to the United States and the United Nations and U.S. ambassadors accredited abroad).

Schoenfeldt, Lyle F. "Data Archives as Resources for Research, Instruction, and Policy Planning." AMERICAN PSYCHOLOGIST 25 (July 1970): 609-16.

Short essay dealing with computer applications, major data archives, advantages and disadvantages of data archives, and data archives as resources for instruction and policy planning. Table 1 (pp. 610-11), lists some thirty major data archives, giving their names, addresses, and types of data and subject matter. Includes such data archives as the Bureau of Applied Social Research, Human Relations Files, International Development Data Bank, Inter-University Consortium for Political Research, Louis Harris Political Data Center, National Opinion Research Center, Roper Public Opinion Research Center, Survey Research Laboratory, and UCLA Political Behavior Archive.

STATESMAN'S YEARBOOK. London: Macmillan, 1864-- . Annual.

Updated yearbook consisting of tables, statistical information, maps, and other data on individual countries and other territories, international organizations, and the like, with comparative statistical tables. Country section alphabetically arranged, providing information on the geography, economy, government, diplomatic representation, and similar matters for individual countries.

WASHINGTON INFORMATION DIRECTORY. Washington, D.C.: Congressional Quarterly, 1975-76-- . Annual (in May).

Includes some fifteen to twenty chapters, including international affairs, national security, Congress and politics, and government personnel and services. Includes a comprehensive table of contents and indexes providing guidance to functional subjects and agencies or organizations. Current bibliography in each chapter.

OTHERS

THE HANDBOOK OF POLITICAL SCIENCE. Edited by Frank I. Greenstein and Nelson W. Polsby. 8 vols. Reading, Mass.: Addison-Wesley, 1975.

A collection of forty-eight articles written by a broad spectrum of authors, exploring a wide range of topics, grouped in the following categories: political science--scope and theory, governmental institutions and processes, policies and policymaking, international politics, and the like. A major segment of the discipline in each volume.

RESEARCH GUIDE IN POLITICAL SCIENCE. Edited by Carl Kalvelage, Morley Segal, and Peter J. Anderson. 2d ed. Morristown, N.J.: General Learning Press, 1976. 224 p.

Guide to source material and library use, primarily for undergraduate students. Part 1 devoted to the nature of research and writing; part 2 provides an annotated listing of basic references including specialized dictionaries, encyclopedias, guides to study, and opinion polls; and part 3 lists additional tools for the political science undergraduate.

SOCIAL SCISEARCH. Philadelphia: Institute for Scientific Information, 1974-- .

An on-line, interactive, interdisciplinary file of social science literature, accompanied by an instant retrieval system, providing ready information from a variety of journals and periodicals. The system furnishes citation searching and full text copy retrieval service. More than 1,400 journals are utilized, supplemented by 1,200 more in the science field where they are deemed to be relevant to social science. The system offers searching capability respecting more than 400,000 items published in recent years and about 7,500 additional items are supplemented each month.

GUIDES TO DISSERTATIONS

Abstracts

DISSERTATION ABSTRACTS INTERNATIONAL: A GUIDE TO DISSERTATIONS AND MONOGRAPHS AVAILABLE ON MICROFILM. Ann Arbor, Mich.: University Microfilms International, 1938-- . Quarterly.

> Began as MICROFILM ABSTRACTS (vols. 1-11), changed to DISSERTATION ABSTRACTS in 1952 (vol. 12), and to its current title in 1969 (vol. 30). Section A on the humanities and social sciences; section B on science and engineering. A compilation of dissertation abstracts arranged in various broad topical groupings, in alphabetical order, containing sections on political science which have subdivisions concerned with general matters, international law and relations, and public administration. Thereunder, dissertations listed alphabetically by name of author, each citation giving the title dissertation supervisor, university, date, and abstract outlining the nature and treatment of the subject.

General Indexes

AMERICAN DOCTORAL DISSERTATIONS. Ann Arbor, Mich.: University Microfilms International, 1961-62-- . Annual.

> Compiled for the Association of Research Libraries. Originally titled INDEX TO AMERICAN DOCTORAL DISSERTATIONS, and changed to its current title in 1964-65. An index to all dissertations accepted by American and Canadian universities during each academic year. Citations arranged by subject categories and alphabetically by the names of universities thereunder, providing the author's name, dissertation title, degree, and date for each entry.

COMPREHENSIVE DISSERTATION INDEX, 1861-1972. 37 vols. Ann Arbor, Mich.: Xerox University Microfilms, 1970.

> An index to dissertations. A cumulative listing arranged topically. Of special interest are vol. 17 (social sciences), vol. 27 (law and political science), vol. 28 (history), and vols. 33-37 (author index). Citations give the author's name, title, degree, year, institution, and number of pages.

DOCTORAL DISSERTATIONS ACCEPTED BY AMERICAN UNIVERSITIES. 22 vols. New York: Wilson, 1933-55. Annual, 1940-41 to 1954-55.

> Compiled for the Association of Research Libraries. Arrangement by major subject, and thereunder by universities, alphabetically arranged, and then by author. Citations give title and date. An index of authors and an alphabetical subject index are provided.

Functional Fields

"Doctoral Dissertations in Political Science." In AMERICAN POLITICAL SCI-
ENCE REVIEW, 1911-67. Annual.

> Entries grouped into two major sections dealing with dissertations
> under preparation or completed subsequent to the previous issue.
> Each major division comprised of a number of topical sections, with
> entries arranged alphabetically by author. Also published sepa-
> rately as a reprint. Generally published in the September issue in
> recent decades. Superseded by the following citation.

"Doctoral Dissertations in Political Science." In PS: NEWSLETTER OF THE
AMERICAN POLITICAL SCIENCE ASSOCIATION. 1968-- . Annual.

> Consists of two sections: "Dissertations-in-Preparation" and "Dis-
> sertations Completed." Each section consists of functional fields--
> which vary over the years--such as foreign and national institu-
> tions and behavior; international law, organization, and politics;
> public policy--functions and content; public administration; and
> United States political institutions, processes, and behavior. En-
> tries arranged alphabetically by name of author, providing the
> dissertation title and the university at which it is written. Usual-
> ly in the fall issue.

POLITICAL SCIENCE: A DISSERTATION BIBLIOGRAPHY. Ann Arbor, Mich.:
University Microfilms International, n.d. 74 p.

> General listing of over fifty-six hundred entries, alphabetically
> arranged by name of author. Each entry in this and the following
> compilations provides the name of the author, title, degree earned,
> granting institution, date of degree, number of pages, and cita-
> tion to DISSERTATION ABSTRACTS INTERNATIONAL (volume, is-
> sue, and page number).

POLITICAL SCIENCE: INTERNATIONAL LAW AND RELATIONS AND PUBLIC
ADMINISTRATION. Ann Arbor, Mich.: University Microfilms International,
n.d. 57 p. Also supplement on INTERNATIONAL LAW AND RELATIONS, n.d. 18 p.

> Consists of two sections: "International Law and Relations" and
> "Public Administration." Contains over twenty-one hundred entries
> in the first section and some sixteen hundred entries on public ad-
> ministration. Supplement contains approximately 425 entries.

UNITED NATIONS: A KEYWORD DISSERTATION BIBLIOGRAPHY. Ann Arbor, Mich.: University Microfilms International, n.d. 41 p.

> Contains citations to about 350 dissertations. First part, pp. 1-34,
> listing dissertations according to key subjects arranged by keywords;
> the second, pp. 35-41, providing a separate listing of author's
> names arranged alphabetically.

UNITED STATES FOREIGN RELATIONS: A CATALOGUE OF DISSERTATIONS.
Ann Arbor, Mich.: University Microfilms International, 1973. 21 p.

> Contains dissertations concerned with U.S. foreign affairs since
> 1900, and includes more than six hundred entries, arranged alpha-
> betically by author, with a subject index, pp. 19-21.

Other such functional dissertation lists are available in the fields of American
history (1492-1789), mass communications, the military, and the like, and the
number of such listings is likely to grow. Individual research service is available through the following:

DATRIX II. Ann Arbor, Mich.: Xerox University Microfilms.

> Mail-order, computerized retrieval service to compile, on specific
> request, a list of dissertations published since 1861 on a specific
> topic or fields to assist the researcher.

SELECTED JOURNALS AND PERIODICALS

The following is a selected list of English-language, primarily American, journals
and periodicals, both current and defunct or superseded, in the fields of administration, diplomacy, foreign affairs, international law and organization, policy science,
politics, world affairs, and area studies, providing materials on diplomatic and U.S.
foreign relations. With a few exceptions, journals and periodicals concerned with
such related fields as economics, geography, history, psychology, public opinion,
and sociology are not included; neither are foreign-language publications, those
concerned primarily with the United Nations, NATO, and other specific international organizations, news magazines, yearbooks, or law reviews; nor are those
that deal largely with military affairs--for such a compilation see the following:

Larson, Arthur D. "Periodicals." In his NATIONAL SECURITY AFFAIRS: A
GUIDE TO INFORMATION SOURCES, pp. 289-93. Management Information
Guide, vol. 27. Detroit: Gale Research Co., 1973.

Additional official Department of State periodicals and journals are listed in
chapter 22.

ADMINISTRATION AND SOCIETY. Beverly Hills, Calif.: Sage, 1969-- .
Quarterly. Formerly JOURNAL OF COMPARATIVE ADMINISTRATION.

ADMINISTRATIVE SCIENCE QUARTERLY. Ithaca, N.Y.: Graduate School of
Business and Public Administration, Cornell University, 1956-- .

AEI FOREIGN POLICY AND DEFENSE REVIEW. Washington, D.C.: American
Enterprise Institute, 1979-- . 6 per yr.

AFRICAN AFFAIRS. London: Royal African Society, 1901-- . Quarterly.

AFRICAN STUDIES. Johannesburg, South Africa: Witwatersrand University Press, 1942-- . Quarterly.

AFRICAN STUDIES REVIEW. East Lansing: African Studies Center, Michigan State University, 1970-- . 3/yr.

ALTERNATIVES: A JOURNAL OF WORLD POLICY. New York: Institute for World Order, 1975-- . Quarterly.

AMERICAN BEHAVIORAL SCIENTIST. Beverly Hills, Calif.: Sage, 1957-- . Bimonthly.

AMERICAN JOURNAL OF COMPARATIVE LAW. Ann Arbor, Mich.: American Association for the Comparative Study of Law, 1952-- . Quarterly.

AMERICAN JOURNAL OF INTERNATIONAL LAW. Washington, D.C.: American Society of International Law, 1907-- . Quarterly.

AMERICAN JOURNAL OF POLITICAL SCIENCE. Detroit: Wayne State University Press for Midwest Political Science Association, 1972-- . Quarterly. Successor to MIDWEST JOURNAL OF POLITICAL SCIENCE, 1957-1972.

AMERICAN POLITICAL SCIENCE REVIEW. Washington, D.C.: American Political Science Association, 1906-- . Quarterly.

AMERICAN POLITICS QUARTERLY. Beverly Hills, Calif.: Sage, 1973-- .

AMERICAN SLAVIC AND EAST EUROPEAN REVIEW. Seattle, Wash.: American Association for the Advancement of Slavic Studies, 1945-61. Semiannual to 1947. Quarterly, 1948-61. Changed to SLAVIC REVIEW in 1961.

AMERICAS. Washington, D.C.: Pan American Union, 1949-- . Monthly.

ANNALS OF THE AMERICAN ACADEMY OF POLITICAL AND SOCIAL SCIENCE. Philadelphia: American Academy of Political and Social Science, 1890-- . Bimonthly.

ANNALS OF THE ORGANIZATION OF AMERICAN STATES. Washington, D.C.: Organization of American States, 1949-- . Quarterly.

ARBITRATION JOURNAL. New York: American Arbitration Association, 1937-- . Quarterly.

ARBITRATOR. London: International Arbitration League, 1872-- . Irregular.

ASIAN FORUM. Washington, D.C.: 1969-- . Quarterly.

ASIAN REVIEW. London: East and West, 1953-- . Quarterly. Incorporates the ASIATIC REVIEW and the JOURNAL OF THE EAST ASIA ASSOCIATION.

ASIAN SURVEY. Berkeley, Calif.: Institute of International Studies, University of California, 1961-- . Monthly.

ASIA QUARTERLY. Brussels: University of Brussels, 1971-- .

ATLANTIC COMMUNITY QUARTERLY. Washington, D.C.: Atlantic Council of the United States, 1963-- .

ATLANTIC MONTHLY. Boston: 1875-- .

ATLANTIC STUDIES. Boulogne-sur-Seine, France: Atlantic Institute, 1964-68. Annual.

AUSTRALIAN JOURNAL OF POLITICS AND HISTORY. Brisbane: University of Queensland, 1955-- . Semiannual.

BEHAVIORAL SCIENCE. Ann Arbor: Mental Health Research Institute, University of Michigan, 1956-- . Bimonthly.

BEHAVIOR SCIENCE RESEARCH. New Haven, Conn.: Human Relations Area Files, 1965-- . Quarterly.

BRITISH JOURNAL OF INTERNATIONAL STUDIES. British International Studies Association, 1975-- . 3/yr.

BRITISH JOURNAL OF POLITICAL SCIENCE. New York: Cambridge University Press, 1971-- . Quarterly.

BULLETIN OF INTERNATIONAL NEWS. London: Royal Institute of International Affairs, 1924-45. Biweekly.

BULLETIN OF PEACE PROPOSALS. Oslo, Norway: International Peace Research Association, 1970-- . Quarterly.

CANADIAN JOURNAL OF ECONOMICS AND POLITICAL SCIENCE. Toronto: University of Toronto Press, 1935-67. Quarterly.

CARIBBEAN STUDIES. Rio Piedras: Institute of Caribbean Studies, University of Puerto Rico, 1961-- . Quarterly.

CHINA QUARTERLY. Paris: Congress for Cultural Freedom, 1960-- .

CHRONOLOGY OF INTERNATIONAL EVENTS AND DOCUMENTS. London: Royal Institute of International Affairs, 1945-- . Bimonthly. Supplement to WORLD TODAY.

COMMENTARY. New York: American Jewish Committee. 1945-- . Monthly.

COMPARATIVE POLITICAL STUDIES. Beverly Hills, Calif.: Sage, 1968-- . Quarterly.

COMPARATIVE STRATEGY: AN INTERNATIONAL JOURNAL. New York: Crane, Russak, 1978-- . Quarterly.

COOPERATION AND CONFLICT: NORDIC JOURNAL OF INTERNATIONAL POLITICS. Oslo, Norway: Nordic Cooperation Committee for the Study of International Politics, 1965-- . Semiannual to 1973. Quarterly, 1974-- .

CURRENT. Washington, D.C.: Heldref, 1960-- . Monthly (combined issues for May-June, July-August).

CURRENT DEVELOPMENTS IN UNITED STATES FOREIGN POLICY: SUMMARY OF EVENTS. Washington, D.C.: Brookings Institution, 1947-52. Ten issues per year. Issued as a supplement to MAJOR PROBLEMS OF UNITED STATES FOREIGN POLICY: A STUDY GUIDE; see separate entry below, p. 104.

CURRENT HISTORY. Philadelphia: Events Publishing Co., 1915-- . Monthly.

CURRENT READINGS IN INTERNATIONAL RELATIONS. Cambridge, Mass.: Massachusetts Institute of Technology, 1947-49. Semiannual.

DAEDALUS: JOURNAL OF THE AMERICAN ACADEMY OF ARTS AND SCIENCES. Cambridge, Mass.: American Academy of Arts and Sciences, Harvard University, 1871-- . Quarterly.

DEPARTMENT OF STATE BULLETIN. Washington, D.C.: U.S. Department of State, 1939-- . Weekly. January 1978-- . Monthly.

DEPARTMENT OF STATE NEWSLETTER. Washington, D.C.: U.S. Department of State, 1961-- . Monthly.

DIPLOMATIC HISTORY. Wilmington, Del.: Society for Historians of American Foreign Relations, 1977-- . Quarterly.

DIPLOMATIST: A REVIEW OF THE DIPLOMATIC AND CONSULAR WORLD. London: 1947-- . Monthly.

DISSENT. New York: 1954-- . Quarterly.

EVALUATION QUARTERLY: A JOURNAL OF APPLIED SOCIAL RESEARCH. Beverly Hills, Calif.: Sage, 1977-- .

EXTERNAL AFFAIRS. Ottawa: Canada, Department of External Affairs, 1948-- . Monthly.

FAR EASTERN QUARTERLY. Ann Arbor, Mich.: Association for Asian Studies, 1941-- .

FAR EASTERN SURVEY. New York: American Institute of Pacific Relations, 1932-61. Biweekly (monthly in summer).

FOREIGN AFFAIRS. New York: Council on Foreign Relations, 1922-- . Quarterly.

FOREIGN POLICY. Washington, D.C.: National Affairs, 1970-- . Quarterly.

FOREIGN POLICY BULLETIN. New York: Foreign Policy Association, 1921-- . Semimonthly.

FOREIGN POLICY REPORTS. New York: Foreign Policy Association, 1925-51. Irregular.

FOREIGN SERVICE JOURNAL. Washington, D.C.: American Foreign Service Association, 1924-- . Monthly.

FORUM. Philadelphia: Events Publishing Co., 1886-1950. Monthly.

GOVERNMENT AND OPPOSITION. London: Government and Opposition, 1965-- . Quarterly.

HARPER'S MAGAZINE. New York: 1850-- . Monthly.

HARVARD STUDIES IN INTERNATIONAL AFFAIRS. Cambridge, Mass.: Committee on International and Regional Studies, Harvard University, 1951-- . Irregular.

HEADLINE SERIES. New York: Foreign Policy Association, 1943-- . Irregular.

Each issue devoted to a particular topic.

HISPANIC-AMERICAN REPORT. Stanford, Calif.: Stanford University, 1948-64. Monthly.

INDIAN JOURNAL OF PUBLIC ADMINISTRATION. New Delhi: Indian Institute of Public Administration, 1955-- . Quarterly.

INDIAN POLITICAL SCIENCE REVIEW. Delhi: Department of Political Science, University of Delhi, 1966-- . Quarterly.

INDIA QUARTERLY. New Delhi: Appadorai, 1945-- .

INTER-AMERICAN. New York: Inter-American, 1942-46. Monthly.

INTER-AMERICAN ECONOMIC AFFAIRS. Washington, D.C.: Institute of Inter-American Studies, 1947-- . Quarterly.

INTERNATIONAL AFFAIRS. London: Royal Institute of International Affairs, 1922-- . Bimonthly to 1939. Quarterly (irregular), 1940-- .

INTERNATIONAL AND COMPARATIVE LAW QUARTERLY. London: Society of Comparative Legislation, 1952-- . Formed by the union of INTERNATIONAL LAW QUARTERLY and JOURNAL OF COMPARATIVE LEGISLATION.

INTERNATIONAL CONCILIATION. New York: Carnegie Endowment for International Peace, 1907-72. Monthly during academic year.

INTERNATIONAL INTERACTIONS: A TRANSNATIONAL MULTIDISCIPLINARY JOURNAL. London: Gordon and Breach Science Publisher, 1975-- . Quarterly. Successor to WAR/PEACE REPORT and NEW PRIORITIES.

INTERNATIONAL JOURNAL. Toronto: Canadian Institute for International Affairs, 1946-- . Quarterly.

INTERNATIONAL JOURNAL OF MIDDLE EAST STUDIES. London: Cambridge University Press, 1970-- . Quarterly.

INTERNATIONAL JOURNAL OF POLITICS. White Plains, N.Y.: International Arts and Sciences Press, 1971-- . Quarterly. Provides English-language translations of foreign-language materials.

INTERNATIONAL ORGANIZATION. Boston: World Peace Foundation, 1947-- . Quarterly.

INTERNATIONAL POLITICAL SCIENCE REVIEW. Beverly Hills, Calif.: Sage, 1980-- . Quarterly.

INTERNATIONAL SECURITY. Boston: Center for Science and International Affairs, Kennedy School of Government, Harvard University, 1976-- . Quarterly.

INTERNATIONAL SOCIAL SCIENCE JOURNAL. Paris: Unesco, 1949-- . Quarterly.

INTERNATIONAL STUDIES QUARTERLY. Beverly Hills, Calif.: Sage for International Studies Association, 1957-- .

INTER-PARLIAMENTARY BULLETIN. Geneva: Bureau of Inter-Parliamentary Union, 1920-- . 5/yr.

INTER-PARLIAMENTARY UNION CONSTITUTIONAL AND PARLIAMENTARY INFORMATION. Geneva: Bureau of Inter-Parliamentary Union, 1950-- . Quarterly.

JERUSALEM JOURNAL OF INTERNATIONAL RELATIONS. New York: Leonard Davis Institute for International Relations and Hebrew University of Jerusalem, 1975-- . Quarterly.

JOURNAL OF ADMINISTRATION OVERSEAS. London: H.M. Stationery Office, 1962-- . Quarterly.

JOURNAL OF AMERICAN STUDIES. New York: British Association for American Studies, 1967-- . Biennial.

JOURNAL OF APPLIED BEHAVIORAL SCIENCE. Washington, D.C.: National Training Laboratories, 1965-- . Quarterly.

JOURNAL OF ASIAN STUDIES. Ann Arbor, Mich.: Association for Asian Studies, 1941-56. Quarterly.

JOURNAL OF CENTRAL EUROPEAN AFFAIRS. Boulder. University of Colorado, 1941-64. Quarterly.

JOURNAL OF COMPARATIVE ADMINISTRATION. Beverly Hills, Calif.: Sage, 1969-74. Quarterly. Superseded by ADMINISTRATION AND SOCIETY.

JOURNAL OF CONFLICT RESOLUTION. Ann Arbor: University of Michigan, 1957-- . Quarterly.

JOURNAL OF CONTEMPORARY HISTORY. London: Weidenfeld and Nicolson, Institute for Advanced Studies in Contemporary History, 1966-- . Quarterly.

JOURNAL OF INTER-AMERICAN STUDIES AND WORLD AFFAIRS. Miami, Fla.: University of Miami, 1959-- . Quarterly.

JOURNAL OF INTERNATIONAL AFFAIRS. New York: Columbia University, 1947-- . Semiannual.

JOURNAL OF LATIN AMERICAN STUDIES. London: Cambridge University Press, 1969-- . Semiannual.

JOURNAL OF MODERN AFRICAN STUDIES. London: Cambridge University Press, 1963-- . Quarterly.

JOURNAL OF PEACE RESEARCH. Oslo, Norway: International Peace Research Association, 1964-- . Quarterly.

JOURNAL OF POLICY MODELING. New York: Elsevier North-Holland for the Society for Policy Modeling, 1978-- . 3/yr.

JOURNAL OF POLITICS. Gainesville, Fla.: Southern Political Science Association, 1939-- . Quarterly.

JOURNAL OF PUBLIC LAW. Atlanta: Emory University Law School, 1952-73. Semiannual.

JOURNAL OF SOUTHERN AFRICAN AFFAIRS. College Park, Md.: Southern African Research Association, 1977-- . Quarterly.

KEESING'S CONTEMPORARY ARCHIVES. Bath, Engl.: Keesing's Publications, 1931-- . Weekly.

LATIN AMERICA TODAY. New York: Latin American Research Bureau, 1951-- . Monthly.

LAW AND CONTEMPORARY PROBLEMS. Durham, N.C.: School of Law, Duke University, 1933-- . Quarterly.

LAW AND SOCIETY REVIEW. Denver: Law and Society Association, 1966-- . 5/yr.

MAJOR PROBLEMS OF UNITED STATES FOREIGN POLICY: A STUDY GUIDE. Washington, D.C.: Brookings Institution, 1947-54. Annual. For some years, supplemented by CURRENT DEVELOPMENTS IN UNITED STATES FOREIGN POLICY: SUMMARY OF EVENTS, see separate entry, p. 100.

MIDDLE EASTERN AFFAIRS. New York: Council for Middle Eastern Affairs, 1950-- . Monthly.

MIDDLE EASTERN STUDIES. London: Frank Cass, 1964-- . 3 per yr.

MIDDLE EAST JOURNAL. Washington, D.C.: Middle East Institute, 1947-- . Quarterly.

MIDWEST JOURNAL OF POLITICAL SCIENCE. Detroit: Midwest Conference of Political Scientists, 1957-72. Quarterly. Superseded by AMERICAN JOURNAL OF POLITICAL SCIENCE.

MODERN ASIAN STUDIES. New York: Cambridge University Press, 1967-- . Quarterly.

ORBIS. Philadelphia: Foreign Policy Research Institute, University of Pennsylvania, 1957-- . Quarterly.

PACIFIC AFFAIRS. New York: Institute of Pacific Relations, 1928-- . Quarterly.

PAN AMERICAN: MAGAZINE OF THE AMERICAS. New York: Famous Features, 1940-- . Monthly.

PAN AMERICAN UNION: BULLETIN. Washington, D.C.: Pan American Union, 1893-1948. Monthly. Superseded by ANNALS OF THE ORGANIZATION OF AMERICAN STATES.

PARLIAMENTARY AFFAIRS. London: Oxford University Press with cooperation of Hansard Society, 1948-- . Quarterly.

POLICY ANALYSIS. Berkeley: University of California Press, 1975-- . Quarterly.

POLICY AND POLITICS. London: Macmillan Journals, 1972-- . Quarterly.

POLICY REVIEW. Washington, D.C.: Heritage Foundation, 1977-- . Quarterly.

POLICY SCIENCES. New York: American Elsevier, 1970-- . Quarterly.

POLICY STUDIES JOURNAL. Urbana, Ill.: Policy Studies Organization, 1972-- . Quarterly.

POLICY STUDIES REVIEW ANNUAL. Beverly Hills, Calif.: Sage, 1977-- .

POLITICAL AFFAIRS. New York: New Century, 1922-- . Monthly.

POLITICAL METHODOLOGY. Los Altos, Calif.: Geron-X Publishers, 1974-- . Quarterly.

POLITICAL QUARTERLY. London: Turnstile, 1930-- .

POLITICAL SCIENCE. Victoria, New Zealand: Political Science Society, Victoria University College, 1948-- . Semiannual.

POLITICAL SCIENCE QUARTERLY. New York: Academy of Political Science, Columbia University, 1886-- .

POLITICAL STUDIES. Oxford: Political Studies Association of the United Kingdom, 1953-- . 8 per yr.

POLITICS AND SOCIETY. Los Altos, Calif.: Geron-X Publishers, 1971-- . Quarterly.

POLITY: JOURNAL OF THE NORTHEASTERN POLITICAL SCIENCE ASSOCIATION. Amherst, Mass.: University of Massachusetts, 1968-- . Quarterly.

PUBLIC ADMINISTRATION REVIEW. Chicago: American Society for Public Administration, 1940-- . Quarterly.

PUBLIC CHOICE. Blacksburg: Center for the Study of Public Choice, Virginia Polytechnic Institute, 1948-- . Quarterly.

PUBLIC INTEREST. New York: National Affairs, 1965-- . Quarterly.

PUBLIC OPINION. Washington, D.C.: American Enterprise Institute, 1978-- . Bimonthly.

PUBLIC OPINION QUARTERLY. New York: American Association for Public Opinion Research, Columbia University Press, 1937-- .

PUBLIC POLICY. Cambridge, Mass.: Harvard College, 1940-- . Quarterly.

REVIEW OF POLITICS. Notre Dame, Ind.: University of Notre Dame, 1939-- . Quarterly.

ROYAL CENTRAL ASIAN SOCIETY JOURNAL. London: Royal Central Asian Society, 1903-- . Quarterly.

SIMULATION. La Jolla, Calif.: Society for Computer Simulation, 1948-- . Monthly.

SIMULATION AND GAMES. Beverly Hills, Calif.: Sage, 1970-- . Quarterly.

SLAVIC REVIEW. Seattle, Wash.: American Association for the Advancement of Slavic Studies, 1961-- . Quarterly.

SLAVONIC AND EAST EUROPEAN REVIEW. New York: Cambridge University Press, 1967-- . 3 per yr.

SOCIAL STUDIES. Philadelphia: McKinley Publishing Co., 1909-- . 8 per yr.

SOUTHWESTERN SOCIAL SCIENCE QUARTERLY. Dallas: Southwestern Social Science Association, 1920-- .

SURVEY OF INTERNATIONAL AFFAIRS. London: Royal Institute of International Affairs, 1920-38. Annual.

SWISS REVIEW OF POLITICS. Zurich: Neue Zuercher Zeitung, 1951-- . Monthly.

TERRORISM: AN INTERNATIONAL JOURNAL. New York: Crane, Russak, 1977-- . Quarterly.

VIRGINIA QUARTERLY REVIEW. Charlottesville: University of Virginia, 1925-- .

VITAL SPEECHES OF THE DAY. New York: City News Publishing Co., 1934-- . Semimonthly.

WAR/PEACE REPORT. New York: 1961-75. Monthly. Superseded by INTERNATIONAL INTERACTIONS

WASHINGTON REVIEW OF STRATEGIC AND INTERNATIONAL STUDIES. New Brunswick, N.J.: Transaction Periodicals Consortium, 1978-- . Quarterly.

WESTERN POLITICAL QUARTERLY. Salt Lake City, Utah: Western Political Science Association and Pacific Northwest Political Science Association, 1948-- . Quarterly.

WORLD AFFAIRS. Toronto: World Affairs Press, 1935-- . Monthly.

WORLD AFFAIRS. Washington, D.C.: American Peace Society, 1834-- . Quarterly.

WORLD AFFAIRS. Wellington, New Zealand: United Nations Association of New Zealand, 1945-- Quarterly.

WORLD AFFAIRS INTERPRETER. Los Angeles: University of Southern California, 1931-55. Quarterly. Title changed to WORLD AFFAIRS QUARTERLY.

WORLD AFFAIRS QUARTERLY. Los Angeles: University of Southern California, 1955-60. Title originally WORLD AFFAIRS INTERPRETER, see preceding entry.

WORLD POLITICS. Princeton, N.J.: Princeton Center of International Studies, 1948-- . Quarterly.

WORLD TODAY. London: Royal Institute of International Affairs, 1945-- . Monthly. Supplemented by CHRONOLOGY OF INTERNATIONAL EVENTS AND DOCUMENTS; see separate entry above, p. 100.

YALE REVIEW. New Haven, Conn.: Tuttle, Morehouse, and Taylor, 1911-- . Quarterly.

Chapter 7

THE PRESIDENCY AND FOREIGN RELATIONS

The presidency is a dynamic office and has been made the subject of extensive literary concern over the years, especially since World War II. The materials contained in this chapter are of various types, including studies of a general, broad scope, those concerned more precisely with executive powers and functions, those that concentrate on the presidency's foreign relations role, the president as commander in chief and diplomat in chief, presidential leadership and image, executive privilege, the relations of the president to Congress, and the vice-presidency. Other matters, including tenure of office, presidential constituencies, impeachment, presidential politics and the like, are not included. Aside from relevant references contained in chapter 6, additional guidance to resources on the presidency may be found in:

Greenstein, Fred I.; Berman, Larry; and Felzenberg, Alvin S.; with Lidtke, Doris. EVOLUTION OF THE MODERN PRESIDENCY: A BIBLIOGRAPHICAL SURVEY. Washington, D.C.: American Enterprise Institute, 1977. Unpaged.

> Consists of 2,504 entries, with author index.

Current essay material is available in the issues of:

PRESIDENTIAL STUDIES QUARTERLY. New York: Center for the Study of the Presidency, 1970-- .

Additional materials on individual presidencies is provided in the following:

THE AMERICAN PRESIDENCY SERIES. Lawrence: Regents Press of Kansas, 1973-- .

> Separate volumes on individual presidencies, dealing with the development and operation of the office, the relations of the President with Congress, the Secretary of State and other executive officers, the media, and others, including foreign diplomats. Several volumes have been published. Eventually expected to include all presidencies from that of George Washington to date.

Gibson, Ronald, ed. NAME AND SUBJECT INDEX TO THE PRESIDENTIAL CHRONOLOGY SERIES, GEORGE WASHINGTON TO GERALD FORD. Dobbs Ferry, N.Y.: Oceana, 1977. 160 p.

> Provides key dates in the lives of the presidents, a personal name and a subject index, bibliography on the presidency, and additional documentation not provided in the individual presidency volumes, cited below.

PRESIDENTIAL CHRONOLOGY SERIES. Dobbs Ferry, N.Y.: Oceana, 1977-- .

> Individual volumes on particular presidencies, providing chronologies of important events and developments, documentary sections, and bibliographies.

U.S. Library of Congress. PRESIDENTIAL INAUGURATIONS: A SELECTED LIST OF REFERENCES. 3d ed. Washington, D.C.: 1969. 230 p.

_____. THE PRESIDENTS OF THE UNITED STATES, 1789-1962: A SELECTED LIST OF REFERENCES. Compiled by Donald H. Mugridge. Washington, D.C.: U.S. Library of Congress, 1963. 159 p.

GENERAL LITERATURE

The following list is representative of the growing literature of a general nature dealing with the presidency. It includes the well-known works of Grover Cleveland, William Howard Taft, and Woodrow Wilson--antedating World War I--as well as those of Louis Brownlow, James MacGregor Burns, Edward S. Corwin, Herman Finer, Sidney Hyman, Louis W. Koenig, Harold J. Laski, George E. Reedy, Arthur M. Schlesinger, Jr., Rexford G. Tugwell, Aaron B. Wildavsky, and others. All of these and most others are twentieth-century contributions. Aside from Finley and Sanderson (1908), a few antedate World War II--Agar, Moley, and Stanwood--but increasing attention has been devoted to the office and its incumbents since the early 1960s.

Some of the remaining studies are generally concerned with the person and/or office of president or chief executive, including Bell, Cunliffe, Egger, Fincher, Hersey, Hyman, Linville, and Warren. Others deal with the presidency in a broader way, such as those of Cornwell, Hess, Hughes, Rossiter, Sheehan, Vinyard, and Warner, with several emphasizing the modern or contemporary presidency--Heller, James, McConnell, Murphy, Polsby, and Thomas. The analyses of Hart, Stanwood, and Thach suggest the importance of the historical aspect of the presidency, whereas those of Dunn and Lubell are more concerned with the future. Some authors introduce a variety of particular perspectives or foci--Barber, Califano, Goebel and Goebel, Hoy and Bernstein, Lorant, Morris, Paolucci, Rankin, Schubert, Sickels, and Smith--or are basically assessorial--such as Coyle, Cronin, Henley, Reedy, and others. The studies of Ford, Small, Tourtellot, and Truman present the views of presidents on the presidency. A few studies review the nature and problems of presidential transition--David and Henry--and, since 1950, more attention has been paid to presidential disability and succession, materials on which are in a separate subsection.

Agar, Herbert. THE PEOPLE'S CHOICE: FROM WASHINGTON TO HARDING. Boston: Houghton Mifflin, 1933. 337 p.

"The American Presidency." CURRENT HISTORY 66 (June 1974): 241-77.

Entire issue--symposium of several articles.

"The American Presidency in the Last Half Century." CURRENT HISTORY 39 (October 1960): 193-236.

Entire issue--symposium of eight articles.

Bach, Stanley, and Sulzner, George T., eds. PERSPECTIVE ON THE PRESIDENCY: A COLLECTION. Lexington, Mass.: Heath, 1974. 432 p. Bib.

Bailey, Harry A., Jr., ed. CLASSICS OF THE AMERICAN PRESIDENCY. Oak Park, Ill.: Moore, 1980.

Forty-two essays by different authors.

Barber, James David. THE PRESIDENTIAL CHARACTER: PREDICTING PERFORMANCE IN THE WHITE HOUSE. Englewood Cliffs, N.J.: Prentice-Hall, 1977. 588 p.

Bell, Jack. THE PRESIDENCY: OFFICE OF POWER. Boston: Allyn and Bacon, 1967. 182 p.

_____. THE SPLENDID MISERY: THE STORY OF THE PRESIDENCY AND POWER POLITICS AT CLOSE RANGE. Garden City, N.Y.: Doubleday, 1960. 474 p.

Dulles, Bloh. MEN OF GOOD INTENTIONS: CRISIS OF THE AMERICAN PRESIDENCY. Garden City, N.Y.: Doubleday, 1960. 234 p.

Brownlow, Louis. THE PRESIDENT AND THE PRESIDENCY. Chicago: Aldine, 1949. 137 p.

Bundy, McGeorge. "The Presidency and Peace." FOREIGN AFFAIRS 42 (April 1964): 353-66.

Burns, James MacGregor. PRESIDENTIAL GOVERNMENT: THE CRUCIBLE OF LEADERSHIP. Boston: Houghton Mifflin, 1966. 366 p.

Califano, Joseph A., Jr. A PRESIDENTIAL NATION. New York: Norton, 1975. 338 p.

Clark, G. Edward. "Executive Branch of the Government: Dynamics in a Cloister." FOREIGN SERVICE JOURNAL 34 (February 1957): 22-23, 48.

Clark, Keith C., and Legere, Laurence J., eds. THE PRESIDENT AND THE MANAGEMENT OF NATIONAL SECURITY: A REPORT BY THE INSTITUTE OF DEFENSE ANALYSIS. New York: Praeger, 1969. 274 p. Bibliog.

Cleveland, Grover. PRESIDENTIAL PROBLEMS. New York: Century, 1904. 281 p.

Congressional Quarterly. PRESIDENCY. Washington, D.C.: 1974-- . Annual.

Cornwell, Elmer E. THE AMERICAN PRESIDENCY: VITAL CENTER. Chicago: Scott, Foresman, 1966. 166 p.

Corwin, Edward S. THE PRESIDENT: OFFICE AND POWERS, 1789-1957: HISTORY AND ANALYSIS OF PRACTICE AND OPINION. 4th ed. New York: New York University Press, 1957. 519 p. Bibliog.

Corwin, Edward S., and Koenig, Louis W. THE PRESIDENCY TODAY. New York: New York University Press, 1956. 139 p.

Coyle, David C. ORDEAL OF THE PRESIDENCY. Washington, D.C.: Public Affairs, 1960. 408 p.

Cronin, Thomas E. THE STATE OF THE PRESIDENCY. Boston: Little, Brown, 1975. 355 p. Bibliog.

Cronin, Thomas E., and Tugwell, Rexford G., eds. THE PRESIDENCY REAPPRAISED. 2d ed. New York: Holt, Rinehart, and Winston, 1977. 384 p.

Cunliffe, Marcus. AMERICAN PRESIDENTS AND THE PRESIDENCY. New York: New American Library, 1958. 192 p.; 2d ed. New York: American Heritage Press, 1972. 446 p. Bibliog.

David, Paul, ed. THE PRESIDENTIAL ELECTION AND TRANSITION, 1960-1961. Washington, D.C.: Brookings Institution, 1961. 353 p.

A DISCUSSION WITH GERALD R. FORD: THE AMERICAN PRESIDENCY. Washington, D.C.: American Enterprise Institute, 1977. 21 p.
    Question and answer symposium, 27 March 1977.

Dunn, Charles W., ed. THE FUTURE OF THE AMERICAN PRESIDENCY. Pennsauken, N.J.: Lehigh Press, 1975. 363 p.

Egger, Rowland A. THE PRESIDENT OF THE UNITED STATES. 2d ed. New York: McGraw-Hill, 1972. 198 p. Bibliog.

Filler, Louis. THE PRESIDENT SPEAKS: FROM WILLIAM McKINLEY TO L.B. JOHNSON. New York: Capricorn, 1965. 416 p.

Fincher, Ernest B. THE PRESIDENT OF THE UNITED STATES. New York: Abelard-Schuman, 1955. 192 p. Bibliog.

Finer, Herman. THE PRESIDENCY: CRISIS AND REGENERATION. Chicago: University of Chicago Press, 1960. 374 p. Bibliog.

Finley, John Huston, and Sanderson, John F. THE AMERICAN EXECUTIVE AND EXECUTIVE METHODS. New York: Century, 1908. 352 p.

Goebel, Dorothy B., and Goebel, Julius, Jr. GENERALS IN THE WHITE HOUSE. Garden City, N.Y.: Doubleday, Doran, 1945. 276 p.

Hart, James. THE AMERICAN PRESIDENCY IN ACTION, 1789: A STUDY IN CONSTITUTIONAL HISTORY. New York: Macmillan, 1948. 256 p.

Heller, Francis H. THE PRESIDENCY: A MODERN PERSPECTIVE. New York: Random House, 1960. 114 p. Bibliog.

Henley, Wallace. THE WHITE HOUSE MYSTIQUE. New York: Revell, 1976. 126 p.

Henry, Laurin L. PRESIDENTIAL TRANSITIONS. Washington, D.C.: Brookings Institution, 1960. 755 p.

    Especially chapters 8, 13, 18, 22, 27, and 36.

        . TRANSFERRING THE PRESIDENCY: VARIATIONS, TRENDS, AND PATTERNS. Washington, D.C.: Brookings Institution, 1958. 194 p.

Hersey, John. THE PRESIDENT. New York: Knopf, 1975. 153 p.

Hess, Stephen. ORGANIZING THE PRESIDENCY. Washington, D.C.: Brookings Institution, 1976. 228 p.

Hill, John Philip. THE FEDERAL EXECUTIVE. Boston: Houghton Mifflin, 1916. 294 p.

Hoxie, Ralph Gordon, ed. THE PRESIDENCY OF THE 1970'S: PROCEEDINGS OF THE 1971 MONTAUK SYMPOSIUM ON THE PRESIDENT OF THE UNITED STATES. New York: Center for the Study of the Presidency, 1973. 196 p.

Hoy, John C., and Bernstein, Melvin H., eds. THE EFFECTIVE PRESIDENT. Pacific Palisades, Calif.: Palisades Publishers, 1976. 189 p.

Hughes, Emmet John. THE LIVING PRESIDENCY: THE RESOURCES AND DILEMMAS OF THE AMERICAN PRESIDENTIAL OFFICE. New York: Coward, McCann, and Geoghegan, 1973. 377 p.

Hyman, Sidney. THE AMERICAN PRESIDENT. New York: Harper, 1954. 342 p.

Especially chapter 12.

———. "To Ease the Burden of the Presidency." NEW YORK TIMES MAGA-ZINE, 23 March 1958, pp. 27, 96-98.

———, ed. "The Office of the American Presidency." ANNALS OF THE AMERICAN ACADEMY OF POLITICAL AND SOCIAL SCIENCE 307 (September 1956): entire issue.

Irish, Marian D. "The Organization Man in the Presidency." JOURNAL OF POLITICS 20 (May 1958): 259-77.

James, Dorothy Buckton. THE CONTEMPORARY PRESIDENCY. New York: Pegasus, 1969. 187 p. 2d ed. New York: Pegasus, 1974. 336 p.

Johnson, Donald B., and Walker, Jack L., eds. THE DYNAMICS OF THE AMERICAN PRESIDENCY. New York: Wiley, 1964. 355 p.

Especially section 11.

Johnson, Walter. 1600 PENNSYLVANIA AVENUE: PRESIDENTS AND THE PEOPLE, 1929-1956. Boston: Little, Brown, 1960. 390 p. Bibliog.

Kallenbach, Joseph E. THE AMERICAN CHIEF EXECUTIVE: THE PRESIDENCY AND THE GOVERNORSHIP. New York: Harper and Row, 1966. 622 p.

Koenig, Louis W. THE CHIEF EXECUTIVE. 3d ed. New York: Harcourt Brace Jovanovich, 1975. 452 p. Bibliog.

Kuie, Vukan. "Theory and Practice of the American Presidency." REVIEW OF POLITICS 23 (July 1961): 307-22.

Lammers, William W. PRESIDENTIAL POLITICS: PATTERNS AND PROSPECTS. New York: Harper and Row, 1976. 310 p. Bibliog.

Emphasis on reform since 1932.

Laski, Harold J. THE AMERICAN PRESIDENCY: AN INTERPRETATION. New York: Harper, 1940. 278 p.

    Especially section 4.

Linville, C.E. THE PRESIDENT OF THE UNITED STATES. New York: Oxford University Press, 1965. 92 p.

Lockwood, Henry C. THE ABOLITION OF THE PRESIDENCY. New York: Worthington, 1884. 331 p.

Lorant, Stefan. THE GLORIOUS BURDEN: THE AMERICAN PRESIDENCY. New York: Harper and Row, 1968. 959 p. Bibliog. Photos.

_____. THE PRESIDENCY: A PICTORIAL HISTORY OF PRESIDENTIAL ELECTIONS FROM WASHINGTON TO TRUMAN. New York: Macmillan, 1951. 775 p. Bibliog.

Loss, Richard. "Dissolving Concepts of the Presidency." POLITICAL SCIENCE REVIEWER 4 (Fall 1974): 133–68.

Lubell, Samuel. THE FUTURE WHILE IT HAPPENED. New York: Norton, 1973. 162 p.

McConnell, Grant. THE MODERN PRESIDENCY. 2d ed. New York: St. Martin's, 1977. 294 p. Bibliog.

Moley, Raymond L. AFTER SEVEN YEARS. New York: Harper, 1939. 446 p.

Morris, Richard B. GREAT PRESIDENTIAL DECISIONS. 2d ed. Philadelphia: Lippincott, 1973. 508 p. Bibliog.

Murphy, Charles J.V. "The White House Since Sputnik." FORTUNE, January 1958, pp. 98–101, 228, 230, 232.

Murphy, John F. THE PINNACLE: THE CONTEMPORARY AMERICAN PRESIDENCY. Philadelphia: Lippincott, 1974. 215 p.

Nathan, Richard P. "The 'Administrative Presidency.'" PUBLIC INTEREST 44 (Summer 1976): 40–54.

Neustadt, Richard E. "The Presidency at Mid-Century." LAW AND CONTEMPORARY PROBLEMS 21 (Autumn 1956): 609–45.

Paolucci, Henry. WAR, PEACE AND THE PRESIDENCY. New York: McGraw-Hill, 1968. 241 p.

Parker, Reginald. "The President as Head of the Executive-Administrative Hierarchy: A Survey." JOURNAL OF PUBLIC LAW 8 (Fall 1959): 437-61.

Patterson, Caleb Perry. "The President as Chief Administrator." JOURNAL OF POLITICS 11 (February 1949): 218-35.

_____. PRESIDENTIAL GOVERNMENT IN THE UNITED STATES: THE UN-WRITTEN CONSTITUTION. Chapel Hill: University of North Carolina Press, 1947. 301 p. Bibliog.

Polsby, Nelson W., ed. THE MODERN PRESIDENCY. New York: Random House, 1973. 236 p.

"The Presidency." AMERICAN HERITAGE 15 (August 1964): 4-112.

Entire issue--16 articles.

"The Presidency in Transition." JOURNAL OF POLITICS 11 (February 1949): 1-256.

Entire issue--introduction with twelve articles.

"The Presidential Office." LAW AND CONTEMPORARY PROBLEMS 21 (Autumn 1956): 607-752.

Entire issue--foreword and seven articles.

Rankin, Robert S., ed. THE PRESIDENCY IN TRANSITION. Gainesville, Fla.: Kallman, 1949. 256 p..

Reedy, George E. THE PRESIDENCY IN FLUX. New York: Columbia University Press, 1973. 133 p.

_____. THE TWILIGHT OF THE PRESIDENCY. New York: World, 1970. 205 p.

_____, ed. THE PRESIDENCY. New York: Arno/New York Times, 1975. 468 p.

Reinfeld, Fred. THE BIGGEST JOB IN THE WORLD: THE AMERICAN PRESIDENCY. New York: Crowell, 1964. 229 p. Bibliog.

Roche, John P., and Levy, Leonard W. THE PRESIDENCY. New York: Harcourt, Brace, and World, 1964. 223 p. Bibliog.

Especially part 2 on the executive branch and foreign policy.

Rossiter, Clinton L. THE AMERICAN PRESIDENCY. 2d ed. New York: Harcourt, Brace, and World, 1960. 281 p. Bibliog.

Especially chapters 1 and 2.

_____. "The American President." YALE REVIEW 37 (Summer 1948): 619-37.

Rusk, Dean. "The President." FOREIGN AFFAIRS 38 (April 1960): 353-69.

Schlesinger, Arthur M., Jr. THE IMPERIAL PRESIDENCY. Boston: Houghton Mifflin, 1973. 505 p.

Schubert, Glendon A., Jr. THE PRESIDENCY IN THE COURTS. Minneapolis: University of Minnesota Press, 1957. 391 p.

Especially chapter 4.

Shannon, William V. "Eisenhower as President: A Critical Appraisal of the Record." COMMENTARY 26 (November 1958): 390-98.

Sheehan, Donald Henry. THE AMERICAN PRESIDENCY. Garden City, N.Y.: Doubleday, 1957. 64 p.

Sickels, Robert J. PRESIDENTIAL TRANSACTIONS. Englewood Cliffs, N.J.: Prentice-Hall, 1974. 184 p.

Interaction of president and other branches of the government.

Small, Norman J. SOME PRESIDENTIAL INTERPRETATIONS OF THE PRESIDENCY. Baltimore: Johns Hopkins Press, 1932. 208 p. Bibliog.

Smith, A. Merriman. THE PRESIDENT IS MANY MEN. New York: Harper, 1948. 269 p.

Sorensen, Theodore C. DECISION-MAKING IN THE WHITE HOUSE: THE OLIVE BRANCH OR THE ARROWS. New York: Columbia University Press, 1963. 94 p.

_____. WATCHMEN IN THE NIGHT: PRESIDENTIAL ACCOUNTABILITY AFTER WATERGATE. Cambridge, Mass.: M.I.T. Press, 1975. 178 p.

Stanwood, Edward. A HISTORY OF THE PRESIDENCY. Revised by Charles K. Bolton. 2 vols. 3d ed. Boston: Houghton Mifflin, 1928.

Sundquist, James L. POLITICS AND POLICY: THE EISENHOWER, KENNEDY, AND JOHNSON YEARS. Washington, D.C.: Brookings Institution, 1968. 560 p.

Presidential policy-making process.

Taft, William Howard. OUR CHIEF MAGISTRATE AND HIS POWERS. New York: Columbia University Press, 1916. 165 p.

Second printing with new foreword, 1925.

Thach, Charles C., Jr. THE CREATION OF THE PRESIDENCY, 1775-1789: A STUDY IN CONSTITUTIONAL HISTORY. Baltimore: Johns Hopkins Press, 1923. Reprint. New York: DaCapo, 1969. 182 p.

Thomas, Norman C., ed. THE PRESIDENCY IN CONTEMPORARY CONTEXT. New York: Dodd, Mead, 1975. 348 p. Bibliog.

Tourtellot, Arthur Bernon. THE PRESIDENTS ON THE PRESIDENCY. Garden City, N.Y.: Doubleday, 1964. 505 p. Bibliog.

Especially chapter 6.

Truman, Harry S. "My View of the Presidency." LOOK, 11 November 1958, pp. 25-31.

Tugwell, Rexford G. THE ENLARGEMENT OF THE PRESIDENCY. Garden City, N.Y.: Doubleday, 1960. 508 p.

Vinyard, Dale. THE PRESIDENCY. New York: Scribner, 1971. 214 p.

Elementary volume on presidency; chapter 6 on foreign relations.

Warner, W. Lloyd, et al. THE AMERICAN FEDERAL EXECUTIVE. New Haven, Conn.: Yale University Press, 1963. 405 p.

Warren, Sidney. "The President in the Constitution." CURRENT HISTORY 25 (September 1953): 133-37.

_____, ed. THE AMERICAN PRESIDENT. Englewood Cliffs, N.J.: Prentice-Hall, 1967. 176 p. Bibliog.

Twenty-seven essays and readings on various aspects of the presidency.

Wildavsky, Aaron B. "Choosing the Lesser Evil: The Policy-Maker and the Problem of Presidential Disability." PARLIAMENTARY AFFAIRS 13 (Winter 1959-60): 25-37.

_____. "The Past and Future Presidency." PUBLIC INTEREST 41 (Fall 1975): 56-76.

_____, ed. PERSPECTIVES ON THE PRESIDENCY. Boston: Little, Brown, 1975. 539 p.

_____. THE PRESIDENCY. Boston: Little, Brown, 1969. 795 p.

Wilson, John Richard Meredith. "Herbert Hoover and the Armed Forces: A Study of Presidential Attitudes and Policy." Ph.D. dissertation, Northwestern University, 1971. 269 p.

Wilson, Woodrow. CONSTITUTIONAL GOVERNMENT IN THE UNITED STATES. New York: Columbia University Press, 1911. 236 p.

Wolfe, Harold. HERBERT HOOVER: PUBLIC SERVANT AND LEADER OF THE LOYAL OPPOSITION--A STUDY OF HIS LIFE AND CAREER. New York: Exposition, 1956. 507 p. Bibliog.

Woodward, Augustus Brevoort. THE PRESIDENCY OF THE UNITED STATES. New York: Harper, 1825. 88 p.

PRESIDENTIAL DISABILITY AND SUCCESSION

The matters of presidential disability and succession have also been given research and literary attention. Additional guidance may be found in the following:

Tomkins, Dorothy L. PRESIDENTIAL SUCCESSION: A BIBLIOGRAPHY. Berkeley and Los Angeles: University of California Press, 1964. 20 p.

The following are representative of these materials, and resources on the vice-presidency are provided separately in the last section of this chapter.

Bartholomew, Paul C. "A Summary View: The Problem of Presidential Disability." AMERICAN BAR ASSOCIATION JOURNAL 44 (June 1958): 542-43, 550.

Bayh, Birch E. ONE HEARTBEAT AWAY: PRESIDENTIAL DISABILITY AND SUCCESSION. Indianapolis: Bobbs Merrill, 1968. 372 p.

Blackman, Paul H. "Presidential Disability and the Bayh Amendment." WESTERN POLITICAL QUARTERLY 20 (June 1967): 440-55.

Brown, E.S., and Silva, Ruth C. "Presidential Succession and Inability." JOURNAL OF POLITICS 11 (February 1949): 236-56.

Brownell, Herbert, Jr. "Presidential Disability: The Need for a Constitutional Amendment." YALE LAW JOURNAL 68 (December 1958): 189-211.

Committee for Economic Development. Research and Policy Committee. PRESIDENTIAL SUCCESSION AND INABILITY: A STATEMENT OF NATIONAL POLICY BY THE RESEARCH AND POLICY COMMITTEE OF THE COMMITTEE FOR ECONOMIC DEVELOPMENT. New York: 1965. 41 p.

Corwin, Edward S. "Presidential 'Inability.'" NATIONAL REVIEW 26 (November 1955): 9-16.

A COUNTRY WITHOUT A MAN: A STUDY OF PRESIDENTIAL DISABILITY. Richmond: Virginia Commission on Constitutional Government, 1965. 15 p.

Feerick, John D. FROM FAILING HANDS: THE STORY OF PRESIDENTIAL SUCCESSION. New York: Fordham University Press, 1965. 368 p. Bibliog.

_____. "Presidential Inability: The Problem and a Solution." AMERICAN BAR ASSOCIATION JOURNAL 50 (April 1964): 321-24.

_____. THE TWENTY-FIFTH AMENDMENT: ITS COMPLETE HISTORY AND EARLIEST APPLICATIONS. New York: Fordham University Press, 1976. 270 p. Bibliog.

Gilliam, Armistead W., and Sloat, Jonathan W. "Presidential Inability: The Problem and a Recommendation." GEORGE WASHINGTON LAW REVIEW 24 (March 1956): 448-64.

Marx, Rudolph. THE HEALTH OF THE PRESIDENTS. New York: Putnam, 1960. 376 p.

Silva, Ruth C. PRESIDENTIAL SUCCESSION. Ann Arbor: University of Michigan Press, 1951. 213 p. Bibliog.

_____. "The Presidential Succession Act of 1947." MICHIGAN LAW REVIEW 47 (February 1949): 451-76.

Wildavsky, Aaron B. "Choosing the Lesser Evil: The Policy Maker and the Problem of Presidential Disability." PARLIAMENTARY AFFAIRS 13 (Winter 1959-60): 25-37.

Wilmerding, Lucius, Jr. "Presidential Inability." POLITICAL SCIENCE QUARTERLY 72 (June 1957): 161-81.

_____. "The Presidential Succession." ATLANTIC MONTHLY, May 1947, pp. 91-97.

CABINET, EXECUTIVE OFFICE, AND PRESIDENTIAL STAFF

Materials included in this section range from Woodrow Wilson's essay on cabinet government to more recent analyses of the executive office (including those of Brownlow, Graham, Hobbs, and Rossiter); the cabinet (such as Fenno, Hinsdale, Horn, Learned, and Patterson); and presidential assistants, advisors, and staffs (Anderson, Bernstein and Woodward, Carey, Coffey, Heinlein, Hobbs, Morstein Marx, Nash, Pearson, Plischke, Price, Sichel, and Silverman). Others employ a more general focus, such as the studies of Bailey, Cronin, Heren, Hess, Hoxie, Johnson, Koenig, Mansfield, Seligman, Sparks, Thomas and Baade, and Thomas and Wolman. A few also address themselves to presidential commissions and task forces (Komarovsky, Marcy, Popper, Sulzner, and Wolanin).

Guidance to additional literature on the Executive Office of the President may be found in the following:

U.S. Bureau of the Budget. EXECUTIVE OFFICE OF THE PRESIDENT: SELECTED REFERENCES. Washington, D.C.: Government Printing Office, 1950. 12 p.

Anderson, Patrick. THE PRESIDENT'S MEN. Garden City, N.Y.: Doubleday, 1968. 420 p.

> On presidential assistants to Presidents Roosevelt, Truman, Eisenhower, Kennedy, and Johnson.

Bailey, Sidney K. "The President and His Political Executives." ANNALS OF THE AMERICAN ACADEMY OF POLITICAL AND SOCIAL SCIENCE 307 (September 1956): 24-36.

Bernstein, Carl, and Woodward, Bob. ALL THE PRESIDENT'S MEN. New York: Simon and Schuster, 1974. 349 p.

Brownlow, Louis, et al. "The Executive Office of the President--A Symposium." PUBLIC ADMINISTRATION REVIEW 1 (Autumn 1940): 101-40.

Carey, William D. "Presidential Staffing in the Sixties and Seventies." PUBLIC ADMINISTRATION REVIEW 29 (September-October 1969): 450-58.

Coffey, Joseph I., and Rock, Vincent P. THE PRESIDENTIAL STAFF. Washington, D.C.: National Planning Association, 1961. 102 p.

Cronin, Thomas E. "The Swelling of the Presidency." SATURDAY REVIEW, February 1973, pp. 30-36.

Cronin, Thomas E., and Greenberg, Sanford, eds. THE PRESIDENTIAL AD-VISORY SYSTEM. New York: Harper and Row, 1969. 375 p. Bibliog.

Fenno, Richard F., Jr. "Now Is the Time for Cabinet Makers." NEW YORK TIMES MAGAZINE, 20 November 1960, pp. 12, 88, 91-94.

_____. THE PRESIDENT'S CABINET: AN ANALYSIS IN THE PERIOD FROM WILSON TO EISENHOWER. Cambridge, Mass.: Harvard University Press, 1959. 325 p.

Graham, George A. "The Presidency and the Executive Office of the President." JOURNAL OF POLITICS 12 (November 1950): 599-621.

Heinlein, J.C. PRESIDENTIAL STAFF AND NATIONAL SECURITY POLICY. Cincinnati: Center for the Study of United States Foreign Policy, University of Cincinnati, 1963. 65 p.

Heren, Louis. "King's Men: A British View of the White House." HARPER'S MAGAZINE, February 1965, pp. 108, 110, 112-16.

Hess, Stephen. ORGANIZING THE PRESIDENCY. Washington, D.C.: Brookings Institution, 1976. 228 p.

Hinsdale, Mary L. A HISTORY OF THE PRESIDENT'S CABINET. Ann Arbor, Mich.: Wahr, 1911. Reprint. New York: Octagon, 1973. 355 p. Bibliog.

Hobbs, Edward H. BEHIND THE PRESIDENT: A STUDY OF EXECUTIVE OFFICE AGENCIES. Washington, D.C.: Public Affairs, 1954. 248 p.

_____. "An Historical Review of Plans for Presidential Staffing." LAW AND CONTEMPORARY PROBLEMS 21 (Autumn 1956): 663-87.

Horn, Stephen. THE CABINET AND CONGRESS. New York: Columbia University Press, 1960. 310 p. Bibliog.

Hoxie, Ralph Gordon. THE WHITE HOUSE ORGANIZATION AND OPERATIONS. New York: Center for the Study of the Presidency, 1971. 218 p.

Hyman, Sidney. "Inside the Kennedy 'Kitchen Cabinet.'" NEW YORK TIMES MAGAZINE, 5 March 1961, pp. 27, 86, 88-89.

Johnson, Richard Tanner. MANAGING THE WHITE HOUSE: AN INTIMATE STUDY OF THE PRESIDENCY. New York: Harper and Row, 1974. 270 p.

Koenig, Louis W. THE INVISIBLE PRESIDENCY. New York: Rinehart, 1960. 438 p. Bibliog.

On selected presidential advisers and confidants.

Komarovsky, Mirra, ed. SOCIOLOGY AND PUBLIC POLICY: THE CASE OF THE PRESIDENTIAL COMMISSIONS. New York: Elsevier, 1975. 183 p.

Kraft, Joseph. "Kennedy's Working Staff." HARPER'S MAGAZINE, December 1962, pp. 29-36.

Learned, Henry B. THE PRESIDENT'S CABINET. New Haven, Conn.: Yale University Press, 1912. 471 p. Bibliog.

Mansfield, Harvey C. "Reorganizing the Federal Executive Branch: The Limits of Institutionalization." LAW AND CONTEMPORARY PROBLEMS 35 (Summer 1970): 461-95.

Marcy, Carl M. PRESIDENTIAL COMMISSIONS. New York: Da Capo, 1945. 141 p.

Morstein Marx, Fritz. THE PRESIDENT AND HIS STAFF SERVICES. Chicago: Public Administration Service, 1947. 26 p.

Nash, Bradley D. STAFFING THE PRESIDENCY. Washington, D.C.: National Planning Association, 1952. 78 p.

Paschal, J. Francis, ed. "The Presidential Office." LAW AND CONTEMPORARY PROBLEMS 21 (Autumn 1956): entire issue.

Patterson, B.H. THE PRESIDENT'S CABINET. ISSUES AND QUESTIONS. Washington, D.C.: American Society for Public Administration, 1976. 116 p.

Pearson, Norman M. "A General Administrative Staff to Aid the President." PUBLIC ADMINISTRATION REVIEW 4 (Spring 1944): 127-47.

Plischke, Elmer. "The President's Inner Foreign Policy Team." REVIEW OF POLITICS 30 (July 1968): 292-307.

Popper, Frank. THE PRESIDENT'S COMMISSIONS. New York: Twentieth Century Fund, 1970. 73 p.

Price, Don K. "Staffing the Presidency." AMERICAN POLITICAL SCIENCE REVIEW 40 (December 1946): 1154-68.

Reagan, Michael D. "Toward Improving National Policy Planning." PUBLIC ADMINISTRATION REVIEW 23 (March 1963): 10-19.

Rossiter, Clinton L. "The Constitutional Significance of the Executive Office of the President." AMERICAN POLITICAL SCIENCE REVIEW 43 (December 1949): 1206-17.

Seligman, Lester G. "Presidential Leadership: The Inner Circle and Institutionalization." JOURNAL OF POLITICS 18 (August 1956): 410-26.

Sichel, Werner, ed. ECONOMIC ADVICE AND EXECUTIVE POLICY: RECOMMENDATIONS FROM PAST MEMBERS OF THE COUNCIL OF ECONOMIC ADVISERS. New York: Praeger, 1978. 128 p.

> Presents alternative perspectives on American food exports as an instrument of U.S. foreign policy.

Silverman, Corinne. THE PRESIDENT'S ECONOMIC ADVISERS. University: University of Alabama Press for Inter-University Case Program, 1959. 18 p.

Sobel, Robert. BIOGRAPHICAL DIRECTORY OF THE U.S. EXECUTIVE BRANCH, 1774-1977. 2d ed. Westport, Conn.: Greenwood, 1977. 503 p.

Sparks, Will. WHO TALKED TO THE PRESIDENT LAST? New York: Norton, 1971. 127 p.

Sulzner, George T. "The Policy Process and the Uses of National Governmental Study Commissions." WESTERN POLITICAL QUARTERLY 24 (September 1971): 438-48.

Thomas, Norman C., and Baade, Hans W., eds. THE INSTITUTIONALIZED PRESIDENCY. Dobbs Ferry, N.Y.: Oceana, 1971. 237 p.

Thomas, Norman C., and Wolman, Harold L. "The Presidency and Policy Formulation: The Task Force Device." PUBLIC ADMINISTRATION REVIEW 29 (September-October 1969): 459-71.

Tugwell, Rexford Guy. "The President and His Helpers: A Review Article." POLITICAL SCIENCE QUARTERLY 82 (June 1967): 253-67.

U.S. Congress. House of Representatives. Committee on the Post Office and Civil Service. A REPORT ON THE GROWTH OF THE EXECUTIVE OFFICE OF THE PRESIDENT, 1955-1973. 92d Cong., 2d sess. Committee Print, no. 19. Washington, D.C.: Government Printing Office, 1972. 39 p.

Wilson, Woodrow. CABINET GOVERNMENT IN THE UNITED STATES. Stamford, Conn.: Overbrook Press for Woodrow Wilson Foundation, 1947. 31 p.

> Republication of article by same title originally published in INTERNATIONAL REVIEW (August 1879).

Wise, Sidney, and Schier, Richard F. THE PRESIDENTIAL OFFICE. New York: Crowell, 1968. 248 p. Bibliog.

Wolanin, Thomas R. PRESIDENTIAL ADVISORY COMMISSIONS: TRUMAN TO NIXON. Madison: University of Wisconsin Press, 1975. 298 p.

Of related concern is the matter of executive advisory and coordinating councils and committees. Aside from the materials on the National Security Council, dealt with separately in chapter 10, and some of those on administration and the bureaucracy included in chapter 13, the following general studies focus on this aspect of the organization and functioning of the executive.

U.S. Congress. House of Representatives. Committee on International Relations and U.S. Congress. Senate. Committee on Foreign Relations. THE ROLE OF ADVISORY COMMITTEES IN U.S. FOREIGN POLICY. 94th Cong., 1st sess. Washington, D.C.: Government Printing Office, 1975. 135 p.

> Prepared by Foreign Affairs Division, Congressional Research Service, Library of Congress. Consists of a report on findings and problem areas, functional analysis of advisory committees, implementation of the Federal Advisory Committee Act, monitoring such committees, and concluding observations. Six appendixes annexed, including a list of advisory committees organized by the agency serviced, and an alphabetical list of such committees.

U.S. Congress. Senate. Committee on Government Operations. Subcommittee on National Security and International Operations. COUNCILS AND COMMITTEES: A SELECTION OF READINGS. 92d Cong., 2d sess. Washington, D.C.: Government Printing Office, 1972. 46 p.

> Provides thirty-five excerpts from the writings of such authors as Homer, Saint Augustine, Machiavelli, Francis Bacon, Benjamin Franklin, Harold Laski, Herbert Hoover, Don K. Price, Robert Lovett, Averell Harriman, and Dean Acheson, on the functioning of councils and committees in the policy process.

POWERS, FUNCTIONS, AND RESPONSIBILITIES

Supplementing any general list of studies on the presidency are many analyses which focus more directly on presidential authority, powers, functions, and responsibilities. These vary from general reviews of the executive position within the separation of powers system to finite treatment of specific activities and functions. A good many of these, though some of them are tangentially related to the conduct of foreign relations, are not systematically included in this section, such as the executive veto authority and law making, appointment and discharge functions, impoundment of funds, and political leadership and partisan activities. This section presents a series of general studies on the presidential role, followed by separate listings of materials on the separation of powers, executive emergency and crisis authority, and presidential war making and war powers. The last of these has attracted considerable literary interest since World War II, especially as a consequence of the Vietnam War and the enactment of the War Powers Act. Materials concerned with the president's general foreign relations authority and his functioning as commander in chief and as diplomat in chief are treated in separate sections of this chapter.

General Studies

Andrews, William G., ed. COORDINATE MAGISTRATES: CONSTITUTIONAL LAW BY CONGRESS AND PRESIDENT. New York: Van Nostrand Reinhold, 1969. 186 p.

Especially chapters 7 and 8.

Binkley, Wilfred E. THE MAN IN THE WHITE HOUSE: HIS POWERS AND DUTIES. Baltimore: Johns Hopkins Press, 1958. 310 p. Bibliog.

Especially chapter 12.

_____. THE POWERS OF THE PRESIDENT: PROBLEMS OF AMERICAN DE-MOCRACY. Garden City, N.Y.: Doubleday, Doran, 1937. 332 p. Bibliog.

Commager, Henry Steele. THE DEFEAT OF AMERICA: PRESIDENTIAL POWER AND THE NATIONAL CHARACTER. 2d ed. New York: Simon and Schuster, 1974. 163 p.

Flanders, Henry. "Power of the President to Appoint Special Diplomatic Agents Without the Advice and Consent of the Senate." AMERICAN LAW REGISTER AND REVIEW 33 (March 1894): 177-89.

Goldsmith, William M. THE GROWTH OF PRESIDENTIAL POWER: A DOCU-MENTED HISTORY. 3 vols. New York: Chelsea House, 1974. 2,342 p. Bibliog.

Goldstein, Sidney Max. THE GROWTH OF THE EXECUTIVE POWER IN THE UNITED STATES. Washington, D.C.: Georgetown University Press, 1938. 14 p. Bibliog.

Griffith, Ernest S. THE AMERICAN PRESIDENCY: THE DILEMMAS OF SHARED POWER AND DIVIDED GOVERNMENT. New York: New York University Press, 1976. 241 p.

Grundstein, Nathan D. "Presidential Power, Administration, and Administrative Law." GEORGE WASHINGTON LAW REVIEW 18 (April 1950): 285-326.

Haight, David E., and Johnston, Larry D., eds. THE PRESIDENT: ROLES AND POWERS. Chicago: Rand McNally, 1965. 400 p.

Hardin, Charles M. PRESIDENTIAL POWER AND ACCOUNTABILITY: TOWARD A NEW CONSTITUTION. Chicago: University of Chicago Press, 1974. 257 p.

Hargrove, Erwin C. THE POWER OF THE MODERN PRESIDENCY. Philadelphia: Temple University Press, 1974. 353 p.

Especially chapters 4 and 5.

Hart, James. THE ORDINANCE MAKING POWER OF THE PRESIDENT. Baltimore: Johns Hopkins University Studies in Historical and Political Science, 1925. Reprint. New York: DaCapo, 1970. 339 p. Bibliog.

Hart, John. "Executive Organization in the USA and the Growth of Presidential Power." PUBLIC ADMINISTRATION (England) 52 (Summer 1974): 179-91.

Hirschfield, Robert S. "The Power of the Contemporary Presidency." PARLIAMENTARY AFFAIRS 14 (Summer 1961): 353-77.

_____. "The Reality of Presidential Power." PARLIAMENTARY AFFAIRS 21 (Autumn 1968): 375-83.

_____, ed. THE POWER OF THE PRESIDENCY: CONCEPTS AND CONTROVERSY. New York: Atherton, 1968. 328 p. Bibliog.

Levine, David D. "The Executive Order: A Form of Presidential Participation in the Legislative Process." Ph.D. dissertation, American University, 1955. 930 p.

Long, Norton. "Reflections on Presidential Power." PUBLIC ADMINISTRATION REVIEW 29 (September-October 1969): 442-50.

Lynn, Naomi B., and McClure, Arthur F. THE FULBRIGHT PREMISE: SENATOR J. WILLIAM FULBRIGHT'S VIEWS ON PRESIDENTIAL POWER. Lewisburg, Pa.: Bucknell University Press, 1973. 224 p. Bibliog.

Milton, George F. THE USE OF PRESIDENTIAL POWER, 1789-1943. Boston: Little, Brown, 1944. Reprint. New York: Octagon, 1965. 349 p.

Mondale, Walter F. THE ACCOUNTABILITY OF POWER: TOWARD A RESPONSIBLE PRESIDENCY. New York: McKay, 1975. 284 p.

Mullen, W.F. PRESIDENTIAL POWER AND POLITICS. New York: St. Martin's, 1976. 294 p. Bibliog.

Neustadt, Richard E. PRESIDENTIAL POWER: THE POLITICS OF LEADERSHIP. New York: Wiley, 1960. 244 p. Bibliog.

_____. PRESIDENTIAL POWER: THE POLITICS OF LEADERSHIP FROM FDR TO CARTER. New York: Wiley, 1980. 304 p.

_____. PRESIDENTIAL POWER: THE POLITICS OF LEADERSHIP WITH REFLECTIONS ON JOHNSON AND NIXON. New York: Wiley, 1976. 324 p.

Nobleman, Eli E. "The Delegation of Presidential Functions: Constitutional and Legal Aspects." ANNALS OF THE AMERICAN ACADEMY OF POLITICAL AND SOCIAL SCIENCE 307 (September 1956): 134-43.

THE POWERS OF THE PRESIDENCY. Cambridge, Mass.: The Roscoe Pound-American Trial Lawyers Foundation, 1977. 102 p.

> Symposium of three essays on "Presidential War Powers" by Raoul Berger, "Presidential Power in Foreign Affairs" by Louis Henkin, and "Towards a Responsible American Presidency" by Phillip B. Kurland.

Schlesinger, Arthur M., Jr. "The Limits and Excesses of Presidential Power." SATURDAY REVIEW, 3 May 1969, pp. 17-19, 61-62.

Strum, Phillippa. PRESIDENTIAL POWER AND AMERICAN DEMOCRACY. Pacific Palisades, Calif.: Goodyear, 1972. 132 p. Bibliog.

Sullivan, Robert R. "The Role of the Presidency in Shaping Lower Level Policy-Making Process." POLITY 3 (Winter 1970): 201-21.

Taft, William Howard. THE PRESIDENCY: ITS DUTIES, ITS POWERS, ITS OPPORTUNITIES, AND ITS LIMITATIONS. New York: Scribner, 1916. 145 p.

> Consists of three lectures.

Westin, Alan F., ed. THE USES OF POWER: SEVEN CASES IN AMERICAN POLITICS. New York: Harcourt, Brace, and World, 1962. 376 p.

> Especially chapter 2, on the presidency.

Worsnop, Richard L. "Presidential Power." EDITORIAL RESEARCH REPORTS 2 (October 1968): 723-40.

Separation of Powers

Cheever, Daniel S., and Haviland, H. Field, Jr. AMERICAN FOREIGN POLICY AND THE SEPARATION OF POWERS. Cambridge, Mass.: Harvard University Press, 1952. 244 p.

Cleveland, Grover. THE INDEPENDENCE OF THE EXECUTIVE. Princeton, N.J.: Princeton University Press, 1913. 82 p.

Corwin, Edward S. PRESIDENTIAL POWER AND THE CONSTITUTION. Edited by R. Loss. Ithaca, N.Y.: Cornell University Press, 1976. 185 p. Bibliog.

Davenport, F.M. "The Growing Power of the Presidency." BOSTON UNIVERSITY LAW REVIEW 14 (June 1934): 655-67.

Fisher, Louis. "The Efficiency Side of Separated Powers." JOURNAL OF AMERICAN STUDIES 5 (August 1971): 113-31.

Frohmayer, D.B. "The Separation of Powers: An Essay in the Vitality of a Constitutional Idea." OREGON LAW REVIEW 52 (Spring 1973): 211-35.

Gibbons, J.J. "The Interdependence of Legitimacy: An Introduction to the Meaning of Separation of Powers." SETON HALL LAW REVIEW 5 (Spring 1974): 435-88.

Levi, Edward H. "Some Aspects of Separation of Powers." COLUMBIA LAW REVIEW 76 (April 1976): 371-91.

McKinley, Charles. "Federal Administrative Pathology and the Separation of Powers." PUBLIC ADMINISTRATION REVIEW 11 (Winter 1951): 18-25.

Merry, Henry J. CONSTITUTIONAL FUNCTION OF PRESIDENTIAL-ADMINISTRATIVE SEPARATION. Washington, D.C.: University Press of America, 1978. 134 p.

Pritchett, C. Herman. "The President and the Supreme Court." JOURNAL OF POLITICS 11 (February 1949): 80-92.

Ratner, Leonard G. "The Coordinated Warmaking Power: Legislative, Executive, and Judicial Roles." SOUTHERN CALIFORNIA LAW REVIEW 44 (Winter 1971): 461-89.

Reveley, W. Taylor III. "Constitutional Allocation of the War Powers Between the President and Congress: 1787-1788." VIRGINIA JOURNAL OF INTERNATIONAL LAW 15 (Fall 1974): 73-147.

Schubert, Glendon A. "Judicial Review of the Subdelegation of Presidential Power." JOURNAL OF POLITICS 12 (November 1950): 668-93.

_____. THE PRESIDENCY IN THE COURTS. Minneapolis: University of Minnesota Press, 1957. Reprint. New York: DaCapo, 1973. 391 p.

Scigliano, Robert G. THE SUPREME COURT AND THE PRESIDENCY. New York: Free Press, 1971. 233 p. Bibliog.

Shaffer, Helen B. "Separation of Powers." EDITORIAL RESEARCH REPORTS 2 (12 September 1973): 691-708.

Wayne, Stephen J. "Checks Without Balances: Containing Prometheus." GEORGE WASHINGTON LAW REVIEW 43 (January 1975): 485-500.

Zurcher, Arnold J. "The Presidency, Congress and Separation of Powers: A Reappraisal." WESTERN POLITICAL QUARTERLY 3 (March 1950): 75-97.

War Making and War Powers

Baldwin, Simeon E. "The Share of the President of the United States in a Declaration of War." AMERICAN JOURNAL OF INTERNATIONAL LAW 12 (January 1918): 1-14.

Berdahl, Clarence A. THE WAR POWERS OF THE EXECUTIVE IN THE UNITED STATES. Urbana: University of Illinois Press, 1921. 296 p. Bibliog.

Brower, Charles N. "Department Gives Views on Proposed War Powers Legislation." DEPARTMENT OF STATE BULLETIN 68 (9 April 1973): 434-39.

_____. "The Great War Powers Debate." INTERNATIONAL LAWYER 7 (October 1973): 746-51.

Campisi, Dominic J. "Honored in the Breach: Presidential Authority to Execute the Laws with Military Force." YALE LAW JOURNAL 83 (November 1973): 130-52.

Coolidge, F.L, Jr., and Sharrow, J.D., eds. "Presidential vs. Congressional War-Making Powers." BOSTON UNIVERSITY LAW REVIEW 50 (1970): 5-116.

Corwin, Edward S. TOTAL WAR AND THE CONSTITUTION. New York: Knopf, 1947. 182 p.

Eagleton, Thomas F. WAR AND PRESIDENTIAL POWER: A CHRONICLE OF CONGRESSIONAL SURRENDER. New York: Liveright, 1974. 240 p. Bibliog.

Ford, Gerald R. THE WAR POWERS RESOLUTION: STRIKING A BALANCE BETWEEN THE EXECUTIVE AND LEGISLATIVE BRANCHES. Reprint, no. 69. Washington, D.C.: American Enterprise Institute, 1977. 7 p.

Text of John Sherman Cooper lecture presented at University of Kentucky, 11 April 1977.

Gelling, Louis. "The Authority of the President to Deploy United States Armed Forces Abroad in Time of Peace." Masters thesis, University of Maryland, 1963. 132 p.

Goldman, Eric F. "The President, the People, and the Power to Make War." AMERICAN HERITAGE 21 (April 1970): 28-35.

Goldwater, Barry M. "The President's Constitutional Primacy in Foreign Relations and National Defense." VIRGINIA JOURNAL OF INTERNATIONAL LAW 13 (1973): 463-89.

Grundstein, Nathan D. PRESIDENTIAL DELEGATION OF AUTHORITY IN WARTIME. Pittsburgh: University of Pittsburgh Press, 1961. 106 p.

_____. "Presidential Subdelegation of Administrative Authority in Wartime." GEORGE WASHINGTON LAW REVIEW 15 (April 1947): 247-83; 16 (April and June 1948): 301-41, 478-507.

Halperin, Morton H. "The President and the Military." FOREIGN AFFAIRS 50 (January 1972): 310-24.

Harris, L. "War Powers of the President." FLORIDA LAW JOURNAL 19 (July 1945): 221-27.

Holt, Pat M. THE WAR POWERS RESOLUTION: THE ROLE OF CONGRESS IN U.S. ARMED INTERVENTION. Washington, D.C.: American Enterprise Institute, 1978. 48 p.

Houghton, Neal D. "War-Making and the Constitution." SOCIAL SCIENCE 39 (April 1964): 67-78.

Javits, Jacob K. WHO MAKES WAR: THE PRESIDENT VERSUS CONGRESS. New York: Morrow, 1973. 300 p. Bibliog.

Jenkins, Gerald L. "The War Powers Resolution: Statutory Limitation on the Commander-in-Chief." HARVARD JOURNAL OF LEGISLATION 11 (February 1974): 181-204.

Keown, Stuart S. "The President, the Congress, and the Power to Declare War." UNIVERSITY OF KANSAS LAW REVIEW 16 (November 1967): 82-97.

Lofgren, Charles A. "War-Making Under the Constitution: The Original Understanding." YALE LAW JOURNAL 81 (March 1972): 672-702.

Monaghan, H.P. "Presidential War-Making." BOSTON UNIVERSITY LAW REVIEW 50 (May 1970): 19-33.

Moore, John N. "The National Executive and the Use of Armed Forces Abroad." NAVAL WAR COLLEGE REVIEW 21 (January 1969): 28-38.

Odell, Talbot. WAR POWERS OF THE PRESIDENT: WAR POWERS OF THE AMERICAN PRESIDENCY, DERIVED FROM THE CONSTITUTION AND STATUTES, AND THEIR HISTORICAL BACKGROUND. Washington, D.C.: Washington Service Bureau, 1942. 31 p.

Patch, Buel W. "The War Powers of the President." EDITORIAL RESEARCH REPORTS 2 (12 September 1940): 147-64.

Potter, Pitman B. "The Power of the President of the United States to Utilize Its Armed Forces Abroad." AMERICAN JOURNAL OF INTERNATIONAL LAW 48 (July 1954): 458-59.

Putney, Albert H. "Executive Assumption of the War Making Power." NATIONAL UNIVERSITY LAW REVIEW, May 1927, pp. 1-41.

Reveley, W. Taylor III. "Constitutional Allocation of the War Powers Between the President and Congress, 1787-1788." VIRGINIA JOURNAL OF INTERNATIONAL LAW 15 (Fall 1974): 73-147.

Scribner, Jeffrey L. "The President Versus Congress on Warmaking Authority." MILITARY REVIEW 52 (April 1972): 87-96.

Shaffer, L.A. "Presidential Power to Make War." INDIANA LAW REVIEW 7 (1974): 900-924.

Sofaer, Abraham D. WAR, FOREIGN AFFAIRS AND CONSTITUTIONAL POWER: THE ORIGINS. Cambridge, Mass.: Ballinger, 1976. 506 p.

Spong, W.B., Jr. "Can Balance Be Restored in the Constitutional War Powers of the President and Congress?" UNIVERSITY OF RICHMOND LAW REVIEW 6 (Fall 1971): 1-47.

Stevenson, J.R. "The Constitution and the President's War Powers." NEW YORK STATE BAR JOURNAL 45 (April 1973): 172-76.

Swisher, Carl B. "The Control of War Preparations in the United States." AMERICAN POLITICAL SCIENCE REVIEW 34 (December 1940): 1085-1103.

Tansill, Charles C. "War Powers of the President of the United States With Special Reference to the Beginning of Hostilities." POLITICAL SCIENCE QUARTERLY 45 (March 1930): 1-55.

U.S. Congress. House of Representatives. Committee on Foreign Affairs. BACKGROUND INFORMATION ON THE USE OF UNITED STATES ARMED FORCES IN FOREIGN COUNTRIES. 91st Cong., 2d sess. Washington, D.C.: Government Printing Office, 1970. 62 p.

> Prepared by Foreign Affairs Division, Legislative Reference Service, Library of Congress, for Foreign Affairs Committee. Consists of analysis and documents.

U.S. Congress. Senate. Committee on Foreign Relations. POWERS OF THE PRESIDENT TO SEND THE ARMED FORCES OUTSIDE THE UNITED STATES. 82d Cong., 1st sess. Washington, D.C.: Government Printing Office, 1951. 27 p.

Wallace, Don, Jr. "The War-Making Powers: A Constitutional Flaw." CORNELL LAW REVIEW 57 (May 1972): 719-76.

Watkins, Arthur V. "War by Executive Order." WESTERN POLITICAL QUARTERLY 4 (December 1951): 539-49.

White, Howard. EXECUTIVE INFLUENCE IN DETERMINING MILITARY POLICY IN THE UNITED STATES. Urbana: University of Illinois Press, 1925. 292 p. Bibliog.

Whiting, William. WAR POWERS UNDER THE CONSTITUTION OF THE UNITED STATES. Boston: Shorey, 1862. Reprint. New York: Da Capo, 1972. 695 p.

> Early treatise on war powers, involving experience during the Civil War.

Wormuth, Francis D. "The Nixon Theory of the War Power: A Critique." CALIFORNIA LAW REVIEW 60 (May 1972): 623-703.

Worsnop, Richard L. "War Powers of the President." EDITORIAL RESEARCH REPORTS 1 (14 March 1966): 183-200.

Emergency and Crisis Authority

Gibson, Rankin M. "The President's Inherent Emergency Powers." FEDERAL BAR JOURNAL 12 (October 1951): 107-51.

Koenig, Louis W. THE PRESIDENCY AND THE CRISIS: POWERS OF THE OF-

FICE FROM THE INVASION OF POLAND TO PEARL HARBOR. New York: King's Crown, 1944. 166 p. Bibliog.

Patch, Buel W. "Emergency Powers of the President." EDITORIAL RESEARCH REPORTS 1 (11 February 1938): 87-100.

Rankin, Robert S., and Dallmayr, Winfried R. FREEDOM AND EMERGENCY POWERS IN THE COLD WAR. New York: Appleton-Century-Crofts, 1964. 277 p.

Rich, Bennett M. THE PRESIDENTS AND CIVIL DISORDER. Washington, D.C.: Brookings Institution, 1941. 235 p. Bibliog.

Roche, John P. "Executive Power and Domestic Emergency: The Quest for Prerogative." WESTERN POLITICAL QUARTERLY 5 (December 1952): 592-618.

Smith, John Malcolm, and Cotter, Cornelius P. POWERS OF THE PRESIDENT DURING CRISES. Washington, D.C.: Public Affairs, 1960. 184 p. Bibliog.

Sturm, Albert L. "Emergencies and the Presidency." JOURNAL OF POLITICS 11 (February 1949): 121-44.

Thompson, Carol. "The Presidency in Crisis: The Emergency Powers of Our Chief Executive and Its Limits." CURRENT HISTORY 8 (January 1945): 33-38.

U.S. Congress. Senate. Special Committee on the Termination of the National Emergency. EMERGENCY POWERS STATUTES: PROVISIONS OF FEDERAL LAWS NOW IN EFFECT DELEGATING TO THE EXECUTIVE EXTRAORDINARY AUTHORITY IN TIME OF NATIONAL EMERGENCY. 93d Cong., 1st sess., committee print. Washington, D.C.: Government Printing Office, 1973. 607 p.

> Provides introductory summary and texts of laws enacted since the 1930s.

FOREIGN RELATIONS

Much of the literature cited elsewhere in this and other chapters concerns the role of the presidency and the chief executive in the conduct of foreign relations. The studies listed below focus specifically on this function. Some of these deal generally with the presidential foreign relations function, including those of Corwin, Garner, Laski, Levitt, McGee, Mason, Robinson, and Stuart. A few emphasize presidential leadership--Driggs, Landecker, Lee, and Rosen--

which also is treated more generally in a later section of this chapter. Occasional studies are more restricted in their treatment, as illustrated by those of Clark and Legere, Divine, Larkin, McClure, Reno, Reston, Schwarzer, and others.

Berger, Raoul. "Presidential Monopoly on Foreign Relations." MICHIGAN LAW REVIEW 71 (November 1972): 1-58.

Clark, Keith C., and Legere, Laurence J., eds. THE PRESIDENT AND THE MANAGEMENT OF NATIONAL SECURITY. New York: Praeger for Institute for Defense Analysis, 1969. 274 p.

Collier, Ellen C. POWERS OF THE PRESIDENT IN THE FIELD OF FOREIGN POLICY. Washington, D.C.: U.S. Library of Congress, 1969. 12 p.

Corwin, Edward S. THE PRESIDENT'S CONTROL OF FOREIGN RELATIONS. Princeton, N.J.: Princeton University Press, 1917. 216 p.

Destler, I.M. PRESIDENTS, BUREAUCRATS, AND FOREIGN POLICY: THE POLITICS OF ORGANIZATIONAL REFORM. Princeton, N.J.: Princeton University Press, 1972. 329 p.

Divine, Robert A. FOREIGN POLICY AND U.S. PRESIDENTIAL ELECTIONS. 2 vols. (1940-1948 and 1952-1960). New York: New Viewpoints, 1974. 353 p. Bibliog.

Driggs, Don W. "The President as Chief Educator in Foreign Affairs." WESTERN POLITICAL QUARTERLY 11 (December 1958): 813-19.

Garner, James W. "Executive Discretion in the Conduct of Foreign Relations." AMERICAN JOURNAL OF INTERNATIONAL LAW 31 (April 1937): 289-93.

Holcombe, Arthur N. "The Impact of Foreign Commitments on the Presidency." In INTERNATIONAL COMMITMENTS AND NATIONAL ADMINISTRATION, pp. 23-38. Charlottesville, Va.: Bureau of Public Administration, University of Virginia, 1949.

Landecker, Manfred. THE PRESIDENT AND PUBLIC OPINION: LEADERSHIP IN FOREIGN AFFAIRS. Washington, D.C.: Public Affairs, 1969. 133 p.

Larkin, John Day. THE PRESIDENT'S CONTROL OF THE TARIFF. Cambridge, Mass.: Harvard University Press, 1936. 207 p.

Laski, Harold J. "The American President and Foreign Relations." JOURNAL OF POLITICS 11 (February 1949): 171-205.

Lee, Jong R. "Presidential Choice: Limits of Leadership in Foreign Policy." Ph.D. dissertation, Yale University, 1975. 389 p.

Levitt, Albert. THE PRESIDENT AND THE INTERNATIONAL AFFAIRS OF THE UNITED STATES. Los Angeles: Parker, 1954. 87 p.

Lynn, Naomi B. "Senator J. William Fulbright's Views on Presidential Power in Foreign Policy." Ph.D. dissertation, University of Kansas, 1970. 287 p.

McClure, Wallace M. "The Presidency and World Affairs: Mobilization of Assistance." JOURNAL OF POLITICS 11 (February 1949): 206-17.

McGee, Gale W. "Executive Power in Foreign Policy-Making: Expansion or Curtailment?" CAPITOL STUDIES 1 (Fall 1972): 3-8.

Mason, John Brown. "The Constitutional Powers of the American President over the Conduct of Foreign Affairs." JAHRBUCH DES OEFFENTLICHEN RECHTS 7 (1958): 73-93.

Myers, David S. "Foreign Affairs and the Presidential Election of 1964." Ph.D. dissertation, University of Maryland, 1967. 290 p.

Nevins, Allan. THE NEW DEAL AND WORLD AFFAIRS: A CHRONICLE OF INTERNATIONAL AFFAIRS, 1933-1945. New Haven, Conn.: Yale University Press, 1950. 332 p.

Perlmutter, Amos. "The Presidential Political Center and Foreign Policy: A Critique of the Revisionist and Bureaucratic-Political Orientations." WORLD POLITICS 27 (October 1974): 87-106.

Reno, Lawson. "The Power of the President to Acquire and Govern Territory." GEORGE WASHINGTON LAW REVIEW 9 (January 1941): 251-85.

Reston, James B. "The Press, the President and Foreign Policy." FOREIGN AFFAIRS 44 (July 1966): 553-73.

Robinson, Edgar E., et al. POWERS OF THE PRESIDENT IN FOREIGN AFFAIRS, 1945-1965: HARRY S. TRUMAN, DWIGHT D. EISENHOWER, JOHN F. KENNEDY, LYNDON B. JOHNSON. San Francisco: Commonwealth Club of California, 1966. 279 p. Bibliog.

Rosen, David J. "Leadership Change and Foreign Policy." Ph.D. dissertation, Rutgers University, 1975. 157 p.

Schwarzer, William W., and Wood, Robert R. "Presidential Power and Aggression Abroad: A Constitutional Dilemma." AMERICAN BAR ASSOCIATION JOURNAL 40 (May 1954): 394-97.

Scott, James Brown. "President Harding's Foreign Policy." AMERICAN JOURNAL OF INTERNATIONAL LAW 15 (July 1921): 409-11.

Stuart, Graham H. "Presidential Control of Foreign Policy." CURRENT HISTORY 22 (April 1952): 207-10.

Wallace, Don, Jr. "The President's Exclusive Foreign Affairs Power Over Foreign Aid." DUKE LAW JOURNAL, April and June 1970, pp. 293-328, 293-494.

A number of general volumes on American foreign relations contain separate chapters dealing with the presidential role in foreign affairs, illustrated by the following:

Allison, Graham, and Szanton, Peter. REMAKING FOREIGN POLICY: THE ORGANIZATIONAL CONNECTION. New York: Basic Books, 1976.

Especially chapter 4.

Bliss, Howard, and Johnson, M. Glen. BEYOND THE WATER'S EDGE: AMERICA'S FOREIGN POLICIES. Philadelphia: Lippincott, 1975.

Especially chapter 5.

Chamberlain, Lawrence H., and Snyder, Richard C., eds. AMERICAN FOREIGN POLICY. New York: Rinehart, 1948.

Especially chapters 2, 3.

Gerberding, William P. UNITED STATES FOREIGN POLICY: PERSPECTIVES AND ANALYSIS. New York: McGraw-Hill, 1966.

Especially chapter 3.

Hickman, Martin B., ed. PROBLEMS OF AMERICAN FOREIGN POLICY. 2d ed. Beverly Hills, Calif.: Glencoe, 1975.

Especially chapter 2.

Irish, Marian D., and Frank, Elke. U.S. FOREIGN POLICY: CONTEXT CONDUCT, CONTENT. New York: Harcourt Brace Jovanovich, 1975.

Especially chapter 5.

McCamy, James L. THE ADMINISTRATION OF AMERICAN FOREIGN AF-
FAIRS. New York: Knopf, 1950.

Especially chapter 7.

Nash, Henry T. AMERICAN FOREIGN POLICY: RESPONSE TO A SENSE
OF THREAT. Rev. ed. Homewood, Ill.: Dorsey, 1978.

Especially chapter 5.

Sapin, Burton M. THE MAKING OF UNITED STATES FOREIGN POLICY.
Washington, D.C.: Praeger for Brookings Institution, 1966.

Especially chapter 4.

Snyder, Richard C., and Furniss, Edgar S., Jr. AMERICAN FOREIGN POLI-
CY: FORMULATION, PRINCIPLES AND PROGRAMS. New York: Rinehart,
1954.

Especially chapter 5.

COMMANDER IN CHIEF

The presidential authority and responsibility as commander in chief are touched
on in a good many studies listed in other sections of this chapter and in chapter 12. The following focus directly on this capacity of the presidency:

Congressional Quarterly. GUIDE TO THE U.S. SUPREME COURT. Washington, D.C.: Congressional Quarterly, 1979.

Section on "The President as Commander in Chief," pages 163-76.

Deutsch, Eberhard P. "The President as Commander in Chief." AMERICAN
BAR ASSOCIATION JOURNAL 57 (January 1971): 27-32.

Fairman, Charles. "The President as Commander-in-Chief." JOURNAL OF
POLITICS 11 (February 1949): 145-70.

Halperin, Morton H. "The President and the Military." FOREIGN AFFAIRS
50 (January 1972): 310-24. Reprint, no. 224. Washington, D.C.: Brookings Institution, 1972.

Haynes, Richard Frederick. THE AWESOME POWER: HARRY S. TRUMAN
AS COMMANDER IN CHIEF. Baton Rouge: Louisiana State University Press,
1973. 359 p. Bibliog.

_____. "Truman as Commander in Chief: A Study of President Harry S. Tru-
man's Concept and Exercise of the Military Function of the Presidency, 1945-

1953." 2 vols. Ph.D. dissertation, Louisiana State University, 1971. 730 p. Bibliog.

Heller, Francis H. "The President as the Commander in Chief." MILITARY REVIEW 42 (September 1962): 5–16.

May, Ernest R., ed. THE ULTIMATE DECISION: THE PRESIDENT AS COM-MANDER IN CHIEF. New York: Braziller, 1960. 290 p. Bibliog.

Potter, Pitman B. "Power of the President of the United States to Utilize Its Armed Forces Abroad." AMERICAN JOURNAL OF INTERNATIONAL LAW 48 (July 1954): 458–59.

Robinson, Donald L. "The President as Commander in Chief." CENTER MAG-AZINE 4 (September–October 1971): 58–67.

Rogers, James G. WORLD POLICING AND THE CONSTITUTION: AN IN-QUIRY INTO THE POWERS OF THE PRESIDENT AND CONGRESS, NINE WARS AND A HUNDRED MILITARY OPERATIONS, 1789–1945. Boston: World Peace Foundation, 1945. 123 p.

Rossiter, Clinton L. THE SUPREME COURT AND THE COMMANDER IN CHIEF. Ithaca, N.Y.: Cornell University Press, 1951. 145 p.

Schaffter, Dorothy, and Matthews, Dorothy M. THE POWERS OF THE PRESI-DENT AS COMMANDER IN CHIEF OF THE ARMY AND NAVY OF THE UNITED STATES. Washington, D.C.: Government Printing Office, 1956. 145 p.

Smith, J. Malcolm, and Jurika, Stephan, Jr. THE PRESIDENT AND NATION-AL SECURITY: HIS ROLE AS COMMANDER IN CHIEF. Dubuque, Iowa: Kendall-Hunt, 1972. 303 p.

U.S. Congress. Senate. Committee on Foreign Relations. DOCUMENTS RE-LATING TO THE WAR POWERS OF CONGRESS, THE PRESIDENT'S AUTHORITY AS COMMANDER IN CHIEF, AND THE WAR IN INDOCHINA. 91st Cong., 2d sess. Washington, D.C.: Government Printing Office, 1970. 252 p.

DIPLOMAT IN CHIEF—SUMMIT DIPLOMACY

Although political principals have engaged in diplomacy throughout history, summit diplomacy as a field of study and research has been given increasing attention since World War II. It involves several distinguishable aspects, including summit policy making and enunciation, diplomatic communications at the chief of state and head of government levels, the use of presidential special diplomatic representatives (earlier referred to as special agents), presidential trips abroad and summit visits to the United States, and summit meetings and conferences. Related materials are provided in other chapters dealing with policy making (chapters 14 and 16), specialized diplomatic officials (chapter 3), diplomatic communications (chapters 17 and 22), and international conferences (chapters 3, 5 [p. 554], and 22 [pp. 593-94]).

Acheson, Dean G. MEETINGS AT THE SUMMIT: A STUDY IN DIPLOMATIC METHOD--AN ADDRESS AT THE UNIVERSITY OF NEW HAMPSHIRE, MAY 8, 1958. Durham: University of New Hampshire, 1958. 27 p.

_____. "Thoughts About Thought in High Places." NEW YORK TIMES MAGAZINE, 11 October 1959, pp. 20, 86-90.

Baker, Ray Stannard. WOODROW WILSON AND WORLD SETTLEMENT: WRITTEN FROM HIS UNPUBLISHED AND PERSONAL MATERIAL. 3 vols. Garden City, N.Y.: Doubleday, Page, 1922.

   On Wilson at the Paris Peace Conference.

Beitzell, Robert Egner. "Major Strategic Conferences of the Allies, 1941-1943: Quadrant, Moscow, Sextant, and Eureka." Ph.D. dissertation, University of North Carolina, 1967. 518 p.

Burke, Lee H. "The Ambassador at Large: A Study in Diplomatic Method." Ph.D. dissertation, University of Maryland, 1971. 311 p. Bibliog.

_____. AMBASSADOR AT LARGE: DIPLOMAT EXTRAORDINARY. The Hague: Nijhoff, 1972. 176 p. Bibliog.

Clemens, Diane Shaver. YALTA. New York: Oxford University Press, 1970. 356 p. Bibliog.

Congressional Quarterly. GUIDE TO THE U.S. SUPREME COURT. Washington, D.C.: Congressional Quarterly, 1979.

   Section on "The President as Architect of Foreign Policy," pages 177-86.

Dichter, Ernest. "The Khrushchev Visit: The Role of Social Research." PROD 3 (September 1959): 17-18.

Eilts, Hermann Frederick. AHMAD BIN NA'AMAN'S MISSION TO THE UNITED STATES IN 1840: THE VOYAGE OF AL-SULTANAH TO NEW YORK CITY. Reprinted from ESSEX INSTITUTE QUARTERLY (October 1962). Middle East Export Press, for Petroleum Development (Omen) Ltd., 1971. 59 p.

   Account of one of earliest summit visits to the United States.

Eubank, Keith. THE SUMMIT CONFERENCES, 1919-1960. Norman: University of Oklahoma Press, 1966. 225 p.

Feis, Herbert. CHURCHILL, ROOSEVELT, STALIN: THE WAR THEY WAGED AND THE PEACE THEY SOUGHT. Princeton, N.J.: Princeton University Press, 1957. 692 p.

Franklin, William M. "Yalta Viewed from Tehran." In SOME PATHWAYS IN TWENTIETH CENTURY HISTORY, edited by Daniel Beaver, pp. 253-301. Detroit: Wayne State University Press, 1969.

Galtung, Johan. "Summit Meetings and International Relations." JOURNAL OF PEACE RESEARCH 1 (1964): 36-54.

George, Alexander L., and George, J.L. WOODROW WILSON AND COLONEL HOUSE: A PERSONALITY STUDY. New York: Day, 1956. 361 p.

Hankey, Maurice. THE SUPREME CONTROL AT THE PARIS PEACE CONFERENCE, 1919: A COMMENTARY. London: Allen and Unwin, 1963. 206 p.

Harries, O. "Faith in the Summit: Some British Attitudes." FOREIGN AFFAIRS 40 (October 1961): 58-70.

Hill, Larry D. "Woodrow Wilson's Executive Agents in Mexico: From the Beginning of his Administration to the Recognition of Venustiano Carranza." 2 vols. Ph.D. dissertation, Louisiana State University, 1971.

Hoska, Lukas E., Jr. "Summit Diplomacy During World War II: The Conferences at Tehran, Yalta, and Potsdam." Ph.D. dissertation, University of Maryland, 1966. 272 p. Bibliog.

India. Information Service. NEHRU VISITS U.S.A. Washington, D.C.: Information Service of India, 1957. 72 p.

Kemp, Arthur. "Summit Conferences in World War II." In ISSUES AND CONFLICTS: STUDIES IN TWENTIETH CENTURY AMERICAN DIPLOMACY, edited by George L. Anderson, pp. 256-83. Lawrence: University of Kansas Press, 1959.

Kertesz, Stephen D. "Summit and Personal Diplomacy." In his THE QUEST FOR PEACE THROUGH DIPLOMACY, pp. 51-61. Englewood Cliffs, N.J.: Prentice-Hall, 1967.

Lansing, Robert. THE BIG FOUR AND OTHERS OF THE PEACE CONFERENCE. Boston: Houghton Mifflin, 1921. 212 p.

Loewenheim, Francis L.; Langley, Harold D.; and Jonas, Manfred, eds. ROOSEVELT AND CHURCHILL: THEIR SECRET WARTIME CORRESPONDENCE. New York: Saturday Review Press, 1975. 805 p. Bibliog.

Martin, Harold H. "New York's Police: Their Greatest Ordeal." SATURDAY EVENING POST, 10 December 1960, pp. 19-21, 67-69.

On providing personal security for Premier Khrushchev during his summit visit.

Mee, Charles L., Jr. MEETING AT POTSDAM. New York: Evans, 1975. 370 p. Bibliog.

Miller, David Hunter. "Some Legal Aspects of the Visit of President Wilson to Paris." HARVARD LAW REVIEW 36 (November 1922): 51-78.

Minger, Ralph Eldin. "Taft's Mission to Japan: A Study in Personal Diplomacy." PACIFIC HISTORICAL REVIEW 30 (August 1961): 279-94.

On Taft's service as a special presidential representative on trips in 1905 and 1907.

Morgenthau, Hans J. "Dilemma of the Summit." NEW YORK TIMES MAGAZINE, 11 November 1962, pp. 25, 117-22.

_____. "Khrushchev's New Cold War Strategy: Prestige Diplomacy." COMMENTARY 28 (November 1959): 381-88.

Morton, Henry C.V. ATLANTIC MEETING. London: Methuen, 1945. 196 p.

On the Atlantic (Argentia/Placentia Bay) meeting of President Franklin D. Roosevelt and Prime Minister Winston Churchill, 1941.

O'Brien, Francis W. THE HOOVER-WILSON WARTIME CORRESPONDENCE, SEPTEMBER 24, 1914 TO NOVEMBER 11, 1918. Ames: Iowa State University Press, 1974. 297 p.

Correspondence between President Wilson and Food Administrator Herbert Hoover.

Plischke, Elmer. "The Eisenhower-Krushchev Visits: Diplomacy at the Summit." MARYLAND MAGAZINE 30 (September-October 1959): 6-9.

_____. "Eisenhower's 'Correspondence Diplomacy' with the Kremlin: Case Study in Summit Diplomatics." JOURNAL OF POLITICS 30 (February 1968): 137-59.

_____. "International Conferencing and the Summit: Macro-Analysis of Presidential Participation." ORBIS 14 (Fall 1970): 673-713.

Includes table of presidential trips abroad for consultation and conferencing, 1905-68, indicating dates, location, type of meeting, and presidential role.

_____. "The President's Right to Go Abroad." ORBIS 15 (Fall 1971): 755-83.

_____. "Recent State Visits to the United States--A Technique of Summit Diplomacy." WORLD AFFAIRS QUARTERLY 29 (October 1958): 223-55.

_____. "Summit Diplomacy." In his CONDUCT OF AMERICAN DIPLOMACY, pp. 43-55. 3d ed. Princeton, N.J.: Van Nostrand, 1967.

_____. "Summit Diplomacy: Its Uses and Limitations." VIRGINIA QUARTERLY REVIEW 48 (Summer 1972): 321-44.

_____. SUMMIT DIPLOMACY: PERSONAL DIPLOMACY OF THE PRESIDENT OF THE UNITED STATES. College Park: Bureau of Governmental Research, University of Maryland, 1958. Reprint. Westport, Conn.: Greenwood, 1974. 125 p.

_____. "The Tortuous Road to the Summit, 1955-1960." ENGLISH-SPEAKING UNION EDITORIAL BACKGROUND FACT SHEET 9 (February 1961): 17.

Richards, James P. REPORT ON THE SURVEY MISSION TO THE FAR EAST AND MIDDLE EAST. Washington, D.C.: Government Printing Office, 1955. 13 p.

On former Congressman Richards's special mission for the president.

Rogers, Lindsay. "Of Summits." FOREIGN AFFAIRS 34 (October 1955): 141-48.

Rusk, Dean. "The Presidency and the Summit." CORONET 50 (June 1961): 70-75.

Excerpts from Rusk's article on "The President," published in FOREIGN AFFAIRS, cited earlier, p. 117.

Sears, Arthur Marsden. "The Search for Peace Through Summit Conferences." Ph.D. dissertation, University of Colorado, 1972. 967 p.

Sherwood, Robert E. ROOSEVELT AND HOPKINS: AN INTIMATE HISTORY. New York: Harper, 1948. 1,002 p.

Smith, A. Merriman. THE PRESIDENT'S ODYSSEY. New York: Harper, 1961. 272 p.

On President Eisenhower's visits abroad.

Smith, Beverly, Jr. "To Cuba with Cal." SATURDAY EVENING POST, 1 February 1958, pp. 16, 17, 76, 78, 79.

> On Calvin Coolidge's trip to Havana to attend an inter-American conference.

"Special Issue Devoted to the Paris Summit Conference." FREE WORLD FORUM 2 (April-May 1960): 69 p.

> Symposium of fifteen articles by individual authors.

Strange, Russell P. "The Atlantic and Arcadia Conferences: The First Two Wartime Meetings of Roosevelt and Churchill." Master's thesis, University of Maryland, 1953. 156 p. Bibliog.

_____. "Atlantic Conference--The First Roosevelt-Churchill Meeting." UNITED STATES NAVAL INSTITUTE PROCEEDINGS 79 (April 1953): 388-97.

"The Summit Via Paris." ROUND TABLE 49 (December 1959): 3-7.

Thorpe, Francis N. "Is the President of the United States Vested With Authority Under the Constitution to Appoint a Special Diplomatic Agent With Paramount Power Without the Advice and Consent of the Senate?" AMERICAN LAW REGISTER AND REVIEW, April 1894, pp. 257-64.

U.S. Congress. Senate. Foreign Relations Committee. BACKGROUND DOCUMENTS ON EVENTS INCIDENT TO THE SUMMIT CONFERENCE. 86th Cong., 2d sess. Washington, D.C.: Government Printing Office, 1960. 75 p.

> This and the following two items relate to the aborted four-power Paris Summit Conference of 1960.

_____. EVENTS INCIDENT TO THE SUMMIT CONFERENCE: HEARINGS, MAY 27, JUNE 1, 2, 1960. 86th Cong., 2d sess. Washington, D.C.: Government Printing Office, 1960. 302 p.

_____. EVENTS RELATING TO THE SUMMIT CONFERENCE: REPORT. 86th Cong., 2d sess. Washington, D.C.: Government Printing Office, 1960. 36 p.

U.S. Department of State. ATLANTIC CONSULTATION: PRESIDENT NIXON IN EUROPE, FEBRUARY 23-MARCH 2, 1969. Washington, D.C.: Government Printing Office, 1969. 44 p.

_____. BACKGROUND OF HEADS OF GOVERNMENT CONFERENCE--1960: PRINCIPAL DOCUMENTS, 1955-1959, WITH NARRATIVE SUMMARY. Washington, D.C.: Government Printing Office, 1960. 478 p.

_____. THE CAMP DAVID SUMMIT. Washington, D.C.: Government Printing Office, 1978. 19 p.

_____. THE GENEVA CONFERENCE OF HEADS OF GOVERNMENT, JULY 18-23, 1955. Washington, D.C.: Government Printing Office, 1955. 88 p.

_____. NORTH ATLANTIC TREATY ORGANIZATION MEETING OF HEADS OF GOVERNMENT--PARIS, DECEMBER 1957: TEXTS OF STATEMENTS. Washington, D.C.: Government Printing Office, 1958. 117 p.

_____. PRESIDENT EISENHOWER'S EUROPEAN TRIP, AUGUST-SEPTEMBER 1959. Washington, D.C.: Government Printing Office, 1959. 36 p.

_____. PRESIDENT NIXON'S VISIT TO POLAND. Washington, D.C.: Government Printing Office, 1972. 13 p.

_____. THE PROMISE OF A NEW ASIA: UNITED STATES POLICY IN THE FAR EAST AS STATED BY PRESIDENT JOHNSON ON HIS PACIFIC JOURNEY. Washington, D.C.: Government Printing Office, 1966. 65 p.

_____. RETURN TO GLASSBORO: PRESIDENT LYNDON B. JOHNSON. Washington, D.C.: Government Printing Office, 1968. 12 p.

_____. TOWARD BETTER UNDERSTANDING: VICE PRESIDENT NIXON'S VISIT TO THE SOVIET UNION AND POLAND. Washington, D.C.: Government Printing Office, 1959. 50 p.

_____. THE WASHINGTON SUMMIT: GENERAL SECRETARY BREZHNEV'S VISIT TO THE UNITED STATES, JUNE 18-25, 1973. Washington, D.C.: Government Printing Office, 1973. 63 p.

U.S. Information Service. JOURNEY TO THE PACIFIC. Washington, D.C.: Government Printing Office, 1966. 64 p.

On President Johnson's summit trip to the Pacific in 1966.

USSR. KHRUSHCHEV IN AMERICA. New York: Crosscurrents Press, 1960. 231 p.

On Khrushchev's summit visit to the United States in 1959.

_____. KHRUSHCHEV IN NEW YORK. New York: Crosscurrents Press, 1960. 286 p.

_____. THREE DOCUMENTS OF CURRENT HISTORY: REPORT BY CHAIRMAN N.S. KHRUSHCHEV ON HIS MEETING WITH PRESIDENT JOHN F. KENNEDY IN VIENNA. New York: Crosscurrents Press, 1961. 36 p.

On Khrushchev's summit meeting with President Kennedy in 1961.

Velie, Lester. "The Week the Hot Line Burned." READER'S DIGEST, August 1969, pp. 37-44.
Use of the hot line during the Mideast crisis of 1967.

Viereck, George S. THE STRANGEST FRIENDSHIP IN HISTORY: WOODROW WILSON AND COLONEL HOUSE. New York: Liveright, 1932. 375 p.

Waples, Douglas. "Publicity versus Diplomacy: Notes on the Reporting of the 'Summit' Conferences." PUBLIC OPINION QUARTERLY 20 (Spring 1956): 308-14.

Wardall, William King. "State Visits: A Technique of United States Summit Diplomacy." Masters thesis, University of Maryland, 1958. 168 p. Bibliog.

Waters, Maurice. "Special Diplomatic Agents of the President." ANNALS OF THE AMERICAN ACADEMY OF POLITICAL AND SOCIAL SCIENCE 307 (September 1956): 124-33.

Wilson, Theodore A. THE FIRST SUMMIT: ROOSEVELT AND CHURCHILL AT PLACENTIA BAY, 1941. Boston: Houghton Mifflin, 1969. 344 p.

Wimer, Kurt. "Wilson and Eisenhower: Two Experiences in Summit Diplomacy." CONTEMPORARY REVIEW 199 (June 1961): 284-95.

Woolsey, Lester H. "The Personal Diplomacy of Colonel House." AMERICAN JOURNAL OF INTERNATIONAL LAW 21 (October 1927): 706-15.

Worsnop, Richard L. "Heads-of-State Diplomacy." EDITORIAL RESEARCH REPORTS 2 (5 December 1962): 873-92.

_____. "Presidential Diplomacy." EDITORIAL RESEARCH REPORTS 11 (24 September 1971): 737-58.

Wriston, Henry M. EXECUTIVE AGENTS IN AMERICAN FOREIGN RELATIONS. Baltimore: Johns Hopkins Press, 1929. 874 p.

_____. "The Special Envoy." FOREIGN AFFAIRS 38 (January 1960): 219-37.

The following, compiled by the Historical Office of the U.S. Department of State (now the Office of the Historian), initially in 1962, revised in 1968, and updated annually thereafter, are of considerable value for the study of presidential trips abroad and summit visits to the United States:

U.S. Department of State. Office of the Historian. LISTS OF VISITS OF FOREIGN CHIEFS OF STATE AND HEADS OF GOVERNMENT TO THE UNITED STATES, 1789-- . Washington, D.C.: 1968-- . Annual.

_____. LISTS OF VISITS OF PRESIDENTS OF THE UNITED STATES TO FOREIGN COUNTRIES, 1789-- . Washington, D.C.: 1968-- . Annual.

> Contain introductory statements, chronological lists of trips and visits, and lists by country to which the president traveled and from which foreign dignitaries came to visit the United States. Includes dates and nature of the trip or visit.

LEADERSHIP AND IMAGE

The following represent the growing literature on presidential leadership, style, and image. The studies of such authors as Brown and Herring are of a general nature; whereas those of Longaker, Nitze, Rienow and Rienow, and Warren emphasize the president's international leadership role; and those of Barber, George, Graber, and Hargrove deal with his character, qualities, and style. Increasing attention is being paid to the president's relations with the media and public opinion, illustrated by the studies of Blaisdell, Cornwell, Greenstein, Hamilton, Landecker, and Mueller, which focus on presidential image and public opinion, and those of Cornwell, Grossman, Minow et al., Morgan, Pollard, Smith, Stein, and Thomas, which review the president's relations with the media. Of special interest to some are the comparative evaluations of presidents, provided in the studies of Bailey, Borden, and Schlesinger.

Bailey, Thomas A. PRESIDENTIAL GREATNESS: THE IMAGE AND THE MAN FROM GEORGE WASHINGTON TO THE PRESENT. New York: Appleton-Century, 1966. 368 p. Bibliog.

> Contains four bibliographies as appendices, including a general chapter bibliography and a separate bibliography of materials on each president from Washington through Kennedy.

Barber, James David. "Classifying and Predicting Presidential Styles: Two 'Weak' Presidents." JOURNAL OF SOCIAL ISSUES 24 (July 1968): 51-80.

> On Presidents Coolidge and Hoover.

_____. THE PRESIDENTIAL CHARACTER: PREDICTING PERFORMANCE IN THE WHITE HOUSE. Englewood Cliffs, N.J.: Prentice-Hall, 1972. 479 p.

Blaisdell, Thomas C., Jr., et al. THE AMERICAN PRESIDENCY IN POLITICAL CARTOONS: 1776-1976. Salt Lake City, Utah: Peregrine Smith, 1976. 278 p.

Borden, Morton, ed. AMERICA'S TEN GREATEST PRESIDENTS. Chicago: Rand McNally, 1961. 269 p. Bibliog.

Brown, Stuart Gerry. THE AMERICAN PRESIDENCY: LEADERSHIP, PARTI-
SANSHIP AND POPULARITY. New York: Macmillan, 1966. 279 p.

Especially part 5.

Cater, D. "The President and the Press." ANNALS OF THE AMERICAN
ACADEMY OF POLITICAL AND SOCIAL SCIENCE 307 (September 1956):
55-65.

Cleveland, Harlan. "The Executive and the Public." ANNALS OF THE
AMERICAN ACADEMY OF POLITICAL AND SOCIAL SCIENCE 307 (September
1956): 37-54.

Cornwell, Elmer E., Jr. THE PRESIDENCY AND THE PRESS. Morristown,
N.J.: General Learning Press, 1974. 32 p.

_____. PRESIDENTIAL LEADERSHIP OF PUBLIC OPINION. Bloomington:
Indiana University Press, 1965. 370 p. Bibliog.

_____. "The Presidential Press Conference: A Study of Institutionalization."
MIDWEST JOURNAL OF POLITICAL SCIENCE 4 (November 1960): 370-89.

Frankel, Max. "The Press and the President." COMMENTARY 52 (July
1971): 6, 8, 10, 12, 16, 18, 20.

George, Alexander L. "Assessing Presidential Character." WORLD POLITICS
26 (January 1974): 234-82.

Graber, Doris A. "Personal Qualities in Presidential Images: The Contribution of the Press." MIDWEST JOURNAL OF POLITICAL SCIENCE 16 (February 1972): 46-76.

Greenstein, Fred I. "Popular Images of the President." AMERICAN JOURNAL
OF PSYCHIATRY 122 (November 1965): 523-29.

Grossman, Michael B., and Rourke, Francis E. "The Media and the Presidency: An Exchange Analysis." POLITICAL SCIENCE QUARTERLY 91 (Fall
1976): 455-70.

Hamilton, Holman. WHITE HOUSE IMAGES AND REALITIES. Gainesville:
University of Florida Press, 1958. 98 p. Bibliog.

Hargrove, Erwin C. PRESIDENTIAL LEADERSHIP, PERSONALITY AND POLITI-
CAL STYLE. New York: Macmillan, 1966. 153 p.

Herring, E. Pendleton. PRESIDENTIAL LEADERSHIP: THE POLITICAL RELATIONS OF CONGRESS AND THE CHIEF EXECUTIVE. New York: Farrar, Straus, and Giroux, 1940. Reprint. Westport, Conn.: Greenwood, 1972. 173 p.

Jacob, Charles E. "The Limits of Presidential Leadership." SOUTH ATLANTIC QUARTERLY 62 (Autumn 1963): 461-73.

Landecker, Manfred. THE PRESIDENT AND PUBLIC OPINION: LEADERSHIP IN FOREIGN AFFAIRS. Washington, D.C.: Public Affairs, 1968. 133 p.

Longaker, Richard P. "President as International Leader." LAW AND CONTEMPORARY PROBLEMS 21 (Autumn 1956): 735-52.

Minow, Newton N.; Martin, John Bartlow; and Mitchell, Lee M. PRESIDENTIAL TELEVISION. New York: Basic Books, 1973. 232 p. Bibliog.

Morgan, Edward P., et al. THE PRESIDENCY AND THE PRESS CONFERENCE. Washington, D.C.: American Enterprise Institute, 1971. 56 p.

Mueller, John E. WAR, PRESIDENTS, AND PUBLIC OPINION. New York: Wiley, 1973. 300 p. Bibliog.

Nitze, Paul H. "The Modern President as a World Figure." ANNALS OF THE AMERICAN ACADEMY OF POLITICAL AND SOCIAL SCIENCE 307 (September 1956): 114-23.

Pollard, James E. THE PRESIDENTS AND THE PRESS. New York: Macmillan, 1947. 866 p.

_____. THE PRESIDENTS AND THE PRESS: TRUMAN TO JOHNSON. Washington, D.C.: Public Affairs, 1947. 125 p.

Price, Don K. "Administrative Leadership." DAEDALUS 90 (Fall 1961): 750-63.

Rienow, R., and Rienow, L.T. THE LONELY QUEST: THE EVOLUTION OF PRESIDENTIAL LEADERSHIP. Chicago: Follett, 1966. 307 p.

Schlesinger, Arthur M., Sr. "Historians Rate U.S. Presidents." LIFE, 1 November 1948, pp. 65-66, 68, 73-74.

_____. "Our Presidents: A Rating by 75 Historians." NEW YORK TIMES MAGAZINE, 29 July 1962, pp. 12-13, 40-41, 43.

Smith, A. Merriman. THANK YOU, MR. PRESIDENT: A WHITE HOUSE NOTEBOOK. New York: Harper, 1946. 304 p.

Spragens, William C. THE PRESIDENCY AND THE MASS MEDIA IN THE AGE OF TELEVISION. Washington, D.C.: University Press of America, 1978. 428 p.

Stein, Meyer L. WHEN PRESIDENTS MEET THE PRESS. New York: Messner, 1969. 190 p. Bibliog.

Thomas, Helen. DATELINE: WHITE HOUSE. New York: Macmillan, 1975. 298 p.

Tobin, Richard Lardner. DECISIONS OF DESTINY. Cleveland: World, 1961. 285 p.

Especially chapter 7 on presidential leadership and image.

Warren, Sidney. THE PRESIDENT AS WORLD LEADER. New York: McGraw-Hill, 1964. 480 p. Bibliog.

Wise, David. "The President and the Press." ATLANTIC MONTHLY, April 1973, pp. 55-64.

EXECUTIVE PRIVILEGE

The matter of executive privilege has evoked increasing concern in the 1960s and 1970s, in part because of the Watergate incident. Much of the writing centers on legal as well as political analysis. Related materials on secrecy in diplomacy are provided in chapter 16. Sources on official foreign relations documentation are discussed in chapter 21 and are listed in chapter 22 and elsewhere in this compilation. Additional guidance on executive privilege may be found in:

Smith, S.C. BIBLIOGRAPHY: EXECUTIVE PRIVILEGE. New Haven, Conn.: Yale Law Library, 1973. 41 p.

Berger, Raoul. EXECUTIVE PRIVILEGE: A CONSTITUTIONAL MYTH. Cambridge, Mass.: Harvard University Press, 1974. 430 p. Bibliog.

_____. "Executive Privilege vs. Congressional Inquiry." UCLA LAW REVIEW 12 (August 1965): 1044-64.

Bishop, Joseph W., Jr. "The Executive's Right to Privacy: An Unresolved Constitutional Question." YALE LAW JOURNAL 66 (February 1957): 477-91.

Breckenridge, Adam C. THE EXECUTIVE PRIVILEGE: PRESIDENTIAL CONTROL OVER INFORMATION. Lincoln: University of Nebraska Press, 1974. 188 p.

Collins, Philip R. "Power of Congressional Committees of Investigation to Obtain Information from the Executive Branch: The Argument for the Executive Branch." GEORGIA LAW JOURNAL 39 (May 1951): 563-98.

Cox, Archibald. "Executive Privilege." UNIVERSITY OF PENNSYLVANIA LAW REVIEW 122 (June 1974): 1383-1438.

Dorsen, N., and Shattuck, J.H.F. "Executive Privilege, the Congress, and the Courts." OHIO STATE LAW JOURNAL 35 (1974): 1-40.

Ervin, Sam J. "Controlling Executive Privilege." LOYOLA LAW REVIEW 20, no. 1 (1974): 11-31.

"Government Privilege Against Disclosure of Official Documents." YALE LAW JOURNAL 58 (May 1949): 993-98.

Kramer, Robert, and Marcuse, Herman. "Executive Privilege: A Study of the Period 1953-1960." GEORGE WASHINGTON LAW REVIEW 29 (April and June 1961): 623-717, 827-916.

McGlaughon, H. King, Jr. "Constitutional Law--Executive Privilege: Tilting the Scales in Favor of Secrecy." NORTH CAROLINA LAW REVIEW 53 (December 1974): 419-30.

Oster, Jon F. "Extension of Executive Privilege to Executive Officers of Government Agencies." MARYLAND LAW REVIEW 20 (Fall 1960): 368-73.

Ramis, Timothy V. "Executive Privileges: What Are the Limits?" OREGON LAW REVIEW 54, no. 1 (1975): 81-103.

Randolph, Robert C., and Smith, Daniel C. "Executive Privilege and the Congressional Right of Inquiry." HARVARD JOURNAL ON LEGISLATION 10 (June 1973): 621-71.

Rourke, Francis E. "Administrative Secrecy: A Congressional Dilemma." AMERICAN POLITICAL SCIENCE REVIEW 54 (September 1960): 684-94.

Schwartz, Bernard. "Executive Privilege and Congressional Investigatory Power." CALIFORNIA LAW REVIEW 47 (March 1959): 3-50.

_____. "Executive Privilege: The Public's Right to Know and Public Interest." FEDERAL BAR JOURNAL 19 (1959): 7-17.

PRESIDENT AND CONGRESS

The constitutional, political, and pragmatic problem of executive-legislative relations has existed and has been researched and addressed in literature since the framing of the American political system. Presidential-Congressional relations in the field of foreign affairs has been particularly acute--involving diplomatic appointments by the president, treaty making, and policy formulation. The following illustrate published materials from the perspective of the executive, which need to be supplemented with the more general resources on the separation of powers and executive privilege, dealt with in earlier sections of this chapter, and those emphasizing the congressional point of view, listed in chapter 8. Additional references dealing with more particularized aspects of the problem are incorporated elsewhere in this compilation, such as the sections devoted to policy formulation (chapter 16), decision making (chapter 14), and treaty and agreement making (chapter 17).

Abshire, David M. FOREIGN POLICY MAKERS: PRESIDENT VS. CONGRESS. Washington, D.C.: Center for Strategic Studies, Georgetown University, 1979. 80 p.

Berger, Raoul. "The President, Congress, and the Courts." YALE LAW JOURNAL 83 (May 1974): 1111-55.

Binkley, Wilfred E. "The President and Congress." JOURNAL OF POLITICS 11 (February 1949): 65-79.

_____. PRESIDENT AND CONGRESS. 3d ed. New York: Knopf, 1947. 312 p. Bibliog.

First published as THE POWERS OF THE PRESIDENT in 1937.

_____. "The Relation of the President to Congress." PARLIAMENTARY AFFAIRS 3 (Winter 1949): 7-20.

Black, Henry Campbell. THE RELATION OF THE EXECUTIVE POWER TO LEGISLATION. Princeton, N.J.: Princeton University Press, 1919. 191 p.

Bolles, Blair. "President, Congress, and Foreign Policy." AMERICAN PERSPECTIVE 2 (March 1949): 491-500.

Bullard, Anthony R. "Harry S. Truman and the Separation of Powers in Foreign Affairs." Ph.D. dissertation, Columbia University, 1972. 321 p.

Chamberlain, Lawrence H. THE PRESIDENT, CONGRESS AND LEGISLATION. Columbia Studies in the Social Sciences. New York: Columbia University Press, 1946. 478 p.

_____. "The President, Congress, and Legislation." POLITICAL SCIENCE QUARTERLY 61 (March 1946): 42-60.

Cotter, Cornelius P. "Administrative Accountability to Congress: The Concurrent Resolution." WESTERN POLITICAL QUARTERLY 9 (December 1956): 955-66.

Driggs, Don Wallace. "Executive-Legislative Relationships and the Control of American Foreign Policy with Respect to Collective Security, 1921-1933." Ph.D. dissertation, Harvard University, 1956. 129 p.

Edwards, George C. III. "Presidential Influence in the House: Presidential Prestige as a Source of Presidential Power." AMERICAN POLITICAL SCIENCE REVIEW 70 (March 1976): 101-13.

Egger, Rowland, and Harris, Joseph P. THE PRESIDENT AND CONGRESS. New York: McGraw-Hill, 1963. 128 p.

Fisher, Louis. PRESIDENT AND CONGRESS: POWER AND POLICY. New York: Free Press, 1972. 347 p. Bibliog.

Folts, David William. "The Role of the President and Congress in the Formulation of United States Economic Policy Towards the Soviet Union, 1947-1968." Ph.D. dissertation, University of Notre Dame, 1971. 314 p.

Holtzman, Abraham. LEGISLATIVE LIAISON: EXECUTIVE LEADERSHIP IN CONGRESS. Chicago: Rand McNally, 1970. 308 p.

Jones, Harry Willmer. "The President, Congress, and Foreign Relations." CALIFORNIA LAW REVIEW 29 (July 1941): 565-85.

Kahro, Karl H. "U.S. Foreign Policy: President and Congress." AUSSEN-POLITIK (English edition) 27 (3d Quarter 1976): 257-72.

Kefauver, Estes. "The Need for Better Executive-Legislative Teamwork in National Government." AMERICAN POLITICAL SCIENCE REVIEW 38 (April 1944): 317-25.

Kesselman, Mark. "Presidential Leadership in Congress on Foreign Policy." MIDWEST JOURNAL OF POLITICAL SCIENCE 5 (August 1961): 284-89.

_____. "Presidential Leadership in Congress on Foreign Policy: A Replication of a Hypothesis." MIDWEST JOURNAL OF POLITICAL SCIENCE 9 (November 1965): 401-6.

Kraines, Oscar. "The President versus Congress: The Keep Commission, 1905–1909. The First Comprehensive Presidential Inquiry Into Administration." WESTERN POLITICAL QUARTERLY 23 (March 1970): 5–54.

Lane, Gary. THE PRESIDENT VERSUS CONGRESS: FREEDOM OF INFORMATION. Washington, D.C.: Lanco, 1971. 61 p.

Lehman, John. THE EXECUTIVE, CONGRESS, AND FOREIGN POLICY. New York: Praeger, 1976. 270 p.

MacLean, Joan Coyne, ed. PRESIDENT AND CONGRESS: THE CONFLICT OF POWERS. Reference Shelf, vol. 27, no. 1. New York: Wilson, 1955. 218 p.

Neustadt, Richard E. "Presidency and Legislation: Planning the President's Program." AMERICAN POLITICAL SCIENCE REVIEW 49 (December 1955): 980–1021.

_____. "Presidency and Legislation: The Growth of Central Clearance." AMERICAN POLITICAL SCIENCE REVIEW 48 (September 1954): 641–71.

Ogul, Morris S. "Reforming Executive-Legislative Relations in the Conduct of American Foreign Policy--The Executive-Legislative Council as a Proposed Solution." Ph.D. dissertation, University of Michigan, 1958. 200 p.

Pepper, George W. FAMILY QUARRELS: THE PRESIDENT, THE SENATE, THE HOUSE. New York: Baker, Voorhis, 1931. 192 p.

Pipe, G. Russell. "Congressional Liaison: The Executive Branch Consolidates Its Relations with Congress." PUBLIC ADMINISTRATION REVIEW 26 (March 1966): 14–24.

Rogers, James G. WORLD POLICING AND THE CONSTITUTION: AN INQUIRY INTO THE POWERS OF THE PRESIDENT AND CONGRESS, NINE WARS AND A HUNDRED MILITARY OPERATIONS, 1789–1945. Boston: World Peace Foundation, 1945. 123 p.

Toma, Peter A. THE POLITICS OF FOOD FOR PEACE: EXECUTIVE-LEGISLATIVE INTERACTION. Tucson: University of Arizona Press, 1967. 195 p.

Truman, David B. "The Presidency and Congressional Leadership: Some Notes on Our Changing Constitution." AMERICAN PHILOSOPHICAL SOCIETY PROCEEDINGS 103 (15 October 1959): 687–92.

White, Howard. "Executive Responsibility to Congress Via Concurrent Resolution." AMERICAN POLITICAL SCIENCE REVIEW 36 (October 1942): 895–900.

Zinn, Charles J. THE VETO POWER OF THE PRESIDENT. Washington, D.C.: Government Printing Office, 1951. 44 p.

VICE-PRESIDENCY

Analytical literature on the vice-presidency is scarce, and that which concerns its foreign relations role is even more limited. A few studies are basic or general, concerned with the office and the incumbents, such as those of Williams as well as Young and Middleton, and that of Hatch and Shoup provides a history of the office. Clinton focuses more specifically on the involvement of the vice-president in foreign affairs. DiSalle and Blochman, Levin, Sindler, and Waugh deal with vice-presidential succession to the presidency, a subject also treated in a separate section of this chapter. Guidance to additional materials on the office may be found in Tomkins. A good deal of literature on individual vice-presidents is available in contemporary journals and periodical articles--not included in this compilation--and in memoirs.

Barzman, Sol. MADMEN AND GENIUSES: THE VICE-PRESIDENTS OF THE UNITED STATES. Chicago: Follett, 1974. 335 p. Bibliog.

Bendiner, Robert. "The Changing Role of the Vice-President." COLLIERS, 17 February 1956, pp. 48-53.

Clinton, John Arthur. "The U.S. Vice President and Foreign Affairs." Masters thesis, University of Maryland, 1963. 161 p. Bibliog.

Curtis, Richard, and Wells, Maggie. NOT EXACTLY A CRIME: OUR VICE PRESIDENTS FROM ADAMS TO AGNEW. New York: Dial, 1972. 202 p.

David, Paul. "The Vice Presidency: Its Institutional Evolution and Contemporary Status." JOURNAL OF POLITICS 29 (November 1967): 721-48.

DiSalle, Michael Vincent, and Blochman, Lawrence G. SECOND CHOICE. New York: Hawthorn, 1966. 253 p.

Dorman, Michael. THE SECOND MAN: THE CHANGING ROLE OF THE VICE-PRESIDENCY. New York: Delacorte, 1968. 305 p. Bibliog.

Durham, G. Homer. "The Vice-Presidency." WESTERN POLITICAL QUARTERLY 1 (September 1948): 311-15.

Feerick, John D. "Vice-Presidency and the Problems of Presidential Succession and Inability." FORDHAM LAW REVIEW 32 (March 1964): 457-98.

Goldbloom, Maurice J. "Must Vice Presidents be Throttlebottoms?" AMERICAN MERCURY 75 (August 1952): 26-34.

Graff, Henry F. "A Heartbeat Away." AMERICAN HERITAGE 15 (August 1964): 81-87.

Harwood, Michael. IN THE SHADOW OF PRESIDENTS: THE AMERICAN VICE PRESIDENCY AND SUCCESSION SYSTEM. Philadelphia: Lippincott, 1966. 239 p. Bibliog.

Hatch, Louis Clinton, and Shoup, Earl L. A HISTORY OF THE VICE PRESIDENCY OF THE UNITED STATES. 2d ed. New York: American Historical Society, 1934. 437 p.

Laird, Archibald. THE NEAR GREAT: CHRONICLE OF THE VICE PRESIDENTS. North Quincy, Mass.: Christopher, 1980. 353 p.

Levin, Peter R. SEVEN BY CHANCE: THE ACCIDENTAL PRESIDENTS. New York: Farrar, Straus, 1948. 374 p. Bibliog.

Rossiter, Clinton L. "The Reform of the Vice-Presidency." POLITICAL SCIENCE QUARTERLY 63 (September 1948): 383-403.

Schlesinger, Arthur M., Jr. "Is the Vice-Presidency Necessary?" ATLANTIC MONTHLY, May 1974, pp. 37-44.

Sindler, Allan P. UNCHOSEN PRESIDENTS: THE VICE-PRESIDENT AND OTHER FRUSTRATIONS OF PRESIDENTIAL SUCCESSION. Berkeley: University of California Press, 1976. 128 p.

Tomkins, Dorothy Louise [Campbell] Culver. THE OFFICE OF VICE PRESIDENT: A SELECTED BIBLIOGRAPHY. Berkeley: Bureau of Public Administration, University of California, 1957. 19 p.

Vexler, Robert I. THE VICE PRESIDENTS: BIOGRAPHICAL SKETCHES OF THE VICE-PRESIDENTS AND CABINET MEMBERS. 2 vols. Dobbs Ferry, N.Y.: Oceana, 1975.

Waugh, Edgar Wiggins. SECOND CONSUL: THE VICE PRESIDENCY--OUR GREATEST POLITICAL PROBLEM. Indianapolis: Bobbs-Merrill, 1956. 244 p.

Williams, Irving G. "The American Vice Presidency." CURRENT HISTORY 66 (June 1974): 254-58.

_____. THE AMERICAN VICE PRESIDENCY: NEW LOOK. Garden City, N.Y.: Doubleday, 1954. 82 p.

_____. "The American Vice-Presidency and Foreign Affairs." WORLD AFFAIRS 120 (Summer 1957): 38-41.

_____. THE RISE OF THE VICE PRESIDENCY. Washington, D.C.: Public Affairs, 1956. 206 p.

Wilmerding, Lucius, Jr. "The Vice Presidency." POLITICAL SCIENCE QUARTERLY 68 (March 1953): 17-51.

Worsnop, Richard L. "Vice Presidency." EDITORIAL RESEARCH REPORTS 2 (11 November 1970): 832-56.

Young, Donald. AMERICAN ROULETTE: THE HISTORY AND DILEMMA OF THE VICE-PRESIDENCY. New York: Holt, Rinehart, and Winston, 1965. 367 p. Bibliog.

Young, Klyde, and Middleton, Lamar. HEIRS APPARENT: THE VICE PRESIDENTS OF THE UNITED STATES. New York: Prentice-Hall, 1948. 314 p. Bibliog.

Chapter 8

CONGRESS AND FOREIGN RELATIONS

Congress shares authority with the executive in the management of foreign relations. The legislative powers of Congress are plenary, and this applies to external as well as internal affairs. Cooperation between the two branches of
government in the matter of legislation is essential, and the president and Congress also interact in other respects. Whereas the president accredits diplomats and consuls, his nominations are subject to Senate confirmation. Congress
must appropriate the funds for the establishment of overseas missions, without
which the diplomatic and consular appointments would be meaningless. The
president is commander in chief of the military forces, but Congress is responsible for establishing them by law. Congress is also constitutionally empowered
to declare war, although in practice it awaits presidential initiative. The
Senate must approve presidential appointments and authorize the ratification
of treaties, and if these involve the expenditure of funds, they are dependent
on congressional authorization and appropriation. Although foreign relations
leadership has traditionally been provided by the president, the Congress plays
a major correlative role in the formulation of policy and the conduct of external affairs.

GENERAL LITERATURE

A great deal of literary interest focuses on Congress and its functions. Much
that has been published since 1960 is of a critical nature. Studies vary from
broad-scale elementary description to penetrating analyses of specific powers
and activities. Though comprehensive in scope and treatment, such literature
may provide useful background for the study of the congressional role in the
foreign relations process.

A selected listing of basic material is provided in this section. It includes a
number of classics, like that of Woodrow Wilson, and a few other volumes
predating World War II--such as Bates, Brown, Luce, McCall, and Moore.
Some studies deal with the nature, organization, and development of Congress--
Chelf, DeGrazia, Griffith, Kefauver and Levin, Peabody, Truman, and Roland
Young. A few emphasize its powers and activities--Barber, Bolton, Fenno,
Lahr and Theis, and McCall--and, more specifically, its investigative function
--Hamilton, McGeary, Taylor, and the compilation of Schlesinger and Bruns.

Still others are concerned with the legislative process--Berman, Burns, Froman, Galloway, Oleszek, Riddick, and Ripley--or with reorganization and reform-- Broughton, Heller, and others. Berger deals with the relations of Congress and and the Supreme Court.

Acheson, Dean. A CITIZEN LOOKS AT CONGRESS. New York: Harper, 1957. 124 p.

American Political Science Association. Committee on Congress. THE REOR-GANIZATION OF CONGRESS. Washington, D.C.: Public Affairs, 1945. 89 p.

Barber, Sotirios A. THE CONSTITUTION AND THE DELEGATION OF CON-GRESSIONAL POWER. Chicago: University of Chicago Press, 1975. 153 p.

Bardach, Eugene. THE IMPLEMENTATION GAME: WHAT HAPPENS AFTER A BILL BECOMES A LAW. Cambridge, Mass.: M.I.T. Press, 1977. 336 p.

Bates, Ernest Sutherland. THE STORY OF CONGRESS, 1789-1935. New York: Harper, 1936. 468 p.

Bendiner, Robert. OBSTACLE COURSE ON CAPITOL HILL. New York: McGraw-Hill, 1964. 221 p. Bibliog.

Berger, R. CONGRESS VS. THE SUPREME COURT. Cambridge, Mass.: Har-vard University Press, 1969. 424 p.

Berman, Daniel M. IN CONGRESS ASSEMBLED: THE LEGISLATIVE PROCESS IN THE NATIONAL GOVERNMENT. New York: Macmillan, 1964. 432 p. Bibliog.

Especially chapter 13.

Bolton, John R. THE LEGISLATIVE VETO: UNSEPARATING THE POWERS. Washington, D.C.: American Enterprise Institute, 1977. 50 p.

Broughton, Philip Stephans. FOR A STRONGER CONGRESS. Publication no. 116. New York: Public Affairs Committee, 1946. 32 p.

Brown, George R. THE LEADERSHIP OF CONGRESS. Indianapolis: Bobbs-Merrill, 1922. 311 p.

Burnham, James. CONGRESS AND THE AMERICAN TRADITION. Chicago: Regnery, 1959. 363 p.

Burns, James McGregor. CONGRESS ON TRIAL: THE LEGISLATIVE PROCESS IN THE ADMINISTRATIVE STATE. New York: Harper, 1949. 224 p.

Chelf, Carl P. CONGRESS IN THE AMERICAN SYSTEM. Chicago: Nelson-Hall, 1977. 257 p. Bibliog.

Clark, Joseph S. CONGRESS: THE SAPLESS BRANCH. New York: Harper and Row, 1965. 266 p.

Informal indictment by a member of the Senate.

Committee for Economic Development. MAKING CONGRESS MORE EFFECTIVE. New York: Committee for Economic Development, 1970. 82 p.

Congressional Quarterly. CONGRESS AND THE NATION: A REVIEW OF GOVERNMENT AND POLITICS SINCE WORLD WAR II. 4 vols. Washington, D.C.: 1965, 1969, 1973, 1977.

Volumes on periods 1945-64, 1965-68, 1969-72, 1973-76. Contain chapters on the presidency, foreign and security policy, and related matters.

_____. GUIDE TO CONGRESS. 2d ed. Washington, D.C.: Congressional Quarterly, 1976. 719 p. Appendices, 293 p.

Especially part II on the powers of Congress, including section on foreign affairs.

_____. INSIDE CONGRESS. 2d ed. Washington, D.C.: 1979. 194 p. Bibliog.

_____. MEMBERS OF CONGRESS SINCE 1789. Washington, D.C.: 1977. 181 p.

Provides basic biographical data on all who served in Congress from 1789 to 1977, and includes statistics on congressional sessions, party affiliation, and leadership.

_____. ORIGINS AND DEVELOPMENT OF CONGRESS. Washington, D.C.: 1976. 325 p. Bibliog.

_____. POWERS OF CONGRESS. Washington, D.C.: 1976. 357 p. Bibliog.

_____. THE WASHINGTON LOBBY. 3d ed. Washington, D.C.: 1979. 232 p.

Davidson, Roger H., and Oleszek, Walter J. CONGRESS AGAINST ITSELF. Bloomington: Indiana University Press, 1977. 306 p. Bibliog.

DeGrazia, Alfred, ed. CONGRESS: THE FIRST BRANCH OF GOVERNMENT. Garden City, N.Y.: Anchor, 1967. 477 p.

Dexter, Lewis A. "What Do Congressmen Hear: The Mail." PUBLIC OPINION QUARTERLY 20 (Spring 1956): 16-27.

Dodd, Lawrence C. CONGRESS AND PUBLIC POLICY. Morristown, N.J.: General Learning Press, 1975. 89 p.

Dodd, Lawrence C., and Oppenheimer, Bruce I., eds. CONGRESS RECONSIDERED. New York: Holt, Rinehart and Winston, 1977. 328 p.

Fenno, Richard F., Jr. THE POWER OF THE PURSE: APPROPRIATIONS POLITICS IN CONGRESS. Boston: Little, Brown, 1966. 704 p.

Froman, Lewis A., Jr. THE CONGRESSIONAL PROCESS: STRATEGIES, RULES AND PROCEDURES. Boston: Little, Brown, 1967. 221 p.

Frye, Alton. A RESPONSIBLE CONGRESS: THE POLITICS OF NATIONAL SECURITY. New York: McGraw-Hill, 1975. 238 p.

Galloway, George B. CONGRESS AT THE CROSSROADS. New York: Crowell, 1946. 374 p.

_____. THE LEGISLATIVE PROCESS IN CONGRESS. New York: Crowell, 1955. 689 p.

Galloway, George B., et al. "Congress--Problem, Diagnosis, Proposals: Second Progress Report of the American Political Science Association's Committee on Congress." AMERICAN POLITICAL SCIENCE REVIEW 36 (October 1942): 1091-1102.

Griffith, Ernest S. CONGRESS: ITS CONTEMPORARY ROLE. 5th ed. New York: New York University Press, 1975. 268 p.

Hamilton, James. THE POWER TO PROBE: A CONTEMPORARY LOOK AT CONGRESSIONAL INVESTIGATIONS. New York: Random House, 1976. 333 p.

Heller, Robert. STRENGTHENING THE CONGRESS: A PROGRESS REPORT. New York: National Planning Association, 1946. 18 p.

Heubel, Edward J. "Reorganization and Reform of Congressional Investigations, 1945-1955." Ph.D. dissertation, University of Minnesota, 1955. 213 p.

Kefauver, Estes, and Levin, Jack. A TWENTIETH CENTURY CONGRESS. New York: Duell, Sloan, and Pearce, 1947. 236 p.

Lahr, Raymond M., and Theis, J. William. CONGRESS: POWER AND PURPOSE ON CAPITOL HILL. Boston: Allyn and Bacon, 1967. 288 p. Bibliog.

Especially chapters 6 and 7.

Landis, James M. "Constitutional Limitations on the Congressional Power of Investigation." HARVARD LAW REVIEW 40 (December 1926): 153-221.

Levantrosser, William F. CONGRESS AND THE CITIZEN SOLDIER: LEGISLATIVE POLICY-MAKING FOR THE FEDERAL ARMED FORCES RESERVE. Columbus: Ohio State University Press, 1967. 267 p. Bibliog.

Luce, Robert. CONGRESS: AN EXPLANATION. Cambridge, Mass.: Harvard University Press, 1926. 154 p.

McCall, Samuel W. THE BUSINESS OF CONGRESS. New York: Columbia University Press, 1911. 215 p.

McGeary, Martin Nelson. THE DEVELOPMENT OF CONGRESSIONAL INVESTIGATIVE POWER. New York: Columbia University Press, 1940. 172 p.

MacRae, Duncan, Jr. DIMENSIONS OF CONGRESSIONAL VOTING. Berkeley: University of California Press, 1958. 390 p.

Meller, Norman. "Legislative Behavior Research." WESTERN POLITICAL QUARTERLY 13 (March 1960): 131-53.

Moore, Joseph West. THE AMERICAN CONGRESS: A HISTORY OF NATIONAL LEGISLATION AND POLITICAL EVENTS, 1774-1895. New York: Harper and Row, 1895. 581 p.

Oleszek, Walter J. CONGRESSIONAL PROCEDURES AND THE POLICY PROCESS. Washington, D.C.: Congressional Quarterly, 1978. 256 p. Bibliog.

Peabody, Robert L. LEADERSHIP IN CONGRESS: STABILITY, SUCCESSION, AND CHANGE. Boston: Little, Brown, 1976. 522 p.

Perkins, John A. "Congressional Self-Improvement." AMERICAN POLITICAL SCIENCE REVIEW 38 (June 1944): 499-511.

Polsby, Nelson W. "Strengthening Congress in National Policy-Making." YALE REVIEW 59 (Summer 1970): 481-97.

Riddick, Floyd M. CONGRESSIONAL PROCEDURE. Boston: Chapman and Grimes, 1941. 387 p.

_____. THE UNITED STATES CONGRESS: ORGANIZATION AND PRO-CEDURE. Manassas, Va.: National Capitol Publishers, 1949. 459 p.

Ripley, Randall B. CONGRESS: PROCESS AND POLICY. 2d ed. New York: Norton, 1978. 448 p. Bibliog.

Schlesinger, Arthur M., Jr., and Bruns, Roger, eds. CONGRESS INVESTI-GATES: A DOCUMENTED HISTORY, 1792-1974. 5 vols. New York: Chelsea House, 1975. 4,103 p.

Schneider, Jerrold E. IDEOLOGICAL COALITIONS IN CONGRESS. Westport, Conn.: Greenwood, 1979. 270 p.

Taylor, Telford. GRAND INQUEST: THE STORY OF CONGRESSIONAL IN-VESTIGATIONS. New York: Simon and Schuster, 1955. 358 p.

Thomas, Elbert D. "How Congress Functions Under Its Reorganization Act." AMERICAN POLITICAL SCIENCE REVIEW 43 (December 1949): 1179-89.

Thomas, Norman C., and Lamb, Karl H. CONGRESS: POLITICS AND PRAC-TICE. New York: Random House, 1964. 143 p.

Torrey, Volta. YOU AND YOUR CONGRESS. New York: Morrow, 1944. 280 p.

Truman, David B., ed. THE CONGRESS AND AMERICA'S FUTURE. 2d ed. Englewood Cliffs, N.J.: Prentice-Hall, 1973. 216 p.

Vogler, David J. THE POLITICS OF CONGRESS. 2d ed. Rockleigh, N.J.: Allyn and Bacon, 1977. 338 p.

Weaver, Warren, Jr. BOTH YOUR HOUSES: THE TRUTH ABOUT CONGRESS. New York: Praeger, 1972. 320 p. Bibliog.

White, Howard. "The Concurrent Resolution in Congress." AMERICAN POLI-TICAL SCIENCE REVIEW 35 (October 1941): 886-89.

Wilson, H. Hubert. CONGRESS: CORRUPTION AND COMPROMISE. New York: Rinehart, 1951. 337 p.

Wilson, Woodrow. CONGRESSIONAL GOVERNMENT: A STUDY IN AMERI-CAN POLITICS. Boston: Houghton Mifflin, 1885. Reprint. Cleveland: Meridian, 1965. 333 p.

Wolfinger, Raymond E., ed. READINGS ON CONGRESS. Englewood Cliffs, N.J.: Prentice-Hall, 1971. 426 p. Bibliog.

Young, Roland A. THE AMERICAN CONGRESS. New York: Harper and Row, 1958. 333 p.

On legislative decision-making process.

_____. THIS IS CONGRESS. New York: Knopf, 1943. 267 p.

Young, William W. "Congressional Investigations of the Federal Administration." Ph.D. dissertation, University of California (Berkeley), 1956. 128 p.

FOREIGN RELATIONS

Published resources on the role and function of Congress in the field of foreign relations have mushroomed since World War II. Because materials that concern the separate houses of Congress, their committees, and their members, as well as a number of case studies, are listed in separate sections later in this chapter, those contained in this section tend to be of a general and inclusive nature. Some touch on legislative-executive interaction, but those that emphasize this relationship are also listed separately later.

Except for a few comprehensive volumes on the congressional role in foreign relations, such as those of Dahl and Robinson, most contributions consist of essays and journal articles, including those contained in the compilation of Kalijarvi and Merrow. Considerable interest centers on the foreign policy-making role of Congress. Among the more unique items are the congressional studies on the legislatively required administrative agency reports on foreign affairs, which serve to inform the Congress and the public and to facilitate congressional oversight of operational activities overseas.

Berry, John M. "Foreign Policymaking and the Congress." EDITORIAL RESEARCH REPORTS 1 (19 April 1967): 283-300.

Bolles, Blair. "Congress and Foreign Policy." FOREIGN POLICY REPORTS 20 (15 January 1945): 266-75.

Bradshaw, Mary E. "Congress and Foreign Policy Since 1900." ANNALS OF THE AMERICAN ACADEMY OF POLITICAL AND SOCIAL SCIENCE 289 (September 1953): 40-48.

Brown, Ben H., Jr. "Congress and the Department of State." ANNALS OF THE AMERICAN ACADEMY OF POLITICAL AND SOCIAL SCIENCE 289 (September 1953): 100-107.

Buckwalter, Doyle W. "The Concurrent Resolution: A Search for Foreign Policy Influence." MIDWEST JOURNAL OF POLITICAL SCIENCE 14 (August 1970): 434-58.

Clark, Joseph S. "The Influence of Congress in the Formulation of Disarmament Policy." ANNALS OF THE AMERICAN ACADEMY OF POLITICAL AND SOCIAL SCIENCE 342 (July 1962): 147-53.

Cohen, Benjamin V. "The Evolving Role of Congress in Foreign Affairs." PROCEEDINGS OF THE AMERICAN PHILOSOPHICAL SOCIETY 92 (October 1948): 211-16.

Colegrove, Kenneth W. "The Role of Congress and Public Opinion in Formulating Foreign Policy." AMERICAN POLITICAL SCIENCE REVIEW 38 (October 1944): 956-69.

Committee for Economic Development. CONGRESSIONAL DECISION MAKING FOR NATIONAL SECURITY: A STATEMENT ON NATIONAL POLICY. New York: 1974. 56 p.

"The Congress and United States Foreign Relations." CONGRESSIONAL DIGEST 30 (February 1951): 35-41, 64.

Congressional Quarterly. GUIDE TO THE U.S. SUPREME COURT. Washington, D.C.: 1979.

In part on the powers of Congress, section on "The Power over Foreign Affairs," pages 105-12.

Dahl, Robert A. CONGRESS AND FOREIGN POLICY. New York: Harcourt Brace, 1950. Rev. ed. New York: Norton, 1964. 305 p. Bibliog.

Elliott, William Y. "Congressional Control over Foreign Policy Commitments." In INTERNATIONAL COMMITMENTS AND NATIONAL ADMINISTRATION, pp. 1-22. Charlottesville, Va.: Bureau of Public Administration, University of Virginia, 1949.

Franck, Thomas M., and Weisband, Edward. FOREIGN POLICY BY CONGRESS. New York: Oxford University Press, 1979. 384 p.

Fry, Alton. RESPONSIBLE CONGRESS: THE POLITICS OF NATIONAL SECURITY. New York: McGraw-Hill For Council on Foreign Relations, 1975. 238 p.

Gibbons, William C. "Political Action Analysis as an Approach to the Study of Congress and Foreign Policy." Ph.D. dissertation, Princeton University, 1961. 323 p.

Goebel, Dorothy B. "Congress and Foreign Relations Before 1900." ANNALS OF THE AMERICAN ACADEMY OF POLITICAL AND SOCIAL SCIENCE 289 (September 1950): 22-39.

Grassmuck, George L. SECTIONAL BIASES IN CONGRESS ON FOREIGN POLICY. Baltimore: Johns Hopkins Press, 1951. 181 p.

Especially chapter 1.

Griffith, Ernest S. "The Place of Congress in Foreign Relations." ANNALS OF THE AMERICAN ACADEMY OF POLITICAL AND SOCIAL SCIENCE 289 (September 1953): 11-21.

Holt, Pat M. THE WAR POWERS RESOLUTION: THE ROLE OF CONGRESS IN U.S. ARMED INTERVENTION. Washington, D.C.: Government Printing Office, 1978. 48 p.

Hughes, Thomas L. "Foreign Policy on Capitol Hill." REPORTER 20 (30 April 1959): 28-31.

Javits, Jacob K. "The Congressional Presence in Foreign Relations." FOREIGN AFFAIRS 48 (January 1970): 221-34.

Kalijarvi, Thorston V., and Merrow, Chester E., eds. "Congress and Foreign Relations." ANNALS OF THE AMERICAN ACADEMY OF POLITICAL AND SOCIAL SCIENCE 289 (September 1953), entire issue.

Consists of nineteen articles, several of which are listed separately in this chapter.

Kissinger, Henry A. "A New National Partnership: Congress and Foreign Policy." VITAL SPEECHES 41 (15 February 1975): 258-62.

Manley, John F. "The Rise of Congress in Foreign Policy-Making." ANNALS OF THE AMERICAN ACADEMY OF POLITICAL AND SOCIAL SCIENCE 397 (September 1971): 60-70.

Marcy, Carl, and Hansen, Morella. "A Note on American Participation in Interparliamentary Meetings." INTERNATIONAL ORGANIZATION 13 (Summer 1959): 431-38.

Millikan, George L. "Congress and the Conduct of Foreign Affairs." AMERICAN FOREIGN SERVICE JOURNAL 27 (January 1950): 11-13.

Morton, Thruston B. "Congress and Foreign Affairs." SOCIAL SCIENCE 30 (October 1955): 236-38.

Munkres, Robert Lee. "The Use of the Congressional Resolution as an Instrument of Influence over Foreign Policy: 1925-1950." Ph.D. dissertation, University of Nebraska, 1956. 243 p.

Perkins, James A. "Congressional Investigations of Matters of International Import." AMERICAN POLITICAL SCIENCE REVIEW 34 (April 1940): 284-94.

Robinson, James A. CONGRESS AND FOREIGN POLICY-MAKING: A STUDY IN LEGISLATIVE INFLUENCE AND INITIATIVE. 2d ed. Homewood, Ill.: Dorsey, 1967. 254 p. Bibliog.

Rosenberg, J.A.; Weinberg, P.; and Pinzler, W.M. "Historical and Structural Limitations on Congressional Abilities to Make Foreign Policy." BOSTON UNIVERSITY LAW REVIEW 50 (1970): 51-77.

Schlesinger, Arthur M., Jr. "Congress and the Making of American Foreign Policy." FOREIGN AFFAIRS 51 (October 1972): 78-113.

Stroud, Virgil. "Congressional Investigations of the Conduct of War." Ph.D. dissertation, New York University, 1955. 396 p.

U.S. Commission on the Organization of the Government for the Conduct of Foreign Policy. "Congress and Executive," "Congressional Survey," and "Congress and National Security." In its COMMISSION ON THE ORGANIZATION OF THE GOVERNMENT FOR THE CONDUCT OF FOREIGN POLICY, JUNE 1975. Appendix, vol. 5, pp. 1-273. Washington, D.C.: Government Printing Office, 1976.

U.S. Congress. CONGRESS, INFORMATION AND FOREIGN AFFAIRS. Washington, D.C.: Government Printing Office, 1978. 103 p.

   Concerns debate of Congress and the executive on the formulation
   of foreign policy.

U.S. Congress. House of Representatives. Committee on Foreign Affairs and U.S. Congress. Senate. Committee on Foreign Relations. IMPROVING THE REPORTING REQUIREMENT SYSTEM IN THE FOREIGN AFFAIRS FIELD. 93d Cong., 2d sess. Washington, D.C.: Government Printing Office, 1974. 104 p.

_____. REQUIRED REPORTS TO CONGRESS IN THE FOREIGN AFFAIRS FIELD. 93d Cong., 1st sess. Washington, D.C.: Government Printing Office, 1973. 427 p

   Comprehensive report on legislative requirements and executive reporting practice, with appendix on guidance to such reports.

U.S. Congress. House of Representatives. Committee on International Relations. CONGRESS AND FOREIGN POLICY. Washington, D.C.: Government Printing Office, 1976. 26 p.

_____. CONGRESS AND FOREIGN POLICY. Washington, D.C.: Government Printing Office, 1975-- . Annual. Var. pag.

U.S. Congress. Senate. Committee on Foreign Relations. SECURITY CLASSIFICATION AS A PROBLEM IN THE CONGRESSIONAL ROLE IN FOREIGN POLICY. 92d Cong., 1st sess. Washington, D.C.: Government Printing Office, 1971. 41 p.

_____. UNITED STATES FOREIGN POLICY OBJECTIVES AND OVERSEAS MILITARY INSTALLATIONS. 96th Cong., 1st sess. Washington, D.C.: Government Printing Office, 1979. 207 p.

Westerfield, H. Bradford. "Congress and Closed Politics in National Security Affairs." ORBIS 10 (Fall 1966): 737-53.

A number of general textbooks on American foreign relations contain separate chapters dealing with the role of Congress, illustrated by the following:

Allison, Graham, and Szanton, Peter. REMAKING FOREIGN POLICY: THE ORGANIZATIONAL CONNECTION. New York: Basic Books, 1976.
    Especially chapter 5.

Bliss, Howard, and Johnson, M. Glen. BEYOND THE WATER'S EDGE: AMERICA'S FOREIGN POLICIES. Philadelphia: Lippincott, 1975.
    Especially chapter 5.

Chamberlain, Lawrence H., and Snyder, Richard C., eds. AMERICAN FOREIGN POLICY. New York: Rinehart, 1948.
    Especially chapters 4, 5.

Gerberding, William P. UNITED STATES FOREIGN POLICY: PERSPECTIVES AND ANALYSIS. New York: McGraw-Hill, 1966.
    Especially chapter 2.

Hickman, Martin B., ed. PROBLEMS OF AMERICAN FOREIGN POLICY. 2d ed. Beverly Hills, Calif.: Glencoe, 1975.
    Especially chapter 3.

Irish, Marian D., and Frank, Elke. U.S. FOREIGN POLICY: CONTEXT, CONDUCT, CONTENT. New York: Harcourt Brace Jovanovich, 1975.
    Especially chapter 7.

Knappen, Marshall. AN INTRODUCTION TO AMERICAN FOREIGN POLICY. New York: Harper, 1956.

Especially chapter 6.

McCamy, James L. THE ADMINISTRATION OF AMERICAN FOREIGN AF-FAIRS. New York: Knopf, 1950.

Especially chapter 14.

Sapin, Burton M. THE MAKING OF UNITED STATES FOREIGN POLICY. Washington, D.C.: Praeger for Brookings Institution, 1966.

Especially chapter 3.

Snyder, Richard C., and Furniss, Edgar S., Jr. AMERICAN FOREIGN POLICY: FORMULATION, PRINCIPLES AND PROGRAMS. New York: Rinehart, 1954.

Especially chapter 10.

HOUSE OF REPRESENTATIVES, SENATE, THEIR COMMITTEES, AND THEIR MEMBERS

A good many additional studies on the Congress are restricted to either the House of Representatives or the Senate, to their committees, and to their members. These are grouped in two categories. The first incorporates the more general literature, and the second is confined specifically to foreign relations.

General

Commentary in general literature is applicable to foreign as well as internal affairs. Some contributions are basic and comprehensive studies on the House of Representatives--including Alexander, Bolling, and Galloway--and the Senate--such as Clark, Harris, Haynes, Preston, Rogers, and White. Others specialize on congressional committees--Dimock, Fenno, Lees, and Morrow--and congressional staffs--Kammerer and Kofmehl. Materials on the committees concerned specifically with foreign relations are listed separately in the next section. A few studies seek to probe the role of the members of Congress, including those of Clapp, Miller, and Tacheron on Congressmen and that of Matthews on Senators. An additional reservoir of information on members of Congress is available in the memoirs and biographies of those who served in the House and Senate.

Acheson, Dean. "My Adventures Among the U.S. Senators." SATURDAY EVENING POST, 1 April 1961, pp. 26-29, 68.

Conclusion of his series entitled "Of Men I Have Known."

Alexander, DeAlva Stanwood. HISTORY AND PROCEDURE OF THE HOUSE OF REPRESENTATIVES. Boston: Houghton Mifflin, 1916. 435 p.

Bolling, Richard. HOUSE OUT OF ORDER. New York: Dutton, 1965. 253 p.

_____. POWER IN THE HOUSE: A HISTORY OF THE LEADERSHIP OF THE HOUSE OF REPRESENTATIVES. New York: Dutton, 1968. 296 p. Bibliog.

Buchanan, William; Eulau, Heinz; Ferguson, LeRoy C.; and Wahlke, John C. "The Legislator as Specialist." WESTERN POLITICAL QUARTERLY 13 (September 1960): 636-51.

Carr, Robert K. THE HOUSE UN-AMERICAN ACTIVITIES COMMITTEE. Ithaca, N.Y.: Cornell University Press, 1952. 489 p.

Clapp, Charles L. THE CONGRESSMAN: HIS WORK AS HE SEES IT. Washington, D.C.: Brookings Institution, 1963. 452 p.

Clark, Joseph S., et al. THE SENATE ESTABLISHMENT. New York: Hill and Wang, 1963. 138 p.

    Concerns complaint by Senators of domination by inner circle.

Dimock, Marshall E. CONGRESSIONAL INVESTIGATING COMMITTEES. Johns Hopkins University Series in Historical and Political Science, series 47, no. 1. Baltimore: Johns Hopkins Press, 1929. 182 p. Bibliog.

Fenno, Richard F., Jr. CONGRESSMEN IN COMMITTEES. Boston: Little, Brown, 1973. 302 p.

Fox, Harrison W., Jr., and Hammond, Susan Webb. CONGRESSIONAL STAFFS: THE INVISIBLE FORCE IN AMERICAN LAWMAKING. Riverside, N.J.: Free Press, 1977. 227 p. Bibliog.

Galloway, George B. "Development of the Committee System in the House of Representatives." AMERICAN HISTORICAL REVIEW 65 (October 1959): 17-30.

_____. HISTORY OF THE HOUSE OF REPRESENTATIVES. New York: Crowell, 1961. 334 p.

Goodwin, George, Jr. Subcommittees: The Miniature Legislatures of Congress." AMERICAN POLITICAL SCIENCE REVIEW 56 (September 1962): 596-604.

Harris, Joseph P. THE ADVICE AND CONSENT OF THE SENATE: A STUDY OF THE CONFIRMATION OF APPOINTMENTS BY THE UNITED STATES SENATE. Berkeley and Los Angeles: University of California Press, 1953. 457 p.

Haynes, George H. THE SENATE OF THE UNITED STATES: ITS HISTORY AND PRACTICE. 2 vols. New York: Russell and Ressell, 1970. 1,118 p. Bibliog.

Hyman, Sidney. "With the Advice and Consent-- ." NEW YORK TIMES MAGAZINE, 5 July 1959, pp. 9, 28, 30.

Jones, Rochelle, and Woll, Peter. THE PRIVATE WORLD OF CONGRESS. Riverside, N.J.: Free Press, 1979. 288 p.

Kammerer, Gladys. CONGRESSIONAL COMMITTEE STAFFING SINCE 1946. Lexington, Ky.: Bureau of Government Research, 1951. 65 p.

_____. THE STAFFING OF THE COMMITTEES OF CONGRESS. Lexington, Ky.: Bureau of Government Research, 1949. 45 p.

Kingdon, John W. CONGRESSMEN'S VOTING DECISIONS. New York: Harper and Row, 1973. 313 p.

Kofmehl, Kenneth Theodore. PROFESSIONAL STAFFS OF CONGRESS. West Lafayette, Ind.: Purdue University Press, 1962. 283 p.

Lees, John O. THE COMMITTEE SYSTEM OF THE UNITED STATES CONGRESS. New York: Humanities Press, 1967. 114 p.

Low, A. Maurice. "The Oligarchy of the Senate." NORTH AMERICAN REVIEW 172 (February 1902): 231-44.

_____. "The Usurped Powers of the Senate." AMERICAN POLITICAL SCIENCE REVIEW 1 (November 1906): 1-16.

McCown, Ada C. THE CONGRESSIONAL CONFERENCE COMMITTEE. New York: Columbia University Studies in the Social Sciences, 1927. 274 p.

MacNeil, Neil. FORGE OF DEMOCRACY: THE HOUSE OF REPRESENTATIVES. New York: McKay, 1963. 496 p. Bibliog.

Matthews, Donald R. UNITED STATES SENATORS AND THEIR WORLD. New York: Vintage; Chapel Hill: University of North Carolina Press, 1960. 303 p.

Miller, Clem, ed. MEMBER OF THE HOUSE: LETTERS OF A CONGRESSMAN. New York: Scribner, 1962. 195 p.

Morrow, William L. CONGRESSIONAL COMMITTEES. New York: Scribner, 1969. 261 p.

Preston, Nathaniel S. THE SENATE INSTITUTION. New York: Van Nostrand Reinhold, 1969. 202 p.

Especially chapters 4, 10, and 11.

Rapoport, Daniel. INSIDE THE HOUSE. Chicago: Follett, 1975. 260 p.

Riddle, Donald H. THE TRUMAN COMMITTEE: A STUDY IN CONGRESSIONAL RESPONSIBILITY. New Brunswick, N.J.: Rutgers University Press, 1964. 207 p. Bibliog.

Robinson, George Lee. "The Development of the Senate Committee System." Ph.D. dissertation, New York University, 1955. 449 p.

Rogers, Lindsay. THE AMERICAN SENATE. New York: Knopf, 1926. 285 p.

Smallwood, Frank. THE JOINT COMMITTEE ON ATOMIC ENERGY: CONGRESSIONAL "WATCHDOG" OF THE ATOM? New York: American Political Science Association, 1960. 22 p.

Steiner, Gilbert Y. THE CONGRESSIONAL CONFERENCE COMMITTEE-- SEVENTIETH TO EIGHTIETH CONGRESSES. Illinois Studies in the Social Sciences, vol. 32, no. 3-4. Urbana: University of Illinois Press, 1951. 185 p. Bibliog.

Tacheron, Donald G., and Udall, Morris K. THE JOB OF A CONGRESSMAN. Indianapolis: Bobbs-Merrill, 1966. 446 p. Bibliog.

U.S. Congress. House of Representatives. Committee on House Administration. HISTORY OF THE UNITED STATES HOUSE OF REPRESENTATIVES. 87th Cong., 1st sess. Washington, D.C.: Government Printing Office, 1962. 216 p.

U.S. Congress. Senate. BIOGRAPHICAL DIRECTORY OF THE AMERICAN CONGRESS, 1774-1971. 92d Cong., 1st sess. Washington, D.C.: Government Printing Office, 1971. 1,972 p.

Watkins, Charles L., and Riddick, Floyd M. SENATE PROCEDURE: PRECEDENTS AND PRACTICES. Washington, D.C.: Government Printing Office, 1958. 674 p.

White, William S. CITADEL: THE STORY OF THE U.S. SENATE. New York: Harper, 1956. 274 p.

Especially chapters 3 and 12.

Foreign Relations

A number of studies deal with the basic foreign relations role of the House of Representatives--such as Carroll--and the Senate--including Colegrove and Jewell. Several others concentrate on the foreign relations committees of the respective chambers, among the better known of which are Westphal on the House Foreign Affairs Committee, and Dennison and Farnsworth on the Senate Foreign Relations Committee. A number of congressional reports on these committees have also been published. A few studies deal with the Senate role in the appointment process--Gallagher, Nigro, and a Senate report on foreign affairs appointments--and on Senate foreign relations research--Halperin and Robinson. The Senate's role in treaty making is dealt with in chapter 17. Occasionally, individual members of Congress are called upon to serve in a formal diplomatic capacity, which is treated at the end of this section.

Andrew, Jean Douglas. "The Effect of Senate Foreign Relations Committee Membership in Terms of Support of Foreign Policy--1946-1966." Ph.D. dissertation, University of Connecticut, 1968. 258 p.

Carroll, Holbert N. THE HOUSE OF REPRESENTATIVES AND FOREIGN AFFAIRS. Pittsburgh: University of Pittsburgh Press, 1958. 365 p. Bibliog. Rev. ed. Boston: Little, Brown, 1966. 386 p. Bibliog.

Challener, Richard D., ed. THE LEGISLATIVE ORIGINS OF AMERICAN FOREIGN POLICY: THE SENATE FOREIGN RELATIONS COMMITTEE IN EXECUTIVE SESSION. 10 vols. New York: Garland, 1978-- .

Each volume to cover a particular chronological period.

Chiperfield, Robert B. "The Committee on Foreign Affairs." ANNALS OF THE AMERICAN ACADEMY OF POLITICAL AND SOCIAL SCIENCE 289 (September 1953): 73-83.

Cole, Wayne S. "Senator Key Pittman and American Neutrality Policies, 1933-1940." MISSISSIPPI VALLEY HISTORICAL REVIEW 46 (March 1960): 644-62.

Colegrove, Kenneth W. THE AMERICAN SENATE AND WORLD PEACE. New York: Vanguard, 1944. 209 p.

Daughan, George C. "From Lodge to Fulbright: The Chairman of the Senate Foreign Relations Committee." Ph.D. dissertation, Howard University, 1968. 235 p.

Dennison, Eleanor E. THE SENATE FOREIGN RELATIONS COMMITTEE. Stanford, Calif.: Stanford University Press, 1942. 201 p. Bibliog.

Farnsworth, David N. "A Comparison of the Senate and Its Foreign Relations Committee on Selected Roll Call Votes." WESTERN POLITICAL QUARTERLY 14 (March 1961): 168-75.

_____. THE SENATE COMMITTEE ON FOREIGN RELATIONS. Illinois Studies in the Social Sciences, no. 49. Urbana: University of Illinois Press, 1961. 189 p. Bibliog.

Gallagher, Hugh G. ADVISE AND OBSTRUCT: THE ROLE OF THE UNITED STATES SENATE IN FOREIGN POLICY DECISIONS. New York: Delacorte, 1969. 338 p. Bibliog.

Gillette, Guy M. "The Senate in Foreign Relations." ANNALS OF THE AMERICAN ACADEMY OF POLITICAL AND SOCIAL SCIENCE 289 (September 1953): 49-57.

Gould, James W. "The Origins of the Senate Committee on Foreign Relations." WESTERN POLITICAL QUARTERLY 12 (September 1959): 670-82.

Halperin, Morton. "Is the Senate's Foreign Relations Research Worthwhile?" AMERICAN BEHAVIORAL SCIENTIST 4 (September 1960): 21-24.

Hauptman, Laurence Marc. "To the Good Neighbor: A Study of the Senate's Role in American Foreign Policy." Ph.D. dissertation, New York University, 1972. 223 p.

Henschel, Richard L. "The Committee on Foreign Relations." WASHINGTON WORLD 4 (13 April 1964): 13-17.

Hill, Norman L. THE NEW DEMOCRACY IN FOREIGN POLICY MAKING. Lincoln: University of Nebraska Press, 1970. 150 p.

    Especially chapter 8 on Senate Foreign Relations Committee.

Hill, Thomas Michael. "The Senate Leadership and International Policy from Lodge to Vandenberg." Ph.D. dissertation, Washington University, 1970. 295 p.

Humphrey, Hubert H. "The Senate in Foreign Policy." FOREIGN AFFAIRS 37 (July 1959): 525-36.

Jewell, Malcolm E. "Evaluating the Decline of Southern Internationalism Through Senatorial Roll Call Votes." JOURNAL OF POLITICS 21 (November 1959): 624-46.

_____. "The Role of Political Parties in the Formation of Foreign Policy in the Senate, 1947-1956." Ph.D. dissertation, Pennsylvania State University, 1958. 451 p.

_____. "The Senate Republican Policy Committee and Foreign Policy." WESTERN POLITICAL QUARTERLY 12 (December 1959): 966-80.

_____. SENATORIAL POLITICS AND FOREIGN POLICY. Lexington: University of Kentucky Press, 1962. 214 p.

Johnson, Victor Charles. "Congress and Foreign Policy: The House Foreign Affairs and Senate Foreign Relations Committees." Ph.D. dissertation, University of Wisconsin (Madison), 1975. 370 p.

Kenworthy, E.W. "The Fulbright Idea of Foreign Policy." NEW YORK TIMES MAGAZINE, 10 May 1959, pp. 10-11, 74, 76, 78.

McConaughy, James L., Jr. "Congressmen and the Pentagon." FORTUNE, April 1958, pp. 156-60, 162, 166, 168.

Mickey, David Hopwood. "Senatorial Participation in Shaping Certain United States Foreign Policies, 1921-1941 (Being Largely a Study of THE CONGRESSIONAL RECORD)." Ph.D. dissertation, University of Nebraska, 1954. 737 p.

Moore, Heyward, Jr. "Congressional Committees and the Formulation of Foreign Aid Policy." Ph.D. dissertation, University of North Carolina (Chapel Hill), 1965. 290 p.

Nigro, Felix A. "Senate's Confirmation and Foreign Policy." JOURNAL OF POLITICS 14 (May 1952): 281-99.

Richards, James P. "The House of Representatives in Foreign Affairs." ANNALS OF THE AMERICAN ACADEMY OF POLITICAL AND SOCIAL SCIENCE 289 (September 1953): 66-72.

Robinson, James A. "Another Look at Senate Research on Foreign Policy." AMERICAN BEHAVIORAL SCIENTIST 4 (November 1960): 12-14.

Rosenau, James N. "Senate Attitudes Toward a Secretary of State." In LEGISLATIVE BEHAVIOR: A READER IN THEORY AND RESEARCH, edited by John C. Wahlke and Heinz Eulau, pp. 333-47. Glencoe, Ill.: Free Press, 1959.

Sparkman, John J. "The Role of the Senate in Determining Foreign Policy." In THE SENATE INSTITUTION, edited by Nathaniel S. Preston, pp. 31-39. New York: Van Nostrand, 1969.

Toulmin, Harry A. DIARY OF DEMOCRACY: THE SENATE WAR INVESTIGATING COMMITTEE. New York: Smith, 1947. 277 p. Bibliog.

U.S. Congress. House of Representatives. Committee on Foreign Affairs. SURVEY OF ACTIVITIES. Washington, D.C.: Government Printing Office, 1950-- .

> Published serially beginning with the 81st Congress. Provides documented survey, arranged by functional topics.

U.S. Congress. Senate. COMMITTEE ON FOREIGN RELATIONS, UNITED STATES SENATE--160TH ANNIVERSARY, 1816-1976. 94th Cong., 2d sess. Washington, D.C.: Government Printing Office, 1976. 74 p. Bibliog.

U.S. Congress. Senate. Committee on Aeronautical and Space Sciences. COMMITTEE ON AERONAUTICAL AND SPACE SCIENCES, UNITED STATES SENATE--1958-1976. 94th Cong., 2d sess. Washington, D.C.: Government Printing Office, 1977. 87 p. Bibliog.

U.S. Congress. Senate. Committee on Foreign Relations. BACKGROUND INFORMATION ON THE COMMITTEE ON FOREIGN RELATIONS, UNITED STATES SENATE. 3d ed. 94th Cong., 1st sess. Washington, D.C.: Government Printing Office, 1975. 84 p. Bibliog.

_____. LEGISLATIVE HISTORY OF THE COMMITTEE ON FOREIGN RELATIONS, UNITED STATES SENATE. Washington, D.C.: Government Printing Office, 1971-- . Biannual (except 88th-90th Congresses in one issue).

_____. THE ROLE OF THE SENATE IN TREATY RATIFICATION: A STAFF MEMORANDUM TO THE COMMITTEE ON FOREIGN RELATIONS. 94th Cong., 1st sess. Washington, D.C.: Government Printing Office, 1977. 78 p.

_____. THE SENATE ROLE IN FOREIGN AFFAIRS APPOINTMENTS. 92d Cong., 1st sess. Washington, D.C.: Government Printing Office, 1971. 76 p.

West, W. Reed. "Senator Taft's Foreign Policy." ATLANTIC MONTHLY, June 1952, pp. 50-52.

Westphal, Albert C.F. THE HOUSE COMMITTEE ON FOREIGN AFFAIRS. New York: Columbia University Press, 1942. 268 p.

White, William S. "The Senators Move in on Our Foreign Policy." HARPER'S MAGAZINE, May 1959, pp. 64-66.

Wickersham, George W. "The Senate and Our Foreign Relations." FOREIGN AFFAIRS 2 (December 1923): 177-92.

Wiley, Alexander. "The Committee on Foreign Relations." ANNALS OF THE AMERICAN ACADEMY OF POLITICAL AND SOCIAL SCIENCE 289 (September 1953): 58-65.

Yang, Ryh-hsiuh. "The Role of Chairman Arthur H. Vandenberg of the Senate Foreign Relations Committee in the 80th Congress, 1947-1948." Ph.D. dissertation, New School for Social Research, 1966. 244 p.

Little literary attention has been paid to the matter of congressmen-diplomats, both currently serving and former members of Congress. Butner's study focuses on the constitutional problems and the usefulness of such appointments in bridging executive-legislative relations, and Gareau deals with one particular type of such appointments.

Butner, John C. "Congressmen-Diplomats: Legislative-Executive Collaboration in the Conduct of American Foreign Relations." Ph.D. dissertation, University of Maryland, 1977. 313 p. Bibliog.

Gareau, Frederick. "Congressional Representatives to the UN General Assembly: 'Corruption' by Foreign Gentry?" ORBIS 21 (Fall 1977): 701-24.

CONGRESS AND THE EXECUTIVE

Executive-legislative relations may be treated from a variety of perspectives. Much literature on the subject views the relationship from that of the executive, and this is listed in chapter 7. A good deal of additional commentary and analysis is included in other studies, such as those dealing with the separation of powers, constitutional prescriptions concerning the making of foreign policy and the administration of foreign relations, decision making (chapter 14), and the negotiation, approval, and ratification of treaties and agreements (chapter 17).

Acheson, Dean. "Legislative-Executive Relations." YALE REVIEW 45 (1956): 481-95.

Barrie, Robert Wesley. "Congress and the Executive: The Making of U.S. Foreign Trade Policy." Ph.D. dissertation, University of Minnesota, 1968. 352 p.

Brown, MacAlistair. "The Demise of State Department Public Opinion Polls: A Study of Legislative Oversight." MIDWEST JOURNAL OF POLITICAL SCIENCE 5 (February 1961): 1-17.

"Congress, the President, and the Power to Commit Troops to Combat." HARVARD LAW REVIEW 81 (June 1968): 1771-1805.

Crabb, Cecil V., Jr., and Holt, Pat M. INVITATION TO STRUGGLE: CONGRESS, THE PRESIDENT, AND FOREIGN POLICY. Washington, D.C.: Congressional Quarterly, 1980. 234 p.

DeGrazia, Alfred. REPUBLIC IN CRISIS: CONGRESS AGAINST THE EXECUTIVE FORCE. New York: Federal Legal Publications, 1965. 303 p.

Dunn, Charles W. "The Congress and the Presidency in Military Crises: A Communications Model." Ph.D. dissertation, Florida State University, 1965. 143 p.

Franck, Thomas M., and Glennon, Michael, eds. U.S. FOREIGN RELATIONS LAW: A DOCUMENTARY STUDY OF CONGRESSIONAL-EXECUTIVE RELATIONS. 5 vols. contemplated. Dobbs Ferry, N.Y.: Oceana, 1979-- .

Ginnane, Robert W. "The Control of Federal Administration by Congressional Resolutions and Committees." HARVARD LAW REVIEW 66 (February 1953): 569-611.

Graebner, Norman A. "Politics in Foreign Policy." CURRENT HISTORY 28 (January 1955): 7-14.

On influence of certain members of Congress on power of executive to conduct foreign affairs.

Harris, Joseph P. CONGRESSIONAL CONTROL OF ADMINISTRATION. Washington, D.C.: Brookings Institution, 1964. 306 p.

Henderson, Thomas A. CONGRESSIONAL OVERSIGHT OF EXECUTIVE AGENCIES: A STORY OF THE HOUSE COMMITTEE ON GOVERNMENT OPERATIONS. University of Florida Monograph Series, no. 40. Gainesville: University of Florida Press, 1970. 74 p.

Hilsman, Roger. "Congressional-Executive Relations and the Foreign Policy Consensus." AMERICAN POLITICAL SCIENCE REVIEW 52 (September 1958): 725-44.

Kampelman, Max M. "Congressional Control vs. Executive Flexibility." PUBLIC ADMINISTRATION REVIEW 18 (Summer 1958): 185-88.

Koenig, Louis W. CONGRESS AND THE PRESIDENT: OFFICIAL MAKERS OF PUBLIC POLICY. Chicago: Scott, Foresman, 1965. 197 p.

Pluralistic nature of policy making, including case studies.

Lehman, John F., Jr. "Functional Analysis of Congress and the Executive in Foreign Policy." Ph.D. dissertation, University of Pennsylvania, 1974. 505 p.

Lowenstein, James G. "The Senate and the Executive." INTERPLAY OF EUROPEAN/AMERICAN AFFAIRS 1 (March 1968): 58-60.

Macmahon, Arthur W. "Congressional Oversight of Administration: The Power of the Purse." POLITICAL SCIENCE QUARTERLY 58 (June and September 1943): 161-90, 380-414.

Mansfield, Harvey C., ed. CONGRESS AGAINST THE PRESIDENT. New York: Academy of Political Science, 1975. 200 p.

Moe, Ronald C., ed. CONGRESS AND THE PRESIDENT: ALLIES AND AD-VERSARIES. Pacific Palisades, Calif.: Goodyear, 1971. 324 p.

Moore, John N. "Contemporary Issues in an Ongoing Debate: The Roles of Congress and the President in Foreign Affairs." INTERNATIONAL LAWYER 7 (October 1973): 733-45.

Ogul, Morris S. CONGRESS OVERSEES THE BUREAUCRACY: STUDIES IN LEGISLATIVE SUPERVISION. Pittsburgh: University of Pittsburgh Press, 1976. 237 p. Bibliog.

Polsby, Nelson W. CONGRESS AND THE PRESIDENCY. 3d ed. Englewood Cliffs, N.J.: Prentice-Hall, 1976. 212 p. Bibliog.

Reed, R.P. "Foreign Policy and the Initiation of War: The Congress and the Presidency in the Dispute over War Powers." POTOMAC REVIEW 6 (1973): 1-29.

Rieselbach, Leroy N. THE ROOTS OF ISOLATIONISM: CONGRESSIONAL VOTING AND PRESIDENTIAL LEADERSHIP IN FOREIGN POLICY. Indiana-polis: Bobbs-Merrill, 1966. 240 p. Bibliog.

Ripley, Randall B., and Franklin, Grace A. CONGRESS, THE BUREAUCRACY, AND PUBLIC POLICY. Rev. ed. Homewood, Ill.: Dorsey, 1980. 262 p. Bibliog.

    Especially chapters 7 and 8.

Robinson, James A. "Process Satisfaction and Policy Approval in State De-partment-Congressional Relations." AMERICAN JOURNAL OF SOCIOLOGY 67 (November 1961): 278-83.

Rourke, Francis E. "Administrative Secrecy: A Congressional Dilemma." AMERICAN POLITICAL SCIENCE REVIEW 54 (September 1960): 684-94.

Ryley, Thomas W. A LITTLE GROUP OF WILLFUL MEN: A STUDY OF CON-GRESSIONAL-PRESIDENTIAL AUTHORITY. Port Washington, N.Y.: National University, 1975. 198 p. Bibliog.

    Especially chapter 1.

Schlesinger, Arthur M., Jr., and DeGrazia, Alfred. CONGRESS AND THE PRESIDENCY: THEIR ROLE IN MODERN TIMES. Washington, D.C.: Ameri-can Enterprise Institute, 1967. 192 p.

Travis, Walter Earl, comp. CONGRESS AND THE PRESIDENT: READINGS IN EX-
ECUTIVE-LEGISLATIVE RELATIONS. New York: Teachers College Press, Columbia
University, 1967. 179 p.

Wilcox, Francis O. CONGRESS, THE EXECUTIVE, AND FOREIGN POLICY.
New York: Harper and Row, 1971. 179 p.

Wolkinson, Herman. "Demands of Congressional Committees for Executive
Papers." FEDERAL BAR JOURNAL 10 (April and July 1949): 103-50, 223-59.

Younger, Irving. "Congressional Investigations and Executive Secrecy: A
Study in the Separation of Powers." UNIVERSITY OF PITTSBURGH LAW RE-
VIEW 20 (June 1959): 755-84.

Zinn, Charles J. EXTENT OF THE CONTROL OF THE EXECUTIVE BY THE
CONGRESS OF THE UNITED STATES. Washington, D.C.: Government
Printing Office, 1962. 37 p.

> Prepared for Senate Committee on Government Operations.

CASE STUDIES

The case studies listed here pose Congress or one of its chambers as central to
the conduct of foreign relations. Much of the case study literature referred to
elsewhere (especially in chapters 14, 15, and 16) also involves Congress and
needs to be consulted to complete the study of literature on the subject.

Ashton, Charles Henry. "Congressional Decision-Making in the Foreign Policy-
Making Process: The Case of the Bokaro Steel Mill Project in Indo-American
Relations." Ph.D. dissertation, University of Pennsylvania, 1972. 383 p.

Bailey, Stephen K., and Samuel, Howard D. CONGRESS AT WORK. New
York: Holt, 1952. 502 p. Reprint. Hamden, Conn.: Archon, 1965.

> Collection of case studies describing Congress in terms of human
> behavior.

Berry, Lee R. "The United States Congress and Cuba: Four Case Studies of
Congressional Influence on American Foreign Policy." Ph.D. dissertation,
Notre Dame University, 1976. 180 p

Craft, James Pressley, Jr. "The Role of Congress in the Determination of
Naval Strategy in Support of United States Foreign Policy, 1956-1966." Ph.D.
dissertation, University of Pennsylvania, 1969. 201 p.

Donovan, John C. "Congress and the Making of Neutrality Legislation, 1935-
1939." Ph.D. dissertation, Howard University, 1949. 134 p.

Duane, Edward Anthony. "Congress and Inter-American Relations, 1961-1965." Ph.D. dissertation, University of Pennsylvania, 1969. 449 p.

Dvorin, Eugene P., ed. THE SENATE'S WAR POWERS: DEBATE ON CAMBODIA FROM THE CONGRESSIONAL RECORD. Chicago: Markham, 1971. 244 p.

Gambrell, Leonard Lee. "The Influence of the Senate Foreign Relations Committee Chairman in the Making of United States Foreign Policy: A Case Analysis." Ph.D. dissertation, University of Virginia, 1971. 378 p.

Garcia, Rogello. "Opposition Within the Senate to American Military Intervention in Nicargua, 1926-1933." Ph.D. dissertation, Columbia University, 1973. 240 p.

Heindel, Richard H.; et al. "The North Atlantic Treaty in the United States Senate." AMERICAN JOURNAL OF INTERNATIONAL LAW 43 (October 1949): 633-65.

Hickey, John. "The Role of the Congress in Foreign Policy: Case--The Cuban Disaster." INTER-AMERICAN ECONOMIC AFFAIRS 14 (Spring 1961): 67-89.

Huitt, Ralph K. "The Congressional Committee: A Case Study." AMERICAN POLITICAL SCIENCE REVIEW 48 (June 1954): 340-65.

Leu, Christopher Amadeus. "Congress and the Role of Private Enterprise in the United States Foreign Assistance Program." Ph.D. dissertation, University of California (Los Angeles), 1973. 426 p.

McCoy, Pressley Crane. "An Analysis of the Debates on Recognition of the Union of Soviet Socialist Republics, in the United States Senate, 1917-1934." Ph.D. dissertation, Northwestern University, 1954. 899 p.

Mangan, Mary. "The Congressional Image of Aid to the Underdeveloped Countries (1949-1959) As Revealed in the Congressional Hearings and Debates." Ph.D. dissertation, Yale University, 1964. 401 p.

Riggs, James Richard. "Congress and the Conduct of the Korean War." Ph.D. dissertation, Purdue University, 1972. 455 p.

Robinson, James A. THE MONRONEY RESOLUTION: CONGRESSIONAL INITIATIVE IN FOREIGN POLICY MAKING. New York: Holt, 1959. 16 p.

Sarros, Panayiotis Peter. "Congress and the New Diplomacy: The Formulation of Mutual Security Policy, 1953-1960." Ph.D. dissertation, Princeton University, 1964. 443 p.

Scowcroft, Brent. "Congress and Foreign Policy: An Examination of Congressional Attitudes Toward the Foreign Aid Programs to Spain and Yugoslavia." Ph.D. dissertation, Columbia University, 1967. 413 p.

Stern, Paula. WATER'S EDGE: DOMESTIC POLITICS AND THE MAKING OF AMERICAN FOREIGN POLICY. Westport, Conn.: Greenwood, 1979. 265 p.

_____. "The Water's Edge: The Jackson Amendment as a Case Study of the Role Domestic Politics Plays in the Creation of American Foreign Policy." Ph.D. dissertation, Tufts University, Fletcher School, 1976.

Thomas, Morgan, with Robert M. Northrup. ATOMIC ENERGY AND CONGRESS. Ann Arbor: University of Michigan Press, 1956. 301 p.

Wiltz, John E. IN SEARCH OF PEACE: THE SENATE MUNITIONS INQUIRY, 1934-1936. Baton Rouge: Louisiana State University Press, 1963. 277 p.

Young, Roland A. CONGRESSIONAL POLITICS IN THE SECOND WORLD WAR. New York: Columbia University Press, 1956. 281 p.

Chapter 9

DEPARTMENT OF STATE AND DIPLOMATIC SERVICE

In the American system, the president enjoys fundamental responsibility in the conduct of foreign relations. The secretary of state is his chief adviser and primary agent, the Department of State constitutes the secretary's staff, and the diplomatic service serves as the field agency. While general policies are determined by Congress and the president, with the counsel of the secretary and Department of State, it is the diplomatic service that executes these policies and programs overseas. Some organizational distinction exists between the organs of government that centrally establish policy and define the objectives and principles of external affairs, on the one hand, and the instrumentality or servicing agency utilized in their achievement, on the other. In many ways, their relations are inseparable, which is reflected in much of the literature on the subject. Nevertheless, some studies treat particularized aspects of this web of institutions, officials, and activities.

Resource material on the Department of State and the diplomatic service of the United States, though less plentiful than that on substantive foreign policy and crisis and other relations, nevertheless is substantial. As noted in chapter 3, it is a great deal more plentiful than English-language publications on the Foreign Offices and diplomatic personnel of other countries. By utilizing official and unofficial resources, analysts are able to become well informed concerning the nature, organization, functioning, and problems of the Department of State and the diplomatic service.

Some published materials on American practice are general and comprehensive in scope, but many are more restricted in focus. Some are descriptive and analytical, others are assessorial (often negatively critical), and still others are reformative in objective. To generalize, since World War II, emphasis is being placed largely on organization and reorganization, management, operations, personnel, and improvement. Although some accounts published in the DEPARTMENT OF STATE BULLETIN, the DEPARTMENT OF STATE NEWS-LETTER, and the FOREIGN SERVICE JOURNAL are listed below, these publications are rich resources for additional, often relatively short, articles on the Department of State and the Foreign Service. Additional guidance to post-World War II official documentation may be found in the following:

U.S. Congress. Senate. Committee on Government Operations. Subcommittee on National Policy Machinery. ORGANIZING FOR NATIONAL SECURITY: A BIBLIOGRAPHY. 86th Cong., 1st sess. Washington, D.C.: Government Printing Office, 1959. 77 p.

Pages 54–57 on "The Department of State."

U.S. Congress. Senate. Committee on Government Operations. Subcommittee on National Security Staffing and Operations. ADMINISTRATION OF NATIONAL SECURITY: A BIBLIOGRAPHY. 87th Cong., 2d sess. Washington, D.C.: Government Printing Office, 1963. 89 p.

Pages 19–20 on "Department of State."

Department of State practice respecting the publication and release of diplomatic documentation and related materials is discussed in part III.

TABLE OF PRESIDENTS AND THEIR SECRETARIES OF STATE

For convenient reference, a table of presidents and their secretaries of state is provided as the first subsection of this chapter.

President	Political Party	Secretary of State	From	To
Cont. Congress		John Jay[1]	Dec. 21, 1784	
Washington	Fed.	John Jay		Mar. 22, 1790
		Thomas Jefferson	Mar. 22, 1790	Dec. 31, 1793
		Edmund Randolph	Jan. 2, 1794	Aug. 20, 1795
		Timothy Pickering[2]	Dec. 10, 1795	
Adams	Fed.	Timothy Pickering		May 12, 1800
		John Marshall	May 12, 1800*	Feb. 4, 1801
Jefferson	Rep.[3]	James Madison	May 2, 1801*	Mar. 3, 1809
Madison	Rep.	Robert Smith	Mar. 6, 1809	April 1, 1811
		James Monroe[4]	Apr. 6, 1811	Sept. 30, 1814
Monroe	Rep.	John Quincy Adams	Sept. 22, 1817*	Mar. 3, 1825
Adams	Rep.	Henry Clay	Mar. 7, 1825*	Mar. 3, 1829
Jackson	Dem.	Martin Van Buren	Mar. 28, 1829*	May 23, 1831
		Edward Livingston	May 24, 1831	May 29, 1833
		Louis McLane	May 29, 1833	June 30, 1834
		John Forsyth	July 1, 1834	
Van Buren	Dem.	John Forsyth		Mar. 3, 1841
Harrison	Whig	Daniel Webster	Mar. 6, 1841*	
Tyler	Whig	Daniel Webster		May 8, 1843
		Abel P. Upshur[5]	July 24, 1843*	Feb. 28, 1844
		John C. Calhoun	Apr. 1, 1844*	
Polk	Dem.	John C. Calhoun		Mar. 10, 1845
		James Buchanan	Mar. 10, 1845	Mar. 7, 1849
Taylor	Whig	John M. Clayton	Mar. 8, 1849	July 22, 1850

President	Party	Secretary of State		
Fillmore	Whig	Daniel Webster	July 23, 1850	Oct. 24, 1852
		Edward Everett	Nov. 6, 1852*	Mar. 3, 1853
Pierce	Dem.	William L. Marcy	Mar. 8, 1853*	Mar. 6, 1857
Buchanan	Dem.	Lewis Cass	Mar. 6, 1857	Dec. 14, 1860
		Jeremiah Black	Dec. 17, 1860*	Mar. 5, 1861
Lincoln	Rep.	William H. Seward	Mar. 6, 1861	
Johnson	Rep.	William H. Seward		Mar. 4, 1869
Grant	Rep.	Elihu B. Washburne	Mar. 5, 1869	Mar. 16, 1869
		Hamilton Fish	Mar. 17, 1869	Mar. 12, 1877
Hayes	Rep.	William M. Evarts	Mar. 12, 1877	Mar. 7, 1881
Garfield	Rep.	James G. Blaine	Mar. 7, 1881	Dec. 19, 1881
Arthur	Rep.	Frederick T. Frelinghuysen	Dec. 19, 1881	Mar. 6, 1885
Cleveland	Dem.	Thomas F. Bayard	Mar. 7, 1885	Mar. 6, 1889
Harrison	Rep.	James G. Blaine	Mar. 7, 1889	June 4, 1892
		John W. Foster	June 29, 1892*	Feb. 23, 1893
Cleveland	Dem.	Walter Q. Gresham	Mar. 7, 1893*	May 28, 1895
		Richard Olney	June 10, 1895*	Mar. 5, 1897
McKinley	Rep.	John Sherman	Mar. 6, 1897	Apr. 27, 1898
		William R. Day	Apr. 28, 1898	Sept. 16, 1898
		John Hay	Sept. 30, 1898*	
T. Roosevelt	Rep.	John Hay		July 1, 1905
		Elihu Root	July 19, 1905*	Jan. 27, 1909
		Robert Bacon	Jan. 27, 1909	Mar. 5, 1909
Taft	Rep.	Philander C. Knox	Mar. 6, 1909	Mar. 5, 1913
Wilson	Dem.	William Jennings Bryan	Mar. 5, 1913	June 9, 1915
		Robert Lansing[6]	June 24, 1915*	Feb. 13, 1920
		Bainbridge Colby	Mar. 23, 1920*	Mar. 4, 1921
Harding	Rep.	Charles E. Hughes	Mar. 5, 1921	
Coolidge	Rep.	Charles E. Hughes		Mar. 4, 1925
		Frank B. Kellogg	Mar. 5, 1925	Mar. 28, 1929

President	Party	Secretary of State	Appointed	Terminated
Hoover	Rep.	Henry L. Stimson	Mar. 28, 1929	Mar. 4, 1933
F.D. Roosevelt	Dem.	Cordell Hull	Mar. 4, 1933	Nov. 30, 1944
		Edward R. Stettinius	Dec. 1, 1944*	
Truman	Dem.	Edward R. Stettinius		June 27, 1945
		James F. Byrnes	July 3, 1945*	Jan. 21, 1947
		George C. Marshall	Jan. 21, 1947	Jan. 20, 1949
		Dean Acheson	Jan. 21, 1949	Jan. 20, 1953
Eisenhower	Rep.	John Foster Dulles	Jan. 21, 1953	Apr. 22, 1959
		Christian A. Herter	Apr. 22, 1959	Jan. 20, 1961
Kennedy	Dem.	Dean Rusk	Jan. 21, 1961	
Johnson	Dem.	Dean Rusk		Jan. 20, 1969
Nixon	Rep.	William P. Rogers	Jan. 22, 1969	Sep. 3, 1973
	Rep.	Henry A. Kissinger	Sep. 22, 1973*	
Ford	Rep.	Henry A. Kissinger		Jan. 20, 1977
Carter	Dem.	Cyrus Vance	Jan. 23, 1977*	Apr. 28, 1980
		Edmund S. Muskie	May 8, 1980	

*During the interim period, while there was no duly commissioned Secretary of State, the office was held ad interim by some other member of the President's Cabinet or by some ranking member of the Department of State, such as the Under Secretary, Assistant Secretary, or, in earlier days, the Chief Clerk.

[1] Originally appointed Secretary of Foreign Affairs by Continental Congress and later served unofficially under the Constitution until Jefferson was appointed Secretary of State.

[2] Also, as Secretary of War, served ad interim, Aug. 20, 1795-Dec. 9, 1795.

[3] The Republican Party (or Republican-Democratic Party) of Jefferson's day was not the precursor of the present Republican Party, which dates from the mid-1850's.

[4] As Secretary of War also served ad interim, Oct. 1, 1814-Feb. 28, 1815.

[5] Also, as Secretary of Navy, served ad interim, June 24, 1843-July 23-1843.

[6] Also served ad interim, June 9, 1915-June 23, 1915.

SECRETARYSHIP OF STATE

The following materials focus on the secretaryship of state as an office and the secretaries as individuals. Before World War II, a standard multivolume compilation of the secretaries of state was provided in:

Bemis, Samuel Flagg, ed. THE AMERICAN SECRETARIES OF STATE AND ⅂ THEIR DIPLOMACY. 10 vols. New York: Knopf, 1927-29.

> Consists of career sketches of individual secretaries of state from Benjamin Franklin to Charles Evans Hughes, with several secretaries included in each volume.

This series is being brought up to date, under the title AMERICAN SECRETARIES OF STATE AND THEIR DIPLOMACY, edited by Robert H. Ferrell, which continues the volume sequence of the Bemis series. The new volumes include the following, given in historical sequence by secretary of state. The series is planned to be continued.

Ferrell, Robert H. FRANK B. KELLOGG AND HENRY L. STIMSON. Vol. 11. New York: Cooper Square, 1963. 360 p.

Pratt, Julius W. CORDELL HULL, 1933-1944. Vols. 12 and 13. New York: Cooper Square, 1964. 840 p.

Walker, Richard L., and Curry, George. EDWARD R. STETTINIUS AND JAMES F. BYRNES. Vol. 14. New York: Cooper Square, 1965. 423 p.

Ferrell, Robert H. GEORGE C. MARSHALL. Vol. 15. New York: Cooper Square, 1965. 326 p. Bibliog. essay.

Smith, Gaddis. DEAN ACHESON. Vol. 16. New York: Cooper Square, 1972. 473 p.

Gerson, Louis L. JOHN FOSTER DULLES. Vol. 17. New York: Cooper Square, 1967. 372 p.

Noble, George Bernard. CHRISTIAN A. HERTER. Vol. 18. New York: Cooper Square, 1970. 333 p.

Also of relevance are such encompassing studies as:

Graebner, Norman A., ed. AN UNCERTAIN TRADITION: AMERICAN SECRETARIES OF STATE IN THE TWENTIETH CENTURY. New York: McGraw-Hill, 1961. 341 p. Bibliog.

Consists of an introductory statement and separate chapters by individual authors on fourteen secretaries of state, from John Hay
to John Foster Dulles.

Heller, David. PATHS OF DIPLOMACY: AMERICA'S SECRETARIES OF
STATE. Philadelphia: Lippincott, 1967. 192 p.

Career sketches of twenty selected secretaries of state, from
Thomas Jefferson to Dean Rusk.

Supplementing these basic surveys, additional biographical, autobiographical,
and memoir literature on individual secretaries of state is provided in part IV.

The following are probing and comprehensive studies of the office of the secretaryship of state:

DeConde, Alexander. THE AMERICAN SECRETARY OF STATE: AN INTER-
PRETATION. New York: Praeger, 1962. 182 p. Bibliog.

Contains chapters dealing with such matters as origins, responsibilities, and powers of the office, qualifications and selection of
the incumbent, and roles of the office, including those of heir
apparent, prime minister, figurehead, partner, statesman, and
administrator.

Hill, Norman L. MR. SECRETARY OF STATE. New York: Random House,
1963. 185 p. Bibliog.

Contains chapters on relation to the president, appointment and
tenure, and the secretary's roles as policy adviser, department
head, manager of congressional relations, framer of public opinion,
traveler, and politician, with analyses of incumbents, the secretary's philosophy, and the nature of his office.

Price, Don K., ed. THE SECRETARY OF STATE. Englewood Cliffs, N.J.:
Prentice-Hall for American Assembly, 1960. 200 p.

Contains chapters by individual authors on a new look at the secretary, his relations with the president, Congress, and the public,
his functions in developing, coordinating, and executing policy,
his management of the Department of State, and his status under
the Constitution.

A few more limited studies of the secretaryship and the secretary of state have
been published, including some on individual incumbents, which are represented
by the following:

"Functions of Secretary of State in National Election." DEPARTMENT OF
STATE BULLETIN 18 (7 November 1948): 587.

Greenberg, Myron Arthur. "The Secretary of State and Secretarial Belief Systems: An Inquiry into the Relationship Between Knowledge and Action." Ph.D. dissertation, University of Cincinnati, 1979. 575 p.

"How the Secretary of State Apportions His Time." DEPARTMENT OF STATE BULLETIN 54 (25 April 1966): 651-54.

Jablon, Howard. "Cordell Hull, The State Department and the Foreign Policy of the First Roosevelt Administration, 1933-1936." Ph.D. dissertation, Rutgers University, 1967. 266 p.

Jackson, Henry M., ed. THE SECRETARY OF STATE AND THE AMBASSADOR: JACKSON SUBCOMMITTEE PAPERS ON THE CONDUCT OF AMERICAN FOREIGN POLICY. New York: Praeger, 1966. 203 p.

Modelski, George. "The Foreign Ministers as a World Elite." PEACE RESEARCH SOCIETY PAPERS (INTERNATIONAL) 14 (1970): 31-46.

Newcomer, James Roger. "Acheson, Dulles, and Rusk: Information, Coherence, and Organization in the Department of State." Ph.D. dissertation, Stanford University, 1976. 690 p.

Perlmutter, Oscar W. "Acheson and the Diplomacy of World War II." WESTERN POLITICAL QUARTERLY 14 (December 1961): 896-911.

Robertson, Charles Langner. "The American Secretary of State: A Study of the Office Under Henry L. Stimson and Cordell Hull." Ph.D. dissertation, Princeton University, 1959. 290 p.

Stupak, Ronald Joseph. "Dean Acheson: The Secretary of State as a Policy-Maker." Ph.D. dissertation, Ohio State University, 1967. 265 p.

_____. THE SHAPING OF FOREIGN POLICY: THE ROLE OF THE SECRETARY OF STATE AS SEEN BY DEAN ACHESON. New York: Odyssey, 1969. 132 p. Bibliog.

Tessendorf, K.C. "Mr. Secretary, May We Have Your Remittance, Please?" FOREIGN SERVICE JOURNAL 47 (August 1970): 39-41.

U.S. Congress. Senate. Committee on Government Operations. Subcommittee on National Security and International Operations. THE SECRETARY OF STATE AND THE PROBLEM OF COORDINATION: NEW DUTIES AND PROCEDURES OF MARCH 4, 1966. 89th Cong., 2d sess. Washington, D.C.: Government Printing Office, 1966. 23 p.

U.S. Congress. Senate. Committee on Government Operations. Subcommittee on National Policy Machinery. ORGANIZING FOR NATIONAL SECURITY:

THE SECRETARY OF STATE AND THE NATIONAL SECURITY POLICY PROCESS.
87th Cong., 1st sess. Washington, D.C.: Government Printing Office, 1961. 10 p.

U.S. Congress. Senate. Committee on Government Operations. Subcommittee on National Security Staffing and Operations. ADMINISTRATION OF NATIONAL SECURITY: THE SECRETARY OF STATE. 88th Cong., 2d sess. Washington, D.C.: Government Printing Office, 1964. 15 p.

U.S. Department of State. THE SECRETARIES OF STATE: PORTRAITS AND BIOGRAPHICAL SKETCHES. Compiled by Lee H. Burke and Jan K. Herman. Washington, D.C.: Government Printing Office, 1978. 125 p.

Wriston, Henry M. "The Secretary of State Abroad." FOREIGN AFFAIRS 34 (July 1956): 523-41.

It may seem strange that former secretaries of state have not contributed significant analytical literature on the office, but a few writings, such as the memoirs of John W. Foster, Henry L. Stimson, Cordell Hull, James F. Byrnes, and others, as well as Dean Acheson's PRESENT AT THE CREATION, cited in chapter 15, p. 337, deal partly with the role of the incumbent in this capacity. In 1970, the secretary of state began to publish a series of annual reports, but these continued for only a short time. In addition to commentary on geographic and functional policy development, these contained analysis of various aspects of the conduct of foreign relations in a special section titled "Management."

U.S. Department of State. UNITED STATES FOREIGN POLICY: A REPORT OF THE SECRETARY OF STATE. Washington, D.C.: Government Printing Office. Vols. for 1969-70, published in 1971, 616 p; for 1971 published in 1972, 604 p.; for 1972 published in 1973, 743 p.

The last of these added an annex, which included a selected list of treaties and agreements consummated during the year, and a list of principal departmental officers.

Summary statements concerning these reports were published as the following, given in chronological sequence:

Rogers, William P. "U.S. Foreign Policy, 1969-70: A Report of the Secretary of State." DEPARTMENT OF STATE BULLETIN 64 (5 April 1971): 465-77.

_____. "U.S. Foreign Policy, 1971: A Report of the Secretary of State." DEPARTMENT OF STATE BULLETIN 66 (27 March 1972): 459-70.

_____. 1973--A YEAR OF BUILDING: INTRODUCTORY COMMENT BY THE SECRETARY OF STATE--THE SECRETARY OF STATE OUTLINES U.S. OBJECTIVES. Washington, D.C.: Government Printing Office, 1973. 26 p.

Reprint of introductory comment, several graphs, and a chronology from 1972 report (UNITED STATES FOREIGN POLICY, cited above).

DEPARTMENT OF STATE

Although it is not always possible to segregate concern with matters of governmental machinery and personnel, the following are largely descriptive and analytical surveys of the Department of State as an institutional agency. A few studies review its historical development.

Hunt, Gaillard. THE DEPARTMENT OF STATE OF THE UNITED STATES: ITS HISTORY AND FUNCTIONS. New Haven, Conn.: Yale University Press, 1914. 459 p.

Michael, William H. HISTORY OF THE DEPARTMENT OF STATE OF THE UNITED STATES: ITS FUNCTIONS AND DUTIES, TOGETHER WITH BIOGRAPHIES OF ITS PRESENT OFFICERS AND SECRETARIES FROM THE BEGINNING. . . . Washington, D.C.: Government Printing Office, 1901. 136 p.

Stuart, Graham H. THE DEPARTMENT OF STATE: A HISTORY OF ITS ORGANIZATION, PROCEDURE, AND PERSONNEL. New York: Crowell, 1949. 517 p.

U.S. Department of State. THE DEPARTMENT OF STATE OF THE UNITED STATES: ITS HISTORY AND FUNCTIONS. Washington, D.C.: Government Printing Office, 1893. 212 p.

For historical treatment, see also the works of Ilchman and Summers listed below, p. 197 and p. 198. Aside from the histories of Hunt and Michael, and the Department of State report on history and functions, a few other earlier general volumes antedate 1945, of which the following are among the better known.

Bendiner, Robert. THE RIDDLE OF THE STATE DEPARTMENT. New York: Farrar and Rinehart, 1942. 231 p.

Hulen, Bertram D. INSIDE THE DEPARTMENT OF STATE. New York: McGraw Hill, 1939. 328 p.

Spaulding, E. Wilder, and Blue, George Verne. THE DEPARTMENT OF STATE OF THE UNITED STATES. Rev. ed. Washington, D.C.: Government Printing Office, 1936. 65 p.

U.S. Department of State. THE DEPARTMENT OF STATE OF THE UNITED STATES. Washington, D.C.: Government Printing Office, 1933. 101 p.

For later publications, see Gerber and Department of State reports
cited below, p. 197 and p. 199.

Books and Monographs

Far more literary attention has been devoted to the subject of the Department
of State since World War II, especially since the 1960s. Occasionally, publications are written by practitioners who serve in Washington and in the field,
such as Ambassadors Ellis Briggs and Charles W. Yost, as well as by departmental officials, including Barron, Campbell, Estes and Lightner, Rostow, and
Simpson. A good many authors tend to be critical and suggest changes and
improvements, such as Barron, Briggs, and Simpson. A comprehensive series
of other evaluative and reformative analyses, produced largely since World
War II, are dealt with separately later in this chapter.

While some analyses are broad in scope, such as Campbell, Elder, and Simpson, a number address themselves to more limited aspects of the subject. These
include studies on elements of organization and administration (Argyris, Leacacos, and the Senate Foreign Relations Committee), specific departmental components (Bacchus, Hoffman, and Summers), and congressional relations (Bruce
and Burke). Somewhat unusual interest has been devoted to the role of lawyers
and the legal adviser in the Department of State--Merrilat, Outland, Stowell,
and a number of articles cited later. The Department of State also has periodically published a series of short monographs, prepared by William Gerber
and others. As a whole, this literature on the Department of State offers a
fairly comprehensive depiction of its nature and operations, and materials cited
in other sections of this compilation relate it to the presidency, the Congress,
and other components of the administrative bureaucracy.

Argyris, Chris. SOME CAUSES OF ORGANIZATIONAL INEFFECTIVENESS
WITHIN THE DEPARTMENT OF STATE. Department of State Publication 8180.
Washington, D.C.: Government Printing Office, 1967. 52 p.

> Produced by Center for International Systems Research as Occa-
> sional Paper no. 2.

Bacchus, William I. FOREIGN POLICY AND THE BUREAUCRATIC PROCESS:
THE STATE DEPARTMENT'S COUNTRY DIRECTOR SYSTEM. Princeton, N.J.:
Princeton University Press, 1974. 350 p. Bibliog.

Baram, Philip J. THE DEPARTMENT OF STATE IN THE MIDDLE EAST, 1919-
1945. Philadelphia: University of Pennsylvania Press, 1978. 343 p.

Barron, Bryton. INSIDE THE STATE DEPARTMENT: A CANDID APPRAISAL
OF THE BUREAUCRACY. New York: Comet, 1956. 178 p.

_____. THE STATE DEPARTMENT: BLUNDERS OR TREASON? Springfield,
Va.: Crestwood, 1965. 189 p.

_____. THE UNTOUCHABLE STATE DEPARTMENT. Springfield, Va.: Crestwood, 1962. 166 p.

Bergman, Helen A. THE COMMUNICATIONS SYSTEM OF THE UNITED STATES DEPARTMENT OF STATE AS IT PERTAINS TO THE FOREIGN SERVICE. Minneapolis: University of Minnesota, 1948. 98 p.

Briggs, Ellis. FAREWELL TO FOGGY BOTTOM: THE REFLECTIONS OF A DIPLOMAT. New York: McKay, 1964. 306 p.

Bruce, Diana Abbey. "The Office of Congressional Relations of the Department of State, 1959-1960." M.A. thesis, University of California (Berkeley), 1961.

Burke, Lee H. "The Department of State's Congressional Relations Office." Research Project, no. 1152. Washington, D.C.: U.S. Department of State, Office of the Historian, 1977. 40 p.

Campbell, John Franklin. THE FOREIGN AFFAIRS FUDGE FACTORY. New York: Basic Books, 1971. 292 p.

Chittick, William O. "The Domestic Information Activities of the Department of State." Ph.D. dissertation, Johns Hopkins University, 1964. 266 p.

_____. STATE DEPARTMENT, PRESS, AND PRESSURE GROUPS: A ROLE ANALYSIS. New York: Wiley Interscience, 1970. 373 p. Bibliog.

Colligan, Francis J. THE IN-SERVICE TRAINING OF CULTURAL RELATIONS OFFICERS: AN OUTLINE GUIDE. Washington, D.C.: Government Printing Office, 1949. 59 p.

David, Joan. INSIDE THE STATE DEPARTMENT: HOW IT WORKS AT HOME AND ABROAD. New York: Manhattan, 1952. 64 p.

Davis, David Howard. "Bureaucratic Exchange in Policy Formulation: The State Department's Relations with Three Domestic Agencies in the Foreign Affairs Arena." Ph.D. dissertation, Johns Hopkins University, 1971. 331 p.

Elder, Robert E. THE POLICY MACHINE: THE DEPARTMENT OF STATE AND AMERICAN FOREIGN POLICY. Syracuse, N.Y.: Syracuse University Press, 1960. 238 p.

Estes, Thomas Stuart, and Lightner, E. Allen, Jr. THE DEPARTMENT OF STATE. New York: Praeger, 1976. 272 p. Bibliog.

Feis, Herbert. SEEN FROM E.A.: THREE INTERNATIONAL EPISODES. New York: Knopf, 1947. 313 p.

Concerns difficulties resulting from organization of World War II period. "E.A." refers to the Office of the Economic Adviser, Department of State.

Frankel, Charles. HIGH ON FOGGY BOTTOM: AN OUTSIDER'S INSIDE VIEW OF THE GOVERNMENT. New York: Harper and Row, 1968. 240 p.

Gerber, William. THE DEPARTMENT OF STATE OF THE UNITED STATES. Washington, D.C.: Government Printing Office, 1942. 91 p. Bibliog.

Also see Spaulding and Blue, cited above, p. 194 and publications of the Department of State, listed below, p. 199.

Hilsman, Roger, Jr. THE POLITICS OF POLICY-MAKING IN DEFENSE AND FOREIGN AFFAIRS. New York: Harper and Row, 1971. 198 p.

Especially chapter 3 on career bureaucrats.

Hoffman, Ralph Nicholas, Jr. "Latin American Diplomacy: The Role of the Assistant Secretary of State, 1957-1969." Ph.D. dissertation, Syracuse University, 1969. 557 p.

Hunt, Gaillard. THE AMERICAN PASSPORT: ITS HISTORY AND A DIGEST OF LAWS, RULINGS, AND REGULATIONS GOVERNING ITS ISSUANCE BY THE DEPARTMENT OF STATE. Washington, D.C.: Government Printing Office, 1898. 233 p.

Ilchman, Warren Frederick. PROFESSIONAL DIPLOMACY IN THE UNITED STATES, 1779-1939: A STUDY IN ADMINISTRATIVE HISTORY. Chicago: University of Chicago Press, 1961. 254 p.

Leacacos, John P. FIRES IN THE IN-BASKET: THE ABC'S OF THE STATE DEPARTMENT. Cleveland: World, 1968. 552 p.

Macmahon, Arthur W. MEMORANDUM ON THE POSTWAR INTERNATIONAL INFORMATION PROGRAM OF THE UNITED STATES. Washington, D.C.: U.S. Department of State, 1945. 135 p.

Especially parts 8 and 9.

Marrow, Alfred Jay. MAKING WAVES IN FOGGY BOTTOM: HOW A NEW AND MORE SCIENTIFIC APPROACH CHANGED THE MANAGEMENT AT THE STATE DEPARTMENT. Washington, D.C.: NTL Institute, 1974. 93 p.

Merillat, Herbert C.L., ed. LEGAL ADVISERS AND FOREIGN AFFAIRS. Dobbs Ferry, N.Y.: Oceana for American Society of International Law, 1964. 162 p.

Mosher, Frederick, and Harr, John Ensor. PROGRAMMING SYSTEMS AND FOREIGN POLICY LEADERSHIP. New York: Oxford University Press, 1970. 261 p.

Outland, John Warner. "Law and the Lawyer in the State Department's Administration of Foreign Policy." Ph.D. dissertation, Syracuse University, 1970. 204 p.

Pritt, Denis N. THE STATE DEPARTMENT AND THE COLD WAR. New York: International Publishers, 1948. 96 p.

Pruitt, Dean G. PROBLEM SOLVING IN THE DEPARTMENT OF STATE. Monograph Series in World Affairs, no. 2. Denver: University of Denver, 1964-65. 56 p.

Rostow, Walt W. VIEW FROM THE SEVENTH FLOOR. New York: Harper and Row, 1964. 178 p.

> Senior officials—above the assistant secretaries—have their offices on the seventh floor of the Department of State headquarters.

Simpson, Smith. THE ANATOMY OF THE STATE DEPARTMENT. Boston: Houghton Mifflin, 1967. 285 p.

Stempel, John D. "Policy/Decision-Making in the Department of State: Vietnamese Problem, 1961-1965." Ph.D. dissertation, University of California (Berkeley), 1965. 361 p.

Stowell, Ellery C. THE ECONOMIC ADVISER OF THE DEPARTMENT OF STATE. Washington, D.C.: Digest Press, 1935. 16 p.

_____. THE LEGAL ADVISER OF THE DEPARTMENT OF STATE. Washington, D.C.: Digest Press, 1936. 53 p.

Summers, Natalia. OUTLINE OF THE FUNCTIONING OF THE OFFICES OF THE DEPARTMENT OF STATE, 1789-1943. Washington, D.C.: U.S. National Archives, Division of Department of State Archives, 1946. 226 p. Bibliog.

Terrell, John Upton. THE UNITED STATES DEPARTMENT OF STATE: A STORY OF DIPLOMATS, EMBASSIES AND FOREIGN POLICY. New York: Duell, Sloan, and Pearce, 1964. 121 p.

> Also deals with diplomatic and consular service.

U.S. Bureau of the Budget. A STUDY OF RELATIONSHIPS BETWEEN THE DEPARTMENTS OF STATE AND COMMERCE. Washington, D.C.: Government Printing Office, 1948. 69 p.

U.S. Congress. Senate. Committee on Foreign Relations. ADDITIONAL MATERIALS ON ADMINISTRATION OF THE DEPARTMENT OF STATE. 87th Cong., 2d sess. Washington, D.C.: Government Printing Office, 1962. 255 p.

Supplement to the following.

_____. ADMINISTRATION OF THE DEPARTMENT OF STATE. 86th Cong., 2d sess. Washington, D.C.: Government Printing Office, 1960. 206 p.

_____. ADMINISTRATION OF THE DEPARTMENT OF STATE AND THE FOREIGN SERVICE, AND ESTABLISHMENT OF A FOREIGN SERVICE ACADEMY. Hearings. 86th Cong., 1st sess. Washington, D.C.: Government Printing Office, 1959. 240 p.

_____. STATE DEPARTMENT EMPLOYEE LOYALTY INVESTIGATION. 81st Cong., 2d sess. Washington, D.C.: Government Printing Office, 1950. 313 p.

U.S. Department of State. THE DEPARTMENT OF STATE, 1930-1955. Washington, D.C.: Government Printing Office, 1955. 66 p.

_____. DEPARTMENT OF STATE--1963: A REPORT TO THE CITIZEN. Washington, D.C.: Government Printing Office, 1963. 151 p.

_____. THE DEPARTMENT OF STATE TODAY. Washington, D.C.: Government Printing Office, 1951. 33 p.

_____. FOREIGN POLICY AND THE DEPARTMENT OF STATE. Washington, D.C.: Government Printing Office, 1976. 30 p.

_____. GUIDEBOOK TO DIPLOMATIC RECEPTION ROOMS IN DEPARTMENT OF STATE. Washington, D.C.: Government Printing Office, 1969. 63 p.

_____. "The Rank of the Counselor Historically in the Department of State." Washington, D.C.: Department of State, 1961. 8 p. with unnumbered supplements.

_____. THE SCIENCE ADVISER OF THE DEPARTMENT OF STATE. Washington, D.C.: Government Printing Office, 1960. 27 p.

_____. THE SEAL OF THE UNITED STATES. Washington, D.C.: Government Printing Office, 1957. 14 p.; also THE GREAT SEAL OF THE UNITED STATES. Washington, D.C.: Government Printing Office, 1976. 8 p.

Department of State is responsible for the official seal of the U.S. government. For discussion of the Department of State seal, see Richard S. Patterson, p. 205, and last section of this chapter, pp. 238-39.

Villard, Henry S. AFFAIRS AT STATE. New York: Crowell, 1965. 254 p.

Willis, Davis K. THE STATE DEPARTMENT. Boston: Christian Science Publishing Society, 1968. 99 p.

> Republication of eleven articles appearing in CHRISTIAN SCIENCE MONITOR.

Yost, Charles W. THE CONDUCT AND MISCONDUCT OF FOREIGN AFFAIRS. New York: Random House, 1972. 234 p.

> Especially chapter 3.

Chapters, Essays, and Journal Literature

Shorter accounts on the Department of State are available as chapters in a variety of books, represented by the following:

Allison, Graham, and Szanton, Peter. REMAKING FOREIGN POLICY: THE ORGANIZATIONAL CONNECTION. New York: Basic Books, 1976.

> Especially chapter 6.

Barber, Hollis W. FOREIGN POLICIES OF THE UNITED STATES. New York: Dryden, 1953.

> Especially chapter 3.

Briggs, Ellis O. ANATOMY OF DIPLOMACY: THE ORIGIN AND EXECUTION OF AMERICAN FOREIGN POLICY. New York: McKay, 1968.

> Especially chapter 4.

Chamberlain, Lawrence H., and Snyder, Richard C. AMERICAN FOREIGN POLICY. New York: Rinehart, 1948.

> Especially chapter 6.

Esterline, John H., and Black, Robert B. INSIDE FOREIGN POLICY: THE DEPARTMENT OF STATE POLITICAL SYSTEM AND ITS SUBSYSTEMS. Palo Alto, Calif.: Mayfield, 1975.

> Especially chapter 5 on the Department of State and chapter 8 on the Arms Control and Disarmament Agency.

Johnson, Richard A. THE ADMINISTRATION OF UNITED STATES FOREIGN POLICY. Austin: University of Texas Press, 1971.

> Especially chapter 10.

McCamy, James L. THE ADMINISTRATION OF AMERICAN FOREIGN AF-
FAIRS. New York: Knopf, 1950.

> Especially chapters 3 and 4.

Moore, John Bassett. A DIGEST OF INTERNATIONAL LAW. Washington,
D.C.: Government Printing Office, 1906.

> Especially vol. 4, pages 780-806.

Murphy, Robert. DIPLOMAT AMONG WARRIORS. Garden City, N.Y.:
Doubleday, 1964.

> Especially chapter 29.

Nash, Henry T. AMERICAN FOREIGN POLICY: RESPONSE TO A SENSE
OF THREAT. Rev. ed. Homewood, Ill.: Dorsey, 1978.

> Especially chapter 4.

Plischke, Elmer. CONDUCT OF AMERICAN DIPLOMACY. 3d ed. Princeton, N.J.: Van Nostrand, 1967.

> Especially chapters 6 and 7.

Sapin, Burton M. THE MAKING OF UNITED STATES FOREIGN POLICY.
Washington, D.C.: Brookings Institution, 1966.

> Especially chapter 5.

Snyder, Richard C., and Furniss, Edgar S., Jr. AMERICAN FOREIGN POLI-
CY: FORMULATION, PRINCIPLES, AND PROGRAMS. New York: Rinehart,
1954.

> Especially chapters 6 and 7.

Stuart, Graham H. AMERICAN DIPLOMATIC AND CONSULAR PRACTICE.
2d ed. New York: Appleton-Century-Crofts, 1952.

> Especially chapters 2 to 4.

Williams, Benjamin H. AMERICAN DIPLOMACY: POLICIES AND PRACTICE.
New York: McGraw-Hill, 1936.

> Especially chapter 24.

Additional shorter accounts on the Department of State and its activities are
provided in a variety of essays and journal articles, as follows:

"Archival and Records Functions Transferred to General Services Administration."
DEPARTMENT OF STATE BULLETIN 22 (24 April 1950): 660.

Bess, Demaree C. "Why Americans Hate the State Department." SATURDAY EVENING POST, 19 August 1950, pp. 77-78, 80, 83.

Bilder, Richard B. "The Office of the Legal Adviser: The State Department Lawyer and Foreign Affairs." AMERICAN JOURNAL OF INTERNATIONAL LAW 56 (July 1962): 633-84.

Blair, William D., Jr. "Department Discusses National Security Information System." DEPARTMENT OF STATE BULLETIN 66 (3 April 1972): 523-25.

Blaney, Harry C. "Global Challenges and the Fudge Factory." FOREIGN SERVICE JOURNAL 51 (September 1974): 13-14, 26.

Bolles, Blair, and Ringwood, O.K.D. "Modern Functions and Tasks of the State Department." FOREIGN POLICY REPORTS 23 (15 August 1947): 144.

Bowie, Robert. "Planning in the Department." FOREIGN SERVICE JOURNAL 38 (March 1961): 20-24.

Testimony by several officials on planning.

Brown, MacAlister. "The Demise of State Department Public Opinion Polls: A Study in Legislative Oversight." MIDWEST JOURNAL OF POLITICAL SCIENCE 5 (February 1961): 1-17.

Burke, Lee H. HOMES OF THE DEPARTMENT OF STATE, 1774-1976: THE BUILDINGS OCCUPIED BY THE DEPARTMENT OF STATE AND ITS PREDECESSORS. Washington, D.C.: Historical Office, U.S. Department of State, 1977. 57 p. Photos.

A comprehensive history of the headquarters of the Department of State, covering two centuries.

_____. "Homes of the Department of State and Its Predecessors: The Story of the Buildings Occupied from 1774-1976." DEPARTMENT OF STATE NEWSLETTER, nos. 172-81 (October 1975-July 1976): no. 172, pp. 22-26; no. 173, pp. 22-24; no. 174, pp. 18-22; no. 175, pp. 17-19; no. 176, pp. 36-39; no. 177, pp. 22-25; no. 178, pp. 38-43; no. 179, pp. 28-32; no. 180, pp. 30-34; no. 181, pp. 30-33.

Republished, with minor changes and corrections, in the preceding item.

Casey, William J. "The Economic Role of the State Department." DEPARTMENT OF STATE BULLETIN 68 (11 June 1973): 849-52.

Clubb, O. Edmund. "Security Risks: National Security and the State Department." FOREIGN SERVICE JOURNAL 50 (December 1973): 13-15.

Coulter, Eliot B. "Visa Work of the Department of State and the Foreign Service." DEPARTMENT OF STATE BULLETIN 21 (10 October 1949): 523-35.

_____. "Visa Work of the Department of State and the Foreign Service." DEPARTMENT OF STATE BULLETIN 28 (2 and 9 February 1953): 195-203, 232-39.

Critchett, Frederick. "The Division of Current Information of the Department of State." CUMULATIVE DIGEST OF INTERNATIONAL LAW AND RELATIONS 2, bulletins 5, 6 (25 January 1932).

Cunningham, John E. "Are We Administering Away Our Effectiveness?" FOREIGN SERVICE JOURNAL 36 (February 1959): 19-21.

"The Department of State, 1930-1955: Expanding Functions and Responsibilities." DEPARTMENT OF STATE BULLETIN 32 (21 and 28 March 1955): 470-86, 528-44.

Destler, I.M. "State and Presidential Leadership." FOREIGN SERVICE JOURNAL 48 (September 1971): 26, 31-32, 43.

Dougall, Richardson, and Patterson, Richard S. "The Numbering of the Secretaries of State." DEPARTMENT OF STATE BULLETIN 41 (20 July 1959): 80-82.

"First Official Intern Program Started." DEPARTMENT OF STATE BULLETIN 21 (26 September 1949): 482.

Garnham, David. "State Department Rigidity: Testing a Hypothetical Hypothesis." INTERNATIONAL STUDIES QUARTERLY 18 (March 1974): 31-39. Bibliog.

Gimlin, Hoyt. "State Department and Policy Making." EDITORIAL RESEARCH REPORTS 1 (26 June 1969): 467-84.

Gordon, Lincoln. "Organization for the Conduct of Foreign Policy." FOREIGN SERVICE JOURNAL 32 (August 1955): 18-20, 46-48.

Graves, Harold N. "State Department--New Model." REPORTER 1 (8 November 1949): 27-29.
    On Dean Acheson's twentieth-century foreign office.

Gross, Ernest A. "Operation of the Legal Adviser's Office." AMERICAN JOURNAL OF INTERNATIONAL LAW 43 (January 1949): 122-27.

Halle, Louis J., Jr. "Significance of the Institute of Inter-American Affairs in the Conduct of U.S. Foreign Policy." DEPARTMENT OF STATE BULLETIN 18 (23 May 1948): 659-62.

Hamilton, William C. "Some Problems of Decision-Making in Foreign Affairs." DEPARTMENT OF STATE BULLETIN 37 (9 September 1957): 432-36.

Hammond, Paul Y. "Foreign Policy-Making and Administrative Politics." WORLD POLITICS 17 (July 1965): 656-71.

Harr, John Ensor. "The Issue of Competence in the State Department." INTERNATIONAL STUDIES QUARTERLY 14 (March 1970): 95-101.

Herring, Hubert C. "The Department of State." HARPER'S MAGAZINE, February 1937, pp. 225-38.

Hopkins, Frank S. "Training Responsibilities in the Department of State." PUBLIC ADMINISTRATION REVIEW 8 (Spring 1948): 119-25.

Immerman, Robert M. "The Formulation and Administration of U.S. Foreign Policy." FOREIGN SERVICE JOURNAL 37 (April 1960): 21-23.

"John Q and the State Department." CONGRESSIONAL DIGEST 29 (April 1950): 100.

Kennan, George F. "America's Administration Response to Its World Problems." DAEDALUS 87 (May 1958): 4-25.

Kennan, George F., et al. "Planning in the Department [of State]." FOREIGN SERVICE JOURNAL 38 (March 1961): 20-24.

> Symposium of former directors of Department of State's Policy Planning Staff, including Kennan, Paul H. Nitze, Robert R. Bowie, and Gerard C. Smith.

Kissinger, Henry A. "Domestic Structure and Foreign Policy." DAEDALUS 95 (Spring 1966): 503-29.

_____. "Secretary Kissinger Announces New Steps for Improvement of Department's Resource Allocation and Personnel Systems." DEPARTMENT OF STATE BULLETIN 73 (21 July 1975): 85-90

Langer, William L. "The Mechanism of American Foreign Policy." INTERNATIONAL AFFAIRS 24 (July 1948): 319-28.

Lee, D.E. "State Department and Foreign Policy." PROCEEDINGS OF THE AMERICAN ACADEMY OF POLITICAL AND SOCIAL SCIENCE 25 (May 1952): 100-108.

McCleod, Scott. "Security in the Department of State." DEPARTMENT OF STATE BULLETIN 30 (29 March 1954): 469-72.

> McCloud, director of the Department of State's security affairs, played an active role in implementing Senator Joseph R. McCarthy's attack on foreign service officers in the 1950s.

"The Machinery of United States Foreign Affairs." WORLD TODAY 8 (February 1952): 52-60.

Maddox, William P. "Foreign Service Institute of the U.S. Department of State." HIGHER EDUCATION 4 (15 October 1947): 37-40.

Martin, Thomas M. "Due Process Invades Foggy Bottom." PROGRESSIVE 38 (March 1974): 13.

Miller, August C. "The New State Department." AMERICAN JOURNAL OF INTERNATIONAL LAW 33 (July 1939): 500-518.

Morgenstern, Oskar. "Decision Theory and the State Department." FOREIGN SERVICE JOURNAL 37 (December 1960): 19-22.

Norton, Henry K. "Foreign Office Organization." ANNALS OF THE AMERICAN ACADEMY OF POLITICAL AND SOCIAL SCIENCE 143, supplement (May 1929): 1-83.

"Operations of the Department of State in Connection with Programs of the Economic Cooperation Administration." DEPARTMENT OF STATE BULLETIN 18 (30 May 1948): 718-19.

"Organization of the Department of State." DEPARTMENT OF STATE BULLETIN 20 (26 June 1949): 835.

Osborne, John. "Is the State Department Manageable?" FORTUNE, March 1957, pp. 110-12, 267-68, 270, 272, 276, 278.

Patterson, Richard S. "The Seal of the Department of State." DEPARTMENT OF STATE BULLETIN 21 (12 December 1949): 894-96.

> Also see Department of State's publications on the official seal, p. 199 and last section of this chapter, pp. 238-39.

Department of State & Diplomatic Service

Peurifoy, John E. "The Department of State: A Reflection of U.S. Leadership." DEPARTMENT OF STATE BULLETIN 21 (31 October 1949): 671-74.

Richardson, Elliot L. "The Office of the Under Secretary for Western Hemisphere Affairs." DEPARTMENT OF STATE BULLETIN 62 (13 April 1970): 498-99.

Rigert, Joseph C. "The Office of the Assistant Secretary of State for Congressional Relations: A Study of an Aspect of Executive-Legislative Relations in the Formulation of Foreign Policy." Masters thesis, Georgetown University, 1959.

Robinson, James A. "Process Satisfaction and Policy Approval in State Department-Congressional Relations." AMERICAN JOURNAL OF SOCIOLOGY 67 (November 1961): 278-83.

Scott, Andrew M. "Environmental Change and Organizational Adaptation: The Problem of the State Department." FOREIGN SERVICE JOURNAL 47 (June 1970): 25-27, 63.

_____. "The Department of State: Formal Organization and Informal Culture." INTERNATIONAL STUDIES QUARTERLY 13 (Spring 1969): 1-18.

Spiers, Ronald I. "International Security Affairs and the Department of State." DEPARTMENT OF STATE BULLETIN 66 (24 April 1972): 591-97.

"Streamlining the Department of State--Process of Making Policy and Translating It Into Action." DEPARTMENT OF STATE BULLETIN 22 (13 Feburary 1950): 235-37.

Stuart, Graham H. "A Streamlined State Department." CURRENT HISTORY 18 (February 1950): 71-75.

Stupak, Ronald J., and McLellan, David S. "The Bankruptcy of Super-Activism and the Resurgence of Diplomacy and the Department of State." FOREIGN SERVICE JOURNAL 52 (April 1975): 23-28.

Sylvester, John, Jr. "Will Candor Survive the Leaking Ship of State?" FOREIGN SERVICE JOURNAL 52 (June 1975): 15-16, 32.

Turpin, William N. "Foreign Relations, Yes; Foreign Policy, No." FOREIGN POLICY 8 (Fall 1972): 50-61.

Tuthill, John W. "Operation Topsy." FOREIGN POLICY 8 (Fall 1972): 62-85.

U.S. Department of State. "The Responsibility of the Office of Assistant Secretary of State for Occupied Areas." In AMERICAN POLICY IN OCCU- PIED AREAS, Department of State Publication 2794, pp. 1-2. Washington, D.C.: Government Printing Office, 1947.

Vogelsang, Sandy. "Feminism in Foggy Bottom: Man's World, Woman's Place?" FOREIGN SERVICE JOURNAL 49 (August 1972): 4, 6, 8, 10-11.

Webb, James E. "Department of State." AIR AFFAIRS 3 (Autumn 1949): 34-43.

_____. "U.S. Organization for the Conduct of Foreign Affairs." DEPART- MENT OF STATE BULLETIN 24 (12 February 1951): 273-76.

Yardley, Edward. "Identification Pass System for the Department of State." FOREIGN SERVICE JOURNAL 18 (October 1941): 554-55.

FOREIGN SERVICE—DIPLOMATIC CORPS

From the outset, the separate diplomatic and consular services of the United States consisted of officials appointed on the basis of the spoils system. Al- though some progress was made by Presidents Theodore Roosevelt and William Howard Taft to introduce the merit principle by executive order, it was not until 1915 that Congress passed a law to establish a career foreign service founded on merit and to systematize personnel classification. The Rogers Act of 1924 amalgamated the separate diplomatic and consular functions and per- sonnel, and subsequent enactments produced additional administrative refine- ments. The current diplomatic and consular personnel system is based on the Foreign Service Act of 1946, as amended and supplemented. Matters of post- World War II administrative and personnel reorganization and reform are dealt with in the following section.

While only occasional literary interest--other than official reports and personal memoirs--was devoted to the matter of diplomatic personnel prior to the twen- tieth century, a substantial quantity of literature has emerged in recent de- cades, especially since World War II. Subjects of concern include such mat- ters as the nature of the personnel systems of the Department of State, the diplomatic and consular services, and other agencies (including those concerned with foreign assistance and information programs), the dichotomy of profession- als as against political appointees, and of generalists versus specialists, the background, qualities, and training of appointees, other standard matters of personnel administration (such as appointment, promotion, salaries and perqui- sites, dismissal, and retirement), and reform and improvement. Aside from some in-house reports that are not widely available, more general studies and memoir commentary listed elsewhere in this compilation, materials on the con- sular function treated in chapter 17, and those on specialized attaches, presi- dential special representatives, and overseas missions which are listed in other chapters, the following illustrate the growing body of resource material on the Foreign Service. Summary guidance is furnished in:

"Bibliography: The American Foreign Service—Its Past, Present, and Future." FOREIGN SERVICE JOURNAL 31 (March 1954): 58-63.

> Consists of sections on history, administration (general, regulations, and training), and activities, listing some 150 references to books, articles, and reports.

Additional guidance, on the issue of the generalist vs. the specialist in the diplomatic service, is available in:

Carlsen, Charles R., ed. BIBLIOGRAPHY: THE GENERALIST AND THE SPECIALIST IN THE U.S. FOREIGN SERVICE. Minneapolis: University of Minnesota, 1965. 57 p.

> Contains annotated bibliography of articles appearing in the DEPARTMENT OF STATE NEWS LETTER, 1960-65, and the FOREIGN SERVICE JOURNAL, 1950-65, arranged chronologically, with general bibliography appended.

Legislation on the Foreign Service

The legal basis of the contemporary professional Foreign Service of the United States consists of the Rogers Act (1924), the Moses-Linthicum Act (1931), and the Foreign Service Act (1946). Among other things, the Rogers Act amalgamated the former diplomatic and consular services into a single, professionalized Foreign Service, and the Moses-Linthicum Act introduced a number of changes respecting organization, management, classification, compensation, and other matters. The Foreign Service Act of 1946, as subsequently amended, constitutes the organic law of the American Foreign Service today.

General background on the historical development of legislation governing the diplomatic and consular services of the United States may be found in the following.

Barnes, William, and Morgan, John Heath. THE FOREIGN SERVICE OF THE UNITED STATES: ORIGINS, DEVELOPMENT, AND FUNCTIONS. Washington, D.C.: Government Printing Office, 1961.

> Part II, "The 19th-Century Foreign Service, 1829-1897," pp. 67-152.

> Part III, "Establishment of the Career Principle, 1897-1917," pp. 153-86.

> Part IV, "Career Consolidation—From World War I to World War II," pp. 187-238.

Plischke, Elmer. CONDUCT OF AMERICAN DIPLOMACY. 3d ed. Princeton, N.J.: Van Nostrand, 1963.

"The Foreign Service," pp. 223-61.

Stuart, Graham H. AMERICAN DIPLOMATIC AND CONSULAR PRACTICE. 2d ed. New York: Appleton-Century-Crofts, 1952.

Chapter 5, "The Development of the American Foreign Service," pp. 81-97.

Chapter 6, "Development of the Foreign Service Since World War I," pp. 98-113.

_____. THE DEPARTMENT OF STATE: A HISTORY OF ITS ORGANIZATION, PROCEDURE, AND PERSONNEL. New York: Macmillan, 1949.

"An Improved Foreign Service," pp. 271-72.

"Maladministration of the Rogers Act," pp. 287-88.

"Kellogg Supports the Foreign Service," pp. 288-89.

"Secretary Byrnes Resigns," pp. 438-41.

Documentary resources concerning the enactment of basic twentieth-century legislation on the diplomatic and consular services of the United States consist of the following (given in chronological sequence)--also see section on "Reorganization and Reform" below.

HEARINGS AND REPORTS

U.S. Congress. House of Representatives. Committee on Foreign Affairs. HEARINGS ON H.R. 17 and H.R. 6357 FOR THE REORGANIZATION AND IMPROVEMENT OF THE FOREIGN SERVICE OF THE UNITED STATES AND FOR OTHER PURPOSES, JANUARY 14-18, 1924. 68th Cong., 1st sess. Washington, D.C.: Government Printing Office, 1924. 226 p.

_____. REORGANIZATION AND IMPROVEMENT OF THE FOREIGN SERVICE OF THE UNITED STATES. A REPORT TO ACCOMPANY HOUSE RESOLUTION 6357. House Report, no. 157. 68th Cong., 1st sess. Washington, D.C.: Government Printing Office, 1924. 18 p.

_____. REORGANIZATION OF THE FOREIGN SERVICE. House Report, no. 2508 to accompany H.R. 6967. 79th Cong., 2d sess. Washington, D.C.: Government Printing Office, 1946. 230 p.

Provides texts of superseded legislation and justification for new enactment.

_____. THE FOREIGN SERVICE ACT OF 1946, AS AMENDED TO OCTOBER 17, 1960. Committee Print. 86th Cong., 2d sess. Washington, D.C.: Government Printing Office, 1960. 200 p.

Department of State & Diplomatic Service

LEGISLATIVE ENACTMENTS

Rogers Act, May 24, 1924   43 U.S. STATUTES AT LARGE 140-46

Moses Linthicum Act, February 23, 1931   46 U.S. STATUTES AT LARGE 1207-17

Foreign Service Act, August 13, 1946   60 U.S. STATUTES AT LARGE 999-1040

CURRENT LEGAL PRESCRIPTIONS

22 U.S. CODE, Chapter 14

LEGISLATION ON FOREIGN RELATIONS--WITH EXPLANATORY NOTES. Chapter on Department of State.

> Gives updated legislation, with supplementary executive orders, and presents comprehensive chronology of citations to the Foreign Service Act of 1946, with its amendments. Full citation to this source is given in chapter 22, p. 453.

Books, Monographs, and Reports

Except for a few studies, such as those of Lay (1925) and Childs (1948), and a number of official reports, little comprehensive literature on the diplomatic corps and the Foreign Service of the United States was published prior to 1950. Since 1960, however, a substantial quantity of such studies (as well as journal literature listed in the following subsection) have been produced. These include basic volumes on diplomats (Waters), analytical surveys of ranking emissaries, largely chiefs of mission (Merli and Wilson, Plischke, and Spaulding), and a series of general studies on the founding and nature of the Foreign Service (Barnes and Morgan, Blancke, Shade, Steiner, Van Dyne, Weil, Werking, and several congressional and Department of State reports). Considerable interest is also devoted to the fundamental matter of careers in the diplomatic service (Angel, Davis, Delaney, Harr, Lavine, Lisagor and Higgins, Neal, and Sapell), as well as the more specific matters of personnel systems and problems (Bahti, Harr, Jones, and Moser), recruitment and training (Fielder and Harris, Sayre and Thurber, and Schulzinger), and diplomatic qualities and character (Andrews, Creaghe, McKibbin, and Walther). Other materials concern more specialized matters, such as studies on women in foreign affairs (Calkin), particular groups of diplomatic officers (Kahn), specialized functional roles (Cardozo and Moss), and the politics of recalling and withholding emissaries (Lent). In addition, some of the items referred to in chapters 2 and 3, as well as much memoir literature, listed in part IV, provide useful resources on the diplomatic service of the United States and its members.

Andrews, Russell P. THE REAMERICANIZATION OF FOREIGN SERVICE OFFICERS. Syracuse, N.Y.: Inter-University Case Program, 1970.

Angel, Juvenal Londono. CAREERS IN THE DIPLOMATIC SERVICE. 4th ed. New York: World Trade Academy Press, 1961. 26 p.

Bahti, James H. "Personnel Integration in the Foreign Service." Ph.D. dissertation, University of Michigan, 1959. 140 p.

Barnes, William, and Morgan, John Heath. THE FOREIGN SERVICE OF THE UNITED STATES: ORIGINS, DEVELOPMENT, AND FUNCTIONS. Washington, D.C.: Government Printing Office, 1961. 430 p. Bibliog.

Blancke, W. Wendell. THE FOREIGN SERVICE OF THE UNITED STATES. New York: Praeger, 1969. 286 p.

Bohlen, Charles E. THE FOREIGN SERVICE AND THE PANORAMA OF CHANGE. Department of State Publication 7223. Washington, D.C.: Government Printing Office. 1961. 18 p. Also in DEPARTMENT OF STATE BULLETIN 44 (19 June 1961): 964-69.

Calkin, Homer L. WOMEN IN THE DEPARTMENT OF STATE: THEIR ROLE IN AMERICAN FOREIGN AFFAIRS. 2d ed. Washington, D.C.: Government Printing Office, 1978. 307 p.

> A history of women in the Department of State and the Foreign Service, with charts and tables.

Cardozo, Michael H. DIPLOMATS IN INTERNATIONAL COOPERATION: STEPCHILDREN OF THE FOREIGN SERVICE. Ithaca, N.Y.: Cornell University Press, 1962. 142 p.

Childs, James Rives. AMERICAN FOREIGN SERVICE. New York: Holt, 1948. 261 p.

Creaghe, John St. George. "Personal Qualities and Effective Diplomatic Negotiations." Ph.D. dissertation, University of Maryland, 1965. 314 p. Bibliog.

Davis, Nathaniel P. FEW DULL MOMENTS: A FOREIGN SERVICE CAREER. Philadelphia: Dunlap, 1967. 158 p.

Delaney, Robert Finley. YOUR FUTURE IN THE FOREIGN SERVICE. New York: Richards Rosen, 1961. 158 p.

Fielder, Frances, and Harris, Godfrey. THE QUEST FOR FOREIGN AFFAIRS OFFICERS--THEIR RECRUITMENT AND SELECTION. New York: Carnegie Endowment, 1966. 63 p.

Harr, John Ensor. THE ANATOMY OF THE FOREIGN SERVICE: A STATISTICAL PROFILE. New York: Carnegie Endowment, 1965. 89 p.

_____. THE DEVELOPMENT OF CAREERS IN THE FOREIGN SERVICE. New York: Carnegie Endowment, 1965. 104 p.

_____. THE PROFESSIONAL DIPLOMAT. Princeton, N.J.: Princeton University Press, 1969. 404 p. Bibliog.

_____. "The Professional Diplomat and the New Diplomacy." Ph.D. dissertation, University of California (Berkeley), 1967. 364 p.

Hilton, Ralph. WORLDWIDE MISSION: THE STORY OF THE UNITED STATES FOREIGN SERVICE. New York: World, 1970. 256 p.

Jones, Arthur G. THE EVOLUTION OF PERSONNEL SYSTEMS FOR U.S. FOREIGN AFFAIRS: A HISTORY OF REFORM EFFORTS. New York: Carnegie Endowment, 1964. 136 p.

Kahn, Ely J., Jr. THE CHINA HANDS: AMERICA'S FOREIGN SERVICE OFFICERS AND WHAT BEFELL THEM. New York: Viking, 1975. 337 p. Bibliog.

Lavine, David. OUTPOSTS OF ADVENTURE: THE STORY OF THE FOREIGN SERVICE. Garden City, N.Y.: Doubleday, 1966. 84 p.

Lay, Tracy H. THE FOREIGN SERVICE OF THE UNITED STATES. New York: Prentice-Hall, 1925. 438 p.

Lent, Ernest S. THE RECALL OR WITHHOLDING OF U.S. AMBASSADORS TO INFLUENCE OTHER GOVERNMENTS OR EXPRESS DISAPPROVAL OF THEIR ACTIONS: SOME SPECIFIC CASES. Washington, D.C.: U.S. Library of Congress, 1969. 12 p.

Linehan, Patrick E. THE FOREIGN SERVICE PERSONNEL SYSTEM: AN ORGANIZATIONAL ANALYSIS. Boulder, Colo.: Westview, 1976. 401 p. Bibliog.

Analysis based on interviews of over 300 Foreign Service officers respecting the needs of the Foreign Service organization and its personnel.

Lisagor, Peter, and Higgins, Marguerite. OVERTIME IN HEAVEN: ADVENTURES IN THE FOREIGN SERVICE. Garden City, N.Y.: Doubleday, 1964. 275 p.

McKibbin, Carroll R. "The Career Structure and Success in the U.S. Foreign Service." Ph.D. dissertation, University of Kansas, 1968. 192 p.

Macomber, William. THE ANGELS' GAME: A HANDBOOK OF MODERN DIPLOMACY. New York: Stein and Day, 1975. 225 p.

Mennis, Bernard. AMERICAN FOREIGN POLICY OFFICIALS: WHO ARE THEY AND WHAT ARE THEY? Columbus: Ohio State University Press, 1971. 210 p. Bibliog.

Merli, Frank J., and Wilson, Theodore A. MAKERS OF AMERICAN DIPLO-MACY: FROM BENJAMIN FRANKLIN TO HENRY KISSINGER. New York: Scribner, 1974. 728 p.

Moser, Martin W. "The Personnel System of the Foreign Service of the United States." Ph.D. dissertation, University of Maryland, 1952. 311 p. Bibliog.

Moss, Michael Alan. "The Ambassador as Advisor and Advocate." Ph.D. dissertation, Yale University, 1966. 240 p.

Neal, Harry Edward. YOUR CAREER IN FOREIGN SERVICE. New York: Messner, 1965. 191 p.

Plischke, Elmer. UNITED STATES DIPLOMATS AND THEIR MISSIONS: A PROFILE OF AMERICAN DIPLOMATIC EMISSARIES SINCE 1778. Washington, D.C.: American Enterprise Institute, 1975. 201 p.

_____, ed. MODERN DIPLOMACY: THE ART AND THE ARTISANS. Washington, D.C.: American Enterprise Institute, 1979. 456 p. Bibliog.

Rinden, Robert W., and Nadler, S.I. LIFE AND LOVE IN THE FOREIGN SERVICE. Washington, D.C.: Foreign Service Journal, 1969. 60 p. Photos.
   Spoof providing series of photographs with humorous captions.

Roudybush, Franklin. AN ANALYSIS OF THE EDUCATIONAL BACKGROUND AND EXPERIENCE OF U.S. FOREIGN SERVICE OFFICERS. Washington, D.C.: George Washington University Press, 1944. 71 p.

Rubottom, Roy R., Jr. THE PEOPLE WHO WAGE THE PEACE. AN ACCOUNT OF THE HISTORY AND MISSION OF THE FOREIGN SERVICE. Washington, D.C.: Government Printing Office, 1958. 15 p.

Sakell, Achilles Nicholas. CAREERS IN THE FOREIGN SERVICE. New York: Walck, 1962. 118 p. Bibliog.

Sayre, Wallace S., and Thurber, Clarence E. TRAINING FOR SPECIALIZED MISSION PERSONNEL. Chicago: Public Administration Service, 1952. 85 p.

Schulzinger, Robert D. "The Making of the Diplomatic Mind: The Training, Outlook, and Style of United States Foreign Service Officers, 1906-1928." Ph.D. dissertation, Yale University, 1971. 362 p.

_____. THE MAKING OF THE DIPLOMATIC MIND: THE TRAINING, OUT-LOOK, AND STYLE OF UNITED STATES FOREIGN SERVICE OFFICERS, 1908-1931. Middletown, Conn.: Wesleyan University Press, 1975. 237 p. Bibliog.

Shade, Chloris. FOREIGN SERVICE. 2d ed. Chicago: Morgan, Dillon, 1940. 23 p.

Spaulding, E. Wilder. AMBASSADORS ORDINARY AND EXTRAORDINARY. Washington, D.C.: Public Affairs Press, 1961. 302 p. Bibliog.

Steiner, Zara S. PRESENT PROBLEMS OF THE FOREIGN SERVICE. Princeton, N.J.: Center of International Studies, Princeton University, 1961. 57 p.

U.S. Congress. House of Representatives. Committee on Foreign Affairs. THE FOREIGN SERVICE: BASIC INFORMATION ON ORGANIZATION, ADMINISTRATION, AND PERSONNEL. 84th Cong., 1st sess. Washington, D.C.: Government Printing Office, 1955. 178 p.

_____. FOREIGN SERVICE OF THE UNITED STATES. Hearings. 68th Cong., 1st sess. Washington, D.C.: Government Printing Office, 1924. 226 p.

On Act of 1924.

U.S. Congress. Senate. Committee on Foreign Relations. FOREIGN SERVICE OF THE UNITED STATES. 69th Cong., 1st sess. Washington, D.C.: Government Printing Office, 1926. 6 p.

_____. RECRUITMENT AND TRAINING FOR THE FOREIGN SERVICE OF THE UNITED STATES. 85th Cong., 2d sess. Washington, D.C.: Government Printing Office, 1958. 197 p.

U.S. Congress. Senate. Committee on Government Operations. Subcommittee on National Security and International Operations. SPECIALISTS AND GENERALISTS: A SELECTION OF READINGS. 90th Cong., 2d sess. Washington, D.C.: Government Printing Office, 1968. 71 p.

Contains thirty readings by individual authors.

U.S. Congress. Senate. Committee on Government Operations. Subcommittee on National Security Staffing and Operations. ADMINISTRATION OF NATIONAL SECURITY: THE AMERICAN AMBASSADOR. 88th Cong., 2d sess. Washington, D.C.: Government Printing Office, 1964. 16 p.

_____. THE AMBASSADOR AND THE PROBLEM OF COORDINATION. 88th Cong., 1st sess. Washington, D.C.: Government Printing Office, 1963. 159 p.

U.S. Department of State. THE AMERICAN AMBASSADOR. Washington, D.C.: Government Printing Office, 1957. 22 p.

_____. CAREER OPPORTUNITIES IN THE U.S. FOREIGN SERVICE. Washington, D.C.: Government Printing Office, 1958. 22 p.

_____. THE FOREIGN SERVICE OFFICER: A CAREER IN THE U.S. DEPARTMENT OF STATE. Washington, D.C.: Government Printing Office, 1963. 36 p.

_____. THE FOREIGN SERVICE OF THE SEVENTIES. Washington, D.C.: Government Printing Office, 1970. 36 p.

_____. THE FOREIGN SERVICE OF THE UNITED STATES. Washington, D.C.: Government Printing Office, 1958. 47 p.

_____. SOME FACTS ABOUT THE FOREIGN SERVICE: A SHORT ACCOUNT OF ITS ORGANIZATION AND DUTIES TOGETHER WITH PERTINENT LAWS AND REGULATIONS. Washington, D.C.: Government Printing Office, 1950. 70 p.

_____. THE U.S. FOREIGN SERVICE: A CAREER FOR AMERICANS. Washington, D.C.: Government Printing Office, 1952. 23 p.

Published from time to time since the 1930s under varying titles.

Van Dyne, Frederick. OUR FOREIGN SERVICE: THE "ABC" OF AMERICAN DIPLOMACY. Rochester, N.Y.: Lawyers Cooperative, 1909. 316 p.

Walther, Regis. ORIENTATIONS AND BEHAVIORAL STYLES OF FOREIGN SERVICE OFFICERS. New York: Carnegie Endowment, 1965. 52 p.

Waters, Maurice. THE AD HOC DIPLOMAT. The Hague: Nijhoff, 1963. 233 p. Bibliog.

Weil, Martin. A PRETTY GOOD CLUB: THE FOUNDING FATHERS OF THE U.S. FOREIGN SERVICE. New York: Norton, 1978. 313 p.

Werking, Richard Hume. THE MASTER ARCHITECTS: BUILDING THE UNITED STATES FOREIGN SERVICE, 1890-1913. Lexington: University of Kentucky Press, 1978. 340 p.

Chapters, Essays, and Journal Literature

Chapters on the Foreign Service and diplomatic personnel are to be found in a number of more general studies, including the following:

Barber, Hollis W. FOREIGN POLICIES OF THE UNITED STATES. New York: Dryden, 1953.

> Especially chapter 3.

Briggs, Ellis O. ANATOMY OF DIPLOMACY: THE ORIGIN AND EXECUTION OF AMERICAN FOREIGN POLICY. New York: McKay, 1968.

> Especially chapters 5, 7, and 8.

Chamberlain, Lawrence H., and Snyder, Richard C. AMERICAN FOREIGN POLICY. New York: Rinehart, 1948.

> Especially chapter 7.

Johnson, Richard A. THE ADMINISTRATION OF UNITED STATES FOREIGN POLICY. Austin: University of Texas Press, 1971.

> Especially chapter 10.

McCamy, James L. THE ADMINISTRATION OF AMERICAN FOREIGN AFFAIRS. New York: Knopf, 1950.

> Especially chapters 8 and 9.

Plischke, Elmer. CONDUCT OF AMERICAN DIPLOMACY. 3d ed. Princeton, N.J.: Van Nostrand, 1967.

> Especially chapter 8.

Snyder, Richard C., and Furniss, Edgar S., Jr. AMERICAN FOREIGN POLICY: FORMULATION, PRINCIPLES, AND PROGRAMS. New York: Rinehart, 1954.

> Especially chapter 8.

Stuart, Graham H. AMERICAN DIPLOMATIC AND CONSULAR PRACTICE. 2d ed. New York: Appleton-Century-Crofts, 1952.

> Especially chapters 5 and 6.

Additional short accounts, often of a specialized and limited nature, are provided in a variety of essays and journal articles, as follows:

"Academic Training For the Foreign Service." DEPARTMENT OF STATE BULLETIN 39 (3 November 1958): 689-92.

> Remarks by President Eisenhower and Under Secretary of State Robert Murphy.

"AFSA [American Foreign Service Association] Recognized as Exclusive Representative for Foreign Service Employees." DEPARTMENT OF STATE NEWSLETTER 142 (February 1973): 15.

Allen, George V. "The Utility of a Trained and Permanent Foreign Service." FOREIGN SERVICE JOURNAL 31 (March 1954): 20-23, 49-50.

Atwater, Elton. "The American Foreign Service Since 1939." AMERICAN JOURNAL OF INTERNATIONAL LAW 41 (January 1947): 73-102.

_____. "Examinations for the American Foreign Service." Washington, D.C.: Digest Press, 1936. 8 p.

Bailey, Thomas A. "A Hall of Fame for American Diplomats." VIRGINIA QUARTERLY REVIEW 36 (Summer 1960): 390-404.

Belmont, Perry. "Ambassadorial Rank for Ministers." CURRENT HISTORY 29 (January 1929): 629-32.

Briggs, Ellis O. "The Sad State of the Department of State: Part I. The Hog-Tied Ambassador." ESQUIRE, September 1963, pp. 100-101.

For part 2 see Mark Epernay below, p. 218.

Brown, R.L. "Rise of the Ambassador." CONTEMPORARY REVIEW 210 (April 1967): 196-200.

Cabot, John M. "Understanding Our Foreign Service." DEPARTMENT OF STATE BULLETIN 30 (8 March 1954): 353-58.

Calvocoressi, P. "The Diplomat." POLITICAL QUARTERLY 28 (October 1957): 352-61.

Cantrell, William A. II. "Culture Shock and the Foreign Service Child." FOREIGN SERVICE JOURNAL 51 (December 1974): 4, 6, 8, 28-29.

Carpenter, W.B. "The Equipment of American Students for Foreign Service." ANNALS OF THE AMERICAN ACADEMY OF POLITICAL AND SOCIAL SCIENCE 122 (November 1925): 124-30.

Carter, Kent C. "Development of the Foreign Service Inspection System." FOREIGN SERVICE JOURNAL 51 (January 1974): 18-20, 25.

Charlick, Carl. "Diplomatic Caretaker." FOREIGN SERVICE JOURNAL 32 (October 1955): 20-23, 40, 42, 44, 46.

Churchill, Malcolm. "What Happened to the Career Foreign Service?" FOREIGN SERVICE JOURNAL 47 (December 1970): 38, 50-52.

Clubb, O. Edmund. "The National Security and Our Foreign Service." NATION, 25 December 1954, pp. 544-47.

Cohen, E.M. "Rank Injustice: The Case for Semiautomatic Promotion of Middle Grade Officers [of the Foreign Service]." FOREIGN SERVICE JOURNAL 49 (August 1972): 17-19, 27-28.

Davis, Nathaniel. "Accelerating Promotion [in the Foreign Service]." FOREIGN SERVICE JOURNAL 51 (October 1974): 16-17, 57.

"Department Announces New Emphasis on Foreign Service Recruitment." DEPARTMENT OF STATE BULLETIN 65 (4 October 1971): 350-61.

Elder, R.E. "A Career Service for USIA?" FOREIGN SERVICE JOURNAL 33 (February 1956): 26-27, 40, 42, 44.

Epernay, Mark. "The Sad State of the Department of State: Part II. The Hog-Wild Machine." ESQUIRE, September 1963, pp. 102-103, 151-53.

For part I see Ellis O. Briggs above, p. 217.

Estes, Thomas S. "Executive and Administrative Assignments for FSO's." FOREIGN SERVICE JOURNAL 29 (March 1952): 26, 48.

Felix, David. "Three Suggestions for Strengthening the Foreign Service." FOREIGN SERVICE JOURNAL 32 (December 1955): 30-31, 42-45.

Ford, Gerald R. "Fiftieth Anniversary of the Foreign Service." DEPARTMENT OF STATE BULLETIN 71 (22 July 1974): 145-47.

"Foreign Service Auxiliary." DEPARTMENT OF STATE BULLETIN 5 (11 October 1941): 283-84.

"Forty Years of the Foreign Service, 1924-1964." DEPARTMENT OF STATE NEWSLETTER, no. 39 (July 1964): entire issue.

Fosdick, Dorothy. "For the Foreign Service--Help Wanted." NEW YORK TIMES MAGAZINE, 20 November 1955, pp. 13, 65-69.

Glassman, Jon D. "The Foreign Service Officer: Observer or Advocate?" FOREIGN SERVICE JOURNAL 47 (May 1970): 29-30, 45.

Grew, Joseph C. "Ambassador Grew on the American Foreign Service." FOREIGN SERVICE JOURNAL 13 (December 1936): 649, 694, 696.

Grover, Jack. ". . . None Is Swifter Than These . . . " DEPARTMENT OF STATE FIELD REPORTER 2 (January-February 1954): 6-11.

Halle, Louis J., Jr. "'Policy Making' and the Career Service." FOREIGN SERVICE JOURNAL 30 (September 1953): 31, 48, 50.

Hannah, Norman B. "Craftsmanship and Responsibility: A Restatement of the Generalist-Specialist Problem." FOREIGN SERVICE JOURNAL 39 (April 1962): 21-24.

Harper, Elizabeth J. THE ROLE OF WOMEN IN INTERNATIONAL DIPLO-MACY. Washington, D.C.: U.S. Department of State, 1972. 8 p.

Harvey, George. "Diplomats of Diplomacy." NORTH AMERICAN REVIEW 199 (February 1914): 161-74.

Henderson, Loy. "The Foreign Service--First Line of Defense." DEPARTMENT OF STATE BULLETIN 32 (23 May 1955): 849-53.

_____. "The Foreign Service as a Career." DEPARTMENT OF STATE BUL-LETIN 32 (18 April 1955): 635-40.

Herz, Martin F. "More on Dissent and Loyalty." FOREIGN SERVICE JOUR-NAL 52 (February 1975): 12-14.

Johnson, R.C. "Recruitment and Training for the Foreign Service of the United States." INDIA QUARTERLY 11 (October-December 1955): 376-81.

Kennan, George F. "Diplomacy as a Profession." FOREIGN SERVICE JOUR-NAL 38 (May 1961): 23-26.

_____. "The Future of Our Professional Diplomacy." FOREIGN AFFAIRS 33 (July 1955): 566-86.

_____. "History and Diplomacy as Viewed by a Diplomatist." REVIEW OF POLITICS 18 (April 1956): 170-77.

_____. "The Needs of the Foreign Service." In THE PUBLIC SERVICE AND UNIVERSITY EDUCATION, edited by Joseph E. McClean, pp. 97 ff. Prince-ton, N.J.: Princeton University Press, 1949.

Kryza, E. Gregory, and Knight, William E. "Management in the Foreign Service." FOREIGN SERVICE JOURNAL 52 (March 1975): 16-18.

Laves, Walter H.C. "Increasing the Number of Americans Potentially Available for Foreign Assignments." AMERICAN POLITICAL SCIENCE REVIEW 47 (September 1953): 798-804.

Lenderking, William R. "Dissent, Disloyalty, and Foreign Service Finkism." FOREIGN SERVICE JOURNAL 51 (May 1974): 13-15.

Luce, Clare Boothe. "The Ambassadorial Issue: Professional or Amateur?" FOREIGN AFFAIRS 36 (October 1957): 105-21.

McCamy, James L., and Corrandini, Alessandro. "The People of the State Department and the Foreign Service." AMERICAN POLITICAL SCIENCE REVIEW 47 (December 1954): 1067-82.

McGhee, George C. "The Changing Role of the American Ambassador." DEPARTMENT OF STATE BULLETIN 46 (25 June 1962): 1007-11.

McNair, Clare H. "Women in the Foreign Service." FOREIGN SERVICE JOURNAL 22 (June 1945): 30-31, 46.

Macomber, William B., Jr. "Department Discusses Grievance Procedures for the Foreign Service." DEPARTMENT OF STATE BULLETIN 67 (30 October 1972): 505-15.

Maddox, William P. "The Foreign Service in Transition." FOREIGN AFFAIRS 25 (January 1947): 303-13.

Martin, James V., Jr. "The Quiet Revolution in the Foreign Service." FOREIGN SERVICE JOURNAL 37 (February 1960): 19-22.

Mendershausen, Horst. "The Diplomat's National and Transnational Commitments." FOREIGN SERVICE JOURNAL 47 (February 1970): 20-22, 31-33.

Morris, Roger. "Clientism in the Foreign Service." FOREIGN SERVICE JOURNAL 51 (February 1974): 24-26, 30-31.

Moss, Ambler H. "The Foreign Service Illusion." FOREIGN SERVICE JOURNAL 49 (June 1972): 6, 8, 10, 12.

Nerval, Richard. "My Diplomatic Education." SATURDAY EVENING POST, 10 February 1923, pp. 8-9, 121-22, 125-26; 3 March 1923, pp. 24-25, 61-62, 64, 67; 17 March 1923, pp. 20-21, 157-58, 160-62; 31 March 1923, pp. 14-15, 123, 125-26, 129-30; 7 April 1923, pp. 23, 196-98, 201-2; 28 April 1923, pp. 19, 113-14, 117-18, 121-22; 12 May 1923, pp. 23, 124, 127, 130, 133; 26 May 1923, pp. 19, 177-78, 180-81; 9 June 1923, pp. 11, 77-

78, 80, 83; 23 June 1923, pp. 22–23, 84, 87, 91; 7 July 1923, pp. 17, 124–26, 128–30; 8 September 1923, pp. 24, 65–66, 69–70, 73.

Nixon, Richard M. "President Nixon Delineates Authority of American Ambassadors." DEPARTMENT OF STATE BULLETIN 62 (12 January 1970): 30–31.
   Presidential letter to all U.S. ambassadors.

Osborne, John. "The Importance of Ambassadors." FORTUNE, April 1957, pp. 146–47, 150–51, 184, 186, 189, 190, 192, 194.

_____. "What's the U.S. Foreign Service Worth?" FORTUNE, May 1957, pp. 154–59, 238, 241–42, 244, 247.

Perry, Jack. "The Present Challenge to the Foreign Service." FOREIGN SERVICE JOURNAL 51 (October 1974): 18–20.

Peters, C. Brooks. "Why Not a Foreign Service Career?" READER'S DIGEST, October 1956, pp. 118–20.

Petrie, Charles. "The Place of the Professional in Modern Diplomacy." QUARTERLY REVIEW 605 (July 1955): 295–308.

Plischke, Elmer. "United States Diplomats Since 1778: Bicentennial Review and Future Projection." WORLD AFFAIRS 138 (Winter 1975–76): 205–18.

Rogers, William P. "The New Foreign Service and the Job of Modern Diplomacy." DEPARTMENT OF STATE BULLETIN 65 (13 December 1971): 675–76.

Rossow, Robert. "The Professionalization of the New Diplomacy." WORLD POLITICS 14 (July 1962): 561–75.

Rubin, Seymour J. "American Diplomacy: The Case for Amateurism." YALE REVIEW 45 (March 1956): 321–35.

Stewart, Irvin. "Congress, the Foreign Service, and Department of State: Personnel Problems." AMERICAN POLITICAL SCIENCE REVIEW 24 (May 1930): 355–66.

Stowell, Ellery C. "The Ban on Alien Marriages in the Foreign Service." AMERICAN JOURNAL OF INTERNATIONAL LAW 31 (January 1937): 91–94.

_____. "Cramping Our Foreign Service." AMERICAN JOURNAL OF INTERNATIONAL LAW 29 (April 1935): 314–17.

_____. "Examinations for the American Foreign Service." AMERICAN JOUR-
NAL OF INTERNATIONAL LAW 24 (July 1930): 577-81.

_____. "The Foreign Service School." AMERICAN JOURNAL OF INTER-
NATIONAL LAW 19 (October 1925): 763-68.

Stuart, Graham H. "A Better Foreign Service." CURRENT HISTORY 21
(September 1951): 148-50.

Thayer, Charles W. "Our Ambassadors: An Intimate Appraisal of the Men
and the System." HARPERS MAGAZINE, September 1959, pp. 29-35.

Tracy, Thomas M. "Automation and the Foreign Service." FOREIGN SERVICE
JOURNAL 48 (February 1971): 21-22.

"The U.S. Foreign Service." FORTUNE, July 1946, pp. 81-87, 198-207.

"The U.S. Foreign Service: A Career for Young Americans." DEPARTMENT
OF STATE BULLETIN 26 (7 April 1952): 549-50.

Ward, Paul V. "Performance Evaluation: The Annual Inventory." FOREIGN
SERVICE JOURNAL 51 (October 1974): 29-31, 52.

Warwick, Donald P. "Performance Appraisal and Promotions in the Foreign
Service." FOREIGN SERVICE JOURNAL 47 (July 1970): 37-41, 45.

Welch, Holmes. "The Real Life of the Foreign Service Officer." HARPER'S
MAGAZINE, March 1962, pp. 82-85.

Whitney, R.F. "State Express." NEW YORK TIMES MAGAZINE, 25 January
1948, pp. 22-24.
    On diplomatic courier service.

Williams, Carman C. "The Wasted Resource: Foreign Service Wives." FOR-
EIGN SERVICE JOURNAL 52 (May 1975): 6-7, 20-21.

Woodward, Clark H. "Relations Between the Navy and the Foreign Service."
AMERICAN JOURNAL OF INTERNATIONAL LAW 33 (April 1939): 283-91.

Wriston, Henry M. "Young Men and the Foreign Service." FOREIGN AF-
FAIRS 33 (October 1954): 28-42.

Zorthian, Barry. "A Press Relations Doctrine for the Foreign Service." FOR-
EIGN SERVICE JOURNAL 48 (February 1971): 20-23, 55-56.

REORGANIZATION AND REFORM

Since World War I and the establishment of the professional Foreign Service, considerable official, quasiofficial, and unofficial attention has been paid to matters of government organization and reorganization, relationship of the Department of State with other administrative agencies, diplomatic personnel and the career Foreign Service, and structural and personnel reform. A number of surveys of these issues and of the literature pertaining to them have been published. General historical development is traced in the following older studies:

Plischke, Elmer. CONDUCT OF AMERICAN DIPLOMACY. New York: Van Nostrand, 1950. 3d ed. Princeton, N.J.: Van Nostrand, 1967.

> Chapter 6, "The Department of State--Development and Organization," pp. 164-97.

> Chapter 7, "Department of State Functions," pp. 198-222.

> Chapter 8, "The Foreign Service," pp. 223-61.

Stuart, Graham H. AMERICAN DIPLOMATIC AND CONSULAR PRACTICE. New York: Appleton-Century-Crofts, 1936. 2d ed. New York: Appleton-Century-Crofts, 1952.

> Chapter 2, "The Department of State--I," pp. 18-37.

> Chapter 3, "The Department of State--II," pp. 38-61.

> Chapter 4, "The Department of State--III," pp. 62-80.

> Chapter 5, "The Development of the American Foreign Service," pp. 81-97.

> Chapter 6, "Development of the Foreign Service Since World War I," pp. 98-113.

_____. THE DEPARTMENT OF STATE: A HISTORY OF ITS ORGANIZATION, PROCEDURE, AND PERSONNEL. New York: Macmillan, 1949. 517 p.

Several others concentrate more precisely on reorganization and reform, and on the literature relating to them, as follows.

Bacchus, William I. "Diplomacy for the 70s: An Afterview and Appraisal." AMERICAN POLITICAL SCIENCE REVIEW 68 (June 1974): 736-48.

> Primarily concerned with reorganization and reform in the early 1970s, but also lists investigations and reports for the period from the early 1950s.

Ball, Harris H., Jr. "An Examination of the Major Efforts for Organizational

Effectiveness in the Department of State from 1924 to 1971." Master's thesis, George Washington University, 1971. 164 p.

> Covers the period from the Rogers Act to the Macomber management reforms.

Dangerfield, Royden J. "Studies in the Administration of U.S. Foreign Affairs." PUBLIC ADMINISTRATION REVIEW 11 (August 1951): 275-82.

> Comprehensive review of three studies on administration of foreign affairs published in 1950 and 1951, with reference to other studies on the subject of administrative reform.

Jones, Arthur G. THE EVOLUTION OF PERSONNEL SYSTEMS FOR U.S. FOREIGN AFFAIRS. A HISTORY OF REFORM EFFORTS. Foreign Affairs Personnel Studies. New York: Carnegie Endowment, 1964. 136 p.

> Primarily concerned with personnel reform in the twentieth century to the mid-1960's. See also p. 230.

Macmahon, Arthur W. ADMINISTRATION IN FOREIGN AFFAIRS. University: University of Alabama Press, 1953. 275 p.

_____. "The Administration of Foreign Affairs." AMERICAN POLITICAL SCIENCE REVIEW 45 (September 1951): 836-66.

> Concerned with reorganization and reform, and literature pertaining to them, for immediate post-World War II period. Also, see additional citations of Macmahon contributions listed below, p. 234.

_____. "International Policy and Governmental Structure." PROCEEDINGS OF THE AMERICAN PHILOSOPHICAL SOCIETY 92 (October 1948): 217-27.

Reorganization Plans and Proposals

The following is a summary list of major twentieth-century official, quasiofficial, and unofficial reviews of foreign relations administrative reorganization and personnel reform, with dates of reports. Most of these reviews are restricted to the Department of State and the Foreign Service, although some-- such as the Hoover Commission, the White House Personnel Task Force, the Jackson Subcommittees of the Senate Committee on Government Operations, and the President's Task Force on Government Organization--are broader in scope. This list does not include the Foreign Service Act of 1946 or individual executive reorganization orders.

National Civil Service Reform League	1919
Commission of Inquiry on Public Service Personnel	1935
President's Committee on Administrative Management	1937

Department of State & Diplomatic Service

Bureau of the Budget	1945
Commission on Organization of the Executive Branch of the Government (First Hoover Commission)	1949
Secretary of State's Advisory Group on Amalgamation of the Department of State and Foreign Service	1949
Secretary of State's Advisory Committee on Personnel (Rowe Committee)	1950
Brookings Institution (first report)	1951
Woodrow Wilson Foundation (Elliott group report)	1952
Department of State's Public Committee on Personnel (Wriston Committee)	1954
White House Personnel Task Force	1954
Commission on Organization of the Executive Branch of the Government (Second Hoover Commission)	1955
Syracuse University	1959
Brookings Institution (second report)	1960
Jackson Subcommittee of Senate Committee on Government Operations	1961
Committee on Foreign Affairs Personnel (Herter Committee)	1962
Jackson Subcommittee of Senate Committee on Government Operations	1965
Carnegie Institution	1964–65
Department of State (Crockett Reforms)	1966
Maxwell Taylor Task Forces	1966
Brookings Institution (Third report)	1966
President's Task Force on Government Organization (Heineman Task Force)	1967
American Foreign Service Association	1968
Institute for Defense Analysis (Keith C. Clark and Laurence J. Legere)	1969
Department of State Management Reform Program (Macomber Program)	1970
Commission on the Organization of the Government for the Conduct of Foreign Policy (Murphy Commission)	1975

The following, listed in chronological sequence, constitute the reports on these reorganization and reform reviews, a number of which, intended for internal governmental use, were not published. Selected additional materials, largely official, although not involving separate or special agency consideration, are also included.

National Civil Service Reform League. REPORT ON THE FOREIGN SERVICE. New York: 1919. 322 p.

Commission of Inquiry on Public Service Personnel. BETTER GOVERNMENT PERSONNEL: REPORT OF THE COMMISSION OF INQUIRY ON PUBLIC SERVICE PERSONNEL. New York: McGraw-Hill, 1935. 86 p.

President's Committee on Administrative Management. PERSONNEL ADMINIS-TRATION IN THE FEDERAL SERVICE. Washington, D.C.: Government Print-ing Office, 1937.

U.S. Bureau of the Budget. "The Organization and Administration of the Department of State." 15 August 1945.

> Unpublished memorandum submitted at the request of Secretary of State James F. Byrnes by the director of the budget.

Foster, Andrew B. "Examination of the Proposal to Combine the Foreign Ser-vice and the Departmental Service." 14 September 1945.

> Unpublished memorandum concerning amalgamating Department of State and Foreign Service personnel systems.

Chapin, Selden. "A Plan for a Single Service Under the Secretary of State." 31 October 1945.

> Unpublished memorandum concerning amalgamating Department of State and Foreign Service personnel systems.

Nelson, O.L. REPORT ON THE ORGANIZATION OF THE DEPARTMENT OF STATE. Washington, D.C.: U.S. Department of State, 1946. 89 p.

U.S. Congress. House of Representatives. Committee on Foreign Affairs. REORGANIZATION OF THE FOREIGN SERVICE. 79th Cong., 2d sess. Washington, D.C.: Government Printing Office, 1946. 230 p.

> Contains texts of superseded legislation and explanation of bill enacted as the Foreign Service Act of 1946.

Peurifoy, John E. "Reorganization of the State Department." 6 May 1948.

> Memorandum to Secretary of State George C. Marshall.

Stein, Harold. THE FOREIGN SERVICE ACT OF 1946. New York: Commit-tee on Public Administration Cases, 1949. 153 p. Also in his PUBLIC AD-MINISTRATION AND POLICY DEVELOPMENT, pp. 661-737. New York: Harcourt, Brace and World, 1952.

> Unofficial analysis.

Brookings Institution. GOVERNMENTAL MECHANISM FOR THE CONDUCT OF UNITED STATES FOREIGN RELATIONS. Washington, D.C.: Brookings Institution, 1949. 58 p. Bibliog.

Unofficial analysis, prepared under direction of Leo Pasvolsky.

Bundy, Harvey H., and Rogers, James G. THE ORGANIZATION OF THE GOVERNMENT FOR THE CONDUCT OF FOREIGN AFFAIRS: A REPORT WITH RECOMMENDATIONS PREPARED FOR THE COMMISSION ON ORGANIZATION OF THE EXECUTIVE BRANCH OF THE GOVERNMENT. Washington, D.C.: Government Printing Office, 1949. 134 p.

Commission on Organization of the Executive Branch of the Government (Hoover Commission). FOREIGN AFFAIRS. Washington, D.C.: Government Printing Office, 1949. 77 p.

General report to Congress of first Hoover Commission.

_____. TASK FORCE REPORT ON FOREIGN AFFAIRS (APPENDIX H). Washington, D.C.: Government Printing Office, 1949. 134 p.

Specialized report prepared by task force headed by Harvey H. Bundy and James Grafton Rogers. Also useful are the mimeographed staff studies and other papers prepared by the task force.

U.S. Congress. House of Representatives. Committee on Foreign Affairs. TO STRENGTHEN AND IMPROVE THE ORGANIZATION AND ADMINISTRATION OF THE DEPARTMENT OF STATE. Hearings. 81st Cong., 1st sess. Washington, D.C.: Government Printing Office, 1949. 80 p.

_____. REORGANIZATION OF THE DEPARTMENT OF STATE. 81st Cong., 1st sess. Washington, D.C.: Government Printing Office, 1949. 17 p.

U.S. Department of State. FACTS AND ISSUES RELATING TO THE AMALGAMATION OF THE DEPARTMENT OF STATE AND THE FOREIGN SERVICE. Washington, D.C.: 1949.

Prepared for secretary of state's Advisory Group on Amalgamation.

U.S. Secretary of State's Advisory Committee on Personnel. AN IMPROVED PERSONNEL SYSTEM FOR THE CONDUCT OF FOREIGN AFFAIRS: A REPORT TO THE SECRETARY OF STATE BY THE SECRETARY'S ADVISORY COMMITTEE ON PERSONNEL. Washington, D.C.: U.S. Department of State, 1950. 43 p. and appendixes.

Rowe Committee Report.

Brookings Institution. THE ADMINISTRATION OF FOREIGN AFFAIRS AND OVERSEAS OPERATIONS. Washington, D.C.: 1951. 30 p.

Prepared for Bureau of the Budget under direction of Leo Pasvolsky and immediate supervision of Paul T. David.

U.S. Congress. House of Representatives. Committee on Foreign Affairs. AN ANALYSIS OF THE PERSONNEL IMPROVEMENT PLAN OF THE DEPART-MENT OF STATE. 82d Cong., 1st sess. Washington, D.C.: Government Printing Office, 1951. 68 p.

Analysis of department's program to implement certain recommendations of the (Rowe) Advisory Committee on Personnel.

U.S. Department of State. "Directive to Improve the Personnel Program of the Department of State and the Unified Foreign Service of the United States." Washington, D.C.: March 1951.

U.S. Congress. Senate. Committee on Government Operations. ADMINISTRATION OF OVERSEAS ACTIVITIES OF THE GOVERNMENT. Hearings. May-June 1951. Washington, D.C.: Government Printing Office, 1951. 79 p.

_____. QUESTIONS AND ANSWERS ON PERSONNEL OPERATIONS UNDER THE SECRETARY'S PERSONNEL IMPROVEMENT DIRECTIVE. 82d Cong., 1st sess. Washington, D.C.: Government Printing Office, August 1951. 31 p.

Consists of some 102 questions and answers concerning the personnel improvement program of 1951.

Elliott, William Yandell, et al. UNITED STATES FOREIGN POLICY: ITS ORGANIZATION AND CONTROL. New York: Columbia University Press, 1952. 288 p.

Prepared by study group of Woodrow Wilson Foundation.

U.S. Department of State. TOWARD A STRONGER FOREIGN SERVICE: REPORT OF THE SECRETARY OF STATE'S PUBLIC COMMITTEE ON PERSONNEL. Washington, D.C.: Government Printing Office, 1954. 70 p.

Wriston Committee report.

White House Personnel Task Force. "A Foreign Affairs Personnel System." Washington, D.C.: 28 October 1954.

Prepared by small group under President's Advisor on Personnel Management Philip Young, and headed by Henry DuFlon.

U.S. Commission on Organization of the Executive Branch of the Government (Hoover Commission). OVERSEAS ECONOMIC OPERATIONS. Washington, D.C.: Government Printing Office, 1955. 854 p.

Report to Congress of Second Hoover Commission.

U.S. Congress. House of Representatives. Committee on Government Operations. ADMINISTRATION OF OVERSEAS PERSONNEL. Hearings. 84th Cong., 1st sess. 4 parts in 2 vols. Washington, D.C.: Government Printing Office, 1955.

Wiley, Alexander. THE UNITED STATES FOREIGN SERVICE. Washington, D.C.: Government Printing Office, 1955. 23 p.

> Report of Sen. Alexander Wiley on visits to certain European posts, August-September 1954.

U.S. Congress. Senate. Committee on Foreign Relations. ADMINISTRATION OF THE DEPARTMENT OF STATE AND THE FOREIGN SERVICE, AND ESTABLISHMENT OF A FOREIGN SERVICE ACADEMY. Hearings. 86th Cong., 1st. sess. Washington, D.C.: Government Printing Office, July 1959. 240 p.

_____. FOREIGN SERVICE ACT AMENDMENTS OF 1959. Report, no. 880. 86th Cong., 1st. sess. Washington, D.C.: Government Printing Office, 1959. 77 p.

Syracuse University. Maxwell Graduate School of Citizenship and Public Affairs. UNITED STATES FOREIGN POLICY: THE OPERATIONAL ASPECTS OF UNITED STATES FOREIGN POLICY. Washington, D.C.: Government Printing Office, November 1959. 73 p.

> Prepared at request of Senate Foreign Relations Committee, 86th Cong., 1st sess.

Haviland, H. Field, Jr., ed. THE FORMULATION AND ADMINISTRATION OF UNITED STATES FOREIGN POLICY. Washington, D.C.: Brookings Institution, 1960. 191 p.

> Second Brookings Institution study.

U.S. Congress. House of Representatives. Committee on Foreign Affairs. THE FOREIGN SERVICE ACT OF 1946 AS AMENDED TO OCTOBER 17, 1960. 86th Cong., 2d sess. Washington, D.C.: Government Printing Office, 1960. 200 p.

U.S. Congress. Senate. Committee on Government Operations. Subcommittee on National Policy Machinery. ORGANIZING FOR NATIONAL SECURITY. 3 vols. Washington, D.C.: Government Printing Office, 1961.

> Jackson Subcommittee reports. Volume 1--hearings; volume 2-- studies and background materials; and volume 3--staff reports and recommendations. Covers more than the Department of State and Foreign Service.

U.S. Department of State. Committee on Foreign Affairs Personnel. PERSONNEL FOR THE NEW DIPLOMACY. Washington, D.C.: Carnegie Endowment, 1962. 161 p.

Herter Committee Report. Prepared at request of Secretary of State Dean Rusk, under auspices of Carnegie Endowment.

Carnegie Endowment also sponsored and published six Foreign Affairs Personnel Studies in 1964–66, as follows. Full citations for these may be found on the page in parentheses.

1. Jones, Arthur G. THE EVOLUTION OF PERSONNEL SYSTEMS FOR U.S. FOREIGN AFFAIRS: A HISTORY OF REPORT EFFORTS. 1964. 136 p. (pp. 212, 224).

2. Elder, Robert E. OVERSEAS REPRESENTATION AND SERVICES FOR FEDERAL DOMESTIC AGENCIES. 1965. 106 p. (p. 372).

3. Harr, John Ensor. THE DEVELOPMENT OF CAREERS IN THE FOREIGN SERVICE. 1965. 104 p. (p. 212).

4. Harr, John Ensor. THE ANATOMY OF THE FOREIGN SERVICE--A STATISTICAL PROFILE. 1965. 89 p. (p. 211).

5. Walther, Regis. ORIENTATIONS AND BEHAVIORAL STYLES OF FOREIGN SERVICE OFFICERS. 1965. 52 p. (p. 215).

6. Fielder, Frances, and Harris, Godfrey. THE QUEST FOR FOREIGN AFFAIRS OFFICERS--THEIR RECRUITMENT AND SELECTION. 1966. 63 p. (p. 211).

U.S. Congress. Senate. Committee on Government Operations. Subcommittee on National Security Staffing and Operations. ADMINISTRATION OF NATIONAL SECURITY. 88th Cong., 1st and 2d sess. Washington, D.C.: Government Printing Office, 1965. 600 p.

Jackson Subcommittee Reports. Includes reports on the secretary of state (1964), on the American ambassador (1964), and on the ambassador and the problem of coordination (1963), cited elsewhere in this chapter, pp. 193, 214–15. Other sections on subjects other than the Department of State and Foreign Service.

Sapin, Burton M. THE MAKING OF UNITED STATES FOREIGN POLICY. Washington, D.C.: Brookings Institution, 1966; New York: Praeger for Brookings Institution, 1966. 425 p.

Unofficial analysis; third Brookings Institution study.

Taylor, Maxwell D. "New System for Coping With Our Overseas Problems." FOREIGN SERVICE JOURNAL 43 (May 1966): 34–36.

Summary of author's thinking regarding interdepartmental coordination for foreign relations. Author worked with four task forces. Also, see Jackson subcommittee report on the ambassador and the problem of coordination, 1963, above.

U.S. Department of State. A MANAGEMENT PROGRAM FOR THE DEPART-
MENT OF STATE, OFFICE OF THE DEPUTY UNDER SECRETARY FOR ADMIN-
ISTRATION. Washington, D.C.: 1966.

> Summary of studies and reforms launched by William J. Crockett,
> 1961-67.

President's Task Force on Government Organization, Washington, D.C., unpublished report, 1 October 1967.

> Prepared by Heineman Task Force.

American Foreign Service Association. TOWARD A MODERN DIPLOMACY:
A REPORT TO THE AMERICAN FOREIGN SERVICE ASSOCIATION. Washington, D.C.: 1968. 185 p.

> Prepared by committee chaired by Ambassador Graham Martin.
> Also summarized in FOREIGN SERVICE JOURNAL 45 (November
> 1968): part 2, separate issue, 60 p.

Clark, Keith C., and Legere, Laurence J., eds. THE PRESIDENT AND THE
MANAGEMENT OF NATIONAL SECURITY. New York: Praeger, 1969. 274 p.

> Review sponsored in 1968 by Institute for Defense Analysis, with
> foundation financing, for new presidential administration.

U.S. Department of State. DIPLOMACY FOR THE 70'S: A PROGRAM OF
MANAGEMENT REFORM FOR THE DEPARTMENT OF STATE. Washington,
D.C.: Government Printing Office, 1970. 610 p.

> Macomber modernization program for Department of State and its
> career professionals, prepared at request of Secretary William P.
> Rogers. Refined compilation of some five hundred recommendations
> systematically development by thirteen Department of State Task
> Forces.

_____. DIPLOMACY FOR THE 70'S: A PROGRAM OF MANAGEMENT RE-
FORM FOR THE DEPARTMENT OF STATE--SUMMARY. Washington, D.C.:
Government Printing Office, 1970. 30 p.

> Summary of preceding item.

"A Schedule for Implementing the Recommendations of the Department of State
Task Forces on Management Reform." DEPARTMENT OF STATE NEWSLETTER,
no. 177 (January 1971): 20-43.

> Summary statement respecting "Management Reform Bulletins" is-
> sued to implement Macomber reforms. A report on the implemen-
> tation process provided in Bacchus, "Diplomacy for the 70s," cited
> earlier, p. 223.

U.S. Congress. Senate. Committee on Foreign Relations. BACKGROUND
MATERIAL ON FOREIGN SERVICE GRIEVANCE PROCEDURES. 92d Cong.,
2d sess. Washington, D.C.: Government Printing Office, 1972. 89 p.

U.S. Commission on the Organization of the Government for the Conduct of
Foreign Policy. COMMISSION ON THE ORGANIZATION OF THE GOVERN-
MENT FOR THE CONDUCT OF FOREIGN POLICY, JUNE 1975. Washing-
ton, D.C.: Government Printing Office, 1975. 278 p. Bibliog.

> Report of the commission chaired by retired Ambassador Robert D.
> Murphy, appointed under congressional authorization. Supple-
> mented with seven volumes containing twenty-five appendixes
> (labeled A to X) published in 1976, concerning, among others,
> such subjects as management of global issues, coordination in
> complex settings, and especially the adequacy of current organi-
> zation for defense and arms control (volume 4, 475 p.) and mak-
> ing organizational change effective, personnel for foreign affairs,
> advisory panels, and budgeting for foreign affairs coordination
> (volume 6, 462 p.). An annex to volume 7 provides a short bib-
> liography on pp. 336-37. Specific appendixes cited elsewhere
> in this compilation, where topically appropriate.

U.S. Congress. House of Representatives. Committee on International Relations. Subcommittee on International Operations. SURVEY OF PROPOSALS
TO REORGANIZE THE U.S. FOREIGN AFFAIRS AGENCIES, 1951-1975.
95th Cong., 1st sess. Washington, D.C.: Government Printing Office, 1977.
70 p.

> Part 1 on public diplomacy.

Reorganization and Reform—Commentary

In addition, many studies prepared by individual authors on the Department of
State and the Foreign Service also touch on questions of structural reorganization and issues of personnel and reform, including those of Barnes and Morgan
(p. 211), Briggs (p. 196 and 200), Campbell (p. 196), Elder (p. 196), Harr
(pp. 211-12), Ilchman (p. 197), Johnson (pp. 200 and 216), Simpson (p. 198),
Yost (p. 200) and others, cited earlier in this chapter. Supplementary materials and commentary on these subjects and pertaining to reports on official and
unofficial investigations are provided in the following:

Acheson, Dean G. "The Eclipse of the State Department." FOREIGN AF-
FAIRS 49 (July 1971): 593-606.

Bacchus, William M. "Obstacles to Reform in Foreign Affairs: The Case of
NSAM [National Security Action Memorandum] 341." ORBIS 18 (Spring
1974): 266-76.

> This memorandum concerned the development of a State Depart-
> ment-centered government-wide coordination system.

Bolles, Blair. "Reorganization of the State Department." FOREIGN POLICY REPORTS 23 (15 August 1947): 134-43.

Cheever, Daniel S., and Haviland, H. Field. "Hoover Commission: A Symposium--Foreign Affairs." AMERICAN POLITICAL SCIENCE REVIEW 43 (October 1949): 966-78.

"Commission on Conduct of Foreign Policy." DEPARTMENT OF STATE BULLETIN 68 (9 April 1973): 425.

On Murphy Commisssion on government organization for the conduct of foreign relations.

Curran, R.T. "The State Department's Revolution in Executive Management." FOREIGN SERVICE JOURNAL 49 (October 1972): 4, 6, 8, 10, 12.

Denby, James O., et al. "Suggestions for Improving the Foreign Service and Its Administration to Meet Its War and Postwar Responsibilities." FOREIGN SERVICE JOURNAL 22 (February-July 1945): 7-10, 12-15, 12-14, 14-17, 12-14, 13-15, in sequential issues.

Contributions by Denby, Edmund Gullion, Edward Trueblood, Perry N. Jester, Selden Chapin, and Ware Adams.

Elliott, William Y. "The Control of Foreign Policy in the United States." POLITICAL QUARTERLY 20 (October 1949): 337-51.

_____. "Governmental Organizations for Foreign Policy Decisions." SOCIAL SCIENCE 30 (October 1955): 209-16.

Evans, A.E. "Reorganization of the American Foreign Service." INTERNATIONAL AFFAIRS 24 (April 1948): 206-17.

Fesler, James W. "Administrative Literature and the Second Hoover Commission Reports." AMERICAN POLITICAL SCIENCE REVIEW 51 (March 1957): 135-57.

"Foreign Service Act of 1946." FOREIGN SERVICE JOURNAL 23 (September 1946): 7-21.

Jackson, Henry M. "Organizing for Survival." FOREIGN AFFAIRS 38 (April 1960): 446-56.

Johnson, Richard A. "A Proposal for Reorganizing the High Command of the Department of State." FOREIGN SERVICE JOURNAL 48 (October 1971): 19-20, 38.

Kennedy, Aubrey L. "Reorganization of the Foreign Service." QUARTERLY REVIEW 566 (October 1945): 397-413.

Laves, Walter H.C., and Wilcox, Francis O. "Organizing the Government for Participation in World Affairs." AMERICAN POLITICAL SCIENCE REVIEW 38 (October 1944): 913-30.

_____. "The Reorganization of the Department of State." AMERICAN PO-LITICAL SCIENCE REVIEW 38 (April 1944): 289-301.

Updated by the following article.

_____. "The State Department Continues Its Reorganization." AMERICAN POLITICAL SCIENCE REVIEW 39 (April 1945): 309-17.

Macmahon, Arthur W. "Administration and Foreign Policy." UNIVERSITY OF ILLINOIS BULLETIN 54, no. 44 (1957): entire issue.

_____. "Function and Area in the Administration of International Affairs." NEW HORIZONS IN PUBLIC ADMINISTRATION, pp. 119-45. University, Ala.: University of Alabama Press, 1945.

Macomber, William B., Jr. "Change in Foggy Bottom: An Anniversary Report on Management Reform and Modernization in the Department of State." DE-PARTMENT OF STATE BULLETIN 66 (14 February 1972): 206-12.

_____. "Diplomacy for the Seventies: A Program of Management Reform for the Department of State." DEPARTMENT OF STATE BULLETIN 63 (28 December 1970): 775-93.

_____. "Management Strategy: A Program for the Seventies." DEPARTMENT OF STATE BULLETIN 62 (2 February 1970): 130-41.

Maddox, William P. "The Foreign Service in Transition." FOREIGN AFFAIRS 25 (January 1947): 303-13.

Mead, Lawrence M. "Foreign Service Reform: A View from HEW." FOREIGN SERVICE JOURNAL 52 (October 1975): 21-24.

"Meeting of Public Committee on Personnel." DEPARTMENT OF STATE BUL-LETIN 33 (26 December 1955): 1053-54.

Mosher, Frederick C. "Personnel Management in Foreign Affairs." PUBLIC PERSONNEL REVIEW 12 (October 1951): 175-86.

_____. "Some Observations About Foreign Service Reform: Famous First Words." PUBLIC ADMINISTRATION REVIEW 29 (November-December 1969): 600-610.

Myers, Denys P., and Ransom, Charles F. "Reorganization of the State Department." AMERICAN JOURNAL OF INTERNATIONAL LAW 31 (October 1937): 713-20.

"On Organizing the Government for the Conduct of Foreign Policy." DEPARTMENT OF STATE NEWSLETTER, no. 153 (February 1974): 6-7.

On Murphy Commission study, requesting suggestions.

"Personnel Improvement Plans Announced." DEPARTMENT OF STATE BULLETIN 24 (30 April 1951): 715-16.

Saltzman, Charles E. "Progress Report on the Wriston Committee Recommendations." FOREIGN SERVICE JOURNAL 32 (January 1955): 18-21, 42.

_____. "The Reorganization of the American Foreign Service." DEPARTMENT OF STATE BULLETIN 31 (27 September 1954): 436-44.

_____. THE REORGANIZATION OF THE AMERICAN FOREIGN SERVICE: INCLUDING STATEMENT ON PERSONNEL INTEGRATION PROGRAM, BY JOHN FOSTER DULLES. Washington, D.C.: Government Printing Office, 1954. 446 p.

Simpson, Smith. "Perceptives of Reform: Part I. The Era of Wilbur Carr." FOREIGN SERVICE JOURNAL 48 (August 1971): 17-19, 41.

_____. "Perspectives of Reform: Part II. The Post-Carr Period." FOREIGN SERVICE JOURNAL 48 (September 1971): 21-25.

_____. "Reform from Within: The Importance of Attitudes." FOREIGN SERVICE JOURNAL 47 (May 1970): 33-34, 47.

Steiner, Zara S. THE STATE DEPARTMENT AND THE FOREIGN SERVICE: THE WRISTON REPORT--FOUR YEARS LATER. Princeton, N.J.: Center of International Studies, Princeton University, 1958. 57 p.

Stern, Thomas. "Management: A New Look." FOREIGN SERVICE JOURNAL 49 (March 1972): 14-15.

Stettinius, Edward R. "Reorganization of the Office of the Foreign Service." DEPARTMENT OF STATE BULLETIN 12 (22 April 1945): 777-84.

Stowell, Ellery C. "The Moses-Linthicum Act on the Foreign Service."
AMERICAN JOURNAL OF INTERNATIONAL LAW 25 (July 1931): 516-20.

> Moses-Linthicum Act of 1931 superseded the Rogers Act of 1924
> as the organic foundation of the Foreign Service.

_____. "Reforms in the State Department and Foreign Service." AMERICAN
JOURNAL OF INTERNATIONAL LAW 22 (July 1928): 606-10.

Walker, Lannon. "Our Foreign Affairs Machinery: Time for an Overhaul."
FOREIGN AFFAIRS 47 (January 1969): 309-20.

> Related to American Foreign Service Association report of 1968.

Warwick, Donald P. "Bureaucratization in the Government Agency: The Case
of the U.S. State Department." SOCIOLOGICAL INQUIRY 44 (Spring 1974):
75-92.

_____. A THEORY OF PUBLIC BUREAUCRACY: POLITICS, PERSONALITY,
AND ORGANIZATION IN THE STATE DEPARTMENT. Cambridge, Mass.:
Harvard University Press, 1975. 242 p. Bibliog.

> Study commissioned by the Department of State.

DEPARTMENT OF STATE AND INTERNATIONAL ORGANIZATIONS

Literature on U.S. field missions and overseas representation is listed separately
in chapter 16, and other materials included elsewhere in this compilation touch
on the nature of, and the mechanism for, administering relationships with the
United Nations and other international organizations, including analyses of
international conferences (chapter 3), the new diplomacy (especially on parliamentary diplomacy contained in the last section of chapter 5), and certain
documentary materials on international conferences and organization (referred
to in chapter 22). The following relate more precisely to U.S. relations with
international organizations, national representation in such diplomatic forums,
and Washington and field operations in the management of national policy and
operations of international organizations, principally the United Nations. The
memoir literature of those who have represented the United States in international organizations also constitutes a useful resource, presented in part IV.

Beichman, Arnold. THE "OTHER" STATE DEPARTMENT: THE UNITED STATES
MISSION TO THE UNITED NATIONS--ITS ROLE IN THE MAKING OF FOR-
EIGN POLICY. New York: Basic Books, 1967. 221 p.

Bloomfield, Lincoln Palmer. "The Department of State and the United Nations." DEPARTMENT OF STATE BULLETIN 23 (20 November 1950): 804-11.

_____. "The Department of State and the United Nations." INTERNA-
TIONAL ORGANIZATION 4 (August 1950): 400-411.

Cheever, Daniel, and Haviland, H. Field, Jr. "The New Diplomacy and World Order." In their ORGANIZING FOR PEACE: INTERNATIONAL ORGANIZATION IN WORLD AFFAIRS, pp. 815-22. Boston: Houghton Mifflin, 1954.

Evans, Luther. THE UNITED STATES AND UNESCO. Dobbs Ferry, N.Y.: Oceana, 1971. 217 p.

Gregoire, Roger. NATIONAL ADMINISTRATION AND INTERNATIONAL ORGANISATIONS. New York: UNESCO Publications Center, 1958. 84 p. Bibliog.

Gross, Franz B., ed. THE UNITED STATES AND THE UNITED NATIONS. Norman: University of Oklahoma Press, 1964. 356 p.

Hyde, James N. "U.S. Participation in the UN." INTERNATIONAL ORGANIZATION 10 (February 1956): 22-34.

MacVane, John. EMBASSY EXTRAORDINARY: THE U.S. MISSION TO THE UNITED NATIONS. Public Affairs Pamphlet, no. 311. New York: Public Affairs Committee, 1961. 28 p.

Meck, J.F., and Koenig, Louis William. THE ADMINISTRATION OF UNITED STATES PARTICIPATION IN INTERNATIONAL ORGANIZATIONS. Washington, D.C.: American Society for Public Administration, 1950. 77 p.

Parker, Chauncey G. "The Ambassadorship to the United Nations." YALE REVIEW 63 (Autumn 1973): 1-9.

Pedersen, Richard F. "National Representation in the United Nations." INTERNATIONAL ORGANIZATION 15 (Spring 1961): 255-66.

Richardson, Channing B. "The United States Mission to the United Nations." INTERNATIONAL ORGANIZATION 7 (February 1953): 22-34.

Summers, Robert E. THE UNITED STATES AND INTERNATIONAL ORGANIZATIONS. New York: Wilson, 1952. 194 p. Bibliog.

U.S. Congress. Senate. Committee on Foreign Relations. Subcommittee on the United Nations Charter. REVIEW OF THE UNITED NATIONS CHARTER. Document, no. 87. 83d Cong., 2d sess. Washington, D.C.: Government Printing Office, 1954. 895 p. Bibliog.

> Especially sections on action in Congress concerning U.S. participation and on representation in the United Nations.

U.S. Department of State. U.S. PARTICIPATION IN THE UN. Washington, D.C.: Government Printing Office, 1946-- . Annual.

> Especially the sections on U.S. participation and on administration and budgeting.

Wilcox, Francis O., and Haviland, H. Field, Jr. THE UNITED STATES AND THE UNITED NATIONS. Baltimore: Johns Hopkins Press, 1961. 188 p.

Zeydel, Walter H., and Chamberlin, Waldo, eds. ENABLING INSTRUMENTS OF MEMBERS OF THE UNITED NATIONS. Part 1: THE UNITED STATES OF AMERICA. New York: Carnegie Endowment, 1951. 126 p.

GREAT SEAL OF THE UNITED STATES

In addition to serving as foreign secretary, from the very outset the secretary of state (and the department) was responsible for a variety of internal or "home" functions. These ranged from issuing patents to publishing census returns and from granting copyrights and handling land patents and petitions for presidential pardons to publishing the acts and resolutions of Congress. As the federal administration proliferated, these functions were transferred to other agencies. One of the important residual domestic responsibilities of the secretary of state is having custody of the official seal of the United States--also known as the "Great Seal"--and imprinting it on public papers, as prescribed by law, to authenticate the presidential signature. For commentary on the official seal and the function of the Department of State in that regard, see the following:

Cigrand, Bernard J. STORY OF THE GREAT SEAL OF THE UNITED STATES; OR, HISTORY OF AMERICAN EMBLEMS. Chicago: Cameron, Amberg, 1903. 544 p.

Hunt, Gaillard. THE HISTORY OF THE SEAL OF THE UNITED STATES. Washington, D.C.: Government Printing Office, 1909. 72 p.

_____. THE SEAL OF THE UNITED STATES: HOW IT WAS DEVELOPED AND ADOPTED. Washington, D.C.: U.S. Department of State, 1892. 32 p.

Lander, E.T. "The Great Seal of the United States." MAGAZINE OF AMERICAN HISTORY 29 (May-June 1893): 471-91.

Lossing, Benson J. "The Great Seal of the United States." HARPER'S NEW MONTHLY MAGAZINE, July 1856, pp. 178-86.

Patterson, Richard S., and Dougall, Richardson. THE EAGLE AND THE SHIELD: A HISTORY OF THE GREAT SEAL OF THE UNITED STATES. Washington, D.C.: Government Printing Office, 1976. 637 p. Bibliog.

U.S. Department of State. THE GREAT SEAL OF THE UNITED STATES.
Washington, D.C.: Government Printing Office, 1976. 8 p.

_____. THE SEAL OF THE UNITED STATES. Washington, D.C.: Government Printing Office, 1957. 14 p.

Earlier editions were published in 1939, 4 p.; 1947, 4 p.; and 1952, 4 p.

Chapter 10

NATIONAL SECURITY COUNCIL SYSTEM

The paramount post-World War II forum of the executive branch of the government concerned with foreign and security policy making at the Cabinet level is the National Security Council. The Second World War demonstrated the desirability, if not the need, for a continuing organizational mechanism to integrate the interests and positions of the Department of State and defense agencies. This task was ascribed to the ad hoc State-War-Navy Coordinating Committee--known as SWNCC, or "Swink"--which was activated in December 1944, at the Assistant Secretary level, to provide coordination for certain military, military government, and civil occupation responsibilities. It was assisted by a directorate and various interdepartmental subcommittees. With the reorganization of the military establishment under the National Security Act of 1947, this agency was changed to the State-Army-Navy-Air Force Coordinating Committee, or SANACC. These two institutions are discussed in the following:

U.S. Department of State. AMERICAN POLICY IN OCCUPIED AREAS. Department of State publication 2794. Washington, D.C.: Government Printing Office, 1947. 31 p.

_____. FOREIGN RELATIONS OF THE UNITED STATES, 1946. Washington, D.C.: Government Printing Office, 1969. Vol. 5, pp. 659-60.

_____. POSTWAR FOREIGN POLICY PREPARATION, 1939-1945. Washington, D.C.: Government Printing Office, 1949, pp. 226, 229, 347-48, 349-50, 368, 369, 370, 371-72, 393.

For unofficial background and commentary, see:

Hayward, Edwin J. "Co-ordination of Military and Civilian Civil Affairs Planning." ANNALS OF THE AMERICAN ACADEMY OF POLITICAL AND SOCIAL SCIENCE 267 (January 1950): 19-27.

In the meantime, a report to the Secretary of the Navy, cited below, recommended the creation of a more formal and permanent coordinating institution of greater stature, and this resulted in the establishment, in 1947, of the National Security Council by the National Security Act. It functions at the Cabinet level and is directly advisory to the president on the integration of foreign, military, and domestic policy relating to national security. As indicated in the literature, presidents tend to view the structuring, procedural institutionalization, functions, and value of the National Security Council system (consisting of the council and its subagencies) in different ways, varying with their preferred professional and personal methods of operation and the types of issues involved--such as crisis handling, contingency planning, long-range policy development, and day-to-day problems. The following official documents are concerned with the establishment of the National Security Council:

U.S. Congress. Senate. Committee on Armed Services. NATIONAL DEFENSE ESTABLISHMENT (UNIFICATION OF THE ARMED SERVICES). Hearings. 80th Cong., 1st sess. Washington, D.C.: Government Printing Office, 1947.

U.S. Congress. Senate. Committee on Naval Affairs. UNIFICATION OF THE WAR AND NAVY DEPARTMENTS AND POSTWAR ORGANIZATION FOR NATIONAL SECURITY. Washington, D.C.: Government Printing Office, 1945. 251 p.

>   Report to Secretary of the Navy James V. Forrestal by Ferdinand Eberstadt, which formally initiated the proposal resulting in the creation of the National Security Council.

Materials on the National Security Council deal with both its structure and functioning. They are largely descriptive, analytical, and evaluative. Additional guidance to literary resources is provided in the following:

U.S. Congress. Senate. Committee on Government Operations. Subcommittee on National Policy Machinery. ORGANIZING FOR NATIONAL SECURITY: A BIBLIOGRAPHY. 86th Cong., 1st sess. Washington, D.C.: Government Printing Office, 1959. 77 p.

>   Especially part 1, B.

U.S. Congress. Senate. Committee on Government Operations. Subcommittee on National Security Staffing and Operations. ADMINISTRATION OF NATIONAL SECURITY: A BIBLIOGRAPHY. 87th Cong., 2d sess. Washington, D.C.: Government Printing Office, 1963. 89 p.

>   Especially part 2.

Because the organization and operation of the National Security Council system changes from president to president, and even during an individual incumbency, literary attention is devoted to an incoming president's initial plans and expectations, subsequent reorganization, and evaluation, with some comparative analysis. Furthermore, because much of the council's work is confidential, little is published or otherwise made systematically available respecting the outcome of its deliberations. Some of the materials listed below are broad in scope (such as the analyses of Clark and Legere, Falk, Heinlein, and Saxon); some emphasize policy making (such as Davis, Snyder, and Souers); and some are historical (such as the Senate study on organizational development published in 1960). Most of the materials deal explicitly with the National Security Council, its subagencies, and its interagency relations. The reports of the Jackson Senate subcommittee and other writings are assessory and reformative. Aside from the materials listed in this chapter, useful contributions may be found in the memoir literature of the presidents and other officials who served on the council and its subsidiaries and in literature on such matters as the presidency, the executive bureaucracy, policy formulation, decision making, and crisis management.

Anderson, Dillon. "The President and National Security." ATLANTIC MONTHLY, January 1956, pp. 42-46.

Bowie, Robert R. "Analysis of Our Policy Machine." NEW YORK TIMES MAGAZINE, 9 March 1958, pp. 16, 68-71.

Bresica, Peter F. "The National Security Council: Integration of American Foreign Policy." JOURNAL OF INTERNATIONAL AFFAIRS 4 (Spring 1950): 74-77.

Clark, Keith C., and Legere, Laurence J., eds. THE PRESIDENT AND THE MANAGEMENT OF NATIONAL SECURITY: A REPORT BY THE INSTITUTE FOR DEFENSE ANALYSIS. New York: Praeger, 1969. 274 p.

Cronin, Thomas E., and Greenberg, Sanford D., eds. THE PRESIDENTIAL ADVISORY SYSTEM. New York: Harper and Row, 1969. 375 p.

    Especially part 3, chapter 2, on the Gaither Committee.

Cutler, Robert. "The Development of the National Security Council." FOR-EIGN AFFAIRS 34 (April 1956): 441-58.

_____. NO TIME FOR REST. Boston: Little, Brown, 1966. 421 p.

    On the role and operation of National Security Council.

Davis, Vincent. "American Military Policy: Decisionmaking in the Executive Branch." NAVAL WAR COLLEGE REVIEW 22 (May 1970): 4-23.

Falk, Stanley L. "The National Security Council under Truman, Eisenhower, and Kennedy." POLITICAL SCIENCE QUARTERLY 79 (September 1964): 403-34.

_____. THE NATIONAL SECURITY STRUCTURE. Washington, D.C.: Indus-trial College of the Armed Forces, 1967. 166 p.

Fischer, John. "Mr. Truman's Politburo." HARPER'S MAGAZINE, June 1951, pp. 29-36.

Hammond, Paul Y. "The National Security Council as a Device for Inter-departmental Coordination: An Interpretation and Appraisal." AMERICAN POLITICAL SCIENCE REVIEW 54 (December 1960): 899-910.

Heinlein, J.C. PRESIDENTIAL STAFF AND NATIONAL SECURITY POLICY. Occasional Papers, no. 2. Cincinnati, Ohio: Center for the Study of United States Foreign Policy, 1963. 65 p.

Jackson, Henry M. "Organizing for Survival." FOREIGN AFFAIRS 38 (April 1960): 446-56.

_____. "To Forge a Strategy for Survival." PUBLIC ADMINISTRATION RE-VIEW 19 (Summer 1959): 157-63.

_____, ed. THE NATIONAL SECURITY COUNCIL: JACKSON SUBCOM-MITTEE PAPERS ON POLICY-MAKING AT THE PRESIDENTIAL LEVEL. New York: Praeger, 1965. 311 p.

Johnson, Robert H. "The National Security Council: The Relevance of Its Past to Its Future." ORBIS 13 (Fall 1969): 709-35.

Kintner, William R. "Organizing for Conflict: A Proposal." ORBIS 2 (Summer 1958): 155-74.

Kirkpatrick, Helen P. "The National Security Council." AMERICAN PER-SPECTIVE 7 (February 1949): 443-50.

Kissinger, Henry A. THE NATIONAL SECURITY COUNCIL. Washington, D.C.: Government Printing Office, 1970. 7 p.

Kolodziej, Edward A. "The National Security Council: Innovations and Impli-cations." PUBLIC ADMINISTRATION REVIEW 29 (November-December 1969): 573-85.

Lay, James S., Jr. "The National Security Council." FOREIGN SERVICE JOURNAL 25 (March 1948): 7-8.

_____. "National Security Council's Role in the U.S. Security and Peace Program." WORLD AFFAIRS 115 (Summer 1952): 37-39.

Leacacos, John P. "Kissinger's Apparat." FOREIGN POLICY 5 (Winter 1971-72): 3-27.

Lee, Gus C. "The Organization for National Security." PUBLIC ADMINIS-
TRATION REVIEW 9 (Winter 1949): 36-50.

Leviero, Anthony H. "Seven Who Guide Our Destiny." NATION'S BUSINESS
41 (December 1953): 32-33, 72-73.

_____. "Untouchable, Unreachable, and Unquotable." NEW YORK TIMES
MAGAZINE, 30 January 1955, pp. 12-13, 53, 56.

Maechling, Charles, Jr. "Foreign Policy-Makers: The Weakest Link?" VIR-
GINIA QUARTERLY REVIEW 52 (Winter 1976): 1-23.
    Analysis of National Security Council system in operation.

Melbourne, Roy M. "Coordination for Action." FOREIGN SERVICE JOURNAL
35 (March 1958): 25, 28-29.

Mendez, Louis G., Jr. "The Soldier and National Security Policy." ARMY
INFORMATION DIGEST 14 (January 1959): 32-39.

Merritt, J.N. "The National Security Council System: Decision-Making In
the Seventies." Thesis, Industrial College of the Armed Forces (Washington,
D.C.), 1970.

Millis, Walter. "The Policymakers." NEW YORK HERALD TRIBUNE, 9 March
1954.

Morgenthau, Hans J. "Can We Entrust Defense to a Committee?" NEW YORK
TIMES MAGAZINE, 7 June 1959, pp. 9, 62-66.

Nihart, Brook. "National Security Council: New Staff System After One
Year." ARMED FORCES JOURNAL 107 (4 April 1970): 25-29.

Perkins, James A. "Administration of the National Security Program." PUB-
LIC ADMINISTRATION REVIEW 13 (Spring 1953): 80-86.

Phillips, Cabell. "The Super-Cabinet for our Security." NEW YORK TIMES
MAGAZINE, 4 April 1954, pp. 14-15, 60, 62-63.

Reston, James. "The Anonymous Advisers." NEW YORK TIMES, 26 June
1958, p. 16.

Roberts, Charles Wesley. LBJ'S INNER CIRCLE. New York: Delacorte, 1965.
223 p.

Roberts, Owen W. "Revitalization of the National Security Council: A Move Toward More Coordination of Foreign Afairs." Thesis, U.S. Air War College, 1969.

Saxon, Thomas J., Jr. "The Evolution of the National Security Council System Under President Nixon." Ph.D. dissertation, University of Maryland, 1971. 444 p. Bibliog.

Scott, Andrew M., and Dawson, Raymond H., eds. READINGS IN THE MAKING OF AMERICAN FOREIGN POLICY. New York: Macmillan, 1965.

Especially part 4, pages 334-78.

"The Security Council at Work: The Commander-in-Chief's Group of Policy Coordinators." REPORTER 1 (10 May 1949): 8-10.

Snyder, William P. MAKING U.S. NATIONAL SECURITY POLICIES. Carlisle Barracks, Pa.: U.S. Army War College, [1971]. 20 p.

Souers, Sidney W. "Policy Formulation for National Security." AMERICAN POLITICAL SCIENCE REVIEW 43 (June 1949): 534-43.

Stanley, Timothy W., and Ransom, Harry Howe. THE NATIONAL SECURITY COUNCIL. Serial, no. 104. Cambridge, Mass.: Harvard Defense Policy Seminar, 1957.

Taylor, Robert C. "The National Security Council, 1969: An Interim Appraisal." Thesis, Industrial College of the Armed Forces (Washington, D.C.), 1970.

Wyeth, George A., Jr. "The National Security Council: Concept of Operations; Organization; Actual Operations." JOURNAL OF INTERNATIONAL AFFAIRS 8 (Spring 1954): 185-95.

In 1970, President Nixon began to issue annual reports on foreign relations. Three were issued, which described the role of the National Security Council during his first administration, as follows:

Nixon, Richard. "The National Security Council System." In his U.S. FOREIGN POLICY FOR THE 1970'S: A NEW STRATEGY FOR PEACE--A REPORT TO THE CONGRESS BY RICHARD NIXON, PRESIDENT OF THE UNITED STATES, FEBRUARY 18, 1970, pp. 17-23. Washington, D.C.: Government Printing Office, 1970. 160 p.

_____. "The National Security Council System." In his U.S. FOREIGN POLICY FOR THE 1970'S: BUILDING FOR PEACE--A REPORT TO THE CON-

GRESS BY RICHARD NIXON, PRESIDENT OF THE UNITED STATES, FEBRUARY 25, 1971, pp. 225-32. Washington, D.C.: Government Printing Office, 1971. 235 p.

_____. "The Policy-Making Process: The NSC System." In his U.S. FOR-EIGN POLICY FOR THE 1970'S: THE EMERGING STRUCTURE OF PEACE--A REPORT TO THE CONGRESS BY RICHARD NIXON, PRESIDENT OF THE UNITED STATES, FEBRUARY 9, 1972, pp. 208-12. Washington, D.C.: Government Printing Office, 1972. 215 p.

Beginning late in the Eisenhower administration, a subcommittee of the Senate Committee on Government Operations, chaired by Henry M. Jackson, reviewed the functioning of the National Security Council system, reflected in several of its reports, as follows:

U.S. Congress. Senate. Committee on Government Operations. Subcommittee on National Policy Machinery. ORGANIZATIONAL HISTORY OF THE NATIONAL SECURITY COUNCIL. 86th Cong., 2d sess. Washington, D.C.: Government Printing Office, 1960. 52 p.

> Surveys the first three phases of National Security Council development through the Eisenhower administration.

_____. ORGANIZING FOR NATIONAL SECURITY. 3 vols. 86th Cong. Washington, D.C.: Government Printing Office, 1961.

> Especially volume 1, HEARINGS, pages 559-910, and volume 3, STAFF REPORTS AND RECOMMENDATIONS, pages 25-40.

_____. ORGANIZING FOR NATIONAL SECURITY: SELECTED MATERIALS. 86th Cong., 2d sess. Washington, D.C.: Government Printing Office, 1960. 180 p.

> Compilation of twenty-one documents, essays, and articles on the National Security Council and other components of the policy-making and implementation process.

U.S. Congress. Senate. Committee on Government Operations. Subcommittee on National Security and International Operations. CONDUCT OF NATIONAL SECURITY POLICY: SELECTED READINGS. 89th Cong., 1st sess. Washington, D.C.: Government Printing Office, 1965. 155 p.

> Compilation of thirteen basic documentary readings.

U.S. Congress. Senate. Committee on Government Operations. Subcommittee on National Security Staffing and Operations. ADMINISTRATION OF NATIONAL SECURITY: SELECTED PAPERS. 87th Cong., 2d sess. Washington, D.C.: Government Printing Office, 1962. 203 p.

> Compilation of twenty-three documentary analyses and other essays tangentially related to the National Security Council system.

Chapter 11

INTELLIGENCE COMMUNITY

It is an axiom of foreign relations that the formulation of policy, the making of decisions, and the nature and essence of resulting policy are not likely to be better than the information on which they are based. Effective foreign relations operation therefore depends upon an adequate and reliable flow of timely and relevant data on which to base national objectives and the courses of action designed to achieve them. The contribution of reporting and intelligence agents and agencies--responsible for the gathering, transmitting, analyzing, assessing, ordering, refining, and verifying of information--can scarcely be overestimated. The intelligence function, concerned with such information gathering and use, is exercised by a network of American administrative agencies, involving not only the Department of State, but also the Commerce, Defense, Justice, Treasury, and other departments and a variety of additional administrative agencies, with the Central Intelligence Agency, administered under the National Security Council, responsible for intelligence coordination and advice to the foreign and security policy system.

Because much of the operation of the intelligence function is not widely publicized, it may be presumed that resource materials respecting its nature, management, and problems are scarce. Aside from those listed below, materials related to the subject are also touched upon in other sections of this compilation, including some of those concerned with decision making (chapter 14), secrecy (chapter 16), information and diplomatic reporting (chapter 17), crises (chapter 18), fiction (chapter 20), and personal experiences and assessments contained in memoirs (part IV). Additional guidance to literary resources on U.S. intelligence activities is provided in:

Blackstock, Paul W., and Schaf, Frank L., Jr., eds. INTELLIGENCE, ESPIONAGE, COUNTERESPIONAGE, AND COVERT OPERATIONS: A GUIDE TO INFORMATION SOURCES. International Relations Information Guide Series, vol. 2. Detroit: Gale Research Co., 1978. 255 p.

Devore, Ronald M. SPIES AND ALL THAT: INTELLIGENCE AGENCIES AND OPERATIONS--A BIBLIOGRAPHY. Los Angeles: Center for the Study of Armament and Disarmament, California State University, 1977. 71 p.

Harris, William Robert. INTELLIGENCE AND NATIONAL SECURITY: A BIBLIOGRAPHY WITH SELECTED ANNOTATIONS. 3 vols. Cambridge, Mass.: n.p., 1968.

U.S. Department of State. INTELLIGENCE: A BIBLIOGRAPHY OF ITS FUNCTIONS, METHODS AND TECHNIQUES. Washington, D.C.: U.S. Department of State, Office of Libraries and Intelligence Acquisition, 1948. 93 p.

Few books were written on the subjects of espionage and American intelligence operations prior to World War II, but the following evidenced some emergent literary interest:

Pratt, Fletcher. SECRET AND URGENT: THE STORY OF CODES AND CIPHERS. Garden City, N.Y.: Blue Ribbon, 1942. 282 p.

Yardley, Herbert O. THE AMERICAN BLACK CHAMBER. Indianapolis: Bobbs-Merrill, 1931. 375 p.
> Story of Department of State code and deciphering work at time of World War I, written by Department of State code clerk.

Since World War II, attention has been paid not only to the intelligence function generally, but also to espionage and the American intelligence community. Materials dealing with the general matter of espionage include such studies as the following:

Copeland, Miles. WITHOUT CLOAK OR DAGGER: THE TRUTH ABOUT THE NEW ESPIONAGE. New York: Simon and Schuster, 1974. 351 p.

Dulles, Allen W., ed. GREAT TRUE SPY STORIES. New York: Harper and Row, 1968. 393 p.

Frewin, Leslie R. THE SPY TRADE: AN ANTHOLOGY OF INTERNATIONAL ESPIONAGE IN FACT AND FICTION. London: Frewin, 1966. 248 p.

Gramont, Sanche de. THE SECRET WAR: THE STORY OF INTERNATIONAL ESPIONAGE SINCE WORLD WAR II. London: Deutsch, 1962. 515 p.

Huss, Pierre J., and Carpozi, George, Jr. RED SPIES IN THE U.N. New York: Coward-McCann, 1965. 287 p.
> Series of case histories of communist clandestine operations in the United States at the United Nations, managed by the Soviet mission to the United Nations.

Jeffreys-Jones, Rhodri. AMERICAN ESPIONAGE: FROM SECRET SERVICE TO CIA. New York: Free Press, 1977. 276 p.

Kahn, David. THE CODEBREAKERS: THE STORY OF SECRET WRITING. London: Weidenfeld and Nicolson, 1967. 1164 p.

Laffin, John. CODES AND CIPHERS: SECRET WRITING THROUGH THE AGES. New York: Abelard-Schuman, 1964. 152 p.

Moore, Dan Tyler, and Waller, Martha. CLOAK AND CIPHER. Indianapolis: Bobbs-Merrill, 1962. 256 p.

Seth, Ronald. SPIES AT WORK: A HISTORY OF ESPIONAGE. London: Owen, 1954. 234 p.

Steele, Alexander. HOW TO SPY ON THE UNITED STATES. New Rochelle, N.Y.: Arlington House, 1975. 185 p.

Thompson, James Westphal, and Padover, Saul K. SECRET DIPLOMACY: ESPIONAGE AND CRYPTOGRAPHY, 1500-1815. New York: Unger, 1963. 290 p. Bibliog.

Tully, Andrew Martin. WHITE TIE AND DAGGER. New York: Morrow, 1967. 257 p.

> On subversive diplomatic and consular service in the United States.

Winterbotham, Frederick William. THE ULTRA SECRET. New York: Harper and Row, 1974. 199 p.

> Reveals intelligence secrets of World War II regarding the breaking of the Nazi radio code.

INTELLIGENCE COMMUNITY, OSS, AND CIA

A number of studies are concerned with the overall intelligence community of the United States and with specific governmental intelligence agencies and units, especially the Office of Strategic Services (OSS), operating during World War II, and the Central Intelligence Agency (CIA), established by the National Security Act of 1947. The following treat the intelligence community as a whole:

Fain, Tyrus G.; Plant, Katharine C.; and Milloy, Ross, comps. THE INTELLIGENCE COMMUNITY: HISTORY, ORGANIZATION, AND ISSUES. Public Documents Series, vol. 1. New York: Bowker, 1977. 1,215 p. Bibliog.

> Consists of three parts, dealing with "History and Structure of the U.S. Foreign Intelligence Community," "Components of the Foreign Intelligence Community," and "Public Issues," with chapter 9 on the intelligence functions of the Department of State.

Kirkpatrick, Lyman B., Jr. THE UNITED STATES INTELLIGENCE COMMU-
NITY: FOREIGN POLICY AND DOMESTIC ACTIVITIES. New York: Hill
and Wang, 1973. 212 p.

MacCloskey, Monro. THE AMERICAN INTELLIGENCE COMMUNITY. New
York: Rosen, 1967. 190 p.

MONOGRAPH ON NATIONAL SECURITY. Providence, R.I.: Brown University, 1976. 141 p.

> Contains 3 articles, each with bibliography: Edmund S. Hawley,
> "The Administration of the Intelligence Community"; Bruce O.
> Riedel, "Intelligence Failures in the October War"; and James A.
> Urry, "Secrecy and the Intelligence Community."

Ransom, Harry Howe. CENTRAL INTELLIGENCE AND NATIONAL SECURITY.
Cambridge, Mass.: Harvard University Press, 1958. 287 p. Bibliog.

_____. THE INTELLIGENCE ESTABLISHMENT. Cambridge, Mass.: Harvard
University Press, 1970. 309 p. Bibliog.

> Revision and enlargement of the author's 1958 study.

Weber, Ralph E. UNITED STATES DIPLOMATIC CODES AND CIPHERS, 1775-
1938. Chicago: New University Press, 1978. 600 p.

Wise, David, and Ross, Thomas B. THE ESPIONAGE ESTABLISHMENT. New
York: Random House, 1967. 308 p.

_____. THE INVISIBLE GOVERNMENT. New York: Random House, 1964.
375 p. Bibliog.

Other studies describe and analyze the Office of Strategic Services (OSS),
which operated during the war years, as follows:

Alsop, Stewart, and Braden, Thomas. SUB ROSA: THE OSS AND AMERICAN
ESPIONAGE. New York: Reynal and Hitchcock, 1946. 237 p.

Dulles, Allen W. THE SECRET SURRENDER. New York: Harper and Row,
1966. 255 p. Bibliog.

> Written by a former agent of OSS, who manipulated action to end
> World War II in Italy.

Ford, Corey, and MacBain, Alastair. CLOAK AND DAGGER: THE SECRET
STORY OF O.S.S. New York: Random House, 1946. 216 p.

Hall, Roger. YOU'RE STEPPING ON MY CLOAK AND DAGGER. New York: Norton, 1957. 219 p.

Humorous recounting concerning the OSS.

Morgan, William J. THE O.S.S. AND I. New York: Norton, 1957. 281 p.

Smith, R. Harris. OSS: THE SECRET HISTORY OF AMERICA'S FIRST CENTRAL INTELLIGENCE AGENCY. Berkeley and Los Angeles: University of California Press, 1972. 470 p.

Since World War II, increasing interest has been devoted to publicizing the operations of the Central Intelligence Agency (CIA), created as part of the American national security system.

Agee, Philip. INSIDE THE COMPANY: CIA DIARY. New York: Stonehill, 1975. 639 p.

Blackstock, Paul W. THE CIA AND THE INTELLIGENCE COMMUNITY. St. Charles, Mo.: Forum, 1974. 15 p.

Buncher, Judith, ed. THE CIA AND THE SECURITY DEBATE, 1971-1975. New York: Facts on File, 1976. 362 p.

Cline, Ray S. SECRETS, SPIES, AND SCHOLARS: BLUEPRINT OF THE ESSENTIAL CIA. Washington, D.C.: Acropolis, 1977. 294 p.

Dulles, Allen W. THE CRAFT OF INTELLIGENCE. New York: Harper and Row, 1963. 277 p. Bibliog.

Written by former director of CIA, 1953-61.

_____. "The Craft of Intelligence." HARPER'S MAGAZINE, April 1963, pp. 127-74.

Frazier, Howard. UNCLOAKING THE CIA. Riverside, N.J.: Free Press, 1978. 304 p.

Harkness, Richard, and Harkness, Gladys. "The Mysterious Doings of CIA." SATURDAY EVENING POST, 30 October 1954, pp. 19-21, 162, 165; 6 November 1954, pp. 34-35, 64, 66, 68; 13 November 1954, pp. 30, 132-34.

Heuer, Richards J., Jr. QUANTITATIVE APPROACHES TO POLITICAL INTELLIGENCE: THE CIA EXPERIENCE. Boulder, Colo.: Westview, 1978. 175 p.

Kim, Young H., ed. THE CENTRAL INTELLIGENCE AGENCY: PROBLEMS OF SECRECY IN A DEMOCRACY. Lexington, Mass.: Heath, 1968. 113 p.

Kirkpatrick, Lyman B., Jr. THE REAL CIA. New York: Macmillan, 1968. 312 p.

McGarvey, Patrick J. C.I.A.: THE MYTH AND THE MADNESS. New York: Saturday Review Press, 1972. 240 p.

Marchetti, Victor, and Marks, John D. THE CIA AND THE CULT OF INTELLIGENCE. New York: Knopf, 1974. 398 p.

Padover, Saul K. EXPERIMENT IN GERMANY: THE STORY OF AN INTELLIGENCE OFFICER. New York: Duell, Sloane, and Pearce, 1946. 400 p.

Raborn, William F. "What's CIA?" U.S. NEWS AND WORLD REPORT, 18 July 1966, pp. 74–80.

Rositzke, Harry. THE CIA'S SECRET OPERATIONS: ESPIONAGE, COUNTERESPIONAGE, AND COVERT ACTION. New York: Reader's Digest Press, 1977. 286 p.

Stockwell, John. IN SEARCH OF ENEMIES: THE CIA STORY. New York: Norton, 1978. 288 p.

Tully, Andrew Martin. CIA: THE INSIDE STORY. New York: Morrow, 1962. 276 p.

OTHER MATERIALS ON INTELLIGENCE FUNCTION

A variety of other, more general materials have been published on intelligence activities. Some of these are contained as chapters or sections in more comprehensive volumes, as follows:

Allison, Graham T., and Szanton, Peter. REMAKING FOREIGN POLICY: THE ORGANIZATIONAL CONNECTION. New York: Basic Books, 1976.

> Especially chapter 9.

Appleton, Sheldon. UNITED STATES FOREIGN POLICY: AN INTRODUCTION WITH CASES. Boston: Little, Brown, 1968.

> Especially chapter 6.

Chamberlain, Lawrence H., and Snyder, Richard C. AMERICAN FOREIGN POLICY. New York: Rinehart, 1948.

Especially chapter 8.

Esterline, John H., and Black, Robert B. INSIDE FOREIGN POLICY. Palo Alto, Calif.: Mayfield, 1975.

Especially chapter 2.

Irish, Marian, and Frank, Elke. U.S. FOREIGN POLICY: CONTEXT, CON-DUCT, CONTENT. New York: Harcourt Brace Jovanovich, 1975.

Section on intelligence and covert operations, pages 482-91.

London, Kurt. THE MAKING OF FOREIGN POLICY: EAST AND WEST. Philadelphia: Lippincott, 1965.

Especially chapter 3.

McCamy, James L. THE ADMINISTRATION OF AMERICAN FOREIGN AF-FAIRS. New York: Knopf, 1950.

Especially chapter 13.

Nash, Henry T. AMERICAN FOREIGN POLICY: RESPONSE TO A SENSE OF THREAT. Rev. ed. Homewood, Ill.: Dorsey, 1978.

Especially chapter 7.

Plischke, Elmer. CONDUCT OF AMERICAN DIPLOMACY. 3d ed. Prince-ton, N.J.: VanNostrand, 1967.

Section on the intelligence community, pages 140-43.

Sapin, Burton M. THE MAKING OF UNITED STATES FOREIGN POLICY. Washington, D.C.: Brookings Institution, 1966.

Especially chapter 10.

Other general materials on the intelligence function, its nature, operation, and restraints are provided in the following. A few are concerned with the intelligence estimates process (Barlow and Knorr), the nature and importance of strategic intelligence (Freedman, Hilsman, Kent, McGovern, and Platt), and the role of intelligence in the policy process (Barnds, Cline, Evans, Hils-man, Holt and van de Velde, Hughes, and Kent). Others deal with govern-mental oversight, supervision, and review, especially the congressional investi-gations and reports. Still others are either more general (Kendall, Kirkpatrick, Nicolson, and Tully) or deal with current status and the future (Pettee and Possony).

Baldwin, Hanson W. "The Growing Risks of Bureaucratic Intelligence." RE-PORTER, 15 August 1963, pp. 48–52.

Barlow, Allen. "The Estimative Process: The Production of National Intelligence Estimates." Master's thesis, Georgetown University, 1967.

Barnds, William J. "Intelligence and Foreign Policy: Dilemmas of a Democracy." FOREIGN AFFAIRS 47 (January 1969): 281–95.

Cline, Ray S. "Policy Without Intelligence." FOREIGN POLICY 17 (Winter 1974–75): 121–35.

Dvornik, Francis. ORIGINS OF INTELLIGENCE SERVICES: THE ANCIENT NEAR EAST, PERSIA, GREECE, ROME, BYZANTIUM, THE ARAB MUSLIM EMPIRES, THE MONGOL EMPIRE, CHINA, MUSCOVY. New Brunswick, N.J.: Rutgers University Press, 1974. 334 p.

Evans, Allan. "Intelligence and Policy Formulation." WORLD POLITICS 12 (October 1959): 84–91.

Freedman, Lawrence. U.S. INTELLIGENCE AND THE SOVIET STRATEGIC THREAT. Boulder, Colo.: Westview, 1978. 235 p. Bibliog.

Growth, A.J. "On the Intelligence Aspects of Personal Diplomacy." ORBIS 7 (Winter 1964): 833–48.

Halperin, Morton H., et al. THE LAWLESS STATE: THE CRIMES OF THE U.S. INTELLIGENCE AGENCIES. New York: Penguin, 1976. 328 p.

Hilsman, Roger, Jr. "Intelligence and Policy Making in Foreign Affairs." WORLD POLITICS 5 (October 1952): 1–45.

_____. STRATEGIC INTELLIGENCE AND NATIONAL DECISIONS. Glencoe, Ill.: Free Press, 1956. 187 p.

Holt, Robert T., and van de Velde, Robert W. STRATEGIC PSYCHOLOGICAL OPERATIONS AND AMERICAN FOREIGN POLICY. Chicago: University of Chicago Press, 1960. 243 p.

Hughes, Thomas L. THE FATE OF FACTS IN A WORLD OF MEN: FOREIGN POLICY AND INTELLIGENCE-MAKING. Headline Series, no. 233. New York: Foreign Policy Association, November 1976.

Kendall, Willmore. "The Function of Intelligence." WORLD POLITICS 1 (July 1949): 542–52.

Kent, Sherman. STRATEGIC INTELLIGENCE FOR AMERICAN WORLD POLICY. Princeton, N.J.: Princeton University Press, 1949. 226 p.

Kirkpatrick, Lyman B. "United States Intelligence." MILITARY REVIEW 41 (May 1961): 18-22.

Knorr, Klaus. "Failures in National Intelligence Estimates: The Case of the Cuban Missiles." WORLD POLITICS 16 (April 1964): 455-67.

_____. FOREIGN INTELLIGENCE AND THE SOCIAL SCIENCES. Princeton, N.J.: Center of International Studies, Princeton University, 1964. 58 p. Bibliog.

Lasswell, Harold D. "The Intelligence Function: Built-In Errors." PROD 3 (September 1959): 3-7.

McGovern, William M. STRATEGIC INTELLIGENCE AND THE SHAPE OF TOMORROW. Foundation for Foreign Affairs Series, no. 5. Chicago: Regnery, 1961. 191 p.

Mackey, James Patrick III. "The Acquisition of Intelligence in the Nuclear Age: Some Political and Strategic Implications." Master's thesis, Georgetown University, 1967.

Nicolson, Harold. "The Easy Chair Intelligence Services: Their Use and Misuse." HARPER'S MAGAZINE, November 1957, pp. 12, 14, 16, 18, 20.

Pettee, George S. THE FUTURE OF AMERICAN SECRET INTELLIGENCE. Washington, D.C.: Infantry Journal Press, 1946. 120 p.

Platt, Washington. NATIONAL CHARACTER IN ACTION: INTELLIGENCE FACTORS IN FOREIGN RELATIONS. New Brunswick, N.J.: Rutgers University Press, 1961. 250 p. Bibliog.

_____. STRATEGIC INTELLIGENCE PRODUCTION: BASIC PRINCIPLES. New York: Praeger, 1957. 302 p.

Possony, Stefan T. "United States Intelligence at the Crossroads." ORBIS 9 (Fall 1965): 587-612.

Ransom, Harry Howe. STRATEGIC INTELLIGENCE. Morristown, N.J.: General Learning Press, 1973. 20 p. Bibliog.

_____. "Strategic Intelligence and Foreign Policy." WORLD POLITICS 27 (October 1974): 131-46.

Tully, Andrew. THE SUPER SPIES. New York: Morrow, 1969. 256 p.

Survey of federal investigative agencies.

U.S. Commission on the Organization of the Government for the Conduct of Foreign Policy. "Intelligence Functions Analysis." In its COMMISSION ON THE ORGANIZATION OF THE GOVERNMENT FOR THE CONDUCT OF FOREIGN POLICY, JUNE 1975, vol. 7, pp. 1-102. Washington, D.C.: Government Printing Office, 1976.

U.S. Congress. House of Representatives. Select Committee on Intelligence. INTELLIGENCE AGENCIES AND ACTIVITIES. Washington, D.C.: Government Printing Office, 1975-76.

Part 1. INTELLIGENCE COSTS AND FISCAL PROCEDURES, 1975. 630 p.

Part 2. THE PERFORMANCE OF THE INTELLIGENCE COMMUNITY, 1975. 306 p.

Part 3. DOMESTIC INTELLIGENCE, 1976. 285 p.

Part 4. COMMITTEE PROCEEDINGS, 1976. 344 p.

Part 5. RISKS AND CONTROL OF FOREIGN INTELLIGENCE, 1976. 468 p.

Part 6. COMMITTEE PROCEEDINGS, II, 1976. 278 p.

U.S. Congress. Senate. Committee on Foreign Relations. DR. KISSINGER'S ROLE IN WIRETAPPING. Hearings. 93d Cong., 2d sess., 1973-74. Washington, D.C.: Government Printing Office, 1974. 409 p.

Hearings held at Henry Kissinger's request.

U.S. Congress. Senate. Select Committee to Study Governmental Operations with Respect to Intelligence Activities. FINAL REPORT OF THE SENATE SELECT COMMITTEE TO STUDY GOVERNMENTAL OPERATIONS WITH RESPECT TO INTELLIGENCE ACTIVITIES. Book 6 on SUPPLEMENTARY REPORTS ON INTELLIGENCE ACTIVITIES. 94th Cong., 2d sess. Washington, D.C.: Government Printing Office, 1976. 378 p.

Chronicles the evolution and organization of U.S. intelligence functions from 1776 to 1975, highlighting major personalities and events that affected American intelligence efforts.

Zacharias, Ellis M. SECRET MISSIONS: THE STORY OF AN INTELLIGENCE OFFICER. New York: Putnam, 1946. 433 p.

Chapter 12

THE MILITARY

Close cooperation between the Department of State, other government agencies concerned with foreign affairs, and the military is essential to the effective conduct of contemporary American foreign relations, and U.S. foreign, security, and military policy making and implementation must be fully coordinated. Often, external policy would be untenable if military as well as diplomatic capabilities were insufficient to implement it. Prior to World War II, interagency collaboration was largely ad hoc, with the Department of State primarily responsible for managing virtually all foreign relations. Since then, U.S. military activities abroad have proliferated, and the defense and military service departments have come to play a far more active part in the foreign affairs process.

This chapter is not intended to provide a definitive listing of materials on the American military. More comprehensive anthologies are available elsewhere. This compilation consists rather of a selection of readily available resources on a limited spectrum of subjects, dealing largely with elements of government organization and the policy process. Subjects encompassed elsewhere--not included in this listing--include such matters as the arms race and arms control, military command and leadership, logistics, weaponry, military law and justice, manpower and conscription, various types of warfare (maritime, land, air, chemical and biological, nuclear, limited, and guerrilla), civil defense, and the like.

Several listings appearing in other chapters of this compilation also relate to military affairs, especially those that deal with specialized attaches (chapter 3), the president as commander in chief (chapter 7), the National Security Council system (chapter 10), the intelligence community (chapter 11), decision making (chapter 14), and crisis handling (chapter 18). Comprehensive guidance to considerable additional materials on the military aspect of foreign relations may be found in the following:

Albion, R.G., ed. NAVAL AND MARITIME HISTORY: AN ANNOTATED BIBLIOGRAPHY. 4th ed. Mystic, Conn.: Munson Institute of American Maritime History, 1973. 370 p.

Burns, Richard Dean, ed. ARMS CONTROL AND DISARMAMENT: A BIB-LIOGRAPHY. Santa Barbara, Calif.: ABC-Clio Press, 1977. 430 p.

Burt, Richard, and Kemp, Geoffrey, eds. CONGRESSIONAL HEARINGS ON AMERICAN DEFENSE POLICY, 1947-1971: AN ANNOTATED BIBLIOGRAPHY. Lawrence: University of Kansas Press, 1974. 377 p.

Gordon, Colin. THE ATLANTIC ALLIANCE: A BIBLIOGRAPHY. London: Francis Pinter, 1978. 232 p.

> Contains some 3,000 items from American, British, Canadian, Scandinavian, Soviet, and West European materials.

Greenwood, John, et al., comps. AMERICAN DEFENSE POLICY SINCE 1945: A PRELIMINARY BIBLIOGRAPHY. Lawrence: University of Kansas Press, 1973. 317 p.

Lang, Kurt, ed. MILITARY INSTITUTIONS AND THE SOCIOLOGY OF WAR: A REVIEW OF THE LITERATURE WITH ANNOTATED BIBLIOGRAPHY. Sage Series on Armed Forces and Society, vol. 3. Beverly Hills, Calif.: Sage, 1972. 337 p. Bibliog.

_____. SOCIOLOGY OF THE MILITARY: A SELECTED AND ANNOTATED BIBLIOGRAPHY. Chicago: Inter-University Seminar on Armed Forces and Society, University of Chicago, 1969. 96 p.

Larson, Arthur D., ed. NATIONAL SECURITY AFFAIRS: A GUIDE TO IN-FORMATION SOURCES. Management Information Guide, vol. 27. Detroit: Gale Research Co., 1973. 411 p.

> Especially sections 3-9 and section 13.

Social Science Research Council. Committee on Civil-Military Relations Re-search. CIVIL-MILITARY RELATIONS: AN ANNOTATED BIBLIOGRAPHY, 1940-1952. New York: Columbia University Press, 1954. 140 p.

U.S. Congress. House of Representatives. Committee on Foreign Affairs. NATIONAL SECURITY AND THE CHANGING WORLD POWER ALIGNMENT: OUTLINE AND BIBLIOGRAPHY. 92d Cong., 2d sess. Washington, D.C.: Government Printing Office, 1972. 22 p.

U.S. Congress. Senate. Committee on Government Operations. Subcommit-tee on National Policy Machinery. ORGANIZING FOR NATIONAL SECURITY: A BIBLIOGRAPHY. 86th Cong., 1st sess. Washington, D.C.: Government Printing Office, 1959. 77 p.

> Especially pages 16-30, 39-40, 58-66, 72-76.

U.S. Congress. Senate. Committee on Government Operations. Subcommittee on National Security Staffing and Operations. ADMINISTRATION OF NATIONAL SECURITY: A BIBLIOGRAPHY. 87th Cong., 2d sess. Washington, D.C.: Government Printing Office, 1963. 89 p.

Especially pages 20-31, 44-47, 71-72.

U.S. Department of the Army. MILITARY POWER AND NATIONAL OBJECTIVES: A SELECTED LIST OF TITLES. Special Bibliography, no. 15. Washington, D.C.: Government Printing Office, 1957. 181 p.

_____. NATIONAL SECURITY, MILITARY POWER, AND THE ROLE OF FORCE IN INTERNATIONAL RELATIONS: A BIBLIOGRAPHIC SURVEY OF LITERATURE. Washington, D.C.: Government Printing Office, 1976. 171 p.

_____. NUCLEAR WEAPONS AND NATO: ANALYTICAL SURVEY OF LITERATURE. Washington, D.C.: Government Printing Office, 1970. 450 p.

_____. NUCLEAR WEAPONS AND THE ATLANTIC ALLIANCE: A BIBLIOGRAPHIC SURVEY. Washington, D.C.: Government Printing Office, 1965. 193 p.

_____. SELECT BIBLIOGRAPHY ON ADMINISTRATIVE ORGANIZATION. Washington, D.C.: Government Printing Office, 1960. 38 p.

_____. UNITED STATES NATIONAL SECURITY. Special Bibliography, no. 7. Washington, D.C.: Government Printing Office, 1956. 218 p.

Wright, Christopher, ed. "Arms Control: Selected Critical Bibliography." DAEDALUS 89 (Fall 1960): 1055-70.

GENERAL LITERATURE

The following provide broad-scale, general materials and background on the military, including such matters as general military history and heritage, the role of the military in American society and politics, military power and the going to war, militarism, the military profession, weapons culture, and a few items on the relation of the military to U.S. diplomacy:

Abrahamsson, Bengt. MILITARY PROFESSIONALIZATION AND POLITICAL POWER. Beverly Hills, Calif.: Sage, 1972. 184 p.

Ackley, Charles Walton. THE MODERN MILITARY IN AMERICAN SOCIETY. Philadelphia: Westminster, 1972. 400 p.

Ambrose, Stephen E., and Barber, James A., Jr., eds. THE MILITARY AND AMERICAN SOCIETY. New York: Free Press, 1972. 332 p.

Binken, Martin, and Back, Shirley J. WOMEN IN THE MILITARY. Washington, D.C.: Brookings Institution, 1977. 134 p.

Blechman, Barry M., and Kaplan, Stephen S. FORCE WITHOUT WAR: U.S. ARMED FORCES AS A POLITICAL INSTRUMENT. Washington, D.C.: Brookings Institution, 1978. 584 p.

Cable, John. GUNBOAT DIPLOMACY. POLITICAL APPLICATION OF LIMITED NAVAL FORCES. New York: Praeger for Institute for Strategic Studies, 1971. 251 p.

Callan, John F., ed. THE MILITARY LAWS OF THE UNITED STATES. Baltimore: Murphy, 1858. 484 p.

Chrysospathis, Spiros. "Diplomacy and Defense." NATO LETTER 10 (September 1962): 2-6.

Clotfelter, James. THE MILITARY IN AMERICAN POLITICS. New York: Harper and Row, 1973. 244 p.

Coffin, Tristram. THE ARMED SOCIETY: MILITARISM IN MODERN AMERICA. Baltimore: Penguin, 1964. 287 p.

_____. THE PASSION OF THE HAWKS: MILITARISM IN MODERN AMERICA. New York: Macmillan, 1964. 280 p.

Coffman, Edward M. THE WAR TO END ALL WARS: THE AMERICAN MILITARY EXPERIENCE IN WORLD WAR I. New York: Oxford University Press, 1968. 412 p. Bibliog.

Cook, Fred J. THE WARFARE STATE. New York: Macmillan, 1962. 376 p. Bibliog.

Davis, Kenneth S. EXPERIENCE OF WAR: THE UNITED STATES IN WORLD WAR II. Garden City, N.Y.: Doubleday, 1965. 704 p. Bibliog.

Derthick, Martha. THE NATIONAL GUARD IN POLITICS. Cambridge, Mass.: Harvard University Press, 1965. 202 p.

Dupuy, R. Ernest, and Dupuy, Trevor N[evitt]. MILITARY HERITAGE OF AMERICA. New York: McGraw-Hill, 1956. 794 p. Bibliog.

Dupuy, Trevor Nevitt. DOCUMENTARY HISTORY OF THE ARMED FORCES OF THE UNITED STATES. 10 vols. Washington, D.C.: University Publications of America, 1978.

Galbraith, John Kenneth. HOW TO CONTROL THE MILITARY. New York: New American Library, 1969. 95 p.

Glass, Robert R., and Davidson, Philip B. INTELLIGENCE IS FOR COMMANDERS. Harrisburg, Pa.: Military Service, 1948. 189 p.

Haas, Ernst B. "The Impact of Modern Weapons on Diplomacy." WORLD AFFAIRS INTERPRETER 23 (Winter 1953): 404-14.

Halle, Louis J. "The Role of Force in Foreign Policy." SOCIAL SCIENCE 30 (October 1955): 203-8.

Henderson, George, ed. HUMAN RELATIONS IN THE MILITARY: PROBLEMS AND PROGRAMS. Chicago: Nelson-Hall, 1975. 291 p. Bibliog.

Herring, Edward P. THE IMPACT OF WAR: OUR AMERICAN DEMOCRACY UNDER ARMS. New York: Farrar and Rinehart, 1941. 306 p. Bibliog.

Horowitz, Robert S. THE RAMPARTS WE WATCH. Derby, Conn.: Monarch, 1964. 190 p.

Huntington, Samuel P., ed. CHANGING PATTERNS OF MILITARY POLITICS. New York: Free Press, 1962. 272 p.

Janowitz, Morris. MILITARY CONFLICT: ESSAYS IN THE INSTITUTIONAL ANALYSIS OF WAR AND PEACE. Beverly Hills, Calif.: Sage, 1975. 320 p.

_____. THE PROFESSIONAL SOLDIER: A SOCIAL AND POLITICAL POR-TRAIT. Glencoe, Ill.: Free Press, 1960. 464 p. Bibliog.

Just, Ward. MILITARY MEN. New York: Knopf, 1970. 256 p. Bibliog.

Karsten, Peter. SOLDIERS AND SOCIETY: THE EFFECTS OF MILITARY SERVICE AND WAR ON AMERICAN LIFE. Westport, Conn.: Greenwood, 1978. 339 p.

Kelleher, Catherine M., ed. POLITICAL-MILITARY SYSTEMS: COMPARATIVE PERSPECTIVES. Beverly Hills, Calif.: Sage, 1974. 306 p.

Knorr, Klaus E. MILITARY POWER AND POTENTIAL. Lexington, Mass.: Heath, 1970. 150 p.

_____. THE WAR POTENTIAL OF NATIONS. Princeton, N.J.: Princeton University Press, 1956. 310 p.

Lapp, Ralph E. ARMS BEYOND DOUBT: A TYRANNY OF WEAPONS TECHNOLOGY. New York: Cowles, 1970. 210 p.

_____. THE WEAPONS CULTURE. New York: Norton, 1968. 230 p.

Leckie, Robert. THE WARS OF AMERICA. New York: Harper and Row, 1968. 1,052 p.

Little, Roger W., ed. A SURVEY OF MILITARY INSTITUTIONS. 2 vols. Chicago: Inter-University Seminar on Armed Forces and Society, 1969.

Loory, Stuart H. DEFEATED: INSIDE AMERICA'S MILITARY MACHINE. New York: Random House, 1973. 405 p.

Lyons, Gene M., and Masland, John W. EDUCATION AND MILITARY LEADERSHIP: A STUDY OF THE R.O.T.C. Princeton, N.J.: Princeton University Press, 1959. 283 p.

Masland, John W. "The National War College and the Administration of Foreign Affairs." PUBLIC ADMINISTRATION REVIEW 12 (Autumn 1952): 267-75.

MILITARY LAWS OF THE UNITED STATES: FROM THE CIVIL WAR THROUGH THE WAR POWERS ACT OF 1973. New York: Arno, 1979.

Continues the series of reprints of laws compiled by Callan, listed above.

Millett, John D. "The War Department in World War II." AMERICAN POLITICAL SCIENCE REVIEW 40 (October 1946): 863-97.

Millis, Walter. ARMS AND MEN: A STUDY IN AMERICAN MILITARY HISTORY. New York: Putnam, 1956. 382 p. Bibliog.

Morgenstern, Oskar. THE QUESTION OF NATIONAL DEFENSE. New York: Vintage, 1961. 328 p.

Murphy, Robert D. "The Soldier and the Diplomat." FOREIGN SERVICE JOURNAL 29 (May 1952): 17-19, 49-50.

Oppenheimer, Martin, ed. THE AMERICAN MILITARY. Chicago: Aldine, 1971. 180 p.

Perlmutter, Amos. THE MILITARY AND POLITICS IN MODERN TIMES: ON PROFESSIONALS, PRAETORIANS, AND REVOLUTIONARY SOLDIERS. New Haven, Conn.: Yale University Press, 1977. 352 p.

Pusey, Merlo J. THE WAY WE GO TO WAR. Boston: Houghton Mifflin, 1969. 202 p.

Quester, George H., ed. SEA POWER IN THE 1970'S: A SYMPOSIUM SPONSORED BY THE CORNELL UNIVERSITY PROGRAM ON PEACE STUDIES. Port Washington, N.Y.: Kennikat, 1975. 248 p.

Reinhardt, George C., and Kintner, William R. THE HAPHAZARD YEARS: HOW AMERICA HAS GONE TO WAR. Garden City, N.Y.: Doubleday, 1960. 242 p.

Russett, Bruce M., ed. PEACE, WAR, AND NUMBERS. Beverly Hills, Calif.: Sage, 1972. 352 p.

Russett, Bruce M., and Stepan, A., eds. MILITARY FORCE AND AMERICAN SOCIETY. New York: Harper and Row, 1973. 371 p.

Sarkisian, Sam C., ed. THE MILITARY-INDUSTRIAL COMPLEX: A REASSESS-MENT. Beverly Hills, Calif.: Sage, 1972. 340 p.

Schelling, Thomas C. ARMS AND INFLUENCE. New Haven, Conn.: Yale University Press for Center for International Affairs, Harvard University, 1966. 293 p.

Schiller, Herbert I., and Phillips, Joseph D. SUPER-STATE: READINGS IN THE MILITARY INDUSTRIAL COMPLEX. Urbana: University of Illinois Press, 1971. 351 p.

Stambuk, George. "American Military Forces Abroad: A Postwar Pattern in International Relations." Ph.D. dissertation, Indiana University, 1961. 328 p.

Stern, Ellen P., ed. THE LIMITS OF MILITARY INTERVENTION. Beverly Hills, Calif.: Sage, 1977. 400 p.

Sternberg, Fritz. THE MILITARY AND INDUSTRIAL REVOLUTION OF OUR TIME. New York: Praeger, 1959. 359 p.

Swomley, John M., Jr. "The Growing Power of the Military." PROGRESSIVE 23 (January 1959): 24-28.

Thayer, George. THE WAR BUSINESS: THE INTERNATIONAL TRADE IN ARMAMENTS. New York: Simon and Schuster, 1969. 417 p.

U.S. Army. Office of Chief of Military History. AMERICAN MILITARY HISTORY. Washington, D.C.: Government Printing Office, 1969. 701 p. Bibliog.

U.S. Congress. House of Representatives. Committee on Foreign Affairs. BACKGROUND INFORMATION ON THE USE OF UNITED STATES ARMED FORCES IN FOREIGN COUNTRIES. House Report no. 127. 82d Cong., 1st sess. Washington, D.C.: Government Printing Office, 1951. 77 p.

Vagts, Alfred. DEFENSE AND DIPLOMACY: THE SOLDIER AND THE CONDUCT OF FOREIGN RELATIONS. New York: King's Crown, 1956. 547 p. Bibliog.

Warner, W. Lloyd, et al. THE AMERICAN FEDERAL EXECUTIVE: A STUDY OF THE SOCIAL AND PERSONAL CHARACTERISTICS OF THE CIVILIAN AND MILITARY LEADERS OF THE UNITED STATES FEDERAL GOVERNMENT. New Haven, Conn.: Yale University Press, 1963. 405 p.

Warren, Earl. "The Bill of Rights and The Military." NEW YORK UNIVERSITY LAW REVIEW 37 (April 1962): 181-203.

Weigley, Russell F. HISTORY OF THE UNITED STATES ARMY. New York: Macmillan, 1967. 688 p.

Zuckerman, Solly. "Judgment and Control in Modern Warfare." FOREIGN AFFAIRS 40 (January 1962): 196-212.

A number of more comprehensive volumes on American foreign relations also contain general chapters on the relationship and importance of the military to the conduct of foreign affairs, as follow:

Allison, Graham T., and Szanton, Peter. REMAKING FOREIGN POLICY: THE ORGANIZATIONAL CONNECTION. New York: Basic Books, 1976.

    Especially chapter 8.

Appleton, Sheldon. UNITED STATES FOREIGN POLICY: AN INTRODUCTION WITH CASES. Boston: Little, Brown, 1968.

    Especially chapter 5.

Chamberlain, Lawrence H., and Snyder, Richard C. AMERICAN FOREIGN POLICY. New York: Rinehart, 1948.

    Especially chapter 9.

McCamy, James L. THE ADMINISTRATION OF AMERICAN FOREIGN AF-
FAIRS. New York: Knopf, 1950.

Especially chapter 10.

Nash, Henry T. AMERICAN FOREIGN POLICY: RESPONSE TO A SENSE
OF THREAT. Rev. ed. Homewood, Ill.: Dorsey, 1978.

Especially chapters 3, 9.

Sapin, Burton M. THE MAKING OF UNITED STATES FOREIGN POLICY.
Washington, D.C.: Brookings Institution, 1966.

Especially chapter 6.

Snyder, Richard C., and Furniss, Edgar S., Jr. AMERICAN FOREIGN POLICY:
FORMULATION, PRINCIPLES, AND PROGRAMS. New York: Rinehart, 1954.

Especially chapter 9.

CIVIL-MILITARY RELATIONS

Historically the relationship of civil and military authority has constituted an
important issue in American constitutional and political development. The following materials focus on this matter as it affects command, policy making,
and pragmatic operational levels. A number of items--including those of Coles,
Hauser, Huntington, Lovell, Millis, Smith, and others--deal with the matter
of civilian control of the military. Additional materials on the president as
commander in chief are presented in chapter 7, and a more comprehensive
listing of materials is contained in the Social Science Research Council bibliography referred to at the beginning of this chapter, p. 260. Guidance to
additional materials may be found in the following:

Larson, Arthur D., ed. CIVIL-MILITARY RELATIONS AND MILITARISM: A
CLASSIFIED BIBLIOGRAPHY COVERING THE UNITED STATES AND OTHER
NATIONS OF THE WORLD, WITH INTRODUCTORY NOTES. Manhattan:
Kansas State University Library, 1971. 113 p.

Bienen, Henry, ed. THE MILITARY INTERVENES: CASE STUDY IN POLITI-
CAL DEVELOPMENT. New York: Russell Sage Foundation, 1968. 175 p.

Cochran, Charles L., ed. CIVIL MILITARY RELATIONS: CHANGING CON-
CEPTS IN THE SEVENTIES. New York: Free Press, 1974. 366 p. Bibliog.

Coles, Harry L., ed. TOTAL WAR AND COLD WAR: PROBLEMS IN CIVIL-
IAN CONTROL OF THE MILITARY. Columbus: Ohio State University Press,
1962. 300 p.

Ekrich, Arthur A. THE CIVILIAN AND THE MILITARY. New York: Oxford University Press, 1956. 340 p. Bibliog.

Finer, Samuel E. THE MAN ON HORSEBACK: THE ROLE OF THE MILITARY IN POLITICS. New York: Praeger, 1962. 268 p. Bibliog.

Flannery, Richard F., Jr. "Civil-Military Relations in Wartime: The United States and the Soviety Union, 1940-1945." Ph.D. dissertation, University of Wisconsin, 1974. 275 p.

Fox, William T.R. "Civilians, Soldiers, and American Military Policy." WORLD POLITICS 7 (April 1955): 402-18.

_____. "Representativeness and Efficiency: Dual Problem of Civil-Military Relations." POLITICAL SCIENCE QUARTERLY 76 (September 1961): 354-66.

Gellermann, Josef E. GENERALS AS STATESMEN. New York: Vantage, 1959. 150 p.

Glick, Edward B. PEACEFUL CONFLICT: THE NON-MILITARY USE OF THE MILITARY. Harrisburg, Pa.: Stackpole, 1967. 223 p. Bibliog.

Goodpaster, Andrew J., and Huntington, Samuel P., in association with Gene A. Sherill and Orville Menard. CIVIL MILITARY RELATIONS. Washington, D.C.: American Enterprise Institute, 1977. 84 p.

Hauser, William L. AMERICA'S ARMY IN CRISIS: A STUDY IN CIVIL-MILITARY RELATIONS. Baltimore: Johns Hopkins Press, 1973. 242 p.

Hoopes, Townsend. "Civilian-Military Balance." YALE REVIEW 43 (December 1953): 218-34.

Howard, Michael. SOLDIERS AND GOVERNMENT. Bloomington: University of Indiana Press, 1959. 192 p.

Huntington, Samuel P. "Civilian Control and the Constitution." AMERICAN POLITICAL SCIENCE REVIEW 50 (September 1956): 676-99.

_____. THE SOLDIER AND THE STATE: THE THEORY AND POLITICS OF CIVIL-MILITARY RELATIONS. Cambridge, Mass.: Belknap Press of Harvard University Press, 1957. 534 p.

Kerwin, Jerome G., ed. CIVIL-MILITARY RELATIONSHIPS IN AMERICAN LIFE. Chicago: University of Chicago Press, 1948. 181 p.

Lovell, John P., and Kronenberg, Philip S. NEW CIVIL-MILITARY RELA-
TIONS: AGONIES OF ADJUSTMENT TO POST-VIETNAM REALITIES. New
York: Dutton, 1973. 352 p.

Lyons, Gene M. "The New Civil-Military Relations." AMERICAN POLITICAL
SCIENCE REVIEW 55 (March 1961): 53–63.

Mansfield, Harvey C. "Civil-Military Relations in the United States." CUR-
RENT HISTORY 38 (April 1960): 228–33.

Marshall, Charles Burton. "Present Day Relationship Between Military Power
and Civil Authority." DEPARTMENT OF STATE BULLETIN 27 (8 September
1952): 348–52.

May, Ernest R. "The Development of Political-Military Consultation in the
United States." POLITICAL SCIENCE QUARTERLY 70 (June 1955): 161–80.

Millis, Walter; Mansfield, Harvey C.; and Stein, Harold. ARMS AND THE
STATE: CIVIL-MILITARY ELEMENTS IN NATIONAL POLICY. New York:
Twentieth Century Fund, 1958. 436 p. Bibliog.

Smith, Louis. AMERICAN DEMOCRACY AND MILITARY POWER: A STUDY
OF CIVIL CONTROL OF THE MILITARY POWER IN THE UNITED STATES.
Chicago: University of Chicago Press, 1951. 370 p.

Spina, Joseph. "The Citizen-Soldier and the Civil-Military Interface: A
Study of Foreign Policy Opinion Circulation by U.S. Military Reserve Officers."
Ph.D. dissertation, Rutgers University, 1976. 237 p.

Stein, Harold, ed. AMERICAN CIVIL-MILITARY DECISIONS: A BOOK OF
CASE STUDIES. University: University of Alabama Press, 1963. 705 p.

MILITARY ORGANIZATION AND ADMINISTRATION

This section provides a limited selection of materials on military organization,
reorganization, institutionalization, and administration. It consists of separate
sections on the secretary of defense and the service secretaries, the chiefs of
staff and Joint Chiefs, the military establishment, the Department of Defense
and the Pentagon, and the development and problems of military organization
and reorganization, together with the roles of a few related agencies.

Secretaries of Defense and the Military Services

Albion, Robert G., and Connery, Robert H. FORRESTAL AND THE NAVY.
New York: Columbia University Press, 1962. 359 p. Bibliog.

Borklund, Carl W. MEN OF THE PENTAGON: FROM FORRESTAL TO McNAMARA. New York: Praeger, 1966. 236 p.

Forrestal, James. THE FORRESTAL DIARIES. Edited by Walter Millis with E.S. Duffield. New York: Viking, 1951. 581 p.

Kaufmann, William W. THE McNAMARA STRATEGY. New York: Harper and Row, 1964. 339 p.

Kugler, Richard L. "The Politics of Restraint: Robert McNamara and the Strategic Nuclear Forces." Ph.D. dissertation, Massachusetts Institute of Technology, 1975.

Leach, W. Barton. "The Job of an American Service Secretary." REVUE MILITAIRE GENERALE, March 1958, pp. 359-89.

McNamara, Robert S. THE ESSENCE OF SECURITY: REFLECTIONS IN OF-FICE. New York: Harper and Row, 1968. 176 p.

Rogow, Arnold A. JAMES FORRESTAL: A STUDY OF PERSONALITY, POLI-TICS, AND POLICY. New York: Macmillan, 1963. 397 p.

Roherty, James M. DECISIONS OF ROBERT S. McNAMARA: A STUDY OF THE ROLE OF SECRETARY OF DEFENSE. Coral Gables, Fla.: University of Miami Press, 1970. 223 p.

Zuckert, Eugene M. "The Service Secretary: Has He a Useful Role?" FOR-EIGN AFFAIRS 44 (April 1966): 458-79.

Chiefs of Staff and the Joint Chiefs

American Enterprise Institute. THE ROLE OF THE JOINT CHIEFS OF STAFF IN NATIONAL POLICY. Washington, D.C.: 1978. 42 p.
    Round table held on August 2, 1978.

Edwards, Earl W. "Secretary of the General Staff or Super-Staff?" MILITARY REVIEW 34 (January 1955): 3-7.

Hittle, J.D. "Military Planning at the Seat of Government." U.S. NAVAL INSTITUTE PROCEEDINGS 83 (July 1957): 713-21.

Korb, Lawrence J. THE JOINT CHIEFS OF STAFF: THE FIRST TWENTY-FIVE YEARS. Bloomington: Indiana University Press, 1976. 210 p.

Nelson, Otto L., Jr. NATIONAL SECURITY AND THE GENERAL STAFF. Washington, D.C.: Infantry Journal Press, 1946. 608 p.

Sulzberger, Arthur O. THE JOINT CHIEFS OF STAFF, 1941-1954. Washington, D.C.: U.S. Marine Corps Institute, 1954. 88 p.

Twining, Nathan F. "The Joint Chiefs of Staff." ORDNANCE 43 (May-June 1959): 898-900.

Watson, Mark Skinner. CHIEF OF STAFF: PREWAR PLANS AND PREPARATIONS. Washington, D.C.: Historical Division, U.S. Department of the Army, 1950. 551 p.

Wermuth, Anthony L. "A General Staff for America in the Sixties." MILITARY REVIEW 39 (February 1960): 11-20.

The Military Establishment

Collins, J. Lawton. "Our Modern Military Establishment." MILITARY REVIEW 42 (September 1962): 17-30.

Frye, William. "National Military Establishment." AMERICAN POLITICAL SCIENCE REVIEW 43 (June 1949): 543-55.

Hammond, Paul Y. ORGANIZING FOR DEFENSE: THE AMERICAN MILITARY ESTABLISHMENT IN THE TWENTIETH CENTURY. Princeton, N.J.: Princeton, University Press, 1961. 403 p.

Janowitz, Morris. SOCIOLOGY AND THE MILITARY ESTABLISHMENT. 3d ed. Beverly Hills, Calif.: Sage, 1974. 159 p.

Moskos, Charles C., Jr., ed. PUBLIC OPINION AND THE MILITARY ESTABLISHMENT. Beverly Hills, Calif.: Sage, 1971. 294 p.

Schratz, Paul Richard. "The U.S. Defense Establishment: Trends in Organizational Structures, Functions, and Interrelationships, 1958-1970." Ph.D. dissertation, Ohio State University, 1972. 586 p.

_____, ed. EVOLUTION OF THE AMERICAN MILITARY ESTABLISHMENT SINCE WORLD WAR II. Lexington, Va.: George C. Marshall Foundation, 1978. 125 p.

U.S. Department of Defense. THE HISTORY OF THE JOINT CHIEFS OF STAFF: THE JOINT CHIEFS OF STAFF AND NATIONAL POLICY. 3 vols. in 4. Wilmington, Del.: Glazier, 1979.

Williams, Thomas H. AMERICANS AT WAR: THE DEVELOPMENT OF THE AMERICAN MILITARY SYSTEM. 2d ed. New York: Collier, 1962. 159 p.

Yarmolinsky, Adam. THE MILITARY ESTABLISHMENT: ITS IMPACT ON AMERICAN SOCIETY. New York: Harper and Row, 1971. 434 p.

Department of Defense and the Pentagon

Borklund, Carl W. THE DEPARTMENT OF DEFENSE. New York: Praeger, 1969. 342 p. Bibliog.

Congressional Quarterly. THE POWER OF THE PENTAGON: THE CREATION, CONTROL AND ACCEPTANCE OF DEFENSE POLICY BY THE U.S. CONGRESS. Washington, D.C.: 1972. 116 p.

Gurney, Gene. THE PENTAGON. New York: Crown, 1964. 146 p.

Kintner, William R., with Joseph I. Coffey and Raymond J. Albright. FORGING A NEW SWORD: A STUDY OF THE DEPARTMENT OF DEFENSE. New York: Harper and Row for Center for International Studies, Massachusetts Institute of Technology, 1958. 238 p.

Mollenhoff, Clark R. THE PENTAGON: POLITICS: PROFITS, AND PLUNDER. New York: Putnam, 1967. 450 p.

Neblett, William H. PENTAGON POLITICS. New York: Pageant, 1953. 131 p.

Nielson, Waldemar A. "Huge, Hidden Impact of the Pentagon." NEW YORK TIMES MAGAZINE, 25 June 1961, pp. 9, 31, 34, 36.

Raymond, Jack. POWER AT THE PENTAGON. New York: Harper and Row, 1964. 363 p. Bibliog.

Tyrell, C. Merton. PENTAGON PARTNERS: THE NEW NOBILITY. New York: Grossman, 1970. 233 p.

Organization, Reorganization, and Administration

Beishline, John R. MILITARY MANAGEMENT FOR NATIONAL DEFENSE. New York: Prentice-Hall, 1950. 289 p.

Bobrow, Davis B., ed. WEAPONS SYSTEMS DECISIONS: POLITICAL AND PSYCHOLOGICAL PERSPECTIVES ON CONTINENTAL DEFENSE. New York: Praeger, 1969. 282 p.

Brannen, Philip Barry. "A Single Service: Perennial Issue in National Defense." U.S. NAVAL INSTITUTE PROCEEDINGS 83 (December 1957): 1280-87.

Brown, Alvin. THE ARMOR OF ORGANIZATION: A RATIONAL PLAN OF ORGANIZATION FOR THE ARMED FORCES AND, AS A PRELIMINARY THERE-TO, AN INQUIRY INTO THE ORIGINS OF EXISTING MILITARY ORGANIZA-TION. New York: Hibbert, 1953. 597 p.

Callan, Robert W., and Kinsella, W.T. THE STRUCTURE AND OPERATION OF TOP-LEVEL MILITARY COMMAND. Santa Barbara, Calif.: General Electric Co., TEMPO, 1962. 76 p.

Coates, Charles H., and Pelligrin, Roland J. MILITARY SOCIOLOGY: A STUDY OF AMERICAN MILITARY INSTITUTIONS AND MILITARY LIFE. University Park, Md.: Social Science, 1965. 424 p. Bibliog.

Cutler, Robert. "Defense Organization at the Policy Level." GENERAL ELECTRIC DEFENSE QUARTERLY 2 (January-March 1959): 8-15.

Davis, Vincent. THE ADMIRALS LOBBY. Chapel Hill: University of North Carolina Press, 1967. 329 p.

Drucker, Peter F. "Defense Organization: New Realities and Old Concepts." GENERAL ELECTRIC DEFENSE QUARTERLY 2 (January-March 1959): 4-7.

Emmerich, Herbert. "Some Notes on Wartime Federal Administration." PUBLIC ADMINISTRATION REVIEW 5 (Winter 1945): 55-61.

Enke, Stephen, ed. DEFENSE MANAGEMENT. Englewood Cliffs, N.J.: Prentice-Hall, 1967. 385 p. Bibliog.

Enthoven, Alain C., and Rowen, H.S. AN ANALYSIS OF DEFENSE ORGA-NIZATION. Research Paper P-1640. Santa Monica, Calif.: Rand, 1959. 55 p.

Enthoven, Alain C., and Smith, K. Wayne. HOW MUCH IS ENOUGH? SHAPING THE DEFENSE PROGRAM, 1961-1969. New York: Harper and Row, 1971. 364 p.

Henry, Andrew F.; Masland, John W.; and Radway, Laurence I. "Armed Forces Unification and the Pentagon Officer." PUBLIC ADMINISTRATION RE-VIEW 15 (Summer 1955): 173-80.

Huie, William B. THE CASE AGAINST THE ADMIRALS: WHY WE MUST HAVE A UNIFIED COMMAND. New York: Dutton, 1946. 216 p.

Huzar, Elias. "Reorganization for National Security." JOURNAL OF POLI-TICS   12 (February 1950): 128-52.

Janowitz, Morris, ed. THE NEW MILITARY: CHANGING PATTERNS OF ORGANIZATION. New York: Russell Sage Foundation, 1964. 369 p.

Kammerer, Gladys M. IMPACT OF WAR ON FEDERAL PERSONNEL ADMINISTRA-TION, 1939-1945. Lexington: University of Kentucky Press, 1951. 372 p.

Mosher, Frederick C. "Old Concepts and New Problems." PUBLIC ADMIN-ISTRATION REVIEW   18 (Summer 1958): 169-75.

Olverson, John B. "Problems of Defense Unification Under the National Secu-rity Act." FEDERAL BAR JOURNAL   18 (January-March 1958): 3-20.

Palmer, John M. AMERICA IN ARMS: THE EXPERIENCE OF THE UNITED STATES WITH MILITARY ORGANIZATION. New Haven, Conn.: Yale Uni-versity Press, 1941. 207 p.

Powers, Patrick W. A GUIDE TO NATIONAL DEFENSE: THE ORGANIZA-TION AND OPERATIONS OF THE U.S. MILITARY ESTABLISHMENT. New York: Praeger, 1964. 326 p. Bibliog.

Ries, John C. THE MANAGEMENT OF DEFENSE: ORGANIZATION AND CONTROL OF THE U.S. ARMED FORCES. Baltimore: Johns Hopkins Press, 1964. 228 p. Bibliog.

Somers, Herman M. PRESIDENTIAL AGENCY: OWMR, THE OFFICE OF WAR MOBILIZATION AND RECONVERSION. Cambridge, Mass.: Harvard Univer-sity Press, 1950. 238 p.

Stewart, Irvin. ORGANIZING SCIENTIFIC RESEARCH FOR WAR: THE AD-MINISTRATIVE HISTORY OF THE OFFICE OF SCIENTIFIC RESEARCH AND DEVELOPMENT. Boston: Little, Brown, 1948. 358 p.

U.S. Bureau of the Budget. THE UNITED STATES AT WAR: DEVELOPMENT AND ADMINISTRATION OF THE WAR PROGRAM BY THE FEDERAL GOVERN-MENT. Washington, D.C.: Government Printing Office, 1946. 555 p.

U.S. Commission on the Organization of the Government for the Conduct of Foreign Policy. "Adequacy of Current Organization: Defense and Arms Con-trol." In its COMMISSION ON THE ORGANIZATION OF THE GOVERN-MENT FOR THE CONDUCT OF FOREIGN POLICY, JUNE 1975, Appendix, vol. 4, pp. 1-475. Washington, D.C.: Government Printing Office, 1976.

White, Leonard D., ed. CIVIL SERVICE IN WARTIME. Chicago: University of Chicago Press, 1945. 253 p.

Yoshpe, Harry B. NATIONAL SECURITY RESOURCES BOARD, 1947-1953: A CASE STUDY IN PEACETIME MOBILIZATION PLANNING. Washington, D.C.: Government Printing Office, 1953. 172 p.

Prepared for Executive Office of the President.

MILITARY-SECURITY-DEFENSE POLICY AND STRATEGY

One of the more important aspects of the military in the conduct of U.S. foreign relations is its foreign and security policy role. Inasmuch as the military has played an increasingly important part in this matter since World War II, special attention needs to be paid to published resources on such subjects as policy making (see also chapter 16), decision making (see also chapter 14), the impact of military doctrine and theory on public policy and external affairs, national security, national strategy and strategic policy, and the basic interaction of foreign and military policy.

Policy Making

Benjamin, Roger W. "Military Influence in Foreign Policy-Making." Ph.D. dissertation, Washington University (St. Louis), 1967. 252 p.

Benjamin, Roger W., and Edinger, Lewis J. "Conditions for Military Control over Foreign Policy Decisions in Major States: An Historical Explanation." JOURNAL OF CONFLICT RESOLUTION 15 (March 1971): 5-31.

Bolles, Blair. "Influence of Armed Forces on U.S. Foreign Policy." FOREIGN POLICY REPORTS 22 (1 October 1946): 170-80.

Bolt, Ernest Collier, Jr. "The War Referendum Approach to Peace in Twentieth Century America: A Study in Foreign Policy Formulation and Military Defense Attitudes." Ph.D. dissertation, University of Georgia, 1966. 401 p.

Bull, Hedley. "Strategic Studies and Its Critics." WORLD POLITICS 20 (July 1968): 593-605.

Caraley, Demetrios. THE POLITICS OF MILITARY UNIFICATION, 1943-1947: A STUDY OF CONFLICT AND THE POLICY PROCESS. New York: Columbia University Press, 1965. 403 p. Bibliog.

Edinger, Lewis J. "Military Leaders and Foreign Policy-Making." AMERICAN POLITICAL SCIENCE REVIEW 57 (June 1963): 392-405.

Giffin, S.F. "Tomorrow's Military Matrix." WORLD POLITICS 14 (April 1962): 433-38.

Herzog, James Henry. "The Role of the United States Navy in the Evolution and Execution of American Foreign Policy Relative to Japan, 1936-1941." Ph.D. dissertation, Brown University, 1963. 224 p.

Hilsman, Roger. THE POLITICS OF POLICY MAKING IN DEFENSE AND FOREIGN AFFAIRS. New York: Harper and Row, 1971. 198 p.

Hoag, Malcolm W. "Some Complexities in Military Planning." WORLD POLITICS 11 (July 1959): 553-76.

Knorr, Klaus E., and Morgenstern, Oskar. POLITICAL CONJECTURE IN MILITARY PLANNING. Princeton, N.J.: Center of International Studies, Princeton University, 1968. 56 p.

Murdock, Clark A. DEFENSE POLICY FORMATION: A COMPARATIVE ANALYSIS OF THE McNAMARA ERA. Albany: State University of New York Press, 1974. 209 p. Bibliog.

Quade, Edward S., and Boucher, W.I., eds. SYSTEMS ANALYSIS AND POLICY PLANNING: APPLICATIONS IN DEFENSE. New York: American Elsevier, 1968. 453 p. Bibliog.

Schlesinger, James R. "Quantitative Analysis and National Security." WORLD POLITICS 15 (January 1963): 295-315.

Decision Making

A more comprehensive listing of materials on the decision-making process, with case studies, is presented in chapter 14. The following list is confined to a few selected items relating specifically to matters especially relevant to the military.

Enthoven, Alain C. "Systems Analysis and Decision Making." MILITARY REVIEW 43 (January 1963): 7-17.

Goldman, Thomas A., ed. COST EFFECTIVENESS ANALYSIS: NEW APPROACHES IN DECISION-MAKING. New York: Praeger, for Washington Operations Research Council, 1967. 231 p. Bibliog.

Hitch, Charles Johnston. DECISION-MAKING FOR DEFENSE. Berkeley: University of California Press, 1965. 83 p.

Hoxie, R. Gordon. COMMAND DECISION AND THE PRESIDENCY: A STUDY IN NATIONAL SECURITY POLICY AND ORGANIZATION. New York: Reader's Digest Press, 1977. 505 p.

Livingston, J. Sterling. "Decision Making in Weapons Development." HAR-VARD BUSINESS REVIEW 36 (January-February 1958): 127-36.

Medaris, John B., and Gordon, Arthur. COUNTDOWN FOR DECISION. New York: Putnam, 1960. 303 p.

Mosher, Frederick C. "Decision-Making in Defense: The Role of Organization." PUBLIC ADMINISTRATION REVIEW 18 (Summer 1958): 169-88.

Quade, Edward S., ed. ANALYSIS FOR MILITARY DECISIONS. Chicago: Rand McNally, 1964. Reprint. New York: American Elsevier, 1970. 382 p. Bibliog.

Stein, Harold, ed. AMERICAN CIVIL-MILITARY DECISIONS: A BOOK OF CASE STUDIES. University: University of Alabama Press, 1963. 705 p.

Military Doctrine and Theory

Bretnor, Reginald. DECISIVE WARFARE: A STUDY IN MILITARY THEORY. Harrisburg, Pa.: Stackpole, 1969. 192 p.

Coats, Wendell J. ARMED FORCE AS POWER: THE THEORY OF WAR RE-CONSIDERED. New York: Exposition, 1967. 432 p. Bibliog.

Garnett, John C., ed. THEORIES OF PEACE AND SECURITY: A READER IN CONTEMPORARY STRATEGIC THOUGHT. New York: St. Martin's, 1970. 272 p. Bibliog.

Millis, Walter, ed. AMERICAN MILITARY THOUGHT. Indianapolis: Bobbs-Merrill, 1966. 554 p. Bibliog.

Smith, Dale O. U.S. MILITARY DOCTRINE: A STUDY AND APPRAISAL. New York: Duell, Sloan, and Pearce, 1955. 256 p.

Weigley, Russell F. TOWARDS AN AMERICAN ARMY: MILITARY THOUGHT FROM WASHINGTON TO MARSHALL. New York: Columbia University Press, 1962. 297 p. Bibliog.

National Strategy and Security

Dorman, James E., Jr. UNITED STATES NATIONAL SECURITY POLICY IN THE DECADE AHEAD. New York: Crane, Russak, 1978. 200 p.

Erickson, John; Crowley, Edward L.; and Galay, Nikolai, eds. THE MILITARY-TECHNICAL REVOLUTION: ITS IMPACT ON STRATEGY AND FOREIGN POLICY. New York: Praeger for Institute for the Study of the USSR (Munich), 1966. 284 p.

Greenfield, Kent R. AMERICAN STRATEGY IN WORLD WAR II: A RECONSIDERATION. Baltimore: Johns Hopkins Press, 1963. 145 p.

Halperin, Morton H. CONTEMPORARY MILITARY STRATEGY. Boston: Little, Brown for Center for International Affairs, Harvard University, 1967. 156 p. Bibliog.

_____. DEFENSE STRATEGIES FOR THE SEVENTIES. Boston: Little, Brown, 1971. 149 p. Bibliog.

Huntington, Samuel P. THE COMMON DEFENSE: STRATEGIC PROBLEMS IN NATIONAL POLITICS. New York: Columbia University Press, 1961. 500 p. Bibliog.

Institute for Strategic Studies (London). PROBLEMS OF MODERN STRATEGY. New York: Praeger, 1970. 219 p. Bibliog.

Jackson, Henry M. FACT, FICTION, AND NATIONAL SECURITY. New York: MacFadden-Bartell, 1964. 128 p.

Kaufmann, William W., ed. MILITARY POLICY AND NATIONAL SECURITY. Princeton, N.J.: Princeton University Press, 1956. 274 p.

Kecskemeti, Paul. STRATEGIC SURRENDER: THE POLITICS OF VICTORY AND DEFEAT. Stanford, Calif.: Stanford University Press, 1958. 287 p.

Kingston-McCloughry, Edgar J. THE SPECTRUM OF STRATEGY: A STUDY OF POLICY AND STRATEGY IN MODERN WAR. London: Cape, 1964. 223 p.

Kintner, William R. PEACE AND THE STRATEGY CONFLICT. New York: Praeger for Foreign Policy Research Institute, University of Pennsylvania, 1967. 264 p.

Kissinger, Henry A. NUCLEAR WEAPONS AND FOREIGN POLICY. New York: Harper for Council on Foreign Relations, 1957. 455 p.

_____, ed. PROBLEMS OF NATIONAL STRATEGY: A BOOK OF READINGS. New York: Praeger, 1965. 477 p.

Kissinger, Henry A., and Brodie, Bernard. BUREAUCRACY, POLITICS, AND STRATEGY. Los Angeles: University of California Press, 1968. 60 p.

Knorr, Klaus E. ON THE USES OF MILITARY POWER IN THE NUCLEAR AGE. Princeton, N.J.: Princeton University Press for Center of International Studies, Princeton University, 1966. 185 p.

_____, ed. HISTORICAL DIMENSIONS OF NATIONAL SECURITY PROBLEMS. Lawrence: University Press of Kansas, 1976. 387 p.

Laird, Melvin R. A HOUSE DIVIDED: AMERICA'S STRATEGY GAP. Chicago: Regnery, 1962. 179 p.

Murphy, Robert D. "Interlocking Elements in Our National Security." DEPARTMENT OF STATE BULLETIN 36 (25 March 1957): 475-79.

Nitze, Paul H. POLITICAL ASPECTS OF A NATIONAL STRATEGY. Washington, D.C.: Washington Center for Foreign Policy Research, Johns Hopkins University, 1960. 23 p.

Radway, Laurence I. THE LIBERAL DEMOCRACY IN WORLD AFFAIRS: FOREIGN POLICY AND NATIONAL DEFENSE. Atlanta: Scott, Foresman, 1969. 207 p.

Rockefeller Brothers Fund. INTERNATIONAL SECURITY: THE MILITARY ASPECT. Garden City, N.Y.: Doubleday, 1958. 63 p.

Sanders, Ralph. THE POLITICS OF DEFENSE ANALYSIS. Port Washington, N.Y.: Dunellen, 1973. 361 p.

Schilling, Warner R.; Hammond, Paul Y.; and Snyder, Glenn H. STRATEGY, POLITICS, AND DEFENSE BUDGETS. New York: Columbia University Press, 1962. 532 p.

Schwarz, Urs. AMERICAN STRATEGY: A NEW PERSPECTIVE--THE GROWTH OF POLITICO-MILITARY THINKING IN THE UNITED STATES. Garden City, N.Y.: Doubleday, 1966. 178 p.

Tarr, David W. AMERICAN STRATEGY IN THE NUCLEAR AGE. New York: Macmillan, 1966. 140 p.

Trager, Frank N., and Kronenberg, Philip S. NATIONAL SECURITY AND AMERICAN SOCIETY: THEORY, PROCESS, AND POLICY. Lawrence: Regents Press of Kansas, 1978. 612 p.

Turner, Gordon B., and Challener, Richard D., eds. NATIONAL SECURITY IN THE NUCLEAR AGE: BASIC FACTS AND THEORIES. New York: Praeger, 1960. 293 p.

Twining, Nathan F. NEITHER LIBERTY NOR SAFETY: A HARD LOOK AT U.S. MILITARY POLICY AND STRATEGY. New York: Holt, Rinehart, and Winston, 1966. 320 p.

Military and Foreign Policy

Abbott, Charles C. THE INTERNATIONAL POSITION AND COMMITMENTS OF THE UNITED STATES. Washington, D.C.: American Enterprise Association, 1953. 36 p.

Andrews, Craig N. FOREIGN POLICY AND THE NEW AMERICAN MILITARY. Beverly Hills, Calif.: Sage, 1974. 46 p.

Baral, Jaya Krishna. THE PENTAGON AND THE MAKING OF U.S. FOREIGN POLICY: A CASE STUDY OF VIETNAM, 1960-1968. Atlantic Highlands, N.J.: Humanities Press, 1978. 333 p.

Beckman, Peter Roane. "The Influence of the American Military Establishment on American Foreign Policy." Ph.D. dissertation, University of Wisconsin (Madison), 1974. 215 p.

Bennett, John Arthur Watson. "An Examination of the Foreign Policy Role of American Military Officers in the Light of Contemporary American Military History." Ph.D. dissertation, American University, 1968. 541 p.

Berger, William Ellsworth. "The Role of the Armed Services in International Policy." Ph.D. dissertation, University of Nebraska, 1956. 296 p.

Bernardo, C. Joseph, and Bacon, Eugene H. AMERICAN MILITARY POLICY: ITS DEVELOPMENT SINCE 1775. 2d ed. Harrisburg, Pa.: Stackpole, 1961. Reprint: Westport, Conn.: Greenwood, 1974. 548 p.

Bletz, Donald F. THE ROLE OF THE MILITARY PROFESSIONAL IN U.S. FOREIGN POLICY. New York: Praeger, 1972. 320 p.

Bobrow, Davis B., ed. COMPONENTS OF DEFENSE POLICY. Chicago: Rand McNally, 1965. 445 p. Bibliog.

Booth, K. NAVIES AND FOREIGN POLICY. New York: Crane, Russak, 1977. 294 p.

Bosch, Juan. PENTAGONISM: A SUBSTITUTE FOR IMPERIALISM. Translated by Helen R. Lane. New York: Grove, 1968. 141 p.

Challener, Richard D. ADMIRALS, GENERALS, AND AMERICAN FOREIGN POLICY: 1898-1914. Princeton, N.J.: Princeton University Press, 1973. 433 p. Bibliog.

Cobb, Stephen Archibald. "The Military-Industrial Complex and Foreign Policy." Ph.D. dissertation, Vanderbilt University, 1971. 134 p.

Donnelly, Charles H. UNITED STATES DEFENSE POLICIES SINCE WORLD WAR II. Washington, D.C.: Government Printing Office, 1957. 87 p. Bibliog.

   Prepared for Legislative Reference Service, U.S. Library of Congress.

Finletter, Thomas K. POWER AND POLICY: U.S. FOREIGN POLICY AND MILITARY POWER IN THE HYDROGEN AGE. New York: Harcourt, Brace, 1954. 408 p.

Furniss, Edgar S. AMERICAN MILITARY POLICY: STRATEGIC ASPECTS OF WORLD POLITICAL GEOGRAPHY. New York: Rinehart, 1957. 494 p. Bibliog.

   Especially chapter 2.

Goldwin, Robert A., ed. AMERICAN ARMED: ESSAYS ON UNITED STATES MILITARY POLICY. Chicago: Rand McNally, 1963. 140 p.

Hammond, Paul Y. "The Effects of Structure on Policy." PUBLIC ADMINIS-TRATION REVIEW 18 (Summer 1958): 175-79.

Johnson, David T., and Schneider, Barry R. CURRENT ISSUES IN U.S. DE-FENSE POLICY. New York: Praeger, 1976. 254 p. Bibliog.

Katzenbach, Edward L., Jr. "Military Policy as a National Issue." CUR-RENT HISTORY 31 (October 1956): 193-98.

Kintner, William R. "War, Politics, and the Military." U.S. NAVAL INSTI-TUTE PROCEEDINGS 77 (February 1951): 129-33.

Masland, John W., and Radway, Laurence I. SOLDIERS AND SCHOLARS: MILITARY EDUCATION AND NATIONAL POLICY. Princeton, N.J.: Princeton University Press, 1957. 530 p.

Murphy, Robert D. "The Interrelationship of Military Power and Foreign Policy." DEPARTMENT OF STATE BULLETIN 31 (30 August 1954): 291-94.

O'Connor, Raymond G., ed. AMERICAN DEFENSE POLICY IN PERSPECTIVE

FROM COLONIAL TIMES TO THE PRESENT. New York: Wiley, 1965. 377 p.

Quester, George H. NUCLEAR DIPLOMACY: THE FIRST TWENTY-FIVE YEARS. New York: Dunellen for Center for International Affairs, Harvard University, 1970. 327 p.

Rakove, Milton L., ed. ARMS AND FOREIGN POLICY IN THE NUCLEAR AGE. Chicago: American Foundation for Continuing Education, 1964. 635 p.

Reinhardt, George C., and Kintner, William R. "Policy: Matrix of Strategy." U.S. NAVAL INSTITUTE PROCEEDINGS 80 (February 1954): 144-55.

Rosenberg, Milton J., ed. BEYOND CONFLICT AND CONTAINMENT: CRITICAL STUDIES OF MILITARY AND FOREIGN POLICY. New Brunswick, N.J.: Transaction, 1972. 341 p.

Sapin, Burton M., ed. CONTEMPORARY AMERICAN FOREIGN AND MILITARY POLICY. Glenview, Ill.: Scott, Foresman, 1970. 185 p.

Sapin, Burton M., and Snyder, Richard C. THE ROLE OF THE MILITARY IN AMERICAN FOREIGN POLICY. Garden City, N.Y.: Doubleday, 1954. 84 p. Bibliog.

Sapin, Burton M.; Snyder, Richard C.; and Bruck, H.W. AN APPROPRIATE ROLE FOR THE MILITARY IN AMERICAN FOREIGN POLICY-MAKING: A RESEARCH NOTE. Princeton, N.J.: Princeton University Press, 1954. 64 p.

Schilling, Warner Roller. "Admirals and Foreign Policy, 1913-1919." Ph.D. dissertation, Yale University, 1954. 375 p.

Skolnikoff, Eugene B. SCIENCE, TECHNOLOGY, AND AMERICAN FOREIGN POLICY. Cambridge, Mass.: M.I.T. Press, 1967. 330 p.

Stanley, Timothy W. AMERICAN DEFENSE AND NATIONAL SECURITY. Washington, D.C.: Public Affairs, 1956. 202 p. Bibliog.

Sunderland, Riley. "The Soldier's Relation to Foreign Policy." U.S. NAVAL INSTITUTE PROCEEDINGS 69 (September 1943): 1170-75.

Trask, David F. THE UNITED STATES IN THE SUPREME WAR COUNCIL: AMERICAN WAR AIMS AND INTER-ALLIED STRATEGY, 1917-1918. Middletown, Conn.: Wesleyan University Press, 1961. 244 p.

Whetten, Lawrence L. CONTEMPORARY AMERICAN FOREIGN POLICY: MINIMAL DIPLOMACY, DEFENSE STRATEGY, AND DETENTE MANAGEMENT. Lexington, Mass.: Lexington Books, 1974. 386 p.

Whitson, William W., ed. FOREIGN POLICY AND U.S. NATIONAL SECU-
RITY. New York: Praeger, 1976. 384 p.

Yarmolinsky, Adam. UNITED STATES MILITARY POWER AND FOREIGN POLI-
CY. Chicago: Center for Policy Study, University of Chicago, 1967. 28 p.

ECONOMIC FACTORS AND MOBILIZATION

Whereas literary resources on U.S. economic policy and development would
fill a substantial library, and although one aspect of foreign economic affairs
is touched on in chapter 17 (section on "Trade and Aid"), the following list
is simply a nucleus of recent materials (since 1950) pertinent to the economic
aspects of the role of the military in the conduct of foreign relations:

Backman, Jules, ed. WAR AND DEFENSE ECONOMICS. New York: Rinehart, 1952. 458 p. Bibliog.

Baldwin, William L. THE STRUCTURE OF THE DEFENSE MARKET, 1955-1964.
Durham, N.C.: Duke University Press, 1967. 249 p.

Campbell, W. Glenn, ed. ECONOMICS OF MOBILIZATION AND WAR.
Homewood, Ill.: Irwin, 1952. 196 p.

Chandler, Lester V., and Wallace, Donald H. ECONOMIC MOBILIZATION
AND STABILIZATION: SELECTED MATERIALS ON THE ECONOMICS OF WAR
AND DEFENSE. New York: Holt, 1951. 610 p.

Clark, John J. THE NEW ECONOMICS OF NATIONAL DEFENSE. New
York: Random House, 1966. 242 p.

Clayton, James I., ed. THE ECONOMIC IMPACT OF THE COLD WAR:
SOURCES AND READINGS. New York: Harcourt, Brace, and World, 1970.
287 p. Bibliog.

Coffey, Kenneth J. MANPOWER FOR MILITARY MOBILIZATION. Washington, D.C.: American Enterprise Institute, 1978. 47 p.

Committee for Economic Development. THE PROBLEM OF NATIONAL SECU-
RITY--SOME ECONOMIC AND ADMINISTRATIVE ASPECTS: A STATEMENT
ON NATIONAL POLICY. New York: 1958. 58 p.

Cooling, Benjamin Franklin, ed. WAR, BUSINESS, AND AMERICAN SOCIETY:
HISTORICAL PERSPECTIVES ON THE MILITARY-INDUSTRIAL COMPLEX. Port
Washington, N.Y.: Kennikat, 1977. 205 p.

Elliott, William Y., et al. THE POLITICAL ECONOMY OF AMERICAN FOREIGN POLICY: ITS CONCEPTS, STRATEGY, AND LIMITS. New York: Holt for Woodrow Wilson Foundation and National Planning Association, 1955. 414 p.

Harris, Seymour E. THE ECONOMICS OF MOBILIZATION AND INFLATION. New York: Norton, 1951. 308 p. Bibliog.

Hitch, Charles J., and McKean, Roland N. THE ECONOMICS OF DEFENSE IN THE NUCLEAR AGE. Cambridge, Mass.: Harvard University Press, 1960. 422 p. Bibliog.

Janeway, Eliot. THE ECONOMICS OF CRISIS: WAR, POLITICS, AND THE DOLLAR. New York: Weybright and Talley, 1968. 317 p. Bibliog.

_____. THE STRUGGLE FOR SURVIVAL: A CHRONICLE OF ECONOMIC MOBILIZATION IN WORLD WAR II. New Haven, Conn.: Yale University Press, 1951. 382 p.

Javits, Jacob K.; Hitch, Charles J.; and Burns, Arthur F. THE DEFENSE SECTOR AND THE AMERICAN ECONOMY. New York: New York University Press, 1968. 100 p.

Koistinen, Paul A.C. "The Hammer and the Sword: Labor, the Military, and Industrial Mobilization, 1920-1945." 2 vols. Ph.D. dissertation, University of California (Berkeley), 1964. 846 p.

Kraut, John A., ed. "Mobilizing American Power for Defense." ACADEMY OF POLITICAL AND SOCIAL SCIENCE PROCEEDINGS 24 (May 1951): 287-439.

McKean, Roland N., ed. ISSUES IN DEFENSE ECONOMICS. New York: National Bureau of Economic Research, 1967. 286 p.

Melman, Seymour. PENTAGON CAPITALISM: THE POLITICAL ECONOMY OF WAR. New York: McGraw-Hill, 1970. 290 p. Bibliog.

Perlo, Victor. MILITARISM AND INDUSTRY: ARMS PROFITEERING IN THE MISSILE AGE. New York: International, 1963. 208 p. Bibliog.

Russett, Bruce M. WHAT PRICE VIGILANCE?: THE BURDENS OF NATIONAL DEFENSE. New Haven, Conn.: Yale University Press, 1970. 261 p.

Schlesinger, James R. THE POLITICAL ECONOMY OF NATIONAL SECURITY: A STUDY OF THE ECONOMIC ASPECTS OF THE CONTEMPORARY POWER STRUGGLE. New York: Praeger, 1960. 292 p.

Scitovsky, Tibor; Shaw, Edward; and Tarshis, Lorie. MOBILIZING RESOURCES FOR WAR: THE ECONOMIC ALTERNATIVES. New York: McGraw-Hill, 1951. 284 p.

Wallace, Donald H. ECONOMIC CONTROLS AND DEFENSE. New York: Twentieth Century Fund, 1953. 260 p.

SCIENCE AND SCIENTISTS

The following list provides a few selected materials on the interrelation of science and technology with the military in the conduct of foreign affairs. Additional materials on scientific interrelations are provided in chapter 17.

Cox, Donald W. AMERICA'S NEW POLICY MAKERS: THE SCIENTISTS' RISE TO POWER. Philadelphia: Chilton, 1964. 298 p. Bibliog.

Gilpin, Robert. AMERICAN SCIENTISTS AND NUCLEAR WEAPONS POLICY. Princeton, N.J.: Princeton University Press, 1962. 352 p.

Knorr, Klaus E., and Morgenstern, Oskar. SCIENCE AND DEFENSE: SOME CRITICAL THOUGHTS ON MILITARY RESEARCH AND DEVELOPMENT. Princeton, N.J.: Center of International Studies, Princeton University, 1965. 58 p.

Mansfield, Edwin, comp. DEFENSE, SCIENCE, AND PUBLIC POLICY. New York: Norton, 1968. 224 p.

Pokrovskii, Georgii I. SCIENCE AND TECHNOLOGY IN CONTEMPORARY WAR. Translated and annotated by Raymond L. Garthoff. New York: Praeger, 1959. 180 p.

Zuckerman, Solly. SCIENTISTS AND WAR: THE IMPACT OF SCIENCE ON MILITARY AND CIVIL AFFAIRS. New York: Harper and Row, 1967. 177 p.

Chapter 13

OTHER AGENCIES AND THE BUREAUCRACY

Paralleling a growing concern with the public policy-making process and the relationship of bureaucratic organization to public policy analysis has been an increasing literary interest in the nature and functioning of bureaucratic organization in the modern political system. Aside from materials devoted to the presidency (chapter 7) and Congress (chapter 8), earlier chapters deal with the Cabinet and Executive Office (chapter 7), the Department of State (chapter 9), the National Security Council (chapter 10), the Intelligence Community (chapter 11), and the military (chapter 12). This chapter, on the other hand, contains references to selected materials concerned primarily with bureaucracy as a collective and integrative mechanism and with the matter of administrative management, as well as illustrative studies on residual government agencies not included elsewhere in this compilation. For a selected list of former and contemporary agencies, see chapter 22, especially section on "Other Departments and Administrative Agencies."

BUREAUCRACY AND ADMINISTRATION

The following materials are essentially of three basic types. Many are descriptive and analytical surveys of the character, functioning, and problems of bureaucracy and bureaucratization. Most of these deal with the subjects in general and are applicable to domestic affairs as well as foreign relations. A few of these deal with reform and reorganization--including Balzano, Brown, Destler, Gawthrop, Mansfield, Merstein Marx, and Pemberton--or with administrative relations with Congress and the courts, exemplified by Freeman, Harris, Shapiro, and Tanenhaus. Others, however, focus more directly on foreign affairs, such as Alger, Davis, Destler, Halperin, Hammon, Kissinger and Brodie, and Rourke. The second category encompasses those publications relating to administrative structuring and management, represented by Emmerich, Gladden, Gulick and Urwick, Kaufman, Landis, Millett, Mosher, Ostrom, Presthus, Redford, Rehfuss, Robbins, Selznick, Simon, Smith, Stein, Waldo, and White. The third group emphasizes the role of particular groups of individuals in the bureaucratic establishment--Dror, Friedman, Gilb, Gilpin, and Primack.

Abrahamsson, Bengt. BUREAUCRACY OR PARTICIPATION: THE LOGIC OF ORGANIZATION. Beverly Hills, Calif.: Sage, 1977. 240 p.

Other Agencies and the Bureaucracy

Albrow, Martin. BUREAUCRACY. New York: Praeger, 1970. 157 p. Bibliog.

Alger, Chadwick F. "The External Bureaucracy in United States Foreign Affairs." ADMINISTRATIVE SCIENCE QUARTERLY 7 (June 1962): 50-78.

American Assembly. THE FEDERAL GOVERNMENT SERVICE: ITS CHARACTER, PRESTIGE, AND PROBLEMS. New York: Columbia University, School of Business, 1954. 189 p.

Anderson, Paul Arthur. BUREAUCRACY, GOAL SEEKING, AND FOREIGN POLICY. Ph.D. dissertation, Ohio State University, 1979. 258 p.

Arkes, Hadley. BUREAUCRACY, THE MARSHALL PLAN, AND THE NATIONAL INTEREST. Princeton, N.J.: Princeton University Press, 1972. 395 p. Bibliog.

Balzano, Michael P. REORGANIZING THE FEDERAL BUREAUCRACY: THE RHETORIC AND THE REALITY. Washington, D.C.: American Enterprise Institute, 1977. 43 p.

Bernstein, Marver H. THE JOB OF THE FEDERAL EXECUTIVE. Washington, D.C.: Brookings Institution, 1958. 241 p. Bibliog.

Blau, Peter Michael. BUREAUCRACY IN MODERN SOCIETY. New York: Random House, 1956. 127 p.

_____. THE DYNAMICS OF BUREAUCRACY: A STUDY OF INTERPERSONAL RELATIONS IN TWO GOVERNMENT AGENCIES. 2d ed. Chicago: University of Chicago Press, 1963. 322 p.

Brown, David S. "The President and the Bureaus: Time for a Renewal of Relationships?" PUBLIC ADMINISTRATION REVIEW 26 (September 1966): 174-82.

Cater, Douglass. THE FOURTH BRANCH OF GOVERNMENT. Boston: Houghton Mifflin, 1959. 194 p.

Committee for Economic Development. IMPROVING EXECUTIVE MANAGEMENT IN THE FEDERAL GOVERNMENT. New York: 1964. 76 p.

Crenson, Matthew A. THE FEDERAL MACHINE: BEGINNINGS OF BUREAUCRACY IN JACKSONIAN AMERICA. Baltimore: Johns Hopkins Press, 1975. 186 p. Bibliog.

Crozier, Michel. THE BUREAUCRATIC PHENOMENON. Chicago: University of Chicago Press, 1964. 320 p.

Davis, David Howard. HOW THE BUREAUCRACY MAKES FOREIGN POLICY: AN EXCHANGE ANALYSIS. Lexington, Mass.: Heath, 1972. 164 p. Bibliog.

Davis, James Warren, Jr. THE NATIONAL EXECUTIVE BRANCH: AN INTRODUCTION. New York: Free Press, 1970. 228 p. Bibliog.

Deitchman, Seymour J. THE BEST-LAID SCHEMES: A TALE OF SOCIAL RESEARCH AND BUREAUCRACY. Cambridge, Mass.: M.I.T. Press, 1976. 483 p.

Destler, I.M. PRESIDENTS, BUREAUCRATS, AND FOREIGN POLICY: THE POLITICS OF ORGANIZATIONAL REFORM. Princeton, N.J.: Princeton University Press, 1972. 329 p.

Downs, Anthony. INSIDE BUREAUCRACY. Santa Monica, Calif.: Rand, 1964. 29 p.

Dror, Yehezkel. "Policy Analysts: A New Professional Role in Government Service." PUBLIC ADMINISTRATION REVIEW 27 (September 1967): 197-203.

Dunn, Delmer D. PUBLIC OFFICIALS AND THE PRESS. Reading, Mass.: Addison-Wesley, 1969. 208 p.

Eisenstadt, Shmuel Noah. "Bureaucracy and Bureaucratization." In his ESSAYS ON COMPARATIVE INSTITUTIONS, pp. 175-271. New York: Wiley, 1965. 376 p.

_____. "Political Struggle in Bureaucratic Societies." WORLD POLITICS 9 (October 1956): 15-36.

Emmerich, Herbert. FEDERAL ORGANIZATION AND ADMINISTRATIVE MANAGEMENT. University: University of Alabama Press, 1971. 304 p.

Etzioni, Amitai. "Authority Structure and Organizational Effectiveness." ADMINISTRATIVE SCIENCE QUARTERLY 4 (June 1959): 43-67.

_____. COMPLEX ORGANIZATIONS: A SOCIOLOGICAL READER. New York: Holt, Rinehart, and Winston, 1961. 497 p.

Feit, Edward. THE ARMED BUREAUCRATS: MILITARY-ADMINISTRATIVE REGIMES AND POLITICAL DEVELOPMENT. Boston: Houghton Mifflin, 1973. 199 p. Bibliog.

Finer, Herman. "Administrative Responsibility in Democratic Government." PUBLIC ADMINISTRATION REVIEW 1 (Summer 1941): 335-50.

Freeman, John Leiper. "The Bureaucracy in Pressure Politics." ANNALS OF THE AMERICAN ACADEMY OF POLITICAL AND SOCIAL SCIENCE 319 (September 1958): 10-19.

_____. THE POLITICAL PROCESS: EXECUTIVE BUREAU-LEGISLATIVE COMMITTEE RELATIONS. 2d ed. New York: Random House, 1965. 146 p.

Fried, Robert C. PERFORMANCE IN AMERICAN BUREAUCRACY. Boston: Little, Brown, 1976. 470 p.

Friedman, Robert S. PROFESSIONALISM: EXPERTISE AND POLICY MAKING. New York: General Learning Press, 1971. 24 p.

Friedman, Robert S.; Klein, Bernard W.; and Romani, John H. "Administrative Agencies and the Publics They Serve." PUBLIC ADMINISTRATION REVIEW 26 (September 1966): 192-204.

Gawthrop, Louis C. BUREAUCRATIC BEHAVIOR IN THE EXECUTIVE BRANCH: AN ANALYSIS OF ORGANIZATIONAL CHANGE. New York: Free Press, 1969. 276 p. Bibliog.

Gellhorn, Ernest. "Adverse Publicity by Administrative Agencies." HARVARD LAW REVIEW 86 (June 1973): 1380-1441.

Gilb, Corinne Lathrop. HIDDEN HIERARCHIES: THE PROFESSIONS AND GOVERNMENT. New York: Harper and Row, 1966. 307 p.

Gilbert, Charles E. "The Framework of Administrative Responsibility." JOURNAL OF POLITICS 21 (August 1959): 373-407.

Gilpin, Robert, and Wright, Christopher, eds. SCIENTISTS AND NATIONAL POLICY-MAKING. New York: Columbia University Press, 1964. 307 p.

Gladden, E.N. A HISTORY OF PUBLIC ADMINISTRATION. 2 vols. London: Frank Cass, 1972. Bibliog.

Glaser, R.S. "On Task Forcing." PUBLIC INTEREST 15 (Spring 1969): 40-45.

Golden, Joseph C. "The Hostile Bureaucracy." WASHINGTONIAN 9 (May 1974): 155-68.

Gulick, Luther H., and Urwick, Lyndall, eds. PAPERS ON THE SCIENCE OF ADMINISTRATION. New York: Institute of Public Administration, Columbia University, 1937. 195 p.

Halberstam, David. THE BEST AND THE BRIGHTEST. New York: Random House, 1972. 688 p. Bibliog.

Halperin, Morton H. BUREAUCRATIC POLITICS AND FOREIGN POLICY. Washington, D.C.: Brookings Institution, 1974. 340 p. Bibliog.

Hammond, Paul Y. "Foreign Policy-Making and Administrative Politics." WORLD POLITICS 17 (July 1965): 656-71.

Harris, Joseph P. CONGRESSIONAL CONTROL OF ADMINISTRATION. Washington, D.C.: Brookings Institution, 1964. 306 p.

Holden, Matthew, Jr. "'Imperialism' in Bureaucracy." AMERICAN POLITICAL SCIENCE REVIEW 60 (December 1966): 943-51.

Hood, Christopher C. THE LIMITS OF ADMINISTRATION. New York: Wiley-Interscience, 1976. 213 p.

Hummel, Ralph P. THE BUREAUCRATIC EXPERIENCE. New York: St. Martin's, 1977. 238 p.

Hyneman, Charles S. BUREAUCRACY IN A DEMOCRACY. New York: Harper, 1950. 586 p.

Jacob, Charles E. POLICY AND BUREAUCRACY. New York: Van Nostrand, 1966. 217 p. Bibliog.

Jansen, Robert B. THE ABC'S OF BUREAUCRACY. Chicago: Nelson-Hall, 1978. 240 p.

Jones, Charles O. AN INTRODUCTION TO THE STUDY OF PUBLIC POLICY. Belmont, Calif.: Wadsworth, 1970. 170 p. 2d ed. N. Scituate, Mass.: Duxbury, 1977. 258 p. Bibliog.

Juran, Joseph M. BUREAUCRACY: A CHALLENGE TO BETTER MANAGEMENT. New York: Harper, 1944. 138 p.

Karas, Thomas Harlan. "Organizational Processes and Foreign Policy Failure: The United States in Vietnam." Ph.D. dissertation, Harvard University, 1971. 299 p.

Kaufman, Herbert. ADMINISTRATIVE FEEDBACK: MONITORING SUBORDINATES' BEHAVIOR. Washington, D.C.: Brookings Institution, 1973. 83 p.

_____. "Emerging Conflicts in the Doctrines of Public Administration." AMERICAN POLITICAL SCIENCE REVIEW 50 (December 1956): 1057-73.

Kissinger, Henry A., and Brodie, Bernard. BUREAUCRACY, POLITICS, AND STRATEGY. Los Angeles: University of California Press, 1968. 60 p.

Krislov, Samuel. REPRESENTATIVE BUREAUCRACY. Englewood Cliffs, N.J.: Prentice-Hall, 1974. 149 p. Bibliog.

Landis, James McCauley. THE ADMINISTRATIVE PROCESS. New Haven, Conn.: Yale University Press, 1938. 160 p.

LaPalombara, Joseph, ed. BUREAUCRACY AND POLITICAL DEVELOPMENT. Princeton, N.J.: Princeton University Press, 1963. 513 p. Bibliog.

Levine, Sol, and White, Paul E. "Exchange as a Conceptual Framework for the Study of Interorganizational Relationships." ADMINISTRATIVE SCIENCE QUARTERLY 5 (March 1961): 583-601.

Macmahon, Arthur W., and Millett, John D. FEDERAL ADMINISTRATORS: A BIOGRAPHICAL APPROACH TO THE PROBLEMS OF DEPARTMENTAL MANAGEMENT. New York: Columbia University Press, 1939. 524 p.

Mann, Dean E. "The Selection of Federal Political Executives." AMERICAN POLITICAL SCIENCE REVIEW 58 (March 1964): 81-99.

Mansfield, Harvey C. "Federal Executive Reorganization: Thirty Years of Experience." PUBLIC ADMINISTRATION REVIEW 29 (July-August 1969): 332-45.

Morstein Marx, Fritz, ed. "Federal Executive Reorganization Re-Examined: A Symposium." AMERICAN POLITICAL SCIENCE REVIEW 40 (December 1946): 1124-68; 41 (February 1947): 48-84.

Mosher, Frederick. AMERICAN PUBLIC ADMINISTRATION: PAST, PRESENT, FUTURE. University: University of Alabama Press, 1975. 298 p.

Murphy, Thomas P.; Nuechterline, Donald E.; and Stupak, Ronald J., eds. THE PRESIDENT'S PROGRAM DIRECTORS: THE ASSISTANT SECRETARIES--A SYMPOSIUM. Charlottesville, Va.: U.S. Civil Service Commission, Federal Executive Institute, 1976. 112 p.

Nadel, Mark V. "The Hidden Dimension of Public Policy: Private Governments and the Policy Making Process." JOURNAL OF POLITICS 37 (February 1975): 2-34.

NEW HORIZONS IN PUBLIC ADMINISTRATION. University: University of Alabama Press, 1945. 145 p.

Niskanen, William A., Jr. BUREAUCRACY AND REPRESENTATIVE GOVERN-MENT. Chicago: Aldine-Atherton, 1971. 241 p. Bibliog.

Ostrom, Vincent. THE INTELLECTUAL CRISIS IN AMERICAN PUBLIC AD-MINISTRATION. University: University of Alabama Press, 1973. 165 p. Bibliog.

Pemberton, William E. BUREAUCRATIC POLITICS: EXECUTIVE REORGANIZA-TION DURING THE TRUMAN ADMINISTRATION. Columbia: University of Missouri Press, 1979. 256 p. Bibliog.

Peters, Charles, and Nelson, Michael, eds. THE CULTURE OF BUREAUCRACY. New York: Holt, Rinehart, and Winston, 1979. 256 p.

Presthus, Robert Vance. BEHAVIORAL APPROACHES TO PUBLIC ADMINIS-TRATION. University: University of Alabama Press, 1965. 158 p.

_____. THE ORGANIZATIONAL SOCIETY: AN ANALYSIS AND A THEORY. New York: Knopf, 1962. 323 p. Bibliog.

Primack, Joel, and von Hippel, Frank. ADVICE AND DISSENT: SCIENTISTS IN THE PUBLIC ARENA. New York: New American Library, 1974. 299 p.

Redford, Emmet S. IDEAL AND PRACTICE IN PUBLIC ADMINISTRATION. University: University of Alabama Press, 1958. 155 p.

Rehfuss, John. PUBLIC ADMINISTRATION AS POLITICAL PROCESS. New York: Scribner, 1973. 247 p.

Robbins, Stephen P. THE ADMINISTRATIVE PROCESS: INTEGRATING THEORY AND PRACTICE. Englewood Cliffs, N.J.: Prentice-Hall, 1976. 494 p. Bibliog.

Rourke, Francis E. BUREAUCRACY, POLITICS AND PUBLIC POLICY. 2d ed. Boston: Little, Brown, 1976. 208 p. Bibliog.

_____. BUREAUCRACY AND FOREIGN POLICY. Baltimore: Johns Hopkins Press, 1972. 80 p.

_____. "Bureaucratic Secrecy and Its Constituents." THE BUREAUCRAT 1 (Summer 1972): 116-21.

_____, ed. BUREAUCRATIC POWER IN NATIONAL POLITICS. 2d ed. Bos-ton: Little Brown, 1972. 418 p.

Saletan, Elma M. "Administrative Trustification." WESTERN POLITICAL QUARTERLY 11 (December 1958): 857-74.

Scnuman, David. BUREAUCRACIES, ORGANIZATIONS, AND ADMINISTRATION: A POLITICAL PRIMER. Riverside, N.J.: Macmillan, 1976. 235 p.

Selznick, Philip. LEADERSHIP IN ADMINISTRATION: A SOCIOLOGICAL INTERPRETATION. Evanston, Ill.: Row, Peterson, 1957. 162 p.

Shafritz, Jay M., and Hyde, Albert C. CLASSICS OF PUBLIC ADMINISTRATION. Oak Park, Ill.: Moore, 1978. 456 p.

This is a symposium of 43 previously published essays by eminent scholars and analysts, arranged chronologically from 1887 to the late 1970s.

Shapiro, Martin. THE SUPREME COURT AND ADMINISTRATIVE AGENCIES. New York: Free Press, 1968. 288 p.

Short, Lloyd M. "An Investigation of the Executive Agencies of the United States Government." AMERICAN POLITICAL SCIENCE REVIEW 33 (February 1939): 60-66.

Simon, Herbert Alexander. ADMINISTRATIVE BEHAVIOR: A STUDY OF DECISION-MAKING PROCESSES IN ADMINISTRATIVE ORGANIZATION. 3d ed. New York: Free Press, 1976. 364 p.

_____. THE NEW SCIENCE OF MANAGEMENT DECISION. New York: Harper and Row, 1960. 50 p.

Smith, Harold Dewey. THE MANAGEMENT OF YOUR GOVERNMENT. New York: McGraw-Hill, 1945. 179 p.

Somers, Herman Miles. "The Federal Bureaucracy and the Change of Administration." AMERICAN POLITICAL SCIENCE REVIEW 48 (March 1954): 131-51.

Stein, Harold, ed. PUBLIC ADMINISTRATION AND POLICY DEVELOPMENT: A CASE BOOK. New York: Harcourt, Brace, 1952. 860 p.

Tanenhaus, Joseph. "Supreme Court Attitudes Toward Federal Administrative Agencies." JOURNAL OF POLITICS 22 (August 1960): 502-24.

Thompson, James D., and McEwen, William J. "Organizational Goals and Environment: Goal-Setting as an Interaction Process." AMERICAN SOCIOLOGICAL REVIEW 23 (February 1958): 23-31.

Truman, David B. THE GOVERNMENTAL PROCESS: POLITICAL INTERESTS AND PUBLIC OPINION. 2d ed. New York: Knopf, 1971. 544 p. Bibliog.

Tuggle, Francis D. ORGANIZATIONAL PROCESSES. Arlington Heights, Ill.: AHM Publishing Co., 1978. 240 p.

U.S. Congress. House of Representatives. Committee on Foreign Affairs. Subcommittee on Foreign Economic Policy. U.S. FOREIGN ECONOMIC POLICY: IMPLICATIONS FOR THE ORGANIZATION OF THE EXECUTIVE BRANCH. 92d Cong., 2d sess. Washington, D.C.: Government Printing Office, 1972. 212 p.

Waldo, Dwight. THE ADMINISTRATIVE STATE: A STUDY OF THE POLITICAL THEORY OF AMERICAN PUBLIC ADMINISTRATION. New York: Ronald, 1948. 227 p. Bibliog.

_____. PERSPECTIVES ON ADMINISTRATION. University: University of Alabama Press, 1956. 143 p.

Wallace, Schuyler C. FEDERAL DEPARTMENTALIZATION: A CRITIQUE OF THEORIES OF ORGANIZATION. New York: Columbia University Press, 1941. 251 p.

Weeks, O.D. "Initiation of Legislation by Administrative Agencies." BROOKLYN LAW REVIEW 9 (January 1940): 117-31.

Whyte, William Hollingsworth. THE ORGANIZATION MAN. New York: Simon and Schuster, 1956. 429 p.

Wildavsky, Aaron. THE POLITICS OF THE BUDGETARY PROCESS. 2d ed. Boston: Little, Brown, 1974. 271 p. Bibliog.

Wilson, James Q. "The Bureaucracy Problem." PUBLIC INTEREST 6 (Winter 1967): 3-9.

Woll, Peter. AMERICAN BUREAUCRACY. 2d ed. New York: Norton, 1977. 260 p. Bibliog.

Woll, Peter, and Jones, Rochelle. "The Bureaucracy as a Check Upon the President." BUREAUCRAT 3 (April 1974): 8-20.

Wynia, Bob L. "Federal Bureaucrats' Attitudes Toward a Democratic Ideology." PUBLIC ADMINISTRATION REVIEW 34 (March-April 1974): 156-62.

TOP-LEVEL ADVISERS AND ASSISTANTS

A few studies deal with presidential advisers and assistants and with other high-level members of the bureaucracy. These supplement the materials listed in other sections of this compilation, especially those on the cabinet, executive office, and the presidential staff (chapter 7), on the secretaryship of state (chapter 9), and on the secretaries of defense and the chiefs of staff (chapter 12).

Anderson, Patrick. THE PRESIDENT'S MEN: WHITE HOUSE ASSISTANTS OF FRANKLIN D. ROOSEVELT, HARRY S. TRUMAN, JOHN F. KENNEDY, AND LYNDON B. JOHNSON. New York: Doubleday, 1968. 420 p.

Beckler, David Z. "The Precarious Life of Science in the White House." DAEDALUS 103 (Summer 1974): 115-34.

Bronk, David W. "Science Advice in the White House: The Genesis of the President's Science Advisers and the National Science Foundation." SCIENCE 186 (11 October 1974): 116-21.

Corson, John Jay, and Paul, R. Shale. MEN NEAR THE TOP: FILLING KEY POSTS IN THE FEDERAL SERVICE. Baltimore: Johns Hopkins Press, 1966. 189 p.

Lyons, Gene M. "The President and His Experts." ANNALS OF THE AMERICAN ACADEMY OF POLITICAL AND SOCIAL SCIENCE 394 (March 1971): 36-45.

Steelman, John R., and Kraeger, H. Dewayne. "The Executive Office as Administrative Coordinator." LAW AND CONTEMPORARY PROBLEMS 21 (Autumn 1956): 688-709.

OTHER GOVERNMENT AGENCIES

The following are largely institutional studies of particular government agencies not treated in other chapters, including such high-level coordinating or advisory agencies as the Office of Management and Budget, Bureau of the Budget, and the Council of Economic Advisers:

Allardice, Corbin, and Trapnell, Edward R. THE ATOMIC ENERGY COMMISSION. New York: Praeger, 1974. 236 p. Bibliog.

Arnow, Kathryn Smul. THE DEPARTMENT OF COMMERCE FIELD SERVICE. The Inter-University Case Program, no. 21. University: University of Alabama Press, 1954. 33 p.

Berman, Larry. THE OFFICE OF MANAGEMENT AND BUDGET AND THE PRESIDENCY, 1921-1979. Princeton, N.J.: Princeton University Press, 1979. 208 p.

Bernhardt, Joshua. THE TARIFF COMMISSION: ITS HISTORY, ACTIVITIES AND ORGANIZATION. New York: Appleton, 1922. 71 p. Bibliog.

Binning, William Charles. "The Role of the Export-Import Bank in Inter-American Affairs." Ph.D. dissertation, University of Notre Dame, 1970. 319 p.

Bombardier, Gary. "The Managerial Function of the OMB: Intergovernmental Relations as a Test Case." PUBLIC POLICY 23 (Summer 1975): 317-54.

Refers to the Office of Management and Budget.

Brundage, Percival Flack. THE BUREAU OF THE BUDGET. New York: Praeger, 1970. 327 p. Bibliog.

Cushman, Robert E. THE INDEPENDENT REGULATORY COMMISSIONS. New York: Oxford University Press, 1941. 780 p.

Dimock, Marshall E. "Government Corporations: A Focus of Policy and Administration." AMERICAN POLITICAL SCIENCE REVIEW 43 (October 1949): 899-921.

Flash, Edward Serrill, Jr. ECONOMIC ADVICE AND PRESIDENTIAL LEADERSHIP: THE COUNCIL OF ECONOMIC ADVISERS. New York: Columbia University Press, 1965. 382 p. Bibliog.

Holt, William Stull. THE FEDERAL TRADE COMMISSION: ITS HISTORY, ACTIVITIES AND ORGANIZATION. New York: Appleton, 1922. 80 p.

Kohlmeier, Louis M., Jr. THE REGULATORS: WATCHDOG AGENCIES AND THE PUBLIC INTEREST. New York: Harper and Row, 1969. 339 p.

Mann, Fritz Karl. "The Government Corporation as a Tool of Foreign Policy." PUBLIC ADMINISTRATION REVIEW 3 (Summer 1943): 194-204.

Morstein Marx, Fritz. "The Bureau of the Budget: Its Evolution and Present Role." AMERICAN POLITICAL SCIENCE REVIEW 39 (August and October 1945): 653-84; 869-98.

Norton, Hugh Stanton. THE COUNCIL OF ECONOMIC ADVISERS: THREE PERIODS OF INFLUENCE. Columbia: Bureau of Business and Economic Research, University of South Carolina, 1973. 72 p. Bibliog.

Nourse, Edwin G., and Gross, Bertram M. "The Role of the Council of Economic Advisers." AMERICAN POLITICAL SCIENCE REVIEW 42 (April 1948): 283-95.

Pearson, Norman M. "The Budget Bureau: From Routine Business to General Staff." PUBLIC ADMINISTRATION REVIEW 3 (Spring 1943): 126-49.

Ripley, Randall B., and Davis, James W. "The Bureau of the Budget and Executive Branch Agencies: Notes on Their Interaction." JOURNAL OF POLITICS 29 (November 1967): 749-69.

Schmeckebier, Laurence Frederick. THE AERONAUTICS BRANCH, DEPARTMENT OF COMMERCE: ITS HISTORY, ACTIVITIES AND ORGANIZATION. Washington, D.C.: Brookings Institution, 1930. 147 p.

Schmeckebier, Laurence Frederick, and Weber, Gustavus A. THE BUREAU OF FOREIGN AND DOMESTIC COMMERCE: ITS HISTORY, ACTIVITIES AND ORGANIZATION. Baltimore: Brookings Institution, 1924. Reprint. Toronto and London: AMS Press, 1973. 180 p.

Short, Lloyd Milton. THE BUREAU OF NAVIGATION: ITS HISTORY, ACTIVITIES AND ORGANIZATION. Baltimore: Johns Hopkins Press, 1923. 124 p. Bibliog.

Smith, Darrell Hevenor. THE UNITED STATES SHIPPING BOARD: ITS HISTORY, ACTIVITIES AND ORGANIZATION. Washington, D.C.: Brookings Institution, 1931. 338 p. Bibliog.

Smith, Darrell Hevenor, and Herring, H. Guy. THE BUREAU OF IMMIGRATION: ITS HISTORY, ACTIVITIES AND ORGANIZATION. Baltimore: Brookings Institution, 1924. Reprint. Toronto and London: AMS Press, 1974. 247 p. Bibliog.

Smith, Darrell Hevenor, and Wilbur, Fred. THE COAST GUARD: ITS HISTORY, ACTIVITIES AND ORGANIZATION. Washington, D.C.: Brookings Institution, 1929. 265 p. Bibliog.

Somers, Herman Miles. PRESIDENTIAL AGENCY: OWMR--THE OFFICE OF WAR MOBILIZATION AND RECONVERSION. Cambridge, Mass.: Harvard University Press, 1950. Reprint. New York: Greenwood, 1969. 238 p.

Weber, Gustavus Adulphus. THE WEATHER BUREAU: ITS HISTORY, ACTIVITIES AND ORGANIZATION. New York: Appleton, 1922. 87 p. Bibliog.

Chapter 14

DECISION MAKING

The decision-making process has become a popular subject for comprehensive and systematic literary scrutiny since World War II. Investigation and analysis focus upon various decision-making activities, viewed from varying perspectives. These range from simple group action to complex business and other private enterprises, involving Congress, the White House, the military forces, and other government agents and agencies, including the framing of foreign policy and the conduct of foreign affairs.

Particularized foci of attention run the gamut from theory formulation to organizational structure and functioning, elemental action and interaction, cause-and-effect relationships, and the role played by individuals within the decision process. Attention is paid to primary and lesser decision makers, as well as to others who contribute to the process. Investigatory treatments also differ, including simple factual and descriptive recounting of developments by means of historical and other case studies, systems analysis, empirical examination of the validity of preconceived hypotheses, and normatively oriented exhortations.

This growing body of literature emphasizes a complex of decision-making components and operational methods, embracing policy formulation, problem solving, group interaction, paradigm devising, theory analysis, and particularly analysis of organizational, structural, bureaucratic, and institutional mechanisms. Relevant literature includes general analyses which transcend international relations, those which focus directly on foreign affairs, and those which emphasize theoretical implications and applications. Additional references related to decision making may be found in materials listed in other sections, including those on the presidency, the National Security Council, the Department of State, the military, the bureaucracy, case studies, policy formulation, and crisis diplomacy.

BIBLIOGRAPHICAL GUIDES

The following provide guidance to published listings of resources on decision making. Additional bibliographies are to be found in specific items, as noted.

Gore, William J., and Silander, Fred S. "A Bibliographical Essay on Decision Making." ADMINISTRATIVE SCIENCE QUARTERLY 4 (1959): 97-121.

Raser, John R. "Personal Characteristics of Political Decision Makers: A Literature Review." PEACE RESEARCH SOCIETY (INTERNATIONAL) PAPERS 5 (1966): 612-82.

Wasserman, Paul, and Silander, Fred S., eds. DECISION-MAKING: AN ANNOTATED BIBLIOGRAPHY. Ithaca, N.Y.: Cornell University Press, 1958. 111 p. Supplement for 1958-63 (1964). 178 p.

GENERAL ANALYSES

Some literary analyses of decision making, such as the following, are of a general nature--that is, not related specifically to foreign relations--and sometimes their scope is broader than governmental decision making. Some authors are specifically concerned with public policy making, such as Anderson, Dror, Edwards and Sharkansky, Hammond, Quade, and Simon. So far as analytical approach is concerned, only a few--Boulding, Kepner, and Oppenheim--emphasize the rational system. Others stress the bureaucratic approach--Allison, Jacob. Still others view the process from the broader political perspective--Goldman, Lerner, Snyder, Sorensen, and Ulmer. A substantial number of studies review decision making in relation to organizational factors and group action, including Alexis and Wilson, Castles, Feldman and Kantor, Fisher, Jones, Maier, Siegel and Fouraker, Taylor, Vroom, and Wood. A good many others focus upon specific aspects, functions, and problems of decision making. These range from matters of probability (Feather), and prediction and conjecture (Churchman, DeJouvenal, and Martino), to communications (Deutsch, Haas), information (Rappaport), discussion (Gouran), ambiguity (Becker and Brownson), conflict and crisis management (Conn, Holsti, Janis and Mann, and Sieber), query analysis (Leys), computerization and gaming (Bremer, Luce), and interorganizational relations (Tuite).

Abercrombie, M.L. Johnson. THE ANATOMY OF JUDGMENT. New York: Basic Books, 1960. 156 p.

Ackoff, Russell L. SCIENTIFIC METHOD: OPTIMIZING APPLIED RESEARCH DECISIONS. New York: Wiley, 1962. 464 p. Bibliog.

Alexis, Marcus, and Wilson, Charles Z. ORGANIZATIONAL DECISION-MAKING. Englewood Cliffs, N.J.: Prentice-Hall, 1967. 447 p. Bibliog.

Allison, Graham T., and Halperin, Morton H. "Bureaucratic Politics: A Paradigm and Some Policy Implications." In THEORY AND POLICY IN INTERNATIONAL RELATIONS, edited by Raymond Tanter and Richard H. Ullman, pp. 40-79. Washington, D.C.: Brookings Institution, 1972.

Anderson, James E. PUBLIC POLICY-MAKING. New York: Praeger, 1975. 178 p.

_____, ed. CASES IN PUBLIC POLICY-MAKING. New York: Praeger, 1976. 329 p. Bibliog.

Anker, James M.; Townsend, John C.; and O'Connor, James P. "A Multivariate Analysis of Decision Making and Related Measures." JOURNAL OF PSYCHOLOGY 55 (January 1963): 211-21.

Axelrod, Robert, ed. STRUCTURE OF DECISION: THE COGNITIVE MAPS OF POLITICAL ELITES. Princeton, N.J.: Princeton University Press, 1976. 404 p.

Bachrach, Peter, and Baratz, Morton S. "Decisions and Non-decisions: An Analytical Framework." AMERICAN POLITICAL SCIENCE REVIEW 57 (September 1963): 632-42.

Bates, James. "A Model for the Science of Decisions." PHILOSOPHY OF SCIENCE 21 (October 1954): 326-39.

Becker, Selwyn W., and Brownson, Fred O. "What Price Ambiguity? Or the Role of Ambiguity in Decision-Making." JOURNAL OF POLITICAL ECONOMICS 72 (February 1964): 62-73.

Boulding, Kenneth. "Decision-Making in the Modern World." In AN OUTLINE OF MAN'S KNOWLEDGE OF THE MODERN WORLD, edited by Lyman Bryson, pp. 418-42. New York: McGraw-Hill, 1960.

_____. "The Ethics of Rational Decision." MANAGEMENT SCIENCE 12 (February 1966): B161-B169.

Bower, Joseph L. "The Role of Conflict in Economic Decision-Making Groups: Some Empirical Results." QUARTERLY JOURNAL OF ECONOMICS 79 (May 1965): 263-77.

Braybrooke, David, and Lindblom, Charles E. A STRATEGY FOR DECISION: POLICY EVALUATION AS A SOCIAL PROCESS. New York: Free Press, 1963. 268 p. Bibliog.

Bremer, Stuart A. SIMULATED WORLDS: A COMPUTER MODEL OF NATIONAL DECISION-MAKING. Princeton, N.J.: Princeton University Press, 1977. 249 p.

Brim, Orville Gilbert, et al. PERSONALITY AND DECISION PROCESSES: STUDIES IN THE SOCIAL PSYCHOLOGY OF THINKING. Stanford, Calif.: Stanford University Press, 1962. 336 p. Bibliog.

Brinkers, Henry S., ed. DECISION-MAKING: CREATIVITY, JUDGMENT, AND SYSTEMS. Columbus: Ohio State University Press, 1972. 276 p. Bibliog.

Bross, Irwin. DESIGN FOR DECISIONS. New York: Macmillan, 1953. Reprint. New York: Free Press, 1965. 276 p. Bibliog.

Castles, Francis G., et al., eds. DECISIONS, ORGANIZATIONS AND SOCIETY. Baltimore: Penguin, 1972. 424 p.

Churchman, Charles West. PREDICTION AND OPTIMAL DECISION. Englewood Cliffs, N.J.: Prentice-Hall, 1961. 394 p. Bibliog.

Conn, Paul H., ed. CONFLICT AND DECISION-MAKING: AN INTRODUCTION TO POLITICAL ANALYSIS. New York: Harper and Row, 1971. 317 p. Bibliog.

Conway, M. Margaret, and Feigert, Frank B. "Decision-Making." In their POLITICAL ANALYSIS: AN INTRODUCTION, pp. 193-220. 2d ed. Rockleigh, N.J.: Allyn and Bacon, 1976. 369 p.

Coombs, Clyde Hamilton, and Pruitt, Dean G. A STUDY OF DECISION MAKING UNDER RISK. Ann Arbor: Willow Run Laboratories, University of Michigan, 1960.

Cooper, Joseph D. THE ART OF DECISION-MAKING. Garden City, N.Y.: Doubleday, 1961. 394 p.

Davidson, Donald, et al. DECISION-MAKING: AN EXPERIMENTAL APPROACH. Stanford, Calif.: Stanford University Press, 1957. 121 p. Bibliog.

DeJouvenal, Bertrand. THE ART OF CONJECTURE. Translated by Nikita Lary. New York: Basic Books, 1967. 307 p.

Deutsch, Karl W. "Communications Models and Decision Systems." In CONTEMPORARY POLITICAL ANALYSIS, edited by James C. Charlesworth, pp. 273-99. New York: Free Press, 1967.

Diesing, Paul. REASON IN SOCIETY: FIVE TYPES OF DECISIONS AND THEIR SOCIAL CONDITIONS. Urbana: University of Illinois Press, 1962. 262 p. Bibliog.

Dror, Yehezkel. PUBLIC POLICYMAKING REEXAMINED. San Francisco: Chandler, 1968. 370 p. Bibliog.

Dumas, Neil S. THE DECISION MAKER'S GUIDE TO APPLIED PLANNING, ORGANIZATION, ADMINISTRATION, RESEARCH, EVALUATION, INFOR-MATION PROCESSING AND ANALYSIS TECHNIQUES. Gainesville: Regional Rehabilitation Research Institute, University of Florida, 1970. 191 p.

Easton, Allan. DECISION MAKING: A SHORT COURSE IN PROBLEM SOLV-ING FOR PROFESSIONALS. Somerset, N.J.: Wiley, 1976.

Edwards, George C. III, and Sharkansky, Ira. THE POLICY PREDICAMENT: MAKING AND IMPLEMENTING PUBLIC POLICY. San Francisco: Freeman, 1978. 336 p.

On rational decision making and constraints on decisions.

Etzioni, Amitai. "Mixed-Scanning: A 'Third' Approach to Decision-Making." PUBLIC ADMINISTRATION REVIEW 27 (December 1967): 385-92.

Feather, N.T. "Subjective Probability and Decisions Under Uncertainty." PSYCHOLOGICAL REVIEW 66, no. 3 (1959): 150-64.

Feldman, Julian, and Kantor, Herschel E. "Organizational Decision-Making." In HANDBOOK OF ORGANIZATIONS, edited by James G. March, pp. 614-49. Chicago: Rand McNally, 1965.

Fisher, B. Aubrey. SMALL GROUP DECISION MAKING: COMMUNICATION AND THE GROUP PROCESS. New York: McGraw-Hill, 1974. 264 p. Bibliog.

Goldman, Ralph M. "Decision Making By American Political Organizations." In his BEHAVIORAL PERSPECTIVES ON AMERICAN POLITICS, pp. 200-40. Homewood, Ill.: Dorsey, 1973.

Gore, William J., and Dyson, J.W., eds. THE MAKING OF DECISIONS: A READER IN ADMINISTRATIVE BEHAVIOR. New York: Free Press, 1964. 440 p.

Gouran, Dennis S. DISCUSSION: THE PROCESS OF GROUP DECISION-MAKING. New York: Harper and Row, 1974. 199 p. Bibliog.

Guilford, J.P. "Intellectual Aspects of Decision Making." In DECISION MAKING AND AGE, edited by A.T. Welford, pp. 82-102. Basel: Karger, 1969.

Haas, Michael. "Communication Factors in Decision Making." PEACE RE-SEARCH SOCIETY PAPERS 12 (1968): 65-86.

Hammond, Kenneth R., ed. JUDGMENT AND DECISION IN PUBLIC POLICY FORMATION. Boulder, Colo.: Westview, 1978. 175 p. Bibliog.

Hoffman, L. Richard. "Conditions for Creative Problem Solving." JOURNAL OF PSYCHOLOGY 52 (October 1961): 429-44.

Holsti, Ole R. "Crisis, Stress, and Decision-Making." INTERNATIONAL SOCIAL SCIENCE JOURNAL 23 (November 1971): 53-67.

Horowitz, Irving Louis, ed. THE USE AND ABUSE OF SOCIAL SCIENCE: BEHAVIORAL SCIENCE AND NATIONAL POLICY MAKING. New Brunswick, N.J.: Transaction Books, 1971. 350 p.

Hovey, Harold A. THE PLANNING-PROGRAMMING-BUDGETING APPROACH TO GOVERNMENT DECISION-MAKING. New York: Praeger, 1968. 264 p.

Jacob, Charles E. POLICY AND BUREAUCRACY. Princeton, N.J.: Van Nostrand, 1966. 271 p. Bibliog.

Janis, Irving L., and Mann, Leon. DECISION MAKING: A PSYCHOLOGICAL ANALYSIS OF CONFLICT, CHOICE, AND COMMITMENT. New York: Free Press, 1977. 488 p. Bibliog.

Jones, William M. ON DECISIONMAKING IN LARGE ORGANIZATIONS. Santa Monica, Calif.: Rand, 1964. 26 p.

Kaysen, Carl. "Model-Makers and Decision-Makers: Economists and the Policy Process." PUBLIC INTEREST 12 (Summer 1968): 80-95.

Kepner, Charles H., and Tregoe, Benjamin R. THE RATIONAL MANAGER: A SYSTEMATIC APPROACH TO PROBLEM SOLVING AND DECISION MAKING. New York: McGraw-Hill, 1965. 275 p. Bibliog.

Lasswell, Harold D. THE DECISION PROCESS: SEVEN CATEGORIES OF FUNCTIONAL ANALYSIS. College Park: Bureau of Governmental Research, University of Maryland, 1956. 23 p.

Lerner, Allan W. THE POLITICS OF DECISIONMAKING: STRATEGY, COOPERATION, AND CONFLICT. Sage Library of Social Science, no. 34. Beverly Hills, Calif.: Sage, 1976. 216 p.

Leys, Wayne A.R. ETHICS FOR POLICY DECISIONS: THE ART OF ASKING DELIBERATIVE QUESTIONS. Englewood Cliffs, N.J.: Prentice-Hall, 1952. 428 p.

Lindblom, Charles E. THE INTELLIGENCE OF DEMOCRACY: DECISION-MAKING THROUGH MUTUAL ADJUSTMENT. New York: Free Press, 1965. 352 p. Bibliog.

_____. THE POLICY-MAKING PROCESS. Englewood Cliffs, N.J.: Prentice-Hall, 1968. 122 p.

_____. "The Science of Muddling Through." PUBLIC ADMINISTRATION REVIEW 19 (Spring 1959): 79-88.

Lindley, Dennis V. MAKING DECISIONS. New York: Wiley Interscience, 1971. 195 p.

Luce, R. Duncan, and Raiffa, Howard. GAMES AND DECISIONS. New York: Wiley, 1957. 509 p. Bibliog.

Lyden, Fremont J.; Shipman, George A.; and Kroll, Morton, eds. POLICIES, DECISIONS, AND ORGANIZATION. New York: Appleton-Century-Crofts, 1969. 387 p.

Maier, Norman Raymond Frederick. PROBLEM-SOLVING AND CREATIVITY IN INDIVIDUALS AND GROUPS. Belmont, Calif.: Brooks-Coles, 1970. 493 p. Bibliog.

_____. PROBLEM-SOLVING DISCUSSIONS AND CONFERENCES: LEADERSHIP METHODS AND SKILLS. New York: McGraw-Hill, 1963. 261 p. Bibliog.

Martino, Joseph P. TECHNOLOGICAL FORECASTING FOR DECISIONMAKING. New York: American Elsevier, 1972. 750 p.

Mason, Richard O. "Dialectics in Decision-Making: A Study in the Use of Counterplanning and Structured Debate in Management Information Systems." Ph.D. dissertation, University of California (Berkeley), 1968. 227 p.

Morell, Robert William. MANAGERIAL DECISION-MAKING: A LOGICAL APPROACH. Milwaukee: Bruce, 1960. 201 p. Bibliog.

Morris, William Thomas. MANAGEMENT FOR ACTION: PSYCHOTECHNICAL DECISION MAKING. Reston, Va.: Reston Publishing Co., 1972. 223 p. Bibliog.

Oppenheim, Felix E. "Rational Choice." JOURNAL OF PHILOSOPHY 50 (June 1953): 341-50.

Quade, Edward S. ANALYSIS FOR PUBLIC DECISIONS. New York: American Elsevier, 1975. 322 p. Bibliog.

Rappaport, Alfred, ed. INFORMATION FOR DECISION MAKING: QUANTITATIVE AND BEHAVIORAL DIMENSIONS. Englewood Cliffs, N.J.: Prentice-Hall, 1970. 447 p. Bibliog.

Rowen, Henry S. "Bargaining Analysis in Government." In THE ADMINISTRATIVE PROCESS AND DEMOCRATIC THEORY, edited by Louis C. Gawthrop, pp. 31-37. Boston: Houghton Mifflin, 1970.

Shelly, Maynard Wolfe, ed. HUMAN JUDGMENTS AND OPTIMALITY. New York: Wiley, 1964. 436 p. Bibliog.

Shklar, Judith. "Decisionism." In NOMOS VII: RATIONAL DECISIONS, edited by Carl J. Friedrich, pp. 3-17. New York: Atherton, 1964.

Sieber, J.E., and Lanyetta, J.T. "Conflict and Conceptual Structure as Determinants of Decision-Making Behavior." JOURNAL OF PERSONALITY 32 (December 1964): 622-41.

Siegel, Sidney. DECISION AND CHOICE: CONTRIBUTIONS OF SIDNEY SIEGEL. Edited by Samuel Messick and Arthur H. Brayfield. New York: McGraw-Hill, 1964. 298 p. Bibliog.

Siegel, Sidney, and Fouraker, Lawrence E. BARGAINING AND GROUP DECISION MAKING. New York: McGraw-Hill, 1960. 132 p.

Siegel, Sidney, et al. CHOICE, STRATEGY, AND UTILITY. New York: McGraw-Hill, 1964. 180 p. Bibliog.

Simon, Herbert A. ADMINISTRATIVE BEHAVIOR: A STUDY OF DECISION-MAKING PROCESSES IN ADMINISTRATIVE ORGANIZATION. 3d ed. New York: Macmillan, 1976. 364 p.

Snyder, Richard C. "Decision Making as an Approach to the Analysis of Political Phenomena." In APPROACHES TO THE STUDY OF POLITICS, edited by Roland Young, pp. 3-38. Evanston, Ill.: Northwestern University Press, 1958.

Sorensen, Theodore C. DECISION-MAKING IN THE WHITE HOUSE. New York: Columbia University Press, 1963. 94 p.

Taylor, Charles W. "Organizing for Consensus in Problem Solving." MANAGEMENT REVIEW 61 (April 1972): 17-25.

_____. PANEL CONSENSUS TECHNIQUE: A NEW APPROACH TO DECISION-MAKING. Carlisle Barracks, Pa.: U.S. Army War College, 1972. 23 p.

_____. PANEL CONSENSUS TECHNIQUE--A NEW APPROACH TO DECISIONMAKING: THE IDEA FUNNEL. Lake City, Fla.: International Creativity Center, 1973. 13 p.

Thayer, Frederick C. "Presidential Policy Processes and 'New Administration': A Search for Revised Paradigms." PUBLIC ADMINISTRATION REVIEW 31 (September-October 1971): 552-61.

Thrall, Robert M., et al. DECISION PROCESSES. New York: Wiley, 1954. 332 p.

Tobin, Richard Lardner. DECISIONS OF DESTINY. Cleveland: World, 1961. 285 p.

Tuite, Matthew; Chisholm, Roger K.; and Radnor, Michael, eds. INTERORGANIZATIONAL DECISION MAKING. Chicago: Aldine, 1972. 298 p.

Ulmer, Sidney, et al. POLITICAL DECISION MAKING. New York: Van Nostrand Reinhold, 1970. 146 p.

Vroom, Victor H.; Grant, Lester D.; and Cotton, Timothy S. "The Consequences of Social Interaction in Group Problem Solving." ORGANIZATIONAL BEHAVIOR AND HUMAN PERFORMANCE 4 (February 1969): 77-95.

Vroom, Victor H., and Yetten, Philip W. LEADERSHIP AND DECISIONMAKING. Pittsburgh: University of Pittsburgh Press, 1973. 233 p. Bibliog.

Wallach, Michael A., and Kogan, Nathaniel. "Aspects of Judgment and Decision-Making: Interrelationships and Change with Age." BEHAVIORAL SCIENCE 6 (January 1961): 23-36.

Wood, Michael T. "Power Relationships and Group Decision Making in Organizations." PSYCHOLOGICAL BULLETIN 79 (May 1973): 280-93.

Ziegler, Raymond J. BUSINESS POLICIES AND DECISION MAKING. New York: Appleton-Century-Crofts, 1966. 260 p. Bibliog.

LEGISLATIVE AND JUDICIAL DECISION MAKING

Though neither general in scope nor related specifically to foreign affairs, the following may nevertheless be of tangential concern and illustrate additional applications of decision-making analysis which are likely to be given increased attention in the future. Studies of legislative decision making as related to external affairs are provided below in the section on foreign relations; see also chapter 8.

Clausen, Aage R. HOW CONGRESSMEN DECIDE: A POLICY FOCUS. New York: St. Martins, 1973. 243 p.

> Especially chapter on "The Policy Dimension Theory of Congressional Decision-Making: Five Major Policy Dimensions."

Committee for Economic Development. CONGRESSIONAL DECISION MAKING FOR NATIONAL SECURITY. New York: 1974. 56 p.

Curtis, Thomas B., et al. DECISION MAKING IN THE U.S. CONGRESS. Regents lecture, 1969. Los Angeles: University of California at Los Angeles, Institute of Government and Public Affairs, 1969. 44 p.

Gallagher, Hugh G. ADVISE AND OBSTRUCT: THE ROLE OF THE UNITED STATES SENATE IN FOREIGN POLICY DECISIONS. New York: Delacorte, 1969. 338 p. Bibliog.

Keefe, William J., and Ogul, Morris S. "The Legislative Structure for Decision-Making." In his THE AMERICAN LEGISLATIVE PROCESS: CONGRESS AND THE STATES, chapter 2. 4th ed. Englewood Cliffs, N.J.: Prentice-Hall, 1977.

Matthews, Donald R., and Stimson, James A. YEAS AND NAYS: NORMAL DECISION-MAKING IN THE U.S. HOUSE OF REPRESENTATIVES. New York: Wiley Interscience, 1975. 190 p.

Rohde, David W., and Spaeth, Harold J. SUPREME COURT DECISION MAKING. San Francisco: Freeman, 1976. 229 p.

Schubert, Glendon. JUDICIAL POLICY MAKING: THE POLITICAL ROLE OF THE COURTS. Chicago: Scott, Foresman, 1965. 224 p.

Spaeth, Harold J. AN INTRODUCTION TO SUPREME COURT DECISION MAKING. Rev. ed. San Francisco: Chandler, 1972. 20 p.

FOREIGN GOVERNMENTS AND AGENCIES

English-language studies of the policy-making and decision-making processes of other governments may be useful for comparative purposes. The number of these is likely to increase in the future.

Adomeit, Hannes, and Boardman, Robert, eds. FOREIGN POLICY MAKING IN COMMUNIST STATES. New York: Praeger, 1979. 208 p.

Brecher, Michael. DECISIONS IN ISRAEL'S FOREIGN POLICY. ·New Haven, Conn.: Yale University Press, 1975. 651 p.

_____. THE FOREIGN POLICY SYSTEM OF ISRAEL: SETTINGS, IMAGES, PROCESS. New Haven, Conn.: Yale University Press, 1972. 693 p.

Clapman, Christopher. FOREIGN POLICY MAKING IN DEVELOPING STATES: A COMPARATIVE APPROACH. Lexington, Mass.: Lexington, 1977. 184 p.

Cohen, Jerome A. DECISION MAKING AND INTERNATIONAL LAW: CHINA'S PRACTICE OF INTERNATIONAL LAW--SOME CASE STUDIES. Cambridge, Mass.: Harvard University Press, 1972. 417 p.

Farrell, R. Barry. "Foreign Policy Formation in the Communist Countries of Eastern Europe." EAST EUROPEAN QUARTERLY 1 (March 1967): 39-74.

Hanf, Kenneth, and Scharpf, Fritz W., eds. INTERORGANIZATIONAL POLICY MAKING: LIMITS TO COORDINATION AND CENTRAL CONTROL. Beverly Hills, Calif.: Sage, 1978. 330 p.

    On intergovernmental policy making and implementation.

Keatinge, Patrick. THE FORMULATION OF IRISH FOREIGN POLICY. Dublin: Institute of Public Administration, 1973. 323 p.

Kelley, Donald R. "Toward a Model of Soviet Decision Making: A Research Note." AMERICAN POLITICAL SCIENCE REVIEW 68 (June 1974): 701-6.

Kirton, John James. "The Conduct and Coordination of Canadian Government Decision-Making Towards the United States." Ph.D. dissertation, Johns Hopkins University, 1977. 364 p.

McLaurin, R.D.; Mughisuddin, Mohammed; and Wagner, Abraham R. FOREIGN POLICY MAKING IN THE MIDDLE EAST. New York: Praeger, 1977. 313 p.

Mayntz, Renate, and Scharpf, Fritz W. POLICY MAKING IN THE GERMAN FEDERAL BUREAUCRACY. New York: American Elsevier, 1975. 183 p.

Pempel, T.J., ed. POLICYMAKING IN CONTEMPORARY JAPAN. Ithaca, N.Y.: Cornell University Press, 1977. 345 p.

Remnek, Richard B., ed. SOCIAL SCIENTISTS AND POLICY MAKING IN THE SOVIET UNION. New York: Praeger, 1977. 144 p. Bibliog.

Sasse, Christoph; Poullet, Edouard; Coombes, David; and Deprez, Gerard. DECISION MAKING IN THE EUROPEAN COMMUNITY. New York: Praeger, 1977. 352 p.

Schwab, Peter. DECISION MAKING IN ETHIOPIA: A STUDY OF THE PO-LITICAL PROCESS. Cranbury, N.J.: Associated University Press, 1972. 201 p. Bibliog.

Sfeir-Younis, Alfredo, and Bromley, Daniel W. DECISION MAKING IN DEVELOPING COUNTRIES: MULTIOBJECTIVE FORMULATION AND EVALUA-TION METHODS. New York: Praeger, 1977. 222 p.

Vital, David. THE MAKING OF BRITISH FOREIGN POLICY. London: Allen and Unwin, 1968. 119 p.

Vogel, Ezra F., ed. MODERN JAPANESE ORGANIZATION AND DECISION MAKING. Berkeley: University of California Press, 1975. 340 p.

Wagner, Abraham R. CRISIS DECISION-MAKING: ISRAEL'S EXPERIENCE IN 1967 AND 1973. New York: Praeger, 1974. 186 p. Bibliog.

Wallace, Helen; Wallace, William; and Webb, Carole, eds. POLICY-MAKING IN THE EUROPEAN COMMUNITIES. Somerset, N.J.: Wiley Interscience, 1977. 341 p.

Wallace, William. THE FOREIGN POLICY PROCESS IN BRITAIN. Reading, Mass.: Allen and Unwin, 1975. 336 p.

Wallace, William, and Paterson, William, eds. FOREIGN POLICY MAKING IN WESTERN EUROPE. Lexington, Mass.: Lexington, 1978. 161 p. Bibliog.

On policy making in Britain, France, Federal Republic of Germany, Belgium, the Netherlands, and Scandinavia.

FOREIGN RELATIONS DECISION MAKING

A distinct literature is also available on the study of decision making in the field of international affairs, emphasizing both the conduct of foreign relations and the formulation of foreign policy. The following are representative of three types of contributions concerned directly with the decision process: broadly oriented volumes and journal articles, chapters or sections of more general volumes on foreign relations and international politics, and items of specialized interest. Additional materials on the less restricted question of the making of foreign policy are listed in chapter 16, section on "Policy Formulation."

Research and literary concern with foreign relations decision making spans a broad spectrum of interests. These range from the pioneering ventures of Richard Snyder and others in the mid-1950s, and the basic views of practitioners like Dean Acheson and Dean Rusk, to a variety of largely unofficial interpretations, refinements, and applications. Psychological aspects are probed by such writers as D'Amato, de Bourbon-Busset, and de Rivera. There are also those analysts who seek to develop and explain particular decision-making systems, including the bureaucratic (David Davis and Alexander George) and the intellectual-rational (Cobbledick, Frankel, and Plischke). Some apply analysis directly to the Department of State (Bowling) and international organizations (Cox and Jacobson, Hadwen and Kaufman, Lindberg, and Lopez); others focus on national security and the military (Halperin, Hammond, Hitch, Quade, and William Snyder). Many discuss systematizing analysis of the decision-making process or design a predictive and planning formula or a viable theory of international relations. Literature on specific case studies and theory building is dealt with separately in subsequent sections of this chapter.

Abel, Theodore. "The Element of Decision in the Pattern of War." AMERICAN SOCIOLOGICAL REVIEW 6 (December 1941): 853-59.

Acheson, Dean G. "Responsibility for Decision in Foreign Policy." YALE REVIEW 44 (Autumn 1954): 1-12.

Bauer, Raymond A.; Pool, Ithiel de Sola; and Dexter, Lewis Anthony. AMERICAN BUSINESS AND PUBLIC POLICY: THE POLITICS OF FOREIGN TRADE. 2d ed. Chicago: Aldine-Atherton, 1972. 499 p. Bibliog.

Bowling, John W. "How We Do Our Thing: Crisis Management." FOREIGN SERVICE JOURNAL 47 (May 1970): 19-21.

_____. "How We Do Our Thing: Innovation." FOREIGN SERVICE JOURNAL 47 (October 1970): 25-27, 55-56.

_____. "How We Do Our Thing: Policy Formulation." FOREIGN SERVICE JOURNAL 47 (January 1970): 19-22, 48.

Braybrooke, David, and Lindblom, Charles E. "Types of Decision Making." In INTERNATIONAL POLITICS AND FOREIGN POLICY, edited by James Rosenau, pp. 207-16. 2d ed. New York: Free Press, 1969.

Cobbledick, James R. CHOICE IN AMERICAN FOREIGN POLICY: OPTIONS FOR THE FUTURE. New York: Crowell, 1973. 282 p.

Especially chapter 1, "The Options Approach: Some Considerations."

Committee for Economic Development. CONGRESSIONAL DECISION MAKING FOR NATIONAL SECURITY. New York: 1974. 29 p.

Coplin, William D., and Rochester, J. Martin. FOREIGN POLICY DECISION-MAKING. Chicago: Markham, 1971. 32 p. Bibliog.

Cox, Robert W., and Jacobson, Harold K. DECISION MAKING IN INTER-
NATIONAL ORGANIZATION. New Haven, Conn.: Yale University Press,
1972. 497 p.

> Deals with the General Agreement on Tariffs and Trade, Interna-
> tional Atomic Energy Agency, International Labor Organization,
> International Monetary Fund, International Telecommunication
> Union, United Nations Educational, Scientific and Cultural Or-
> ganization, United Nations Conference on Trade and Development,
> and World Health Organization.

Crabb, Cecil V., Jr. "Public Opinion and Decision Making." In his
AMERICAN FOREIGN POLICY IN THE NUCLEAR AGE, pp. 129-51. 2d ed.
New York: Harper and Row, 1965.

> This was redesigned as "The Public Context of Foreign Policy."
> Chapter 7 of ibid, pp. 145-73. 3d ed. 1972.

D'Amato, Anthony A. "Psychological Constructs in Foreign Policy Prediction."
JOURNAL OF CONFLICT RESOLUTION 11 (September 1967): 294-311.

Davis, David Howard. HOW THE BUREAUCRACY MAKES FOREIGN POLICY:
AN EXCHANGE ANALYSIS. Lexington, Mass.: Heath, 1972. 164 p. Bibliog.

Davis, Vincent. "American Military Policy: Decision-Making in the Executive
Branch." NAVAL WAR COLLEGE REVIEW 22 (May 1970): 4-23.

de Bourbon-Busset, Jacques. "Decision-Making in Foreign Policy." In DIPLO-
MACY IN A CHANGING WORLD, edited by Stephen D. Kertesz and M.A.
Fitzsimons, pp. 77-100. Notre Dame, Ind.: University of Notre Dame Press, 1959.

_____. "How Decisions Are Made in Foreign Policy: Psychology in Interna-
tional Relations." REVIEW OF POLITICS 20 (October 1958): 591-614.

de Rivera, Joseph H. THE PSYCHOLOGICAL DIMENSION OF FOREIGN
POLICY. Columbus, Ohio: Merrill, 1968. 441 p.

Deutsch, Karl W. "Another Look at the National Decision System." In his
THE ANALYSIS OF INTERNATIONAL RELATIONS, pp. 101-10. Englewood
Cliffs, N.J.: Prentice-Hall, 1968.

Donovan, John C. THE COLD WAR: A POLICY-MAKING ELITE. Lexington,
Mass.: Heath, 1974. 294 p.

Druzhinin, V.V., and Kontorov, D.S. DECISIONMAKING AND AUTOMA-
TION: CONCEPT, ALGORITHM, DECISION (A SOVIET VIEW). Moscow:

1972. Translated and published under the auspices of the U.S. Air Force. Washington, D.C.: Government Printing Office, 1975. 296 p.

Frankel, Joseph. THE MAKING OF FOREIGN POLICY: AN ANALYSIS OF DECISION MAKING. New York: Oxford University Press, 1963. 231 p.

_____. "Rational Decision-Making in Foreign Policy." YEARBOOK OF WORLD AFFAIRS 14 (1960): 40-66.

_____. "Towards a Decision-Making Model in Foreign Policy." POLITICAL STUDIES 7 (February 1959): 1-11.

Fuchs, Kenneth R. "Foreign Policy Decision-Maker Lines." Ph.D. dissertation, State University of New York (Buffalo), 1974. 365 p.

George, Alexander L. "The Case for Multiple Advocacy in Making Foreign Policy." AMERICAN POLITICAL SCIENCE REVIEW 66 (September 1972): 751-95.

_____. "The 'Operational Code': A Neglected Approach to the Study of Political Leaders and Decision-Making." INTERNATIONAL STUDIES QUARTERLY 13 (June 1969): 190-222.

Geyer, Alan Francis. "American Protestantism and World Politics, 1898-1960: A Typological Approach to the Functions of Religion in the Decision Making Processes of Foreign Policy." Ph.D. dissertation, Boston University, 1961. 462 p.

Hadwen, John G., and Kaufmann, Johan. HOW UNITED NATIONS DECISIONS ARE MADE. Leiden, The Netherlands: Sijthoff, 1960. 144 p.

Halper, Thomas. FOREIGN POLICY CRISES: APPEARANCE AND REALITY IN DECISIONMAKING. Columbus, Ohio: Merrill, 1971. 235 p. Bibliog.

Halperin, Morton H. NATIONAL SECURITY POLICY-MAKING: ANALYSES, CASES, AND PROPOSALS. Lexington, Mass.: Lexington, 1975. 191 p.

_____. "Why Bureaucrats Play Games." FOREIGN POLICY 5 (May 1971): 70-90.

Halperin Morton H., with assistance of Priscilla Clapp and Arnold Kanter. BUREAUCRATIC POLITICS AND FOREIGN POLICY. Washington, D.C.: Brookings Institution, 1974. 340 p. Bibliog.

Hamilton, William C. "Some Problems of Decision-Making in Foreign Affairs." DEPARTMENT OF STATE BULLETIN 37 (9 September 1957): 432-36.

Hammond, Paul Y. "A Functional Analysis of Defense Department Decision-Making in the McNamara Administration." AMERICAN POLITICAL SCIENCE REVIEW 62 (March 1968): 57-69.

Hilsman, Roger, Jr. STRATEGIC INTELLIGENCE AND NATIONAL DECISIONS. Glencoe, Ill.: Free Press, 1956. 187 p.

Hitch, Charles J. DECISION MAKING FOR DEFENSE. Berkeley and Los Angeles: University of California Press, 1966. 83 p.

Hoerch, H., and Lavin, M.M. SIMULATION OF DECISION MAKING IN CRISES: THREE MANUAL GAMING EXPERIMENTS. Rand Memorandum 4202-PR. Santa Monica, Calif.: Rand, 1964.

Holsti, Ole R. "Perceptions of Time and Alternatives as Factors in Crisis Decision-Making." PEACE RESEARCH SOCIETY PAPERS 3 (1964): 79-120.

Hopkins, Raymond, and Mansbach, Richard W. STRUCTURE AND PROCESS IN INTERNATIONAL POLITICS. New York: Harper and Row, 1973.

Chapter 8 on decision making.

Janis, Irving L. VICTIMS OF GROUPTHINK: A PSYCHOLOGICAL STUDY OF FOREIGN-POLICY DECISIONS AND FIASCOS. Boston: Houghton Mifflin, 1972. 258 p. Bibliog.

Jervis, Robert. "Hypotheses on Misperception." In INTERNATIONAL POLITICS AND FOREIGN POLICY, edited by James Rosenau, pp. 239-54. 2d ed. New York: Free Press, 1969.

Kissinger, Henry A. "Domestic Structure and Foreign Policy." DAEDALUS 95 (Spring 1966): 503-29.

Landheer, Bartholomeus. ETHICAL VALUES IN INTERNATIONAL DECISION MAKING. The Hague: Nijhoff, 1960. 103 p.

Lentner, Howard H. "Decisions." In his FOREIGN POLICY ANALYSIS: A COMPARATIVE AND CONCEPTUAL APPROACH, pp. 173-97. Columbus, Ohio: Merrill, 1974.

Lindberg, Leon N. "Decisionmaking and Integration in the European Community." INTERNATIONAL ORGANIZATION 19 (Winter 1965): 56-80.

Lopez, George A. "Correlates of the Decision-Making Authority of Secretaries-General: A Comparative Analysis of Intergovernmental Organizations." Ph.D. dissertation, Syracuse University, 1975. 190 p.

Lovell, John P. FOREIGN POLICY IN PERSPECTIVE: STRATEGY, ADAPTATION, DECISION MAKING. New York: Holt, Rinehart, and Winston, 1970. 370 p. Bibliog.

Mennis, Bernard. "An Empirical Analysis of the Background and Political Preferences of American Foreign Policy Decision-Makers." Ph.D. dissertation, University of Michigan, 1967. 236 p.

North, Robert C. "Decision-Making in Crises: An Introduction." JOURNAL OF CONFLICT RESOLUTION 6 (September 1962): 197-200.

Pettman, Ralph. "On Method and Against It: The Decisionmaking Process." In his HUMAN BEHAVIOR AND WORLD POLITICS, pp. 23-64. London: Macmillan, 1975.

Plischke, Elmer. FOREIGN RELATIONS DECISIONMAKING: OPTIONS ANALYSIS. Beirut, Lebanon: Catholic Press for Institute of Middle Eastern and North African Affairs, 1973. 52 p. Bibliog.

_____. "Intellectual Dimensions of Foreign Relations Decisionmaking." In FOREIGN POLICY ANALYSIS, edited by Richard L. Merritt, pp. 63-71. Lexington, Mass.: Lexington Books, 1975. Reprinted from POLICY STUDIES JOURNAL 3 (Winter 1974): 155-58.

Pruitt, Dean G. "Definition of the Situation as a Determinant of International Action." In INTERNATIONAL BEHAVIOR: A SOCIAL PSYCHOLOGICAL ANALYSIS, edited by Herbert Kelman, pp. 391-432. New York: Holt, Rinehart, and Winston, 1965.

Quade, Edward S., ed. ANALYSIS FOR MILITARY DECISIONS. New York: American Elsevier, 1970. 382 p. Bibliog.

Rosecrance, Richard, and Mueller, J.E. "Decision-Making and the Quantitative Analysis of International Relations." YEARBOOK OF WORLD AFFAIRS 21 (1967): 1-19.

Rosenau, James N. "The Premises and Promises of Decision-Making Analysis." In CONTEMPORARY POLITICAL ANALYSIS, edited by James C. Charlesworth, pp. 189-211. New York: Free Press, 1967.

_____, ed. "Decision Making and Decision Makers." In his INTERNATIONAL POLITICS AND FOREIGN POLICY, pp. 199-254. 2d ed. New York: Free Press, 1969.

Rusk, Dean. "The Anatomy of Foreign Policy Decisions." DEPARTMENT OF STATE BULLETIN 52 (27 September 1965): 502-9.

Schwebel, Stephen M., ed. THE EFFECTIVENESS OF INTERNATIONAL DECISIONS. Leiden: Sijthoff; Dobbs Ferry, N.Y.: Oceana, 1971. 538 p. Bibliog.

Scott, Andrew M. "Decision-Making." In his THE FUNCTIONING OF THE INTERNATIONAL POLITICAL SYSTEM, pp. 80-105. New York: Macmillan, 1967.

Shapiro, Michael J., and Bonham, G. Matthew. "Cognitive Process and Foreign Policy Decision-Making." INTERNATIONAL STUDIES QUARTERLY 17 (June 1973): 147-74.

Sidjanski, Dusan, ed. POLITICAL DECISION-MAKING PROCESSES: STUDIES IN NATIONAL, COMPARATIVE, AND INTERNATIONAL POLITICS. San Francisco: Jossey-Bass, 1973. 237 p. Bibliog.

Snyder, Richard C.; Bruck, H.W.; and Sapin, Burton M. DECISION-MAKING AS AN APPROACH TO THE STUDY OF INTERNATIONAL POLITICS. Princeton, N.J.: Princeton University Press, 1954. 120 p.

_____, eds. FOREIGN POLICY DECISION MAKING: AN APPROACH TO THE STUDY OF INTERNATIONAL POLITICS. New York: Free Press, 1962. 274 p.

Snyder, Richard C., and Furniss, Edgar S., Jr. "The Decision Making Process." In their AMERICAN FOREIGN POLICY: FORMULATION, PRINCIPLES, AND PROGRAMS, pp. 89-133. New York: Rinehart, 1954.

Snyder, Richard C., and Robinson, James A. NATIONAL AND INTERNATIONAL DECISION-MAKING. Report to Committee on Research for Peace. New York: Institute for International Order, 1961. 228 p. Bibliog.

Snyder, William P. MAKING U.S. NATIONAL SECURITY POLICIES. Carlisle Barracks, Pa.: U.S. Army War College, 1971. 20 p.

Stichting, Grotius S. ETHICAL VALUES IN INTERNATIONAL DECISION-MAKING. The Hague: Nijhoff, 1960. 103 p.

Toma, Peter A., and Gyorgy, Andrew. "The Decision Makers." In their BASIC ISSUES IN INTERNATIONAL RELATIONS, pp. 305-46. New York: Allyn and Bacon, 1967.

United Nations Association of the United States of America. FOREIGN POLICY DECISION MAKING: THE NEW DIMENSIONS. New York: U.N. Association of the USA in cooperation with the Carnegie Endowment for International Peace, 1973. 103 p.

U.S. Commission on the Organization of the Government for the Conduct of Foreign Policy. "The Use of Information." In its COMMISSION ON THE ORGANIZATION OF THE GOVERNMENT FOR THE CONDUCT OF FOREIGN POLICY, JUNE, 1975, vol. 2, pp. 7-136. Washington, D.C.: Government Printing Office, 1976.

Relates information to decision-making process.

Wiegle, Thomas C. "Decision-Making in an International Crisis: Some Biological Factors." INTERNATIONAL STUDIES QUARTERLY 17 (September 1973): 295-335. Bibliog.

CASE STUDIES

Decision-making analysis is increasingly being applied to specific policy determinations, as illustrated by the following. Some studies pertain to territorial crisis situations, such as Azerbaijan (Irani), Cuba (Allison), Korea (Paige, Snyder), and Vietnam (Gelb, Thompson). Additional and more general literature on crisis management is provided in chapter 18. Other case studies relate to policy formulation respecting relations with particular countries or territories, such as those of Backer, Baron, Leader , Mahood, Moorsteen, Plischke, Sanchez, Sigal, and Towell. Special interest also is centered upon weaponry matters, including the development and use of nuclear bombs, represented by the contributions of Amrine, Art, Batchelder, Chayes, Dyer, Fogelman, Halperin, Schilling, Schoenberger, Stimson, and Wilson. A few publications deal with questions of foreign aid and assistance--Ahmad, Biglow, Dawson, Randall, Jones, and Sylvan. Occasionally, attention is paid to such historic events as decisions respecting American independence (Pole) and the outbreak of war in 1914 (Farrar). Although most compilations of case studies of U.S. foreign relations, as noted in chapter 15, are more general in scope, some attempt has been made to produce collections of decision-making case studies as well--Caputo, Morris, Rostow, Stein, and Strauss. Additional related materials may be found in chapter 12 on the military.

Ahmad, Zubair. "The United States Decision on Military Aid to Pakistan." Ph.D. dissertation, University of Pennsylvania, 1975. 309 p.

Allison, Graham T. "Conceptual Models and the Cuban Missile Crisis." AMERICAN POLITICAL SCIENCE REVIEW 63 (September 1969): 689-718.

_____. ESSENCE OF DECISION: EXPLAINING THE CUBAN MISSILE CRISIS. Boston: Little, Brown, 1971. 338 p.

Amrine, Michael. THE GREAT DECISION: THE SECRET HISTORY OF THE ATOMIC BOMB. New York: Putnam, 1959. 251 p.

Art, Robert J. THE TFX DECISION: McNAMARA AND THE MILITARY. Boston: Little, Brown, 1968. 202 p. Bibliog.

Ashton, Charles Henry. "Congressional Decision-Making in the Foreign Policy-Making Process: The Case of the Bokaro Steel Mill Project in Indo-American Relations." Ph.D. dissertation, University of Pennsylvania, 1972. 383 p.

Backer, John H. THE DECISION TO DIVIDE GERMANY: AMERICAN FOREIGN POLICY IN TRANSITION. Durham, N.C.: Duke University Press, 1978. 212 p.

Baron, Dona Gene. "Policy for 'Paradise': A Study of United States Decision-Making Processes Respecting the Trust Territories of the Pacific Islands and the Impact Thereupon of United Nations Oversight." Ph.D. dissertation, Columbia University, 1973. 670 p.

Batchelder, Robert C. THE IRREVERSIBLE DECISION, 1939-1950. New York: Macmillan, 1961. Boston: Houghton Mifflin, 1962. 306 p.

Especially section on decision regarding dropping of atom bombs on Japan, pp. 190-210.

Berkowitz, Morton; Bock, P.G.; and Fuccillo, Vincent J. THE POLITICS OF AMERICAN FOREIGN POLICY: THE SOCIAL CONTEXT OF DECISIONS. Englewood Cliffs, N.J.: Prentice-Hall, 1977. 310 p.

Chapters 2-12 constitute decision-making case studies.

Biglow, Frank William. "The Alliance for Progress, the OAS, and the Kennedy Administration: A Decision-Making Study of United States Foreign Policy Objectives in Latin America, 1960-1963." Ph.D. dissertation, University of California (Berkeley), 1972.

Bottome, Edgar M. THE MISSILE GAP: A STUDY OF THE FORMULATION OF MILITARY AND POLITICAL POLICY. Rutherford, N.J.: Fairleigh Dickinson University Press, 1971. 265 p. Bibliog.

Caputo, David A., ed. THE POLITICS OF POLICY MAKING IN AMERICA: FIVE CASE STUDIES. San Francisco: Freeman, 1977. 189 p.

One of case studies concerned with decision making respecting foreign relations.

Chayes, Abram, and Wiesner, Jerome B. ABM: AN EVALUATION OF THE DECISION TO DEPLOY AN ANTI-BALLISTIC MISSILE SYSTEM. New York: Harper and Row, 1969. 282 p.

Daniels, Roger. THE DECISION TO RELOCATE THE JAPANESE AMERICANS. Philadelphia: Lippincott, 1975. 135 p.

Dawson, Raymond Howard. THE DECISION TO AID RUSSIA, 1941: FOREIGN POLICY AND DOMESTIC POLITICS. Chapel Hill: University of North Carolina Press, 1959. 315 p. Bibliog.

_____. "The United States Decision to Aid Soviet Russia in 1941: Foreign Policy and Domestic Politics." Ph.D. dissertation, University of North Carolina (Chapel Hill), 1958. 479 p.

Dyer, Philip Wadsworth. "The Decisions to Make and Deploy Tactical Nuclear Weapons: A Case Study in the Foreign Policy Process." Ph.D. dissertation, Indiana University, 1970. 258 p.

Farrar, L.L. "The Limits of Choice: July 1914 Reconsidered." JOURNAL OF CONFLICT RESOLUTION 16 (March 1972): 1-23.

Fogelman, Edwin. HIROSHIMA: THE DECISION TO USE THE A-BOMB. New York: Scribner, 1964. 116 p.

Garfield, Gene Jensen. "The Truman Policy in Indochina: A Study in Decision-Making." Ph.D. dissertation, Southern Illinois University, 1972. 384 p.

Gelb, Leslie H. VIETNAM: THE SYSTEM WORKED. Washington, D.C.: Brookings Institution, 1971. 17 p. Reprinted from FOREIGN POLICY 3 (Summer 1971): 140-67.

Halperin, Morton H. "The Decision to Deploy the ABM: Bureaucratic and Domestic Politics in the Johnson Administration." WORLD POLITICS 25 (October 1972): 62-95.

Halperin, Morton H., and Kanter, Arnold, eds. READINGS IN AMERICAN FOREIGN POLICY: A BUREAUCRATIC PERSPECTIVE. Boston: Little, Brown, 1973. 434 p. Bibliog.

   Series of case studies contained in parts 2 and 3, pages 172-350.

Irani, Robert Ghobad. AMERICAN DIPLOMACY: AN OPTIONS ANALYSIS OF THE AZERBAIJAN CRISIS, 1945-1946. Beirut, Lebanon: Institute of Middle Eastern and North African Affairs, 1978. 94 p.

_____. "The Azerbaijan Crisis, 1945-1946: An Options Analysis of United States Policy." Ph.D. dissertation, University of Maryland, 1973. 495 p. Bibliog.

Jones, Joseph Marion. THE FIFTEEN WEEKS--FEBRUARY 21-JUNE 5, 1947. New York: Viking, 1955. 296 p.

   On decisions to put Truman Doctrine and Marshall Plan into effect.

Decision Making

Jones, Randall J., Jr. "American Policy Toward Generalized Tariff Preferences for Developing Countries: The Punta del Este Decision of 1967." Ph.D.
dissertation, University of Texas (Austin), 1974. 321 p.

Kahn, Gilbert N. "Pressure Group Influence on Foreign Policy Decision Making: A Case Study of the United States Efforts to Join the World Court, 1935."
Ph.D. dissertation, New York University, 1972. 288 p.

Leader, Stefan H. "Intellectual Processes in Foreign Policy Decision-Making:
The Case of German-American Relations, 1933-1941." Ph.D. dissertation,
State University of New York (Buffalo), 1971. 238 p.

Lepper, Mary M. FOREIGN POLICY FORMULATION: A CASE STUDY OF
THE NUCLEAR TEST BAN TREATY OF 1963. Columbus, Ohio: Merrill, 1971.
191 p. Bibliog.

Mahood, Harry Richard. "The St. Lawrence Seaway Bill of 1954: A Case
Study of Decision-Making in American Foreign Policy." Ph.D. dissertation,
University of Illinois, 1960. 180 p.

Moorsteen, Richard, and Abramowitz, Morton. REMAKING CHINA POLICY:
UNITED STATES-CHINA RELATIONS AND GOVERNMENTAL DECISIONMAK-
ING. Cambridge, Mass.: Harvard University Press, 1971. 136 p.

Morris, Richard Brandon, ed. GREAT PRESIDENTIAL DECISIONS: STATE
PAPERS THAT CHANGED THE COURSE OF HISTORY. Rev. ed. New York:
Harper and Row, 1973. 508 p. Bibliog.

Paige, Glenn D. THE KOREA DECISION (JUNE 24-30, 1950). New York:
Free Press, 1968. 394 p. Bibliog.

Plischke, Elmer. "Resolving the 'Berlin Question'--An Options Analysis."
WORLD AFFAIRS 131 (July-September 1968): 91-100.

_____. "Reunifying Germany--An Options Analysis." WORLD AFFAIRS 132
(June 1969): 28-38.

_____. "United States Southeast Asian Policy--An Options Analysis." SO-
CIAL STUDIES (North Carolina) 18 (Fall 1971): 18-31.

_____. "West German Foreign and Defense Policy." ORBIS 12 (Winter
1969): 1098-1136.

Pole, Jack Richon. THE DECISION FOR AMERICAN INDEPENDENCE. Philadelphia: Lippincott, 1975. 124 p.

Rimkus, Raymond Alston. "The Cuban Missile Crisis: A Decision-Making Analysis of the Quarantine Policy With Special Emphasis Upon the Implication for Decision-Making Theory." Ph.D. dissertation, University of Oklahoma, 1972. 255 p.

Rosenthal, Glenda. THE MEN BEHIND THE DECISIONS: CASES IN EURO-PEAN POLICY-MAKING. Lexington, Mass.: Lexington Books, 1975. 176 p.

Rostow, Walt W. THE DIFFUSION OF POWER: AN ESSAY IN RECENT HISTORY. New York: Macmillan, 1972. 739 p.

>   On men and decisions that shaped America's role in the world, 1957-72.

Sanchez, Jose Manuel. "U.S. Intervention in the Caribbean: 1954-1965: Decision-Making and the Information Input." Ph.D. dissertation, Columbia University, 1972.

Schilling, Warner R. "The H-Bomb Decision: How to Decide Without Actually Choosing." POLITICAL SCIENCE QUARTERLY 76 (March 1961): 24-46.

Schoenberger, Walter S. DECISION OF DESTINY. Athens: Ohio University Press, 1970. 330 p. Bibliog.

>   On use of the atomic bomb.

_____. "The Decision to Use the Atomic Bomb and Its Political and Moral Consequences." Ph.D. dissertation, Tufts University, Fletcher School, 1963. 116 p.

Short, Frisco W.; Head, Richard G.; and McFarlane, Robert C. CRISIS RE-SOLUTION: PRESIDENTIAL DECISION MAKING IN THE MAYAGUEZ AND KOREAN CONFRONTATIONS. Boulder, Colo.: Westview, 1978. 300 p. Bibliog.

Sigal, Leon V. "The 'Rational Policy' Model and the Formosa Straits Crisis." INTERNATIONAL STUDIES QUARTERLY 14 (June 1970): 121-56.

Skillern, William Gustaf. "An Analysis of the Decision-Making Process in the Cuban Missile Crisis." Ph.D. dissertation, University of Idaho, 1971. 337 p.

Snyder, Richard C., and Paige, Glenn D. "The United States Decision to Resist Aggression in Korea: The Application of an Analytic Scheme." AD-MINISTRATIVE SCIENCE QUARTERLY 3 (December 1958): 341-78.

Stein, Harold, ed. AMERICAN CIVIL-MILITARY DECISIONS: A BOOK OF CASE STUDIES. University: University of Alabama Press, 1963. 705 p.

Steinbrunner, John D. "The Mind and Milieu of Policy-Makers: A Case Study of the MLF." Ph.D. dissertation, M.I.T., 1968. 231 p.

> Multilateral nuclear force was considered as a NATO joint strategic plan in the mid-1960s.

Stempel, John Dallas. "Policy/Decision Making in the Department of State: The Vietnamese Problem, 1961-1965." Ph.D. dissertation, University of California (Berkeley), 1965. 361 p.

Stimson, Henry L. "Decision to Use the Atomic Bomb." HARPER'S MAGAZINE, February 1947, pp. 97-107.

Strauss, Lewis L. MEN AND DECISIONS. New York: Doubleday, 1962. 468 p. Bibliog.

Sylvan, Donald Avery. "Models of Foreign Policy Choice: The Case of Foreign Assistance to Developing Nations." Ph.D. dissertation, University of Minnesota, 1974. 210 p.

Thompson, James C., Jr. "How Could Vietnam Happen? An Autopsy." ATLANTIC MONTHLY, April 1968, pp. 47-53.

Towell, William P. "Cognitive Complexity of a Foreign Policy Decision-Maker Under Conditions of Rising Threat: Joseph Grew and U.S.-Japan Relations, 1938-1941." Ph.D. dissertation, University of Illinois (Urbana), 1975. 198 p.

Trotter, Richard Gordon. "The Cuban Missile Crisis: An Analysis of Policy Formulation in Terms of Current Decision Making Theory." Ph.D. dissertation, University of Pennsylvania, 1970. 257 p.

Truitt, Wesley Byron. "The Troops to Europe Decision: The Process, Politics, and Diplomacy of a Strategic Commitment." Ph.D. dissertation, Columbia University, 1968. 557 p.

U.S. Congress. House of Representatives. Committee on International Relations. GREAT DECISIONS ON U.S. FOREIGN POLICY. 94th Cong., 1st sess. Washington, D.C.: Government Printing Office, 1975. 29 p.

> Testimony on such diverse topics as the world food problem, the Soviet Union, nuclear proliferation, the oceans, and the world economy.

White, Irvin L. DECISION-MAKING FOR SPACE: LAW AND POLITICS IN AIR, SEA, AND OUTER SPACE. Lafayette, Ind.: Purdue University Studies, 1970. 277 p. Bibliog.

Wilson, Richard Lee. "Bureaucratic Power in Foreign Policy Decision Making: The Manhattan District Triumvirate and the U.S. Nuclear Monopoly." Ph.D. dissertation, Johns Hopkins University, 1972. 584 p.

Winham, Gilbert Rathbone. "An Analysis of Foreign Aid Decision-Making: The Case of the Marshall Plan." Ph.D. dissertation, University of North Carolina (Chapel Hill), 1968. 195 p.

DECISION-MAKING THEORY

Some of the analyses listed above involve decision-making theory or hypothetical aspects of the decisional process, such as the publications of de Rivera, Frankel, Richard Snyder, and others, pp. 312, 313, 316. In addition, the following are representative essays in the developing literature on the analysis and evaluation of decision-making theory:

Alger, Chadwick F. "Decision-Making Theory and Human Conflict." In THE NATURE OF HUMAN CONFLICT, edited by Elton B. McNeil, pp. 274-92. Englewood Cliffs, N.J.: Prentice-Hall, 1965.

Bower, Joseph L. "Descriptive Decision Theory from the 'Administrative Viewpoints.'" In THE STUDY OF POLICY FORMATION, edited by Raymond A. Bauer and Kenneth J. Gergen, pp. 103-48. New York: Free Press, 1968.

Cartwright, D., and Festinger, L.A. "A Quantitative Theory of Decisions." PSYCHOLOGICAL REVIEW 50 (November 1943): 595-622.

Chernoff, Herman, and Moses, Lincoln E. ELEMENTARY DECISION THEORY. New York: Wiley, 1959. 364 p. Bibliog.

Dennis, Jack S. "Theories of Decision-Making in Political Science." Ph.D. dissertation, University of Chicago, 1962. 278 p.

Dyckman, John W. "Planning and Decision Theory." AMERICAN INSTITUTE OF PLANNERS 27 (November 1961): 335-45.

Edwards, Ward. "The Theory of Decision-Making." PSYCHOLOGICAL BULLE-TIN 51 (July 1954): 380-417.

Fagot, R.F. "A Theory of Decision-Making." Ph.D. dissertation, Stanford University, 1956. 121 p.

Gorman, Robert A. "On the Inadequacies of Non-Philosophical Political Science: A Critical Analysis of Decision-Making Theory." INTERNATIONAL STUDIES QUARTERLY 14 (December 1970): 395-411.

Kadish, Mortimer R. "Toward a Theory of Decision." Ph.D. dissertation, Columbia University, 1950. 225 p.

Lee, Wayne. DECISION THEORY AND HUMAN BEHAVIOR. New York: Wiley, 1971. 353 p. Bibliog.

Morgan, Patrick M. "A System, A System, The Kingdom Is a System." In his THEORIES AND APPROACHES TO INTERNATIONAL POLITICS: WHAT ARE WE TO THINK?, pp. 137-59. San Ramon, Calif.: Consensus, 1972.

On decision making as theory.

Nagel, Stuart S., and Neef, Marian G. DECISION THEORY AND THE LEGAL PROCESS. Lexington, Mass.: Lexington Books, 1979. 294 p. Bibliog.

Patchen, Martin. "Decision Theory in the Study of National Action: Problems and a Proposal." JOURNAL OF CONFLICT RESOLUTION 9 (June 1965): 165-76.

Pollard, William E., and Mitchell, Terrence R. "Decision Theory Analysis and Social Power." PSYCHOLOGICAL BULLETIN 78 (December 1972): 433-46.

Robinson, James A., and Majak, R. Roger. "The Theory of Decision-Making." In CONTEMPORARY POLITICAL ANALYSIS, edited by James C. Charlesworth, pp. 175-88. New York: Free Press, 1967.

Robinson, James A., and Snyder, Richard C. "Decision-Making in International Politics." In INTERNATIONAL BEHAVIOR: A SOCIAL-PSYCHOLOGICAL ANALYSIS, edited by Herbert Kelman, pp. 435-63. New York: Holt, Rinehart, and Winston, 1965.

Rogers, Robert C. "The Intellectual Dimension of Foreign Relations Decision-Making." Master's thesis, University of Maryland, 1972. 192 p. Bibliog.

Shubik, Martin. "Studies and Theories of Decision Making." ADMINISTRATIVE SCIENCE QUARTERLY 3 (December 1958): 289-306.

Steinbrunner, John D. THE CYBERNETIC THEORY OF DECISION: NEW DIMENSIONS OF POLITICAL ANALYSIS. Princeton, N.J.: Princeton University Press, 1974. 366 p. Bibliog.

White, Douglas J. DECISION THEORY. Chicago: Aldine, 1969; London: Allen and Unwin, 1969. 185 p. Bibliog.

Chapter 15

GENERAL STUDIES ON CONDUCT OF

U.S. FOREIGN RELATIONS

Supplementing the extensive resource materials on the presidency, the Congress, foreign relations decision making and policy formulation, the biographies and memoirs of individuals, and especially the materials on the secretary and Department of State and the diplomatic and consular services, the bulk of official literature on the conduct of foreign relations consists essentially of four basic types. These include general surveys, collections of readings and documents, case studies, and a host of specialized monographs. The materials incorporated into this chapter tend to be more general than most of those listed in other chapters devoted to more delimited and precise subjects. Some overlapping, however, is unavoidable.

GENERAL SURVEYS

The following are merely suggestive of the general literature, broad in scope and often in comprehension, and sometimes intended for use as textbooks that deal with the conduct of U.S. foreign relations. A few analyses, such as the following which antedate World War II, are regarded as pioneering volumes in this field:

Foster, John W. THE PRACTICE OF DIPLOMACY AS ILLUSTRATED IN THE FOREIGN RELATIONS OF THE UNITED STATES. Boston: Houghton Mifflin, 1906. 401 p. Bibliog.

Mathews, John M. AMERICAN FOREIGN RELATIONS: CONDUCT AND POLICIES. New York: Century, 1928. 2d ed. New York: Appleton-Century-Crofts, 1938. 766 p.

Part 2, chapters 10-29, on conduct of foreign relations.

_____. THE CONDUCT OF AMERICAN FOREIGN RELATIONS. New York: Century, 1922. 353 p.

Poole, DeWitt C. THE CONDUCT OF FOREIGN RELATIONS UNDER MODERN DEMOCRATIC CONDITIONS. New Haven, Conn.: Yale University Press, 1924. 208 p.

    Especially chapters 1-5.

Schuyler, Eugene. AMERICAN DIPLOMACY AND THE FURTHERANCE OF COMMERCE. New York: Scribners, 1886. 469 p.

Stuart, Graham H. AMERICAN DIPLOMATIC AND CONSULAR PRACTICE. New York: Appleton-Century-Crofts, 1936. 560 p. 2d ed. New York: Appleton-Century-Crofts, 1952. 477 p. Bibliog.

Williams, Benjamin H. AMERICAN DIPLOMACY: POLICIES AND PRACTICE. New York: McGraw-Hill, 1936. 517 p. Bibliog.

    Especially chapters 21-25.

Wright, Quincy. THE CONTROL OF AMERICAN FOREIGN RELATIONS. New York: Macmillan, 1922. 412 p.

Literary interest in the conduct of U.S. foreign relations has accelerated since World War II. For some years, the works of Graham, McCamy, Plischke, and Stuart (second edition) were numbered among the principal basic studies on the conduct of American diplomacy. McCamy emphasized the bureaucratic and administrative approach, Stuart focussed on fundamental diplomatic and consular affairs, and Plischke, parallelling the earlier works of Mathews, Williams, and Wright, employed a more encompassing approach, including broad-scale treatment of treaty making, international conferences, and parliamentary diplomacy. In the 1960s and 1970s, these were supplemented by the analyses of such authors as Armacost, Elliott, Jacobson and Zimmermann, Johnson, Kertesz, Macmahon, and others. In the meantime, a series of studies on the governmental mechanism for the administration of foreign relations was produced by Allison and Szanton, Bundy and Rogers, David, Haviland, and Sapin, largely concerned with reform and reorganization. Beginning in the 1960s, a number of diplomatic careerists have also contributed to this basic literature, including Ambassadors Briggs and Yost.

Much of this general literature emphasizes the legal, organizational, and institutional aspects of foreign policy making and implementation, including considerations of administrative structure, reorganization, and functioning. Additional information concerning these matters may be found in studies on the presidency, Congress, the Department of State, the National Security Council, foreign policy making, and decision making, which are listed in other chapters.

A number of studies are concerned specifically with constitutional problems in the foreign relations process. Aside from those listed elsewhere, as in the section on the separation of powers (chapter 7) and on treaty making (chapter 17), see those of Bishop, Fulbright, Henkin, Levitan, Potter, Sherwood, Wilcox and Frank, and others, listed below.

Allison, Graham, and Szanton, Peter. REMAKING FOREIGN POLICY: THE ORGANIZATIONAL CONNECTION. New York: Basic Books, 1976. 238 p.

Armacost, Michael H. THE FOREIGN RELATIONS OF THE UNITED STATES. Belmont, Calif.: Dickenson, 1969. 244 p. Bibliog.

Bishop, William W., Jr. "The Structure of Federal Power over Foreign Affairs." MINNESOTA LAW REVIEW 36 (March 1952): 299-322.

Briggs, Ellis O. ANATOMY OF DIPLOMACY: THE ORIGIN AND EXECUTION OF AMERICAN FOREIGN POLICY. New York: McKay, 1968. 248 p.

Brookings Institution. GOVERNMENTAL MECHANISM FOR THE CONDUCT OF UNITED STATES FOREIGN RELATIONS. Washington, D.C.: 1949. 58 p. Bibliog.

Bundy, Harvey H., and Rogers, James G. THE ORGANIZATION OF THE GOVERNMENT FOR THE CONDUCT OF FOREIGN AFFAIRS: A REPORT WITH RECOMMENDATIONS PREPARED FOR THE COMMISSION ON ORGANIZATION OF THE EXECUTIVE BRANCH OF THE GOVERNMENT. Washington, D.C.: Government Printing Office, 1949. 134 p.

David, Paul T., and staff. THE ADMINISTRATION OF FOREIGN AFFAIRS AND OVERSEAS OPERATIONS. Washington, D.C.: Brookings Institution, 1951. 380 p.

    Report prepared for U.S. Bureau of the Budget, Executive Office of the President.

Elliott, William Y., et al. UNITED STATES FOREIGN POLICY: ITS ORGANIZATION AND CONTROL. New York: Columbia University Press, 1952. 288 p.

Etzold, Thomas H. THE CONDUCT OF AMERICAN FOREIGN RELATIONS: THE OTHER SIDE OF DIPLOMACY. New York: New Viewpoints, Watts, 1977. 159 p. Bibliog.

Fulbright, J. William. "American Foreign Policy in the 20th Century Under an 18th Century Constitution." CORNELL LAW REVIEW 47 (Fall 1961): 1-13.

Graham, Malbone W. AMERICAN DIPLOMACY IN THE INTERNATIONAL COMMUNITY. Baltimore: Johns Hopkins Press, 1948. 279 p.

Haviland, H. Field, Jr., ed. THE FORMULATION AND ADMINISTRATION OF UNITED STATES FOREIGN POLICY. Washington, D.C.: Brookings Institution, 1960. 191 p.

Henkin, Louis. FOREIGN AFFAIRS AND THE CONSTITUTION. Mineola, N.Y.: Foundation Press, 1972. 553 p.

Jacobson, Harold Karan, and Zimmerman, William, eds. THE SHAPING OF FOREIGN POLICY. New York: Atherton, 1969. 214 p.

Johnson, Richard A. THE ADMINISTRATION OF UNITED STATES FOREIGN POLICY. Austin: University of Texas Press, 1971. 415 p.

Kertesz, Stephen D., ed. AMERICAN DIPLOMACY IN A NEW ERA. Notre Dame, Ind.: University of Notre Dame Press, 1961. 601 p.

Levitan, David M. "Constitutional Developments in the Control of Foreign Affairs: A Quest for Democratic Control." JOURNAL OF POLITICS 7 (February 1945): 58-92.

_____. "The Foreign Relations Power: An Analysis of Mr. Justice Sutherland's Theory." YALE LAW JOURNAL 55 (April 1946): 467-97.

McCamy, James L. THE ADMINISTRATION OF AMERICAN FOREIGN AFFAIRS. New York: Knopf, 1950. 364 p.

_____. CONDUCT OF THE NEW DIPLOMACY. New York: Harper and Row, 1964. 303 p. Bibliog.

Macmahon, Arthur W. "Administration and Foreign Policy." UNIVERSITY OF ILLINOIS BULLETIN 54, no. 44 (1957): entire issue.

_____. ADMINISTRATION IN FOREIGN AFFAIRS. University: University of Alabama Press, 1953. 275 p.

_____. "Functions and Area in the Administration of International Affairs." In NEW HORIZONS IN PUBLIC ADMINISTRATION, pp. 119-45. University: University of Alabama Press, 1945.

Myers, Denys P. "The Control of Foreign Relations." AMERICAN POLITICAL SCIENCE REVIEW 11 (February 1917): 24-58.

 Largely on general aspects of control, not restricted to the American process.

Plischke, Elmer. CONDUCT OF AMERICAN DIPLOMACY. 1st ed. New York: Van Nostrand, 1952. 3d ed. Princeton, N.J.: Van Nostrand, 1967. 677 p. Bibliog.

_____, ed. MODERN DIPLOMACY: THE ART AND THE ARTISANS. Washington, D.C.: American Enterprise Institute, 1979. 456 p. Bibliog.

Potter, Pitman B. "Control of American Diplomacy." INDIA QUARTERLY 6 (June 1950): 162-78.

Sapin, Burton M. THE MAKING OF UNITED STATES FOREIGN POLICY. Washington, D.C.: Praeger for Brookings Institution, 1966. 425 p.

Sherwood, Foster H. "Foreign Relations and the Constitution." WESTERN POLITICAL QUARTERLY 1 (December 1948): 386-99.

U.S. Congress. Senate. Committee on Foreign Relations. UNITED STATES FOREIGN POLICY: THE FORMULATION AND ADMINISTRATION OF UNITED STATES FOREIGN POLICY. 86th Cong., 2d sess. Washington, D.C.: Government Printing Office, 1960. 191 p.

> Prepared by Brookings Institution; see Haviland above, p. 229.

Westerfield, H. Bradford. THE INSTRUMENTS OF AMERICA'S FOREIGN POLICY. New York: Crowell, 1963. 538 p. Bibliog.

Wilcox, Francis O., and Frank, Richard A., eds. THE CONSTITUTION AND THE CONDUCT OF FOREIGN POLICY. New York: Praeger, 1976. 145 p.

Yost, Charles W. THE CONDUCT AND MISCONDUCT OF FOREIGN AFFAIRS. New York: Random House, 1972. 234 p.

As might be expected, many volumes which deal primarily with substantive foreign policy or the general external relations of the United States devote some, though more limited, attention to the conduct of diplomatic relations. In addition to the textbooks listed in chapter 2, such partial treatment is also provided in the following:

Barber, Hollis W. FOREIGN POLICIES OF THE UNITED STATES. New York: Dryden, 1953. 614 p.

> Especially chapters 1-3.

Bliss, Howard, and Johnson, M. Glen. BEYOND THE WATER'S EDGE: AMERICA'S FOREIGN POLICIES. Philadelphia: Lippincott, 1975. 272 p.

> Especially chapters 1, 5-9.

Crabb, Cecil V., Jr. AMERICAN FOREIGN POLICY IN THE NUCLEAR AGE. 3d ed. New York: Harper and Row, 1972. 528 p. Bibliog.

> Especially chapters 3-7.

Furniss, Edgar S., Jr., and Snyder, Richard C. AN INTRODUCTION TO AMERICAN FOREIGN POLICY. New York: Rinehart, 1955. 252 p. Bibliog.

Especially chapters 1, 5-6.

Gange, John. AMERICAN FOREIGN RELATIONS: PERMANENT PROBLEMS AND CHANGING POLICIES. New York: Ronald, 1959. 593 p. Bibliog.

Especially chapters 1-6, 13.

Gerberding, William P. UNITED STATES FOREIGN POLICY: PERSPECTIVES AND ANALYSIS. New York: McGraw-Hill, 1966. 383 p. Bibliog.

Especially chapters 2-3.

Hickman, Martin B., ed. PROBLEMS OF AMERICAN FOREIGN POLICY. 2d ed. Beverly Hills, Calif.: Glencoe, 1975. 206 p.

Especially chapters 2-4.

Irish, Marian D., and Frank, Elke. U.S. FOREIGN POLICY: CONTEXT, CONDUCT, CONTENT. New York: Harcourt Brace Jovanovich, 1975. 562 p. Bibliog.

Especially chapters 4-9.

Kegley, Charles W., Jr., and Wittkopf, Eugene R. AMERICAN FOREIGN POLICY: PATTERN AND PROCESS. New York: St. Martin's, 1979. 544 p.

Especially chapters 9-13.

Knappen, Marshall. AN INTRODUCTION TO AMERICAN FOREIGN POLICY. New York: Harper, 1956. 593 p.

Especially chapters 3-6, 16.

Lerche, Charles O., Jr. FOREIGN POLICY OF THE AMERICAN PEOPLE. 3d ed. Englewood Cliffs, N.J.: Prentice-Hall, 1967. 524 p. Bibliog.

Especially chapter 2.

Manning, Bayless. THE CONDUCT OF UNITED STATES FOREIGN POLICY IN THE NATION'S THIRD CENTURY. Headline Series, no. 231. New York: Foreign Policy Association, 1976. 80 p. Bibliog.

Especially pp. 50-78.

Nash, Henry T. AMERICAN FOREIGN POLICY: CHANGING PERSPECTIVES ON NATIONAL SECURITY. Rev. ed. Homewood, Ill.: Dorsey, 1978. 394 p.

Especially chapters 1, 2, 4-7.

_____. AMERICAN FOREIGN POLICY: RESPONSE TO A SENSE OF THREAT. Homewood, Ill.: Dorsey, 1973. 247 p.

  Especially chapters 1, 3-5.

Rainey, Gene E. PATTERNS OF AMERICAN FOREIGN POLICY. Boston: Allyn and Bacon, 1975. 405 p.

  Especially chapters 1, 5-12, 17.

Snyder, Richard C., and Furniss, Edgar S., Jr. AMERICAN FOREIGN POLICY: FORMULATION, PRINCIPLES, AND PROGRAMS. New York: Rinehart, 1954. 846 p. Bibliog.

  Especially chapters 3-13, 16.

Stupak, Ronald J. AMERICAN FOREIGN POLICY: ASSUMPTIONS, PROCESSES, AND PROJECTIONS. New York: Harper and Row, 1976. 243 p. Bibliog.

  Especially chapter 2.

COLLECTIONS AND READINGS

The contribution of collections of readings to this general and basic literature is reflected in the following anthologies. Generally, these contain descriptive and analytical readings respecting substantive foreign policy and the development of relations of the United States with other powers. However, Ransom's readings are more concerned with the essence or nature of foreign policy than with its substantive content, Halperin emphasizes the bureaucratic impact on policy making and implementation, and Scott and Dawson deal solely and entirely with various aspects of the conduct of foreign relations. Most of these compilations were published in the 1950s and 1960s, and this format appears to be declining in popularity as a foreign relations resource, except for anthologies of systematic analysis. Much the same is true of collections and readings in the field of international politics, except for those concerned with more specific subjects, such as theories of international relations, national strategy, power politics, disarmament, and the like.

Chamberlain, Lawrence H., and Snyder, Richard C., eds. AMERICAN FOREIGN POLICY. New York: Rinehart, 1948. 862 p. Bibliog.

  Especially chapters 1-15.

Cohen, Bernard C., ed. FOREIGN POLICY IN AMERICAN GOVERNMENT. Boston: Little, Brown, 1965. 204 p.

  Especially chapters 3-12.

Goldwin, Robert A., and Clor, Harry M., eds. READINGS IN AMERICAN DIPLOMACY. New York: Oxford University Press, 1971. 721 p.

Especially chapters 1 and 10.

Gordon, Morton, and Vines, Kenneth N., eds. THEORY AND PRACTICE OF AMERICAN FOREIGN POLICY. New York: Crowell, 1955. 562 p. Bibliog.

Especially chapters 3-4.

Graebner, Norman A., ed. IDEAS AND DIPLOMACY: READINGS IN THE INTELLECTUAL TRADITION OF AMERICAN FOREIGN POLICY. New York: Oxford University Press, 1964. 892 p.

Especially chapter 1.

Halperin, Morton H., and Kanter, Arnold, eds. READINGS IN AMERICAN FOREIGN POLICY: A BUREAUCRATIC PERSPECTIVE. Boston: Little, Brown, 1973. 434 p. Bibliog.

Jacobson, Harold Karan, ed. AMERICA'S FOREIGN POLICY. 2d ed. New York: Random House, 1965. 782 p.

Especially chapters 1-4.

Leonard, L. Larry, ed. ELEMENTS OF AMERICAN FOREIGN POLICY. New York: McGraw-Hill, 1953. 611 p. Bibliog.

Especially parts 1-3, pp. 1-214.

Needler, Martin C., ed. DIMENSIONS OF AMERICAN FOREIGN POLICY: READINGS AND DOCUMENTS. Princeton, N.J.: Van Nostrand, 1966. 372 p.

Especially chapters 1-2.

Ransom, Harry Howe, ed. AN AMERICAN FOREIGN POLICY READER. New York: Crowell, 1965. 690 p. Bibliog.

Especially chapters 1 and 7.

Rappaport, Armin, ed. ISSUES IN AMERICAN DIPLOMACY. 2 vols. New York: Macmillan, 1965. 394 p., 412 p.

Especially vol. 1, chapters 1-2.

Rosenau, James N., ed. INTERNATIONAL POLITICS AND FOREIGN POLICY: A READER IN RESEARCH AND THEORY. 2d ed. New York: Free Press, 740 p.

Scott, Andrew M., and Dawson, Raymond H., eds. READINGS IN THE MAKING OF AMERICAN FOREIGN POLICY. New York: Macmillan, 1965. 551 p. Bibliog.

UNOFFICIAL COMPILATIONS OF DOCUMENTS

As with most compilations of readings, the single-volume, broad-scale unofficial collections of illustrative documents primarily portray substantive policy, and they often are chronologically arranged. Because some of them are intended as textbooks, they are more directly related to the unfolding of diplomatic history as normally conceived than to the principles of the conduct of foreign relations. This literature, which was most popular in the 1950s and 1960s, although Bartlett's first edition was published in 1947, is represented by the following. Citations to official compilations of documents are provided in chapter 22.

Bartlett, Ruhl J., ed. THE RECORD OF AMERICAN DIPLOMACY: DOCUMENTS AND READINGS IN THE HISTORY OF AMERICAN FOREIGN RELATIONS. 4th ed. New York: Knopf, 1964. 892 p. Bibliog.

Brockway, Thomas P., ed. BASIC DOCUMENTS IN UNITED STATES FOREIGN POLICY. Princeton, N.J.: Van Nostrand, 1957. 191 p.

Divine, Robert A., ed. AMERICAN FOREIGN POLICY. New York: Meridian, 1960. 318 p.

 Contains documents and commentary.

Goebel, Dorothy Burne, ed. AMERICAN FOREIGN POLICY: A DOCUMENTARY SURVEY, 1776-1960. New York: Holt, Rinehart, and Winston, 1961. 458 p.

Guerrant, Edward O., ed. MODERN AMERICAN DIPLOMACY. Albuquerque: University of New Mexico Press, 1954. 318 p. Bibliog.

Paterson, Thomas G. MAJOR PROBLEMS IN AMERICAN FOREIGN POLICY: DOCUMENTS AND ESSAYS. 2 vols. Lexington, Mass.: Heath, 1978.

 Vol. 1 to 1914, and vol. 2 since 1914.

Rappaport, Armin, ed. SOURCES IN AMERICAN DIPLOMACY. New York: Macmillan, 1966. 367 p.

Snyder, Louis L., ed. FIFTY MAJOR DOCUMENTS OF THE NINETEENTH CENTURY. New York: Van Nostrand, 1955. 191 p.

_____. FIFTY MAJOR DOCUMENTS OF THE TWENTIETH CENTURY. New York: Van Nostrand, 1955. 185 p.

Williams, William Appleman, ed. THE SHAPING OF AMERICAN DIPLO-
MACY: READINGS AND DOCUMENTS IN AMERICAN FOREIGN RELATIONS,
1750-1955. Chicago: Rand McNally, 1956. 1,130 p.

Woodrow Wilson Foundation. OFFICIAL DOCUMENTS: TEXTS OF SELECTED
DOCUMENTS ON U.S. FOREIGN POLICY, 1918-1952. New York: Woodrow Wilson Foundation, 1952. 76 p.

Documentary collections restricted entirely to the foreign relations process--as
distinguished from declaratory statements and substantive policy--are rare.
The following provide illustrative documents, including some facsimiles, on
constitutional prescriptions, organization for the conduct of foreign relations,
diplomatic and consular credentials, privileges and immunities, international
conferences and the functioning of parliamentary diplomacy, treaty making,
processes for the resolution of disputes, and the handling of international conflict and the going to and termination of war.

Harmon, Robert B. THE ART AND PRACTICE OF DIPLOMACY: A SELECTED
AND ANNOTATED GUIDE. Metuchen, N.J.: Scarecrow, 1971.

> Especially chapter 7, "Diplomatic Documents and Organization,"
> pp. 212-92.

Plischke, Elmer. CONDUCT OF AMERICAN DIPLOMACY. 3d ed. Princeton, N.J.: Van Nostrand, 1976.

> See appendix, pp. 600-623.

_____. INTERNATIONAL RELATIONS: BASIC DOCUMENTS. 2d ed.
Princeton, N.J.: Van Nostrand, 1962. 194 p.

> Especially chapters 1-6, 9, and 11.

A few compilers, such as the following, have produced single unofficial volumes of documentary collections on specific aspects of foreign relations. Additional comprehensive unofficial and official collections of documents concerned
with policy statements, diplomatic communications, treaties, and other matters
are provided in chapter 22.

Elliot, Jonathan, ed. THE AMERICAN DIPLOMATIC CODE . . . 1778-1834.
2 vols. Washington, D.C.: J. Elliott, Jr., 1834.

> Consists of treaties, conventions, judicial decisions, summary of
> law of nations, and diplomatic manual applicable to the United
> States.

Feller, Abraham H., and Hudson, Manley O., eds. A COLLECTION OF THE
DIPLOMATIC AND CONSULAR LAWS AND REGULATIONS OF VARIOUS
COUNTRIES. 2 vols. Washington, D.C.: Carnegie Endowment, 1933.

Special mention needs to be made of the following periodic and systematic unofficial compilation:

Council on Foreign Relations. DOCUMENTS ON AMERICAN FOREIGN RE-LATIONS. New York: Harper for Council on Foreign Relations, 1939-- . Annual.

> Prepared by various compilers. Initially published by World Peace Foundation, Boston, and later Princeton, N.J. Since 1952, published by Council on Foreign Relations. Sections and subsections devoted to various aspects of the conduct of foreign affairs and to specific geographic areas. Includes official statements, reports, press releases, addresses, legislation, diplomatic communications, treaties and agreements, and similar diplomatic instruments.

CASE STUDIES

Quantitatively, the production of case study literature concerned with U.S. foreign relations is substantial, has been mushrooming in recent decades, and is especially appealing to the writers of doctoral dissertations. Much of this literature constitutes diplomatic history or, if otherwise oriented, emphasizes substantive policy and general state interaction rather than emphasizing matters of diplomatic process. Understandably, aside from a few anthologies listed below, such studies are primarily ad hoc. They concentrate on specific examples of policy formulation, decision making, and the handling of negotiable problems, rather than being systematic or inclusive compilations. In addition to the analyses of these and related matters, a good many concern particular treaty negotiations (such as the host of studies on negotiating the Versailles Treaty and the World War II peace settlement as well as similar recountings of the making of other treaties) and recent regionally oriented crisis situations. Extensive listings of such case study materials are provided in chapters 8, 14, 16-18, and elsewhere in this compilation. The following, therefore, is largely a residual list representing collections of case studies and a few isolated analyses of factors or issues involving the case study approach.

Overall, much case study literature concerns the framing of policy rather than the systematic analysis of the functions of diplomats in the field, except for the recountings and reflections of practitioners in their memoirs, which are listed in part IV. This area of planned production of selected case studies, with emphasis focussed more directly on the pragmatic functioning of the diplomatic processes, on the implementation of policy, and on the responsibilities and activities of diplomats and consuls, warrants considerably more scholarly and literary attention.

Appleton, Sheldon. UNITED STATES FOREIGN POLICY: AN INTRODUCTION WITH CASES. Boston: Little, Brown, 1968. 624 p.

> Analysis of particular aspects of U.S. foreign relations, with seventeen case studies.

Bemis, Samuel Flagg. THE DIPLOMACY OF THE AMERICAN REVOLUTION. Bloomington: Indiana University Press, 1957. 293 p.

Dulles, Allen W. THE SECRET SURRENDER. New York: Harper and Row, 1966. 255 p. Bibliog.

On intelligence activities to produce the Italian surrender in World War II.

Graber, Doris A. PUBLIC OPINION, THE PRESIDENT, AND FOREIGN POLICY: FOUR CASE STUDIES FROM THE FORMATIVE YEARS. New York: Holt, Rinehart, and Winston, 1968. 374 p.

McKenna, Joseph Charles. DIPLOMATIC PROTEST IN FOREIGN POLICY: ANALYSIS AND CASE STUDIES. Chicago: Loyola University Press, 1962. 222 p.

Matecki, B.E. ESTABLISHMENT OF THE INTERNATIONAL FINANCE CORPORATION AND UNITED STATES POLICY: A CASE STUDY IN INTERNATIONAL ORGANIZATION. New York: Praeger, 1957. 194 p.

Pratt, James W. "Leadership Relations in U.S. Foreign Policy Making: Case Studies, 1947-1950." Ph.D. dissertation, Columbia University, 1963. 397 p.

Rosenau, James N. NATIONAL LEADERSHIP AND FOREIGN POLICY: A CASE STUDY IN THE MOBILIZATION OF PUBLIC SUPPORT. Princeton, N.J.: Princeton University Press, 1963. 409 p.

Stein, Harold, ed. AMERICAN CIVIL-MILITARY DECISIONS: A BOOK OF CASE STUDIES. University: University of Alabama Press, 1963. 705 p.

Teaf, Howard M., and Franck, Peter G., eds. HAND ACROSS FRONTIERS: CASE STUDIES IN TECHNICAL COOPERATION. Ithaca, N.Y.: Cornell University Press, 1955. 579 p.

PERSPECTIVES, METHODS, OBJECTIVES, AND OTHER ANALYSES

There are a good many additional studies relating to the American foreign relations process which, though neither of the same breadth of scope as many of the volumes listed above nor as delimited in specialized approach as those contained in the categories which follow in chapters 16 and 17, nevertheless contribute to the study and analysis of the field. The following are merely suggestive of such contributions, but they parallel and supplement the materials listed in chapter 2 and the last section of chapter 3, which deal with diplomacy in general, as well as other portions of this compilation:

Acheson, Dean G. PRESENT AT THE CREATION: MY YEARS IN THE STATE DEPARTMENT. New York: Norton, 1969. 798 p.

Alger, Chadwick F. "The Role of the Private Expert in the Conduct of American Foreign Affairs." Ph.D. dissertation, Princeton University, 1958. 399 p.

Armstrong, Hamilton Fish, ed. FIFTY YEARS OF FOREIGN AFFAIRS. New York: Praeger, 1972. 501 p.

Compilation of thirty-one articles (selected from among twenty-six hundred) published in the FOREIGN AFFAIRS journal over the years, issued as an anniversary volume.

Beloff, Max. FOREIGN POLICY AND THE DEMOCRATIC PROCESS. Baltimore: Johns Hopkins Press, 1955. 134 p.

Berle, Adolph A., Jr. TIDES OF CRISIS: A PRIMER OF FOREIGN RELATIONS. New York: Reynal, 1957. 328 p.

Cleveland, Harlan. MANAGING U.S. FOREIGN POLICY IN A LEADERLESS WORLD. New York: Bernard M. Baruch College, 1975. 16 p.

Divine, Robert A., ed. AMERICAN FOREIGN POLICY SINCE 1945. Chicago: Quadrangle, 1969. 248 p.

Series of articles published in NEW YORK TIMES MAGAZINE, 1945-67.

Ekirch, Arthur A., Jr. IDEAS, IDEALS, AND AMERICAN DIPLOMACY: A HISTORY OF THEIR GROWTH AND INTERACTION. New York: Appleton, 1966. 205 p.

Farer, Tom J. TOWARD HUMANITARIAN DIPLOMACY: A PRIMER FOR POLICY. New York: New York University Press, 1980. 288 p.

Ferrell, Robert H. AMERICAN DIPLOMACY IN THE GREAT DEPRESSION. New Haven, Conn.: Yale University Press, 1957. 319 p.

Foreign Policy Association. A CARTOON HISTORY OF UNITED STATES FOREIGN POLICY: 1776-1976. New York: Morrow, 1976. 210 p.

Frankel, Charles. MORALITY AND U.S. FOREIGN POLICY. Headline Series, no. 224. New York: Foreign Policy Association, 1975. 63 p.

Gardner, Lloyd C. ARCHITECTS OF ILLUSION: MEN AND IDEAS IN AMERICAN FOREIGN POLICY, 1941-1949. New York: New Viewpoints, 1970. 379 p.

Grenville, John A.S., and Young, George Berkeley. POLITICS, STRATEGY, AND AMERICAN DIPLOMACY: STUDIES IN FOREIGN POLICY, 1783-1917. New Haven, Conn.: Yale University Press, 1966. 370 p.

Ilchman, Warren Frederick. PROFESSIONAL DIPLOMACY IN THE UNITED STATES, 1779-1939: A STUDY IN ADMINISTRATIVE HISTORY. Chicago: University of Chicago Press, 1961. 254 p.

Kennan, George. REALITIES OF AMERICAN FOREIGN POLICY. Princeton, N.J.: Princeton University Press, 1954. 119 p.

Lefever, Ernest W. ETHICS AND UNITED STATES FOREIGN POLICY. New York: Meridian, 1957. 199 p. Bibliog.

Lowenheim, Francis L., ed. THE HISTORIAN AND THE DIPLOMAT: THE ROLE OF HISTORY AND HISTORIANS IN AMERICAN FOREIGN POLICY. New York: Harper, 1967. 213 p.

May, Ernest R. LESSONS OF THE PAST: THE USE AND MISUSE OF HISTORY IN AMERICAN FOREIGN POLICY. New York: Oxford University Press, 1974. 220 p. Bibliog.

Moore, John Bassett. THE PRINCIPLES OF AMERICAN DIPLOMACY. New York: Harper, 1918. 476 p.

Mowrer, Paul S. OUR FOREIGN AFFAIRS: A STUDY IN NATIONAL INTEREST AND THE NEW DIPLOMACY. New York: Dutton, 1924. 348 p.

Needler, Martin C. UNDERSTANDING FOREIGN POLICY. New York: Holt, Rinehart, and Winston, 1966. 280 p.

> Especially chapter 3.

Parenti, Michael J. TRENDS AND TRAGEDIES IN AMERICAN FOREIGN POLICY. Boston: Little, Brown, 1971. 228 p.

Pearson, Drew, and Brown, Constantine. THE AMERICAN DIPLOMATIC GAME. Garden City, N.Y.: Doubleday, Doran, 1935. 398 p.

Perkins, Dexter. THE AMERICAN APPROACH TO FOREIGN POLICY. Cambridge, Mass.: Harvard University Press, 1952. 195 p.

> On moral and intellectual components of American tradition in foreign relations.

Ponsonby, Arthur. DEMOCRACY AND DIPLOMACY: A PLEA FOR POPULAR CONTROL OF FOREIGN POLICY. London: Methuen, 1915. 198 p.

Simpson, Smith. THE CRISIS IN THE AMERICAN DIPLOMACY: A SHOT ACROSS THE BOW OF THE STATE DEPARTMENT. North Quincy, Mass.: Christopher, 1979. 324 p.

_____, ed. "Resources and Needs of American Diplomacy." ANNALS OF THE AMERICAN ACADEMY OF POLITICAL AND SOCIAL SCIENCE 380 (November 1968): 1-144.

Stebbins, Phillip Eugene. "A History of the Role of the United States Supreme Court in Foreign Policy." Ph.D. dissertation, Ohio State University, 1966. 205 p.

Stoke, Harold Walter. THE FOREIGN RELATIONS OF THE FEDERAL STATE. Johns Hopkins Studies in Historical and Political Science, New Series. Baltimore: Johns Hopkins Press, 1931. 245 p.

Sulzberger, Cyrus L. WHAT'S WRONG WITH U.S. FOREIGN POLICY? New York: Harcourt, Brace, 1959. 255 p.

Thompson, Kenneth W. AMERICAN DIPLOMACY AND EMERGENT PATTERNS. New York: New York University Press, 1962. 273 p. Bibliog.

Trilateral Commission. TRILATERAL COMMISSION TASK FORCE REPORTS. 14 reports In 2 vols. New York: New York University Press, 1977, 1978. 209 p., 303 p.

> The unofficial Trilateral Commission, launched in 1973, concentrated on developing closer relations of the United States, Canada, Japan, and Western Europe. Each task force study was undertaken by three authors from Japan, North America, and Europe, assisted by a wide range of consultants.

U.S. Congress. House of Representatives. Committee on Foreign Affairs. THE FUTURE OF UNITED STATES PUBLIC DIPLOMACY. 90th Cong., 2d sess., 1968. Washington, D.C.: Government Printing Office, 1968. 175 p.

U.S. Congress. Senate. Committee on Government Operations. Subcommittee on National Security and International Operations. PLANNING-PROGRAMMING-BUDGETING. 90th and 91st Cong. Washington, D.C.: Government Printing Office, 1967-69.

> Series of studies, Including PPBS AND FOREIGN AFFAIRS and OFFICIAL DOCUMENTS, relevant to the administration of foreign affairs.

U.S. Congress. Senate. Committee on Government Operations. Subcommittee on National Security Staffing. ADMINISTRATION OF NATIONAL SECURITY: SELECTED PAPERS. 87th Cong., 2d sess. Washington, D.C.: Government Printing Office, 1962. 203 p.

Weisband, Edward. THE IDEOLOGY OF AMERICAN FOREIGN POLICY: A PARADIGM OF LOCKIAN LIBERALISM. Beverly Hills, Calif.: Sage, 1973. 69 p.

Wriston, Henry M. DIPLOMACY IN A DEMOCRACY. New York: Harper, 1956. 115 p.

Wu, Ting-fang. AMERICA AND THE AMERICANS FROM A CHINESE POINT OF VIEW. London: Duckworth, 1914. 267 p.

Chapter 16

SPECIALIZED ASPECTS OF CONDUCT OF

U.S. FOREIGN RELATIONS

This chapter includes publications on a number of specialized aspects of American foreign relations warranting separate emphasis. These include policy formulation, the role and impact of public opinion, the media, and interest groups (including political parties) on external affairs, secrecy vs. openness of diplomacy in a democratic society, and the nature and function of diplomatic and consular field missions and overseas representation. The following chapter is devoted to additional functional aspects of the diplomatic process.

As reflected in the literature, each of the four subjects included in this chapter has been given serious attention. The first three--policy making, public opinion and the media, and secrecy--have become the subjects of extensive analysis in recent decades. On the other hand, the matter of field missions and their operations (distinguished from central or headquarters management and administration), though fundamental to diplomatic and consular relations, appears to arouse less literary concern, and needs to be supplemented with the recountings of practitioners as contained in diplomatic memoirs and biographies. Materials on the role of private individuals are given in the last section.

POLICY FORMULATION

Most of the general literature on U.S. foreign relations that is concerned with organizational and institutional components of the government dealing with diplomacy and the conduct of external affairs (chapters 7-9), and especially that which focuses on decision making (chapter 14) and systematic foreign relations analysis (chapter 19), as well as many autobiographies and memoirs (part IV), touches upon some features of, or experience with, foreign policy formulation. The following list, however, represents the literature which exemplifies individual treatment from a broad perspective respecting the making (and in some cases, implementation) of foreign policy, and this literature is generally less concerned with the technicalities and intellectual or rational aspects of decision making. Some of the materials included are generic or even abstract in their approach, some fuse institutional with other elements of the policy process, and others stress particular influences and ingredients. These materials vary in their approach from the theoretical to the historical or descriptive, from the empirical to the normative, and from the elementary and rudimentary to the sophisticated and technically analytical. A few are sufficiently comprehensive to also be included in other categories, and several constitute chapters of larger studies.

Alsop, Joseph, and Alsop, Stewart. "How Our Foreign Policy is Made." SATURDAY EVENING POST, 30 April 1949, pp. 30-31, 113-16.

Baldwin, David A. "Making American Foreign Policy: A Review." JOURNAL OF CONFLICT RESOLUTION 12 (September 1968): 386-92.

Bauer, Raymond Alexander, and Gergen, Kenneth J., eds. THE STUDY OF POLICY FORMATION. New York: Free Press, 1968. 392 p.

Beichman, Arnold. THE "OTHER" STATE DEPARTMENT: THE UNITED STATES MISSION TO THE UNITED NATIONS--ITS ROLE IN THE MAKING OF FOR-EIGN POLICY. New York: Basic Books, 1967. 221 p.

Berding, Andrew Henry Thomas. FOREIGN AFFAIRS AND YOU! HOW AMERICAN FOREIGN POLICY IS MADE AND WHAT IT MEANS TO YOU. Garden City, N.Y.: Doubleday, 1962. 264 p.

_____. THE MAKING OF FOREIGN POLICY. Washington, D.C.: Potomac, 1956. 264 p. Bibliog.

Berkowitz, Morton; Bock, P.G.; and Fuccillo, Vincent J. THE POLITICS OF AMERICAN FOREIGN POLICY: THE SOCIAL CONTEXT OF DECISIONS. Englewood Cliffs, N.J.: Prentice-Hall, 1977. 310 p.

Chapters 1, 13, and 14 on the foreign policy process.

Bloomfield, Lincoln P. THE FOREIGN POLICY PROCESS: MAKING THEORY RELEVANT. Beverly Hills, Calif.: Sage, 1974. 60 p.

Bolles, Blair. WHO MAKES OUR FOREIGN POLICY? Headline Series, no. 62. New York: Foreign Policy Association, 1947. 86 p.

Bowie, Robert R. "Analysis of Our Policy Machine." NEW YORK TIMES MAGAZINE, 9 March 1958, pp. 16, 68-71.

_____. "Formulation of American Foreign Policy." ANNALS OF THE AMERI-CAN ACADEMY OF POLITICAL AND SOCIAL SCIENCE 330 (July 1960): 1-10.

Churchill, Janice. "U.S. Policy Formulation: A Case Study of Fisheries Juris-diction." Ph.D. dissertation, American University, 1974. 163 p.

Cobbledick, James. R. "Policy Process in American Government." In his CHOICE IN AMERICAN FOREIGN POLICY: OPTIONS FOR THE FUTURE, pp. 20-44. New York: Crowell, 1973.

Cohen, Stephen D., and Bergsten, C. Fred. THE MAKING OF UNITED STATES INTERNATIONAL ECONOMIC POLICY: PRINCIPLES, PROBLEMS, AND PROPOSALS FOR REFORM. New York: Praeger, 1977. 236 p.

Dahl, Robert A. "A New Pattern in Policy Making." In his CONGRESS AND FOREIGN POLICY, pp. 123-264. 2d ed. New York: Norton, 1964.

Davis, David H. HOW THE BUREAUCRACY MAKES FOREIGN POLICY: AN EXCHANGE ANALYSIS. Lexington, Mass.: Heath, 1972. 164 p.

Dulles, Eleanor Lansing. AMERICAN FOREIGN POLICY IN THE MAKING. New York: Harper and Row, 1968. 370 p. Bibliog.

Edinger, Lewis J. "Military Leaders and Foreign Policy-Making." AMERICAN POLITICAL SCIENCE REVIEW 57 (June 1963): 392-405.

Fox, Douglas M., comp. THE POLITICS OF U.S. FOREIGN POLICY MAKING: A READER. Pacific Palisades, Calif.: Goodyear, 1971. 353 p.

Frankel, Joseph. THE MAKING OF FOREIGN POLICY: AN ANALYSIS OF DECISION MAKING. New York: Oxford University Press, 1963. 231 p.

Friedrich, Carl J. FOREIGN POLICY IN THE MAKING. New York: Norton, 1938. 296 p.

Fulbright, J. William. "What Makes U.S. Foreign Policy." REPORTER 20 (14 May 1959): 18-21.

Furniss, Edgar S., Jr., and Snyder, Richard C. "The Problem of Policy Making." In their AN INTRODUCTION TO AMERICAN FOREIGN POLICY, pp. 203-38. New York: Rinehart, 1955.

Gange, John. "Foreign Policy Formulation in America." In his AMERICAN FOREIGN RELATIONS: PERMANENT PROBLEMS AND CHANGING POLICIES, pp. 541-73. New York: Ronald, 1959.

Gilboa, Eytan. "The Scholar and the Foreign Policy Maker in the United States." Ph.D. dissertation, Harvard University, 1974.

Gordon, Morton, and Vines, Kenneth N., eds. "The Formation of American Foreign Policy." In their THEORY AND PRACTICE OF AMERICAN FOREIGN POLICY, pp. 252-336. New York: Crowell, 1955.

Halperin, Morton H. "The Gaither Committee and the Policy Process." WORLD POLITICS 13 (April 1961): 360–84.

Hammond, Paul Y. FOREIGN POLICYMAKING: PLURALISTIC POLITICS OR UNITARY ANALYSIS? Santa Monica, Calif.: Rand, 1965. 33 p. Bibliog.

Hartmann, Frederick H. THE NEW AGE OF AMERICAN FOREIGN POLICY. New York: Macmillan, 1970. 399 p. Bibliog.

  Especially part 2 on policy making.

Haviland, H. Field, Jr. THE FORMULATION AND ADMINISTRATION OF UNITED STATES FOREIGN POLICY. Washington, D.C.: Brookings Institution, 1960. 191 p. Also published as U.S. Congress. Senate. Foreign Relations Committee. UNITED STATES FOREIGN POLICY: THE FORMULATION AND ADMINISTRATION OF UNITED STATES FOREIGN POLICY. 86th Cong., 2d sess. Washington, D.C.: Government Printing Office, 1946. 191 p.

Henderson, Loy W. FOREIGN POLICIES: THEIR FORMULATION AND ENFORCEMENT. Washington, D.C.: Government Printing Office, 1946. 20 p.

Hilsman, Roger, Jr. "The Foreign Policy Consensus: An Interim Research Report." JOURNAL OF CONFLICT RESOLUTION 3 (December 1959): 361–82.

_____. THE POLITICS OF POLICY MAKING IN DEFENSE AND FOREIGN AFFAIRS. New York: Harper and Row, 1971. 198 p.

Holsti, Kalevi J. INTERNATIONAL POLITICS: A FRAMEWORK FOR ANALYSIS. Englewood Cliffs, N.J.: Prentice-Hall, 1967.

  Chapters 5 and 6 on foreign policy making.

Hughes, Thomas L. "Policy-Making in a World Turned Upside Down." FOREIGN AFFAIRS 45 (January 1967): 202-14.

Huntington, Samuel P. "Strategic Planning and the Political Process." FOREIGN AFFAIRS 38 (January 1960): 285-300.

Immerman, Robert M. "The Formulation and Administration of U.S. Foreign Policy." FOREIGN SERVICE JOURNAL 37 (April 1960): 21-23.

Irish, Marian, and Frank, Elke. "The Nature of Policy Making." In their U.S. FOREIGN POLICY: CONTEXT, CONDUCT, CONTENT, pp. 313-54. New York: Harcourt Brace Jovanovich, 1975.

Jacobson, Harold K., and Zimmermann, William, eds. THE SHAPING OF FOREIGN POLICY. New York: Atherton, 1969. 214 p.

Kegley, Charles W., Jr., and Wittkopf, Eugene R. AMERICAN FOREIGN POLICY: PATTERN AND PROCESS. New York: St. Martin's, 1979. 512 p.

Especially chapters 9-11.

Kissinger, Henry A. "The Policymaker and the Intellectual." REPORTER 20 (5 March 1959): 30-35.

KNOWLEDGE AND POLICY. THE UNCERTAIN CONNECTION. Washington, D.C.: National Academy of Sciences, 1978. 184 p.

Contains individual papers by authors with variety of backgrounds and areas of specialization.

Leonard, L. Larry. "The Making of American Foreign Policy." In his ELE-MENTS OF AMERICAN FOREIGN POLICY, pp. 89-214. New York: McGraw-Hill, 1953.

Lindblom, Charles E. THE POLICY-MAKING PROCESS. Englewood Cliffs, N.J.: Prentice-Hall, 1968. 122 p.

Lindsay, Franklin A. "Program Planning: The Missing Element." FOREIGN AFFAIRS 39 (January 1961): 279-90.

London, Kurt. HOW FOREIGN POLICY IS MADE. New York: Van Nostrand, 1949. 277 p. Bibliog.

_____. THE MAKING OF FOREIGN POLICY--EAST AND WEST. Philadel-phia: Lippincott, 1965. 358 p. Bibliog.

Marshall, Charles B. "The Making of Foreign Policy in the United States." In ESSAYS IN POLITICAL SCIENCE, edited by Edward H. Buehrig, pp. 37-60. Bloomington: Indiana University Press, 1966.

Modelski, George A. A THEORY OF FOREIGN POLICY. New York: Prae-ger, for Center of International Studies, Princeton University, 1962. 152 p.

Morgan, George Allen. "Planning in Foreign Affairs: The State of the Art." FOREIGN AFFAIRS 39 (January 1961): 271-78.

Needler, Martin C. "The Making and Execution of Policy." In his DIMEN-SIONS OF AMERICAN FOREIGN POLICY: READINGS AND DOCUMENTS, pp. 357-72. Princeton, N.J.: Van Nostrand, 1966.

Ogburn, Charles, Jr. "The Flow of Policymaking in the Department of State." In THE FORMULATION AND ADMINISTRATION OF UNITED STATES FOREIGN POLICY, edited by H. Field Haviland, Jr., pp. 172-77. Washington, D.C.: Brookings Institution, 1960.

Padgett, Edward Riddle. "The Role of the Minority Party in Bipartisan Foreign Policy Formulation in the United States, 1945-1955." Ph.D. dissertation, University of Maryland, 1957. 405 p. Bibliog.

Philipose, Thomas. "The 'Loyal Opposition': Republican Leaders and Foreign Policy, 1943-1946." Ph.D. dissertation, University of Denver, 1972. 295 p.

Polk, William R. "The Scholar and the Administrator in International Affairs." BULLETIN OF ATOMIC SCIENTISTS 22 (March 1966): 2-8.

> On interplay of academia in the international affairs policymaking arena.

Rainey, Gene E. "Foreign Policymaking and Implementation." In his PATTERNS OF AMERICAN FOREIGN POLICY, pp. 139-229. Boston: Allyn and Bacon, 1975.

Ripley, Randall B., and Franklin, Grace A., eds. POLICY-MAKING IN THE FEDERAL EXECUTIVE BRANCH. New York: Free Press, 1975. 224 p. Bibliog.

> Analyzes who makes policy in the executive branch.

Rostow, Walt W. "The Planning of Foreign Policy." DEPARTMENT OF STATE NEWSLETTER 38 (June 1964): 3-5, 45.

Rothstein, Robert L. PLANNING, PREDICTION, AND POLICYMAKING IN FOREIGN AFFAIRS: THEORY AND PRACTICE. Boston: Little, Brown, 1972. 215 p.

> Especially chapter 2 on policy planning.

Rusk, Dean. "The Formulation of Foreign Policy." DEPARTMENT OF STATE BULLETIN 44 (20 March 1961): 395-99. Reproduced in U.S. Department of State. AMERICAN FOREIGN POLICY: CURRENT DOCUMENTS, 1961, pp. 22-28. Washington, D.C.: Government Printing Office, 1965.

Sapin, Burton M. THE MAKING OF UNITED STATES FOREIGN POLICY. Washington, D.C.: Brookings Institution, 1966; New York: Praeger, 1966. 415 p.

_____, ed. "Formulating and Implementing National Policy." In his CONTEMPORARY AMERICAN FOREIGN AND MILITARY POLICY, pp. 82-135. Glenview, Ill.: Scott, Foresman, 1970.

Spanier, John W., and Uslaner, Eric M. HOW AMERICAN FOREIGN POLI-
CY IS MADE. New York: Holt, Rinehart, and Winston, 1978. 192 p.

U.S. Commission on the Organization of the Government for the Conduct of
Foreign Policy. "Policy Planning." In its COMMISSION ON THE ORGANI-
ZATION OF THE GOVERNMENT FOR THE CONDUCT OF FOREIGN POLICY,
JUNE 1975, appendix, vol. 2, pp. 209-35. Washington, D.C.: Government
Printing Office, 1976.

Vile, M.J.C. "The Formation and Execution of Policy in the United States."
POLITICAL QUARTERLY 33 (Spring 1962): 160-71.

Wendzel, Robert L. INTERNATIONAL RELATIONS: A POLICYMAKER FOCUS.
New York: Wiley, 1977. 286 p.

Especially chapters 2, 4-6.

Case Studies

In addition to the compilations of case studies referred to in chapter 15, those
concerned more precisely with analysis of the decision-making process listed in
chapter 14, and those that deal with crises contained in chapter 18, the following represent discussion of case studies of policy formulation and implementation:

Barnes, Harley H. "The U.S. Policy-Making Process: The Nuclear Non-Pro-
liferation Treaty of 1968." Ph.D. dissertation, Rutgers University, 1976. 563 p.

Beard, Charles A. AMERICAN FOREIGN POLICY IN THE MAKING, 1932-
1940: A STUDY IN RESPONSIBILITIES. New Haven, Conn.: Yale University Press, 1946. 336 p.

Beard, Edmund. DEVELOPING THE ICBM: A STUDY IN BUREAUCRATIC
POLITICS. New York: Columbia University Press, 1976. 273 p. Bibliog.

Cohen, Bernard C. THE POLITICAL PROCESS AND FOREIGN POLICY: THE
MAKING OF THE JAPANESE PEACE SETTLEMENT. Princeton, N.J.: Princeton University Press, 1957. 293 p.

Haendel, Dan. THE PROCESS OF POLICY FORMATION: U.S. FOREIGN
POLICY IN THE INDO-PAKISTANI WAR OF 1971. Boulder, Colo.: Westview, 1978. 448 p. Bibliog.

Johnson, James Herbert. "The Marshall Plan: A Case Study in American
Foreign Policy Formulation and Implementation." Ph.D. dissertation, University
of Oklahoma, 1966. 362 p.

Lepper, Mary M. FOREIGN POLICY FORMULATION: A CASE STUDY OF THE NUCLEAR TEST BAN TREATY OF 1963. Columbus, Ohio: Merrill, 1971. 191 p. Bibliog.

May, Ernest R. THE MAKING OF THE MONROE DOCTRINE. Cambridge, Mass.: Harvard University Press, 1979. 224 p.

Oliver, James Knowles. "United States Foreign Policy Formulation and the Budgetary Process in the 1960's." Ph.D. dissertation, American University, 1970. 416 p.

Pratt, James Worthington. "Leadership Relations in United States Foreign Policy Making: Case Studies, 1947-1950." Ph.D. dissertation, Columbia University, 1963. 397 p.

Terchek, Ronald J. THE MAKING OF THE TEST BAN TREATY. The Hague: Nijhoff, 1970. 211 p.

_____. "The Making of the Test Ban Treaty in the United States." Ph.D. dissertation, University of Maryland, 1965. 382 p. Bibliog.

Winkler, Fred Herbert. "The United States and the World Disarmament Conference, 1926-1935: A Study of the Formulation of Foreign Policy." Ph.D. dissertation, Northwestern University, 1957. 366 p.

Wood, Bryce. THE MAKING OF THE GOOD NEIGHBOR POLICY. New York: Columbia University Press, 1961. 438 p.

Yizhar, Michael. "The Eisenhower Doctrine: A Case Study of American Foreign Policy Formulation and Implementation." Ph.D. dissertation, New School for Social Research, 1969. 257 p.

PUBLIC OPINION, THE MEDIA, INTEREST GROUPS, AND POLITICAL PARTIES

A good deal of information is available on the overall interrelationship between public opinion and government operation and policy. A few studies of the more restricted role of public opinion in the conduct of foreign relations were produced prior to World War II, such as the contributions of Arthur Ponsonby (1915) and Quincy Wright (1933). It was not until the 1940s and 1950s, however, with the emergence of such volumes as Gabriel A. Almond's THE AMERICAN PEOPLE AND FOREIGN POLICY, Thomas A. Bailey's THE MAN IN THE STREET, Harold D. Lasswell's PUBLIC OPINION IN WAR AND PEACE, Walter Lippmann's republished PUBLIC OPINION, Lester Markel's PUBLIC OPINION AND FOREIGN POLICY, and George Seldes's THE PEOPLE DON'T KNOW, that major attention was centered on the subject. In relating interest and timing, much the same may be said of literary attention paid to the role of the media in foreign relations opinion formation, except that it appears to be generating its momentum more recently. The following selections exemplify these developments so far as the United States is concerned. Additional publications, dealing with the interest groups as they impinge upon the formation of opinion and influence foreign affairs and dealing with political parties (including bipartisanship) are contained in separate subsections below. Studies on programs for the export of information and propaganda as well as psychological warfare, on the other hand, are dealt with in chapter 17. Moreover, some standard texts and other general volumes on American foreign relations, including some of those listed in chapter 15, also contain chapters or sections on the matter of public opinion.

Additional guidance to literature on the matter of the public's right to know and the role of the media may be found in the following:

Boston Public Library. THE PUBLIC INTEREST AND THE RIGHT TO KNOW-- ACCESS TO GOVERNMENT INFORMATION AND THE ROLE OF THE PRESS: A SELECTIVE BIBLIOGRAPHICAL GUIDE. Boston: 1971. 59 p.

The People and Public Opinion

The following emphasize public opinion generally, the attitudes and role of the American public, communications flow, opinion polls, and the impact of the public and its opinion on public policy:

Abravanel, Martin Don. "Affect, Belief, and International Affairs: Soviet-American Competition and the National Images of Mass Publics." Ph.D. dissertation, University of Wisconsin, 1971. 415 p.

Albig, William. MODERN PUBLIC OPINION. New York: McGraw-Hill, 1956. 518 p.

Allard, Winston. "Congressional Attitudes Toward Public Opinion." JOURNALISM QUARTERLY 18 (March 1941): 47-50.

Almond, Gabriel A. THE AMERICAN PEOPLE AND FOREIGN POLICY. New York: Praeger, 1950. Reprint. New York: Praeger, 1960. 269 p. Bibliog.

Bailey, Thomas A. THE MAN IN THE STREET: THE IMPACT OF AMERICAN PUBLIC OPINION ON FOREIGN POLICY. New York: Macmillan, 1948. 334 p. Bibliog.

Barrett, Edward W. "The American People's Part in U.S. Foreign Policy." DEPARTMENT OF STATE BULLETIN 22 (24 April 1950): 646-49.

Beloff, Max. FOREIGN POLICY AND THE DEMOCRATIC PROCESS. Baltimore: Johns Hopkins Press, 1955. 134 p.

Berelson, Bernard, and Janowitz, Morris, eds. READER IN PUBLIC OPINION AND COMMUNICATION. Glencoe, Ill.: Free Press, 1953; 2d ed. New York: Free Press, 1966. 788 p. Bibliog.

Bryce, James. "Popular Control of Foreign Policy and the Morality of States." In his INTERNATIONAL RELATIONS, pp. 176-205. New York: Macmillan, 1922.

Buchanan, William, and Cantril, Hadley. HOW NATIONS SEE EACH OTHER: A STUDY IN PUBLIC OPINION. Urbana: University of Illinois Press, 1953. 220 p.

Carlson, Robert O. COMMUNICATIONS AND PUBLIC OPINION: A PUBLIC OPINION QUARTERLY READER. New York: Praeger, 1975. 642 p.

Caspary, William R. "The 'Mood Theory': A Study of Public Opinion and Foreign Policy." AMERICAN POLITICAL SCIENCE REVIEW 64 (June 1970): 536-47.

Chandler, Geoffrey. "American Opinion and Foreign Policy." INTERNATIONAL AFFAIRS 31 (October 1955): 447-58.

Chapin, Richard E. MASS COMMUNICATIONS: A STATISTICAL ANALYSIS. East Lansing: Michigan State University Press, 1957. 148 p.

Chasteen, Robert James. "American Foreign Aid and Public Opinion, 1945-1952." Ph.D. dissertation, University of North Carolina (Chapel Hill), 1958. 425 p.

Cohen, Bernard C. CITIZEN EDUCATION IN WORLD AFFAIRS. Princeton, N.J.: Center of International Studies, Princeton University, 1953. 145 p.

_____. THE PUBLIC'S IMPACT ON FOREIGN POLICY. Boston: Little, Brown, 1973. 221 p.

Cottrell, Leonard S., Jr., and Eberhart, Sylvia. AMERICAN OPINION ON WORLD AFFAIRS IN THE ATOMIC AGE. Princeton, N.J.: Princeton University Press, 1948. 152 p.

Culbert, David Holbrook. "Tantalus' Dilemma: Public Opinion, Six Radio Commentators, and Foreign Affairs, 1935-1941." Ph.D. dissertation, Northwestern University, 1970. 684 p.

Cutler, Neal E. "Generational Succession as a Source of Foreign Policy Attitudes: A Cohort Analysis of American Opinion, 1946-1966." JOURNAL OF PEACE RESEARCH 7, no. 1 (1970): 33-47.

Davis, Elmer. "Vox Populi and Foreign Policy." HARPER'S MAGAZINE, June 1952, pp. 66-73.

Dean, Vera M. "U.S. Foreign Policy and the Voter." FOREIGN POLICY REPORTS 20 (15 September 1944): 150-64.

DeFleur, Melvin L., and Larsen, Otto N. THE FLOW OF INFORMATION: AN EXPERIMENT IN MASS COMMUNICATION. New York: Harper, 1958. 302 p.

Devine, Donald J. THE ATTENTIVE PUBLIC: POLYARCHICAL DEMOCRACY. Chicago: Rand McNally, 1970. 146 p.

Elder, Robert. "The Public Studies Division of the Department of State: Public Opinion Analysts in the Formulation and Conduct of American Foreign Policy." WESTERN POLITICAL QUARTERLY 10 (December 1957): 783-92.

Erikson, Robert S., and Luttbeg, Norman R. AMERICAN PUBLIC OPINION: ITS ORIGINS, CONTENT, AND IMPACT. New York: Wiley, 1973. 343 p.

Fagan, Richard R. "Some Assessments and Uses of Public Opinion in Diplomacy." PUBLIC OPINION QUARTERLY 24 (Fall 1960): 448-57.

Feld, M.D. "Political Policy and Persuasion: The Role of Communications from Political Leaders." JOURNAL OF CONFLICT RESOLUTION 2 (March 1958): 78-89.

Foster, Harry Schuyler. "Registering Public Opinion." DEPARTMENT OF STATE BULLETIN 28 (18 May 1953): 712-14.

_____. "Role of the Public in U.S. Foreign Relations." DEPARTMENT OF STATE BULLETIN 43 (28 November 1960): 823-31.

_____. THE ROLE OF THE PUBLIC IN UNITED STATES FOREIGN RELATIONS. Washington, D.C.: U.S. Department of State, 1961. 20 p.

Free, Lloyd A., and Cantril, Hadley. THE POLITICAL BELIEFS OF AMERICANS: A STUDY OF PUBLIC OPINION. New Brunswick, N.J.: Rutgers University Press, 1967. 239 p.

Graber, Doris A. PUBLIC OPINION, THE PRESIDENT, AND FOREIGN POLICY: FOUR CASE STUDIES FROM THE FORMATIVE YEARS. New York: Holt, Rinehart, and Winston, 1968. 374 p.

Hanes, John W., Jr. "The Citizen and Foreign Policy." DEPARTMENT OF STATE BULLETIN 42 (16 May 1960): 791-97.

Hero, Alfred O. OPINION LEADERS IN AMERICAN COMMUNITIES. Studies in Citizen Participation in International Relations, vol. 6. Boston: World Peace Foundation, 1959. 67 p.

Hilsman, Roger, Jr. "The Foreign-Policy Consensus: An Interim Research Report." JOURNAL OF CONFLICT RESOLUTION 3 (December 1959): 361-82.

Hohenberg, John. BETWEEN TWO WORLDS: POLICY, PRESS, AND PUBLIC OPINION IN ASIAN-AMERICAN RELATIONS. New York: Praeger, 1967. 507 p.

Hoyt, Edwin P. AMERICAN ATTITUDE: THE STORY OF THE MAKING OF FOREIGN POLICY IN THE UNITED STATES. New York: Abelard-Schuman, 1970. 254 p. Bibliog.

Ippolito, Dennis S.; Walker, Thomas G.; and Kolson, Kenneth L. PUBLIC OPINION AND RESPONSIBLE DEMOCRACY. Englewood Cliffs, N.J.: Prentice-Hall, 1976. 330 p. Bibliog.

Irish, Marian D. "Public Opinion and American Foreign Policy: The Quemoy Crisis of 1958." POLITICAL QUARTERLY 31 (April-June 1960): 151-62.

Jacobs, Norman, ed. "Government and Public Opinion." In his MAKING FOREIGN POLICY IN A NUCLEAR AGE, pp. 3-63. New York: Foreign Policy Association, 1965.

Juergensmeyer, John Eli. "Democracy's Diplomacy: The People-to-People Program: A Study of Attempts to Focus the Effects of Private Contacts in International Politics." Ph.D. dissertation, Princeton University, 1960. 637 p.

Katz, Daniel, ed. PUBLIC OPINION AND PROPAGANDA: A BOOK OF READINGS. New York: Dryden, 1954. 779 p.

Katz, Elihu, and Lazarsfeld, Paul. PERSONAL INFLUENCE: THE PART PLAYED BY PEOPLE IN THE FLOW OF MASS COMMUNICATIONS. Glencoe, Ill.: Free Press, 1955. 400 p.

Keller, Suzanne. "Diplomacy and Communication." PUBLIC OPINION QUARTERLY 20 (Spring 1956): 176-82.

Kennan, George F. CURRENT PROBLEMS IN THE CONDUCT OF FOREIGN POLICY. Department of State Publication 3862. Washington, D.C.: U.S. Department of State, 1950. 16 p.

Klingberg, Frank L. "The Historical Alternation of Moods in American Foreign Policy." WORLD POLITICS 4 (January 1952): 239-73.

Kriesberg, Martin. "What Congressmen and Administrators Think of the Polls." PUBLIC OPINION QUARTERLY 9 (Fall 1945): 333-37.

Landecker, Manfred. THE PRESIDENT AND PUBLIC OPINION: LEADERSHIP IN FOREIGN AFFAIRS. Washington, D.C.: Public Affairs, 1968. 133 p.

Lane, Robert E., and Sears, David O. PUBLIC OPINION. Englewood Cliffs, N.J.: Prentice-Hall, 1964. 120 p.

Lasswell, Harold D. PUBLIC OPINION IN WAR AND PEACE: HOW AMERICANS MAKE UP THEIR MINDS. Washington, D.C.: National Education Association, 1943. 68 p. Bibliog.

Laudon, Kenneth C. COMMUNICATIONS TECHNOLOGY AND DEMOCRATIC PARTICIPATION. New York: Praeger, 1977. 128 p.

Laulicht, Jerome. "Public Opinion and Foreign Policy Decisions." JOURNAL OF PEACE RESEARCH 2, no. 2 (1965): 147-60.

Lehman, Robert G. AMERICAN INSTITUTIONS, POLITICAL OPINION, AND PUBLIC POLICY. New York: Holt, Rinehart, and Winston, 1976. 256 p. Bibliog.

Levering, Ralph B. THE PUBLIC AND AMERICAN FOREIGN POLICY, 1918-1978. New York: Morrow for Foreign Policy Association, 1978. 160 p. Bibliog.

Lippmann, Walter. PUBLIC OPINION. New York: Macmillan, 1922. Reprint. New York: Free Press, 1949. 451 p.

_____. PUBLIC OPINION AND FOREIGN POLICY IN THE UNITED STATES. London: Allen and Unwin, 1952. 52 p.

Lipset, Seymour M. "Doves, Hawks, and Polls." ENCOUNTER 27 (October 1966): 38-45.

Lowell, Abbott Lawrence. PUBLIC OPINION AND POPULAR GOVERNMENT. New York: Longmans, Green, 1913. 415 p.

Luttbeg, Norman R., ed. PUBLIC OPINION AND PUBLIC POLICY: MODELS OF POLITICAL LINKAGE. Rev. ed. Homewood, Ill.: Dorsey, 1974. 489 p.

Manning, Robert J. "People and Policy." DEPARTMENT OF STATE BULLETIN 49 (21 October 1963): 639-44.

Markel, Lester, et al. PUBLIC OPINION AND FOREIGN POLICY. New York: Harper, 1949. 227 p.

Marshall, James. "Citizen Diplomacy." AMERICAN POLITICAL SCIENCE REVIEW 43 (February 1949): 83-90.

Miller, Warren E. "Voting and Foreign Policy." In DOMESTIC SOURCES OF FOREIGN POLICY, edited by James N. Rosenau, pp. 213-30. New York: Free Press, 1967.

Mitchell, William C. PUBLIC CHOICE IN AMERICA. Chicago: Markham, 1971. 396 p. Bibliog.

Monroe, Alan D. PUBLIC OPINION IN AMERICA. New York: Dodd, Mead, 1975. 296 p.

Mueller, John E. WAR, PRESIDENTS AND PUBLIC OPINION. New York: Wiley, 1973. 300 p. Bibliog.

Nossiter, Bernard D. THE MYTHMAKERS. Boston: Houghton Mifflin, 1964. 244 p.

Padover, Saul Kussiel. UNITED STATES FOREIGN POLICY AND PUBLIC OPINION. New York: Foreign Policy Association, 1958. 57 p. Bibliog.

Penikis, J. John. "Foreign Opinion and American Foreign Policy: The Orientations of American Foreign Policy-Makers Toward Non-Governmental Opinion Abroad." Ph.D. dissertation, University of Wisconsin, 1974. 303 p.

Perkins, Dexter. FOREIGN POLICY AND THE AMERICAN SPIRIT. Edited by Glyndon G. Van Deusen and Richard C. Wade. Ithaca, N.Y.: Cornell University Press, 1957. 254 p.

Ponsonby, Arthur. DEMOCRACY AND DIPLOMACY: A PLEA FOR POPULAR CONTROL OF FOREIGN POLICY. London: Methuen, 1915. 198 p.

Rielly, John E. AMERICAN PUBLIC OPINION AND U.S. FOREIGN POLICY, 1975. Chicago: Chicago Council on Foreign Relations, 1975. 29 p.

Riesman, David. "Private People and Public Policy." BULLETIN OF THE ATOMIC SCIENTISTS 15 (May 1959): 203-8.

Robinson, John P. PUBLIC INFORMATION ABOUT WORLD AFFAIRS. 1967. Reprint. Ann Arbor: Institute of Social Research, University of Michigan, 1971. 69 p. Bibliog.

Rogers, William C.; Stuhler, Barbara; and Koenig, Donald. "A Comparison of Informed and General Public Opinion on U.S. Foreign Policy." PUBLIC OPINION QUARTERLY 31 (Summer 1967): 242-52.

Roper, Elmo. "American Attitudes on World Organization." PUBLIC OPINION QUARTERLY 17 (Winter 1953): 405-42.

Rosenau, James N. THE ATTENTIVE PUBLIC AND FOREIGN POLICY: A THEORY OF GROWTH AND SOME NEW EVIDENCE. Princeton, N.J.: Center of International Studies, Princeton University, 1968. 48 p.

_____. "Consensus, Leadership and Foreign Policy." SAIS [School for Advanced International Studies] REVIEW 6 (Winter 1962): 3-10.

_____. NATIONAL LEADERSHIP AND FOREIGN POLICY: A CASE STUDY IN THE MOBILIZATION OF PUBLIC SUPPORT. Princeton, N.J.: Princeton University Press, 1963. 409 p.

> Concerns conference on foreign aspects of U.S. national security, Washington, D.C., 1958.

_____. PUBLIC OPINION AND FOREIGN POLICY. New York: Random House, 1961. 118 p. Bibliog.

_____. "Public Protest, Political Leadership and Diplomatic Strategy." ORBIS 14 (Fall 1970): 557-71.

Russell, Francis H. "The Function of Public Opinion Analysis in the Formulation of Foreign Policy." DEPARTMENT OF STATE BULLETIN 20 (6 March 1949): 275-77, 303.

Smith, Paul. "Opinions, Publics, and World Affairs in the United States." WESTERN POLITICAL QUARTERLY 14 (September 1961): 698-714.

Stoudinger, Susan. "A Cross-National Analysis of Selected Correlates of Foreign Policy Opinion Holding." Ph.D. dissertation, Indiana University, 1970. 252 p.

Truman, David B. THE GOVERNMENT PROCESS: POLITICAL INTERESTS AND PUBLIC OPINION. New York: Knopf, 1955. 560 p. Bibliog.

Truman, Harry S. "Public Opinion and American Foreign Policy." DEPARTMENT OF STATE BULLETIN 21 (1 August 1949): 145-47.

Wanger, Walter F. "Donald Duck and Diplomacy." PUBLIC OPINION QUARTERLY 14 (Fall 1950): 443-52.

Specialized Aspects of Conduct

Weissberg, Robert. PUBLIC OPINION AND POPULAR GOVERNMENT. Englewood Cliffs, N.J.: Prentice-Hall, 1976. 269 p. Bibliog.

Wheeler, Michael. LIES, DAMN LIES, AND STATISTICS: THE MANIPULA-TION OF PUBLIC OPINION IN AMERICA. New York: Liveright, 1976. 336 p.

Wright, Quincy, ed. PUBLIC OPINION AND WORLD POLITICS. Chicago: University of Chicago Press, 1933. 236 p.

Wriston, Henry M. "The Fabric of American Opinion on Foreign Affairs." INTERNATIONAL AFFAIRS 28 (April 1952): 144-55.

The Media

The following represent the emerging literature on the media--still principally the press--and their impact on public policy and foreign relations:

Abrams, Floyd, et al. FREEDOM OF THE PRESS. Washington, D.C.: American Enterprise Institute, 1976. 101 p.

> Symposium, with William Ruckelshaus and Elie Abel as moderators.

Alsop, Joseph, and Alsop, Stewart. THE REPORTER'S TRADE. New York: Reynal, 1958. 377 p.

> Especially chapters 3 and 4, devoted to reporting about foreign affairs and national defense.

American Enterprise Institute. THE PRESS AND PUBLIC POLICY. Washington, D.C.: American Enterprise Institute, 1979. 43 p.

> American Enterprise Institute Forum, January 10, 1979.

Aronson, James. THE PRESS AND THE COLD WAR. Indianapolis: Bobbs-Merrill, 1970. 308 p.

Bagdikian, Ben H. THE INFORMATION MACHINES: THEIR IMPACT ON MEN AND THE MEDIA. New York: Harper and Row, 1971. 359 p.

Baldwin, Hanson W. "Managed News: Our Peacetime Censorship." ATLANTIC MONTHLY, April 1963, pp. 53-59.

Batscha, Robert M. FOREIGN AFFAIRS NEWS AND THE BROADCAST JOUR-NALIST. New York: Praeger, 1975. 254 p. Bibliog.

Cater, Douglass. THE FOURTH BRANCH OF GOVERNMENT. Boston: Houghton Mifflin, 1959. 194 p.

On the role the press plays in the formulation of public policy.

Chafee, Zechariah. GOVERNMENT AND MASS COMMUNICATIONS. 2 vols. Chicago: University of Chicago Press, 1947.

Chase, Harold W., and Lerman, Allen H., eds. KENNEDY AND THE PRESS: THE NEWS CONFERENCES. New York: Crowell, 1965. 555 p.

Chittick, William O. STATE DEPARTMENT, PRESS, AND PRESSURE GROUPS: A ROLE ANALYSIS. New York: Wiley Interscience, 1970. 373 p. Bibliog.

Cohen, Bernard C. THE PRESS AND FOREIGN POLICY. Princeton, N.J.: Princeton University Press, 1963. 288 p.

_____. "The Press and Foreign Policy in the United States." JOURNAL OF INTERNATIONAL AFFAIRS 10, no. 2 (1956): 128-37.

Dunn, Delmer D. PUBLIC OFFICIALS AND THE PRESS. Reading, Mass.: Addison-Wesley, 1969. 208 p.

English, Cary Clyde. "United States Media Diplomacy: Problems in the Politics of Administration." Ph.D. dissertation, Emory University, 1968. 332 p.

Hero, Alfred O. MASS MEDIA AND WORLD AFFAIRS. Boston: World Peace Foundation, 1959. 187 p.

Jones, Paul. "Diplomacy by Press Release May Not Be the Last Word." SATURDAY EVENING POST, 20 May 1950, p. 12.

Osgood, Einar. "Factors Influencing the Flow of News." JOURNAL OF PEACE RESEARCH 1 (1965): 39-63.

Read, William H. AMERICA'S MASS MEDIA MERCHANTS. Baltimore: Johns Hopkins Press, 1977. 209 p.

Reston, James B. THE ARTILLERY OF THE PRESS: ITS INFLUENCE ON AMERICAN FOREIGN POLICY. New York: Harper and Row, 1967. 116 p.

Rivers, William L. THE OPINIONMAKERS: AN INSIDE VIEW OF THE WASHINGTON PRESS CORPS. Boston: Beacon, 1965. 207 p.

Rosten, Leo G. THE WASHINGTON CORRESPONDENTS. New York: Harcourt, Brace, 1937. 436 p. Bibliog.

Rubin, Bernard. MEDIA, POLITICS, AND DEMOCRACY. New York: Oxford University Press, 1977. 208 p.

Schiller, Herbert I. MASS COMMUNICATION AND AMERICAN EMPIRE. New York: Kelley, 1969. 170 p.

_____. THE MIND MANAGERS. Boston: Beacon, 1973. 214 p.

Schramm, Wilbur, and Roberts, Donald F., eds. THE PROCESS AND EFFECTS OF MASS COMMUNICATION. Rev. ed. Urbana: University of Illinois Press, 1971. 997 p. Bibliog.

Seiden, Martin H. WHO CONTROLS THE MASS MEDIA?: POPULAR MYTHS AND ECONOMIC REALITIES. New York: Basic Books, 1974. 246 p.

Seldes, George. THE PEOPLE DON'T KNOW: THE AMERICAN PRESS AND THE COLD WAR. New York: Gaer, 1949. 342 p.

Seymour-Uere, Colin. THE POLITICAL IMPACT OF MASS MEDIA. Beverly Hills, Calif.: Sage, 1974. 296 p.

Stein, Robert. MEDIA POWER: WHO IS SHAPING YOUR PICTURE OF THE WORLD? Boston: Houghton Mifflin, 1972. 265 p.

Sterling, Christopher H., and Haight, Timothy. THE MASS MEDIA: ASPEN GUIDE TO COMMUNICATION INDUSTRY TRENDS. New York: Praeger, 1977. 288 p.

Tunstall, Jeremy. THE MEDIA ARE AMERICAN. New York: Columbia University Press, 1977. 352 p. Bibliog.

Interest Groups

The impact of interest groups (other than political parties) on public affairs and opinion has evoked some attention since World War II, illustrated by the following. Important areas of particularized interest group influence and action on external policy and relations remain to be explored and assessed. Some are touched upon, however, in the more comprehensive and general studies on the subject, which, although not included here, may be consulted with profit.

Adler, Kenneth P., and Bobrow, Davis. "Interest and Influence in Foreign Affairs." PUBLIC OPINION QUARTERLY 20 (Spring 1956): 89-101.

Bachrack, Stanley D. THE COMMITTEE OF ONE MILLION: "CHINA LOBBY" POLITICS, 1953-1971. New York: Columbia University Press, 1976. 371 p. Bibliog.

Baker, Roscoe. THE AMERICAN LEGION AND AMERICAN FOREIGN POLICY. New York: Bookman, 1954. 329 p.

Balboni, Alan. "The Study of the Efforts of the American Zionists to Influence the Formulation and Conduct of U.S. Foreign Policy During the Roosevelt, Truman, and Eisenhower Administrations." Ph.D. dissertation, Brown University, 1973. 261 p.

Bauer, Raymond A.; Pool, Ithiel de Sola; and Dexter, Louis A. AMERICAN BUSINESS AND PUBLIC POLICY: THE POLITICS OF FOREIGN TRADE. 2d ed. Chicago: Aldine-Atherton, 1972. 499 p. Bibliog.

Berry, Jeffrey M. LOBBYING FOR THE PEOPLE: THE POLITICAL BEHAVIOR OF PUBLIC INTEREST GROUPS. Princeton, N.J.: Princeton University Press, 1977. 336 p.

Blaisdell, Donald C. "Pressure Groups, Foreign Policy, and International Politics." ANNALS OF THE AMERICAN ACADEMY OF POLITICAL AND SOCIAL SCIENCE 319 (September 1958): 149-57.

Burdette, Franklin L. "Influence of Noncongressional Pressure on Foreign Policy." ANNALS OF THE AMERICAN ACADEMY OF POLITICAL AND SOCIAL SCIENCE 289 (September 1953): 92-99.

Cohen, Bernard C. THE INFLUENCE OF NON-GOVERNMENTAL GROUPS ON FOREIGN POLICY-MAKING. Boston: World Peace Foundation, 1959. 26 p. Bibliog.

Conlin, Joseph R., ed. AMERICAN ANTI-WAR MOVEMENTS. Beverly Hills, Calif.: Glencoe, 1968. 163 p.

Crawford, Kenneth G. THE PRESSURE BOYS: THE INSIDE STORY OF LOB-BYING IN AMERICA. New York: Messner, 1939. 308 p.

Davis, Vincent. THE ADMIRALS' LOBBY. Chapel Hill: University of North Carolina Press, 1967. 329 p.

Derthick, Martha. THE NATIONAL GUARD IN POLITICS. Cambridge, Mass.: Harvard University Press, 1965. 201 p.

Edelman, Murray. "Labor's Influence in Foreign Policy." LABOR LAW JOURNAL 5 (May 1954): 323-29.

Emeny, Brooks. "Non-Governmental Organizations in International Affairs." SOCIAL SCIENCE 30 (October 1955): 239-43.

"Foreign Lobbyists: The Hidden Pressures to Sway U.S. Policy." NEWSWEEK, 30 July 1962, pp. 18-22.

Foreign Policy Association. FOREIGN POLICY: THE NATIONAL INTEREST AND SPECIAL INTERESTS. New York: 1976.

Fuchs, Lawrence H. "Minority Groups and Foreign Policy." POLITICAL SCIENCE QUARTERLY 74 (June 1959): 161-75.

Fuess, John C. "World Labor and American Foreign Policy." YALE REVIEW 43 (Spring 1954): 437-43.

Gable, Richard W. "Interest Groups as Policy Shapers." ANNALS OF THE AMERICAN ACADEMY OF POLITICAL AND SOCIAL SCIENCE 319 (September 1958): 84-93.

Gershman, Carl. THE FOREIGN POLICY OF AMERICAN LABOR. Beverly Hills, Calif.: Sage, 1975. 82 p.

Gerson, L.L. THE HYPHENATE IN RECENT AMERICAN POLITICS AND DEMOCRACY. Lawrence: University of Kansas Press, 1964. 325 p.

Geyer, Alan Francis. "American Protestantism and World Politics, 1898-1960: A Typological Approach to the Functions of Religion in the Decision Making Processes of Foreign Policy." Ph.D. dissertation, Boston University, 1961. 462 p.

Grabill, Joseph Leon. "Missionaries and Conflict: Their Influence Upon American Relations with the Near East, 1914-1927." Ph.D. dissertation, Indiana University, 1964. 254 p.

Green, Mark J. THE OTHER GOVERNMENT: THE UNSEEN POWER OF WASHINGTON LAWYERS. New York: Grossman, 1975. 318 p.

Hadwiger, Don Frank. "Farm Organizations and United States Foreign Trade Policy, 1946-1955." Ph.D. dissertation, State University of Iowa, 1956. 286 p.

Hennessy, Bernard. "A Case Study of Intra-Pressure Group Conflicts: The United World Federalists." JOURNAL OF POLITICS 16 (February 1954): 76-95.

Hero, Alfred O., Jr. AMERICAN RELIGIOUS GROUPS VIEW FOREIGN POLICY: TRENDS IN RANK-IN-FILE OPINION, 1957-1969. Durham, N.C.: Duke University Press, 1973. 552 p.

_____. THE SOUTHERNER AND WORLD POLITICS. Baton Rouge: Louisiana State University Press, 1965. 676 p.

Huff, Earl Dean. "A Study of a Successful Interest Group: The American Zionist Movement." WESTERN POLITICAL QUARTERLY 25 (March 1972): 109-24.

_____. "Zionist Influences Upon U.S. Foreign Policy: A Study of American Policy Toward the Middle East from the Time of the Struggle for Israel to the Sinai Conflict." Ph.D. dissertation, University of Idaho, 1971. 303 p.

Hughes, Barry B. THE DOMESTIC CONTEXT OF AMERICAN FOREIGN POLICY. San Francisco: Freeman, 1978. 240 p.

On public and interest groups.

Hutchins, Lavern C. THE JOHN BIRCH SOCIETY AND UNITED STATES FOREIGN POLICY. New York: Pageant, 1968. 295 p.

Kahn, Gilbert N. "Pressure Group Influence on Foreign Policy Decision Making: A Case Study of the United States Efforts to Join the World Court, 1935." Ph.D. dissertation: New York University, 1972. 288 p.

Koen, Ross Y., ed. THE CHINA LOBBY IN AMERICAN POLITICS. New York: Harper, 1974. 279 p. Bibliog.

Kraft, Joseph. "School for Statesmen." HARPER'S MAGAZINE, July 1958, pp. 64-68.

On the Council on Foreign Relations.

Lall, Betty Goetz. "The Foreign Policy Program of the League of Women Voters of the United States: Methods of Influencing Government Action, Effects on Public Opinion, and Evaluation of Results." Ph.D. dissertation, University of Minnesota, 1964. 421 p.

Larson, Simeon. LABOR AND FOREIGN POLICY: GOMPERS, THE AFL, AND THE FIRST WORLD WAR, 1914-1918. Rutherford, N.J.: Fairleigh Dickinson University Press, 1975. 176 p. Bibliog.

_____. "Trade Union Impact on United States Foreign Policy, 1914-1918." Ph.D. dissertation, New School for Social Research, 1971. 230 p.

Lefever, Ernest Warren. "Protestants and United States Foreign Policy, 1925-1954: A Study of the Response of National Protestant Leaders to the Issues and Direction of U.S. Foreign Policy and of the Theoretical Assumptions which Underlay that Response." Ph.D. dissertation, Yale University, 1956. 335 p.

McLellan, David S., and Woodhouse, Charles E. "The Business Elite and Foreign Policy." WESTERN POLITICAL QUARTERLY 13 (March 1960): 172-90.

_____. "Businessmen and Foreign Policy." SOUTHWESTERN SOCIAL SCIENCE QUARTERLY 39 (March 1959): 283-90.

Melone, Albert P. LAWYERS, PUBLIC POLICY AND INTEREST GROUP POLITICS. Washington, D.C.: University Press of America, 1977. 265 p.

Milbrath, Lester W. "Interest Groups and Foreign Policy." In DOMESTIC SOURCES OF FOREIGN POLICY, edited by James N. Rosenau, pp. 231-51. New York: Free Press, 1967.

_____. THE WASHINGTON LOBBYISTS. Chicago: Rand McNally, 1963. 431 p. Bibliog.

Murphy, Robert D. "Labor's Concern with Foreign Affairs." DEPARTMENT OF STATE BULLETIN 32 (17 January 1955): 84-86.

Ogene, Francis C. "Group Interests and United States Foreign Policy on African Issues." Ph.D. dissertation, Case Western Reserve University, 1971. 403 p.

Ornstein, Norman J., and Elder, Shirley. INTEREST GROUPS, LOBBYING AND POLICYMAKING. Washington, D.C.: Congressional Quarterly, 1978. 245 p.

Panzella, Emmett E. "The Atlantic Union Committee: A Study of Pressure Groups in Foreign Policy." Ph.D. dissertation, Kent State University, 1969. 328 p.

Paterson, Thomas Graham. "The Economic Cold War: American Business and Economic Foreign Policy, 1945-1950." Ph.D. dissertation, University of California (Berkeley), 1968. 494 p.

Pye, Lucian W. "Effects of Legislative and Administrative Accessibility on Interest Group Politics." PROD 1 (January 1958): 11-13.

Radosh, Ronald. AMERICAN LABOR AND UNITED STATES FOREIGN POLICY. New York: Random House, 1969. 463 p.

Said, Abdul Aziz, and Simmons, Luiz A., eds. ETHNICITY AND U.S. FOREIGN POLICY. New Brunswick, N.J.: Transaction, 1976. 241 p. Bibliog.

Savord, Ruth, and Wasson, Donald, comps. AMERICAN AGENCIES INTERESTED IN INTERNATIONAL AFFAIRS. New York: Council on Foreign Relations, 1948. 195 p.

Snetsinger, John. TRUMAN, THE JEWISH VOTE, AND THE CREATION OF ISRAEL. Stanford, Calif.: Hoover Institution, 1974. 208 p.

Sprout, Harold H. "Pressure Groups and Foreign Policies." ANNALS OF THE AMERICAN ACADEMY OF POLITICAL AND SOCIAL SCIENCE 179 (May 1935): 114-23.

Stevens, Richard P. AMERICAN ZIONISM AND U.S. FOREIGN POLICY, 1942-1947. New York: Pageant, 1962. 227 p. Bibliog.

Trice, Robert H., Jr. "Domestic Political Interests and American Policy in the Middle East: Pro-Israel, Pro-Arab, and Corporate Non-Governmental Actors and the Making of American Foreign Policy." Ph.D. dissertation, University of Wisconsin (Madison), 1974. 506 p.

U.S. Congress. Senate. Committee on Foreign Relations. ACTIVITIES OF NONDIPLOMATIC REPRESENTATIVES OF FOREIGN PRINCIPALS IN THE UNITED STATES. Hearings. 13 pts. 88th Cong., 1st sess. Washington, D.C.: Government Printing Office, 1963.

Welch, Susan Kay. "Groups and Foreign Policy Decisions: The Case of Indochina, 1950-1956." Ph.D. dissertation, University of Illinois (Urbana-Champaign), 1970. 476 p.

Welles, Sumner. "Pressure Groups and Foreign Policy." ATLANTIC MONTHLY, November 1947, pp. 63-67.

Whiteford, Daniel Francis. "The American Legion and American Foreign Policy, 1950-1963." Ph.D. dissertation, University of Maryland, 1967. 352 p.

Wilson, Bonnie Salango. "The Methodist Foreign Policy Response, 1939-1964: A Case Study In Churches and Foreign Policy in the United States." Ph.D. dissertation, Johns Hopkins University (School of Advanced International Studies), 1970. 595 p.

Wilson, Joan Hoff. AMERICAN BUSINESS AND FOREIGN POLICY, 1920-1933. Boston: Beacon, 1971. 339 p. Bibliog.

Windmueller, Steven F. "United States Foreign Policy in the Middle East and the American Jewish Community." Ph.D. dissertation, University of Pennsylvania, 1973. 440 p.

Windmuller, John P. FOREIGN AFFAIRS AND THE AFL-CIO. Reprint Series, no. 44. Ithaca, N.Y.: New York State School of Industrial and Labor Relations, 1956. 14 p.

Reprinted from INDUSTRIAL AND LABOR RELATIONS REVIEW, April 1956, pages 419-32.

_____. "The Foreign Policy Conflict in American Labor." POLITICAL SCIENCE QUARTERLY 82 (June 1967): 205-34.

Wooten, Graham. INTEREST GROUPS. Englewood Cliffs, N.J.: Prentice-Hall, 1970. 116 p. Bibliog.

Zeigler, Harmon L., and Peak, G. Wayne. INTEREST GROUPS IN AMERICAN SOCIETY. 2d ed. Englewood Cliffs, N.J.: Prentice-Hall, 1972. 309 p. Bibliog.

Political Parties, Partisans, and Bipartisanship

The following selections represent published resources on the relationship between political parties and foreign relations. Following World War II, special attention centered on analyzing the nature and operation of bipartisanship. Additional material on the impact of parties on the foreign affairs of the United States may be found in other sections of this compilation, particularly those dealing with the president, Congress, their interaction, and the bureaucracy.

Acheson, Dean G. "Parties and Foreign Policy." HARPER'S MAGAZINE, November 1955, pp. 29-34.

Armstrong, Hamilton Fish. "Foreign Policy and Party Politics." ATLANTIC MONTHLY, April 1947, pp. 56-63.

Belknap, George, and Campbell, Angus. "Political Party Identification and Attitudes Toward Foreign Policy." PUBLIC OPINION QUARTERLY 15 (Winter 1951): 601-23.

"Bipartisanship in the Balance." CONGRESSIONAL DIGEST 29 (February 1950): 36.

Bolles, Blair. "Bipartisanship in American Foreign Policy." FOREIGN POLICY REPORTS 24 (1 January 1949): 190-99.

Burns, James MacGregor. "Bipartisanship and the Weakness of the Party System." AMERICAN PERSPECTIVE 4 (Spring 1950): 164-74.

Crabb, Cecil V., Jr. BIPARTISAN FOREIGN POLICY: MYTH OR REALITY. Evanston, Ill.: Row, Peterson, 1957. 278 p. Bibliog.

Davileck, Richard E. A LOYAL OPPOSITION IN TIME OF WAR: THE RE-PUBLICAN PARTY AND THE POLITICS OF FOREIGN POLICY FROM PEARL HARBOR TO YALTA. Westport, Conn.: Greenwood, 1976. 239 p.

Donovan, John C. "The Political Party and Foreign Policy-Making." WORLD AFFAIRS QUARTERLY 28 (Spring 1957): 62-75.

Fulbright, J. William. "Bipartisanship Is a Two-Way Street." REPORTER 11 (16 December 1954): 8-11.

Graham, Charles John. "Republican Foreign Policy, 1939-1952." Ph.D. dissertation, University of Illinois, 1955. 334 p.

Gross, Ernest A. "What Is A Bipartisan Foreign Policy?" DEPARTMENT OF STATE BULLETIN 21 (3 October 1949): 504-5.

Kefauver, Estes, and Smith, H.A. "Can Bipartisanship be Restored in Foreign Policy?" FOREIGN POLICY BULLETIN 33 (15 June 1954): 4-6.

Peterson, Walfred Hugo. "The Foreign Policy and Foreign Policy Theory of the American Socialist Party, 1901-1920." Ph.D. dissertation, University of Minnesota, 1957. 517 p.

Poole, Walter Sloan. "The Quest for a Republican Foreign Policy: 1941-1951." Ph.D. dissertation, University of Pennsylvania, 1968. 436 p.

Raymond, Orin R. "The American Communist Party and United States 'Imperial-ism,' 1920-1928: Application of Doctrine." Ph.D. dissertation, Harvard University, 1971. 299 p.

Seager, Robert II. "The Progressives and American Foreign Policy, 1898-1917: An Analysis of the Attitudes of the Leaders of the Progressive Movement Toward External Affairs." 2 vols. Ph.D. dissertation, Ohio State University, 1956.

Shapiro, Martin. "Bipartisanship and the Foreign Policy-Making Process." In PUBLIC POLICY 10, edited by Carl J. Friedrich and Seymour Harris, pp. 206-38. Cambridge, Mass.: Harvard University Press, 1960.

Silverman, Sheldon Arnold. "At the Water's Edge: Arthur Vandenberg and the Foundation of American Bipartisan Foreign Policy." Ph.D. dissertation, University of California (Los Angeles), 1966. 314 p.

Smith, George H.E. "Bipartisan Foreign Policy in Partisan Politics." AMERICAN PERSPECTIVE 4 (Spring 1950): 157-69.

Tucker, Robert W. THE RADICAL LEFT AND AMERICAN FOREIGN POLICY.

Baltimore: Johns Hopkins Press, 1971. 156 p.

Vandenberg, Arthur H. "Bipartisan Foreign Policy." VITAL SPEECHES 15 (15 October 1948): 11–14.

Westerfield, H. Bradford. FOREIGN POLICY AND PARTY POLITICS: PEARL HARBOR TO KOREA. New Haven, Conn.: Yale University Press, 1955. 448 p. Bibliog.

Williams, Benjamin H. "Bipartisanship in American Foreign Policy." ANNALS OF THE AMERICAN ACADEMY OF POLITICAL AND SOCIAL SCIENCE 259 (September 1948): 136–43.

Ziegler, John Alan. "The Progressive's Views on Foreign Affairs, 1909–1941: A Case Study of Liberal Economic Isolationism." Ph.D. dissertation, Syracuse University, 1970. 375 p.

SECRECY IN DIPLOMACY

The debate on the degree of openness of foreign relations essential to the proper functioning of democratic institutions and the amount of confidentiality requisite for the effective conduct of relations with other countries has raged since the establishment of representative government. This debate has been waged in the United States for two centuries, and, since World War I, it has involved both national and international dimensions.

The internal aspect of the issue concerns the authority and action of the executive branch of the government (the presidency, White House, Department of State, and diplomats in the field) vis-a-vis the Congress, the media, and the people. In part, this contest hinges on openness respecting not only the essence or nature of foreign policy and the end products of diplomatic conversations and negotiations but also on the processes of implementing policy and consummating agreements. In the post-World War II era, the debate was extended, as attention came to be centered more directly on the making of policy during its formulation, even before it is determined. This internal level of debate, pertaining to the legal and political role of the executive branch and the application of constraints upon it, received increased literary attention following both World Wars I and II, with the policy-making element attracting considerable interest especially since the 1960s.

The second level of debate involves the international aspect of openness in the diplomacy of the United States and other countries in dealing with each other and the more general question of secrecy of governments and diplomatic forums in the international environment. It was these components of the issue to which, in the first of his Fourteen Points, Woodrow Wilson addressed his proposal for "open covenants . . . openly arrived at." The problem was muddied by the conflicting views of political principals, parliamentarians, diplomatic practitioners, journalists, and academicians. Despite the fact that, in certain limited respects--with the systematic publication of treaties and agreements in multinational compilations and with multipartite parliamentary institutionalization in the League of Nations system--

diplomacy became more open after World War I, few governments, if any, have achieved the degree of openness established by the United States. The debate nevertheless continues, as evidenced by the following selected materials. Other publications and commentary concerning the publication and public availability of U.S. documentary and other resources is dealt with in some detail later, in part III.

Barker, Carol M., and Fox, Matthew H. CLASSIFIED FILES: THE YELLOWING PAGES--A REPORT ON SCHOLARS' ACCESS TO GOVERNMENT DOCUMENTS. New York: Twentieth Century Fund, 1972. 115 p. Bibliog.

Blanchard, Paul. THE RIGHT TO READ: THE BATTLE AGAINST CENSORSHIP. Boston: Beacon, 1935. 339 p.

Borah, William E. "The Perils of Secret Treaty Making." FORUM 60 (December 1918): 657-68.

_____. "Results of Secrecy." SUNSET 48 (February 1922): 30-31.

Briareus. "Suggestion for Open Diplomacy." NATION, 28 December 1918, pp. 801-2.

Chesterton, G.K. "The Real Secret Diplomacy." NORTH AMERICAN REVIEW 207 (April 1918): 505-15.

Claude, Inis L., Jr. THE IMPACT OF PUBLIC OPINION UPON FOREIGN POLICY AND DIPLOMACY: OPEN DIPLOMACY REVISITED. The Hague: Mouton, 1965. 21 p. Reprint, no. 1. Ann Arbor: International Organization Program, University of Michigan, n.d. 21 p.

Eller, George. SECRET DIPLOMACY. London: Swift, 1912. 214 p.

Franck, Thomas M., and Weisband, Edward, eds. SECRECY AND FOREIGN POLICY. New York: Oxford University Press, 1974. 453 p.

Galnoor, Itzhak, ed. GOVERNMENT SECRECY IN DEMOCRACIES. New York: Harper and Row, 1976. 317 p.

Goldberg, Arthur J. "Public Diplomacy at the U.N." DEPARTMENT OF STATE BULLETIN 57 (28 August 1967): 262-65.

Address of 27 July 1967.

Gordon, Andrew C., and Heinz, John P. PUBLIC ACCESS TO INFORMATION. New Brunswick, N.J.: Transaction, 1978. 400 p.

Halle, Louis J. "Case for Quiet Diplomacy." NEW YORK TIMES MAGA-ZINE, 11 September 1960, p. 31.

Halperin, Morton H., and Hoffman, Daniel N. TOP SECRET: NATIONAL SECURITY AND THE RIGHT TO KNOW. New York: Simon and Schuster, 1977. 128 p.

Hammarskjold, Dag. "The Element of Privacy in Peacemaking." VITAL SPEECES 24 (15 March 1958): 337-39.

Hudson, Manley O. "The 'Injunction of Secrecy' With Respect to American Treaties." AMERICAN JOURNAL OF INTERNATIONAL LAW 23 (April 1929): 329-35.

Johnson, M.B. GOVERNMENT SECRECY CONTROVERSY: A DISPUTE IN-VOLVING THE GOVERNMENT AND THE PRESS IN THE EISENHOWER, KEN-NEDY, AND JOHNSON ADMINISTRATIONS. New York: Vantage, 1967. 136 p.

Jorden, William J. "Quiet Diplomacy of Our Moscow Spokesman." NEW YORK TIMES MAGAZINE, 26 January 1958, pp. 11, 56-57.

Kirkpatrick, Ivone. "Open Covenants But Unopenly Arrived At." NEW YORK TIMES MAGAZINE, 15 May 1960, pp. 19, 108-9.

Laise, Carol C. DEPARTMENT DISCUSSES RECENT STEPS TO IMPROVE ITS DECLASSIFICATION PROGRAMS. Washington, D.C.: Government Printing Office, 1974. 7 p.

_____. DEPARTMENT GIVES VIEWS ON PROPOSED AMENDMENTS TO FREEDOM OF INFORMATION ACT. Washington, D.C.: Government Printing Office, 1974. 8 p.

"The Limits to Secrecy." COMMONWEAL 81 (12 February 1965): 627-28.

Low, Maurice A. "The Vice of Secret Diplomacy." NORTH AMERICAN REVIEW 207 (February 1918): 209-20.

Macdonell, John. "Secret or Constructive Diplomacy." CONTEMPORARY REVIEW 109 (June 1916): 718-24.

McGuire, Martin C. SECRECY AND THE ARMS RACE. Cambridge, Mass.: Harvard University Press, 1965. 249 p.

Mansfield, Mike. "Open Agreements Privately Made." NEW YORK TIMES MAGAZINE, 26 January 1958, pp. 10, 34, 36, 38.

Middleton, Drew. "Open Covenants Unopenly Arrived At." NEW YORK TIMES MAGAZINE, 27 February 1955, pp. 13, 31, 33. Reply by James Deutsch. "Unopen Diplomacy." NEW YORK TIMES MAGAZINE, 13 March 1955, p. 4.

Mollenhoff, Clark R. "Secrecy, Classified Information, and Executive Privilege." In THE PRESS IN WASHINGTON, edited by Ray E. Hiebert, pp. 197-216. New York: Dodd, Mead, 1966.

"More Light on Open Diplomacy." NEW REPUBLIC, 27 August 1919, pp. 106-7. Reply. "Even More Secretive: Reply to More Light on Open Diplomacy." NEW REPUBLIC, 3 December 1919, pp. 25-26.

"More or Less Secret Diplomacy?" ROTARIAN 84 (May 1954): 12-14.

Consists of "Open Diplomacy in U.N." by Carlos Romulo vs. "Open Covenants--Someday!" by Tom Benson.

Moss, John E. "The Crisis of Secrecy." BULLETIN OF THE ATOMIC SCIENTISTS 17 (January 1961): 8-11.

Namier, Lewis B. "Diplomacy, Secret and Open." NINETEENTH CENTURY 123 (January 1938): 36-45.

Nicolson, Harold. "An Open Look at Secret Diplomacy." NEW YORK TIMES MAGAZINE, 13 September 1953, pp. 17, 34, 47-48.

"Open Diplomacy at Last." NEW REPUBLIC, 3 May 1919, pp. 4-5.

Plischke, Elmer. "A More Open Diplomacy vs. Greater Secrecy." FOREIGN SERVICE JOURNAL 34 (April 1957): 31-34.

_____, ed. "Democratic and Open Diplomacy." In his MODERN DIPLOMACY: THE ART AND THE ARTISANS, pp. 99-149. Washington, D.C.: American Enterprise Institute, 1979.

Punke, Harold H. "Secret Diplomacy and American Democracy." SOCIAL STUDIES 47 (March 1956): 83-88.

Ransom, Harry Howe. GOVERNMENT SECRECY AND NATIONAL SECURITY: AN ANALYSIS. Serial, no. 123. Boston: Harvard Defense Seminar, 1958.

Reinsch, Paul S. SECRET DIPLOMACY: HOW FAR CAN IT BE ELIMINATED? New York: Harcourt, Brace, 1922. 231 p. Bibliog.

Rogers, Lindsay. "How Open Can Diplomacy Get?" REPORTER 14 (26 January 1956): 42-43.

"The Role of Secrecy in the Conduct of Foreign Policy." AMERICAN JOURNAL OF INTERNATIONAL LAW, PROCEEDINGS 66 (September 1972): 61-78.

> Round table at sixty-sixth annual meeting, participated in by Bayless Manning, chairman, Max Frankel, Phil G. Goulding, Carl Marcy, and Harry C. McPherson.

Rourke, Francis E. SECRECY AND PUBLICITY: DILEMMAS OF DEMOCRACY. Baltimore: Johns Hopkins Press, 1961. 236 p.

Rowat, Donald C., ed. ADMINISTRATIVE SECRECY IN DEVELOPED COUNTRIES. New York: Columbia University Press, 1978. 350 p.

> Comparative surveys of 12 countries--including the United States--concerning public access to information held by government agencies.

Rusk, Dean. "Secretary of State Cites Value of Privacy in Use of Diplomatic Channel." DEPARTMENT OF STATE BULLETIN 44 (13 February 1961): 214.

Schurman, Franz. THE LOGIC OF WORLD POWER: SECRECY AND FOREIGN POLICY. New York: Pantheon, 1974. 593 p.

"Secret and Open Diplomacy?" SENIOR SCHOLASTIC 66 (13 April 1955): 7-8.

"Secret Diplomacy." NATION, 30 December 1915, pp. 765.

"Secret Diplomacy at Geneva." FORTNIGHTLY REVIEW 125 (April 1926): 454-61.

"Secret Diplomacy at Work." LIVING AGE 295 (24 November 1917): 493-95.

Shils, Edward A. THE TORMENT OF SECRECY: THE BACKGROUND AND CONSEQUENCES OF AMERICAN SECURITY POLICIES. Glencoe, Ill.: Free Press, 1956. 238 p.

Sigal, Leon V. "Official Secrecy and Informal Communication in Congressional Bureaucratic Relations." POLITICAL SCIENCE QUARTERLY 90 (Spring 1975): 71-92.

"That Secret Diplomacy Was Stuffy, But It Kept Wars Down to Size." SATUR-
DAY EVENING POST, 7 February 1953, p. 12.

Thompson, James Westphal, and Padover, Saul K. SECRET DIPLOMACY: ES-
PIONAGE AND CRYPTOGRAPHY, 1500-1815. New York: Unger, 1963.
290 p. Bibliog.

U.S. Congress. Senate. Committee on Government Operations. Subcommit-
tee on Intergovernmental Relations. GOVERNMENT SECRECY. Hearings.
May and June 1974. 93d Cong., 2d sess. Washington, D.C.: Government
Printing Office, 1974. 908 p.

"U.S. Secrets: Too Hot to Print?--Diplomatic Papers." U.S. NEWS AND
WORLD REPORT, 26 March 1954, pp. 48, 50, 52.

Wiggins, James R. FREEDOM OR SECRECY. New York: Oxford University
Press, 1956; rev. ed., 1964. 242 p.

Wilson, P.W. "Open Methods in Modern Diplomacy." CURRENT HISTORY
35 (October 1931): 85-90.

Wise, David. THE POLITICS OF LYING: GOVERNMENT DECEPTION,
SECRECY, AND POWER. New York: Random House, 1973. 415 p. Bibliog.

Zilliachus, Konni. MIRROR OF THE PAST: A HISTORY OF SECRET DIPLO-
MACY. New York: Current Books, 1946. 362 p.

FIELD MISSIONS AND OVERSEAS REPRESENTATION

Materials on the organization and functions of diplomatic and consular field
missions are far from abundant, and comprehensive analyses of their internal
politics, inter- and intra-agency operations, and coordination problems are even
scarcer. Some information on these and other aspects of field operations, such
as relations with and impact upon host governments, institutions, and peoples
may be gleaned from memoir literature. Materials on information, assistance,
and other operational programs abroad are to be found in specific literature on
these more restricted subjects, some of which are listed in chapter 17, and
publications on the diplomatic service, the military, and the intelligence community are presented in chapters 9, 11, and 12. The following items, many
of a general nature and some constituting segments of broad-scope volumes,
deal with various selected aspects of U.S. foreign relations field missions and
with overseas representation and representatives.

Alger, Chadwick, and Brams, Steven J. "Patterns of Representation in National Capitals and International Organizations." WORLD POLITICS 19 (July
1967): 646-63.

Specialized Aspects of Conduct

American Assembly. THE REPRESENTATION OF THE UNITED STATES ABROAD. New York: American Assembly, Columbia University, 1956. 217 p.

Baer, Peter R. THE ROLE OF A NATIONAL DELEGATION IN THE GENERAL ASSEMBLY. New York: Carnegie Endowment, 1970.

Barnett, Vincent M., Jr., ed. THE REPRESENTATION OF THE UNITED STATES ABROAD. New York: Praeger, 1965. 251 p.

Revision of American Assembly entry above.

Beichman, Arnold. THE "OTHER" STATE DEPARTMENT: THE UNITED STATES MISSION TO THE UNITED NATIONS--ITS ROLE IN THE MAKING OF FOREIGN POLICY. New York: Basic Books, 1967. 221 p.

Bishop, D.G. THE ADMINISTRATION OF UNITED STATES FOREIGN POLICY THROUGH THE UNITED NATIONS. Dobbs Ferry, N.Y.: Oceana, 1967. 112 p.

Cleveland, Harlan; Mangone, Gerard J.; and Adams, John Clarke. THE OVERSEAS AMERICANS. New York: McGraw-Hill, 1960. 316 p.

Cleveland, Harlan, and Mangone, Gerard J., eds. THE ART OF OVERSEAS-MANSHIP: AMERICANS AT WORK ABROAD. Syracuse, N.Y.: Syracuse University Press, 1957. 150 p.

Curti, Merle E., and Birr, Kendall. PRELUDE TO POINT FOUR: AMERICAN TECHNICAL MISSIONS OVERSEAS, 1838-1938. Madison: University of Wisconsin Press, 1954. 284 p.

Elder, Robert E. OVERSEAS REPRESENTATION AND SERVICES FOR FEDERAL DOMESTIC AGENCIES. New York: Carnegie Endowment, 1965. 106 p.

Esterline, John H., and Black, Robert B. "The United States Diplomatic Field Mission: A Cluster of Power Centers." In their INSIDE FOREIGN POLICY: THE DEPARTMENT OF STATE POLITICAL SYSTEM AND ITS SUBSYSTEMS, pp. 65-105. Palo Alto, Calif.: Mayfield, 1975.

Etzold, Thomas H. THE CONDUCT OF AMERICAN FOREIGN RELATIONS: THE OTHER SIDE OF DIPLOMACY. New York: New Viewpoints, Watts, 1977. 159 p. Bibliog.

Especially chapter 4, which, though titled "Conducting Foreign Relations," deals with diplomatic missions abroad.

Hero, Alfred O., Jr. AMERICANS IN WORLD AFFAIRS. Boston: World Peace Foundation, 1959. 165 p.

Juergensmeyer, John Eli. "Democracy's Diplomacy: The People-to-People Program--A Study of Attempts to Focus the Effects of Private Contacts in International Politics." Ph.D. dissertation, Princeton University, 1960. 637 p.

McCamy, James L. "War Agencies Abroad" and "Postwar Work Abroad." In his THE ADMINISTRATION OF AMERICAN FOREIGN AFFAIRS. Chapter 10, pp. 227-44; chapter 12, pp. 271-80. New York: Knopf, 1950.

MacVane, John. EMBASSY EXTRAORDINARY: THE U.S. MISSION TO THE UNITED NATIONS. Public Affairs Pamphlet, no. 311. New York: Public Affairs Committee, 1961. 28 p.

Plischke, Elmer. "The Overseas Establishment." In his CONDUCT OF AMERICAN DIPLOMACY, pp. 262-90. 3d ed. Princeton, N.J.: Van Nos-. trand, 1967.

Sapin, Burton M. "Field Missions." In his THE MAKING OF UNITED STATES FOREIGN POLICY, pp. 246-86. Washington, D.C.: Brookings Institution, 1966; New York: Praeger, 1966.

Sayre, Wallace S., and Thurber, Clarence E. TRAINING FOR SPECIALIZED MISSION PERSONNEL. Chicago: Public Administration Service, 1952. 85 p.

Scott, Andrew M., and Dawson, Raymond H., eds. "The Overseas Administration of American Foreign Policy." In their READINGS IN THE MAKING OF AMERICAN FOREIGN POLICY, pp. 507-44. New York: Macmillan, 1965.

Snyder, Richard C., and Furniss, Edgar S., Jr. "Representation of the United States Abroad." In their AMERICAN FOREIGN POLICY: FORMULATION, PRINCIPLES, AND PROGRAMS, pp. 310-44. New York: Rinehart, 1954.

Spector, Paul, and Preston, Harley O. WORKING EFFECTIVELY OVERSEAS. Washington, D.C.: Institute for International Service, 1961. 179 p.

Prepared for the Peace Corps.

Stuart, Graham H. "The American Embassy in Paris." CURRENT HISTORY 21 (October 1951): 220-24.

_____. "The American Government Establishment in Paris." In his AMERICAN DIPLOMATIC AND CONSULAR PRACTICE, pp. 394-416. 2d ed. New York: Appleton-Century-Crofts, 1952.

Thayer, Charles W. "How to Organize an Embassy: American Embassy in Russia." ATLANTIC MONTHLY, November 1950, pp. 58-60.

U.S. Congress. Senate. Committee on Foreign Relations. THE AMERICAN OVERSEAS. Hearing. 86th Cong., 1st sess., 18 February 1959. Washington, D.C.: Government Printing Office, 1959. 48 p.

U.S. Department of State. THE COUNTRY TEAM: AN ILLUSTRATED PROFILE OF OUR AMERICAN MISSIONS ABROAD. Washington, D.C.: Government Printing Office, 1967. 70 p.

"U.S. Embassy, New Model--In Rome." FORTUNE, February 1950, pp. 102-9, 122, 126, 128.

Winfield, Louise. LIVING OVERSEAS. Washington, D.C.: Public Affairs, 1962. 237 p.

The following provide legal analysis of U.S. practice respecting its diplomats and their missions in the field:

Hackworth, Green H. DIGEST OF INTERNATIONAL LAW. Washington, D.C.: Government Printing Office, 1943. Vol. 4, pp. 393-459.

Moore, John Bassett. A DIGEST OF INTERNATIONAL LAW. Washington, D.C.: Government Printing Office, 1906. Vol. 4, pp. 425-630.

Whiteman, Marjorie M. DIGEST OF INTERNATIONAL LAW. Washington, D.C.: Government Printing Office, 1970. Vol. 7, pp. 1-504.

PRIVATE INDIVIDUALS—THE LOGAN ACT

On January 30, 1799, Congress passed the Logan Act, prohibiting unauthorized private citizens from engaging in self-constituted diplomatic relations, including "correspondence or intercourse with any foreign government." As amended, this act remains in the statutes of the United States and renders violators subject to fine and imprisonment. See UNITED STATES CODE, Title 18, Par. 953. For commentary on the Logan Act, see the following:

Bailey, Thomas A. A DIPLOMATIC HISTORY OF THE AMERICAN PEOPLE. 9th ed. New York: Appleton-Century-Crofts, 1974. Pp. 96, 804, 873.

Hackworth, Green H. DIGEST OF INTERNATIONAL LAW. Washington, D.C.: Government Printing Office, 1942. Vol. 4, pp. 609-11.

Kelsey, Hope. "Unauthorized Diplomatic Intercourse by American Citizens with Foreign Powers: The Logan Law, and the William C. Bullitt Incident." CUMULATIVE DIGEST OF INTERNATIONAL LAW AND RELATIONS 3 (25 February 1933): 26-32.

Moore, John Bassett. A DIGEST OF INTERNATIONAL LAW. Washington, D.C.: Vol. 4, pp. 448-50.

Plischke, Elmer. CONDUCT OF AMERICAN DIPLOMACY. 3d ed. Princeton, N.J.: Van Nostrand, 1963. Pp. 100-102.

Vagts, Detlev F. "The Logan Act: Paper Tiger or Sleeping Giant?" AMERICAN JOURNAL OF INTERNATIONAL LAW 60 (April 1966): 268-302.

Whiteman, Marjorie M. DIGEST OF INTERNATIONAL LAW. Washington, D.C.: Government Printing Office, 1970. Vol. 7, p. 194.

The more general matter of unofficial, little publicized undertakings behind the scenes in international affairs, including the role of private citizens, is discussed in the following.

Berman, Maureen R., and Johnson, Joseph E., eds. UNOFFICIAL DIPLOMATS. New York: Columbia University Press, 1977. 268 p.

Chapter 17

FUNCTIONAL SPECIALIZED ASPECTS OF
U.S. FOREIGN RELATIONS

Functional aspects of U.S. foreign relations warranting separate treatment include information and propaganda activities abroad, diplomatic communication and reporting, treaty and agreement making, international trade and assistance, cultural and scientific affairs, and the protection of citizens and their interests in foreign lands as well as of third countries. Literary interest in the diplomatic reporting function and assistance to nationals appears to be modest, but additional information concerning them is contained in diplomatic memoirs (part IV) and in compilations of official documentation (part III). On the other hand, considerable descriptive and analytical literature is being published on international trade and aid relations, on overseas information programs, and especially on treaty making, because of its complex internal as well as international ramifications. Many of these published studies are of recent vintage, evidencing increasing concern with these aspects of American foreign relations, but the matter of diplomatic reporting—unlike other primary diplomatic functions such as representation and negotiation—seems to appeal primarily to professional practitioners. Treaty making, by way of comparison, is of continuing concern to political leaders, constitutional and international lawyers, academicians, journalists, interest groups, and others.

INFORMATION, PROPAGANDA, AND PSYCHOLOGICAL WARFARE

The matter of international communication, external information programs, propaganda, and psychological warfare is broad and many-faceted and involves a substantial and growing literature. The following illustrate these published resources, which, except for a few studies, like those of Bernays and Riegel, have been produced largely since World War II. A few analyses deal with international communication, such as those written by Berlo and Schramm, which supplement studies on diplomatic and international communication listed elsewhere in this compilation, especially in the following section and in chapter 13. Some materials deal with the American information program, including those on the U.S. Information Agency (Bogart, Dizard, Elder, Esterline and Black, Henderson, Rubin, Stephens, and Thompson), the Voice of America (Benton, Pirsein), and Radio Free Europe (Holt). Others are more precisely concerned with propaganda, such as Akzin, Bernays, Brown, Dunn, Fulbright, Grothe, Harter and Sullivan, Joyce, Lambert, Lerner, Martin, Murty, Peterson, and Whitaker. Still others focus upon psychological warfare, as is the case with Daugherty, Holt and Van de Velde, Linebarger, Lerner, Margolin, Qualter, and Summers. To these may be added a few case studies, written by Lerner (Germany), Renick (Korea), Sorenson (World War II), and Whitton (cold war). Additional general materials dealing with such related subjects as public opinion, the media, and interest groups, together with their relation to the foreign relations process, are dealt with in the preceding chapter. Political warfare, including the cold war, is treated in chapter 18.

Akzin, Benjamin. PROPAGANDA BY DIPLOMATS. Washington, D.C.: Digest, 1936. 22 p.

Allen, George V. "U.S. Information Program." DEPARTMENT OF STATE BULLETIN 19 (18 July 1948): 88-91.

Barrett, Edward W. TRUTH IS OUR WEAPON. New York: Funk and Wagnalls, 1953. 355 p. Bibliog.

Benton, William. "Can America Afford to be Silent?" DEPARTMENT OF STATE BULLETIN 14 (6 and 13 January 1946): 7-10.

_____. THE VOICE OF AMERICA. New York: Harper and Row, 1961. 204 p.

Berlo, David Kenneth. THE PROCESS OF COMMUNICATION: AN INTRODUCTION TO THEORY AND PRACTICE. New York: Holt, Rinehart, and Winston, 1960.

     Especially chapters 3, 6-8.

Bernays, Edward L. PROPAGANDA. New York: Liveright, 1928. 159 p.

Bogart, Leo. PREMISES FOR PROPAGANDA: THE UNITED STATES INFORMATION AGENCIES OPERATING ASSUMPTIONS IN THE COLD WAR. Abbreviated by Agnes Bogart. New York: Free Press, 1976. 250 p. Bibliog.

Brown, James Alexander Campbell. TECHNIQUES OF PERSUASION: FROM PROPAGANDA TO BRAINWASHING. Baltimore: Penguin, 1963. 325 p. Bibliog.

Carr, Edward Hallett. "Propaganda and Power." YALE REVIEW 42 (September 1952): 1-9.

Carroll, Wallace. PERSUADE OR PERISH. Boston: Houghton Mifflin, 1948. 392 p.

Cater, Douglass. THE FOURTH BRANCH OF GOVERNMENT. Boston: Houghton Mifflin, 1959. 194 p.

Commager, Henry S., ed. AMERICA IN PERSPECTIVE: THE UNITED STATES THROUGH FOREIGN EYES. New York: Random House, 1947. 389 p. Bibliog.

Creel, George. HOW WE ADVERTISED AMERICA: THE FIRST TELLING OF THE AMAZING STORY OF THE COMMITTEE ON PUBLIC INFORMATION THAT CARRIED THE GOSPEL OF AMERICANISM TO EVERY CORNER OF THE GLOBE. New York: Harper, 1920. 466 p.

Daugherty, William E., with Janowitz, Morris. A PSYCHOLOGICAL WARFARE CASEBOOK. Baltimore: Johns Hopkins Press, 1958. 880 p. Bibliog.

Dizard, Wilson Paul. THE STRATEGY OF TRUTH: THE STORY OF THE U.S. INFORMATION SERVICE. Washington, D.C.: Public Affairs, 1961. 213 p. Bibliog.

Dunn, Frederick S. WAR AND THE MINDS OF MEN. New York: Harper and Row, 1950. 115 p.

Elder, Robert. THE INFORMATION MACHINE: THE UNITED STATES INFORMATION AGENCY AND AMERICAN FOREIGN POLICY. Syracuse, N.Y.: Syracuse University Press, 1968. 356 p.

Elliel, Jacques. PROPAGANDA: THE FORMATION OF MEN'S ATTITUDES. Translated by Konrad Kellen and Jean Lerner. New York: Knopf, 1965. 320 p. Bibliog.

Esterline, John H., and Black, Robert B. INSIDE FOREIGN POLICY: THE DEPARTMENT OF STATE POLITICAL SYSTEM AND ITS SUBSYSTEMS. Palo Alto, Calif.: Mayfield, 1975.

   Chapters 5-7 deal with the U.S. Information Agency.

Fulbright, J. William. THE PENTAGON PROPAGANDA MACHINE. New York: Liveright, 1970. 166 p.

Gardner, Lloyd C. ARCHITECTS OF ILLUSION: MEN AND IDEAS IN AMERICAN FOREIGN POLICY, 1941-1949. Chicago: Quadrangle, 1970. 365 p. Bibliog.

Goodfriend, Arthur. THE TWISTED IMAGE. New York: St. Martin's, 1965. 264 p.

Gordon, George N., and Falk, Irving A. THE WAR OF IDEAS: AMERICA'S INTERNATIONAL IDENTITY CRISIS. New York: Hastings, 1973. 362 p. Bibliog.

Goulding, Phil G. CONFIRM OR DENY: INFORMING THE PEOPLE ON NATIONAL SECURITY. New York: Harper and Row, 1970. 369 p.

Grothe, Peter. TO WIN THE MINDS OF MEN. Palo Alto, Calif.: Pacific Books, 1958. 241 p.

Harter, Donald Lincoln, and Sullivan, John. PROPAGANDA HANDBOOK. Philadelphia: Twentieth Century, 1953. 440 p.

Henderson, John William. THE UNITED STATES INFORMATION AGENCY. New York: Praeger, 1969. 324 p. Bibliog.

Holt, Robert T. RADIO FREE EUROPE. Minneapolis: University of Minnesota Press, 1958. 249 p. Bibliog.

Holt, Robert T., and Van de Velde, Robert W. STRATEGIC PSYCHOLOGICAL OPERATIONS AND AMERICAN FOREIGN POLICY. Chicago: University of Chicago Press, 1960. 249 p.

Joyce, Walter. THE PROPAGANDA GAP. New York: Harper and Row, 1963. 144 p.

Katz, Daniel, ed. PUBLIC OPINION AND PROPAGANDA: A BOOK OF READINGS. New York: Dryden, 1954. 779 p.

Keller, Suzanne. "Diplomacy and Communication." PUBLIC OPINION QUARTERLY 20 (September 1956): 176-82.

Keogh, James. "Information and Modern Diplomacy." DEPARTMENT OF STATE BULLETIN 70 (21 January 1974): 57-63.

Lambert, Richard S. PROPAGANDA. London: Nelson, 1938. 162 p.

Lasswell, Harold D. "The Theory of Political Propaganda." AMERICAN POLITICAL SCIENCE REVIEW 21 (August 1927): 627-31.

Lavine, Harold, and Wechsler, James. WAR PROPAGANDA AND THE UNITED STATES. New Haven, Conn.: Yale University Press, 1940. Reprint. New York: Garland, 1972. 363 p.

Lerner, Daniel. SYKEWAR: PSYCHOLOGICAL WARFARE AGAINST GER-MANY. New York: Stewart, 1949. 463 p.

_____, ed. PROPAGANDA IN WAR AND CRISIS: MATERIALS FOR AMERI-CAN POLICY. New York: Stewart, 1951. 500 p. Bibliog.

Linebarger, Paul M.A. PSYCHOLOGICAL WARFARE. New York: Duell, Sloan, Pearce, 1948. 318 p.

McGaffin, William, and Knoll, Erwin. ANYTHING BUT THE TRUTH: THE CREDIBILITY GAP--HOW THE NEWS IS MANAGED IN WASHINGTON. New York: Putnam, 1968. 250 p.

Margolin, Leo Jay. PAPER BULLETS--A BRIEF STORY OF PSYCHOLOGICAL WARFARE IN WORLD WAR II. New York: Froben, 1946. 150 p.

Martin, Leslie John. INTERNATIONAL PROPAGANDA: ITS LEGAL AND DIPLOMATIC CONTROL. Minneapolis: University of Minnesota Press, 1958. 284 p.

Meyerhoff, Arthur E. THE STRATEGY OF PERSUASION: THE USE OF AD-VERTISING SKILLS IN FIGHTING THE COLD WAR. New York: Coward-McCann, 1965. 191 p. Bibliog.

Minor, Dale. THE INFORMATION WAR. New York: Hawthorn, 1970. 212 p. Bibliog.

Morgan, Thomas B. AMONG THE ANTI-AMERICANS. New York: Holt, Rinehart, and Winston, 1967. 211 p.

Mosher, Frederick, and Harr, John E. PROGRAMMING SYSTEMS AND FOR-EIGN AFFAIRS LEADERSHIP: AN ATTEMPTED INNOVATION. New York: Oxford University Press, 1970. 261 p.

Murty, Bhagevatala S. PROPAGANDA AND WORLD PUBLIC ORDER: THE LEGAL REGULATION OF THE IDEOLOGICAL INSTRUMENT OF COERCION. New Haven, Conn.: Yale University Press, 1968. 310 p.

Peterson, Horace Cornelius. PROPAGANDA FOR WAR: THE CAMPAIGN AGAINST AMERICAN NEUTRALITY, 1914-1917. Port Washington, N.Y.: Kennikat, 1939. 357 p.

Pirsein, Robert William. "The Voice of America: A History of the Interna-tional Broadcasting Activities of the United States Government, 1940-1962." Ph.D. dissertation, Northwestern University, 1970. 603 p.

Ponsonby, Arthur P. FALSEHOOD IN WAR-TIME: CONTAINING AN AS-SORTMENT OF LIES CIRCULATED THROUGHOUT THE NATIONS DURING THE GREAT WAR. London: Allen and Unwin, 1928. 192 p.

Qualter, Terence H. PROPAGANDA AND PSYCHOLOGICAL WARFARE. New York: Random House, 1962. 176 p. Bibliog.

Renick, Roderick Dhu, Jr. "Political Communication: A Case Study of the United States Propaganda in North and South Korea." Ph.D. dissertation, Tulane University, 1971. 256 p.

Riegel, Oscar Wetherhold. MOBILIZING FOR CHAOS: THE STORY OF THE NEW PROPAGANDA. New Haven, Conn.: Yale University Press, 1934. 231 p.

Rubin, Ronald I. THE OBJECTIVES OF THE U.S. INFORMATION AGENCY: CONTROVERSIES AND ANALYSIS. New York: Praeger, 1968. 251 p. Bibliog.

Schramm, Wilbur. THE PROCESS AND EFFECTS OF MASS COMMUNICATION. Urbana: University of Illinois Press, 1965. 586 p. Bibliog.

　　　Especially pp. 156-206, 429-562.

Schroder, Harold M.; Driver, Michael J.; and Streufert, Siegfried. HUMAN INFORMATION PROCESSING. New York: Holt, Rinehart, and Winston, 1967. 224 p. Bibliog.

Smith, Chitra M.; Winograd, Berton; and Jwaideh, Alice R. INTERNATIONAL COMMUNICATION AND POLITICAL WARFARE: AN ANNOTATED BIBLIOG-RAPHY. Santa Monica, Calif.: Rand, 1952. 508 p.

Sorenson, Thomas C. THE WORD WAR: THE STORY OF AMERICAN PROPA-GANDA. New York: Harper and Row, 1968. 337 p.

Stearns, Monteagle. "Democratic Diplomacy and the Role of Propaganda." FOREIGN SERVICE JOURNAL 30 (October 1953): 24, 25, 62-64.

Stephens, Oren. FACTS TO A CANDID WORLD: AMERICA'S OVERSEAS IN-FORMATION PROGRAM. Stanford, Calif.: Stanford University Press, 1955. 164 p. Bibliog.

Summers, Robert E., ed. AMERICA'S WEAPONS OF PSYCHOLOGICAL WAR-FARE. New York: Wilson, 1951. 206 p. Bibliog.

Thomson, Charles A.H. OVERSEAS INFORMATION SERVICE OF THE UNITED STATES GOVERNMENT. Washington, D.C.: Brookings Institution, 1948. 397 p.

U.S. Congress. House of Representatives. Committee on Foreign Affairs. Subcommittee on International Organizations and Movements. WINNING THE COLD WAR: THE U.S. IDEOLOGICAL OFFENSIVE. 88th Cong., 1st and 2d sess. Washington, D.C.: Government Printing Office, 1963-64. 1,097 p.

U.S. Department of State. OVERSEAS INFORMATION PROGRAMS OF THE UNITED STATES GOVERNMENT: A BIBLIOGRAPHY OF SELECTED MATERIALS WITH ANNOTATIONS. Washington, D.C.: Government Printing Office, 1951. 34 p.

U.S. Library of Congress. Legislative Reference Service. THE U.S. IDEO-LOGICAL EFFORT: GOVERNMENT AGENCIES AND PROGRAMS. Washington, D.C.: Government Printing Office, 1964. 22 p.

Westerfield, H. Bradford. THE INSTRUMENTS OF AMERICAN FOREIGN POLICY. New York: Crowell, 1963. 538 p. Bibliog.

   Especially part 3, pages 241-60, on the informational arm of policy.

Whitaker, Urban George, Jr., ed. PROPAGANDA AND INTERNATIONAL RELATIONS. 2d ed. San Francisco: Chandler, 1962. 246 p. Bibliog.

Whitton, John Boardman, ed. PROPAGANDA AND COLD WAR. Washington, D.C.: Public Affairs, 1963. 119 p. Bibliog.

   Princeton University symposium.

Winkler, Allan M. THE POLITICS OF PROPAGANDA: THE OFFICE OF WAR INFORMATION, 1942-1945. New Haven, Conn.: Yale University Press, 1978. 240 p.

In addition to the studies of Creel, Goodfriend, and others, which touch on the subject, the following focuses directly on the relation of diplomacy and the image of the United States abroad.

U.S. Congress. House of Representatives. Committee on Foreign Affairs. Subcommittee on International Organizations and Movements. THE FUTURE OF UNITED STATES PUBLIC DIPLOMACY: REPORT NO. 6 ON WINNING THE COLD WAR--THE U.S. IDEOLOGICAL OFFENSIVE. 90th Cong., 2d sess. Committee Print. Washington, D.C.: Government Printing Office, 1968. 175 p.

   Deals with image building, development of public diplomacy, and the importance of communications in international relations.

DIPLOMATIC COMMUNICATIONS AND REPORTING

Interest and publication concerning the process and problems of diplomatic com-
munication--with the Department of State, the governments of host countries,
and within and among overseas missions--and diplomatic reporting, which are
among the major traditional functions of diplomats, appears to be negligible.
The following items may be supplemented, however, with descriptive analyses
appearing as experiential chronicling in memoirs, limited-scope items published
in the DEPARTMENT OF STATE NEWSLETTER and the FOREIGN SERVICE
JOURNAL, and isolated short statements incorporated into more general volumes. Additionally, commentary respecting and compilations of diplomatic
communications, including messages and reports to and from the field, are
treated separately in part III, and materials on international communication
in general are provided in chapter 19 on systematic analysis.

Blair, William D., Jr. "Communication: The Weak Link in Our Foreign Relations." DEPARTMENT OF STATE BULLETIN 63 (9 November 1970): 580-86.

Cochran, William P., Jr. "A Diplomat's Moments of Truth." FOREIGN SER-
VICE JOURNAL 30 (September 1953): 23, 62.

On fundamentals of political reporting.

Collins, Michael. "Communicating About Foreign Policy." DEPARTMENT OF
STATE BULLETIN 62 (23 March 1970): 393-96.

Cooper, James Ford. "Toward Professional Political Analysis in Foreign Service
Reporting." FOREIGN SERVICE JOURNAL 48 (February 1971): 24-27.

Hall, Harold E. "The Job of Economic Reporting." FOREIGN SERVICE JOUR-
NAL 32 (April 1955): 24-25, 46-47.

Hanson, Betty Crump. "American Diplomatic Reporting from the Soviet Union,
1934-1941." Ph.D. dissertation, Columbia University, 1966. 369 p.

Kattenburg, Paul M. "Some Comments on Observation, Analysis and Appraisal
in Diplomacy." Paper presented at annual meeting of American Political Science Association, Chicago, September 1971. In AN INTRODUCTION TO
DIPLOMATIC PRACTICE, edited by John J. Hurley, Jr., pp. 1-23. Washington, D.C.: Foreign Service Institute, U.S. Department of State, 1971.

London, Kurt. "Diplomatic Communications." In his HOW FOREIGN POLICY
IS MADE, pp. 194-202. New York: Van Nostrand, 1949.

Plischke, Elmer. "Diplomatic Reporting." In his CONDUCT OF AMERICAN
DIPLOMACY, pp. 317-19. 3d ed. Princeton, N.J.: Van Nostrand, 1967.

Schreiner, George Abel. CABLES AND WIRELESS AND THEIR ROLE IN FOR-
EIGN RELATIONS OF THE UNITED STATES. Boston: Stratford, 1924. 269 p.

Swayne, Kingdon W. "Horse and Buggy Political Science in the Jet Age."
FOREIGN SERVICE JOURNAL 45 (March 1968): 17-19, 46.

_____. "The Reporting Function in American Diplomacy." Paper presented
at annual meeting of American Political Science Association, September 1971,
at Chicago. In AN INTRODUCTION TO DIPLOMATIC PRACTICE, edited
by John J. Hurley, Jr., pp. 1-37. Washington, D.C.: Foreign Service
Institute, U.S. Department of State, 1971.

U.S. Commission on the Organization of the Government for the Conduct of
Foreign Policy. "Field Reporting." In its COMMISSION ON THE ORGANI-
ZATION OF THE GOVERNMENT FOR THE CONDUCT OF FOREIGN POLICY,
JUNE 1975, appendix, vol. 2, pp. 137-207. Washington, D.C.: Govern-
ment Printing Office, 1976.

Official commentary on diplomatic correspondence and communications as well
as official documents are provided in the following:

Hackworth, Green H. DIGEST OF INTERNATIONAL LAW. Washington, D.C.:
Government Printing Office, 1943. Vol. 4, pp. 604-32 and 652-54.

Moore, John Bassett. A DIGEST OF INTERNATIONAL LAW. Washington,
D.C.: Government Printing Office, 1906. Vol. 4, pp. 680-726.

Whiteman, Marjorie M. DIGEST OF INTERNATIONAL LAW. Washington,
D.C.: Government Printing Office, 1970. Vol. 7, pp. 174-88 and 502-4.

TREATY AND AGREEMENT MAKING

Whether conventional diplomacy or the international conference is relied upon
as the means, the concluding of an international treaty or agreement constitutes a paragon of foreign relations and, therefore, imbues this aspect of the
diplomatic process with special significance warranting separate consideration.
Both the procedures and the end results of treaty making are important and
have attracted considerable literary inquiry and analysis. The resulting commitments contained in treaties and agreements may shape the course of foreign
policies and international events, evoke or avert war, ameliorate or resolve
disputes, transfer territories and peoples, create international law, bring new
states into the community of nations, or affect interrelations in various other
respects. At the same time, even the very procedure of treaty making is
central to the conduct of foreign relations, because it may condition, and at
times perhaps virtually determine, the complex affairs of states. This is particularly true where internal constitutional and political limitations provide
potent constraints on treaty involvement, as is the case with the United States.

The consummation of treaties and agreements entails several major phases, each of which attracts literary attention. These include negotiation and signature, legislative approval, ratification, exchange of ratifications, proclamation or promulgation, registration and publication, implementation, interpretation, and supercession or termination. Some of these steps are primarily of national concern, some are international, and some may be both.

Because of the constitutional issues relating to executive-legislative relations in the American treaty process and the legal and pragmatic delineation of treaties vs. agreements, and in view of periodic reconsideration of these constitutional matters as well as movements to amend the treaty authority in the United States, reflected in a number of "great debates," much American literature concentrates on these problems and developments. Moreover, analysis of treaty making impinges upon several intellectual disciplines and warrants a variety of research approaches: historical, political, legal, and others.

As a consequence, materials concerned with treaty and agreement making comprise a complex package ranging from process to outcome, from consummation to effectuation, from juridical determinations to institutional procedures, and from geographic (spatial) application to functional content. The following, illustrating such published materials, reflect both the internal and external dimensions of the process and include a number of case studies, but they do not include collections of the texts of treaties and agreements or compilations concerned with their status, which are dealt with in chapter 22.

The following resources consist of a variety of interests and treatments. Some are substantial and comprehensive analyses, several of which antedate World War I, including those of Butler, Crandall, Devlin, and Tucker. Borchard, Catudal, McClure, and McDougal launched renewed interest in analysis at the time of World War II, and, in 1960, these were augmented by the contributions of Blix and Byrd. Quincy Wright's briefer essays spanned a period of more than three decades. Considerable attention has been devoted to the treaty-making role of the Senate, exemplified by the studies of Collier, Dangerfield, Fleming, Hayden, Holt, McClendon, and others. Some analysts, like Cleary, Lodge, Sayre, and Trani, produced case studies; additional treaty-making case studies are listed in chapter 16, section on policy formulation-- such as the contributions of Barnes, Cohen, Lepper, and Terchek, pp. 347, 348. Still other authors were concerned with more precise aspects of the treaty process, including general procedure (Plischke), unperfected treaties (Wiktor), ratification (Camara, Jones, U.S. Senate, and Wilcox), proclamation (Reiff), revision (Hoyt), the legal nature and effect of treaties and agreements (Allen, Anderson, Elias, Harvard Research, and Hendry), and constitutional reform (Bricker, Dulles, Holman, MacBride, Morley, Richberg, and Sutherland).

Allen, Florence E. THE TREATY AS AN INSTRUMENT OF LEGISLATION. New York: Macmillan, 1952. 114 p.

Anderson, Chander P. "The Extent and Limitations of the Treaty-Making Power Under the Constitution." AMERICAN JOURNAL OF INTERNATIONAL LAW 1 (July 1907): 636-70.

_____. "Treaties as Domestic Law." AMERICAN JOURNAL OF INTERNA-TIONAL LAW 29 (July 1935): 472-76.

Arnold, Ralph, ed. TREATY-MAKING PROCEDURE: A COMPARATIVE STUDY OF THE METHODS OBTAINING IN DIFFERENT STATES. London: Oxford University Press, 1933. 78 p.

Barnett, James F. "International Agreements Without the Advice and Consent of the Senate." YALE LAW JOURNAL 15 (November and December 1905): 18-27, 63-82.

Beilenson, Laurence A. THE TREATY TRAP: A HISTORY OF THE PERFOR-MANCE OF POLITICAL TREATIES BY THE UNITED STATES AND EUROPEAN NATIONS. Washington, D.C.: Public Affairs, 1969. 344 p. Bibliog.

   Prepared for Foreign Policy Research Institute, University of Penn-sylvania.

Blix, Hans. TREATY MAKING POWER. New York: Praeger, 1960. 414 p. Bibliog.

Borah, William E. "The Perils of Secret Treaty Making." FORUM 60 (December 1918): 657-68.

Borchard, Edwin M. "The Proposed Constitutional Amendment on Treaty-Making." AMERICAN JOURNAL OF INTERNATIONAL LAW 39 (July 1945): 537-41.

_____. "Shall the Executive Agreement Replace the Treaty?" AMERICAN JOURNAL OF INTERNATIONAL LAW 38 (October 1944): 637-43. Also YALE LAW JOURNAL 53 (1943-44): 664-83.

_____. "Treaties and Executive Agreements." AMERICAN POLITICAL SCI-ENCE REVIEW 40 (August 1946): 729-39.

_____. "Treaties and Executive Agreements--A Reply." YALE LAW JOUR-NAL 54 (June 1945): 616-64.

Bot, B.R. NONRECOGNITION AND TREATY RELATIONS. Dobbs Ferry, N.Y.: Oceana, 1968. 286 p. Bibliog.

Brandon, Michael. "Analysis of the Terms 'Treaty' and 'International Agree-ment' for Purposes of Registration Under Article 102 of the United Nations Charter." AMERICAN JOURNAL OF INTERNATIONAL LAW 47 (January 1953): 49-69.

Bricker, John W. "Making Treaties and Other International Agreements." ANNALS OF THE AMERICAN ACADEMY OF POLITICAL AND SOCIAL SCIENCE 289 (September 1953): 134-44.

Butler, Charles Henry. THE TREATY-MAKING POWER OF THE UNITED STATES. 2 vols. New York: Banks, 1902.

Byrd, Elbert M., Jr. TREATIES AND EXECUTIVE AGREEMENTS IN THE UNITED STATES: THEIR SEPARATE ROLES AND LIMITATIONS. The Hague: Nijhoff, 1960. 276 p. Bibliog.

Call, J.L. "Government by Decree Through Executive Agreement." BAYLOR LAW REVIEW 6 (Spring 1954): 277-90.

Camara, Jose S. THE RATIFICATION OF INTERNATIONAL TREATIES. Toronto: Ontario Publishing Co., 1949. 173 p. Bibliog.

Catudal, Honore Marcel. "Executive Agreement: A Supplement to the Treaty-Making Procedure." GEORGE WASHINGTON LAW REVIEW 10 (1941-42): 653-69.

_____. "Executive Agreement or Treaty?" JOURNAL OF POLITICS 10 (February 1948): 168-78.

Chadee, Zechariah, Jr. "Amending the Constitution to Cripple Treaties." LOUISIANA LAW REVIEW 12 (May 1952): 345-82.

Chamberlain, Lawrence H., and Snyder, Richard C. "The President; Treaties and Executive Agreements." In their AMERICAN FOREIGN POLICY, pp. 57-87. New York: Rinehart, 1948.

Chang, Yi-Ting. THE INTERPRETATION OF TREATIES BY JUDICIAL TRIBUNALS. New York: Columbia University Studies in the Social Sciences, 1933. 196 p.

Cleary, Robert Edward. "Executive Agreements in the Conduct of United States Foreign Policy: A Case Study--the Destroyer-Base Deal." Ph.D. dissertation, Rutgers University, 1962. 299 p.

Cohen, Benjamin V. "Some Comments on the Bricker Amendment." NORTHWESTERN UNIVERSITY LAW REVIEW 48 (May-June 1953): 185-96.

Cohen, R. "Self-Executing Executive Agreements: A Separation of Powers Problem." BUFFALO LAW REVIEW 24 (Fall 1974): 137-58.

Collier, Ellen C. THE MEANING OF "ADVICE AND CONSENT OF THE SENATE" IN THE TREATY-MAKING PROCESS. Washington, D.C.: U.S. Library of Congress, 1969. 50 p.

_____. THE TREATY-MAKING POWER IN THE CONSTITUTION: A SUMMARY OF THE HISTORY RELATING TO THE NON-INCLUSION OF THE HOUSE OF REPRESENTATIVES. Washington, D.C.: U.S. Library of Congress, 1967. 20 p.

Crandall, Samuel B. TREATIES, THEIR MAKING AND ENFORCEMENT. New York: Columbia University Studies in History, Economics, and Public Law, 1904. 2d ed. Washington, D.C.: Byrne, 1916. 663 p.

Dangerfield, Royden J. IN DEFENSE OF THE SENATE: A STUDY IN TREATY-MAKING. Norman: University of Oklahoma Press, 1933. 365 p. Bibliog.

Davis, John William. THE TREATY-MAKING POWER IN THE UNITED STATES. London: Oxford University Press, 1920. 18 p.

Dean, Arthur H. "The Bricker Amendment and Authority Over Foreign Affairs." FOREIGN AFFAIRS 32 (October 1953): 1-19.

Devlin, Robert T. THE TREATY POWER UNDER THE CONSTITUTION OF THE UNITED STATES. San Francisco: Bancroft-Whitney, 1908. 864 p.

Deyrup, Thorold J. "Executive Agreements Under the Bricker Amendment." SOCIAL RESEARCH 20 (Winter 1953): 379-98.

Dickey, John S. "Our Treaty Procedure Versus Our Foreign Policies." FOREIGN AFFAIRS 25 (April 1947): 357-77.

Dillard, Hardy C. "The Treaty-Making Controversy: Substance and Shadow." VIRGINIA QUARTERLY REVIEW 30 (Spring 1954): 178-91.

Dulles, John Foster. "The Making of Treaties and Executive Agreements." DEPARTMENT OF STATE BULLETIN 28 (20 April 1953): 591-95.

Elias, Taslim Olawale. THE MODERN LAW OF TREATIES. Dobbs Ferry, N.Y.: Oceana, 1974. 272 p. Bibliog.

Feidler, Ernest R., and Dwan, Ralph H. "The Extent of the Treaty-Making Power." GEORGETOWN LAW JOURNAL 28 (November 1939): 184-97.

Finch, George A. "The Need to Restrain the Treaty-Making Power of the United States Within Constitutional Limits." AMERICAN JOURNAL OF INTERNATIONAL LAW 48 (January 1954): 57-82.

Fitzpatrick, W.H. "Government by Treaty." VITAL SPEECES 16 (1 August 1950): 633-35.

Fleming, Denna F. "The Advice of the Senate in Treaty Making." CURRENT HISTORY 32 (April-September 1930): 1090-94.

_____. "The Role of the Senate in Treaty-Making: A Survey of Four Decades." AMERICAN POLITICAL SCIENCE REVIEW 28 (August 1934): 583-98.

_____. THE TREATY VETO OF THE AMERICAN SENATE. New York: Putnam, 1930. 325 p.

Forkusch, M.D. "Treaties and Executive Agreements." CHICAGO-KENT LAW REVIEW 32 (June 1954): 201-25.

Foster, John W. "The Treaty-Making Power Under the Constitution." YALE LAW JOURNAL 11 (December 1901): 69-79.

Fraser, Henry S. "Constitutional Scope of Treaties and Executive Agreements." AMERICAN BAR ASSOCIATION JOURNAL 31 (June 1945): 286-89.

Garner, James W. "Acts and Joint Resolutions of Congress as Substitutions for Treaties." AMERICAN JOURNAL OF INTERNATIONAL LAW 29 (July 1935): 482-88.

Harris, Lester. "Treaties Under the Constitution and International Law." DICKINSON LAW REVIEW 54 (June 1950): 417-31.

Harvard Research in International Law. "The Law of Treaties." AMERICAN JOURNAL OF INTERNATIONAL LAW 29 (October 1935): supplement, 653-1240. Bibliog. (pp. 671-85).

Hawkins, Harry Calvin. COMMERCIAL TREATIES AND AGREEMENTS: PRINCIPLES AND PRACTICE. New York: Rinehart, 1951. 254 p.

Hayden, Ralson. THE SENATE AND TREATIES, 1789-1817. New York: Macmillan, 1920. 237 p. Bibliog.

Hendry, James McCleod. TREATIES AND FEDERAL CONSTITUTIONS. Washington, D.C.: Public Affairs, 1955. 186 p.

Henkin, Louis. "Treaty Makers and the Law Makers: The Law of the Land and Foreign Relations." UNIVERSITY OF PENNSYLVANIA LAW REVIEW 107 (May 1959): 903-36.

Herter, Christian A. "Relation of the House of Representatives to the Making and Implementing of Treaties." PROCEEDINGS OF THE AMERICAN SOCIETY OF INTERNATIONAL LAW, 1951, pp. 55-65.

Hill, Sidney B. "Treaty Making Power of the United States: A Bibliographical Guide." THE RECORD (of the Association of the Bar of the City of New York) 9 (February 1954): 1-23.

Holloway, Kaye. MODERN TRENDS IN TREATY LAW. Dobbs Ferry, N.Y.: Oceana, 1967. 737 p. Bibliog.

Holman, Frank E. "Need for a Constitutional Amendment on Treaties and Executive Agreements." WASHINGTON UNIVERSITY LAW QUARTERLY, December 1955, pp. 340-54.

_____. STORY OF THE "BRICKER" AMENDMENT. New York: Committee for Constitutional Government, 1954. 179 p. Bibliog.

Holt, W. Stull. TREATIES DEFEATED BY THE SENATE. Baltimore: Johns Hopkins Press, 1933. Reprint. Gloucester, Mass.: Smith, 1964. 328 p. Bibliog.

Hoyt, Edwin C. THE UNANIMITY RULE IN THE REVISION OF TREATIES: A REEXAMINATION. The Hague: Nijhoff, 1959. 264 p. Bibliog.

Hudson, Manley O. "The 'Injunction of Secrecy' With Respect to American Treaties." AMERICAN JOURNAL OF INTERNATIONAL LAW 23 (April 1929): 329-35.

Hyde, Charles C. "Agreements of the United States Other Than Treaties." THE GREEN BAG 17 (April 1905): 229-38.

Johnson, Loch, and McCormick, James M. "The Making of International Agreements: A Reappraisal of Congressional Involvement." JOURNAL OF POLITICS 40 (May 1978): 468-78.

Jones, John Mervyn. "Constitutional Limitations on the Treatymaking Power." AMERICAN JOURNAL OF INTERNATIONAL LAW 35 (July 1941): 462-81.

_____. FULL POWERS AND RATIFICATION: A STUDY IN THE DEVELOPMENT OF TREATY-MAKING PROCEDURE. Cambridge, Mass.: Harvard University Press, 1946. 182 p.

Law, Alton D. INTERNATIONAL COMMODITY AGREEMENTS: SETTING, PERFORMANCE AND PROSPECTS. Lexington, Mass.: Lexington Books, 1975. 144 p.

Layton, Robert. "The Effect of Measures Short of War on Treaties." UNIVERSITY OF CHICAGO LAW REVIEW 30 (Autumn 1962): 96-119.

Lesser, Stanley T. "Treaty Provisions Dealing with the Status of Pre-War Bilateral Treaties." MICHIGAN LAW REVIEW 51 (February 1953): 573-82.

Levitan, David M. "Constitutional Developments in the Control of Foreign Affairs: A Quest for Democratic Control." JOURNAL OF POLITICS 7 (February 1945): 58-92.

_____. "Executive Agreements: A Study of the Executive in the Control of the Foreign Relations of the United States." ILLINOIS LAW REVIEW 35 (December 1940): 365-95.

Linthicum, J.C. "The Committee on Foreign Affairs of the House of Representatives and the Treaty-Making Power." In PROCEEDINGS OF THE AMERICAN SOCIETY OF INTERNATIONAL LAW, pp. 249-56. Washington, D.C.: American Society of International Law, 1932.

Lodge, Henry Cabot. THE SENATE AND THE LEAGUE OF NATIONS. New York: Scribner, 1925. 424 p.

MacBridge, Roger L. TREATIES VERSUS THE CONSTITUTION. Caldwell, Idaho: Caxton, 1955. 89 p.

McClendon, R. Earl. "Origin of the Two-Thirds Rule in Senate Action Upon Treaties." AMERICAN HISTORICAL REVIEW 36 (July 1931): 768-72.

_____. "The Two-Thirds Rule in Senate Action Upon Treaties, 1789-1901." AMERICAN JOURNAL OF INTERNATIONAL LAW 26 (January 1932): 37-56.

McClure, Wallace M. INTERNATIONAL EXECUTIVE AGREEMENTS: DEMOCRATIC PROCEDURE UNDER THE CONSTITUTION OF THE UNITED STATES. New York: Columbia University Press, 1941. 449 p. Bibliog.

McDougal, Myres [S.], and Lans, Asher. "Treaties and Congressional-Executive or Presidential Agreements: Interchangeable Instruments of National Policy." YALE LAW JOURNAL 54 (March and June 1945): 181-351, 534-615. Also in STUDIES IN WORLD PUBLIC ORDER by Myres S. McDougal et al., pp. 404-717. New Haven, Conn.: Yale University Press, 1960.

McLaughlin, C.H. "The Scope of the Treaty Power in the United States." MINNESOTA LAW REVIEW 42 (April 1958): 709-71, and 43 (March 1959): 651-725.

McNair, Arnold D. THE LAW OF TREATIES. Oxford: Clarendon, 1961. 789 p.

Mathews, Craig. "The Constitutional Power of the President to Conclude International Agreements." YALE LAW JOURNAL 64 (January 1955): 345-89.

Mathews, John M. "The Treaty Making Power: General Principles," "The Treaty Making Power: Practical Operation," and "Agreement Making Power." In his AMERICAN FOREIGN RELATIONS: CONDUCT AND POLICIES, pp. 495-548. Rev. ed. New York: Appleton-Century-Crofts, 1938.

Mikell, William E. "The Extent of the Treatymaking Power of the United States of America." UNIVERSITY OF PENNSYLVANIA LAW REVIEW 57 (April 1909): 435-58.

Morley, Felix. TREATY LAW AND THE CONSTITUTION: A STUDY OF THE BRICKER AMENDMENT. Washington, D.C.: American Enterprise Association, 1953. 52 p.

Nelson, Randall H. "Legislative Participation in the Treaty and Agreement Making Process." WESTERN POLITICAL QUARTERLY 13 (March 1960): 154-71.

Oliver, Covey T. "Treaties, the Senate, and the Constitution: Some Current Questions." AMERICAN JOURNAL OF INTERNATIONAL LAW 51 (July 1957): 606-11.

Phleger, Herman. UNITED STATES TREATIES: RECENT DEVELOPMENTS. Washington, D.C.: Government Printing Office, 1956. 20 p.

Plischke, Elmer. "Treaty-Making." In his INTERNATIONAL RELATIONS: BASIC DOCUMENTS, pp. 24-37. 2d ed. Princeton, N.J.: Van Nostrand, 1962.

_____. "Treaty-Making," "Executive Agreements," and "Execution, Interpretation, and Termination of Treaties and Agreements." In his CONDUCT OF AMERICAN DIPLOMACY, pp. 370-468. 3d ed. Princeton, N.J.: Van Nostrand, 1967.

Potter, Pitman B. "Inhibitions Upon the Treaty-Making Power of the United States." AMERICAN JOURNAL OF INTERNATIONAL LAW 28 (July 1934): 456-74.

Preuss, Lawrence. "On Amending the Treaty-Making Power: A Comparative Study of the Problem of Self-Executing Treaties." MICHIGAN LAW REVIEW 51 (June 1953): 1117-42.

Reiff, Henry. "The Proclaiming of Treaties in the United States." AMERICAN JOURNAL OF INTERNATIONAL LAW 30 (January 1936): 63-79.

_____. "The Proclaiming of Treaties in the United States." AMERICAN JOURNAL OF INTERNATIONAL LAW 44 (July 1950): 572-76.

Richberg, Donald R. "The Bricker Amendment and the Treaty Power." VIRGINIA LAW REVIEW 39 (October 1953): 753-64.

Sayre, Francis B. "The Constitutionality of the Trade Agreements Act." COLUMBIA LAW REVIEW 39 (May 1939): 751-75.

_____. HOW TRADE AGREEMENTS ARE MADE. Department of State Publication, no. 1152. Washington, D.C.: Government Printing Office, 1938. 16 p.

_____. "How Trade Agreements Are Made." FOREIGN AFFAIRS 16 (April 1938): 417-29.

_____. THE WAY FORWARD: THE AMERICAN TRADE AGREEMENTS AND PROGRAMS. New York: Macmillan, 1939. 230 p.

Schubert, Glendon A., Jr. "Politics and the Constitution: The Bricker Amendment During 1953." JOURNAL OF POLITICS 16 (May 1954): 257-98.

Simpson, William H. "Legal Aspects of Executive Agreements." IOWA LAW REVIEW 24 (November 1938): 67-88.

_____. The Use of Executive Agreements in the Settlement of International Reclamation." DETROIT LAW REVIEW 8 (June 1938): 23-28.

Sinclair, Ian McTaggert. THE VIENNA CONVENTION OF THE LAW OF TREATIES. Dobbs Ferry, N.Y.: Oceana, 1973. 150 p.

Sinha, Bhek Pati. UNILATERAL DENUNCIATION OF TREATY BECAUSE OF PRIOR VIOLATIONS OF OBLIGATIONS BY OTHER PARTY. The Hague: Nijhoff, 1966. 232 p. Bibliog.

Sprout, Harold H. "The Storm Center in Treaty-Making." AMERICAN SCHOLAR 7 (Spring 1938): 211-22.

Sutherland, Arthur E., Jr. "The Flag, the Constitution, and International Agreements." HARVARD LAW REVIEW 68 (June 1955): 1374-81.

_____. "Restricting the Treaty Power." HARVARD LAW REVIEW 65 (June 1952): 1305-38.

Tansill, Charles C. "The Treaty-Making Power of the Senate." AMERICAN JOURNAL OF INTERNATIONAL LAW 18 (July 1924): 459-82.

Tobin, Harold J. THE TERMINATION OF MULTIPARTITE TREATIES. New York: Columbia University Studies in the Social Sciences, 1933. 323 p.

Todd, Harry S. "The President's Power to Make International Agreements." CONSTITUTIONAL REVIEW 11 (July 1927): 160-73.

Toscano, Mario. THE HISTORY OF TREATIES AND INTERNATIONAL POLITICS: THE DOCUMENTARY AND MEMOIR SOURCES. Baltimore: Johns Hopkins Press, 1966. 685 p.

Part 1 on sources and part 2 on publication of the sources.

Trani, Eugene Paul. THE TREATY OF PORTSMOUTH: AN ADVENTURE IN AMERICAN DIPLOMACY. Lexington: University of Kentucky Press, 1969. 194 p.

_____. "The Treaty of Portsmouth: An Adventure in Rooseveltian Diplomacy." Ph.D. dissertation, Indiana University, 1966. 220 p.

"Treaties and Executive Agreements." PROCEEDINGS OF THE AMERICAN SOCIETY OF INTERNATIONAL LAW, 1977, pp. 235-58.

Comments by Monroe Leigh, James T. Scholbert, Michael J. Glennon, Richard R. Baxter, Arthur W. Rovine, and Thomas M. Franck from a 1977 symposium in San Francisco.

"Treaty Process." CONGRESSIONAL DIGEST 28 (June 1949): 168-75.

Tucker, Henry St. George. LIMITATIONS ON THE TREATY-MAKING POWER UNDER THE CONSTITUTION OF THE UNITED STATES. Boston: Little, Brown, 1915. 444 p.

U.S. Congress. Senate. Committee on Foreign Relations. INTERNATIONAL AGREEMENTS: AN ANALYSIS OF EXECUTIVE REGULATIONS AND PRACTICES. Committee Print. 95th Cong., 1st sess. Washington, D.C.: Government Printing Office, 1977. 73 p.

_____. THE ROLE OF THE SENATE IN TREATY RATIFICATION: A STAFF MEMORANDUM TO THE COMMITTEE ON FOREIGN RELATIONS. Committee Print. 95th Cong., 1st sess. Washington, D.C.: Government Printing Office, 1977. 78 p.

U.S. Department of State. COMMERCIAL TREATY PROGRAM OF THE UNITED STATES. Washington, D.C.: 1958. 8 p.

Webb, R.E. "Treaty-Making and the President's Obligation to Seek the Advice and Consent of the Senate with Special Reference to the Vietnam Peace Negotiation." OHIO STATE LAW JOURNAL 31 (Summer 1970): 490-515.

Whittington, William V. THE MAKING OF TREATIES AND INTERNATIONAL AGREEMENTS AND THE WORK OF THE TREATY DIVISION OF THE DEPARTMENT OF STATE. Washington, D.C.: Government Printing Office, 1938. 33 p.

    Address delivered to Conference of Teachers of International Law, 29 April 1938.

Whitton, John B., and Fowler, J. Edward. "Bricker Amendment: Fallacies and Dangers." AMERICAN JOURNAL OF INTERNATIONAL LAW 48 (January 1954): 25-56.

Wiktor, Christian L. UNPERFECTED TREATIES OF THE UNITED STATES OF AMERICA. 5 vols. to date. Dobbs Ferry, N.Y.: Oceana, 1976-- .

Wilcox, Francis O. THE RATIFICATION OF INTERNATIONAL CONVENTIONS. London: Allen and Unwin, 1935. 349 p. Bibliog.

Williams, Benjamin H. "Treaties and Executive Agreements." In his AMERICAN DIPLOMACY: POLICIES AND PRACTICE, pp. 425-49. New York: McGraw-Hill, 1936.

Wilson, Robert R. THE INTERNATIONAL LAW STANDARD IN TREATIES OF THE UNITED STATES. Cambridge, Mass.: Harvard University Press, 1953. 321 p.

Wright, Quincy. "Congress and the Treaty-Making Power." PROCEEDINGS OF THE AMERICAN SOCIETY OF INTERNATIONAL LAW 46 (April 1952): 43-58.

    . "The Constitutionality of Treaties." AMERICAN JOURNAL OF INTERNATIONAL LAW 13 (April 1919): 242-66.

    . "The Power to Make International Agreements." In his THE CONTROL OF AMERICAN FOREIGN RELATIONS, pp. 230-62. New York: Macmillan, 1922.

    . "Treaties and the Constitutional Separation of Powers in the United States." AMERICAN JOURNAL OF INTERNATIONAL LAW 12 (January 1918): 64-95.

_____. "The United States and International Agreements." AMERICAN JOURNAL OF INTERNATIONAL LAW 38 (July 1944): 341-55.

_____. "The United States and International Agreements." INTERNATIONAL CONCILIATION, no. 411 (May 1945): 379-98.

Official commentary on the legal and political aspects of treaty making, both internal and international, is provided in the following:

Hackworth, Green H. DIGEST OF INTERNATIONAL LAW. Washington, D.C.: Government Printing Office, 1942. Vol. 5, Chapter 16, pp. 1-433.

Moore, John Bassett. A DIGEST OF INTERNATIONAL LAW. Washington, D.C.: Government Printing Office, 1906. Vol. 5, pp. 155-387.

Whiteman, Marjorie M. DIGEST OF INTERNATIONAL LAW. Washington, D.C.: Government Printing Office, 1970. Vol. 14, Chapter 42, pp. 1-510.

TRADE AND AID

Literature and other resources on trade and aid are freely available, ranging from general, broad-scale to more finite and specialized analyses. Most of the materials listed below have been published since World War II, and they are primarily monographs on policy, administration, programs, and issues relating to foreign trade and commerce, economic development and technical assistance, the Hull Trade Agreements, Lend-Lease, the Marshall Plan, Point Four, AID, the Peace Corps, the Alliance for Progress, U.S. relations with the General Agreement on Tariffs and Trade (GATT), and other aspects of foreign economic relations.

Earlier policy and developments are treated in the pre-World War I studies of Kropotkin (1902), Schuyler (1886), and Washburne (1905); the interwar analyses of Buell, Culbertson, Sayre, and Snyder; as well as others concerned with the Hull Trade Agreements program--Chu and Schatz. Those of Herring and Stettinius deal specifically with the World War II Lend-Lease program. Most publications since 1945, however, deal either with general policy and programmatic affairs or with particular aspects or types of aid and assistance. These include, for example, studies on the Marshall Plan (Arkes, Edelstein, Harriman, Price, T. Wilson, and Winham), the Truman Doctrine (Weiner), Point Four (Curti and Kendall, Daniels, and Warne), technical assistance (Beaulac, Byrnes, Domergue, and Poats), the Kennedy Round (Evans, Preeg), the Tokyo Round (Cline), the Peace Corps (Balzano, Fuchs, Hapgood, and Lowther and Lucas), and the Alliance for Progress (Douglas Brown, Dreier, Levinson and de Onis, and Rogers). An increasing number of authors, including the writers of a good many doctoral dissertations, elect to develop case studies in this field, represented by Dawson (Russia); Beaulac, Deaton, Frederick, Jaquette, and Stottlemire (Latin America); Jordan, Martin, Montgomery, Stillman,

Van Wagoner, and Wolf (Asia); and Doku and McMurtry (Africa). Several studies review the role of Congress, including Barrie, Leu, Mangan, and Scowcroft. A few, addressing themselves to special considerations, may be worthy of note, such as Brady's study of the USAID adviser and Snyder's analysis of the most-favored-nation principle.

For probing studies of general U.S. economic policy, the international banks and development associations, other multilateral financial institutions, commercial development, relations with the developing countries, and the nature, problems, and management of multinational and transnational corporations, a wealth of additional sources are available and need to be consulted.

Some additional bibliographical guidance is available in the following:

Amstutz, Mark R., ed. ECONOMICS AND FOREIGN POLICY: A GUIDE TO INFORMATION SOURCES. International Relations Information Guide Series, vol. 7. Detroit: Gale Research Co., 1977. 179 p.

Hazelwood, Arthur. THE ECONOMICS OF DEVELOPMENT: AN ANNOTATED LIST OF BOOKS AND ARTICLES PUBLISHED 1958-1962. London: Oxford University Press, 1964. 104 p.

U.S. Department of State. Division of Library and Reference Services. POINT FOUR, FAR EAST: A SELECTED BIBLIOGRAPHY OF STUDIES ON ECONOMICALLY UNDERDEVELOPED COUNTRIES. Bibliography, no. 57. Washington, D.C.: 1951. 46 p.

U.S. Library of Congress. Reference Service. A COLLECTION OF EXCERPTS AND A BIBLIOGRAPHY RELATIVE TO UNITED STATES FOREIGN AID. Senate Document No. 62, 85th Cong., 1st sess. Washington, D.C.: Government Printing Office, 1957. 39 p. Bibliog., pp. 35-39.

_____ . WHAT SHOULD BE THE FOREIGN AID POLICY OF THE UNITED STATES? A COLLECTION OF EXCERPTS AND A BIBLIOGRAPHY RELATIVE TO UNITED STATES FOREIGN AID. Senate Document No. 89, 89th Cong., 2d sess. Washington, D.C.: Government Printing Office, 1966. 261 p. Bibliog., pp. 247-61.

Adams, Frederick C. ECONOMIC DIPLOMACY: THE EXPORT-IMPORT BANK AND AMERICAN FOREIGN POLICY, 1934-1939. Columbia: Missouri University Press, 1976. 289 p. Bibliog.

Arkes, Hadley. BUREAUCRACY, THE MARSHALL PLAN, AND THE NATIONAL INTEREST. Princeton, N.J.: Princeton University Press, 1973. 395 p. Bibliog.

Arnold, Harry J.P. AID FOR DEVELOPMENT. Chester Spring, Pa.: Dufour, 1966. 256 p.

Asher, Robert E. DEVELOPMENT ASSISTANCE IN THE SEVENTIES: ALTERNATIVES FOR THE UNITED STATES. Washington, D.C.: Brookings Institution, 1970. 248 p.

Atlantic Council of the United States. GATT PLUS--A PROPOSAL FOR TRADE REFORM: WITH THE TEXT OF THE GENERAL AGREEMENT. New York: Praeger, 1976. 208 p.

Baldwin, David A. ECONOMIC DEVELOPMENT AND AMERICAN FOREIGN POLICY, 1943-1962. Chicago: University of Chicago Press, 1966. 291 p. Bibliog.

_____. FOREIGN AID AND AMERICAN FOREIGN POLICY: A DOCUMENTARY ANALYSIS. New York: Praeger, 1966. 261 p. Bibliog.

Especially chapter 7.

Balzano, Michael P. THE PEACE CORPS: MYTHS AND PROSPECTS. Washington, D.C.: American Enterprise Institute, 1978. 21 p.

Banfield, Edward C. AMERICAN FOREIGN AID DOCTRINES. Washington, D.C.: American Enterprise Institute, 1963. 69 p. Bibliog.

Baranyai, Leopold, and Mills, J.C. INTERNATIONAL COMMODITY AGREEMENTS. New York: Committee for Economic Development, 1963. 190 p. Bibliog.

Barrie, Robert Wesley. "Congress and the Executive: The Making of U.S. Foreign Trade Policy." Ph.D. dissertation, University of Minnesota, 1968. 352 p.

Bauer, Raymond A.; Pool, Ithiel de Sola; and Dexter, Louis A. AMERICAN BUSINESS AND PUBLIC POLICY: THE POLITICS OF FOREIGN TRADE. 2d ed. Chicago: Aldine-Atherton, 1972. 499 p. Bibliog.

Beaulac, Willard L. A DIPLOMAT LOOKS AT AID TO LATIN AMERICA. Carbondale: Southern Illinois University Press, 1970. 148 p.

_____. "Technical Cooperation as an Instrument of Foreign Policy--No Substitute for Traditional Diplomacy." DEPARTMENT OF STATE BULLETIN 32 (13 June 1955): 964-69.

Benham, Frederic. ECONOMIC AID TO UNDERDEVELOPED COUNTRIES. New York: Oxford University Press, 1961. 121 p.

Bergsten, C. Fred, and Krause, Lawrence B. WORLD POLITICS AND INTER-NATIONAL ECONOMICS. Washington, D.C.: Brookings Institution, 1975. 359 p. Bibliog.

Bhatachurya, Anindya K. FOREIGN TRADE AND INTERNATIONAL DEVELOP-MENT. Lexington, Mass.: Lexington, 1976. 107 p.

Bingham, Jonathan B. SHIRT-SLEEVE DIPLOMACY: POINT 4 IN ACTION. New York: Day, 1954. 303 p.

Black, Eugene R. THE DIPLOMACY OF ECONOMIC DEVELOPMENT. Cambridge, Mass.: Harvard University Press, 1960. 74 p.

Black, Lloyd D. THE STRATEGY OF FOREIGN AID. New York: Van Nostrand, 1968. 176 p.

Blessing, James A. "The Cut-Off of Foreign Aid by the United States: A Survey and Analysis." Ph.D. dissertation, State University of New York (Albany), 1975. 261 p.

Bonello, Frank, and Swartz, Thomas, eds. ALTERNATIVE DIRECTIONS IN ECONOMIC POLICY. Notre Dame, Ind.: University of Notre Dame Press, 1978. 183 p.

Brady, James Reginald. "Problems of Implementing American Foreign Assistance Projects: Perceptions of the USAID Advisor." Ph.D. dissertation, University of Michigan, 1971. 294 p.

Brookstone, Jeffrey M. THE MULTINATIONAL BUSINESSMAN AND FOREIGN POLICY: ENTREPRENEURIAL POLITICS IN EAST-WEST TRADE AND INVEST-MENT. New York: Praeger, 1976. 183 p. Bibliog.

Brown, Douglas A. "Three Perspectives on U.S. Foreign Aid: Explaining the Alliance for Progress." Ph.D. dissertation, University of Oregon, 1974. 195 p.

Brown, George Thompson, Jr. "Foreign Policy Legitimation: The Case of American Foreign Aid, 1947-1971." Ph.D. dissertation, University of Virginia, 1971. 429 p.

Brown, Lester Russell. SEEDS OF CHANGE: THE GREEN REVOLUTION AND DEVELOPMENT IN THE 1970S. New York: Praeger, 1970. 205 p. Bibliog.

Brown, William Adams, and Opie, Redvers. AMERICAN FOREIGN ASSIS-TANCE. Washington, D.C.: Brookings Institution, 1953. 615 p. Bibliog.

Buchanan, Norman S., and Ellis, Howard S. APPROACHES TO ECONOMIC DEVELOPMENT. New York: Twentieth Century Fund, 1955. 494 p.

Buell, Raymond Leslie. THE HULL TRADE AGREEMENT PROGRAM AND THE AMERICAN SYSTEM. New York: Foreign Policy Association, 1938. 45 p.

Byrnes, Francis C. AMERICANS IN TECHNICAL ASSISTANCE: A STUDY OF ATTITUDES AND RESPONSES TO THEIR ROLE ABROAD. New York: Praeger, 1965. 156 p.

Calleo, David P., and Rowland, Benjamin M[oore]. AMERICA AND THE WORLD POLITICAL ECONOMY: ATLANTIC DREAMS AND NATIONAL REALITIES. Bloomington: Indiana University Press, 1973. 371 p. Bibliog.

Cardozo, Michael H. DIPLOMATS IN INTERNATIONAL COOPERATION: STEPCHILDREN OF THE FOREIGN SERVICE. Ithaca, N.Y.: Cornell University Press, 1962. 142 p.

Castle, Eugene W. BILLIONS, BLUNDERS AND BALONEY. New York: Devin-Adair, 1955. 278 p.

On foreign aid programs in the 1950s.

Chasteen, Robert James. "American Foreign Aid and Public Opinion, 1945-1952." Ph.D. dissertation, University of North Carolina (Chapel Hill), 1958. 425 p.

Chu, Power Yung-Chao. "A History of the Hull Trade Program, 1934-1939." Ph.D. dissertation, Columbia University, 1957. 443 p.

Cline, William R., et al. TRADE NEGOTIATIONS IN THE TOKYO ROUND: A QUANTITATIVE ASSESSMENT. Washington, D.C.: Brookings Institution, 1978. 314 p.

Coffin, Frank M. WITNESS FOR AID. Boston: Houghton Mifflin, 1964. 273 p.

Cohen, Benjamin J., ed. AMERICAN FOREIGN ECONOMIC POLICY. New York: Harper and Row, 1968. 442 p. Bibliog.

Committee for Economic Development. TRADE POLICY TOWARD LOW-INCOME COUNTRIES. New York: 1967. 44 p.

Coutris, Andreas Nicolaos. "Government Policy-Making and Economic Development." Ph.D. dissertation, Howard University, 1975. 197 p.

Crook, Elizabeth Fletcher. "Political Development as a Program Objective of U.S. Foreign Assistance: Title IX of the 1966 Foreign Assistance Act." Ph.D. dissertation, Tufts University, Fletcher School, 1970. 336 p.

Culbertson, William Smith. INTERNATIONAL ECONOMIC POLICIES: A SURVEY OF THE ECONOMICS OF DIPLOMACY. New York: Appleton, 1925. 575 p.

_____. RECIPROCITY: A NATIONAL POLICY FOR FOREIGN TRADE. New York: Whittlesey House and McGraw-Hill, 1937. 298 p.

Curti, Merle E., and Kendall, Birr. PRELUDE TO POINT FOUR: AMERICAN TECHNICAL MISSIONS OVERSEAS, 1838-1938. Madison: University of Wisconsin Press, 1954. 284 p.

Daniels, Walter M., ed. THE POINT FOUR PROGRAM. New York: Wilson, 1951. 207 p. Bibliog.

Darken, Arthur Humbert. "The Struggle Over Foreign Aid: Major Issues and Competing Theories in the Formulation of United States Foreign Aid Policy." Ph.D. dissertation, Columbia University, 1964. 358 p.

Dawson, Raymond H. THE DECISION TO AID RUSSIA, 1941: FOREIGN POLICY AND DOMESTIC POLITICS. Chapel Hill: University of North Carolina Press, 1959. 315 p. Bibliog.

Deaton, Ronny H. "The Impact of United States Private Investment, Aid, and Trade Policies Toward Brazil During the Alliance for Progress." Ph.D. dissertation, University of Kansas, 1973. 274 p.

Denoon, David B.H. "Aid: High Politics, Technocracy, or Farce?" Ph.D. dissertation, M.I.T., 1975.

Diebold, William, Jr. DOLLARS, JOBS, TRADE AND AID. Headline Series, no. 213. New York: Foreign Policy Association, 1972. 71 p. Bibliog.

_____. THE UNITED STATES AND THE INDUSTRIAL WORLD. New York: Praeger, 1972. 463 p.

Doku, Maurice Kojo. "Economics, Foreign Aid, and Foreign Policy: Case Studies in Three Contiguous West African Countries." Ph.D. dissertation, Claremont Graduate School, 1972. 138 p.

Domergue, Maurice. TECHNICAL ASSISTANCE: THEORY, PRACTICE, AND POLICIES. New York: Praeger, 1968. 196 p. Bibliog.

Dreier, John C. THE ALLIANCE FOR PROGRESS: PROBLEMS AND PERSPEC-
TIVES. Baltimore: Johns Hopkins Press, 1962. 146 p.

Edelstein, Alex S. "The Marshall Plan Information Program in Western Europe
as an Instrument of United States Foreign Policy, 1948-1952." Ph.D. dissertation, University of Minnesota, 1958. 468 p.

Erasmus, Charles J. MAN TAKES CONTROL: CULTURAL DEVELOPMENT
AND AMERICAN AID. Minneapolis: University of Minnesota Press, 1961.
365 p. Bibliog.

Erickson, Bonnie H. INTERNATIONAL NETWORKS: THE STRUCTURED WEBS
OF DIPLOMACY AND TRADE. Beverly Hills, Calif.: Sage, 1975. 56 p.

Esterline, John H., and Black, Robert B. INSIDE FOREIGN POLICY: THE
DEPARTMENT OF STATE POLITICAL SYSTEM AND ITS SUBSYSTEMS. Palo
Alto, Calif.: Mayfield, 1975.

    Chapters 8-9 on AID and foreign assistance.

Evans, John W. THE KENNEDY ROUND IN AMERICAN TRADE POLICY:
THE TWILIGHT OF THE GATT? Cambridge, Mass.: Harvard University Press,
1971. 383 p. Bibliog.

Feis, Herbert. FOREIGN AID AND FOREIGN POLICY. New York: St.
Martin's, 1964. 246 p.

Ferkiss, Victor C. FOREIGN AID: MORAL AND POLITICAL ASPECTS.
Special Studies, no. 110. New York: Council on Religion and International
Affairs, 1965. 48 p.

Foreign Policy Association. UNDERSTANDING FOREIGN AID. New York:
1963. 63 p.

Fraenkel, Richard; Hadwinger, Don Frank; and Browne, William P., eds.
AMERICAN AGRICULTURE AND U.S. FOREIGN POLICY. New York: Praeger, 1979. 206 p.

Frank, Charles R., Jr. FOREIGN TRADE AND DOMESTIC AID. Washington,
D.C.: Brookings Institution, 1977. 180 p.

Frederick, Richard Gordon. "United States Foreign Aid to Bolivia, 1953-1972."
Ph.D. dissertation, University of Maryland, 1976. 316 p. Bibliog.

Fuchs, Lawrence H. "THOSE PECULIAR AMERICANS": THE PEACE CORPS
AND AMERICAN NATIONAL CHARACTER. New York: Meredith, 1967.
232 p.

Gardner, Lloyd C. ECONOMIC ASPECTS OF NEW DEAL DIPLOMACY. Madison: University of Wisconsin Press, 1964. 409 p. Bibliog.

Gardner, Richard N. STERLING-DOLLAR DIPLOMACY IN CURRENT PERSPECTIVE. 3d ed. New York: Columbia University Press, 1980. 480 p.

George, James Herbert, Jr. "United States Postwar Relief Planning: The First Phase, 1940-1943." Ph.D. dissertation, University of Wisconsin, 1970. 347 p.

Goldwin, Robert A., ed. WHY FOREIGN AID? Chicago: Rand McNally, 1963. 140 p.

Gustafson, Milton Odell. "Congress and Foreign Aid: The First Phase, 1943-1947." Ph.D. dissertation, University of Nebraska, 1966. 326 p.

Hapgood, David, and Bennett, Meridian. AGENTS OF CHANGE: A CLOSE LOOK AT THE PEACE CORPS. Boston: Little, Brown, 1968. 244 p.

Harriman, W. Averell. UNITED STATES PRESIDENT'S COMMITTEE ON FOREIGN AID: EUROPEAN RECOVERY AND AMERICAN AID--A REPORT. Washington, D.C.: Government Printing Office, 1947. 286 p.

Hartmann, Christian David. "Local Currency Programs and United States Foreign Policies." Ph.D. dissertation, Columbia University, 1962. 570 p.

Hayes, Louis Dean. "Policy Making and Problem Perception: The 1965 Foreign Assistance Act." Ph.D. dissertation, University of Arizona, 1966. 278 p.

Hayter, Teresa. AID AS IMPERIALISM. Baltimore: Penguin, 1971. 222 p. Bibliog.

Herring, George Cyril, Jr. "Experiment in Foreign Aid: Lend-Lease, 1941-1945." Ph.D. dissertation, University of Virginia, 1965. 494 p.

Heusman, Charles Richard. RICH AGAINST POOR: THE REALITY OF AID. Baltimore: Penguin, 1975. 293 p.

Hoffman, Paul G. "The Role of the Economic Cooperation Administration in National Administration." In INTERNATIONAL COMMITMENTS AND NATIONAL ADMINISTRATION, pp. 73-90. Charlottesville, Va.: Bureau of Public Administration, University of Virginia, 1949.

Hudson, Michael. SUPER IMPERIALISM: THE ECONOMIC STRATEGY OF AMERICAN EMPIRE. New York: Holt, Rinehart and Winston, 1972. 304 p.

Hunter, Robert E., and Rielly, John E., eds. DEVELOPMENT TODAY: A NEW LOOK AT U.S. RELATIONS WITH THE POOR COUNTRIES. New York: Praeger, 1972. 286 p. Bibliog.

Seminar papers presented to Overseas Development Council.

Jameson, Kenneth, and Skurski, Roger. U.S. TRADE IN THE SIXTIES AND SEVENTIES. Lexington, Mass.: Lexington Books, 1974. 137 p. Bibliog.

Jaquette, Jane. "The Impact of the U.S. on Peruvian Development Policy." Ph.D. dissertation, Cornell University, 1971. 314 p.

Jordan, Amos A., Jr. FOREIGN AID AND THE DEFENSE OF SOUTHEAST ASIA. New York: Praeger, 1962. 272 p.

Kaplan, Jacob. THE CHALLENGE OF FOREIGN AID. New York: Praeger, 1967. 405 p.

Kato, Masakatsu. "U.S. Aid and Economic Development: A Comparative Analysis of the Priority of the Development Goal." Ph.D. dissertation, University of Rochester, 1976. 76 p.

Kenen, Peter B. GIANT AMONG NATIONS: PROBLEMS IN UNITED STATES FOREIGN ECONOMIC POLICY. Chicago: Rand McNally, 1963. 249 p. Bibliog.

Kim, Young Hum. "Technical Assistance Programs of the United Nations and of the United States: A Comparative Study." Ph.D. dissertation, University of Southern California, 1961. 454 p.

Kimball, Warren Forbes. "'The Most Unsordid Act': Lend-Lease, 1941." Ph.D. dissertation, Georgetown University, 1968. 549 p.

_____. THE MOST UNSORDID ACT: LEND-LEASE, 1939-1941. Baltimore: Johns Hopkins Press, 1969. 281 p. Bibliog.

Kindleberger, Charles P. AMERICA IN THE WORLD ECONOMY. Headline Series, no. 237. New York: Foreign Policy Association, 1977.

Krause, Walter. ECONOMIC DEVELOPMENT: THE UNDERDEVELOPED WORLD AND AMERICAN INTEREST. San Francisco: Wadsworth, 1961. 524 p. Bibliog.

Kropotkin, Petr Alexsieevich. MUTUAL AID: A FACTOR OF EVOLUTION. London: Heinemann, 1902. Reprint. New York: Knopf, 1925. 348 p.

Kutger, Joseph Peter. "The Military Assistance Program: Symphysis of United States Foreign and Military Policies." Ph.D. dissertation, University of Colorado, 1961. 472 p.

Leu, Christopher Amadeus. "Congress and the Role of Private Enterprise in the United States Foreign Assistance Program." Ph.D. dissertation, University of California (Los Angeles), 1973. 426 p.

Levinson, Jerome, and de Onis, Juande. THE ALLIANCE THAT LOST ITS WAY: A CRITICAL REPORT ON THE ALLIANCE FOR PROGRESS. Chicago: Quadrangle, 1970. 381 p.

Liska, George. THE NEW STATECRAFT: FOREIGN AID IN AMERICAN FOREIGN POLICY. Chicago: University of Chicago Press, 1960. 246 p. Bibliog.

Loeber, Thomas S. FOREIGN AID: OUR TRAGIC EXPERIMENT. New York: Norton, 1961. 139 p.

Lowther, Kevin, and Lucas, C. Payne. KEEPING KENNEDY'S PROMISE: THE PEACE CORPS--UNMET HOPE OF THE NEW FRONTIER. Boulder, Colo.: Westview, 1978. 153 p.

McMurtry, Virginia A. "Foreign Aid and Political Development: The American Experience in West Africa." Ph.D. dissertation, University of Wisconsin, 1974. 562 p.

Maheshwari, Bhanwar Lal. "Foreign Aid and the Policy Process: A Study of the Struggle Over Foreign Aid in Congress, 1961-1965." Ph.D. dissertation, University of Pennsylvania, 1966. 318 p.

Mangan, Sister Mary. "The Congressional Image of Aid to the Underdeveloped Countries (1949-1959) as Revealed in the Congressional Hearings." Ph.D. dissertation, Yale University, 1964. 401 p.

Martin, James R. "Institutionalization and Professionalization of the Republic of Korea Army: The Impact of United States Military Assistance Through Development of a Military Schools System." Ph.D. dissertation, Harvard University, 1973.

Marvel, William Worthington. "Foreign Aid and United States Security: A Study of Demands on the Postwar Assistance Programs." Ph.D. dissertation, Princeton University, 1951. 774 p.

Mason, Edward S. FOREIGN AID AND FOREIGN POLICY. New York: Harper and Row, 1964. 118 p.

Meier, Gerald M. PROBLEMS OF COOPERATION FOR DEVELOPMENT. New York: Oxford University Press, 1974. 249 p.

_____. PROBLEMS OF TRADE POLICY. New York: Oxford University Press, 1973. 288 p.

Meltzer, Ronald Ira. "The Politics of Policy Reversal: The American Response to the Issue of Granting Trade Preferences to Developing Countries, 1964-1967." Ph.D. dissertation, Columbia University, 1975. 333 p.

Millikan, Max. AMERICAN FOREIGN AID: STRATEGY FOR THE 1970'S. New York: Foreign Policy Association, 1969. 63 p. Bibliog.

Monroe, Wilbur F. THE NEW INTERNATIONALISM: STRATEGY AND INITIATIVES FOR U.S. FOREIGN ECONOMIC POLICY. Lexington, Mass.: Lexington Books, 1976. 238 p.

Montgomery, John Dickey. FOREIGN AID IN INTERNATIONAL POLITICS. Englewood Cliffs, N.J.: Prentice-Hall, 1967. 118 p. Bibliog.

_____. THE POLITICS OF FOREIGN AID: AMERICAN EXPERIENCE IN SOUTHEAST ASIA. New York: Praeger for Council on Foreign Relations, 1962. 336 p. Bibliog.

Morley, Lorna, and Morley, Felix. THE PATCHWORK HISTORY OF FOREIGN AID. Washington, D.C.: American Enterprise Institute, 1961. 55 p.

Nelson, Donald Marr. ARSENAL OF DEMOCRACY: THE STORY OF AMERICAN WAR PRODUCTION. New York: Harcourt, Brace, 1946. 439 p.

Nelson, Joan M. AID, INFLUENCE AND FOREIGN POLICY. New York: Macmillan, 1968. 149 p.

O'Leary, Michael Kent. THE POLITICS OF AMERICAN FOREIGN AID. New York: Atherton, 1967. 172 p.

Packenham, Robert A. LIBERAL AMERICA AND THE THIRD WORLD: POLITICAL DEVELOPMENT IDEAS IN FOREIGN AID AND SOCIAL SCIENCE. Princeton, N.J.: Princeton University Press, 1973. 395 p.

Palmer, John D. "Presidential Leadership and Foreign Economic Aid." Ph.D. dissertation, University of Texas, 1965. 338 p.

Parks, Wallace J. UNITED STATES ADMINISTRATION OF ITS INTERNATIONAL ECONOMIC AFFAIRS. Baltimore: Johns Hopkins Press, 1951. 315 p.

Pearson, James Constantine. THE RECIPROCAL TRADE AGREEMENTS PRO-GRAM: THE POLICY OF THE UNITED STATES AND ITS EFFECTIVENESS. Washington, D.C.: Catholic University Press, 1942. 328 p.

Pincus, John. TRADE, AID AND DEVELOPMENT. New York: McGraw-Hill, 1967. 400 p. Bibliog.

Poats, Rutherford M. TECHNOLOGY FOR DEVELOPING NATIONS: NEW DIRECTIONS FOR U.S. TECHNICAL ASSISTANCE. Washington, D.C.: Brookings Institution, 1972. 255 p.

Preeg, Ernest H. ECONOMIC BLOCS AND U.S. FOREIGN POLICY. Washington, D.C.: National Planning Association, 1974. 198 p.

_____. TRADERS AND DIPLOMATS: AN ANALYSIS OF THE KENNEDY ROUND OF NEGOTIATIONS UNDER THE GENERAL AGREEMENT OF TARIFFS AND TRADE. Washington, D.C.: Brookings Institution, 1970. 320 p.

Price, Harry B. THE MARSHALL PLAN AND ITS MEANING. Ithaca, N.Y.: Cornell University Press, 1955. 424 p.

Proxmire, William. UNCLE SAM: THE LAST OF THE BIG-TIME SPENDERS. New York: Simon and Schuster, 1972. 275 p.

Raichur, Satish, and Liske, Craig, eds. THE POLITICS OF AID, TRADE, AND INVESTMENTS. New York: Wiley, Halsted, 1976. 218 p.

Rice, Andrew Eliot. "Building a Constituency for the Foreign Aid Program: The Record of the Eisenhower Years." Ph.D. dissertation, Syracuse University, 1963. 225 p.

Rogers, William D. THE TWILIGHT STRUGGLE: THE ALLIANCE FOR PROGRESS AND THE POLITICS OF DEVELOPMENT IN LATIN AMERICA. New York: Random House, 1967. 301 p.

Rowland, Benjamin Moore. "Commercial Conflict and Foreign Policy: A Study in Anglo-American Relations, 1932-1938." Ph.D. dissertation, Johns Hopkins University (SAIS), 1975. 443 p.

Sayre, Francis B. HOW TRADE AGREEMENTS ARE MADE. Department of State Publication, no. 1152. Washington, D.C.: Government Printing Office, 1938. 16 p.

_____. "How Trade Agreements Are Made." FOREIGN AFFAIRS 16 (April 1938): 417-29.

_____. THE WAY FORWARD: THE AMERICAN TRADE AGREEMENTS PRO-GRAM. New York: Macmillan, 1939. 230 p.

Schatz, Arthur William. "Cordell Hull and the Struggle for the Reciprocal Trade Agreements Program, 1932-1940." Ph.D. dissertation, University of Oregon, 1965. 377 p.

Schultz, George P., and Dam, Kenneth W. ECONOMIC POLICY BEYOND THE HEADLINES. New York: Norton, 1977. 225 p.

Schuyler, Eugene. AMERICAN DIPLOMACY AND THE FURTHERANCE OF COMMERCE. New York: Scribner, 1886. 469 p.

Scowcroft, Brent. "Congress and Foreign Policy: An Examination of Congressional Attitudes Toward the Foreign Aid Programs to Spain and Yugoslavia." Ph.D. dissertation, Columbia University, 1967. 413 p.

Sheaffer, James Martin. "United States Foreign Aid: The Additional Goals." Ph.D. dissertation, University of Iowa, 1971. 253 p.

Shonfield, Andrew. THE ATTACK ON WORLD POVERTY. New York: Random House, 1960. 296 p. Bibliog.

Snyder, Richard C. THE MOST-FAVORED-NATION CLAUSE. New York: King's Crown, 1948. 264 p. Bibliog.

Spero, Joan Edelman. THE POLITICS OF INTERNATIONAL ECONOMIC RE-LATIONS. New York: St. Martin's, 1977. 326 p.

Stanley, Timothy W., et al. RAW MATERIALS AND FOREIGN POLICY. Boulder, Colo.: Westview, 1977. 416 p.

Steel, Ronald Leslie, ed. UNITED STATES FOREIGN TRADE POLICY. New York: Wilson, 1962. 200 p. Bibliog.

Stettinius, Edward Reilly, Jr. LEND-LEASE: WEAPON FOR VICTORY. New York: Macmillan, 1944. 358 p.

Stillman, James Peter. "Foreign Aid, Ideology and Bureaucratic Politics: The Bolaro Steel Mill and Indian-American Relations." Ph.D. dissertation, Columbia University, 1975.. 429 p.

Stottlemire, Marvin Glenn. "Measuring Foreign Policy: Determinants of U.S. Military Assistance to Latin America." Ph.D. dissertation, Rice Institute, 1975. 181 p.

Sumberg, Theodore A. FOREIGN AID AS MORAL OBLIGATION? Beverly Hills, Calif.: Sage, 1973. 72 p.

Tendler, Judith. INSIDE FOREIGN AID. Baltimore: Johns Hopkins Press, 1975. 140 p. Bibliog.

Thompson, Kenneth W. FOREIGN ASSISTANCE: A VIEW FROM THE PRIVATE SECTOR. South Bend, Ind.: Notre Dame University Press, 1972. 160 p.

Thorp, Willard Long. THE REALITY OF FOREIGN AID. New York: Praeger for Council on Foreign Relations, 1971. 370 p.

_____. TRADE, AID, OR WHAT? Baltimore: Johns Hopkins Press, 1954. 224 p.

U.S. Commission on International Trade and Investment Policy. UNITED STATES INTERNATIONAL ECONOMIC POLICY IN AN INTERDEPENDENT WORLD: REPORT TO THE PRESIDENT. 3 vols. Washington, D.C.: Government Printing Office, 1971.

Volume 1 constitutes report to the president (394 p.) and volumes 2 and 3 consist of papers submitted to the commission (1,544 p.).

U.S. Commission on the Organization of the Government for the Conduct of Foreign Policy. "Case Studies on U.S. Foreign Economic Policy, 1965-1974," "Conduct of Routine Economic Relations," and "Foreign Economic Policy." In its COMMISSION ON THE ORGANIZATION OF THE GOVERNMENT FOR THE CONDUCT OF FOREIGN POLICY, JUNE 1975. Appendix, vol. 3, pp. 1-344. Washington, D.C.: Government Printing Office, 1976.

U.S. International Trade Commission. INTERNATIONAL COMMODITY AGREEMENTS. Washington, D.C.: Government Printing Office, 1975. 189 p.

Report on negotiating and operating commodity agreements on cocoa, coffee, sugar, tin, and wheat, and on legal basis for such agreements.

U.S. Library of Congress. Legislative Reference Service. U.S. FOREIGN AID: ITS PURPOSES, SCOPE, ADMINISTRATION, AND RELATED INFORMATION. Washington, D.C.: Government Printing Office, 1959. 117 p.

Prepared by Library of Congress for House of Representatives, House Document 116, 86th Cong., 1st sess.

Van Wagoner, Robert Norton. "The Agency for International Development and Its Effect on Pakistan as a Developing Nation." Ph.D. dissertation, University of Idaho, 1972. 371 p.

Walters, R.S. AMERICAN AND SOVIET AID: A COMPARATIVE ANALYSIS. Pittsburgh: University of Pittsburgh Press, 1970. 299 p.

Warne, William Elmo. MISSION FOR PEACE: POINT FOUR IN IRAN. Indianapolis: Bobbs-Merrill, 1956. 320 p.

Washburne, Elihu Benjamin. AMERICA'S AID TO GERMANY IN 1870-71. St. Louis: N.p., 1905. 463 p.

Weiner, Bernard. "The Truman Doctrine: Background and Presentation." Ph.D. dissertation, Claremont Colleges, 1967. 303 p.

Westwood, Andrew F. FOREIGN AID IN A FOREIGN POLICY FRAMEWORK. Washington, D.C.: Brookings Institution, 1966. 115 p.

White, John Alexander. THE POLITICS OF FOREIGN AID. New York: St. Martin's, 1974. 315 p. Bibliog.

Wiggins, James W., and Schoeck, Helmut, eds. FOREIGN AID REEXAMINED: A CRITICAL APPRAISAL. Washington, D.C.: Public Affairs, 1958. 250 p. Bibliog.

Wilson, Joan Hoff. AMERICAN BUSINESS AND FOREIGN POLICY, 1920-1933. Lexington: University of Kentucky Press, 1971. 339 p.

Wilson, Theodore A. THE MARSHALL PLAN: AN ATLANTIC VENTURE OF 1947-51. Headline Series, no. 236. New York: Foreign Policy Association, 1977. 64 p.

Winham, Gilbert Rathbone. "An Analysis of Foreign Aid Decision-Making: The Case of the Marshall Plan." Ph.D. dissertation, University of North Carolina (Chapel Hill), 1968. 195 p.

Wittkopf, Eugene R. "The Distribution of Foreign Aid in Comparative Perspective: An Empirical Study of the Flow of Foreign Economic Assistance, 1961-1967." Ph.D. dissertation, Syracuse University, 1971. 266 p.

_____. WESTERN BILATERAL AID ALLOCATIONS: A COMPARATIVE STUDY OF RECIPIENT STATE ATTRIBUTES AND AID RECEIVED. Professional Papers in International Studies. Beverly Hills, Calif.: Sage, 1972. 62 p. Bibliog.

Wolf, Charles, Jr. FOREIGN AID: THEORY AND PRACTICE IN SOUTHERN ASIA. Princeton, N.J.: Princeton University Press, 1960. 442 p.

Yeager, Leland B., and Tuerck, David G. FOREIGN TRADE AND U.S. POLICY: THE CASE FOR FREE INTERNATIONAL TRADE. New York: Praeger, 1976. 312 p.

Zupnick, Elliott. PRIMER OF U.S. FOREIGN ECONOMIC POLICY. New York: Foreign Policy Association, 1965. 64 p.

CULTURAL, EDUCATIONAL, SCIENTIFIC, AND TECHNOLOGICAL RELATIONS

Interest and action respecting the international aspects of cultural, educational, and scientific affairs has developed since World War II. Although literary attention has been focused largely on the multipartite agencies concerned with these matters--such as the United Nations, its Educational, Scientific and Cultural Organization (UNESCO), and related regional agencies--and, in recent years, on cross-cultural relations, some attention is also centered on U.S. programs and activities in these fields, represented by the following:

Basiuk, Victor. TECHNOLOGY, WORLD POLITICS AND AMERICAN POLICY. New York: Columbia University Press, 1977. 409 p.

Blum, Robert, ed. CULTURAL AFFAIRS AND FOREIGN RELATIONS. Englewood Cliffs, N.J.: Prentice-Hall, 1963. 184 p.

Braisted, Paul J., ed. CULTURAL AFFAIRS AND FOREIGN RELATIONS. Washington, D.C.: Columbia Book Co. for American Assembly, 1968. 211 p.

Colligan, Francis J. "Twenty Years After: Two Decades of Government Sponsored Cultural Relations." DEPARTMENT OF STATE BULLETIN 39 (21 July 1958): 112-20.

Coombs, Philip H. THE FOURTH DIMENSION IN FOREIGN POLICY: EDUCATIONAL AND CULTURAL AFFAIRS. New York: Harper and Row, 1964. 158 p.

CULTURAL AFFAIRS AND FOREIGN RELATIONS. Report of the Pacific Northwest Assembly. Eugene: University of Oregon, 1963. 28 p.

Deibel, Terry L., and Roberts, Walter R. CULTURE AND INFORMATION: TWO FOREIGN POLICY FUNCTIONS. Beverly Hills, Calif.: Sage, 1976. 62 p.

Erasmus, Charles J. MAN TAKES CONTROL: CULTURAL DEVELOPMENT AND AMERICAN AID. Minneapolis: University of Minnesota Press, 1961. 365 p. Bibliog.

Flack, Michael J. "Cultural Diplomacy: Blindspot in International Affairs Textbooks." INTERNATIONAL EDUCATIONAL AND CULTURAL EXCHANGE 8 (Winter 1972/73): 11-18.

Frankel, Charles. THE NEGLECTED ASPECT OF FOREIGN AFFAIRS: AMERICAN EDUCATIONAL AND CULTURAL POLICY ABROAD. Washington, D.C.: Brookings Institution, 1965. 156 p.

Gilpin, Robert. AMERICAN SCIENTISTS AND NUCLEAR WEAPONS POLICY. Princeton, N.J.: Princeton University Press, 1962. 352 p.

Granger, John Van Nuys. TECHNOLOGY AND INTERNATIONAL RELATIONS. San Francisco: Freeman, 1979. 202 p.

Hayden, Eric W. TECHNOLOGY TRANSFER TO EAST EUROPE: UNITED STATES CORPORATE EXPERIENCE. New York: Praeger, 1976. 152 p.

Heald, Morrell, and Kaplan, Lawrence S. CULTURE AND DIPLOMACY: THE AMERICAN EXPERIENCE. Westport, Conn.: Greenwood, 1977. 361 p.

Jacobson, Harold K., and Stein, Eric. DIPLOMATS, SCIENTISTS, AND POLITICIANS: THE UNITED STATES AND THE NUCLEAR BAN NEGOTIATIONS. Ann Arbor: University of Michigan Press, 1966. 538 p.

Keniston, Hayward. "Cultural Relations and International Understanding." AMERICAN PHILOSOPHICAL SOCIETY PROCEEDINGS 92 (8 March 1948): 37-40.

Laves, Walter H.C., and Thomson, Charles A.H. CULTURAL RELATIONS AND UNITED STATES FOREIGN POLICY. Bloomington: Indiana University Press, 1963. 227 p. Bibliog.

Margolis, Howard. TECHNICAL ADVICE ON POLICY ISSUES. Beverly Hills, Calif.: Sage, 1973. 57 p.

Nau, Henry R. TECHNOLOGY TRANSFER AND U.S. FOREIGN POLICY. New York: Praeger, 1976. 325 p. Bibliog.

Nostrand, Howard Lee. THE CULTURAL ATTACHE. New Haven, Conn.: Hazen Foundation, n.d. 45 p.

Organization for Economic Cooperation and Development. TECHNOLOGY ON TRIAL: PUBLIC PARTICIPATION IN DECISION-MAKING RELATED TO SCIENCE AND TECHNOLOGY. Paris: OECD, 1979. 122 p.

Rogers, William P. "Growing Ties Between Science and Foreign Policy." DEPARTMENT OF STATE BULLETIN 64 (14 June 1971): 766-68.

_____. "U.S. Foreign Policy in a Technological Age." DEPARTMENT OF STATE BULLETIN 64 (15 February 1971): 198-202.

Schulman, Lawrence Daniel. "United States Government Educational, Literary, and Artistic Cultural Exchange Programs, 1948-1958, as a Technique of American Diplomacy." Ph.D. dissertation, New York University, 1967. 244 p.

Shuster, George Nauman. CULTURAL COOPERATION AND THE PEACE: THE DIFFICULTIES AND OBJECTIVES OF INTERNATIONAL CULTURAL UNDERSTANDING. Milwaukee, Wis.: Bruce, 1953. 80 p.

Skolnikoff, Eugene B. SCIENCE, TECHNOLOGY, AND AMERICAN FOREIGN POLICY. Cambridge, Mass.: M.I.T. Press, 1967. 330 p.

Snyder, Harold E. WHEN PEOPLE SPEAK TO PEOPLES: AN ACTION GUIDE TO INTERNATIONAL CULTURAL RELATIONS FOR AMERICAN ORGANIZATIONS, INSTITUTIONS, AND INDIVIDUALS. Washington, D.C.: American Council on Education, 1953. 206 p.

Stevenson, Adlai E. "Science, Diplomacy, and Peace." DEPARTMENT OF STATE BULLETIN 45 (4 September 1961): 402-7.

Thayer, Robert H. "Cultural Diplomacy and the Development of Mutual Understanding." DEPARTMENT OF STATE BULLETIN 41 (31 August 1959): 310-16.

U.S. Congress. House of Representatives. Committee on Foreign Affairs. Subcommittee on National Security Policy and Scientific Developments. SCIENCE, TECHNOLOGY, AND AMERICAN DIPLOMACY: THE POLITICAL LEGACY OF THE INTERNATIONAL GEOPHYSICAL YEAR. 93d Cong., 1st sess. Washington, D.C.: Government Printing Office, 1973. 64 p.

U.S. Department of State. THE AMERICAN CULTURAL ATTACHE. Washington, D.C.: Government Printing Office, 1957. 23 p.

_____. THE SCIENCE ADVISER OF THE DEPARTMENT OF STATE. Washington, D.C.: Government Printing Office, 1960. 27 p.
        Includes section on science attaches.

_____. TECHNOLOGY AND FOREIGN AFFAIRS. Washington, D.C.: Government Printing Office, 1976. 335 p.

U.S. Library of Congress. Congressional Research Service. SCIENCE, TECHNOLOGY, AND AMERICAN DIPLOMACY: SCIENCE, TECHNOLOGY, AND DIPLOMACY IN THE AGE OF INTERDEPENDENCE. Washington, D.C.: Government Printing Office, 1976. 492 p.

Wachs, Melvin Walter. "The Forge of Power: American International Science Policy and Its Administration." Ph.D. dissertation, American University, 1968. 328 p.

Wohlstetter, Albert. "Scientists, Seers and Strategy." FOREIGN AFFAIRS 41 (April 1963): 466-78.

Additional bibliographical guidance may be found in the following:

Caldwell, Lynton K., ed. SCIENCE, TECHNOLOGY, AND PUBLIC POLICY: A SELECTED AND ANNOTATED BIBLIOGRAPHY. 3 vols. Bloomington: Department of Government, Indiana University, 1968-70.

   Includes English-language literature from 1945 to 1970.

Knezo, Genevieve Johanna, ed. SCIENCE, TECHNOLOGY, AND AMERICAN DIPLOMACY: A SELECTED, ANNOTATED BIBLIOGRAPHY OF ARTICLES, BOOKS, DOCUMENTS, PERIODICALS, AND REFERENCE GUIDES. Washington, D.C.: Government Printing Office, 1970. 69 p.

Rettig, Richard A. BIBLIOGRAPHY ON SCIENCE AND WORLD AFFAIRS. Washington, D.C.: Department of State, 1965. 179 p.

Veenhoven, William A., ed. CASE STUDIES ON HUMAN RIGHTS AND FUNDAMENTAL FREEDOMS. 5 vols. The Hague: Nijhoff, 1975-1976.

   Comprehensive compilation of articles on human rights, discrimination, and injustice.

CONSULAR AFFAIRS

Consular practice, closely related to diplomacy throughout history, was well established by the time the United States achieved independence. Inasmuch as it involves the exercise of governmental responsibilities within the territory of foreign states, it requires their express authorization, which generally is achieved by mutual, usually bilateral, agreements in the nature of commercial or consular conventions, literature of which is referred to in chapter 22.

Consular officials, unlike diplomats, are concerned primarily with serving the interests of private individuals and concerns, and their functions are similar to those of a local negotiator, a shipping official, a notary public and justice of the peace, a reporter and information analyst, and an agent of postal, immigration, citizenship, commercial, treasury, and related affairs. The overseas missions in which they serve rank as consulates general, consulates, and consular agencies. Although initially consular officials were distinguished from the diplomatic corps in American practice, they were amalgamated in 1924 and are currently part of the Foreign Service, treated in chapter 9. In addition to materials concerning consular agents and their activities referred to elsewhere in this compilation--especially in chapters 2, 3, 9, and 15-17, as well as in the experiential chronicling contained in memoirs--the following deal specifically with consular matters:

Briggs, Herbert W. "American Consular Rights in Communist China." AMERICAN JOURNAL OF INTERNATIONAL LAW 44 (April 1950): 243-58.

Cahier, Philippe, and Lee, Luke T. "Vienna Conventions on Diplomatic and Consular Relations." INTERNATIONAL CONCILIATION, no. 571 (January 1969): 1-76.

Carr, Wilbur J. "American Consular Service." AMERICAN JOURNAL OF INTERNATIONAL LAW 1 (October 1907): 891-913.

"Despatches from the United States Consulate in New Orleans, 1801-1803." AMERICAN HISTORICAL REVIEW 32 (July 1927): 801-24 and 33 (January 1928): 331-59.

Dinstein, Yoram. CONSULAR IMMUNITY FROM JUDICIAL PROCESS: WITH PARTICULAR REFERENCE TO ISRAEL. Jerusalem: Institute for Legislative Research and Comparative Law, 1966. 89 p.

Etzold, Thomas H. "Understanding Consular Diplomacy." FOREIGN SERVICE JOURNAL 52 (March 1975): 10-12.

Feller, Abraham H., and Hudson, Manley O., eds. A COLLECTION OF THE DIPLOMATIC AND CONSULAR LAWS AND REGULATIONS OF VARIOUS COUNTRIES. 2 vols. Washington, D.C.: Carnegie Endowment, 1933.

Gauss, Clarence Edward. A NOTARIAL MANUAL FOR CONSULAR OFFICERS. Washington, D.C.: Government Printing Office, 1921. 84 p.

Harvard Research in International Law. "The Legal Position and Functions of Consuls." AMERICAN JOURNAL OF INTERNATIONAL LAW, SUPPLEMENT 26 (April 1932): 189-499.

Hinckley, Frank E. AMERICAN CONSULAR JURISDICTION IN THE ORIENT. Washington, D.C.: Lowdermilk, 1906. 283 p.

Johnson, Emory R. "The Early History of the United States Consular Service, 1776-1792." POLITICAL SCIENCE QUARTERLY 13 (March 1898): 19-40.

Jones, Chester Lloyd. THE CONSULAR SERVICE OF THE UNITED STATES: ITS HISTORY AND ACTIVITIES. Series in Political Economy and Public Law, no. 18. Philadelphia: University of Pennsylvania, 1906. 126 p.

Jones, R.L. "America's First Consular Convention." SOUTHWESTERN SO-CIAL SCIENCE QUARTERLY 13 (December 1932): 250-63.

Lee, Luke Tsung-Chou. CONSULAR LAW AND PRACTICE. New York: Praeger, 1961. 431 p.

Ludwig, Ernest. CONSULAR TREATY RIGHTS AND COMMENTS ON THE "MOST FAVORED NATION" CLAUSE. Akron, Ohio: New Werner, 1913. 239 p.

Marx, Walter J. "The Consular Service of the United States." DEPARTMENT OF STATE BULLETIN 33 (19 September 1955): 447-48, 450-54.

Murphy, George H. DIGEST OF CIRCULAR INSTRUCTIONS TO CONSULAR OFFICERS. 2 vols. Washington, D.C.: Government Printing Office, 1904-1906.

Nichols, Roy F. "Trade Relations and the Establishment of United States Con-sulates in Spanish America, 1779-1809." HISPANIC AMERICAN HISTORICAL REVIEW 13 (August 1933): 289-313.

Plischke, Elmer. CONDUCT OF AMERICAN DIPLOMACY. 3d ed. Prince-ton, N.J.: Van Nostrand, 1967.

> Especially "Consular Establishments," pages 272-75, "The Consular Mission," pages 305-11, "Consular Functions," pages 323-33, and "Consular Privileges and Immunities," pages 346-51.

Puente, Julius I. THE FOREIGN CONSUL: HIS JURIDICAL STATUS IN THE UNITED STATES. Chicago: B.J. Smith, 1926. 157 p.

Ravndal, Gabriel Bie. THE ORIGIN OF THE CAPITULATIONS AND OF THE CONSULAR INSTITUTION, BY AMERICAN CONSUL GENERAL AT CONSTAN-TINOPLE. Washington, D.C.: Government Printing Office, 1921. 112 p.

Ritchie, John Alexander. "The Consular Function: The Stepchild of United States Foreign Policy Administration." Ph.D. dissertation, Southern Illinois University, 1969. 348 p.

Scidmore, George Hawthorne. OUTLINE LECTURES ON THE HISTORY, OR-GANIZATION, JURISDICTION, AND PRACTICE OF THE MINISTERIAL AND CONSULAR COURTS OF THE UNITED STATES OF AMERICA IN JAPAN. Tokyo: Igerisu Horitsu Gakko, 1887. 245 p.

Serpell, David R. "American Consular Activities in Egypt, 1849–1863." JOURNAL OF MODERN HISTORY 10 (September 1938): 344–63.

Sheppard, Eli T. AMERICAN CONSULAR SERVICE. Berkeley: University of California Press, 1901. 457 p.

Stewart, Irvin. CONSULAR PRIVILEGES AND IMMUNITIES. New York: Columbia University Press, 1926. 216 p. Bibliog.

Stock, Leo Francis, ed. CONSULAR RELATIONS BETWEEN THE UNITED STATES AND THE PAPAL STATES: INSTRUCTIONS AND DESPATCHES. Washington, D.C.: American Catholic Historical Association, 1945. 467 p.

Stowell, Ellery C. CONSULAR CASES AND OPINIONS. Washington, D.C.: Byrne, 1909. 811 p.

Stuart, Graham H. AMERICAN DIPLOMATIC AND CONSULAR PRACTICE. 2d ed. New York: Appleton-Century-Crofts, 1952. 477 p.

Especially chapters 16–21.

U.S. Department of State. THE AMERICAN CONSUL. Washington, D.C.: Government Printing Office, 1955. 14 p.

_____. REPORTS FROM CONSULAR OFFICERS OF THE UNITED STATES GIVING AN ACCOUNT OF EACH CONSULATE AND CONSULAR AGENCY . . . . Senate Document, no. 411. 57th Cong., 1st sess. Washington, D.C.: Government Printing Office, 1902. 738 p.

Survey of all U.S. consular establishments at the turn of the century.

_____. THE UNITED STATES CONSULAR SYSTEM: A MANUAL FOR CONSULS AND ALSO FOR MERCHANTS, SHIPOWNERS AND MASTERS IN THEIR CONSULAR TRANSACTIONS; COMPRISING THE INSTRUCTIONS OF THE DEPARTMENT OF STATE IN REGARD TO CONSULAR EMOLUMENTS, DUTIES, PRIVILEGES, AND LIABILITIES. Washington, D.C.: Government Printing Office, 1856. 347 p.

Warden, David B. ON THE ORIGIN, NATURE, PROGRESS, AND INFLUENCE OF CONSULAR ESTABLISHMENTS. Paris: Smith, 1813. 331 p.

Legal prescriptions in and official commentary on U.S. practice concerning consuls and their activities over the years are provided in:

Hackworth, Green H. DIGEST OF INTERNATIONAL LAW. Washington, D.C.: Government Printing Office, 1943. Vol. 4, pp. 655–947.

Moore, John Bassett. A DIGEST OF INTERNATIONAL LAW. Washington, D.C.: Government Printing Office, 1906. Vol. 2, pp. 751-55; vol. 5, pp. 1-154.

Whiteman, Marjorie M. DIGEST OF INTERNATIONAL LAW. Washington, D.C.: Government Printing Office, 1970. Vol. 7, Chapter 18, pp. 505-870.

PROTECTION OF CITIZENS AND THEIR INTERESTS ABROAD

Diplomatic and consular establishments have traditionally been responsible, within certain limits, for protecting and servicing American nationals and their interests abroad. This function has received some, but only modest, literary treatment, exemplified by the following, which may be supplemented with specific accounts related in memoirs, selected official documents, and short commentaries contained in a few of the more general volumes on foreign relations.

Borchard, Edwin Montefiore. "Basic Elements of Diplomatic Protection of Citizens Abroad." AMERICAN JOURNAL OF INTERNATIONAL LAW 7 (July 1913): 497-520.

_____. THE DIPLOMATIC PROTECTION OF CITIZENS ABROAD: OR, THE LAW OF INTERNATIONAL CLAIMS. New York: Banks, 1915. Reissue. New York: Banks, 1928. 988 p. Bibliog.

Clark, Joshua Reuben. RIGHT TO PROTECT CITIZENS IN FOREIGN COUNTRIES BY LANDING FORCES. Washington, D.C.: U.S. Department of State, 1912. 70 p. Rev. ed. Washington, D.C.: U.S. Department of State, 1929. 78 p.

Crosswell, Carol M. PROTECTION OF INTERNATIONAL PERSONNEL ABROAD. Dobbs Ferry, N.Y.: Oceana, 1952. 198 p.

Dunn, Frederick Sherwood. THE DIPLOMATIC PROTECTION OF AMERICANS IN MEXICO. Mexico in International Finance and Diplomacy, Vol. 2. New York: Columbia University Press, 1933. 439 p.

_____. THE PROTECTION OF NATIONALS: A STUDY IN THE APPLICATION OF INTERNATIONAL LAW. Baltimore: Johns Hopkins Press, 1932. 228 p.

Mander, Linden A. "The Protection of Nationals Abroad: Their Property and Investments." In his FOUNDATIONS OF MODERN WORLD SOCIETY, pp. 553-600. 2d ed. Stanford, Calif.: Stanford University Press, 1947.

Offutt, Milton. THE PROTECTION OF CITIZENS ABROAD BY THE ARMED FORCES OF THE UNITED STATES. Baltimore: Johns Hopkins Press, 1928. 170 p. Bibliog.

Plischke, Elmer. "Protection of and Services for American Nationals." In his CONDUCT OF AMERICAN DIPLOMACY, pp. 319-21. 3d ed. Princeton, N.J.: Van Nostrand, 1967.

Root, Elihu. "The Basis of Protection to Citizens Residing Abroad." AMERICAN JOURNAL OF INTERNATIONAL LAW 4 (July 1910): 517-28.

Stuart, Graham H. "Consular Services Rendered to Nationals." In his AMERICAN DIPLOMATIC AND CONSULAR PRACTICE, pp. 322-48. 2d ed. New York: Appleton-Century-Crofts, 1952.

PROTECTION OF THIRD COUNTRY INTERESTS

The matter of third country representation and protection of the interests of one foreign country in another, admittedly a narrowly specialized aspect of diplomatic practice, is important to governments, especially in times of crisis and war, and may become increasingly necessary in the relations of the growing number of microstates and other small countries in dealing diplomatically with foreign governments. This aspect of foreign relations is dealt with in some of the general literature on international law, but it is rarely accorded survey treatment as a function of the diplomatic process. The study of William M. Franklin remains the only comprehensive treatment of American practice through World War II.

Escher, Alfred. DER SCHUTZ DER STAATSANGEHOERIGEN IM AUSLAND DURCH FREMDE GESANDSCHAFTEN UND KONSULATE. Aarau, Switzerland: Saarlaender, 1928.

Franklin, William M. PROTECTION OF FOREIGN INTERESTS: A STUDY IN DIPLOMATIC AND CONSULAR PRACTICE. Washington, D.C.: Government Printing Office, 1947. 328 p.

Harris, William R. UNITED STATES PARTICIPATION IN THE RELIEF OF INTERNATIONAL DISASTERS. Santa Monica, Calif.: Rand, 1976. 18 p.

Plischke, Elmer. "Protection of the Interests of Third States." In his CONDUCT OF AMERICAN DIPLOMACY, pp. 321-22. 3d ed. Princeton, N.J.: Van Nostrand, 1967.

Stuart, Graham H. "Protection of Citizens of Third Powers" and "Care of Foreign Legations." In his AMERICAN DIPLOMATIC AND CONSULAR PRACTICE, pp. 201-4. 2d ed. New York: Appleton-Century-Crofts, 1952.

Whiteman, Marjorie M. DIGEST OF INTERNATIONAL LAW. Washington, D.C.: Government Printing Office, 1970. Vol. 7, pp. 448-64.

Chapter 18

CRISIS DIPLOMACY:

PEACEKEEPING AND CRISIS MANAGEMENT

The international environment is inherently competitive, often even in cases in which two or more states seek identical goals. In pursuing their respective interests and objectives and in designing and implementing their foreign policies, states often differ and compete with one another, sometimes to the point of controversy, confrontation, crisis, and ultimately the use of force. The peace-war relationship, as a matter of both state practice and analytical inquiry, consists less of a simple juxtaposition of tranquility vs. warfare than of a broad spectrum of amicable and hostile components. Relations may be friendly and cooperative, controversial though peaceful, or hostile though short of formal violence; or they may degenerate to formally declared or undeclared war, although most resort to open aggression and hostilities in the form of undeclared war. In its various forms, diplomacy constitutes the primary bridge for not only sustaining peaceful cooperation, but also for resolving differences, settling disputes, ameliorating crises, maintaining interaction short of the use of force, and delimiting, containing, and terminating hostilities once they have begun.

The quest for preserving amity, international tranquility, and interstate equilibrium has engrossed philosophers, analysts, and statesmen since the dawn of history. Earlier writings tended to be somewhat simplistic, addressing themselves to generic causes (such as nationalism, imperialism, and militarism) and to proposing solutions (including territorial and organizational integration, establishing a rule of law, and the outlawry of war). In recent decades, while such analyses continue to be produced, interest also has come to be focused on a variety of refinements and related matters, such as limited warfare, nuclear weaponry, nonmilitary war (including the cold war), and the positive process of promoting peace. In addition, supplementing continuing traditional study of peacekeeping, greater attention is being devoted to the systematic study of interrelations involving conflict resolution and crisis handling.

This chapter provides a selective listing of published materials, primarily monographs, on the general nature and status of peace and war, the cold war, international conflict and crisis, the peaceful settlement of disputes, and the concept of peaceful change.

PEACE AND WAR

This section provides guidance to general materials on peace, the use of force, war, and the termination of hostilities. Some attention is paid to sources concerned with peacemaking (though not with the negotiation of particular war-terminating settlements or peace treaties) and with limited or small wars, but not with such specific types as guerilla, insurgency, counterinsurgency, chemical, biological, nuclear, and other precise forms of warfare. Reference to materials on these and similar matters, including deterrance, disarmament and arms control, and the laws of war and neutrality, may be found in other compilations.

A number of studies included in this section are classics, such as that of Von Clausewitz, or are otherwise regarded as basic contributions, including those of writers like Aron, Buchan, and Wright. Some analysts stress the positive process and problems of waging peace, represented by Beaton, Douglas, Etzioni, Johnson, Melman, Mitrany, Rappard, Rathbone, John Strachey, and Swan. The evolution or history of warfare as a sociopolitical process appears to have gained increasing literary support in recent decades, illustrated by the works of Clarkson and Cochran, Hinsley, Knapp, Montross, Otterbein, Ten Eyck, Toynbee, and others. Although peace and war have been among the favored subjects of philosophers, historians, lawyers, and political scientists, a growing interest in psychological and other social science aspects has emerged, as indicated by the contributions of Bramson and Goethals, Coblentz, Farrar, Frank, Fried, Glover, Janowitz, May, Pear, Frank Richardson, Rummel, Speier, and Alix Strachey. The studies of Aron, Burton, Falk and Mendlovitz, Ginsberg, Horowitz, and Waltz evidence growing theoretical analysis. A good many others, such as those of Brownlie, Grob, Kotzsch, and Larson, cope with the concepts of peace and war in international law. Major concern is also centered on moral considerations, reflected in the works of Bainton, Butterfield, Falk, Isbell, Nagle, O'Brien, Potter, and Wasserstrom. Some authors probe the causes or roots of war, including Barnet, Bernard, Blainey, Graham, Mills, Pruitt and Snyder, Singer, Lewis Richardson, Stoessinger, Alix Strachey, and Wallace. Others concentrate on small or limited wars, such as Bloomfield and Leiss, Calwell, Deitchman, Eckstein, Halperin, Knorr and Read, McClintock, Modelski, Nickerson, and Osgood. A few are concerned with the concept of total war--Aron and Veale. Some address themselves to the termination of hostilities--Foster and Brewer, Fox, Ikle, Opie, and Phillipson.

Additional materials, listed separately at the end of this section, relate to peacekeeping and peace research. The systematic study of peace has become a major research interest, as evidenced by many of the articles appearing in the JOURNAL OF PEACE RESEARCH, the JOURNAL OF CONFLICT RESOLUTION, COOPERATION AND CONFLICT, BULLETIN OF THE ATOMIC SCIENTISTS, and elsewhere. For a comprehensive list of journals and periodicals, see the last section of chapter 6. Also of interest is the series of individual "Conflict Studies" published since 1969 by the Institute for the Study of Conflict (London), and similar agencies concerned with conflict analysis.

Angell, Norman. THE GREAT ILLUSION. New York: Putnam, 1933. 308 p.

Angell, Robert C. PEACE ON THE MARCH: TRANSNATIONAL PARTICIPA-TION. New York: Van Nostrand Reinhold, 1969. 205 p.

Aron, Raymond. THE CENTURY OF TOTAL WAR. Garden City, N.Y.: Doubleday, 1954. 379 p.

_____. ON WAR. Translated by Terence Kilmartin. Garden City, N.Y.: Doubleday, 1959. 163 p.

_____. PEACE AND WAR: A THEORY OF INTERNATIONAL RELATIONS. Garden City, N.Y.: Doubleday, 1973. 468 p.

_____. WAR AND INDUSTRIAL SOCIETY. London: Oxford University Press, 1958. 63 p.

Bainton, Roland H. CHRISTIAN ATTITUDES TOWARD WAR AND PEACE: A HISTORICAL SURVEY AND CRITICAL RE-EVALUATION. New York: Abingdon, 1960. 299 p. Bibliog.

Barnet, Richard J. ROOTS OF WAR: THE MEN AND INSTITUTIONS BE-HIND U.S. FOREIGN POLICY. New York: Atheneum, 1972. 350 p.

Beaton, Leonard. THE STRUGGLE FOR PEACE. New York: Praeger, 1966. 118 p.

Beitz, Charles R., and Herman, Theodore, eds. PEACE AND WAR. San Francisco: Freeman, 1973. 435 p.

Bernal, John D. WORLD WITHOUT WAR. New York: Monthly Review, 1950. 300 p. Bibliog.

Bernard, Luther L. WAR AND ITS CAUSES. New York: Holt, 1944. 479 p. Bibliog.

Bigelow, Robert. THE DAWN WARRIORS: MAN'S EVOLUTION TOWARD PEACE. Boston: Little, Brown, 1969. 277 p. Bibliog.

Blainey, Geoffrey. THE CAUSES OF WAR. New York: Free Press, 1973. 278 p.

Bloomfield, Lincoln P., and Leiss, Amelia C. CONTROLLING SMALL WARS: A STRATEGY FOR THE 1970'S. New York: Knopf, 1969. 431 p.

Bottome, Edgar M. THE BALANCE OF TERROR: A GUIDE TO THE ARMS RACE. Boston: Beacon, 1971. 215 p.

Boulding, Kenneth E. THE ECONOMICS OF PEACE. New York: Prentice-Hall, 1945. 278 p.

_____. STABLE PEACE. Austin: University of Texas Press, 1978. 155 p.

_____, ed. PEACE AND THE WAR INDUSTRY. Chicago: Aldine, 1970. 159 p. Bibliog.

Bramson, Leon, and Goethals, George W., eds. WAR: STUDIES FROM PSYCHOLOGY, SOCIOLOGY, ANTHROPOLOGY. 2d ed. New York: Basic Books, 1968. 438 p. Bibliog.

Brodie, Bernard. WAR AND POLITICS. New York: Macmillan, 1973. 514 p.

Brownlie, Ian. INTERNATIONAL LAW AND THE USE OF FORCE BY STATES. London: Oxford University Press, 1963. 532 p. Bibliog.

Buchan, Alastair. WAR IN MODERN SOCIETY: AN INTRODUCTION. New York: Harper and Row, 1968. 207 p. Bibliog.

Burton, John W. PEACE THEORY: PRECONDITIONS OF DISARMAMENT. New York: Knopf, 1962. 201 p.

Butler, Nicholas Murray. WHY WAR?: ESSAYS AND ADDRESSES ON WAR AND PEACE. New York: Scribner, 1940. Reprint. Port Washington, N.Y.: Kennikat, 1969. 323 p.

Butterfield, Herbert. CHRISTIANITY, DIPLOMACY AND WAR. New York: Abingdon-Cokesbury, 1953. 125 p.

_____. INTERNATIONAL CONFLICT IN THE TWENTIETH CENTURY: A CHRISTIAN VIEW. New York: Harper, 1960. 123 p.

Callwell, Charles E. SMALL WARS: THEIR PRINCIPLES AND PRACTICE. 3d ed. London: Harrison, 1906. 559 p.

Caspary, William R. "Richardson's Model of Arms Races: Description, Critique, and an Alternative Model." INTERNATIONAL STUDIES QUARTERLY 11 (March 1967): 63-88.

Clark, George N. THE CYCLE OF WAR AND PEACE IN MODERN HISTORY. Cambridge: Cambridge University Press, 1949. 28 p.

Clark, Grenville. A PLAN FOR PEACE. New York: Harper, 1950. 83 p.

Clarke, Ignatius F. VOICES PROPHESYING WAR, 1763-1948. New York: Oxford University Press, 1966. 254 p. Bibliog.

Clarkson, Jesse D., and Cochran, Thomas C., eds. WAR AS A SOCIAL IN-STITUTION: THE HISTORIAN'S PERSPECTIVE. New York: Columbia University Press, 1941. 333 p.

Coblentz, Stanton A. FROM ARROW TO ATOM BOMB: THE PSYCHOLOGICAL HISTORY OF WAR. New York: Beechhurst, 1953. 539 p. Bibliog.

Coudenhove-Kalergi, Richard N. FROM WAR TO PEACE. London: Cape, 1959. 224 p.

Craig, Gordon A. WAR, POLITICS, AND DIPLOMACY: SELECTED ESSAYS. New York: Praeger, 1966. 297 p.

Davie, Maurice Rea. THE EVOLUTION OF WAR: A STUDY OF ITS ROLE IN EARLY SOCIETIES. New Haven, Conn.: Yale University Press, 1929. 391 p.

Deitchman, Seymour J. LIMITED WAR AND AMERICAN DEFENSE POLICY. 2d ed. Cambridge, Mass.: M.I.T. Press, 1969. 302 p. Bibliog.

Douglas, William O. INTERNATIONAL DISSENT: SIX STEPS TOWARDS WORLD PEACE. New York: Random House, 1971. 155 p. Bibliog.

Dunn, Frederick S. WAR AND THE MINDS OF MEN. New York: Harper for Council on Foreign Relations, 1950. 115 p.

Eckstein, Harry, ed. INTERNAL WAR: PROBLEMS AND APPROACHES. New York: Free Press, 1964. 339 p. Bibliog.

Etzioni, Amitai. THE HARD WAY TO PEACE: A NEW STRATEGY. New York: Crowell-Collier, 1962. 285 p.

Falk, Richard A. LAW, MORALITY, AND WAR IN THE CONTEMPORARY WORLD. New York: Praeger for Center of International Studies, Princeton University, 1963. 120 p.

Falk, Richard A., and Mendlovitz, Saul H., eds. TOWARD A THEORY OF WAR PREVENTION. New York: World Law Fund, 1966. 394 p.

Farrar, L.L., Jr., ed. WAR: A HISTORICAL, POLITICAL, AND SOCIAL STUDY. Santa Barbara, Calif.: ABC-Clio Press, 1978. 285 p.

Foster, James L., and Brewer, Garry D. AND THE CLOCKS WERE STRIKING THIRTEEN: THE TERMINATION OF WAR. Santa Monica, Calif.: Rand, 1976. 26 p.

Fox, William T.R., ed. "How Wars End." ANNALS OF THE AMERICAN ACADEMY OF POLITICAL AND SOCIAL SCIENCE 392 (November 1970): 1-172.

Frank, Jerome D. SANITY AND SURVIVAL: PSYCHOLOGICAL ASPECTS OF WAR AND PEACE. New York: Random House, 1967. 330 p. Bibliog.

Fried, Morton; Harris, Marvin; and Murphy, Robert, eds. WAR: THE ANTHROPOLOGY OF ARMED CONFLICT AND AGGRESSION. Garden City, N.Y.: American Museum of Natural History, 1968. 262 p. Bibliog.

Galtung, Johan. PEACE, WAR, AND DEFENSE. Copenhagen: Christian Ejlers, 1976. 472 p.

Gillett, Nicholas. MEN AGAINST WAR. London: Gollancz, 1965. 144 p. Bibliog.

Ginsberg, Robert, ed. THE CRITIQUE OF WAR: CONTEMPORARY PHILOSOPHICAL EXPLORATIONS. Chicago: Regnery, 1969. 360 p. Bibliog.

Glover, Edward. WAR, SADISM, AND PACIFISM: FURTHER ESSAYS ON GROUP PSYCHOLOGY AND WAR. London: Allen and Unwin, 1947. 292 p.

Graham, Thomas F. ANATOMY OF AGGRESSION: BASES OF WAR. Akron, Ohio: Danner, 1968. 171 p. Bibliog.

Grob, Fritz. THE RELATIVITY OF WAR AND PEACE: A STUDY IN LAW, HISTORY, AND POLITICS. New Haven, Conn.: Yale University Press, 1949. 402 p. Bibliog.

Halperin, Morton H. LIMITED WAR IN THE NUCLEAR AGE. New York: Wiley, 1963. 191 p. Bibliog.

Hancock, William K. FOUR STUDIES OF WAR AND PEACE IN THIS CENTURY. Cambridge: Cambridge University Press, 1961. 129 p.

Heilbrunn, Otto. CONVENTIONAL WARFARE IN THE NUCLEAR AGE. New York: Praeger, 1965. 164 p. Bibliog.

Herring, Edward Pendleton. THE IMPACT OF WAR: OUR AMERICAN DE-MOCRACY UNDER ARMS. New York: Farrar and Rinehart, 1941. 306 p. Bibliog.

Herzog, Arthur. THE WAR-PEACE ESTABLISHMENT. New York: Harper and Row, 1965. 271 p.

Hindmarsh, Albert E. FORCE IN PEACE: FORCE SHORT OF WAR IN INTER-NATIONAL RELATIONS. Cambridge, Mass.: Harvard University Press, 1933. 249 p. Bibliog.

Hinsley, Francis Harry. POWER AND THE PURSUIT OF PEACE: THEORY AND PRACTICE IN THE HISTORY OF RELATIONS BETWEEN STATES. Cambridge: Cambridge University Press, 1963. 416 p.

Holcombe, Arthur N. A STRATEGY OF PEACE IN A CHANGING WORLD. Cambridge, Mass.: Harvard University Press, 1967. 332 p.

Hollins, Elizabeth J., ed. PEACE IS POSSIBLE: A READER FOR LAYMEN. New York: Grossman, 1966. 340 p. Bibliog.

Horowitz, Irving L. THE IDEA OF WAR AND PEACE IN CONTEMPORARY PHILOSOPHY. New York: Paine-Whitman, 1957. 224 p.

Howard, John R. FOURTEEN DECISIONS FOR UNDECLARED WAR. Washington, D.C.: University Press of America, 1978. 172 p.

   Treats U.S. involvement In undeclared wars, from the eighteenth century to Vietnam.

Hughes, H. Stuart. AN APPROACH TO PEACE, AND OTHER ESSAYS. New York: Atheneum, 1962. 204 p.

Ikle, Fred Charles. EVERY WAR MUST END. New York: Columbia University Press, 1971. 160 p.

Isbell, Allen C. WAR AND CONSCIENCE. Abilene, Kans.: Biblical Research, 1966. 221 p. Bibliog.

Janowitz, Morris. MILITARY CONFLICT: ESSAYS IN THE INSTITUTIONAL ANALYSIS OF WAR AND PEACE. Beverly Hills, Calif.: Sage, 1975. 320 p.

Johnson, L. Gunnar. CONFLICTING CONCEPTS OF PEACE IN CONTEMPO-RARY PEACE STUDIES. Beverly Hills, Calif.: Sage, 1976. 63 p.

Kahn, Herman. ON THERMONUCLEAR WAR. Princeton, N.J.: Princeton University Press, 1960. 651 p.

Kintner, William R. THE NEW FRONTIER OF WAR: POLITICAL WARFARE, PRESENT AND FUTURE. Chicago: Regnery, 1962. 362 p. Bibliog.

Knapp, Wilfred. A HISTORY OF WAR AND PEACE, 1939-1965. New York: Oxford University Press, 1967. 639 p. Bibliog.

Knorr, Klaus E. THE WAR POTENTIAL OF NATIONS. Princeton, N.J.: Princeton University Press, 1956. 310 p.

Knorr, Klaus E., and Read, Thornton, eds. LIMITED STRATEGIC WAR. New York: Praeger for Center of International Studies, Princeton University, 1962. 258 p.

Kolko, Gabriel. THE POLITICS OF WAR: THE WORLD AND UNITED STATES FOREIGN POLICY, 1943-1945. New York: Random House, 1968. 685 p.

Kotzsch, Lothar. THE CONCEPT OF WAR IN CONTEMPORARY HISTORY AND INTERNATIONAL LAW. Geneva: Droz, 1956. 310 p. Bibliog.

Lapp, Ralph E. THE WEAPONS CULTURE. Baltimore: Penguin, 1969. 236 p.

Larson, Arthur, ed. A WARLESS WORLD. New York: McGraw-Hill, 1963. 209 p.

_____. WHEN NATIONS DISAGREE: A HANDBOOK ON PEACE THROUGH LAW. Baton Rouge: Louisiana State University Press, 1961. 251 p.

Lasley, John W. THE WAR SYSTEM AND YOU. 2d ed. Chapel Hill, N.C.: Institute for International Studies, 1965. 262 p.

Lasswell, Harold D. "'Inevitable' Wars: A Problem in the Control of Long-Range Expectations." WORLD POLITICS 2 (October 1949): 1-39.

Lentz, Theodore F. TOWARDS A SCIENCE OF PEACE: TURNING POINT IN HUMAN DESTINY. New York: Bookman, 1955. 194 p.

Lider, Julian. ON THE NATURE OF WAR. Farnsbourough, Engl.: Saxon House, 1977. 409 p. Bibliog.

Lipsky, Mortimer. QUEST FOR PEACE: THE STORY OF THE NOBEL AWARD. South Brunswick, N.J.: Barnes, 1966. 281 p.

Lonsdale, Kathleen. IS PEACE POSSIBLE? Harmondsworth, Engl.: Penguin, 1957. 126 p.

Luard, Evan. PEACE AND OPINION. New York: Oxford University Press, 1962. 170 p.

McClintock, Robert. THE MEANING OF LIMITED WAR. Boston: Houghton Mifflin, 1967. 239 p. Bibliog.

McDonald, John D. STRATEGY IN POKER, BUSINESS AND WAR. New York: Norton, 1950. 128 p. Bibliog.

Mahan, Alfred T. ARMAMENTS AND ARBITRATION: OR THE PLACE OF FORCE IN THE INTERNATIONAL RELATIONS OF STATES. New York: Garland, 1912. 772 p.

Martin, Charles E. THE POLITICS OF PEACE. Stanford, Calif.: Stanford University Press, 1929. 458 p.

May, Mark A. A SOCIAL PSYCHOLOGY OF WAR AND PEACE. London: Oxford University Press, 1943. 284 p.

Melman, Seymour. THE PEACE RACE. New York: Braziller, 1962. 152 p.

Middleton, Drew. CAN AMERICA WIN THE NEXT WAR? New York: Scribner, 1975. 271 p.

Midlarsky, Manus I. ON WAR: POLITICAL VIOLENCE IN THE INTERNATIONAL SYSTEM. New York: Free Press, 1975. 229 p.

Miksche, Ferdinand O. SECRET FORCES: THE TECHNIQUE OF UNDERGROUND MOVEMENTS. London: Faber and Faber, 1950. 181 p.

Miller, Lynn H. "The Contemporary Significance of the Doctrine of Just War." WORLD POLITICS 16 (January 1964): 254-86.

Millis, Walter. PERMANENT PEACE. Santa Barbara, Calif.: Center for the Study of Democratic Institutions, 1961. 31 p.

Millis, Walter, and Real, James. THE ABOLITION OF WAR. New York: Macmillan, 1963. 217 p.

Millis, Walter, et al. A WORLD WITHOUT WAR. New York: Washington Square, 1962. 182 p.

Mills, C. Wright. THE CAUSES OF WORLD WAR THREE. New York: Simon and Schuster, 1958. 172 p.

Mitrany, David. A WORKING PEACE SYSTEM. Chicago: Quadrangle, 1966. 211 p.

Modelski, George A. THE INTERNATIONAL RELATIONS OF INTERNAL WAR. Princeton, N.J.: Center of International Studies, Princeton University, 1961. 24 p.

Montross, Lynn. WAR THROUGH THE AGES. 3d ed. New York: Harper, 1960. 1,063 p. Bibliog.

Murty, K. Satchidananda, and Bouquet, A.C. STUDIES IN THE PROBLEMS OF PEACE. New York: Asia Publishing House, 1960. 375 p.

Nagle, William J., ed. MORALITY AND MODERN WARFARE: THE STATE OF THE QUESTION. Baltimore: Halicon, 1960. 168 p.

Nelson, Keith L., and Olin, Spencer C. Jr. WHY WAR?: IDEOLOGY, THEORY, AND HISTORY. Berkeley: University of California Press, 1979. 184 p.

Nickerson, Hoffman. CAN WE LIMIT WAR? New York: Stokes, 1934. 317 p.

Northedge, F.S., ed. THE USE OF FORCE IN INTERNATIONAL RELATIONS. New York: Free Press, 1974. 258 p. Bibliog.

    Classical approach to the matter of warfare.

O'Brien, William V. WAR AND/OR SURVIVAL. Garden City, N.Y.: Doubleday, 1969. 289 p.

Opie, Redvers, et al. THE SEARCH FOR PEACE SETTLEMENTS. Washington, D.C.: Brookings Institution, 1951. 366 p.

Osgood, Robert E. AN ALTERNATIVE TO WAR OR SURRENDER. Urbana: University of Illinois Press, 1962. 183 p.

_____. LIMITED WAR: THE CHALLENGE TO AMERICAN STRATEGY. Chicago: University of Chicago Press, 1957. 315 p. Bibliog.

Otterbein, Keith F. THE EVOLUTION OF WAR: A CROSS-CULTURAL STUDY. n.p.: HRAF (Human Relations Area Files Press), 1970. 165 p. Bibliog.

Payne, James L. THE AMERICAN THREAT: THE FEAR OF WAR AS AN INSTRUMENT OF FOREIGN POLICY. Chicago: Markham, 1970. 241 p.

"Peace Research." INTERNATIONAL SOCIAL SCIENCE JOURNAL 17, no. 3 (1965): 395-501.

Symposium of several articles by individual authors.

Pear, Tom H., ed. PSYCHOLOGICAL FACTORS OF PEACE AND WAR. New York: Philosophical Library, 1950. 262 p. Bibliog.

Phillipson, Coleman. TERMINATION OF WAR AND TREATIES OF PEACE. New York: Dutton, 1916. 486 p.

Pillar, Paul Roy. "Negotiating Peace: The Making of Armistice Agreements." Ph.D. dissertation, Princeton University, 1978. 527 p.

Pompe, Cornelis A. AGGRESSIVE WAR: AN INTERNATIONAL CRIME. The Hague: Nijhoff, 1953. 382 p. Bibliog.

Potter, Ralph B. WAR AND MORAL DISCOURSE. Richmond, Va.: Knox, 1969. 123 p. Bibliog.

Preston, Richard A., and Wise, Sydney F. MEN IN ARMS: A HISTORY OF WARFARE AND ITS INTERRELATIONSHIPS WITH WESTERN SOCIETY. 4th ed. New York: Holt, Rinehart, and Winston, 1979. 472 p.

Pruitt, Dean G., and Snyder, Richard C., eds. THEORY AND RESEARCH ON THE CAUSES OF WAR. Englewood Cliffs, N.J.: Prentice-Hall, 1969. 314 p. Bibliog.

Ramsey, Paul. THE JUST WAR: FORCE AND POLITICAL RESPONSIBILITY. New York: Scribner, 1968. 554 p.

Rappard, William E. THE QUEST FOR PEACE SINCE THE WORLD WAR. Cambridge, Mass.: Harvard University Press, 1940. 516 p.

Rathbone, Eleanor F. WAR CAN BE AVERTED: THE ACHIEVABILITY OF COLLECTIVE SECURITY. London: Gollancz, 1938. 221 p.

Reves, Emery. THE ANATOMY OF PEACE. 10th ed. New York: Harper, 1945. 275 p.

Richardson, Frank M. FIGHTING SPIRIT: PSYCHOLOGICAL FACTORS IN WAR. New York: Crane, Russak, 1978. 196 p. London: Cooper, 1978. 189 p. Bibliog.

Richardson, Lewis Fry. ARMS AND INSECURITY: A MATHEMATICAL STUDY OF THE CAUSES AND ORIGINS OF WAR. Edited by Nicolas Rashevsky and Ernesto Trucco. Pittsburgh: Boxwood, 1960. 307 p. Bibliog.

Rikon, Irving. PEACE AS IT CAN BE. New York: Philosophical Library, 1970. 188 p.

Rummel, R.J. UNDERSTANDING CONFLICT AND WAR. Beverly Hills, Calif.: Sage, 1977. 200 p.

_____, ed. WAR, POWER, PEACE. Beverly Hills, Calif.: Sage, 1979. 450 p.

Russett, Bruce M., ed. PEACE, WAR AND NUMBERS. Beverly Hills, Calif.: Sage, 1972. 352 p. Bibliog.

   Collection of empirical papers on hypotheses about causes and control of international violent conflict.

Schweitzer, Albert. PEACE OR ATOMIC WAR? New York: Holt, 1958. 47 p.

Shotwell, James T. WAR AS AN INSTRUMENT OF NATIONAL POLICY AND ITS RENUNCIATION IN THE PACT OF PARIS. New York: Harcourt, Brace, 1929. 310 p.

Simpson, B. Mitchell III. WAR, STRATEGY, AND MARITIME POWER. New Brunswick, N.J.: Rutgers University Press, 1977. 356 p.

Singer, J. David, ed. THE CORRELATES OF WAR: RESEARCH ORIGINS AND RATIONALE. Riverside, N.J.: Free Press, 1978. 432 p. Bibliog.

   First of two volumes.

Singer, J. David, and Small, Melvin. THE WAGES OF WAR, 1816-1965: A STATISTICAL HANDBOOK. New York: Wiley, 1972. 419 p. Bibliog.

Singer, J. David, et al., eds. EXPLAINING WAR: CAUSES AND CORRELATES OF WAR. Beverly Hills, Calif.: Sage, 1979. 312 p.

   Presents results of Correlates of War project to lay foundations for a science of peace and war.

Slick, Tom. PERMANENT PEACE: A CHECK AND BALANCE PLAN. Englewood Cliffs, N.J.: Prentice Hall, 1958. 191 p.

Smoke, Richard. WAR: CONTROLLING ESCALATION. Cambridge, Mass.: Harvard University Press, 1977. 419 p.

Speier, Hans. SOCIAL ORDER AND RISKS OF WAR: PAPERS IN POLITICAL SOCIOLOGY. New York: Stewart, 1952. 497 p. Bibliog.

Speier, Hans, and Kahler, Alfred, eds. WAR IN OUR TIME. New York: Norton, 1939. 362 p.

Starke, Joseph G. AN INTRODUCTION TO THE SCIENCE OF PEACE (IRENOLOGY). Leiden, The Netherlands: Sijthoff, 1968. 216 p. Bibliog.

Stockholm International Peace Research Institute. ARMS CONTROL: A SURVEY AND APPRAISAL OF MULTILATERAL AGREEMENTS. London: Taylor and Francis, 1978. 238 p.

Stoessinger, John G. WHY NATIONS GO TO WAR. 2d ed. New York: St. Martin's, 1978. 200 p.

Strachey, Alix. THE UNCONSCIOUS MOTIVES OF WAR: A PSYCHO-ANALYTICAL CONTRIBUTION. London: Allen and Unwin, 1957. 283 p.

Strachey, John. ON THE PREVENTION OF WAR. New York: St. Martin's, 1963. 334 p.

Sutton, Antony. WARS AND REVOLUTIONS: A COMPREHENSIVE LIST OF CONFLICTS, INCLUDING FATALITIES. Part 1, 1820-1900; Part 2, 1900-1972. Stanford, Calif.: Hoover Institution, 1971, 1973. 161 p., 206 p.

Swan, Herbert L. POSITIVE PEACEFARE: THE NEGLECTED ART OF WAGING PEACE. New York: Vantage, 1966. 149 p.

Ten Eyck, John C. THE LAW OF DIMINISHING WAR POWER, FROM TROY TO VIETNAM. New York: Pageant, 1970. 273 p. Bibliog.

Thayer, G. THE WAR BUSINESS: THE INTERNATIONAL TRADE IN ARMAMENTS. New York: Simon and Schuster, 1969. 417 p.

Thomas, Norman M. THE PREREQUISITES FOR PEACE. New York: Norton, 1959. 189 p.

Tillema, Herbert K. APPEAL TO FORCE: AMERICAN MILITARY INTERVENTION IN THE ERA OF CONTAINMENT. New York: Crowell, 1973. 260 p. Bibliog.

Timasheff, Nicholas S. WAR AND REVOLUTION. Edited and preface by Joseph F. Scheuer. New York: Sheed and Ward, 1965. 339 p. Bibliog.

Toynbee, Arnold J. WAR AND CIVILIZATION: FROM A STUDY OF HISTORY. Edited by Albert V. Fowler. New York: Oxford University Press for Royal Institute of International Affairs, 1950. 165 p.

Turney-High, Harry H. PRIMITIVE WAR: ITS PRACTICE AND CONCEPTS. Columbia: University of South Carolina Press, 1949. 277 p. Bibliog.

Veale, Frederick J.P. ADVANCE TO BARBARISM: THE DEVELOPMENT OF TOTAL WARFARE FROM SARAJEVO TO HIROSHIMA. 2d ed. London: Mitre, 1968. 363 p. Bibliog.

Von Clausewitz, Karl. ON WAR. Translated by J.J. Graham. Introduction and notes by F.N. Maude. 3 vols. Rev. ed. New York: Barnes and Noble, 1956.

Waitley, Douglas. THE WAR MAKERS. Washington, D.C.: Luce, 1971. 302 p. Bibliog.

Wallace, Victor H., ed. PATHS TO PEACE: A STUDY OF WAR, ITS CAUSES AND PREVENTION. New York: Cambridge University Press, 1957. 397 p.

Waltz, Kenneth N. MAN, THE STATE, AND WAR: A THEORETICAL ANALYSIS. New York: Columbia University Press, 1959. 263 p. Bibliog.

Wasserstrom, Richard A., ed. WAR AND MORALITY. Belmont, Calif.: Wadsworth, 1970. 136 p. Bibliog.

Wehberg, Hans. THE OUTLAWRY OF WAR. Washington, D.C.: Carnegie Endowment for International Peace, 1931. 149 p.

Wells, John M., and Wilhelm, Maria, eds. THE PEOPLE VS. PRESIDENTIAL WAR. New York: Dunellen, 1970. 199 p.

Wheeler-Bennet, J.W. INFORMATION ON THE RENUNCIATION OF WAR, 1927-1928. London: Allen and Unwin, 1928. 191 p.

Wright, Quincy. A STUDY OF WAR. 2d ed. Chicago: University of Chicago Press, 1965. 1637 p. Bibliog.

_____, ed. PREVENTING WORLD WAR III: SOME PROPOSALS. New York: Simon and Schuster, 1962. 460 p. Bibliog.

Ziegler, David W. WAR, PEACE, AND INTERNATIONAL POLITICS. Boston: Little, Brown, 1977. 444 p.

Ziegler, Janet. WORLD WAR II: A BIBLIOGRAPHY OF BOOKS IN ENGLISH, 1945-1965. Stanford, Calif.: Hoover Institution, 1971. 194 p.

Official commentary on U.S. practice, concerned with the legal and political aspects of warfare, is provided in the following:

Hackworth, Green H. DIGEST OF INTERNATIONAL LAW. Washington, D.C.: Government Printing Office, 1943. Vol. 6, Chapters 20 and 21, pp. 161-655.

Moore, John Bassett. A DIGEST OF INTERNATIONAL LAW. Washington, D.C.: Government Printing Office, 1906. Vol. 7, pp. 152-1109.

Whiteman, Marjorie M. DIGEST OF INTERNATIONAL LAW. Washington, D.C.: Government Printing Office, 1967. Vol. 10, Chapters 29 and 30, pp. 1-790.

Peacekeeping

Cox, Arthur M. PROSPECTS FOR PEACEKEEPING. Washington, D.C.: Brookings Institution, 1967. 178 p.

James, Alan. THE POLITICS OF PEACE-KEEPING. New York: Praeger for Institute of Strategic Studies, 1969. 452 p. Bibliog.

Pikus, Robert, and Woito, Robert. TO END WAR: AN INTRODUCTION TO THE IDEAS, BOOKS, ORGANIZATIONS, WORK, THAT CAN HELP. 3d ed. Berkeley, Calif.: World Without War Council, 1970. 261 p. Bibliog.

Rikhye, Indar Jit; Harbottle, Michael; and Egge, Bjorn. THE THIN BLUE LINE: INTERNATIONAL PEACEKEEPING AND ITS FUTURE. New Haven, Conn.: Yale University Press, 1974. 353 p. Bibliog.

Shore, William I. FACT-FINDING IN THE MAINTENANCE OF INTERNA TIONAL PEACE. Dobbs Ferry, N.Y.: Oceana, 1970. 183 p. Bibliog.

Smith, Gordon S. A SELECTED BIBLIOGRAPHY ON PEACE KEEPING. 2d ed. Ottawa: Department of National Defense, Canada, 1966. 35 p.

Veblen, Thorstein. AN INQUIRY INTO THE NATURE OF PEACE AND THE TERMS OF ITS PERPETUATION. New York: Viking, 1945. 367 p.

Wainhouse, David W., et al. INTERNATIONAL PEACEKEEPING AT THE CROSSROADS: NATIONAL SUPPORT--EXPERIENCE AND PROSPECTS. Baltimore: Johns Hopkins University Press, 1973. 634 p.

Young, Oran R. TRENDS IN INTERNATIONAL PEACEKEEPING. Princeton, N.J.: Center of International Studies, Princeton University, 1966. 45 p.

Peace Research

Dedring, Juergen. RECENT ADVANCES IN PEACE AND CONFLICT RESEARCH. Sage Library of Social Research, vol. 27. Beverly Hills, Calif.: Sage, 1976. 249 p.

Galtung, Johan. PEACE: RESEARCH, EDUCATION, ACTION. Copenhagen: Christian Ejlers, 1975. 406 p.

Mahendra, Kumar. CURRENT PEACE RESEARCH AND INDIA. Varanasi, India: Gandhian Institute of Studies, 1968.. 147 p.

Newcombe, Hanna, and Newcombe, Alan. PEACE RESEARCH AROUND THE WORLD. Oakville: Canadian Peace Research Institute, 1969. 275 p.

Niezing, Johan. SOCIOLOGY, WAR AND DISARMAMENT: STUDIES IN PEACE RESEARCH. Rotterdam, The Netherlands: Rotterdam University, 1970. 131 p. Bibliog.

Oppenheimer, Martin. "The Directions of Peace Research: Conflict or Consensus." JOURNAL OF HUMAN RELATIONS 13 (3d Quarter 1965): 314-19.

Roelling, Bert V.A. "National and International Peace Research." INTERNATIONAL SOCIAL SCIENCE JOURNAL 17, no. 3 (1965): 487-501.

Waskow, Arthur I. THE WORRIED MAN'S GUIDE TO WORLD PEACE: A PEACE RESEARCH INSTITUTE HANDBOOK. Garden City, N.Y.: Anchor, 1963. 219 p.

Wehr, Paul, and Washburn, Michael. PEACE AND WORLD ORDER SYSTEMS: TEACHING AND RESEARCH. Beverly Hills, Calif.: Sage, 1976. 255 p.

Wright, Quincy, et al. RESEARCH FOR PEACE. Amsterdam: North Holland for Institute for Social Research, Oslo, 1954. 296 p.

Additional guidance to materials on peace research may be found in the following:

Cook, Blanche Wieser, ed. BIBLIOGRAPHY ON PEACE RESEARCH IN HISTORY. Santa Barbara, Calif.: ABC-Clio Press, 1969. 72 p.

Durkee, Kinde, comp. PEACE RESEARCH: DEFINITIONS AND OBJECTIVES-- A BIBLIOGRAPHY. Los Angeles: Center for the Study of Armament and Disarmament, 1976. 28 p.

Gray, Charles; Gray, Leslie; and Gregory, Glenn, comps. A BIBLIOGRAPHY OF PEACE RESEARCH: INDEXED BY KEY WORDS. Eugene, Oreg.: General Research Analysis Methods, 1968. 164 p.

COLD WAR

The mid-twentieth-century cold war naturally evoked a substantial amount of research and literary attention. This section lists a selection of published materials of concern to analysts of American foreign relations. As might be expected, much interest has concentrated on the origins of the cold war, represented by the studies of Feis, Fleming, Gaddis, Gardner, Herz, Maddox, Marzani, Nagai and Iriye, Paterson, and Yergin. Others are more concerned with its development and history, such as those of Fontaine, Graebner, Halle, Hammond, Ingram, Kaplan, Lukacs, McLellan, Marshall, Seabury, Siracusa, and Winks. Some emphasize various specialized or limited aspects of the cold war, including those of Aronson, Clayton, Gamson and Modigliani, Gati, Kennan, Meyerhoff, Seldes, and Whitton, as well as those which focus specifically on U.S. containment policy. Although many general studies include appraisal of the cold war in American and world relations, a few concentrate specifically on its assessment, such as those of Luard, Schuman, and Wilson.

Alperovitz, Gar, ed. COLD WAR ESSAYS. Garden City, N.Y.: Anchor, 1970. 150 p. Bibliog.

Aptheker, Herbert. AMERICAN FOREIGN POLICY AND THE COLD WAR. New York: New Century, 1962. 416 p.

Aronson, James. THE PRESS AND THE COLD WAR. Indianapolis: Bobbs-Merrill, 1970. 308 p. Bibliog.

Barnet, Richard J., and Raskin, Marcus G. AFTER 20 YEARS: ALTERNATIVES TO THE COLD WAR IN EUROPE. New York: Random House, 1965. 243 p.

Betts, Richard K. SOLDIERS, STATESMEN, AND COLD WAR CRISES. Cambridge, Mass.: Harvard University Press, 1977. 292 p. Bibliog.

Brzezinski, Zbigniew. "How the Cold War Was Played." FOREIGN AFFAIRS 51 (October 1972): 181-209.

Chandler, Harriette L. "Soviet Russia as Seen Through the Eyes of American Policy Makers, 1943-1945: The Problems of Assessing Soviet Policy on the Eve of the Cold War." Ph.D. dissertation: Clark University, 1973. 548 p.

Clayton, James L., ed. THE ECONOMIC IMPACT OF THE COLD WAR: SOURCES AND READINGS. New York: Harcourt, Brace, and World, 1970. 287 p. Bibliog.

Davis, Lynn Etheridge. THE COLD WAR BEGINS: SOVIET-AMERICAN CON-
FLICT OVER EASTERN EUROPE. Princeton, N.J.: Princeton University Press,
1974. 427 p. Bibliog.

_____. "United States Policy Toward Eastern Europe, 1941-1945: The Escala-
tion of Conflict and Commitment." Ph.D. dissertation, Columbia University,
1971. 298 p.

Deutcher, Isaac. THE GREAT CONTEST: RUSSIA AND THE WEST. New
York: Oxford University Press, 1960. 143 p.

Donnelly, Desmond. STRUGGLE FOR THE WORLD: THE COLD WAR, 1917-
1965. New York: St. Martin's, 1965. 511 p. Bibliog.

Feis, Herbert. FROM TRUST TO TERROR: THE ONSET OF THE COLD WAR,
1945-1950. New York: Norton, 1970. 428 p. Bibliog.

Fischer, Louis. RUSSIA, AMERICA, AND THE WORLD. New York: Harper,
1961. 244 p.

Fleming, Denna F. THE COLD WAR AND ITS ORIGINS, 1917-1960. 2 vols.
Garden City, N.Y.: Doubleday, 1961.

Fontaine, Andre. HISTORY OF THE COLD WAR. Translated by D.D. Paige
and R. Bruce. 2 vols. New York: Pantheon, 1968-69. Bibliog.

Freeland, Richard Middleton. "Cold War Mobilization." Ph.D. dissertation,
University of Pennsylvania, 1969. 564 p.

Gaddis, John Lewis. THE UNITED STATES AND THE ORIGINS OF THE
COLD WAR: 1941-1947. New York: Columbia University Press, 1972.
396 p. Bibliog.

Gamson, W.A., and Modigliani, A. UNTANGLING THE COLD WAR: A
STRATEGY FOR TESTING RIVAL THEORIES. Boston: Little, Brown, 1971. 217 p.

Gardner, Lloyd C.; Schlesinger, Arthur, Jr.; and Morgenthau, Hans J. THE
ORIGINS OF THE COLD WAR. Waltham, Mass.: Ginn-Blaisdell, 1970.
122 p. Bibliog.

Gati, Charles, ed. CAGING THE BEAR: CONTAINMENT AND THE COLD
WAR. Indianapolis: Bobbs-Merrill, 1974. 228 p.

Graebner, Norman A. "The Cold War: An American View." INTERNATION-
AL JOURNAL 15 (Spring 1960): 95-112.

_____. COLD WAR DIPLOMACY: AMERICA'S FOREIGN POLICY, 1945-1975. 2d ed. New York: Van Nostrand, 1977. 248 p. Bibliog.

_____. "Cold War Origins and the Continuing Debate: A Review of Recent Literature." JOURNAL OF CONFLICT RESOLUTION 13 (March 1969): 123-38.

_____, ed. THE COLD WAR: A CONFLICT OF IDEOLOGY AND POWER. 2d ed. Lexington, Mass.: Heath, 1976. 206 p. Bibliog.

Gray, Robert Curtis. "The Social Construction of the Cold War: Image and Process in Soviet-American Relations, 1941-1947." Ph.D. dissertation, University of Texas (Austin), 1975. 543 p.

Halle, Louis J. THE COLD WAR AS HISTORY. New York: Harper and Row, 1967. 434 p. Bibliog.

Hammond, Paul Y. COLD WAR AND DETENTE: THE AMERICAN FOREIGN POLICY PROCESS SINCE 1945. New York: Harcourt Brace Jovanovich, 1975. 370 p.
        Revision of THE COLD WAR YEARS, 1969.

Herz, Martin F. BEGINNINGS OF THE COLD WAR. Bloomington: Indiana University Press, 1966. 214 p. Bibliog.

Higgins, H. THE COLD WAR. New York: Barnes and Noble, 1974. 141 p.

Horowitz, David. THE FREE WORLD COLOSSUS: A CRITIQUE OF AMERICAN FOREIGN POLICY IN THE COLD WAR. New York: Hill and Wang, 1965. 451 p. Bibliog.

_____. FROM YALTA TO VIETNAM: AMERICAN FOREIGN POLICY IN THE COLD WAR. 2d ed. Harmondsworth, Engl.: Penguin, 1969. 465 p. Bibliog.

Ingram, Kenneth. HISTORY OF THE COLD WAR. New York: Philosophical Library, 1955. 239 p.

Jeevan Reddy, B.P. MODERN POWER POLITICS: COLD WAR--A STUDY. Madras, India: Orient Longman, 1970. 268 p. Bibliog.

Jefferson, Charles James. "Bureaucracy, Diplomacy and the Origins of the Cold War." Ph.D. dissertation, Claremont University, 1975. 479 p.

Kaplan, Morton A. THE LIFE AND DEATH OF THE COLD WAR: SELECTED STUDIES IN POSTWAR STATECRAFT. Chicago: Nelson-Hall, 1976. 384 p.

Series of the author's own accounts of the politics of the cold war.

Kennan, George F. "After the Cold War: American Foreign Policy in the 1970's." FOREIGN AFFAIRS 51 (October 1972): 210-27.

_____. RUSSIA, THE ATOM, AND THE WEST. New York: Harper, 1958. 116 p.

LaFeber, Walter. AMERICA, RUSSIA, AND THE COLD WAR, 1945-1971. 3d ed. New York: Wiley, 1976. 328 p. Bibliog.

_____, ed. AMERICA IN THE COLD WAR: TWENTY YEARS OF REVOLU-TIONS AND RESPONSE, 1947-1967. New York: Wiley, 1969. 232 p. Bibliog.

Lerche, Charles O., Jr. THE COLD WAR AND AFTER. Englewood Cliffs, N.J.: Prentice-Hall, 1965. 150 p. Bibliog.

Lippmann, Walter. THE COLD WAR: A STUDY IN U.S. FOREIGN POLICY. New York: Harper, 1947. 62 p.

Luard, Evan, ed. THE COLD WAR: A REAPPRAISAL. New York: Praeger, 1964. 347 p. Bibliog.

Lukacs, John A. A NEW HISTORY OF THE COLD WAR. 3d ed. Garden City, N.Y.: Doubleday, 1966. 426 p.

McInnis, Edgar. THE ATLANTIC TRIANGLE AND THE COLD WAR. Toronto: University of Toronto Press, 1959. 163 p.

McLellan, David S. THE COLD WAR IN TRANSITION. New York: Mac-millan, 1966. 149 p.

Maddox, Robert J. THE NEW LEFT AND THE ORIGINS OF THE COLD WAR. Princeton, N.J.: Princeton University Press, 1973. 169 p.

Marshall, Charles Burton. THE COLD WAR: A CONCISE HISTORY. New York: Watts, 1965. 104 p.

Marzani, Carl. WE CAN BE FRIENDS: ORIGINS OF THE COLD WAR. New York: Topical, 1952. 380 p.

Meyerhoff, Arthur E. THE STRATEGY OF PERSUASION: THE USE OF ADVER-TISING SKILLS IN FIGHTING THE COLD WAR. New York: Coward-McCann, 1965. 191 p. Bibliog.

Miller, Lynn H., ed. REFLECTIONS ON THE COLD WAR: A QUARTER CENTURY OF AMERICAN FOREIGN POLICY. Philadelphia: Temple University Press, 1974. 207 p.

Morray, Joseph P. FROM YALTA TO DISARMAMENT: COLD WAR DEBATE. New York: Monthly Review Press, 1961. 368 p.

Nagai, Yonosuke, and Iriye, Akira, eds. THE ORIGINS OF THE COLD WAR IN ASIA. New York: Columbia University Press, 1977. 448 p. Bibliog.

O'Connor, John F. COLD WAR AND LIBERATION. New York: Vantage, 1961. 611 p.

Paterson, Thomas G. SOVIET-AMERICAN CONFRONTATION: POSTWAR RECONSTRUCTION AND THE ORIGINS OF THE COLD WAR. Baltimore: Johns Hopkins Press, 1973. 287 p. Bibliog.

_____, ed. COLD WAR CRITICS: ALTERNATIVES TO AMERICAN FOREIGN POLICY IN THE TRUMAN YEARS. New York: New Viewpoints, 1971. 312 p.

_____, ed. CONTAINMENT AND THE COLD WAR: AMERICAN FOREIGN POLICY SINCE 1945. Reading, Mass.: Addison-Wesley, 1973. 250 p. Bibliog.

_____, ed. THE ORIGINS OF THE COLD WAR. Lexington, Mass.: Heath, 1970. 126 p. Bibliog.

Perla, Leo. CAN WE END THE COLD WAR? A STUDY IN AMERICAN FOREIGN POLICY. New York: Macmillan, 1960. 251 p.

Potichnyj, Peter J., and Shapiro, Jane P., eds. FROM THE COLD WAR TO DETENTE. New York: Praeger, 1976. 238 p.

Ransom, Harry Howe. CAN AMERICAN DEMOCRACY SURVIVE COLD WAR? New York: Doubleday, 1963. 270 p.

Rees, David. THE AGE OF CONTAINMENT: THE COLD WAR, 1945-1965. New York: St. Martin's, 1967. 156 p. Bibliog.

Roberts, Henry L. RUSSIA AND AMERICA: DANGERS AND PROSPECTS. New York: Harper for Council on Foreign Relations, 1956. 251 p.

Ross, Hugh, ed. THE COLD WAR: CONTAINMENT AND ITS CRITICS. Chicago: Rand McNally, 1963. 53 p. Bibliog.

Schuman, Frederick L. THE COLD WAR: RETROSPECT AND PROSPECT. Baton Rouge: Louisiana State University Press, 1962. 104 p. Bibliog.

Seabury, Paul. THE RISE AND DECLINE OF THE COLD WAR. New York: Basic Books, 1967. 171 p. Bibliog.

Seldes, George. THE PEOPLE DON'T KNOW: THE AMERICAN PRESS AND THE COLD WAR. New York: Gaer, 1949. 342 p.

Seton-Watson, Hugh. NEITHER WAR NOR PEACE. THE STRUGGLE FOR POWER IN THE POSTWAR WORLD. London: Methuen, 1960. 504 p. Bibliog.

Sheldon, Della W., ed. DIMENSIONS OF DETENTE. New York: Praeger, 1978. 240 p.

Sherwin, Martin J. "The Atomic Bomb and the Origins of the Cold War: U.S. Atomic-Energy Policy and Diplomacy, 1941-1945." AMERICAN HISTORICAL REVIEW 78 (October 1973): 945-68.

Shulman, Marshall D. BEYOND THE COLD WAR. New Haven, Conn.: Yale University Press for Council on Foreign Relations, 1966. 111 p.

Siracusa, Joseph M., ed. THE AMERICAN DIPLOMATIC REVOLUTION: A DOCUMENTARY HISTORY OF THE COLD WAR, 1941-47. Pt. Washington, N.Y.: Kennikat, 1977. 263 p.

Siracusa, Joseph M., and Barclay, Glen St. John, eds. THE IMPACT OF THE COLD WAR: RECONSIDERATIONS. Pt. Washington, N.Y.: Kennikat, 1977. 208 p.

Steele, George, and Kircher, Paul. THE CRISIS WE FACE: AUTOMATION AND THE COLD WAR. New York: McGraw-Hill, 1960. 220 p.

Thomas, Brian. "What's Left of the Cold War?" POLITICAL QUARTERLY 40 (April-June 1969): 173-86.

Thompson, Kenneth W. INTERPRETERS AND CRITICS OF THE COLD WAR. Washington, D.C.: University of America Press, 1978. 113 p.
    Analyzes the views of Reinhold Niebuhr, Walter Lippmann, George F. Kennan, and Hans J. Morgenthau.

Timberlake, Charles E., ed. DETENTE: A DOCUMENTARY RECORD. New York: Praeger, 1978. 256 p.

Trefousse, Hans Louis, ed. THE COLD WAR: A BOOK OF DOCUMENTS. New York: Putnam, 1965. 296 p. Bibliog.

Ulam, Adam B. THE RIVALS: AMERICA AND RUSSIA SINCE WORLD WAR II. New York: Viking, 1971. 405 p.

Underhill, William Robert. "Public Address: Its Role in the Cold War, 1945-1951." Ph.D. dissertation, Northwestern University, 1955. 510 p.

Walton, Richard J. COLD WAR AND COUNTERREVOLUTION: THE FOREIGN POLICY OF JOHN F. KENNEDY. New York: Viking, 1972. 250 p. Bibliog.

_____. HENRY WALLACE, HARRY TRUMAN, AND THE COLD WAR. New York: Viking, 1976. 388 p. Bibliog.

White, Ralph K. "The Cold War and the Modal Philosophy." JOURNAL OF CONFLICT RESOLUTION 2 (March 1958): 43-50.

Whitton, John B., ed. PROPAGANDA AND THE COLD WAR. Washington, D.C.: Public Affairs, 1963. 119 p. Bibliog.

Wilson, Thomas W., Jr. COLD WAR AND COMMON SENSE. Greenwich, Conn.: New York Graphic Society, 1962. 211 p.

Winks, Robin W. THE COLD WAR: FROM YALTA TO CUBA. New York: Macmillan, 1964. 106 p. Bibliog.

Wolfers, Arnold, ed. ALLIANCE POLICY IN THE COLD WAR. Baltimore: Johns Hopkins Press, 1959. 314 p.

Yergin, Daniel. SHATTERED PEACE: THE ORIGINS OF THE COLD WAR AND THE NATIONAL SECURITY STATE. Boston: Houghton Mifflin, 1977. 526 p.

Coexistence and Detente

Additional materials on the cold war emphasize such specific relations as coexistence and detente, as follow:

Berzins, Alfred. THE TWO FACES OF COEXISTENCE. New York: Speller, 1967. 335 p. Bibliog.

Brandt, Willy. THE ORDEAL OF COEXISTENCE. Cambridge, Mass.: Harvard University Press, 1963. 112 p.

Collier, David S., and Glaser, Kurt, eds. THE CONDITIONS FOR PEACE IN EUROPE: PROBLEMS OF DETENTE AND SECURITY. Washington, D.C.: Public Affairs for Foundation for Foreign Affairs, Chicago, 1969. 204 p.

Dulles, Eleanor, and Crane, Robert D., eds. DETENTE: COLD WAR STRATE-GIES IN TRANSITION. New York: Praeger for Center for Strategic Studies, Georgetown University, 1965. 307 p.

Gaitskell, Hugh T.N. THE CHALLENGE OF COEXISTENCE. Cambridge, Mass.: Harvard University Press, 1957. 114 p.

Gehlen, Michael P. THE POLITICS OF COEXISTENCE: SOVIET METHODS AND MOTIVES. Bloomington: Indiana University Press, 1967. 334 p.

Kennan, George F. "Peaceful Coexistence: A Western View." FOREIGN AFFAIRS 38 (January 1960): 171-90.

Kim, Young Hum, ed. PATTERNS OF COMPETITIVE COEXISTENCE: USA VS. USSR. New York: Putnam, 1966. 484 p. Bibliog.

Kulski, Wladyslaw W. PEACEFUL CO-EXISTENCE: AN ANALYSIS OF SO-VIET FOREIGN POLICY. Chicago: Regnery, 1959. 662 p. Bibliog.

Lindsay, Michael. IS PEACEFUL COEXISTENCE POSSIBLE? East Lansing: Michigan State University Press, 1960. 252 p.

McWhinney, Edward. "PEACEFUL COEXISTENCE" AND SOVIET-WESTERN INTERNATIONAL LAW. Leiden, The Netherlands: Sijthoff, 1964. 135 p.

_____, ed. LAW, FOREIGN POLICY, AND THE EAST-WEST DETENTE. Toronto: University of Toronto Press, 1964. 123 p. Bibliog.

Pranger, Robert J., ed. DETENTE AND DEFENSE: A READER. Washington, D.C.: American Enterprise Institute, 1976. 445 p.

Sakharov, Andrei D. PROGRESS, COEXISTENCE AND INTELLECTUAL FREE-DOM. Translated by New York Times staff. New York: Norton, 1968. 158 p.

Scott, John. POLITICAL WARFARE: A GUIDE TO COMPETITIVE COEXIST-ENCE. New York: Day, 1955. 256 p.

Slessor, John C. WHAT PRICE COEXISTENCE? A POLICY FOR THE WEST-ERN ALLIANCE. New York: Praeger, 1961. 153 p.

Stanley, Timothy W., and Whitt, Darnell M. DETENTE DIPLOMACY: UNITED STATES AND EUROPEAN SECURITY IN THE 1970'S. Cambridge, Mass.: University Press of Cambridge, 1970. 170 p.

ISSUES, CONFLICTS, CONFRONTATION, AND CRISES

This section presents materials concerned with the nature of confrontation and conflict as well as crisis diplomacy. These subjects have attracted considerable research and literary interest in recent decades, and they are being increasingly subjected to systematic analytical scrutiny. The following inventory consists of materials of a general or functionally specialized nature, but it does not include citations to sources on specific confrontations and crises. Materials concerned with conflict resolution and peaceful settlement are dealt with separately in the following section.

Anderson, George L., ed. ISSUES AND CONFLICTS: STUDIES IN TWENTIETH CENTURY AMERICAN DIPLOMACY. Lawrence: University of Kansas Press, 1959. 374 p.

Arnold, G.L. THE PATTERN OF WORLD CONFLICT. New York: Dial, 1955. 250 p.

Aubert, Vilhelm. "Competition and Dissensus: Two Types of Conflict and of Conflict Resolution." JOURNAL OF CONFLICT RESOLUTION 7, no. 1 (1963): 26-42.

Bell, Coral. THE CONVENTIONS OF CRISIS: A STUDY IN DIPLOMATIC MANAGEMENT. New York: Oxford University Press for the Royal Institute of International Affairs, 1971. 131 p. Bibliog.

Berle, Adolf A., Jr. TIDES OF CRISIS: A PRIMER OF FOREIGN RELATIONS. New York: Reynal, 1957. 328 p.

Boulding, Kenneth. CONFLICT AND DEFENSE: A GENERAL THEORY. New York: Harper and Row, 1962. 349 p.

Buchan, Alastair. CRISIS MANAGEMENT: THE NEW DIPLOMACY. Boulogne-sur-Seine, France: Atlantic Institute, 1966. 63 p.

Butterworth, Robert Lyle, with Scranton, Margaret E. MANAGING INTER-STATE CONFLICT, 1945-74: DATA WITH SYNOPSIS. Pittsburgh: Center for International Study, University of Pittsburgh, 1976. 535 p. Bibliog.

Carr, Edward Hallett. THE TWENTY YEARS' CRISIS, 1919-1939. 2d ed. London: Macmillan, 1940. 312 p.

Cleveland, Harland. "Crisis Diplomacy." FOREIGN AFFAIRS 41 (July 1963): 638-49.

Cohen, Raymond. THREAT PERCEPTION IN INTERNATIONAL CRISIS. Madison: University of Wisconsin Press, 1979. 224 p.

Donelan, M., and Grieve, M. INTERNATIONAL DISPUTES: CASE HIS-
TORIES, 1945-70. New York: St. Martin's, 1973. 286 p.

East, Maurice A., and Gregg, Phillip M. "Factors Influencing Cooperation
and Conflict in the International System." INTERNATIONAL STUDIES QUAR-
TERLY 11 (September 1967): 244-69.

Eldridge, Albert F. IMAGES OF CONFLICT. New York: St. Martin's,
1978. 275 p.

Etzioni, Amitai. "On Self-Encapsulating Conflicts." JOURNAL OF CON-
FLICT RESOLUTION 8 (September 1964): 242-55.

Falkowski, Lawrence. PRESIDENTS, SECRETARIES OF STATE, AND CRISES IN
U.S. FOREIGN RELATIONS. Boulder, Colo.: Westview, 1978. 200 p.

Ferris, Wayne H. THE POWER CAPABILITIES OF NATION STATES: INTER-
NATIONAL CONFLICT AND WAR. Lexington, Mass.: Lexington Books,
1973. 192 p.

Fisher, Roger D. INTERNATIONAL CONFLICT FOR BEGINNERS. New York:
Harper and Row, 1969. 231 p.

_____, ed. INTERNATIONAL CONFLICT AND BEHAVIORAL SCIENCE:
THE CRAIGVILLE PAPERS. New York: Basic Book, 1964. 290 p.

Frei, Daniel, ed. INTERNATIONAL CRISES AND CRISIS MANAGEMENT:
AN EAST-WEST SYMPOSIUM. New York: Praeger, 1979. 160 p.

Gavin, James M. CRISIS NOW. New York: Random House, 1968. 184 p.

Giffin, Sidney F. THE CRISIS GAME: SIMULATING INTERNATIONAL CON-
FLICT. Garden City, N.Y.: Doubleday, 1965. 191 p. Bibliog.

Graber, Doris Appel. CRISIS DIPLOMACY: A HISTORY OF U.S. INTER-
VENTION POLICIES AND PRACTICES. Washington, D.C.: Public Affairs,
1959. 402 p. Bibliog.

Haas, Ernst B., et al. CONFLICT MANAGEMENT BY INTERNATIONAL OR-
GANIZATIONS. Morristown, N.J.: General Learning Press, 1972. 66 p.
Bibliog.

Halper, Thomas. "Appearance and Reality in Five American Foreign Policy
Crises." Ph.D. dissertation, Vanderbilt University, 1970. 512 p.

_____. FOREIGN POLICY CRISES: APPEARANCE AND REALITY IN DECISION-MAKING. Columbus, Ohio: Merrill, 1971. 235 p. Bibliog.

Henderson, Gordon Grant. "International Law in American Foreign Policy: A Study of the Role of International Law in the Making of National Policy in Ten Disputes Between the United States and Great Britain in the Period 1919 to 1930." Ph.D. dissertation, Columbia University, 1962. 924 p.

Hermann, Charles F. CRISIS IN FOREIGN POLICY: A SIMULATION ANALYSIS. Indianapolis: Bobbs-Merrill, 1969. 234 p.

_____. "International Crisis As a Situation Variable." In INTERNATIONAL POLITICS AND FOREIGN POLICY, edited by James N. Rosenau, pp. 409-21. 2d ed. New York: Free Press, 1969.

_____, ed. INTERNATIONAL CRISES: INSIGHTS FROM BEHAVIORAL RESEARCH. New York: Free Press, 1972. 334 p.

Holsti, Ole R. CRISIS ESCALATION WAR. Montreal: McGill-Queens University Press, 1972. 268 p.

Howe, Jonathan Trumbull. MULTICRISES: SEA POWER AND GLOBAL POLITICS IN THE MISSILE AGE. Cambridge: M.I.T. Press, 1971. 416 p.

International Sociological Association, comp. THE NATURE OF CONFLICT: STUDIES ON THE SOCIOLOGICAL ASPECTS OF INTERNATIONAL TENSIONS. Paris: UNESCO, 1957. 314 p. Bibliog.

Janeway, Eliot. THE ECONOMICS OF CRISIS: WAR, POLITICS, AND THE DOLLAR. London: Staples, 1968. 307 p.

Kahn, Herman. ON ESCALATION: METAPHORS AND SCENARIOS. New York: Praeger, 1965. 308 p.

Kim, Young Hum, comp. TWENTY YEARS OF CRISES: THE COLD WAR ERA. Englewood Cliffs, N.J.: Prentice-Hall, 1968. 297 p. Bibliog.

Kleiman, Robert. ATLANTIC CRISIS: AMERICAN DIPLOMACY CONFRONTS A RESURGENT EUROPE. New York: Norton, 1964. 158 p.

Likert, R., and Likert, J.G. NEW WAYS OF MANAGING CONFLICT. New York: McGraw-Hill, 1976. 376 p.

General analysis on problem solving.

Lockhart, Charles. BARGAINING IN INTERNATIONAL CONFLICTS. New York: Columbia University Press, 1979. 224 p.

Applies bargaining theory to conflict management.

Luard, Evan. CONFLICT AND PEACE IN THE MODERN INTERNATIONAL SYSTEM. Boston: Little, Brown, 1968. 343 p. Bibliog.

McClelland, Charles. "The Acute International Crisis." WORLD POLITICS 14 (October 1961): 182-204.

McClelland, Charles, and Hoggard, Gary D. "Conflict Patterns in the Inter-actions Among Nations." In INTERNATIONAL POLITICS AND FOREIGN POLICY, edited by James N. Rosenau, pp. 711-24. New York: Free Press, 1969.

McKenna, Joseph C. DIPLOMATIC PROTEST IN FOREIGN POLICY: ANALY-SIS AND CASE STUDIES. Chicago: Loyola University Press, 1962. 222 p.

McNeil, Elton B. THE NATURE OF HUMAN CONFLICT. Englewood Cliffs, N.J.: Prentice-Hall, 1965. 315 p.

Mandel, Robert M. PERCEPTION, DECISION MAKING AND CONFLICT. Washington, D.C.: University Press of America, 1978. 168 p.

_____. "Political Gaming and Crisis Foreign Policymaking." Ph.D. disserta-tion, Yale University, 1976. 216 p.

Nixon, Richard M. SIX CRISES. Garden City, N.Y.: Doubleday, 1962. 460 p.

Concerns crises in American politics, several of which involved foreign affairs.

North, Robert C.; Holsti, Ole R.; Zaninovich, M.G.; and Zinnes, Dina A. CONTENT ANALYSIS: A HANDBOOK WITH APPLICATIONS FOR THE STUDY OF INTERNATIONAL CRISIS. Evanston, Ill.: Northwestern University Press, 1963. 182 p. Bibliog.

North, Robert C.; Koch, Howard E., Jr.; and Zinnes, Dina A. "The Inte-grative Functions of Conflict." JOURNAL OF CONFLICT RESOLUTION 4 (September 1960): 355-74.

Northedge, F., and Donelan, M. INTERNATIONAL DISPUTES: THE POLITI-CAL ASPECTS. New York: St. Martin's, 1971. 348 p.

Phillips, Warren, and Rimkunas, Richard. "The Concept of Crisis in International Politics." College Park: Department of Government and Politics, University of Maryland, 1976. 45 p. Mimeographed.

Prepared with support of the Defense Advanced Research Projects Agency, U.S. Department of Defense.

Pool, Ithiel de Sola, and Kessler, Allen. "The Kaiser, the Tsar, and the Computer: Information in a Crisis." AMERICAN BEHAVIORAL SCIENTIST 8 (May 1965): 31-38.

Richardson, Lewis F. STATISTICS OF DEADLY QUARRELS. Edited by Quincy Wright and C.C. Lienau. Pittsburgh: Boxwood, 1960. 373 p. Bibliog.

Rummel, Rudolph J. "Dimensions of Conflict Behavior Within and Between Nations." GENERAL SYSTEMS YEARBOOK 8 (1963): 1-50.

_____. "The Relationship Between National Attributes and Foreign Conflict Behavior." In QUANTITATIVE INTERNATIONAL POLITICS: INSIGHTS AND EVIDENCE, edited by J. David Singer, pp. 187-214. New York: Free Press, 1968.

Schelling, Thomas C. THE ROLE OF THEORY IN THE STUDY OF CONFLICT. Santa Monica, Calif.: Rand, 1960. 48 p.

_____. THE STRATEGY OF CONFLICT. New York: Oxford University Press, 1960. 309 p.

Scott, Andrew M. THE FUNCTIONING OF THE INTERNATIONAL POLITICAL SYSTEM. New York: Macmillan, 1967. 244 p. Bibliog.

Especially chapters 9, and 10, pp. 158-71, on international conflict.

Snyder, Glenn H., and Diesing, Paul. CONFLICT AMONG NATIONS: BARGAINING, DECISION MAKING, AND SYSTEM STRUCTURE IN INTERNATIONAL CRISES. Princeton, N.J.: Princeton University Press, 1977. 616 p.

Stagner, Ross. PSYCHOLOGICAL ASPECTS OF INTERNATIONAL CONFLICT. Belmont, Calif.: Brooks-Cole, 1967. 234 p. Bibliog.

Steibel, Gerald Lee. "Crisis Management." In his DETENTE: PROMISES AND PITFALLS, pp. 26-33. New York: Crane, Russak, 1975.

Stone, Julius. LEGAL CONTROLS OF INTERNATIONAL CONFLICT: A TREATISE ON THE DYNAMICS OF DISPUTES AND WAR-LAW. New York: Garland, 1973. 851 p.

Crisis Diplomacy

Strausz-Hupe, Robert, et al. PROTRACTED CONFLICT. New York: Harper, 1959. 229 p.

Thompson, James Clay. "Disaster in Foreign Policy: Organization Response to Failure." Ph.D. dissertation: University of Michigan, 1975. 201 p.

Thompson, Kenneth W. POLITICAL REALISM AND THE CRISIS OF WORLD POLITICS: AN AMERICAN APPROACH TO FOREIGN POLICY. Princeton, N.J.: Princeton University Press, 1960. 261 p. Bibliog.

Trivers, Howard. THREE CRISES IN AMERICAN FOREIGN AFFAIRS AND A CONTINUING REVOLUTION. Carbondale: Southern Illinois University Press, 1972. 220 p.

Vincent, Jack E. PREDICTING CONFLICT AND COOPERATION IN THE INTERNATIONAL RELATIONS SYSTEM. Washington, D.C.: University Press of America, 1976. 249 p.

Weede, Erich. "Conflict Behavior of Nation-States." JOURNAL OF PEACE RESEARCH 7, no. 3 (1970): 229-35.

Weintal, Edward, and Bartlett, Charles W. FACING THE BRINK: AN INTIMATE STUDY OF CRISIS DIPLOMACY. New York: Scribner, 1967. 248 p.

Wilkenfeld, Jonathan. "Domestic and Foreign Conflict Behavior of Nations." JOURNAL OF PEACE RESEARCH 5, no. 1 (1968): 56-69.

_____, ed. CONFLICT BEHAVIOR AND LINKAGE POLITICS. New York: McKay, 1973. 388 p. Bibliog.

Williams, Philip. CRISIS MANAGEMENT: CONFLICT, CONFRONTATION, AND DIPLOMACY. New York: Wiley Interscience, 1976. 230 p. Bibliog.

Wolfers, Arnold. DISCORD AND COLLABORATION: ESSAYS ON INTERNATIONAL POLITICS. Baltimore: Johns Hopkins Press, 1962. 283 p.

Wright, Quincy. "The Escalation of International Conflicts." JOURNAL OF CONFLICT RESOLUTION 9 (December 1965): 434-49.

Young, Oran R. THE POLITICS OF FORCE: BARGAINING DURING INTERNATIONAL CRISES. Princeton, N.J.: Princeton University Press, 1968. 438 p.

Young, Robert A., ed. "International Crises: Progress and Prospects for Applied Forecasting and Management." INTERNATIONAL STUDIES QUARTERLY 21 (March 1977): 3-248.

Symposium of nine articles prepared as Defense Advanced Research Agency Project.

Zinnes, Dina A. "A Comparison of Hostile Behavior of Decision-Makers in Simulate and Historical Data." WORLD POLITICS 18 (April 1966): 474-502.

PEACEFUL SETTLEMENT

Over the years, a variety of diplomatic and adjudicatory techniques have been devised to facilitate the amicable resolution of conflicts and crises among nation-states. Prior to World War II, these were called methods and processes of peaceful settlement. Subsequently, when research and analytical concern with the subject intensified, more systematic consideration was undertaken under the guise of conflict resolution and crisis management. Aside from the use of traditional diplomatic negotiation--still the most basic technique for resolving international differences and settling disputes--historically, the principal methods of peaceful settlement included good offices, mediation, and arbitration. In the nineteenth century, various forms of conciliation (including "cooling-off" arrangements) and international arbitration were developed, and, in the twentieth century, a good deal of conciliation and adjudication were turned over to permanent international facilities, including the Hague Tribunal, the League of Nations, the United Nations, the World Court, and other global and regional agencies.

This section contains general and basic materials on peaceful settlement, conflict resolution, and crisis handling, as well as on the spectrum of specific methods and processes. However, it does not include materials on the permanent global and regional international organizations and institutions, or on collective security. Specific peaceful settlement processes are treated in the studies of such writers as Anand, Bar-Yaacov, Deutsch, Edmead, Jackson, Jenks, Katz, Pechota, Simpson, and Young. Related materials on negotiation and international conferences are provided in chapter 3, on treaty making in chapter 17, and on interstate bargaining in chapter 19.

Almond, Nina, and Lutz, Ralph H. AN INTRODUCTION TO A BIBLIOGRAPHY OF THE PARIS PEACE CONFERENCE. Stanford, Calif.: Hoover Institution, 1935. 32 p.

American Arbitration Association. NEW STRATEGIES FOR PEACEFUL RESOLUTION OF INTERNATIONAL BUSINESS DISPUTES. Dobbs Ferry, N.Y.: Oceana, 1972. 252 p.

Anand, Ram Prakash. STUDIES IN INTERNATIONAL ADJUDICATION. Dobbs Ferry, N.Y.: Oceana, 1969. 298 p. Bibliog.

Bailey, Sydney. PEACEFUL SETTLEMENT OF DISPUTES: IDEAS AND PROPOSALS FOR RESEARCH. New York: UNITAR, United Nations, 1970. 67 p.

Bar-Yaacov, Nissim. THE HANDLING OF INTERNATIONAL DISPUTES BY MEANS OF INQUIRY. New York: Oxford University Press, 1974. 370 p.

Barkum, Michael. "Conflict Resolution Through Implicit Mediation." JOURNAL OF CONFLICT RESOLUTION 8 (June 1964): 121-30.

Bloomfield, Lincoln, and Beattie, Robert. "Computers and Policy-Making: the CASCON Experiment." JOURNAL OF CONFLICT RESOLUTION 15 (March 1971): 33-46.

Borchard, Edwin M. DISTINCTION BETWEEN LEGAL AND POLITICAL QUESTIONS. Washington, D.C.: Government Printing Office, 1924. 6 p.

Burton, John W. "Resolution of Conflict." INTERNATIONAL STUDIES QUARTERLY 16 (March 1972): 5-29.

Carlston, Kenneth S. THE PROCESS OF INTERNATIONAL ARBITRATION. New York: Columbia University Press, 1946. 318 p. Bibliog.

Carroll, Bernice A. "How Wars End: An Analysis of Some Current Hypotheses." JOURNAL OF PEACE RESEARCH 6, no. 4 (1969): 295-321.

Chase, Stuart. ROADS TO AGREEMENT: SUCCESSFUL METHODS IN THE SCIENCE OF HUMAN RELATIONS. New York: Harper, 1951. 250 p.

Coser, Lewis A. "The Termination of Conflict." JOURNAL OF CONFLICT RESOLUTION 5 (December 1961): 347-53.

Cukwurah, A.O. THE SETTLEMENT OF BOUNDARY DISPUTES IN INTERNATIONAL LAW. Dobbs Ferry, N.Y.: Oceana, 1967. 320 p.

Deutsch, Morton. THE RESOLUTION OF CONFLICT: CONSTRUCTIVE AND DESTRUCTIVE PROCESSES. New Haven, Conn.: Yale University Press, 1973. 420 p. Bibliog.

Edmead, Frank. ANALYSIS AND PREDICTION IN INTERNATIONAL MEDIATION. New York: UNITAR, United Nations, 1971. 50 p.

Fenwick, Charles O. "Inter-American Regional Procedures for the Settlement of Disputes." INTERNATIONAL ORGANIZATION 10 (February 1956): 12-21.

Fox, William T.R. "The Varieties of Diplomacy: They Provide a Means of Adjusting Disputes Among Nations." WORLDVIEW 2 (August 1959): 3-6.

Friesen, George F. "The Politics of Peacemaking: French-American Relations, 1944-1950." Ph.D. dissertation, Harvard University, 1973.

Galtung, Johan. "Institutionalized Conflict Resolution." JOURNAL OF PEACE RESEARCH 2, no. 4 (1965): 348-97.

Goodrich, Leland M. "The Peaceful Settlement of Disputes." JOURNAL OF INTERNATIONAL AFFAIRS 9, no. 2 (1955): 12-20.

Hilsman, Roger, Jr. "The Foreign Policy Consensus: An Interim Research Report." JOURNAL OF CONFLICT RESOLUTION 3 (December 1959): 361-82.

Holsti, K.J. "Resolving International Conflicts: A Taxonomy of Behavior and Some Figures on Procedures." JOURNAL OF CONFLICT RESOLUTION 10 (September 1966): 272-96.

Jackson, Elmore. MEETING OF MINDS: A WAY TO PEACE THROUGH MEDIATION. New York: McGraw-Hill, 1952. 200 p.

Jackson, William D. "The National Conciliator in an International Organization: A United Nations Case Study." Ph.D. dissertation: University of Virginia, 1972. 308 p.

Jenks, Clarence W. THE PROSPECTS OF INTERNATIONAL ADJUDICATION. Dobbs Ferry, N.Y.: Oceana, 1964. 805 p.

Katz, Milton. THE RELEVANCE OF INTERNATIONAL ADJUDICATION. Cambridge, Mass.: Harvard University Press, 1968. 165 p.

Kellog, Frank B. THE SETTLEMENT OF INTERNATIONAL CONTROVERSIES BY PACIFIC MEANS. Address by Secretary of State delivered before World Alliance for International Friendship, at New York, 11 November 1928. Washington, D.C.: Department of State, 1928. 10 p.

Luard, Evan. "Conciliation and Deterrence: A Comparison of Political Strategies in the Interwar and Postwar Periods." WORLD POLITICS 19 (January 1967): 167-89.

Miller, Linda B., ed. DYNAMICS OF WORLD POLITICS: STUDIES IN THE RESOLUTION OF CONFLICT. Englewood Cliffs, N.J.: Prentice-Hall, 1968. 294 p.
    Includes selected case studies.

Morris, Robert C. INTERNATIONAL ARBITRATION AND PROCEDURE. New Haven, Conn.: Yale University Press, 1911. 238 p.

Morse, Oliver. "Methods of Pacific Settlement of International Disputes: Difficulties and Revision." BROOKLYN LAW REVIEW 25 (December 1958): 21-32.

Parodi, Alexandre. "Pacific Settlement of Disputes." INTERNATIONAL CONCILIATION, no. 445 (November 1948): 616-32.

Pechota, Vratislav. COMPLEMENTARY STRUCTURES OF THIRD-PARTY SETTLEMENT OF INTERNATIONAL DISPUTES. New York: UNITAR, United Nations, 1971. 63 p.

_____. THE QUIET APPROACH: A STUDY OF THE GOOD OFFICES EXERCISED BY THE UNITED NATIONS SECRETARY-GENERAL IN THE CAUSE OF PEACE. New York: UNITAR, United Nations, 1972. 92 p.

Podell, Jerome E., and Knapp, William M. "The Effect of Mediation on the Perceived Firmness of the Opponent." JOURNAL OF CONFLICT RESOLUTION 13 (December 1969): 511-20.

Porshalt, Lars. "On Methods of Conflict and Prevention." JOURNAL OF PEACE RESEARCH 3, no. 2 (1966): 178-93.

Ralston, Jackson H. INTERNATIONAL ARBITRATION FROM ATHENS TO LOCARNO. Stanford, Calif.: Stanford University Press, 1929. 417 p. Bibliog.

Randle, Robert F. THE ORIGINS OF PEACE: A STUDY OF PEACEMAKING AND THE STRUCTURE OF PEACE SETTLEMENTS. New York: Free Press, 1973. 550 p. Bibliog.

Rothstein, Robert. "Domestic Politics and Peacemaking: Reconciling Incompatible Imperatives." ANNALS OF THE AMERICAN ACADEMY OF POLITICAL AND SOCIAL SCIENCE 392 (November 1970): 62-75.

Simpson, John L., and Fox, Hazel. INTERNATIONAL ARBITRATION: LAW AND PRACTICE. New York: Praeger, 1959. 330 p. Bibliog.

Smith, David S., ed. with assistance of Robert F. Randle. FROM WAR TO PEACE: ESSAYS IN PEACEMAKING AND WAR TERMINATION. International Fellows Program Series. New York: Columbia University, 1974. 311 p.

"Techniques of Mediation and Conciliation." INTERNATIONAL SOCIAL SCIENCE BULLETIN 10, no. 4 (1958): entire issue.

Wetter, J. Gillis, ed. THE INTERNATIONAL ARBITRAL PROCESS: PUBLIC AND PRIVATE. 4 vols. projected. Dobbs Ferry, N.Y.: Oceana, 1979-- .

Williams, John Fischer. "Justiciable and Other Disputes." AMERICAN JOURNAL OF INTERNATIONAL LAW 26 (January 1932): 31-36.

Yarrow, C.H. Mike. QUAKER EXPERIENCES IN INTERNATIONAL CONCI-LIATION. New Haven, Conn.: Yale University Press, 1978. 352 p.

Young, Oran R. THE INTERMEDIARIES: THIRD PARTIES IN INTERNATIONAL CRISES. Princeton, N.J.: Princeton University Press, 1967. 427 p. Bibliog.

Official commentary on the legal and political aspects of peaceful settlement of international disputes is provided in the following:

Hackworth, Green H. "Modes of Redress." In his DIGEST OF INTERNA-TIONAL LAW, vol. 6, pp. 1-159. Washington, D.C.: Government Printing Office, 1943.

Moore, John Bassett. A DIGEST OF INTERNATIONAL LAW. Washington, D.C.: Government Printing Office, 1906. Vol. 7, pp. 1-103.

Whiteman, Marjorie M. DIGEST OF INTERNATIONAL LAW. Washington, D.C.: Government Printing Office, 1971. Vol. 12, pp. 894-1152.

Supplementing the extensive library of monographic and essay materials on specific forms of peaceful settlement, the following illustrate the textbook chapters available on the overall process since World War II:

Ball, M. Margaret, and Killough, Hugh B. "Pacific Settlement of Internation-al Disputes." In their INTERNATIONAL RELATIONS, pp. 155-72. New York: Ronald, 1956.

Greene, Fred. "The Peaceful Settlement of Disputes and Conflicts." In his DYNAMICS OF INTERNATIONAL RELATIONS, pp. 553-79. New York: Holt, Rinehart, and Winston, 1964.

Hartmann, Frederick H. "Case Studies in the Settlement of Disputes." In his THE RELATIONS OF NATIONS, pp. 211-31. 5th ed. New York: Macmil-lan, 1978.

Lerche, Charles O., Jr. PRINCIPLES OF INTERNATIONAL POLITICS. New York: Oxford University Press, 1956.

    Especially chapters 6-8.

Palmer, Norman D., and Perkins, Howard C. "Collective Security and Peace-ful Settlement." In their INTERNATIONAL RELATIONS, pp. 238-65. 3d ed. Boston: Houghton Mifflin, 1969.

Schleicher, Charles P. "Peaceful Settlement and Change in International Society." In his INTERNATIONAL RELATIONS: COOPERATION AND CONFLICT, pp. 214-27. Englewood Cliffs, N.J.: Prentice-Hall, 1962.

Schuman, Frederick L. "The Settlement of Disputes." In his INTERNATIONAL POLITICS, pp. 149-69. 7th ed. New York: McGraw-Hill, 1969.

Van Dyke, Vernon. "Diplomacy and the Settling of International Disputes." In his INTERNATIONAL POLITICS, pp. 272-97. 3d ed. New York: Appleton-Century-Crofts, 1972.

PEACEFUL CHANGE

The concept of peaceful change--that is, negotiating modification amicably to accommodate changing realities in the interrelations of states--is central to peacekeeping in all its forms and, therefore, is as ancient as political societies and institutions in the international environment. Nevertheless, following World War I, peaceful change became the subject of special interest and literary concern, related in part to the expected functioning of the League of Nations and expanded international conferences. A few studies are still produced under this general concept, but, since World War II, more attention has been paid to other forms of peacekeeping, especially conflict resolution and crisis handling.

Bloomfield, Lincoln P. EVOLUTION OR REVOLUTION? THE UNITED NATIONS AND THE PROBLEM OF PEACEFUL TERRITORIAL CHANGE. Cambridge, Mass.: Harvard University Press, 1957. 220 p.

Cruttwell, Charles R.M.F. A HISTORY OF PEACEFUL CHANGE IN THE MODERN WORLD. New York: Oxford University Press, 1937. 221 p.

Dunn, Frederick Sherwood. PEACEFUL CHANGE: A STUDY IN INTERNATIONAL PROCEDURES. New York: Council on Foreign Relations, 1937. 156 p.

Manning, Charles Anthony W., ed. PEACEFUL CHANGE: AN INTERNATIONAL PROBLEM. New York: Macmillan, 1937. Reprint. New York: Garland, 1972. 193 p.

Morgenthau, Hans J. "Peaceful Change." In his POLITICS AMONG NATIONS: THE STRUGGLE FOR POWER AND PEACE, pp. 428-35. 5th ed. New York: Knopf, 1973.

Price, Peter. POWER AND THE LAW: A STUDY IN PEACEFUL CHANGE, WITH SPECIAL REFERENCE TO THE BRITISH COMMONWEALTH AND THE UNITED NATIONS. Geneva: Droz, 1954. 155 p. Bibliog.

Tomkins, E. Berkeley, ed. PEACEFUL CHANGE IN MODERN SOCIETY.
Stanford, Calif.: Hoover Institution, 1971. 158 p.

Chapter 19

SYSTEMATIC AND THEORETICAL

FOREIGN RELATIONS ANALYSIS

While theoretical and systematic analysis of political institutions and processes dates back to ancient times, and important literary contributions have been produced through the centuries, interest in this subject has mushroomed since World War II. Frontiers have been identified and broached not only by the classics of Plato, Aristotle, and more recent philosophers, but also by a grow-ing number of twentieth-century analysts, such as George Catlin and Charles Merriam and, more recently, Robert A. Dahl, Karl Deutsch, David Easton, Carl Friedrich, Morton Kaplan, Harold Lasswell, Quincy Wright, and others. As a consequence, a substantial literature has emerged that seeks to treat poli-tics, international relations, and foreign policy and affairs as laboratory sub-jects, amenable to scientific and theoretical scrutiny, rather than to simple historical description and commentary on institutional structuring and operation.

This chapter contains references to materials that relate the conduct of Ameri-can foreign affairs to broader areas of knowledge and concern, such as inter-national relations and the more general field of politics. It include materials on political analysis and systems, theories of politics and international rela-tions, and methods and levels of analysis. For convenience, they are grouped into four main categories: those of a general, basic, and broad theoretical nature; those concerned with international systems (and subsystems) together with systems analysis; others dealing more specifically with foreign affairs analy-sis; and those which emphasize certain limited functional approaches, compo-nents, and methods.

Materials contained in a number of other chapters are closely related, espe-cially those concerned with diplomacy as a political process (chapters 2 and 5), foreign and military policy making (chapters 12 and 16), decision making (chapter 14), and crisis diplomacy (chapter 18). Other matters dealt with elsewhere that are also relevant to specific components of this chapter include negotiation, international conferences, presidential leadership and image, in-telligence and information, public opinion, diplomatic communications, and the like. Additional essay materials on policy studies may be found in such periodicals as FOREIGN POLICY, INTERNATIONAL AFFAIRS: A MONTHLY JOURNAL OF POLICY ANALYSIS, POLICY ANALYSIS, POLICY AND POLI-TICS. POLICY REVIEW, POLICY SCIENCES, POLICY STUDIES JOURNAL, and POLICY STUDIES: REVIEW ANNUAL; STUDIES IN FOREIGN POLICY of the American Enterprise Institute for Public Policy Research; as well as the following Sage publications: INTERNATIONAL YEARBOOK OF FOREIGN POLICY STUDIES, PROFESSIONAL PAPERS IN ADMINISTRATIVE AND POLICY STUDIES, PROFESSIONAL PAPERS IN INTERNATIONAL STUDIES, and YEAR-BOOKS IN POLITICS AND PUBLIC POLICY. For a comprehensive list of journals and periodicals, see the last section of chapter 6.

GENERAL AND THEORETICAL

This section contains references to basic and general systematic and theoretical analyses, commentary on or about theory and theories, analytical approaches to conceptualization and inquiry, problems of theory building and assessment, and similar matters of fundamental scope and treatment. Materials in the fields of politics in general, political science as an academic discipline, and international relations as both a matter of pragmatic state practice and an academic subject are included. Those materials that are concerned with international systems, foreign relations analysis and behavior, and certain specific theoretical approaches are dealt with later in this chapter and in other chapters.

Almond, Gabriel A. "Political Theory and Political Science." AMERICAN POLITICAL SCIENCE REVIEW 60 (December 1966): 869-79.

Anderson, James E. PUBLIC POLICY-MAKING. 2d ed. New York: Holt, Rinehart/ and Winston, 1978. 220 p. Bibliog.

Apter, David E. "Theory and the Study of Politics." AMERICAN POLITICAL SCIENCE REVIEW 51 (September 1957): 747-62.

Bluhm, William T. THEORIES OF THE POLITICAL SYSTEM: CLASSICS OF POLITICAL THOUGHT AND MODERN POLITICAL ANALYSIS. 2d ed. Engle-wood Cliffs, N.J.: Prentice-Hall, 1971. 562 p.

Boasson, Charles. APPROACHES TO THE STUDY OF INTERNATIONAL RELA-TIONS. Assen, The Netherlands: Van Gorcum, 1963. 100 p.

Bowman, Lewis, and Boynton, G.R. POLITICAL BEHAVIOR AND PUBLIC OPINION: COMPARATIVE ANALYSIS. Englewood Cliffs, N.J.: Prentice-Hall, 1974. 499 p.

Bull, Hedley. "International Theory: A Case for A Classical Approach." In CONTENDING APPROACHES TO INTERNATIONAL POLITICS, edited by Klaus Knorr and James N. Rosenau, pp. 20-38. Princeton, N.J.: Princeton University Press, 1969.

Burton, John W. INTERNATIONAL RELATIONS: A GENERAL THEORY. Cambridge: Cambridge University Press, 1965. 288 p. Bibliog.

Catlin, George E.G. THE SCIENCE AND METHOD OF POLITICS. Hamden, Conn.: Archon, 1964. 360 p.

Charlesworth, James C., ed. CONTEMPORARY POLITICAL ANALYSIS. New York: Free Press, 1967. 380 p.

Christiansen, Bjorn. ATTITUDES TOWARDS FOREIGN AFFAIRS AS A FUNC-TION OF PERSONALITY. Oslo: Oslo University Press, 1959. 283 p. Bibliog.

Coplin, William D. INTRODUCTION TO INTERNATIONAL POLITICS: A THEORETICAL OVERVIEW. Chicago: Markham, 1971. 391 p. Bibliog.

Especially "Classifying Foreign Policy Activities," pages 126–40.

Crabb, Cecil V., Jr. POLICY-MAKERS AND CRITICS: CONFLICTING THEORIES OF AMERICAN FOREIGN POLICY. New York: Praeger, 1976. 322 p. Bibliog.

Crawford, Elisabeth T., and Biderman, Albert D., eds. SOCIAL SCIENTISTS AND INTERNATIONAL AFFAIRS: A CASE FOR A SOCIOLOGY OF SOCIAL SCIENCE. New York: Wiley, 1969. 333 p. Bibliog.

Dahl, Robert A. MODERN POLITICAL ANALYSIS. 3d ed. Englewood Cliffs, N.J.: Prentice-Hall, 1976. 176 p.

Delbeare, Kenneth M., ed. PUBLIC POLICY EVALUATION. Beverly Hills, Calif.: Sage, 1975. 286 p. Bibliog.

Deutsch, Karl W. THE ANALYSIS OF INTERNATIONAL RELATIONS. Engle-wood Cliffs, N.J.: Prentice-Hall, 1968. 214 p.

_____. POLITICAL COMMUNITY AT THE INTERNATIONAL LEVEL: PROB-LEMS OF DEFINITION AND MEASUREMENT. Garden City, N.Y.: Double-day, 1954. 70 p. Bibliog.

_____. "Toward an Inventory of Basic Trends and Patterns in Comparative and International Politics." In INTERNATIONAL POLITICS AND FOREIGN POLICY: A READER IN RESEARCH AND THEORY, edited by James N. Rose-nau, pp. 498–512. 2d ed. New York: Free Press, 1969.

Dewey, John. THE QUEST FOR CERTAINTY: A STUDY OF THE RELATION OF KNOWLEDGE AND ACTION. New York: Putnam, 1960. 318 p.

Dye, Thomas R. POLICY ANALYSIS: WHAT GOVERNMENTS DO, WHY THEY DO IT, AND WHAT DIFFERENCE IT MAKES. University: University of Alabama Press, 1976. 122 p.

_____. UNDERSTANDING PUBLIC POLICY. 3d ed. Englewood Cliffs, N.J.: Prentice-Hall, 1978. 350 p.

Easton, David A. A FRAMEWORK FOR POLITICAL ANALYSIS. Englewood Cliffs, N.J.: Prentice-Hall, 1965. 143 p.

_____. THE POLITICAL SYSTEM: AN INQUIRY INTO THE STATE OF POLITICAL SCIENCE. New York: Knopf, 1953. 330 p.

Etzioni, Amitai. A COMPARATIVE ANALYSIS OF COMPLEX ORGANIZA-TIONS: ON POWER, INVOLVEMENT, AND THEIR CORRELATES. New York: Free Press, 1961. 366 p. Bibliog.

_____. "The Epigenesis of Communities at the International Level." AMERI-CAN JOURNAL OF SOCIOLOGY 68 (January 1963): 407-21.

_____. MODERN ORGANIZATIONS. Englewood Cliffs, N.J.: Prentice-Hall, 1964. 120 p. Bibliog.

Eulau, Heinz. MICRO-MACRO POLITICAL ANALYSIS: ACCENTS OF IN-QUIRY. Chicago: Aldine, 1969. 400 p.

Festinger, Leon. A THEORY OF COGNITIVE DISSONANCE. Stanford, Calif.: Stanford University Press, 1962. 291 p.

Fox, William T.R., ed. THEORETICAL ASPECTS OF INTERNATIONAL RELA-TIONS. Notre Dame, Ind.: University of Notre Dame Press, 1959. 118 p.

Friedrich, Carl J. MAN AND HIS GOVERNMENT: AN EMPIRICAL THEORY OF POLITICS. New York: McGraw-Hill, 1963. 737 p. Bibliog.

Frohock, Fred M. THE NATURE OF POLITICAL INQUIRY. Homewood, Ill.: Dorsey, 1967. 218 p. Bibliog.

_____. PUBLIC POLICY: SCOPE AND LOGIC. Englewood Cliffs, N.J.: Prentice-Hall, 1979. 332 p.

Gurr, Ted Robert. POLITIMETRICS: AN INTRODUCTION TO QUANTITATIVE MACROPOLITICS. Englewood Cliffs, N.J.: Prentice-Hall, 1972. 214 p.

Haas, Ernst B. BEYOND THE NATION STATE: FUNCTIONALISM AND IN-TERNATIONAL ORGANIZATION. Stanford, Calif.: Stanford University Press, 1964. 595 p. Bibliog.

Hacker, Andrew. POLITICAL THEORY: PHILOSOPHY, IDEOLOGY, SCI-ENCE. New York: Macmillan, 1961. 612 p.

Harrison, Horace V., ed. THE ROLE OF THEORY IN INTERNATIONAL RELATIONS. Princeton, N.J.: Van Nostrand, 1964. 118 p.

Hilton, Gordon. INTERMEDIATE POLIMETRICS. New York: Columbia University Press, 1976. 282 p.

Hoffman, Stanley. CONTEMPORARY THEORY IN INTERNATIONAL RELATIONS. Englewood Cliffs, N.J.: Prentice-Hall, 1960. 293 p. Bibliog.

_____. "International Relations: The Long Road to Theory." WORLD POLITICS 11 (April 1959): 346-77.

Holsti, K.J. INTERNATIONAL POLITICS: A FRAMEWORK FOR ANALYSIS. 3d ed. Englewood Cliffs, N.J.: Prentice-Hall, 1977. 544 p.

Hopkins, Raymond, and Mansbach, Richard W. STRUCTURE AND PROCESS IN INTERNATIONAL POLITICS. New York: Harper and Row, 1973. 498 p.

Hyneman, Charles S. THE STUDY OF POLITICS: THE PRESENT STATE OF AMERICAN POLITICAL SCIENCE. Urbana: University of Illinois Press, 1959. 232 p. Bibliog.

Jacob, Philip E., and Toscano, James V., eds. THE INTEGRATION OF POLITICAL COMMUNITIES. Philadelphia: Lippincott, 1964. 314 p.

Jones, Charles O. AN INTRODUCTION TO THE STUDY OF PUBLIC POLICY. 2d ed. North Scituate, Mass.: Duxbury, 1977. 258 p.

Jones, Charles O., and Thomas, Robert D. PUBLIC POLICY MAKING IN A FEDERAL SYSTEM. Beverly Hills, Calif.: Sage, 1976. 288 p.

Kaplan, Abraham D.H. THE CONDUCT OF INQUIRY: METHODOLOGY FOR BEHAVIORAL SCIENCE. San Francisco: Chandler, 1964. 428 p. Bibliog.

Kaplan, Morton A. "Is International Relations a Discipline?" JOURNAL OF POLITICS 23 (August 1961): 462-76.

_____. "The New Great Debate: Traditionalism vs. Science in International Relations." WORLD POLITICS 19 (October 1966): 1-20.

_____. SYSTEM AND PROCESS IN INTERNATIONAL POLITICS. New York: Wiley, 1957. 283 p.

_____, ed. NEW APPROACHES TO INTERNATIONAL RELATIONS. New York: St. Martin's, 1968. 518 p.

_____. THE REVOLUTION IN POLITICS. New York: Wiley, 1962. 477 p.

_____. TOWARDS PROFESSIONALISM IN INTERNATIONAL THEORY: MACRO-SYSTEM ANALYSIS. New York: Free Press, 1979. 288 p.

Kindleberger, Charles P. "Scientific International Politics." WORLD POLITICS 11 (October 1958): 83-88.
    Review article.

Klineberg, Otto. THE HUMAN DIMENSION IN INTERNATIONAL RELATIONS. New York: Holt, Rinehart, and Winston, 1964. 173 p. Bibliog.

Knorr, Klaus, and Rosenau, James N., eds. CONTENDING APPROACHES TO INTERNATIONAL POLITICS. Princeton, N.J.: Princeton University Press, 1969. 297 p.

Kolb, Eugene J., and Kolb, Alma. A FRAMEWORK FOR POLITICAL ANALYSIS. Englewood Cliffs, N.J.: Prentice-Hall, 1978. 320 p.

La Palombara, Joseph, ed. BUREAUCRACY AND POLITICAL DEVELOPMENT. Princeton, N.J.: Princeton University Press, 1963. 487 p. Bibliog.

Lasswell, Harold D. THE FUTURE OF POLITICAL SCIENCE. New York: Atherton, 1963. 256 p. Bibliog.

_____. PSYCHOPATHOLOGY AND POLITICS. Chicago: University of Chicago Press, 1934. 285 p. Bibliog.

Lasswell, Harold D., and Kaplan, Abraham D.H. POWER AND SOCIETY: A FRAMEWORK FOR POLITICAL INQUIRY. New Haven, Conn.: Yale University Press, 1950. 295 p. Bibliog.

Laszlo, Ervin. INTRODUCTION TO SYSTEMS PHILOSOPHY: TOWARD A NEW PARADIGM OF CONTEMPORARY THOUGHT. New York: Gordon and Beach, 1972. 328 p. Bibliog.

Lerner, Daniel, and Lasswell, Harold D. THE POLICY SCIENCES: RECENT DEVELOPMENTS IN SCOPE AND METHOD. Stanford, Calif.: Stanford University Press, 1951. 844 p. Bibliog.

Levi, Werner. "The Concept of Integration in Research on Peace." BACK-GROUND 9 (August 1965): 111-26.

Lijphart, Arend. "The Structure of the Theoretical Revolution in International Relations." INTERNATIONAL STUDIES QUARTERLY 18 (March 1974): 41-74.

Likert, Rensis, and Lippitt, Ronald. "The Utilization of Social Science." In RESEARCH METHODS IN THE BEHAVIORAL SCIENCES, edited by Leon Festinger and Daniel Katz, pp. 581-646. New York: Holt, Rinehart, and Winston, 1953.

Lindblom, Charles E. "Policy Analysis." AMERICAN ECONOMIC REVIEW 48 (June 1958): 298-312.

Liska, George. INTERNATIONAL EQUILIBRIUM: A THEORETICAL ESSAY ON THE POLITICS AND ORGANIZATION OF SECURITY. Cambridge, Mass.: Harvard University Press, 1957. 223 p.

Lynch, Thomas D. POLICY ANALYSIS IN PUBLIC POLICYMAKING. Lexington, Mass.: Lexington Books, 1975. 130 p. Bibliog.

    Especially chapter 6 on policy analysis and public policy making.

McClelland, Charles A. "The Function of Theory in International Relations." JOURNAL OF CONFLICT RESOLUTION 4 (September 1960): 303-36.

_____. THEORY AND THE INTERNATIONAL SYSTEM. New York: Macmillan, 1966. 138 p. Bibliog.

McCleslry, Herbert. "Concerning Strategies for a Science of International Politics." WORLD POLITICS 8 (January 1956): 281-95.

McDonald, Neil A. POLITICS: A STUDY OF CONTROL BEHAVIOR. New Brunswick, N.J.: Rutgers University Press, 1965. 264 p. Bibliog.

McGowan, Patrick J. "Problems in the Construction of Positive Foreign Policy Theory." In COMPARING FOREIGN POLICIES, edited by James N. Rosenau, pp. 25-44. New York: Halsted, 1974.

_____. "Toward a Dynamic Theory of Foreign Policy." Syracuse, N.Y.: Comparative International Studies Project, International Relations Program, Maxwell School, Syracuse University, 1971. Mimeographed.

May, Judith V., and Wildavsky, Aaron B., eds. THE POLICY CYCLE. Beverly Hills, Calif.: Sage, 1978. 332 p.

Meehan, Eugene. THE THEORY AND METHOD OF POLITICAL ANALYSIS. Homewood, Ill.: Dorsey, 1965. 277 p.

Merriam, Charles E. SYSTEMATIC POLITICS. Chicago: University of Chicago Press, 1945. 349 p.

Modelski, George A. A THEORY OF FOREIGN POLICY. New York: Praeger, 1962. 152 p.

Moore, David William. "Governmental and Societal Influences on Foreign Policy: A Partial Examination of Rosenau's Adaptation Model." Ph.D. dissertation, Ohio State University, 1970. 109 p.

Morgan, Patrick M. THEORIES AND APPROACHES TO INTERNATIONAL POLITICS: WHAT ARE WE TO THINK. San Ramon, Calif.: Consensus, 1972. 282 p.

Mueller, John E., ed. APPROACHES TO MEASUREMENT IN INTERNATIONAL RELATIONS: A NON-EVANGELICAL SURVEY. New York: Appleton-Century-Crofts, 1969. 311 p.

Nachmias, David. PUBLIC POLICY EVALUATION: APPROACHES AND METHODS. New York: St. Martin's, 1978. 200 p.

Nagel, Stuart S. POLICY STUDIES IN AMERICA AND ELSEWHERE. Lexington, Mass.: Lexington Books, 1975. 256 p.

    Especially chapters 1-5 on general approaches and chapter 10 on
    foreign policy.

Plano, Jack C., and Riggs, Robert E. DICTIONARY OF POLITICAL ANALYSIS. Hinsdale, Ill.: Dryden, 1973. 114 p. Bibliog.

Polsby, Nelson W.; Dentler, Robert A.; and Smith, Paul A. POLITICS AND SOCIAL LIFE: AN INTRODUCTION TO POLITICAL BEHAVIOR. Boston: Houghton Mifflin, 1963. 879 p. Bibliog.

Pool, Ithiel de Sola, ed. CONTEMPORARY POLITICAL SCIENCE: TOWARD EMPIRICAL THEORY. New York: McGraw-Hill, 1967. 276 p.

Rae, Douglas W., and Eismeier, Theodore J., eds. PUBLIC POLICY AND PUBLIC CHOICE. Beverly Hills, Calif.: Sage, 1979. 284 p.

Ranney, Austin. ESSAYS ON THE BEHAVIORAL STUDY OF POLITICS. Urbana: University of Illinois Press, 1962. 251 p.

Ransom, Harry Howe. "International Relations." In POLITICAL SCIENCE: ADVANCE OF THE DISCIPLINE, edited by Marian D. Irish, pp. 55-81. Englewood Cliffs, N.J.: Prentice-Hall, 1968. Reprinted from JOURNAL OF POLITICS 30 (May 1968): 345-71.

Rice, Stuart Arthur. QUANTITATIVE METHODS IN POLITICS. New York: Knopf, 1928. 331 p.

Riker, William H. THE THEORY OF POLITICAL COALITIONS. New Haven, Conn.: Yale University Press, 1962. 300 p.

Rivlin, Alice M. SYSTEMATIC THINKING FOR SOCIAL ACTION. Washington, D.C.: Brookings Institution, 1971. 150 p.

Rosecrance, Richard N. "Categories, Concepts and Reasoning in the Study of International Relations." BEHAVIORAL SCIENCE 6 (July 1961): 222-31.

Roseman, Cyril; Mayo, Charles G.; and Collinge, F.B., eds. DIMENSIONS OF POLITICAL ANALYSIS: AN INTRODUCTION TO THE CONTEMPORARY STUDY OF POLITICS. Englewood Cliffs, N.J.: Prentice-Hall, 1966. 368 p.

Rosenau, James N. THE ADAPTATION OF NATIONAL SOCIETIES: A THEORY OF POLITICAL SYSTEM BEHAVIOR AND TRANSFORMATION. New York: McCaleb-Seiler, 1970. 28 p. Bibliog.

_____, ed. INTERNATIONAL POLITICS AND FOREIGN POLICY: A READER IN RESEARCH AND THEORY. 2d ed. New York: Free Press, 1969. 740 p.

Rosenau, James N.; Davis, Vincent; and East, Maurice A., eds. THE ANALYSIS OF INTERNATIONAL POLITICS. New York: Free Press, 1972. 397 p.

Rummel, Rudolph J. THE DIMENSIONS OF NATIONS. Beverly Hills, Calif.: Sage, 1972. 512 p. Bibliog.

Russell, Frank M. THEORIES OF INTERNATIONAL RELATIONS. New York: Appleton-Century-Crofts, 1936. 651 p.

Russett, Bruce M. TRENDS IN WORLD POLITICS. New York: Macmillan, 1965. 156 p.

Schaar, John H., and Wolin, Sheldon S. "Essays on the Scientific Study of Politics: A Critique." AMERICAN POLITICAL SCIENCE REVIEW 57 (March 1963): 125-50.

A review essay, with responses, pages 151-60.

Scott, Andrew M. THE FUNCTIONING OF THE INTERNATIONAL POLITI-
CAL SYSTEM. New York: Macmillan, 1967. 244 p. Bibliog.

Simmons, Richard E. MANAGING BEHAVIORAL PROCESSES: APPLICATIONS
OF THEORY AND RESEARCH. Arlington Heights, Ill.: AHM Publishing Co.,
1978. 264 p.

Simon, Herbert A. ADMINISTRATIVE BEHAVIOR: A STUDY IN DECISION-
MAKING PROCESSES IN ADMINISTRATIVE ORGANIZATION. 3d ed. New
York: Macmillan, 1976. 364 p.

Singer, J. David. "Data-Making in International Relations." BEHAVIORAL
SCIENCE 10 (January 1965): 68-80.

_____. A GENERAL-SYSTEMS TAXONOMY FOR POLITICAL SCIENCE.
New York: General Learning Press, 1971. 24 p.

_____. "Inter-Nation Influence: A Formal Model." AMERICAN POLITICAL
SCIENCE REVIEW 57 (June 1963): 420-30.

_____. "The Level-of-Analysis Problem in International Relations." In THE
INTERNATIONAL SYSTEM: THEORETICAL ESSAYS, edited by Klaus Knorr
and Sidney Verba, pp. 77-92. Princeton, N.J.: Princeton University Press,
1961.

_____. "The Relevance of the Behavioral Sciences to the Study of Interna-
tional Relations." BEHAVIORAL SCIENCE 6 (October 1961): 324-35.

_____, ed. QUANTITATIVE INTERNATIONAL POLITICS: INSIGHTS AND
EVIDENCE. New York: Free Press, 1968. 394 p. Bibliog.

Smith, David G. "Political Science and Political Theory." AMERICAN
POLITICAL SCIENCE REVIEW 51 (September 1957): 734-46.

Somit, Albert, and Tanenhaus, Joseph. AMERICAN POLITICAL SCIENCE:
A PROFILE OF A DISCIPLINE. New York: Atherton, 1964. 173 p.

Sonderman, Fred A. "The Linkage Between Foreign and International Politics."
In INTERNATIONAL POLITICS AND FOREIGN POLICY: A READER IN RE-
SEARCH AND THEORY, edited by James N. Rosenau, pp. 8-17. New York:
Free Press, 1961.

Sorauf, Frank [Francis] J. PERSPECTIVES ON POLITICAL SCIENCE. Columbus, Ohio: Merrill, 1966. 85 p. Bibliog.

Spanier, John W. GAMES NATIONS PLAY: ANALYZING INTERNATIONAL POLITICS. 3d ed. New York: Holt, Rinehart, and Winston/Praeger, 1978. 628 p. Bibliog.

Starling, Grover. THE POLITICS AND ECONOMICS OF PUBLIC POLICY: AN INTRODUCTORY ANALYSIS WITH CASES. Homewood, Ill.: Dorsey, 1979. 727 p. Bibliog.

> Part 1 contains 10 chapters on analysis in general while part 2 consists of case studies--especially chapter 10 which is on foreign policy in an era of interdependency.

Sterling, Richard W. MACROPOLITICS: INTERNATIONAL RELATIONS IN A GLOBAL SOCIETY. New York: Knopf, 1974. 648 p. Bibliog.

Storing, Herbert J., ed. ESSAYS ON THE SCIENTIFIC STUDY OF POLITICS. New York: Holt, Rinehart, and Winston, 1962. 333 p.

Straussman, Jeffrey D. THE LIMITS OF TECHNOCRATIC POLITICS. New Brunswick, N.J.: Transaction, 1978. 250 p. Bibliog.

Thompson, Kenneth W. POLITICAL REALISM AND THE CRISIS OF WORLD POLITICS: AN AMERICAN APPROACH TO FOREIGN POLICY. Princeton, N.J.: Princeton University Press, 1960. 261 p.

Thorson, Thomas Landon. "Political Values and Analytic Philosophy." JOURNAL OF POLITICS 23 (November 1961): 711-24.

Tufte, Edward F. DATA ANALYSIS FOR POLITICS AND POLICY. Englewood Cliffs, N.J.: Prentice-Hall, 1974. 179 p.

Van Dyke, Vernon. POLITICAL SCIENCE: A PHILOSOPHICAL ANALYSIS. Stanford, Calif.: Stanford University Press, 1960. 235 p.

Voegelin, Eric. THE NEW SCIENCE OF POLITICS: AN INTRODUCTION. Chicago: University of Chicago Press, 1952. 193 p.

Waldo, Dwight. POLITICAL SCIENCE IN THE UNITED STATES OF AMERICA: A TREND REPORT. Paris: UNESCO, 1956. 84 p.

Weldon, Thomas Dewar. THE VOCABULARY OF POLITICS. Baltimore: Penguin, 1953. 199 p.

Wright, Quincy. PROBLEMS OF STABILITY AND PROGRESS IN INTERNATIONAL RELATIONS. Berkeley and Los Angeles: University of California Press, 1954. 378 p. Bibliog.

_____. THE STUDY OF INTERNATIONAL RELATIONS. New York: Appleton-Century-Crofts, 1955. 642 p.

Young, Oran R. "Interdependencies in World Politics." INTERNATIONAL JOURNAL 24 (Autumn 1969): 726-50.

Young, Roland A., ed. APPROACHES TO THE STUDY OF POLITICS: TWENTY-TWO CONTEMPORARY ESSAYS EXPLORING THE NATURE OF POLITICS AND METHODS BY WHICH IT CAN BE STUDIED. Evanston, Ill.: Northwestern University Press, 1958. 382 p.

Zawodny, J.K. GUIDE TO THE STUDY OF INTERNATIONAL RELATIONS. San Francisco: Chandler, 1966. 151 p.

Zinnes, Dina A., and Gillespie, John V. MATHEMATICAL MODELS AND INTERNATIONAL RELATIONS. New York: Praeger, 1976. 397 p.

INTERNATIONAL SYSTEMS AND SYSTEMS ANALYSIS

Materials listed in this section are concerned largely with analysis of the political (including the international) system and subsystems and with systems analysis as a research and theoretical approach to systematic inquiry. Emphasizing the latter, no attempt is made to provide comprehensive guidance to literature on the United Nations and other pragmatic integrative international systems, which lies beyond the scope of this compilation. U.S. institutional and other relations with such organizations are dealt with elsewhere.

Ake, Claude. "Political Integration and Political Stability: A Hypothesis." WORLD POLITICS 19 (April 1967): 486-99.

Almond, Gabriel A. "A Developmental Approach to Political Systems." WORLD POLITICS 17 (January 1965): 183-214.

Berlinski, David. ON SYSTEMS ANALYSIS: AN ESSAY CONCERNING THE LIMITATIONS OF SOME MATHEMATICAL METHODS IN THE SOCIAL, POLITICAL, AND BIOLOGICAL SCIENCES. Cambridge: M.I.T. Press, 1976. 186 p.

Bertelsen, Judy S. NONSTATE NATIONS IN INTERNATIONAL POLITICS: COMPARATIVE SYSTEM ANALYSIS. New York: Praeger, 1976. 272 p.

Brams, Steven J. "Transaction Flows in the International System." AMERICAN POLITICAL SCIENCE REVIEW 60 (December 1966): 880-97.

Chadwick, Richard W. "A Partial Model of National Political-Economic Systems: Evaluation by Causal Inference." JOURNAL OF PEACE RESEARCH 7, no. 2 (1970): 121-31.

Coplin, William D. "International Law and Assumptions About the State System." WORLD POLITICS 17 (July 1965): 615-34.

Deutsch, Karl W., and Singer, J. David. "Multipolar Power Systems and International Stability." WORLD POLITICS 16 (April 1964): 390-406.

Easton, David A. "An Approach to the Analysis of Politcal Systems." WORLD POLITICS 9 (April 1957): 383-400.

_____. A SYSTEMS ANALYSIS OF POLITICAL LIFE. New York: Wiley, 1968. 507 p.

Enthoven, Alain C. "Systems Analysis and Decision Making." MILITARY REVIEW 43 (January 1963): 7-17.

Galtung, Johan. "On the Future of the International System." JOURNAL OF PEACE RESEARCH 4, no. 4 (1967): 305-33.

Goodman, Jay S. "The Concept of 'System' in International Relations Thoery." BACKGROUND 8 (February 1965): 257-68.

Graymer, Leroy, ed. SYSTEMS AND ACTORS IN INTERNATIONAL POLITICS. Scranton, Pa.: Chandler, 1971. 210 p. Bibliog.

Haas, Ernst B. COLLECTIVE SECURITY AND THE FUTURE INTERNATIONAL SYSTEM. Denver: University of Denver, 1968. 117 p. Bibliog.

Hanreider, Wolfram F. "Actor Objectives in International Systems." JOURNAL OF POLITICS 27 (February 1965): 109-32.

_____. FOREIGN POLICIES AND THE INTERNATIONAL SYSTEM: A THEORETICAL INTRODUCTION. New York: General Learning Press, 1971. 24 p. Bibliog.

_____. "The International System: Bipolar or Multibloc?" JOURNAL OF CONFLICT RESOLUTION 9 (September 1965): 299-308.

Hoffman, Stanley. "International Systems and International Law." WORLD POLITICS 14 (October 1961): 205-37.

Hoos, Ida R. SYSTEMS ANALYSIS IN PUBLIC POLICY: A CRITIQUE. Berkeley: University of California Press, 1972. 259 p.

Jacobsen, Kurt. "Sponsorships in the United Nations: A System Analysis." JOURNAL OF PEACE RESEARCH 6, no. 3 (1969): 235-56.

Johnson, Richard A.; Kast, Fremont E.; and Rosenzweig, James E. THE THEORY AND MANAGEMENT OF SYSTEMS. 3d ed. New York: McGraw-Hill, 1973. 539 p. Bibliog.

Kaiser, Karl. "The Interaction of Regional Subsystems: Some Preliminary Notes on Recurrent Patterns and the Role of Superpowers." WORLD POLITICS 21 (October 1968): 84-107.

Kalleberg, Arthur L. "The Logic of Comparison: A Methodological Note on the Comparative Study of Political Systems." WORLD POLITICS 19 (October 1966): 69-82.

Kaplan, Morton A., ed. GREAT ISSUES OF INTERNATIONAL POLITICS: THE INTERNATIONAL SYSTEM AND NATIONAL POLICY. Chicago: Aldine, 1970. 432 p. Bibliog.

Kelly, George A., and Miller, Linda B. INTERNAL WAR AND INTERNATIONAL SYSTEMS: PERSPECTIVES ON METHOD. Cambridge, Mass.: Center for International Affairs, Harvard University, 1969. 40 p. Bibliog.

Knorr, Klaus, and Verba, Sidney, eds. THE INTERNATIONAL SYSTEM: THEORETICAL ESSAYS. Princeton, N.J.: Princeton University Press, 1961. 237 p. Also published in WORLD POLITICS 14 (October 1961): 1-237.

McClelland, Charles A. THEORY AND THE INTERNATIONAL SYSTEM. New York: Macmillan, 1966. 138 p. Bibliog.

Masters, Roger D. "World Politics as a Primitive Political System." WORLD POLITICS 16 (July 1964): 595-619.

Meadows, Paul. "Models, Systems and Science." AMERICAN SOCIOLOGICAL REVIEW 22 (Feburary 1957): 3-9.

Mitchell, John D. "Cross-Cutting Memberships, Integration, and the International System." JOURNAL OF CONFLICT RESOLUTION 14 (March 1970): 49-55.

Modelski, George. "Agraria and Industria: Two Models of the International System." WORLD POLITICS 14 (October 1961): 118-43.

Mosher, Frederick C., and Harr, John Ensor. PROGRAMMING SYSTEMS AND FOREIGN AFFAIRS LEADERSHIP: AN ATTEMPTED INNOVATION. New York: Oxford University Press, 1970. 261 p.

Plischke, Elmer, ed. SYSTEMS OF INTEGRATING THE INTERNATIONAL COMMUNITY. Princeton, N.J.: Van Nostrand, 1964. 198 p.

Riggs, Fred W. "International Relations as a Prismatic System." In THE INTERNATIONAL SYSTEM: THEORETICAL ESSAYS, edited by Klaus Knorr and Sidney Verba, pp. 144-81. Princeton, N.J.: Princeton University Press, 1961. Also published in WORLD POLITICS 14 (October 1961): 144-81.

Rosecrance, Richard N. ACTION AND REACTION IN WORLD POLITICS: INTERNATIONAL SYSTEMS IN PERSPECTIVE. Boston: Little, Brown, 1963. 314 p.

Rosenau, James N. "Transforming the International System: Small Increments Along a Vast Periphery." WORLD POLITICS 18 (April 1966): 525-45.

_____, ed. INTERNATIONAL POLITICS AND FOREIGN POLICY: A READER IN RESEARCH AND THEORY. Rev. ed. New York: Free Press, 1969. 740 p.

_____. LINKAGE POLITICS: ESSAYS ON THE CONVERGENCE OF NATIONAL AND INTERNATIONAL SYSTEMS. New York: Free Press, 1969. 352 p. Bibliog.

_____. OF BOUNDARIES AND BRIDGES: A REPORT ON A CONFERENCE ON THE INTERDEPENDENCIES OF NATIONAL AND INTERNATIONAL POLITICAL SYSTEMS, MARCH 4-6, 1966. Princeton, N.J.: Center of International Studies, Princeton University, 1967. 66 p.

Russett, Bruce M. INTERNATIONAL REGIONS AND THE INTERNATIONAL SYSTEM: A STUDY IN POLITICAL ECOLOGY. Chicago: Rand McNally, 1967. 252 p. Bibliog.

Scott, Andrew M. "Challenge and Response: A Tool for Analysis of International Affairs." REVIEW OF POLITICS 18 (April 1965): 207-26.

Singer, J. David, and Small, Melvin. "The Composition and Status Ordering of the International System: 1815-1940." WORLD POLITICS 18 (January 1966): 236-82.

Sjoberg, Gideon. "Contradictory Functional Requirements and Social Systems." JOURNAL OF CONFLICT RESOLUTION 4 (June 1960): 198-208.

Spiro, Herbert J. WORLD POLITICS: THE GLOBAL SYSTEM. Homewood, Ill.: Dorsey, 1966. 345 p. Bibliog.

Vayrynen, Raimo. "Stratification in the System of International Organizations." JOURNAL OF PEACE RESEARCH 7, no. 4 (1970): 291-309.

Verba, Sidney. "Assumptions of Rationality and Non-Rationality in Models of the International System." WORLD POLITICS 14 (October 1961): 93-117.

Weltman, John Jay. SYSTEMS THEORY IN INTERNATIONAL RELATIONS: A STUDY IN METAPHORIC HYPERTROPHY. Lexington, Mass.: Lexington Books, 1973. 112 p.

Wohlstetter, Albert. "Theory and Opposed Systems Design." JOURNAL OF CONFLICT RESOLUTION 12 (September 1968): 302-31.

Young, Oran R. "Political Discontinuities in the International System." WORLD POLITICS 20 (April 1968): 369-92.

_____. A SYSTEMATIC APPROACH TO INTERNATIONAL POLITICS. Princeton, N.J.: Princeton University Press, 1968. 67 p. Bibliog.

FOREIGN AFFAIRS

This section provides references to materials dealing systematically with the foreign relations of nation-states as actors in the international environment and, consequently, with the interaction of international and foreign relations. So far as foreign policy is concerned, these materials are more pertinent to theories about policy, analyses of the foreign policy concept, foreign relations behavior, and comparative foreign relations than to the pragmatic conduct of U.S. foreign affairs--dealt with elsewhere in considerable detail--or to the substance of American foreign policy.

Foreign Relations Analysis and Analytical Techniques

Andriole, Stephen J. "Public Policy Relevance and Contemporary Social Scientific Inquiry: The Case of Foreign Policy Analysis." Ph.D. dissertation, University of Maryland, 1974. 334 p.

Bandyopadhaya, Jayantanuja. "Making of Foreign Policy: A Tentative Subsystematic Model for South Asia." SOUTH ASIAN STUDIES 3 (July 1968): 27-39.

Bell, Harry H. "Modern Analytical Techniques." FOREIGN SERVICE JOURNAL 38 (October 1961): 23-25.

Bernstein, Robert A., and Weldon, Peter D. "A Structural Approach to the Analysis of International Relations." JOURNAL OF CONFLICT RESOLUTION 12 (June 1968): 159-81.

Brodin, Katarina. "Belief Systems, Doctrines, and Foreign Policy." CO-OPERATION AND CONFLICT 7, no. 2 (1972): 97-112.

Cannon, Jessica C. "Conceptual and Empirical Analysis of the Policy Implementation Process." Ph.D. dissertation, Ohio State University, 1976. 161 p.

Chittick, William O. THE ANALYSIS OF FOREIGN POLICY OUTPUTS. Columbus, Ohio: Merrill, 1975. 245 p.

Coplin, William D.; O'Leary, Michael K.; and McGowan, Patrick. AMERICAN FOREIGN POLICY: AN INTRODUCTION TO ANALYSIS AND EVALUATION. North Scituate, Mass.: Duxbury, 1974. 270 p. Bibliog.

Crabb, Cecil V., Jr. POLICY-MAKERS AND CRITICS: CONFLICTING THEORIES OF AMERICAN FOREIGN POLICY. New York: Holt, Rinehart, and Winston, 1976. 336 p. Bibliog.

Diebold, John. "Computers, Program Management, and Foreign Affairs." FOREIGN AFFAIRS 45 (October 1966): 125-34.

Eaton, Joseph W. "Symbolic and Substantive Evaluative Research." ADMINISTRATIVE SCIENCE QUARTERLY 6 (March 1962): 421-42.

Finnegan, Richard B. "International Relations: The Disputed Search for Method." REVIEW OF POLITICS 34 (January 1972): 40-66.

Gange, John. UNIVERSITY RESEARCH ON INTERNATIONAL AFFAIRS. Washington, D.C.: American Council on Education, 1958. 141 p.

Gross, Feliks. FOREIGN POLICY ANALYSIS. New York: Philosophical Library, 1954. 179 p.

Hammond, Paul Y. "The Political Order and the Burden of External Relations." WORLD POLITICS 19 (April 1967): 443-64.

Hanreider, Wolfram F. "Compatibility and Consensus: A Proposal for the Conceptual Linkage of External and Internal Dimensions of Foreign Policy." AMERICAN POLITICAL SCIENCE REVIEW 61 (December 1967): 971-88.

Hermann, Charles F. "What Is A Foreign Policy Event?" In COMPARATIVE FOREIGN POLICY: THEORETICAL ESSAYS, edited by Wolfram F. Hanreider, pp. 295-321. New York: McKay, 1971.

Hilsman, Roger, Jr. "The Foreign Policy Consensus: An Interim Research Report." JOURNAL OF CONFLICT RESOLUTION 3 (December 1959): 361-82.

Holsti, K.J. "National Role Conceptions in the Study of Foreign Policy." INTERNATIONAL STUDIES QUARTERLY 14 (September 1970): 233-309.

Hughes, Thomas L. "Relativity in Foreign Politics." FOREIGN AFFAIRS 45 (July 1967): 670-83.

Jones, Roy E. ANALYSING FOREIGN POLICY: AN INTRODUCTION TO SOME CONCEPTUAL PROBLEMS. New York: Humanities, 1967. 101 p. Bibliog.

Kegley, Charles W., Jr. A GENERAL EMPIRICAL TYPOLOGY OF FOREIGN POLICY BEHAVIOR. Beverly Hills, Calif.: Sage, 1973. 75 p.

_____. "Toward the Construction of an Empirically Grounded Typology of Foreign Policy Output Behavior." Ph.D. dissertation, Syracuse University, 1971. 416 p.

Levinson, Daniel J. "Authoritarian Personality and Foreign Policy." JOURNAL OF CONFLICT RESOLUTION 1 (March 1957): 37-47.

March, James G. "An Introduction to the Theory and Measurement of Influence." AMERICAN POLITICAL SCIENCE REVIEW 49 (June 1955): 431-51.

May, Ernest R. "The Nature of Foreign Policy: The Calculated Versus the Axiomatic." DAEDALUS 91 (Fall 1962): 653-67.

Merritt, Richard L., ed. FOREIGN POLICY ANALYSIS. Lexington, Mass.: Lexington Books, 1975. 176 p.

O'Leary, Michael K., and Coplin, William D. QUANTITATIVE TECHNIQUES IN FOREIGN POLICY ANALYSIS AND FORECASTING. New York: Praeger, 1975. 201 p.

Pruitt, Dean G. "Definition of the Situation as a Determinant of International Action." In INTERNATIONAL BEHAVIOR: A SOCIAL-PSYCHOLOGICAL ANALYSIS, edited by Herbert C. Kelman, pp. 391-434. New York: Holt, Rinehart, and Winston, 1965.

Rosenau, James N. "The External Environment as a Variable in Foreign Policy Analysis." In THE ANALYSIS OF INTERNATIONAL POLITICS, edited by James N. Rosenau, Vincent Davis, and Maurice A. East, pp. 145-63. New York: Free Press, 1972.

_____. "Paradigm Lost: Five Actors in Search of the Interactive Effects of Domestic and Foreign Affairs." POLICY SCIENCES 4 (December 1973): 415-36.

_____. "Pre-Theories and Theories of Foreign Policy." In APPROACHES TO COMPARATIVE INTERNATIONAL POLITICS, edited by Robert Barry Farrell, pp. 27-92. Evanston, Ill.: Northwestern University Press, 1966.

_____, ed. DOMESTIC SOURCES OF FOREIGN POLICY. New York: Free Press, 1967. 340 p.

_____. THE SCIENTIFIC STUDY OF FOREIGN POLICY. New York: Free Press, 1971. 472 p.

Roskin, Michael. "From Pearl Harbor to Vietnam: Shifting Generational Paradigms and Foreign Policy." POLITICAL SCIENCE QUARTERLY 89 (September 1974): 563-88.

Salmore, Stephen A. "Foreign Policy and National Attributes: A Multi-Variate Analysis." Ph.D. dissertation, Princeton University, 1972. 289 p.

Savage, Richard, and Deutsch, Karl W. "A Statistical Model of the Gross Analysis of Transaction Flows." ECONOMETRICA 28 (July 1960): 551-72.

Schelling, Thomas C. "PPBS and Foreign Affairs." PUBLIC INTEREST 11 (Spring 1968): 26-36.

Schilling, Warner R. "The Clarification of Ends, or, Which Interest Is the National." WORLD POLITICS 8 (July 1956): 566-78.

Singer, J. David. THE SCIENTIFIC STUDY OF POLITICS: AN APPROACH TO FOREIGN POLICY ANALYSIS. Morristown, N.J.: General Learning, 1972. 32 p. Bibliog.

Snyder, Richard C. "The Nature of Foreign Policy." SOCIAL SCIENCE 27 (April 1952): 61-69.

U.S. Commission on the Organization of the Government for the Conduct of Foreign Policy. "Analytic Techniques for Foreign Affairs." In its COMMISSION ON THE ORGANIZATION OF THE GOVERNMENT FOR THE CONDUCT OF FOREIGN POLICY, JUNE 1975, appendix, vol. 2, pp. 237-59. Washington, D.C.: Government Printing Office, 1976.

Vayrynen, Raimo. "Notes on Foreign Policy Research." COOPERATION AND CONFLICT 7, no. 2 (1972): 87-96.

Vocke, William C., ed. AMERICAN FOREIGN POLICY: AN ANALYTIC APPROACH. New York: Free Press, 1976. 330 p. Bibliog.

Zimmerman, William. "Issue Area and Foreign Policy Process: A Research Note in Search of a General Theory." AMERICAN POLITICAL SCIENCE REVIEW 67 (December 1973): 1204-12.

Zinnes, Dina A. CONTEMPORARY RESEARCH IN INTERNATIONAL RELATIONS: A PERSPECTIVE AND A CRITICAL ASSESSMENT. New York: Free Press, 1976. 477 p. Bibliog.

Behavior and Foreign Relations

Blong, Clair Karl. "External Penetration and Foreign Policy Behavior." Ph.D. dissertation, University of Maryland, 1975. 184 p. Bibliog.

Brecher, Michael; Steinberg, Blema; and Stein, Janice. "A Framework for Research on Foreign Policy Behavior." JOURNAL OF CONFLICT RESOLUTION 13 (March 1969): 75-101.

Chadwick, Richard W. "An Inductive, Empirical Analysis of Intra- and International Behavior, Aimed at a Partial Extension of Inter-Nation Simulation Theory." JOURNAL OF PEACE RESEARCH 6, no. 3 (1969): 193-214.

Corning, Peter A. "Some Biological Bases of Behavior and Some Implications for Political Science." WORLD POLITICS 23 (April 1971): 321-70.

East, Maurice A. "Size and Foreign Policy Behavior: A Test of Two Models." WORLD POLITICS 25 (July 1973): 556-76.

Emshoff, James R., and Ackoff, Russell L. "Explanatory Models of Interactive Choice Behavior." JOURNAL OF CONFLICT RESOLUTION 14 (March 1970): 77-89.

Eulau, Heinz. THE BEHAVIORAL PERSUASION IN POLITICS. New York: Random House, 1963. 141 p.

Harsanyi, John C. "Rational-Choice Models of Political Behavior vs. Functionalist and Conformist Theories." WORLD POLITICS 21 (July 1969): 513-38.

Hayes, Louis D., and Hedlund, Ronald D., eds. THE CONDUCT OF POLITICAL INQUIRY: BEHAVIORAL POLITICAL ANALYSIS. Englewood Cliffs, N.J.: Prentice-Hall, 1970. 255 p.

Kelman, Herbert C., ed. INTERNATIONAL BEHAVIOR: A SOCIAL PSYCHOLOGICAL ANALYSIS. New York: Holt, Rinehart, and Winston, 1965. 626 p.

Lasswell, Harold D. THE ANALYSIS OF POLITICAL BEHAVIOR: AN EMPIRI-CAL APPROACH. London: Routledge and Paul, 1947. Reprint. Hamden, Conn.: Archon, 1966. 314 p.

Lutzker, Daniel R. "Internationalism as a Predictor of Cooperative Behavior." JOURNAL OF CONFLICT RESOLUTION 4 (December 1960): 426-30.

Nieburg, Harold L. POLITICAL VIOLENCE: THE BEHAVIORAL PROCESS. New York: St. Martin's, 1969. 184 p. Bibliog.

Rummel, R.J. "Dimensions of Conflict Behavior Within Nations, 1946-59." JOURNAL OF CONFLICT RESOLUTION 10 (March 1966): 65-73.

_____. "Some Attributes and Behavioral Patterns of Nations." JOURNAL OF PEACE RESEARCH 4, no. 2 (1967): 196-206.

_____. "Some Dimensions in the Foreign Behavior of Nations." JOURNAL OF PEACE RESEARCH 3, no. 3 (1966): 201-24.

_____. "Some Empirical Findings on Nations and Their Behavior." WORLD POLITICS 21 (January 1969): 226-41.

Sibley, Mulford Q. "The Limitations of Behavioralism." In THE LIMITS OF BEHAVIORALISM IN POLITICAL SCIENCE, edited by James C. Charlesworth, pp. 68-93. Philadelphia: American Academy of Political and Social Science, 1962.

Singer, J. David, ed. HUMAN BEHAVIOR AND INTERNATIONAL POLITICS: CONTRIBUTIONS FROM THE SOCIAL-PSYCHOLOGICAL SCIENCES. Chicago: Rand McNally, 1965. 466 p. Bibliog.

Terhune, Kenneth W. "From National Character to National Behavior: A Reformulation." JOURNAL OF CONFLICT RESOLUTION 14 (June 1970): 203-63.

Comparative Foreign Relations

Almond, Gabriel A. COMPARATIVE POLITICS: A DEVELOPMENTAL AP-PROACH. Boston: Little, Brown, 1966. 348 p.

_____, ed. COMPARATIVE POLITICS TODAY: A WORLD VIEW. Boston: Little, Brown, 1974. 477 p. Bibliog.

Ashford, Douglas E., ed. COMPARING PUBLIC POLICIES: NEW CONCEPTS AND METHODS. Beverly Hills, Calif.: Sage, 1978. 254 p. Bibliog.

Black, C.E. THE DYNAMICS OF MODERNIZATION: A STUDY OF COM-PARATIVE HISTORY. New York: Harper and Row, 1966. 207 p. Bibliog.

Chittick, William O., and Jenkins, Jerry B. "Studying Foreign Policy Comparatively: Reconceptualizing the Sources of Foreign Policy Behavior." In IN SEARCH OF GLOBAL PATTERNS, edited by James N. Rosenau, pp. 281-91. New York: Free Press, 1975.

Falkowski, Lawrence. "Foreign Policy Flexibility: A Comparative Analysis." Ph.D. dissertation, Rutgers University, 1976. 231 p.

Farrell, Robert Barry. APPROACHES TO COMPARATIVE AND INTERNATION-AL POLITICS. Evanston, Ill.: Northwestern University Press, 1966. 368 p.

Hanreider, Wolfram F., ed. COMPARATIVE FOREIGN POLICY: THEORETI-CAL ESSAYS. New York: McKay, 1971. 402 p.

Hermann, Charles F. "Policy Classification: A Key to the Comparative Study of Foreign Policy." In THE ANALYSIS OF INTERNATIONAL POLITICS, edited by James N. Rosenau, Vincent Davis, and Maurice A. East, pp. 58-79. New York: Free Press, 1972.

Holt, Robert T., and Turner, John E. THE POLITICAL BASIS OF ECONOMIC DEVELOPMENT: AN EXPLORATION IN COMPARATIVE POLITICAL ANALY-SIS. Princeton, N.J.: Van Nostrand, 1966. 410 p.

Kalleberg, Arthur L. "The Logic of Comparison: A Methodological Note on the Comparative Study of Political Systems." WORLD POLITICS 19 (October 1966): 69-82.

Kim, Sehwan. "A Synthetic Theory of Actor Objectives for the Comparative Study of Foreign Policy." Ph.D. dissertation, University of Maryland, 1975. 357 p. Bibliog.

Lentner, Howard H. FOREIGN POLICY ANALYSIS: A COMPARATIVE AND CONCEPTUAL APPROACH. Columbus, Ohio: Merrill, 1974. 295 p. Bibliog.

Liske, Craig, et al. COMPARATIVE PUBLIC POLICY: ISSUES, THEORIES, AND METHODS. New York: Halsted, 1975. 300 p. Bibliog.

McGowan, Patrick J. "Theoretical Approaches to the Comparative Study of Foreign Policy." Ph.D. dissertation, Northwestern University, 1970. 441 p.

McGowan, Patrick J., and O'Leary, Michael K. COMPARATIVE FOREIGN POLICY ANALYSIS MATERIALS. Chicago: Markham, 1971. 45 p.

McGowan, Patrick J., and Shapiro, Howard B. THE COMPARATIVE STUDY OF FOREIGN POLICY: A SURVEY OF SCIENTIFIC FINDINGS. Sage Library of Social Science, vol. 4. Beverly Hills, Calif.: Sage, 1973. 256 p.

Findings from some two hundred empirical studies.

Merritt, Richard L., and Rokkan, Stein, eds. COMPARING NATIONS: THE USE OF QUANTITATIVE DATA IN CROSS-NATIONAL RESEARCH. New Haven, Conn.: Yale University Press, 1966. 584 p. Bibliog.

Neubauer, Deane E., and Kastner, Lawrence D. "The Study of Compliance Maintenance as a Strategy for Comparative Research." WORLD POLITICS 21 (July 1969): 629-40.

Palmer, Monte, and Thompson, William R. COMPARATIVE ANALYSIS OF POLITICS. Itasca, Ill.: Peacock, 1978. 317 p.

Diverse approaches to comparative analysis of politics.

Rosenau, James N., ed. COMPARING FOREIGN POLICIES: THEORIES, FINDINGS, AND METHODS. New York: Halsted, 1974. 442 p.

Rustow, Dankwart A. "New Horizons for Comparative Politics." WORLD POLITICS 9 (July 1957): 530-49.

Salamon, Lester M. "Comparative History and the Theory of Modernization." WORLD POLITICS 23 (October 1970): 83-103.

Waltz, Kenneth Neal. FOREIGN POLICY AND DEMOCRATIC POLITICS: THE AMERICAN AND BRITISH EXPERIENCE. Boston: Little, Brown, 1967. 331 p.

Wilkinson, David O. COMPARATIVE FOREIGN RELATIONS: FRAMEWORK AND METHODS. Belmont, Calif.: Dickenson, 1969. 191 p.

FUNCTIONAL APPROACHES, COMPONENTS, AND METHODS

Materials included in this section, many of which are related to other sections of this and other chapters, are grouped into the following categories: leadership and elites, image and perception, planning and prediction, communication, bargaining, simulation and gaming, and cybernetics. Together with other materials, such as those on decision making, conflict resolution, peacekeeping, and crisis management, each of these subjects has engendered an articulate following, relating investigation and explication to either theory development or systematic analysis. Some of the subjects dealt with below are related to chapters 3 (section on negotiation), 7 (presidential leadership and image), 12 (military-security policy making), and 17 (communications). Additional essay literature on the subjects contained in this section is available in the issues of

such periodicals as the JOURNAL OF CONFLICT RESOLUTION and the JOUR-
NAL OF PEACE RESEARCH.

Leadership and Elites

Angell, Robert C.; Dunham, Vera S.; and Singer, J. David. "Social Values
and Foreign Policy Attitudes of Soviet and American Elites." JOURNAL OF
CONFLICT RESOLUTION 8 (December 1964): 329-491.

Brewer, Thomas L. FOREIGN POLICY SITUATIONS: AMERICAN ELITE RE-
SPONSES TO VARIATIONS IN THREAT, TIME, AND SURPRISE. Beverly
Hills, Calif.: Sage, 1972. 62 p. Bibliog.

_____. "Issue and Context Variations in Foreign Policy: Effects on American
Elite Behavior." JOURNAL OF CONFLICT RESOLUTION 17 (March 1973):
89-111.

_____. "Issue Type and Context in American Foreign Policy-Making: An
Analysis of Elite Behavior in Sixty-Five European Integration and Atlantic Al-
liance Cases, 1949-1968." Ph.D. dissertation, State University of New York
(Buffalo), 1971. 286 p.

Burns, James MacGregor. LEADERSHIP. New York: Harper and Row, 1978.
530 p.

Dahl, Robert A. "A Critique of the Ruling Elite Model." AMERICAN PO-
LITICAL SCIENCE REVIEW 52 (June 1958): 463-69.

Donovan, John C. THE COLD WARRIORS: A POLICY-MAKING ELITE. Lexington, Mass.: Heath, 1974. 294 p.

Etzioni, Amitai. POLITICAL UNIFICATION: A COMPARATIVE STUDY OF
LEADERS AND FORCES. New York: Holt, Rinehart, and Winston, 1965.
346 p.

Gould, Jay M. THE TECHNICAL ELITE. New York: Kelley, 1966. 178 p.

Hveem, Helge. "Foreign Policy Thinking in the Elite and the General Popula-
tion." JOURNAL OF PEACE RESEARCH 5, no. 2 (1968): 146-70.

Lapp, Ralph E. THE NEW PRIESTHOOD: THE SCIENTIFIC ELITE AND THE
USES OF POWER. New York: Harper and Row, 1965. 244 p.

McClosky, Herbert. "Perspectives on Personality and Foreign Policy." WORLD
POLITICS 13 (October 1961): 129-39.

Mills, C. Wright. THE POWER ELITE. New York: Oxford University Press, 1956. 423 p.

Modelski, George. "The World's Foreign Ministers: A Political Elite." JOURNAL OF CONFLICT RESOLUTION 14 (June 1970): 135-75.

Mosher, Frederick, and Harr, John E. PROGRAMMING SYSTEMS AND FOR-EIGN AFFAIRS LEADERSHIP: AN ATTEMPTED INNOVATION. New York: Oxford University Press, 1970. 261 p.

Rosenau, James N. NATIONAL LEADERSHIP AND FOREIGN POLICY: A CASE STUDY IN THE MOBILIZATION OF PUBLIC SUPPORT. Princeton, N.J.: Princeton University Press, 1963. 409 p.

Verba, Sidney. SMALL GROUPS AND POLITICAL BEHAVIOR: A STUDY OF LEADERSHIP. Princeton, N.J.: Princeton University Press, 1961. 273 p. Bibliog.

Image and Perception

Abell, Peter, and Jenkins, Robin. "Perception and Structural Balance of Part of the International System of Nations." JOURNAL OF PEACE RESEARCH 4, no. 1 (1967): 76-82.

Bauer, Raymond A. "Problems of Perception and the Relations Between the United States and the Soviet Union." JOURNAL OF CONFLICT RESOLUTION 5 (September 1961): 223-29.

Bjerstedt, Ake. "'Ego-Involved World-Mindedness,' Nationality Images, and Methods of Research: A Methodological Note." JOURNAL OF CONFLICT RESOLUTION 4 (June 1960): 185-92.

Boulding, Kenneth E. "National Images and International Systems." JOURNAL OF CONFLICT RESOLUTION 3 (June 1959): 120-31.

Gilbert, Stephen P. SOVIET IMAGES OF AMERICA. New York: Crane, Russak, 1977. 167 p.

Holsti, Ole R. "The Belief System and National Images: A Case Study." JOURNAL OF CONFLICT RESOLUTION 6 (September 1962): 244-52.

Jervis, Robert. "Hypotheses on Misperception." WORLD POLITICS 20 (April 1968): 454-79.

_____. THE LOGIC OF IMAGES IN INTERNATIONAL RELATIONS. Princeton, N.J.: Princeton University Press, 1970. 281 p. Bibliog.

_____. PERCEPTION AND MISPERCEPTION IN INTERNATIONAL POLITICS. Riverside, N.J.: Library of Political and International Affairs, 1976. 445 p. Bibliog.

Lumsden, Malvern. "Perception and Information in Strategic Thinking." JOURNAL OF PEACE RESEARCH 3, no. 3 (1966): 257-77.

McGuire, William J. "Cognitive Consistency and Attitude Change." JOURNAL OF ABNORMAL AND SOCIAL PSYCHOLOGY 60, no. 3 (1960): 345-53.

Niemela, Pirkko, et al. "A Study in Intergroup Perception Stereotypy." JOURNAL OF PEACE RESEARCH 6, no. 1 (1969): 57-64.

Nimmo, Dan. POPULAR IMAGES OF POLITICS. Englewood Cliffs, N.J.: Prentice-Hall, 1974. 184 p.

Rapoport, Anatol. THE BIG TWO: SOVIET-AMERICAN PERCEPTIONS OF FOREIGN POLICY. New York: Pegasus, 1971. 249 p. Bibliog.

Welch, William. AMERICAN IMAGES OF SOVIET FOREIGN POLICY: AN INQUIRY INTO RECENT APPRAISALS FROM THE ACADEMIC COMMUNITY. New Haven, Conn.: Yale University Press, 1970. 316 p. Bibliog.

Planning and Prediction

Choucri, Nazli, and Robinson, Thomas W. FORECASTING IN INTERNATIONAL RELATIONS: THEORY, METHODS, PROBLEMS, PROSPECTS. San Francisco: Freeman, 1978. 468 p. Bibliog.

   Symposium on forecasting held at Yale University in 1973.

D'Amato, Anthony A. "Psychological Constructs in Foreign Policy Prediction." JOURNAL OF CONFLICT RESOLUTION 11 (September 1967): 294-311.

Ferkiss, Victor C. FUTUROLOGY: PROMISE, PERFORMANCE, PROSPECTS. Beverly Hills, Calif.: Sage, 1977. 66 p. Bibliog.

Friedmann, John. "A Conceptual Model for the Analysis of Planning Behavior." ADMINISTRATIVE SCIENCE QUARTERLY 12 (September 1967): 225-52.

Lindsay, Franklin A. "Program Planning: The Missing Element." FOREIGN AFFAIRS 39 (January 1961): 279-90.

Mahoney, Roberty Byrne, Jr. "Predicting the Foreign Behaviors of Nations: A Comparison of Internal and External Determinants." Ph.D. dissertation, Northwestern University, 1974. 352 p.

Morgan, George A. "Planning in Foreign Affairs: The State of the Art." FOREIGN AFFAIRS 39 (January 1961): 271-78.

Rothstein, Robert L. PLANNING, PREDICTION, AND POLICYMAKING IN FOREIGN AFFAIRS: THEORY AND PRACTICE. Boston: Little, Brown, 1972. 214 p.

Wright, Quincy. ON PREDICTING INTERNATIONAL RELATIONS: THE YEAR 2000. Denver: University of Denver, 1969. 42 p. Bibliog.

Communication

Berlo, David K. THE PROCESS OF COMMUNICATION: AN INTRODUCTION TO THEORY AND PRACTICE. New York: Holt, Rinehart, and Winston, 1960. 318 p. Bibliog.

Casmir, Fred L., ed. INTERCULTURAL AND INTERNATIONAL COMMUNICA-TION. Washington, D.C.: University Press of America, 1978. 834 p.

Chaffee, Steven H., ed. POLITICAL COMMUNICATION: ISSUES AND STRATEGIES FOR RESEARCH. Sage Annual Reviews of Communication, vol. 4. Beverly Hills, Calif.: Sage, 1975. 320 p.

Davison, W. Phillip. INTERNATIONAL POLITICAL COMMUNICATION. New York: Praeger, 1965. 404 p.

_____. MASS COMMUNICATION AND CONFLICT RESOLUTION: THE ROLE OF THE INFORMATION MEDIA IN THE ADVANCEMENT OF INTER-NATIONAL UNDERSTANDING. New York: Praeger, 1974. 155 p.

Deutsch, Karl W. THE NERVES OF GOVERNMENT: MODELS OF POLITICAL COMMUNICATION AND CONTROL. New York: Free Press, 1966. 316 p. Bibliog.

Feld, M.D. "Political Policy and Persuasion: The Role of Communications from Political Leaders." JOURNAL OF CONFLICT RESOLUTION 2 (March 1958): 78-89.

Merritt, Richard L., ed. COMMUNICATION IN INTERNATIONAL POLITICS. Urbana: University of Illinois Press, 1972. 461 p.

Phillips, Warren R. "International Communications." In INTERNATIONAL SYSTEMS: A BEHAVIORAL APPROACH, edited by Michael Haas, pp. 177-201. New York: Chandler, 1974.

Pool, Ithiel de Sola. COMMUNICATION AND VALUES IN RELATION TO WAR AND PEACE. New York: Institute for International Order, 1961. 69 p. Bibliog.

Report to Committee on Research for Peace.

Pye, Lucian W., ed. COMMUNICATION AND POLITICAL DEVELOPMENT. Princeton, N.J.: Princeton University Press, 1963. 381 p. Bibliog.

Studies in political development.

Speier, Hans. "International Political Communication: Elite vs. Mass." WORLD POLITICS 4 (April 1952): 305-17.

Bargaining

Coddington, Alan. "Game Theory, Bargaining Theory, and Strategic Reasoning." JOURNAL OF PEACE RESEARCH 4, no. 1 (1967): 39-45.

Deutsch, Morton, and Krauss, Robert M. "Studies of Interpersonal Bargaining." JOURNAL OF CONFLICT RESOLUTION 6 (March 1962): 52-76.

Harsanyi, John C. "Bargaining in Ignorance of the Opponent's Utility Function." JOURNAL OF CONFLICT RESOLUTION 6 (March 1962): 29-38.

Jensen, Lloyd. "Military Capabilities and Bargaining Behavior." JOURNAL OF CONFLICT RESOLUTION 9 (June 1965): 155-63.

_____. "Soviet-American Bargaining Behavior in the Postwar Disarmament Negotiations." JOURNAL OF CONFLICT RESOLUTION 7 (September 1963): 522-41.

Meeker, Robert J., and Shure, Gerald H. "Pacifist Bargaining Tactics: Some 'Outsider' Influences." JOURNAL OF CONFLICT RESOLUTION 13 (December 1969): 487-93.

Meeker, Robert J.; Shure, Gerald H.; and Moore, W.H., Jr. "Real-Time Computer Studies of Bargaining Behavior: The Effects of Threat Upon Bargaining." PROCEEDINGS, AMERICAN FEDERATION OF INFORMATION PROCESSING SOCIETIES CONFERENCE 25 (1964): 115-23.

Pen, Jan. "A General Theory of Bargaining." AMERICAN ECONOMIC REVIEW 42 (March 1952): 24-42.

Schelling, Thomas C. "Bargaining, Communication, and Limited War." JOURNAL OF CONFLICT RESOLUTION 1 (March 1957): 19-36.

_____. "Experimental Games and Bargaining Theory." WORLD POLITICS 14 (October 1961): 47-68.

Singer, Eugene. "A Bargaining Model for Disarmament Negotiations." JOURNAL OF CONFLICT RESOLUTION 7 (March 1963): 21-25.

Smith, William P., and Emmons, Timothy D. "Outcome Information and Competitiveness in Interpersonal Bargaining." JOURNAL OF CONFLICT RESOLUTION 13 (June 1969): 262-70.

Sullivan, Michael P. "International Bargaining Behavior." INTERNATIONAL STUDIES QUARTERLY 15 (September 1971): 359-82.

Thibaut, John. "The Development of Contractual Norms in Bargaining: Replication and Variation." JOURNAL OF CONFLICT RESOLUTION 12 (March 1968): 102-12.

Young, Oran R. THE POLITICS OF FORCE: BARGAINING DURING INTERNATIONAL CRISES. Princeton, N.J.: Princeton University Press, 1968. 438 p.

Simulation, Games, and Game Theory

Bloomfield, Lincoln P. "Political Gaming." U.S. NAVAL INSTITUTE PROCEEDINGS 86 (September 1960): 51-64.

Bloomfield, Lincoln P., and Padelford, Norman J. "Three Experiments in Political Gaming." AMERICAN POLITICAL SCIENCE REVIEW 53 (December 1959): 1105-15.

Brams, Steven J. GAME THEORY AND POLITICS. New York: Free Press, 1975. 212 p. Bibliog.

Cohen, Bernard C. "Political Gaming in the Classroom." JOURNAL OF POLITICS 24 (May 1962): 367-81.

Conrath, David W. "Experience as a Factor in Experimental Gaming Behavior." JOURNAL OF CONFLICT RESOLUTION 14 (June 1970): 195-202.

Copeland, Miles. THE GAME OF NATIONS: THE AMORALITY OF POWER POLITICS. New York: Simon and Schuster, 1969. 318 p.

Coplin, William D. "Inter-Nation Simulation and Contemporary Theories of International Relations." AMERICAN POLITICAL SCIENCE REVIEW 60 (September 1966): 562-78.

Davis, John B., Jr. THE USE OF GAMING AS AN AID IN THE EXAMINA-
TION OF NATIONAL SECURITY PROBLEMS OF A POLITICAL NATURE.
Washington, D.C.: National War College, 1964. 62 p.

Deutsch, Morton, et al. "Strategies of Inducing Cooperation: An Experimental Study." JOURNAL OF CONFLICT RESOLUTION 11 (September 1967):
345-60.

Evans, George William III; Wallace, Graham F.; and Sutherland, Georgia L.
SIMULATION USING DIGITAL COMPUTERS. Englewood Cliffs, N.J.: Prentice-Hall, 1965. 198 p.

Giffin, Sidney F. THE CRISIS GAME: SIMULATING INTERNATIONAL CON-
FLICT. Garden City, N.Y.: Doubleday, 1965. 191 p. Bibliog.

Goldhamer, Herbert, and Speier, Hans. "Some Observations on Political
Gaming." WORLD POLITICS 12 (October 1959): 71-83.

Guetzkow, Harold S., et al. SIMULATION IN INTERNATIONAL RELATIONS:
DEVELOPMENTS FOR RESEARCH AND TRAINING. Englewood Cliffs, N.J.:
Prentice-Hall, 1963. 248 p.

_____, ed. SIMULATION IN SOCIAL SCIENCE: READINGS. Englewood
Cliffs, N.J.: Prentice-Hall, 1962. 199 p. Bibliog.

Harsanyi, John C. "On the Rationality Postulates Underlying the Theory of
Cooperative Games." JOURNAL OF CONFLICT RESOLUTION 5 (June 1961):
179-96.

Hermann, Charles F. CRISES IN FOREIGN POLICY: A SIMULATION ANALY-
SIS. Indianapolis: Bobbs-Merrill, 1969. 234 p.

Hermann, Charles F., and Hermann, Margaret G. "An Attempt to Simulate
the Outbreak of World War I." AMERICAN POLITICAL SCIENCE REVIEW 61
(June 1967): 400-416.

Kinley, Holly J. "Development of Strategies in a Simulation and International
Revolutionary Conflict." AMERICAN BEHAVIORAL SCIENTIST 10 (November
1966): 5-9.

Kuhn, Harold W. "Game Theory and Models of Negotiation." JOURNAL OF
CONFLICT RESOLUTION 6 (March 1962): 1-4.

Luce, Robert Duncan, and Raiffa, Howard. GAMES AND DECISIONS: IN-
TRODUCTION AND CRITICAL SURVEY. New York: Wiley, 1957. 509 p.
Bibliog.

Study of Behavioral Models Project, Bureau of Applied Social Research, Columbia University.

McClintock, Charles G., and McNeel, Steven P. "Reward Level and Game Playing Behavior." JOURNAL OF CONFLICT RESOLUTION 10 (March 1966): 98-102.

Morschauer, Joseph. HOW TO PLAY WAR GAMES IN MINIATURE. New York: Walker, 1962. 134 p.

Nardin, Terry, and Cutler, Neal E. "Reliability and Validity of Some Patterns of International Interaction in an Inter-Nation Simulation." JOURNAL OF PEACE RESEARCH 6, no. 1 (1969): 1-12.

Quandt, Richard E. "On the Use of Game Models in Theories of International Relations." WORLD POLITICS 14 (October 1961): 69-76.

Rapoport, Anatol. FIGHTS, GAMES, AND DEBATES. Ann Arbor: University of Michigan Press, 1960. 400 p. Bibliog.

_____. N-PERSON GAME THEORY: CONCEPTS AND APPLICATIONS. Ann Arbor: University of Michigan Press, 1970. 331 p. Bibliog.

_____. "Prospects for Experimental Games." JOURNAL OF CONFLICT RESOLUTION 12 (December 1968): 461-70.

Robinson, James A., et al. "Teaching with Inter-Nation Simulation and Case Studies." AMERICAN POLITICAL SCIENCE REVIEW 60 (March 1966): 53-65.

Schelling, Thomas C. "Experimental Games and Bargaining Theory." WORLD POLITICS 14 (October 1961): 47-68.

_____. "Game Theory and the Study of Ethical Systems." JOURNAL OF CONFLICT RESOLUTION 12 (March 1968): 34-44.

_____. "The Strategy of Conflict: Prospectus for a Reorientation of Game Theory." JOURNAL OF CONFLICT RESOLUTION 2 (September 1958): 203-64.

Shubik, Martin, ed. GAME THEORY AND RELATED APPROACHES TO SOCIAL BEHAVIOR. New York: Wiley, 1964. 390 p. Bibliog.

_____. READINGS IN GAME THEORY AND POLITICAL BEHAVIOR. Garden City, N.Y.: Doubleday, 1954. 74 p.

Specht, Robert Dickerson. WAR GAMES. Report P-1041. Santa Monica, Calif.: Rand, 1957. 19 p.

Swingle, Paul G. "The Effects of the Win-Loss Difference Upon Cooperative Responding in a 'Dangerous' Game." JOURNAL OF CONFLICT RESOLUTION 11 (June 1967): 214-22.

Verba, Sidney. "Simulation, Reality, and Theory in International Relations." WORLD POLITICS 16 (April 1964): 490-519.

Vincent, Jack E., and Tindell, James O. "Alternative Cooperative Strategies in a Bargaining Game." JOURNAL OF CONFLICT RESOLUTION 13 (December 1969): 494-510.

Willis, Richard H., and Joseph, Myron L. "Bargaining Behavior: 'Prominence' as a Predictor of the Outcome of Games of Agreement." JOURNAL OF CONFLICT RESOLUTION 3 (June 1959): 102-13.

Wilson, Andrew. THE BOMB AND THE COMPUTER: WARGAMING FROM ANCIENT CHINESE MAPBOARD TO ATOMIC COMPUTER. New York: Delacorte, 1969. 218 p.

Zellner, Arnold. "War and Peace: A Fantasy in Game Theory?" JOURNAL OF CONFLICT RESOLUTION 6 (March 1962): 39-41.

Zinnes, Dina A. "A Comparison of Hostile Behavior of Decision-Makers in Simulate and Historical Data." WORLD POLITICS 18 (April 1966): 474-502.

Cybernetics

Ashby, William Ross. AN INTRODUCTION TO CYBERNETICS. New York: Wiley, 1956. 295 p.

Hammond, Kenneth R., and Brehmer, Berndt. COGNITION, QUARRELS, AND CYBERNETICS. Boulder: Institute of Behavioral Science, University of Colorado, 1969. 13 p. Bibliog.

Janda, Kenneth. DATA PROCESSING: APPLICATIONS TO POLITICAL RESEARCH. 2d ed. Evanston, Ill.: Northwestern University Press, 1969. 294 p.

Porter, Arthur. CYBERNETICS SIMPLIFIED. New York: Barnes and Noble, 1969. 159 p. Bibliog.

Retzlaff, Ralph H. "The Use of Aggregate Data in Comparative Political Analysis." JOURNAL OF POLITICS 27 (November 1965): 797-817.

Wiener, Norbert. CYBERNETICS: OR, CONTROL AND COMMUNICATION IN THE ANIMAL AND THE MACHINE. 2d ed. New York: M.I.T. Press, 1961. 212 p.

DATA BANKS

Useful data banks have been compiled by the International Data Library and Reference Service (University of California, Berkeley), the Inter-University Consortium for Political Research (University of Michigan), the Yale Political Data Program, the Roper Institute, and others. Selected published general data sources and compilations are cited in chapter 6.

Chapter 20

FICTION

A unique category of diplomatic literature--sometimes exciting and possibly useful though less pertinent to the serious study of the foreign relations process-- consists of fiction. As a resource, it is neither highly developed quantitatively nor generally well known. The following are merely suggestive of such publications concerning diplomats and foreign affairs appearing in the English language, most of which concern the United States. Only a few of these have been written by Department of State officers and American diplomats, such as Paul H. Bonner, John Franklin Carter, John Kenneth Galbraith, Howard R. Simpson, Charles W. Thayer, and Herbert O. Yardley. Also see James River Childs, p. 625.

Aldridge, James. THE DIPLOMAT. Boston: Little, Brown, 1950. 631 p.

> British diplomatic involvement and intrigue concerning Soviet action and policy in Azerbaijan, Iran.

Bonner, Paul H. AMBASSADOR EXTRAORDINARY. New York: Scribner, 1962. 306 p.

> Concerns diplomatic relations with fictitious Latin American country.

_____. SPQR: A ROMANCE. New York: Scribner, 1952. 325 p.

> Concerns young American diplomatic officer in Italy.

Brome, Vincent. THE AMBASSADOR AND THE SPY. New York: Crown, 1973. 245 p.

> Centers on a British spy and the mystery and intrigue surrounding the British embassy in a fictitious country.

Burdick, Eugene, and Wheeler, Harvey. FAIL-SAFE. New York: Dell, 1963. 285 p.

> Involves presidential direct communications with Moscow via the hot line to cope with crisis resulting from mechanical failure which sent U.S. atomic bombers to Soviet Union at fifteen hundred miles per hour with no chance of recalling them.

Byrne, Lawrence. THE AMERICAN AMBASSADOR. New York: Scribner, 1917. 301 p.

About fictional U.S. diplomat in Europe.

Carter, John Franklin ["Diplomat"]. CORPSE ON THE WHITE HOUSE LAWN. New York: Covici, Friede, 1931. 274 p.

Involves the exploits of a diplomatic detective in a lively, somewhat humorous recounting.

_____. MURDER IN THE EMBASSY. New York: Cape and Smith, 1930. 250 p.

Concerns murder of Japanese prince at Japanese embassy in Washington, delicate negotiations, and apprehension of the murderer.

_____. MURDER IN THE STATE DEPARTMENT. New York: Cape and Smith, 1930. 253 p.

Concerns murder of an under secretary of state, revealing some shady activities of diplomats involved in a conspiracy against the U.S. government.

Condon, Richard. THE MANCHURIAN CANDIDATE. New York: Signet, 1959. 351 p.

Spy story concerning Korean war veteran, brainwashed while imprisoned in Communist China, and Communist assassination plot he is programmed for in the United States.

Deiss, Jay. A WASHINGTON STORY. New York: Duell, Sloan, and Pearce, 1950. 313 p.

Congressional investigation of diplomatic official for possible Communist sympathy.

Drury, Allen. ADVISE AND CONSENT: A NOVEL OF WASHINGTON POLITICS. Garden City, N.Y.: Doubleday, 1959. 616 p.

A novel of political intrigue and action in the national capital, involving haggling over presidential appointments, and involving secretary of state and Senate Foreign Relations Committee.

Frank, Pat. AN AFFAIR OF STATE. Philadelphia: Lippincott, 1948. 256 p.

Experiences of prospective diplomatic officer.

Galbraith, John Kenneth. THE TRIUMPH: A NOVEL OF MODERN DIPLOMACY. Boston: Houghton Mifflin, 1968. 239 p.

Role of Department of State during revolution in fictional South American country.

Grady, James. SHADOW OF THE CONDOR. New York: Putnam, 1975. 287 p.

Continues exploits of agent "Condor," described in following item.

_____. SIX DAYS OF THE CONDOR. New York: Norton, 1974. 192 p.

Lone survivor of CIA agency mass murder becomes object of an intense manhunt and struggles to penetrate the plot; involves National Security Council and other high echelons of government.

Greene, Graham. THE HONORARY CONSUL. New York: Simon and Schuster, 1973. 315 p.

Account of politically motivated kidnapping of a minor British official near Argentina's Paraguayan border.

_____. THE QUIET AMERICAN. New York: Viking, 1956. 249 p.

U.S. secret agent and his activities in Southeast Asia.

Hall, Gertrude. AURORA THE MAGNIFICENT. New York: Century, 1917. 437 p.

Exploits of U.S. consul in Florence.

Harper, David. HIJACKED. New York: Dodd, Mead, 1970. 211 p.

Concerns bomb threat scrawled in lipstick on washroom mirror, launching crisis which involves the U.S. Air Force, the FBI, and the American ambassador in Moscow, as the plane is forced to fly to the Soviet Union.

Hoyt, Nancy. CAREER MAN. New York: Doubleday, Doran, 1933. 271 p.

Life of minor American diplomatic official in The Hague.

Kelly, Judith. A DIPLOMATIC INCIDENT. Boston: Houghton Mifflin, 1949. 277 p.

State Department official's involvement with Soviet anti-Stalin underground.

Kennedy, Jay Richard. THE CHAIRMAN. New York: Signet, 1969. 240 p.

CIA operative sent on a secret mission to Communist China, not realizing he is a walking time bomb intended to assassinate Chinese leader.

Keyes, Frances Parkinson. THE GREAT TRADITION. New York: Messner, 1939. 477 p.

About fictional U.S. minister to the Netherlands.

Fiction

_____. PARTS UNKNOWN. Cleveland: World, 1938. 429 p.

Concerns American consul and his family in La Paz.

Laumer, Keith. GALACTIC DIPLOMAT. Garden City, N.Y.: Doubleday, 1965. 227 p.

Satirical science fiction adventure of disillusioned diplomat of Corps Diplomatique Terrestrienne, among world's distant future, to maintain a state of tension short of interplanetary war.

Lederer, William J., and Burdick, Eugene. THE UGLY AMERICAN. New York: Norton, 1958. 285 p.

American diplomacy during cold war in Southeast Asia, involving diplomatic and military agents.

Miller, Merle. THE SURE THING. New York: Sloan, 1949. 341 p.

About Department of State official who loses position for alleged Communist ties.

Plum, Mary. STATE DEPARTMENT CAT. Garden City, N.Y.: Doubleday, Doran, 1945. 208 p.

Spy story involving appointment of prospective diplomatic officer.

Robertson, Constance. SALUTE TO THE HERO. New York: Farrar and Rinehart, 1942. 597 p.

Fictional U.S. diplomat in United Kingdom.

Sanders, Leonard. THE HAMLET WARNING. New York: Scribner, 1976. 280 p.

About former CIA agent, involved in mission during Dominican revolution, who works to prevent terrorist group from detonating a nuclear bomb.

Scott, John Reed. THE CAB OF THE SLEEPING HORSE. New York: Putnam, 1916. 369 p.

Concerns Department of State officials capturing foreign spies.

Sergel, Christopher. THE MOUSE THAT ROARED. Chicago: Dramatic Publishing Co., 1970. 100 p.

A play concerning an imaginary, nearly bankrupt country that declares war on the United States with the intent of losing in order to reap the benefits bestowed by the United States on its vanquished opponents.

Sutton, Jefferson. THE MISSILE LORDS. New York: Dell, 1963. 286 p.

Suspense story involving behind-the-scene deliberations by those making decisions respecting American nuclear weapons and security policy.

Thayer, Charles W. CHECKPOINT. New York: Harper and Row, 1964. 303 p.

Suspense story concerning Allied occupation of Berlin following World War II involving American diplomatic troubleshooter.

_____. MOSCOW INTERLUDE. New York: Harper, 1962. 338 p.

Espionage and conflict centering on an American attache and his Russian wife some years after Stalin's reign of terror.

Theroux, Paul. THE CONSUL'S FILE. Boston: Houghton Mifflin, 1977. 209 p.

Contains twenty short stories from the perspective of a village in modern Malaysia, on the road between Kuala Lumpur and Singapore.

Uris, Leon. TOPAZ. New York: McGraw-Hill, 1967. Reprint. New York: Bantam, 1968. 405 p.

Blend of fact and fiction, involving diplomacy, espionage, and intrigue; French diplomat serving U.S. foreign relations interests in revolutionary Cuba.

Vidal, Gore. THE SEASON OF COMFORT. New York: Dutton, 1949. 253 p.

Experiences of wife of minor Department of State officer who becomes an ambassador.

Walder, Francis. THE NEGOTIATORS. New York: McDowell, Obolensky, 1959. Translated by Denise Folliot from original SAINT-GERMAIN OU LA NEGOCIATION. Paris: Gallimard, 1958. 166 p.

Fifteenth-century negotiations between Catherine de Medici and Admiral de Coligny.

West, Morris L. THE AMBASSADOR. New York: Morrow, 1965. 275 p.

Experiences of U.S. ambassador in South Vietnam.

Wheeler, Keith. THE LAST MAYDAY. Garden City, N.Y.: Doubleday, 1968. 333 p.

Fiction

Suspense story about international crisis involving U.S. rescue of
the dethroned Soviet party leader seeking asylum in the West,
with White House–Kremlin hot line exchanges.

Wright, Austin Tappan. ISLANDIA. New York: Farrar and Rinehart, 1942.
1018 p.

Life of U.S. consul in fictional country.

Yardley, Herbert O. RED SUN OF NIPPON. New York: Longmans, Green,
1934. 247 p.

Department of State and intrigue. War averted by out-maneuver-
ing bureaucratic superiors and foreign agents.

Aside from the fashion in which the president and other political leaders are
introduced into such fiction, a number of novels center largely on the presidential role in foreign affairs. The following, generally involving suspense
and clandestine situations or major international crisis, illustrate such recent
literature:

Anderson, Patrick. THE APPROACH TO KINGS. Garden City, N.Y.:
Doubleday, 1970. 373 p.

Among other actions, the president becomes involved in scuttling
a dictatorial reformer in a mythical Latin American country.

Harrington, William. THE JUPITER CRISIS. New York: McKay, 1971. 345 p.

American president blackmailed by Soviet agents to force conflict
between the United States and China.

Hirschfeld, Burt. MOMENT OF POWER. New York: Avon, 1975. 447 p.

Dangerous president unmasked as imposter planted by China in
White House after the real president abducted while on a clandestine tryst, in order to force conflict between the United States
and the Soviet Union.

Knebel, Fletcher. NIGHT OF CAMP DAVID. New York: Harper and Row,
1965. 336 p.

About paranoid president, schizophrenic about American security,
ordering surveillance of other American public officials.

_____. TRESPASS. Garden City, N.Y.: Doubleday, 1969. 371 p.

About fictional president berating director of FBI for placing minority group under surveillance.

_____. VANISHED. New York: Doubleday, 1968. 407 p.

President faced with impeachment while his special envoy drops out of sight to organize an international conference of scientists on island of Tristan da Cunha, with the intent of forcing their governments to renounce aggressive war.

Knebel, Fletcher, and Bailey, Charles W. II. SEVEN DAYS IN MAY. New York: Bantam, 1963. 372 p.

Suspense story about Joint Chiefs of Staff plotting to take over the government of the United States.

Marlowe, Stephen. THE SUMMIT. New York: Signet/New American Library, 1970. 301 p.

Suspense story concerning presidential summit meeting with Soviet premier at Geneva.

Pearson, Drew. THE PRESIDENT. Garden City, N.Y.: Doubleday, 1970. 470 p.

Bureaucratic (including foreign relations) interaction related to Impeachment of activist liberal president by congressional reactionaries.

Safire, William. FULL DISCLOSURE. New York: Doubleday, 1977. 525 p.

American president blinded by assassination attempt in Russia. Involves resulting diplomacy and politicking to obtain his resignation.

Serling, Robert J. THE PRESIDENT'S PLANE IS MISSING. Garden City, N.Y.: Doubleday, 1967. 297 p.

Presumably killed in crash of Air Force One, the president involved in secret negotiations with Soviet leaders aimed at deterring China from aggressive war.

Most diplomats turned author and authors appointed to diplomatic assignments who produce fiction and short stories, however, appear to prefer alternative subjects. Among the better known and most prolific of these writers who served in American diplomatic appointments, some of whom authored best sellers and occasionally even a classic, include James Fenimore Cooper, Maurice Francis Egan, Nathaniel Hawthorne, William Dean Howells, Washington Irving, Thomas Nelson Page, James G. Thurber, Lew Wallace, and Brand Whitlock. Others who contributed fictional literature include Richard Washburn Child, Theodore S. Fay, Gideon H. Hollister, Henry van Dyke, and Charles A. Washburn. A number of diplomats published fiction under pseudonyms, such as John Franklin Carter (using the pen names of Jay Franklin and "Diplomat"), James Rives Childs (Henry Filmer), John Kenneth Galbraith (Mark Epernay and Julian K. Prescott), and Frederic J. Stimson (J.S. Dale). One of the more remarkable

illustrations of an author-diplomat employing pseudonyms was John Russell Cor-
yell, who wrote the Nick Carter detective stories and others under various
names: Julia Edwards, Geraldine Fleming, and Margaret Grant. A few diplo-
mat-authors were playwrights--George H. Boker, Clare Boothe Luce, Meredith
Nicholson, Bayard Taylor, Henry van Dyke, and Lew Wallace--and still others
wrote poetry. For additional listings and commentary, see:

Boyce, Richard Fyfe, and Boyce, Katherine Randall. AMERICAN FOREIGN
SERVICE AUTHORS: A BIBLIOGRAPHY. Metuchen, N.J.: Scarecrow, 1973.
321 p.

Plischke, Elmer. "Diplomats as Authors." In his UNITED STATES DIPLOMATS
AND THEIR MISSIONS: A PROFILE OF AMERICAN DIPLOMATIC EMISSARIES
SINCE 1778, pp. 117-30. Washington, D.C.: American Enterprise Institute,
1975.

A guide to half a century of related fiction, though not restricted to foreign
relations, is identified and surveyed in:

Linebarger, Genevieve C. "The Federal Government in the American Novel,
1900-1950." Ph.D. dissertation, University of Maryland, 1953. 501 p. Bibliog.

Part III

OFFICIAL SOURCES AND RESOURCES

Some of the materials incorporated into earlier chapters constitute documents, reports, and analyses produced by or related to official sources and resources. These are grouped functionally into sections according to the subjects to which they pertain. The two chapters embodied in this part deal with aggregate official information, documentation, and resources, and provide systematic reference to certain categories of relevant official materials. Chapter 21 describes and analyzes the nature of and problems related to the production, availability, and publication of such resources, and chapter 22 discusses and lists selected categories of published materials and archives. These need to be supplemented with certain groups of monographs, articles, and reports treated earlier, especially those that provide unofficial bibliographical guidance (chapter 6), constitute unofficial compilations of documents (chapter 15), and deal with Department of State and Foreign Service reorganization and reform (chapter 9) and secrecy in diplomacy (chapter 16).

Chapter 21

U.S. FOREIGN RELATIONS DOCUMENTATION—
AN ANALYSIS

Despite widespread public debate, and contrary to popular belief and the allegations of an insatiable press and certain elements of the academic world, the government of the United States pursues a liberal revelation and publication policy for its foreign relations documentation, a practice begun early in the nineteenth century. The inventory of regularized and ad hoc official publications on the conduct of foreign relations, together with those on the essence of foreign policy, is impressive, and the opening of American diplomatic archival documentation, though not immediate, has been systematized and comprehensive.

Since the establishment of the American republic, a great debate has raged over government secrecy in general and, more precisely, the issue of confidentiality in its diplomacy. This has flowed, in part, from an abiding popular suspicion of both governance and governors, from the role of the public and the information media in the American political process, and from the very nature of the democratic system. This dispute has been waged in waves, cresting in the twentieth century at the time of World War I and Woodrow Wilson's plea for "open covenants . . . openly arrived at," following World War II in connection with the Yalta agreements, the proposals to amend the president's treaty making authority in the 1950s, the Freedom of Information Act deliberations, and subsequently in relation to presidential war-making powers, executive privilege, and the publication of the "Pentagon Papers" and similar journalistic revelations.

This debate on confidentiality in foreign relations has proliferated to distinguish "open covenants" from "openly arrived at" and policy making from policy implementation. It has engendered spirited dialogue with respect to the security classification system for information and documents, established policy vs. contingency planning, and confidentiality of information vs. confidentiality of relations. It also raises issues concerning the proprieties of the "injunction to secrecy," executive privilege, the immune sources of the press and other media, news management, planned and uncontrolled leaks and "leakeries," and government public relations, press conferences, official releases, and "backgrounders." It all boils down to the fundamental issue of the public's "right to know"--what and when--as against the public's "need to know"--why.

Not all foreign affairs information or documentation becomes publicly available either immediately or automatically, and the problems involved in revelation and publication are often misunderstood and unappreciated. The crucial issues center upon the question: what should be made public (or released)--to what depth, when, by whom, to whom, and in what forum and format? The basic problem is epitomized by the appellation "secret diplomacy," which automatically evokes an unfavorable perception and a negative response, and which therefore has been called "quiet diplomacy" by Dag Hammarskjöld and others.

The matter of confidentiality requires a rational as well as rationalized compromise between the extremes of complete secrecy and immediate, wholesale revelation. Central is the alignment of the public interest, from the point of view of the individual member of the polity (his right and need to know), with the collective national concern, from the perspective of the aggregate community (its right or need to determine the nature and degree of revelation). Resolution of this juxtaposition of the interests of individuals within the community as against those of the community comprised of those individuals must, at best, accommodate both, must entail realistic compromise, and is not likely to satisfy fully the extreme of either. In 1972, modifying the documentary classification system of the United States, the president declared: "Clearly, the two principles of an informed public and of confidentiality within the Government are irreconcilable in their purest forms, and a balance must be struck between them" (White House Release, 8 March 1972, p.2).

To understand the intricacies of this problem, several interrelated sets of differentiating factors must be considered. These include distinguishing among: (1) information and documentation, (2) various basic methods of placing them in the public domain (including documentary availability, release, and publication), (3) fundamental components of the foreign relations process (including the separable elements of policy making, policy objectives and substance, and policy implementation), (4) levels of international and intragovernmental penetration, and (5) categories of security classification.

"INFORMATION" AND "DOCUMENTATION"—"RELEASE" AND "PUBLICATION"

The concepts "information" and "documentation" need to be clearly differentiated. The former is the more general and inclusive. It is essentially equatable with knowledge, usually communicable, and embraces not only written and printed documentation, but also oral information as well as pictorial, graphic, film and filmstrip, audiotape, and other forms of material that convey verifiable perceptions, facts, proof, or evidence. The term "documents" is more restrictive, connoting the nonoral forms of these materials. Often, information is publicly available, though not in its documentary form, and sometimes it is released even before it is reduced to documentary form.

In considering methods whereby information and documentary materials enter the public domain, including distinctions among "availability," "release," "dissemination," and "publication" of knowledge and documents, a number of concepts need to be understood. Some are fairly obvious, others are more subtle, and still others tend to be imprecise and confusing. The terms "records" and "papers" are often used interchangeably with "documents," although the concept "records" is broader in scope than the other two and, together with "materials," is used as the most generic expression. In essence, "records" encompass books, papers, maps, photographs, charts, and other documentary materials or copies thereof, regardless of physical form and characteristics. Technically, "non-textual" may be differentiated from "textual" records on the basis of content and format. "Papers" and "documents" are distinguished in that they are generally in written (or, in some cases, graphic or pictorial) form, as differentiated from oral documentation, and, although a "document," in its broadest sense, may be any written or graphic instrument that conveys information or proof, often the term is applied to the final version of an official "paper." "Archives," on the other hand, are all those records which are deliberately set aside, usually for long-range preservation.

The titles of certain categories of diplomatic records and documents, by way of comparison, are fairly precise, such as the various types of instruments employed in diplomacy, including the "aide mémoire," "circular note," "communiqué," "declaration," "final act," "note verbale," "procès verbal," "protocol," and "ultimatum." The same may be said of such documentation forms as the "letter," "despatch," "memorandum," "note," "airgram," and "telegram." This also is the case with formal diplomatic credentials, including the "exequatur," "full power," and "letter of credence." The meaning of "drafts" (including the distinction between the "initial," "original," or "preliminary" as against the "final" draft), distinguishable from "final copies" of papers or documents and of "working papers" involved in producing "end-product" documents in their ultimate, official versions, is also readily comprehensible.

It is more difficult, however, to differentiate precisely the meaning of "publication" and "publishing" as applied to government documents and records. "To publish," by definition, means "to make public" or "to divulge," and, while this is normally assumed to apply to the issuance of printed or processed materials, in reality it may also denote the revealing of information in oral as well as written form. "Publication" pertains to the act of publishing but traditionally is reserved for the issuance to the public of material in written or graphic rather than oral form. The dissemination of information in an oral fashion is characterized rather by the words "announcement," "divulgement," and "revelation," whereas the terms "dissemination," "issuance," and "release" may refer to both oral and written information and documentation. When made available or disseminated, such information and documents are said to be "in the public domain." Written publications, as distinct from oral information, may be "printed" or "processed" (i.e., mimeographed, photocopied, or otherwise reproduced), whereas "original" (inceptive or primigenial) documents usually are handwritten, typewritten, teletyped, or in the form of telegrams.

A final, important distinction to be noted is that documents and information may be "publicly available" even though they are neither published nor overtly issued publicly in some other form. Such documents and information may be said to be "available," but the initiative to acquire or extract them is up to the user, and they are potentially in the public domain, even if unused.

The delineation between "published," "disseminated," and "available" documents and information, therefore, may occasion some confusion, and caution must be exercised in evaluating degrees of confidentiality and openness respecting them. That which is explicitly published or disseminated is clearly made public, while that which is available but unused is neither secret nor overtly in the public domain. By comparison, the distinction between "open" and "closed" documentation and between "classified" and "unclassified" materials—both of which sets of differentiations are discussed later--is fairly precise, at least so far as general categories are concerned. At this point, suffice it to say that both published and unpublished records, as well as both documents and information, may be either classified or unclassified.

In short, appreciation of distinctions among these concepts and practices is essential to adjudging the problem of secrecy vs. openness as it relates to the use of foreign relations information and records. It must be realized that, so far as official sources and resources are concerned, a great deal more information is available than is reduced to documentary form, that considerably more documentation is publicly available than has been published by the government, and that far more has been published, disseminated in some other fashion, or produced in a refined manner primarily for internal use than is reproduced in printed version. On the other hand, substantial documentation and information are obtainable in some organized or collated form, even though unpublished, to supplement the basic raw records of the Department of State and other government agencies.

FOREIGN RELATIONS POLICY MAKING, SUBSTANCE, AND IMPLEMENTATION

To cope with the problem of the availability of foreign relations resources, it also is imperative to understand that, while much of the information and documentation which flow from official sources are intended to be made public when perfected, it may be that what goes into perfecting them is not everybody's business--at least not immediately. The consummated needs to be clearly distinguished from the pending. On the one hand, there is the determined objective, the decided policy, or the completed action. These need to be differentiated from the initiatives and proposals raised and discarded, the diplomatic methods, plans, and tactics pursued to gain ends, and the functioning of policy formulation and negotiatory procedures, as well as intergovernmental deliberation and bargaining while in progress to achieve the diplomatic end products desired. Such differentiations apply to both the processes of policy making respecting important and sensitive foreign relations matters and to the forging of end products in the field. They also relate to aligning interagency positions and relations respecting them.

Policy making internally and negotiation externally, by their very nature, involve advocacies, consideration and determination of options, the exercise of choice, and the fixing of priorities. To be fruitful, these normally entail adjustment, accommodation, bargaining, compromise, and concession. Distinctions respecting information and documentation--so far as confidentiality and revelation are concerned--clearly need to be drawn between three components of foreign relations: policy making, policy essence, and policy implementation. Delving deeper, additional discrimination must be made between policy making centrally and in the field, between policy which is substantive and that which is procedural, and between policy implementation at the national capital and through diplomatic agents or missions abroad. Discretion needs to be exercised in applying qualities of confidentiality and revelation to each of these subaspects of the foreign relations process. The amount of openness is greater with respect to some, and the need for constraint may be far more necessary for others. They can scarcely be regarded as equals under the generic designation "diplomacy."

Generally end-product foreign policy is made public relatively early in the United States, especially if it is self-executing and may be enunciated unilaterally. On the other hand, it if requires negotiation with other governments, sometimes basic policy but more often supportive subpolicy, which may be modified by international bargaining and compromise, together with diplomatic strategies, tactics, and the process of deliberation, tends to be withheld pending its consummation and outcome.

Governments, like other human institutions, usually are least willing to divulge information and documents at an early date respecting the details of their internal policy-making process. At the same time, since World War II, it is often this very element of foreign relations--rather than the substance of policy or the results of negotiation--which appears to be especially challenged on grounds of government secretiveness or the unavailability of information and documentation. The issue tends to become whether the right to know exceeds the realm of policy essence and negotiated consequences, and it extends to the detailed processes of policy formulation and implementation and to whether these should be publicized even before decisions are made or actions are taken.

PRELIMINARY VS. END PRODUCT DOCUMENTATION

Another consideration central to the concerns of the user of foreign relations information and documentation is the distinction between diplomatic end products and those which are initiatory, preliminary, or otherwise contributory to the eventuating decision, policy, action, or document. In terms of elementary logic, this is a relatively simple proposition, while, on examination, because of the varying, interrelated degrees of "end-productiveness" at differing stages of the process, it frequently becomes surprisingly intricate.

For example, a treaty draft proposal originating in a subelement of the Department of State, while propositional and initiatory with respect to that which follows, may actually be an end product of the deliberation that precedes it. Within the department, it then becomes the basis for intragency consideration at upper levels of the administrative hierarchy, and in this consideration it loses its earlier character as an end product. Discussion, refinement, and modification may remold it into a departmental end product, which then becomes initiatory in interdepartmental negotiation, producing a still later end product version. As consideration moves up to the White House level, including, possibly, National Security Council or cabinet deliberation, it undergoes another stage of transition from draft to end product, eventually taking on the character of the resultant U.S. draft treaty.

Within the international forum, however, the American proposal reverts to draft status. At the same time, other states may engage in similar deliberations producing their own national draft documents. An intermediate stage may involve the interchange by governments of formal or informal comments on individual national proposals, sometimes resulting in modifications and the preparation of new, more highly refined national versions, which become the end products of this phase of the evolution. These treaty drafts (and some may have become joint propositions) may then be dealt with collectively in differing ways. If the objective is a multipartite treaty, for purposes of illustration, negotiations could be direct and bilateral (which tends to be exceptional) or they may be simultaneous and multilateral (as is the common practice for such a treaty), and procedures for the two processes would vary. In the case of the multipartite convention negotiated at a multilateral conference, the various national drafts may all be regarded as initiatory proposals, or one of them may be made the basic negotiating version with the others viewed as proposals for modifying the working draft. The conference may fragment the composite into segments, each of which is negotiated into end product form by a separate committee. These partial end products would need to be integrated by a coordinating facility, producing its amalgamated, multipartite end product. The latter, finally, becomes the proposal considered (and possibly amended) in plenary session, the resulting version of which eventually becomes the conference end product--and the ultimate end product of the entire process, providing no textual changes are produced by interpretations, reservations, and amendments during national government review and ratification.

Even in this generalized illustration (and a good deal of diplomacy is far more intricate and may range over a span of years rather than weeks or months), it is possible to identify at least seven major stages of "end–productiveness," and to argue for the automatic publication of foreign relations end products raises serious questions of delineation among the respective stages in such a process and of the probable effects of premature release or publication at each stage on the likelihood of gaining the objectives sought. Discretion needs to be exercised, and determinations must safeguard the viability and success of the venture. In general, however, the closer the end product is to the conclusion of the proceeding and the effectuation of its implementation, the more likely is its public divulgence, providing this violates neither the security of the United States nor the confidence of other governments.

At some half-dozen points in this illutration, the end product of one phase of consideration becomes the draft basis of the next. Often, ideas, suggestions, comments, reactions to comments, and alternatives may be proposed, adopted, and negotiated, modifying that which was previously deemed to constitute an end product. The contributing materials and documents and information concerning them, leading to the final end product, may therefore be massive--illustrated by the thirteen volumes of selected and published documentation (nearly

twelve thousand pages) on the Paris Peace Conference following World War I--
and much of the material may be inconsequential, ineffective, unproductive,
or even trivial. Some of the documentation may not materially influence the
process, and some may raise alternatives that are never forcefully advocated
or conscientiously considered. A key issue involved in appraising the interrelation of such a mass of documentation, so far as depth of documentary and
information penetration is concerned, centers on the realistic determination of
a cutoff line below which materials--even those of a preliminary end product
nature during the preparatory stages--may not be automatically put into the
public domain at an early date.

Assuming that not all documentation is expected to be systematically published,
or even to be made publicly available immediately, discretion respecting selection must be exercised. This determination must bridge four sets of factors,
namely: recency, the degree of "end-productiveness" of the documentation,
the level of penetration into the foreign relations process (including policy
making, document devisement, intragovernmental and international discussion,
and negotiation), and the relationship of revelation to the needs of both public
knowledge and national expediency. Decision on the drawing of a rational
dividing line within the parameters of these demands and needs is far from
simple. Furthermore, it must take into account the relations of the United
States with other governments, which are likely to be sensitive to, if not critical of, the revelation by a foreign government of their policies, roles, and
concessions, without their consent, and it must protect pending negotiations
which may be compromised or otherwise disaffected by premature disclosure of
too great a depth.

Moreover, the definitive compilation and total immediate informational and
documentary revelation may not really be indispensable to the establishment
of essential truth. The true account, or a system of published documentation
which enables its user to project an accurate chronicle of the verities, may
be more vital than early definitive revelation and singularly preferable to complete secrecy. The prime difficulty is to define reasonable, workable, and
acceptable criteria for fixing the demarcation line which satisfies the needs
not only of scholarly researchers, the press, and the public, but also of the
government, and yet avoids implications of unessential secretiveness and appel-
lations of incredibility. A secondary difficulty is the establishment of a general acceptance of the fact that neither the information media (given their
biases and special interests), nor the scholars (given theirs), nor the public at
large (given its), is necessarily better qualified than the government to fix such
delineations in the interests of both the people and the polity. In short, in
this regard the best system is bound to be imperfect, and the resolution of the
problem is essentially one of prescribing operational principles as liberally as
is reasonable and implementing them in as generous as well as realistic a fashion as possible.

CLASSIFICATION OF INFORMATION AND DOCUMENTATION

Additionally, it is essential to understand the practice and problem of security "classification" and other systems of designating the treatment of information and documents, which affects directly the availability of foreign relations resources. In essence, a document is classified--and thereby restricted to use by those who are authorized access to it--because of the information it contains. Not all information incorporated in a document may in and of itself be classified, but it becomes classified by virtue of embodiment within an instrument that contains some classified content. Different portions of the information included in a single document may warrant varying degrees or levels of classification, and in the past, the document as a whole has usually been ascribed the classification of the most highly classified information it contains.

Sometimes, however, a document is classified not particularly because of the information contained therein, but simply because it reflects the intention at the time of withholding from the public domain the very existence of the document. Ventures in policy initiation prior to determination, policy formulation during the decision-making process, and diplomatic negotiation prior to reaching international understanding and agreement--together with the information and documents relating to them--are usually regarded by governments as being privileged and currently unavailable, and generally, therefore, they are classified.

Confidential information and documentation are normally sought to be safeguarded by what is broadly termed security classification. More precisely, in the United States they are reserved or vouchsafed, by Executive Order, when they require protection in the interest of "national security." In 1954, the attorney general advised the Department of State that defense classifications may be interpreted "to include the safeguarding of information and material" developed in the course of the conduct of foreign affairs "whenever it appears that the effect of the unauthorized disclosure of such information or material upon international relations or upon policies being pursued through diplomatic channels could result in serious damage to the Nation" (Department of State, FOREIGN AFFAIRS MANUAL, vol. 5, 1969, sec. 911.2). This extended the applicability of classification considerably beyond strictly defined security or defense considerations, and it was confirmed by Executive Order 11652 in 1972 and 12065 of 1978. The Freedom of Information Act of 1966, discussed later, also recognized the necessity for the government to withhold from public disclosure certain categories of information and records, including, but not restricted to, those whose disclosure would result in a "clearly unwarranted invasion of personal privacy" or would "violated a privileged relationship."

The three primary security classification categories, in descending order, are designated "Top Secret," "Secret," and "Confidential," which the Executive Order 12065 of 1978 defined as follows:

> "Top Secret" shall be applied only to information, the unauthorized disclosure of which reasonably could be expected to cause exceptionally grave damage to the national security.

> "Secret" shall be applied only to information, the unauthorized disclosure of which reasonably could be expected to cause serious damage to the national security.

"Confidential" shall be applied to information, the unauthorized disclosure of which reasonably could be expected to cause identifiable damage to the national security.

These categories were essentially the same as those specified in the Executive Order of 1972, but, in 1978, it was stipulated that the "damage to the national security" must be "identifiable" by the classifying authority.

Other materials are nonclassified, but they are not formally designated "unclassified" except in certain specific cases. Some years ago, the lowest ranking classification category--designated "Restricted"--was eliminated, but the appellation "Limited Official Use" was created to identify nonclassified information which required physical protection comparable to that given Confidential material in order to safeguard it from unauthorized access. This administrative control designation, as it was called, was applied by the Department of State to information received through privileged sources, specific references to the contents of diplomatic pouches, certain personnel, medical, investigative, commercial, and financial records, and other similar material. Another such administrative designation--"Official Use Only"--applied where operational principles warranted more expeditious transmission, wider distribution, and less secure storage. Under the 1978 Executive Order, such designations may no longer be employed to identify classified information.

Additional systems of designation are employed to limit access and distribution, to assign attention priorities, and for other reasons. For example, the characterization "Eyes Only" restricts distribution of documents, regardless of security classification, to a specially delimited group of officials. Priority designations for purposes of decision and action are also employed by the Department of State. In ascending order of urgency, they are "Routine," "Priority," "Immediate," and "Flash." Admittedly unique, the World War II communications between President Roosevelt, Prime Minister Churchill, and Premier Stalin bore some interesting designations. Because of their content, it may be presumed that utmost security precautions were maintained in their preparation, transmission, and custody. Most of them were marked "Personal" and either "Secret" or "Top Secret," a good many were designated "Urgent" or "Priority," and occasionally they were regarded as being "Private." One message of Prime Minister Churchill to Premier Stalin in 1945 even carried the distinction of being denominated "Personal, Most Secret, and Quite Private."

Information, and a document based thereon, which is "in confidence," needs to be distinguished from that which is "Confidential" or otherwise restricted for security reasons under the established classification system. Information which is held to be in confidence need not necessarily involve security or defense constraints, but simply evidences that a particular matter or document is not to be publicized at the moment, or that, while the information is not intended to be withheld, its source is not to be revealed, or that it is otherwise deemed to be "privileged." This is particularly important in the field of diplomacy, because much of the documentation involves foreign governments to which the American security classification and the release and publication systems do not apply, and which are entitled to expect their trust and confidence to be maintained. This imbues many diplomatic documents with a unique quality, which is recognized in the Executive Order of 1978.

A number of difficulties flow from the nature and operation of the classification system. Fundamental is the practice of employing a single set of designations founded largely on national security requirements for classification purposes rather than separate sets of firm and well-structured designations for this and for other purposes, including the "in confidence," "limited official use," raw intelligence documentation, and other categories. Inasmuch as the objectives, the intentions, and the degree of willingness to frame and attribute the information and the documents containing it vary, control of and flow into the public domain might best be managed and liberalized by separate sets of designations and procedures. In other words, the lowering or declassification of foreign relations materials, which were highly classified initially to prevent undermining the government's international negotiating posture rather than to protect the physical security of the nation, might be facilitated if they bore a different set of classification designations. For example, a treaty draft might be classified, not because revelation would threaten U.S. security, but merely to maintain its confidentiality during the bargaining process. A special classification designation for such documents might render reclassification and declassification easier if the system were not related to national security considerations.

A second problem is the devisement of methods for distinguishing levels of classification or other confidentiality distinctions for segments of information and documents, in order to avoid overrestricting those portions to which the higher levels of classification need not apply. Overclassification results from an attitude of resolving doubt in favor of classification at the highest requisite or justifiable level (i.e., "when in doubt--classify"), from the practice of classifying an entire document in accordance with the most highly classified information within it even though much of the content could be unclassified and in some cases may already be in the public domain, and from the disposition to classify a complete package of documents, an extensive compilation, or a comprehensive account in accordance with its most highly classified component. The 1978 Executive Order introduced the principle of identifying those portions of documents which are classified.

To induce greater restraint in classification practices, a number of additional reforms were introduced in the Executive Orders of 1972 and 1978. For example, to reduce the amount of material that may be classified, the number of executive departments and agencies authorized to employ classification designations and the number of individual officials within these agencies who are empowered to classify documents and information were circumscribed. The burden of proof was reversed, requiring that each official be held personally accountable for the propriety of the classifications attributed to him, authorizing administrative sanctions against such officials for repeated abuses, and empowering the National Security Council to provide overall policy direction for the program and a special administrative agency to monitor the implementation of the rules.

Much overclassification also has resulted from the condition that, while particular information and documents may be properly classified initially, in the course of time--and in certain cases this may actually be very short--the need for maintaining the original classification, or to continue any classification at all, may cease to exist. Resolution of this problem requires either an automatic system of reclassification-declassification, by which designations are arbitrarily reduced or eliminated entirely on a fixed time schedule, or a system of wholesale, periodic review and reclassification-declassification in accordance with explicit guidelines. A third possibility is a system of initial double classification under which the classifier ascribes two designations, the first of which has a time limit affixed, following which the document automatically permutes to a lower classification or becomes unclassified. Although such methods appear to be reasonable and manageable, and while each has its exponents, each also is fraught with difficulties and disadvantages.

All of these procedures have been used by the United States for its foreign relations documentation. Double or multiple classification and selective declassification are implied, so that documents and materials may be downgraded or declassified in advance or by overt reclassification by the agency applying the original classification. In addition, a wholesale and automatic schedule of downgrading and declassification is prescribed. Under the arrangement of the 1972 Executive Order, "Confidential" material became automatically declassified at the end of six years; "Secret" documents were required to be automatically downgraded to "Confidential" at the end of the second full calendar year and declassified in eight years; and "Top Secret" information and material were required to be downgraded to "Secret" in two years, to "Confidential" in the fourth year, and to be declassified at the end of ten years. The 1978 Executive Order further liberalized the process, providing that each classified document would be ascribed a date for its automatic declassification which could not exceed six years, although it could be downgraded or declassified at an earlier date. It is noteworthy, however, that certain categories of information and documentation are exempted from this arrangement, such as materials furnished by, or produced pursuant to written arrangements requiring confidentiality with foreign governments and international organizations and those specifically protected by U.S. statute.

A final overclassification problem results simply from the fact that the government itself is responsible for classification and declassification. In the past, it has tended to pursue a conservative, protective, and reluctant attitude toward maximal classification. Presumably, the changes instituted in the 1970s were intended to overcome this difficulty, to reduce classification both quantitatively and qualitatively, and to establish a systematic method of declassification. Essential caveats, such as exemptions to the automatic declassification schedule, however, leave considerable room for continued classification. An ultimate safeguard exists in the 1978 requirement for automatic review of information and documentation, with declassification at the end of twenty years, and in the application of this principle beyond the Department of State to other executive agencies, thereby rendering it universally applicable for U.S. government documentation.

Documentation—An Analysis

Parallelling the liberalizing Executive Orders of the 1970s, the Freedom of Information Act, which became effective in 1967, provided a special mechanism for rendering individual documents publicly available pursuant to specific request. This enactment required that the documents sought be easily identifiable and that the Department of State or other responsible agency might deny the request if the documents remain classified or fall into certain exempted categories. The act was not intended to produce the release of large batches of documents, but it does enable the researcher to obtain copies of particular, readily identifiable documents at nominal cost. When a classified document is requested under the Freedom of Information Act, its classification status is reviewed to determine whether the request can be accommodated. Individual documents, which may not be published by the Department of State, may thus be made available to the researcher long before departmental files are opened to public use or are transferred to the National Archives.

DOCUMENTATION INVOLVING FOREIGN GOVERNMENTS

So far as U.S. foreign relations are concerned, a final distinction must be drawn between information and documents that flow from and directly concern only the United States as compared with those that implicate a foreign government--as initiator, sender, recipient, commentator, or negotiating party. In keeping with historical practice, the Department of State cannot, on its own authority and without violating the mutuality of confidence and undermining its international reliability and credibility, reveal or publish information or documents that directly involve foreign powers. Sometimes, while it may be anxious to publish and may actually compile and prepare resulting materials for the press, the Department of State must stand by awaiting acquiescence from abroad, and securing such "clearance" may be delicate and time consuming.

A unilateral policy statement, a telegram from the Department of State to the head of an American diplomatic mission abroad, a national treaty draft, a report to Washington from a field mission, and the like are publishable without foreign approval. On the other hand, unpublished incoming messages from the Foreign Ministries of other countries, memoranda of discussions or negotiations with foreign emissaries, exchanges of views and documentary comments thereon, inquiries to the United States and foreign responses to American queries, and similar documentation involving other countries, according to the rules of the game, may be published by the United States only with the consent of the specific foreign governments concerned.

Even though the Department of State publishes such documentation more systematically, in greater overall depth, and more expeditiously than other powers, care is exercised not to violate this arrangement. In part, this accounts for the delay of some of its publication. It is virtually axiomatic that a government which rapidly publishes diplomatic documentation involving another country without clearance either has no such understood gentlemen's agreement with the other country (that, in fact, it is an adversary, if not an enemy) or, more probably, it publishes not so much to inform its own public as to gain international propaganda advantage.

AVAILABILITY OF UNPUBLISHED INFORMATION AND DOCUMENTATION

Unpublished foreign relations information and documentation are basically of two types--information and materials that are available, though unpublished, and those that are classified or otherwise unavailable. The mass of Department of State records and documents are located in the Department and in the National Archives--and their depositories--and they fall into two basic groupings --the "open" and the "closed" categories.

Under an earlier traditional "thirty-year rule," the documents remained under Department of State control for thirty years and generally were then transferred to the National Archives, where they became available to the public. Foreign relations records physically located in the Department of State and American missions abroad were closed to en masse access by nonofficial users in advance of the publication of the official diplomatic documentation of the United States, titled FOREIGN RELATIONS OF THE UNITED STATES, listed in the following chapter. The beginning date of the closed period was advanced automatically as the annual FOREIGN RELATIONS volumes were released.

These practices have been changed under the 1978 twenty-year rule and the Freedom of Information Act. Except for records involving foreign governments --the availability of which remain under the earlier thirty-year rule--availability of documentation now is less related to the publication of FOREIGN RELATIONS and the transfer of records to the National Archives. Such transfers still tend to be made at about thirty years and involve blocs of documentation. The preponderance of such foreign relations documentation held by the National Archives is publicly available. However, much of that in the Department of State is also obtainable under Freedom of Information Act procedures, but, because of physical access problems, it is not readily accessible to massive public usage.

Under the Freedom of Information Act, copies of identifiable, unclassified foreign relations records, even within the twenty-year "closed" period, may be obtained by the outsider (although he may not personally go through the files). This must be done in accordance with a fixed request and search procedure and at the requester's cost in keeping with a nominal, prescribed schedule of fees for search, true copy certification, and reproduction. Consequently, substantial quantities of materials are available during this "closed" period, and the Executive Order of 1978 specifically authorizes the granting of conditional access even to classified information for historical research purposes.

At times, special releases of documentation may hasten this process. For example, on January 21, 1972, the Department of State announced the en bloc declassification and opening of its foreign relations records for the years 1942 to 1945, through the World War II period. Inasmuch as the British government took similar action for its records, the Department also opened most of its files of formerly classified papers of British origin for this period.

In short, established American procedure provides an automatic method for opening the mass of U.S. foreign relations documentary materials to public scrutiny and usage. By comparison with other governments, this is one of the most liberal and systematized arrangements. According to a report of the Department of State, PUBLIC AVAILABILITY OF DIPLOMATIC ARCHIVES, 1976 (see p. 550), of approximately 120 countries surveyed, the diplomatic records of more than half were found to be largely inaccessible. Some twenty specifically prohibit public access or make no provision for the availability of their records, and nearly thirty governments stipulated no established policy regarding the matter, which means that their documents may be assumed not to be public. It is possible, however, that under appropriate circumstances, bona fide researchers might have access for limited purposes under specified restrictions, and then most likely only with respect to nonsensitive matters. An additional twenty-two governments had no fixed policy on the matter other than to stipulate that the foreign ministry, the national archives, or some other agency could authorize specific individuals to use particular documents on a limited basis. The largest single category consisted of those forty-seven governments which fix particular dates for the opening of their records. Two forms of this arrangement are employed, namely, that by which documents are opened automatically at the end of a prescribed number of years, and that which fixes a specific date as the dividing point, with records subsequent to these dates not being available. Sixteen governments use the basic fifty-year period for the opening of their diplomatic archives, which appears to be the most common but declining practice for automatic opening of foreign relations archives. Nine governments use the thirty-year arrangement. Aside from the United States, which commenced this practice in the 1920s, these include Great Britain, which changed from fifty to thirty years in 1968, and Australia, Ghana, Guyana, India, Israel, Peru, and Tanzania. Others vary from one hundred years (the Vatican) to twenty-five and even as low as twenty years. Only a small number of governments use the fixed cutoff date arrangement. For example, the records of Portugal are open to inspection prior to 1851, Spain uses the year 1900, Luxembourg uses 1914, Thailand uses 1932, and several states employ dates relating to World War II, including Germany and Japan, whose records are generally closed after 1945.

Analysis of comparative governmental practices also reveals that important distinctions are made not only between classified and unclassified documents, but also as to whether the researcher is a national or a foreigner, whether bona fide research is involved or simply general availability to the public, and among open, restricted, and closed periods. Availability normally is freer when the documents are under the control of the national archives of a country than when they are in the foreign ministry.

An earlier report of the Department of State ("Public Availability of Diplomatic Archives in the United States and Certain Foreign Countries," 1961), surveyed the practices of seventy-five foreign governments with respect to the systematic serial publication of their diplomatic papers. It reveals that no country other than the United States had a comparable ongoing, long range, and comprehensive publication program for its foreign relations documentation. As a matter of fact, two-thirds had no publication system or plans whatsoever. Some governments undertook the publication on a regularized basis of only their treaties, agreements, laws, and ordinances. A few issued selected diplomatic papers in annual Foreign Ministry reports or periodical bulletins of various types, a half dozen had published extensive collections for limited earlier periods or for specific situations (such as World War I), and some governments contributed to the "rainbow books"--usually referred to as "white papers" despite the color of their jackets.

"FOREIGN RELATIONS OF THE UNITED STATES" SERIES

To summarize U.S. practice, foreign relations documentation generally is de-classified and made publicly available in twenty years or less. In addition, as documents are published in the FOREIGN RELATIONS series, not only are they declassified and entered into the public domain on a regularized basis, but the bulk raw materials from which they are taken become readily available as they are transferred to the National Archives.

Nevertheless, a few types of documents remain unpublished, whether they bear security classification or not. The preface to the FOREIGN RELATIONS vol-umes indicates that certain categories of materials may be omitted in order to avoid publication of matters which would tend to impede current diplomatic negotiations or other official business, to condense the record and avoid repeti-tion of unnecessary details, to preserve the confidence reposed in the Depart-ment of State by individuals and foreign governments, to avoid giving needless offense to other nationalities or individuals, and to eliminate personal opinions presented in dispatches and not acted upon by the Department of State (except that, in connection with major decisions, it is intended, where possible, to show the alternatives presented to the Department before decisions were made).

In preparing the volumes of FOREIGN RELATIONS for publication, the Depart-ment of State refers to appropriate policy officers of the department and to other U.S. government agencies those papers that require policy clearance--which means declassification if necessary--and it refers to individual foreign governments requests for permission to print as part of the diplomatic documen-tation those previously unpublished documents which were originated by such governments. Similarly, foreign relations records originated by a foreign govern-ment or another agency of the U.S. government, and not yet published or opened to access by that government or agency, are not made publicly avail-able by the Department of State without the consent of the government or agency concerned.

Serious difficulties are encountered in obtaining such consent to publication, and the Department of State has been plagued by delays in gaining requisite clearances. Moreover, in the post-World War II period, greater clearance difficulty is encountered with respect to special types of records, such as those involving intelligence matters, the National Security Council, and crisis diplo-macy. Whereas refined intelligence reports may, in the course of time, be made available or published, it is unlikely that the bulk of raw intelligence materials (which may reveal precise intelligence sources or methods) will flow freely into the public domain. These were explicitly reserved by the Executive Order of 1972, and the 1978 directive broadened this to provide that information concerning "intelligence activities, sources or methods" could remain classified if it "continues to meet the classification requirements . . . despite the passage of time" (Executive Order 12065).

Special problems characterize the documents of the National Security Council. By their very nature, they may be deemed to require more protracted confidentiality because of the matters to which they pertain, because many are preliminary to decision making, and because many relate to contingency considerations which never materialize so that they address probabilities or possibilities, often inchoate, the revelation of which may be deemed detrimental to U.S. diplomacy. Assurance of early publication might very well inhibit the very documentation of such considerations. In addition, records of the National Security Council introduce a unique problem in that, technically, clearance is required both of the individual officials or agencies represented in its deliberations and of the council, as a collective interdepartmental agency. This is tantamount to requiring multiple clearance, and at any given moment the current National Security Council is likely to be reluctant to authorize publication or access to its highly classified documentation. This special problem within the broader issue of the availability and publication of foreign relations materials needs to be faced, and a formula needs to be generated for releasing this important category of documentation. It is clear, however, that its resolution lies beyond the authority simply of the Department of State. Recognizing this, the president instructed not only the National Security Council, but also the Central Intelligence Agency and the Defense Department, to cooperate in expediting the publication by the Department of State of the FOREIGN RELATIONS series on a twenty-year cycle, and the declassification rules of 1978 may help to ameliorate this problem.

Certain categories of documents may remain unavailable indefinitely, beyond the commencement of the open period. Examples include specific types of personnel and medical records, which are withheld because they contain private or personal information which, if disclosed, would amount to an invasion of the privacy of the persons concerned, and investigative records, because they are compiled for the enforcement of law or in preparation of government litigation and adjudicative proceedings. These remain unavailable to the public even if transferred to the National Archives.

In the past, telegrams and cryptographic information were given special protection by government regulations, but this was changed in 1978. After World War II, under Executive Order 10501 of 1953, classified telegrams were not to be referred to, paraphrased, downgraded, declassified, or disseminated, except in accordance with prescribed controls issued by the head of the originating government agency. Furthermore, classified telegrams transmitted over cryptographic systems were required to be handled in accordance with the regulations of the transmitting agency. Executive Order 11652 of 1972 continued to exempt cryptographic information and materials from the revised classification system. This arrangement created an exceptional problem, because these restrictions were patently designed to protect the system of communications rather than the information they contained. As a result, while the information itself could be unclassified or eventually declassified, the nature of the original documentary form in which it was contained could prevent its entering the public domain unless it was converted into some other documentary or oral form or unless security ceased to be essential to its telegraphic or cryptographic form. This exemption was omitted in the 1978 Executive Order 12065.

The foreign relations documentation which remains unavailable and unpublished in the long run is quantitatively small but qualitatively may range from the important to the unimportant for purposes of essaying the essential truth. Restrictions flow from obvious necessity (such as specific covert intelligence sources or clearance by foreign governments of their communications) to problems of interpreting the rules (such as determining which revelation would impede current negotiations, would give needless offense to other nations, would constitute an invasion of personal privacy, or would violate trust reposed in the United States by a foreign government). Nevertheless, the bulk of foreign relations documents enter the public domain eventually--automatically after twenty years or, in the case of documents involving foreign governments, after thirty years). They may become accessible earlier, as they are automatically or systematically declassified, or when they are published in FOREIGN RELATIONS and other periodic and ad hoc publications, or they may be made available on a limited basis for bona fide research in other ways, or, if they are final end products or otherwise unclassified, at a still earlier date.

In the past, the specific aspects of the problem of revelation which appear to have been most seriously questioned--aside from the application of the security classification system--were the fixed-time rule and the delay in publishing the FOREIGN RELATIONS volumes. Proposals to modify the traditional thirty-year rule have been freely made, ranging from contentions that all confidentiality should be eliminated, to those which propose advancing the opening date on the basis of historical events, to those continuing the automatic aspect but shortening the number of years to twenty (as in the 1978 Executive Order), fifteen, or even eight (to cover a presidential administration of two terms). Serious consideration needs to be given to both the criteria and the rationale on which any availability or publication program is based, and such determination would need to be founded on a careful analysis and appreciation of all factors and interests involved. The changes instituted in 1978 reflect a determined effort to liberalize documentary availability.

Additional advantage to the researcher would be gained from advancing the publication schedule of the FOREIGN RELATIONS series. Such publication essentially constitutes a planned process of surveying massive documentary resources and putting extensive portions of them into the public domain on a systematic and liberal basis, while simultaneously placing the residuum of the documentary resources from which they are extracted generally into the available though unpublished category. In principle, the fundamental difficulties with this publication venture are four-fold: the growing mass of documentary materials to be examined, the quantity of documents to be published in the series, the depth to which they penetrate, and the time lag between publication and the date to which they pertain. In practice, the problem is one of funds, personnel to handle the assignment, and the cost of publication.

Documentation—An Analysis

The documentation of the Department of State has increased substantially by comparison with earlier times. The total quantity of departmental official resources amounts to approximately 275,000 cubic feet of documentation. Of this massive reservoir, nearly 125,000 cubic feet of records are to be found in the Department of State, including its central files and its operational and staff bureaus and offices, together with the overseas diplomatic and consular missions and posts. Because they have not been archivally refined, duplication exists. State Department records increase by an average of 5 to 10 percent each year. It is a simple matter of arithmetic to conclude, therefore, that some 2,000 to 3,000 cubic feet of such unrefined documentation would need to be surveyed per year in order to produce the annual contribution to the FOREIGN RELATIONS series.

Initially, commencing in the 1860s, one or two volumes per year sufficed for the important documentation concerning all countries and issues. Beginning with 1932, five or more volumes have been needed for each year, and for the years since World War II, this increased to from eight to eleven volumes per year. A few years ago, the Department of State concluded that it would be called upon to produce a published, high-quality collection of ten volumes per year, each averaging one thousand pages--or one hundred volumes consisting of one hundred thousand pages per decade. Subsequently, this goal was reduced to some six to eight volumes per year, and, more recently, because of increasing costs, it has been suggested that this quota be reduced still further.

On the matter of the depth of penetration, it need only be added that the deeper the penetration, particularly in the policy-making function (as distinct from the end product policy and the policy implementation), together with the closer to currency, the more difficult it is to obtain requisite publication clearances--inside the Department, from other U.S. agencies, and from foreign governments. On the other hand, the shallower the penetration, the less complete will inclusion be. Compromise between this factor of depth of penetration and currency of publication, therefore, is essential, and the potential user can scarcely have it both ways. The choice is between the earlier, less inclusive compilation, or one which, while more definitive, is also more delayed.

When FOREIGN RELATIONS was first published, each volume was issued shortly after the year to which it pertained. The lag was only a year or two, but this gradually eroded, to a fifteen-year delay by the end of World War I, to twenty years by 1960, and, by the early 1970s, it exceeded twenty-five years, and the prospects of preventing this delayed production schedule from slipping even more appeared murky. In 1962, the secretary of state officially set the publication time lapse at twenty years, except in exceptional circumstances, but this schedule was not maintained, in part because of the size of the documentary resources and the clearance problem, but also because of budgetary and personnel restrictions. In March 1972, the president issued directives to the secretary of state and the heads of other relevant agencies to cooperate in returning to the twenty-year standard, but this also proved to be optimistic. Success in achieving and maintaining this rate of production would depend upon an enlightened attitude respecting the role and value of the published FOREIGN RELATIONS series, adequate staffing for the task, and accommodation for the exigencies of depth of penetration and clearance. A supplementary way of helping to reduce the degree of confidentiality would be to extend the publication of ad hoc studies and documentary compilations, including selected case studies of both crisis situations and a broad spectrum of other functional and areal matters, such as more reports on important international conferences, reports on participation in international organizations (in addition to the United Nations), analyses of the diplomatic function, and various occasional studies and materials.

Despite existing shortcomings, the American venture offers a sophisticated, high quality, carefully managed, sagacious, increasingly liberalized, and relatively inexpensive system of diplomatic information and documentary revelation and publication. It has been well tested over the years--for more than a century in the case of the FOREIGN RELATIONS series--and has produced a library of convenient, basic diplomatic sources and resources. Problems of classification, fixing delineations for depth of penetration into the national policy-making process and for the degree of "end-productiveness" of documentation to be released into the public domain, and compromise between the relatively comprehensive as against the less definitive though earlier special compilations and studies are not insuperable, and pragmatic solutions can be found. This would go a long way to bridge the gap between the essential truth now and the definitive truth later and to satisfy both the legitimate needs of the government and the information and resource requirements of the citizenry.

Chapter 22

COMPILATIONS AND OTHER OFFICIAL

PUBLICATIONS AND RESOURCES

This chapter provides general guidance to selected official, largely published documentation useful for the study of the conduct of American foreign relations. It lists basic guides and indexes to government documents and publications, principally those of the president, Congress, the Department of State, and its affiliated agencies, as well as to documentary resources on various functional subjects, such as treaties and agreements, international conferences, arms control and disarmament, and regional background studies. A listing of selected unofficial collections of documents is appended. Additional official documents that relate to specific subjects treated in sections of other chapters are incorporated into those sections. This chapter is comprehensive with respect to certain types of research materials, including published collections of diplomatic correspondence and the texts of treaties and agreements, but it needs to be supplemented from the listings of other chapters for particularized functional topics.

GENERAL BIBLIOGRAPHICAL GUIDANCE AND SOURCES

The following provide general guidance to government documentation and resources. Guidance to more specific topics, including the conduct of foreign relations, the Department of State, the Foreign Service, and various functional subjects are provided in other sections of this compilation.

Official Guides to Government Publications and Documents

Arrangement in this section is generally chronological.

A DESCRIPTIVE CATALOGUE OF THE GOVERNMENT PUBLICATIONS OF THE UNITED STATES, SEPTEMBER 5, 1774-MARCH 4, 1881. Compiled by Benjamin Perley Poore. Washington, D.C.: Government Printing Office, 1885. 1,392 p.

An extensive compilation of titles of government publications, chronologically arranged, with an alphabetical index.

COMPREHENSIVE INDEX OF THE PUBLICATIONS OF THE UNITED STATES

GOVERNMENT, 1889-93. Compiled by John G. Ames. Washington, D.C.: Government Printing Office, 1894. 480 p.

Arranged alphabetically by subject, with an indication of the individual or agency initiating the document or of its classification as a congressional document.

COMPREHENSIVE INDEX TO THE PUBLICATIONS OF THE UNITED STATES GOVERNMENT, 1881-1893. Compiled by John G. Ames. 2d ed. 2 vols. Washington, D.C.: Government Printing Office, 1905. 1,590 p.

Augments the preceding index to fill in the period between Poore's CATALOGUE and 1893, when the superintendent of documents' CATALOGUE commenced, as indicated below.

CATALOGUE OF THE PUBLIC DOCUMENTS. 25 vols. Washington, D.C.: Government Printing Office, 1896-1944.

Prepared by the superintendent of documents. Full title of each volume refers to the particular Congress and to the publications of the departments of the government of the United States. Covers the period from 1893 to 1940. A catalog of congressional and executive documents, arranged alphabetically by subject.

CHECKLIST OF UNITED STATES PUBLIC DOCUMENTS, 1789-1909. Washington, D.C.: Government Printing Office, 1911. 1,707 p.

Contains lists of congressional documents to 1908, and departmental and administrative publications to the end of 1909. Congressional documents listed chronologically by sessions, and departmental publications listed alphabetically by department. Earlier versions published by the Interior Department in 1892 and by the superintendent of documents in 1895.

MONTHLY CATALOGUE OF UNITED STATES GOVERNMENT PUBLICATIONS. Washington, D.C.: Government Printing Office, 1895-- . Monthly.

A monthly listing of the voluminous documentation of the U.S. government. Items arranged alphabetically by the name of the issuing agency or author, and thereunder alphabetically by the title of the publication.

UNITED STATES GOVERNMENT PUBLICATIONS MONTHLY CATALOGUE: DECENNIAL CUMULATIVE INDEX, 1941-1950. Washington, D.C.: Government Printing Office, 1953. 1,848 p.

Cumulated index to the monthly issues of the CATALOGUE from January 1941 to December 1950.

GOVERNMENT PUBLICATIONS: A GUIDE TO BIBLIOGRAPHIC TOOLS. Compiled by Vladimir M. Palic. 4th ed. Washington, D.C.: U.S. Library of Congress, 1975. 441 p.

Supersedes GOVERNMENT DOCUMENT BIBLIOGRAPHY IN THE
UNITED STATES AND ELSEWHERE. Compiled by James B. Childs.
3d ed. Washington, D.C.: U.S. Library of Congress, 1942.
78 p.

Current topical listings of the publications of the U.S. Government Printing
Office are provided in more than 270 SUBJECT BIBLIOGRAPHIES, formerly
titled PRICE LISTS. These are revised and republished periodically, and they
are available, without charge, from the Superintendent of Documents, Washington, D.C. 20402. Aside from those concerned with FOREIGN AFFAIRS
OF THE UNITED STATES (SB 75) and FOREIGN RELATIONS OF THE UNITED
STATES (SB 210), the following are among those most relevant to the conduct
of U.S. foreign affairs:

AMERICA IN SPACE	SB 20
AREA HANDBOOKS	SB 166
ATOMIC ENERGY AND NUCLEAR POWER	SB 200
CUSTOMS, IMMUNIZATION, AND PASSPORTS PUBLICATIONS	SB 27
DIGESTS OF UNITED STATES PRACTICE IN INTER- NATIONAL LAW AND DIGEST OF INTERNATIONAL LAW	SB 185
DISARMAMENT AND ARMS CONTROL	SB 127
FOREIGN INVESTMENTS	SB 275
FOREIGN TRADE AND TARIFF	SB 123
HISTORICAL HANDBOOK SERIES	SB 16
IMMIGRATION, NATURALIZATION, AND CITIZENSHIP	SB 69
INTELLIGENCE ACTIVITIES	SB 272
NATIONAL AND WORLD ECONOMY	SB 97
NATIONAL DEFENSE AND SECURITY PUBLICATIONS	SB 153
POLITICAL ACTIVITIES	SB 136
PRESIDENTS OF THE UNITED STATES	SB 106
TREATIES AND OTHER INTERNATIONAL AGREEMENTS OF THE UNITED STATES	SB 191
UNITED STATES AND FOREIGN MAPS	SB 102

Other Guides to and Commentary on Official Documentation

Bemis, Samuel Flagg, and Griffin, Grace Gardner, eds. GUIDE TO THE DIP-
LOMATIC HISTORY OF THE UNITED STATES. Washington, D.C.: Government
Printing Office, 1935. 979 p.

Covers the period from the Revolution to 1921.

Boyd, Anne Morris, and Rips, Rae Elizabeth. UNITED STATES GOVERNMENT
PUBLICATIONS. 3d ed. New York: Wilson, 1949. 627 p.

Buchanan, William Wallace, and Kanely, Edna A. CUMULATIVE SUBJECT
INDEX TO THE MONTHLY CATALOGUE OF UNITED STATES GOVERNMENT

PUBLICATIONS, 1900–1971. 15 vols. Washington, D.C., and Arlington, Va.: Carrollton Press, 1975.

Burke, John Gordon, and Wilson, Carol Dugan. THE MONTHLY CATALOGUE OF U.S. GOVERNMENT PUBLICATIONS: AN INTRODUCTION TO ITS USES. Hamden, Conn.: Shoe String, 1973. 113 p. Bibliog.

Childs, James B. "United States of America Official Publications." ANNALS OF LIBRARY SCIENCE (of Indian National Scientific Documentation Center, New Delhi) 9 (June 1962): 84–91.

Clarke, Edith E. GUIDE TO THE USE OF UNITED STATES GOVERNMENT PUBLICATIONS. Boston: Faxon, 1919. 308 p.

Conover, Helen F., ed. A GUIDE TO BIBLIOGRAPHIC TOOLS FOR RESEARCH IN FOREIGN AFFAIRS. 2d ed. Washington, D.C.: U.S. Library of Congress, 1958. 160 p.

House, Peter W., and Jones, David W., Jr. GETTING IT OFF THE SHELF: A METHODOLOGY FOR IMPLEMENTING FEDERAL RESEARCH. Boulder, Colo.: Westview, 1977. 304 p.

Leidy, William Philip. A POPULAR GUIDE TO GOVERNMENT PUBLICATIONS. 4th ed. New York: Columbia University Press, 1976. 440 p.

Linebarger, Genevieve Collins, et al. WASHINGTON SOURCES IN INTERNATIONAL AFFAIRS. College Park: Bureau of Governmental Research, University of Maryland, 1951. 54 p.

Lowenstein, Linda, ed. GOVERNMENT RESOURCES AVAILABLE FOR FOREIGN AFFAIRS RESEARCH. Washington, D.C.: Office of External Research, U.S. Department of State, 1965. 56 p.

Morehead, Joe. INTRODUCTION TO UNITED STATES PUBLIC DOCUMENTS. Littleton, Colo.: Libraries Unlimited, 1975. 289 p.

Patch, Buel W. "Access to Official Papers and Information." EDITORIAL RESEARCH REPORTS 1 (24 June 1953): 417–33.

Plischke, Elmer, ed. AMERICAN FOREIGN RELATIONS: A BIBLIOGRAPHY OF OFFICIAL SOURCES. College Park: Bureau of Governmental Research, University of Maryland, 1955. Reprint. New York: Johnson Reprint Corp., 1966. 71 p.

Schmeckebier, Laurence F., and Eastin, Roy B. GOVERNMENT PUBLICA-
TIONS AND THEIR USE. 2d ed. Washington, D.C.: Brookings Institution,
1969. 502 p.

U.S. Congress. Senate. Committee on Government Operations. Subcommittee on National Policy Machinery. ORGANIZING FOR NATIONAL SECU-
RITY: A BIBLIOGRAPHY. 86th Cong., 1st sess. Washington, D.C.: Government Printing Office, 1959. 77 p.

> Especially pp. 47–76.

U.S. Congress. Senate. Committee on Government Operations. Subcommittee
on National Security Staffing and Operations. ADMINISTRATION OF NATION-
AL SECURITY: A BIBLIOGRAPHY. 88th Cong., 1st sess. Washington, D.C.:
Government Printing Office, 1963. 89 p.

> See table of contents for guidance to government publications,
> which are dispersed in each major section of this compilation.

Diplomatic Missions, Washington, D.C.

Foreign diplomatic missions in Washington, D.C., usually have collections of
documents, and some of them maintain libraries containing such materials as
legislative debates, files of legislation, government reports, yearbooks, periodicals, files of newspapers, newspaper clippings concerning the respective
countries, informational booklets, maps, posters, and published volumes concerning foreign countries. For an official listing of foreign diplomatic missions,
see the DIPLOMATIC LIST, cited below in section on "Diplomatic and Consular Missions and Officials," p. 560.

Additional Bibliographies and Publications of a General Nature

Corwin, Edward S., comp. THE CONSTITUTION OF THE UNITED STATES OF
AMERICA: ANALYSIS AND INTERPRETATION. Prepared by the Legislative
Reference Service, U.S. Library of Congress. Washington, D.C.: Government
Printing Office, 1953. 1,361 p.

> Explanation of the Constitution, article by article, and section by
> section, with reference to court decisions bearing upon its inter-
> pretation. Useful for an understanding of the foreign relations
> provisions of the Constitution.

Schellenberg, Theodore R. THE MANAGEMENT OF ARCHIVES. New York:
Columbia University Press, 1965. 383 p.

> Directed primarily to custodians of research material, deals with
> principles and techniques related to the arrangement and descrip-
> tion of textual, cartographic, and pictorial records. Useful back-
> ground to the researcher.

U.S. Library of Congress. AMERICAN HISTORY AND CIVILIZATION: A LIST OF GUIDES AND ANNOTATED OR SELECTIVE BIBLIOGRAPHIES. Compiled by Donald H. Mugridge. 2d ed. Washington, D.C.: Government Printing Office, 1951. 18 p.

_____. LIBRARY OF CONGRESS: PUBLICATIONS IN PRINT. Washington, D.C.: Government Printing Office, 1952-- . Annual since 1959.

> Contains variety of bibliographies, calendars, catalogs, checklists, directories, guides, indexes, registers, other materials (archives, papers, manuscripts, and publications), as well as analyses of various subjects.

U.S. National Archives and Records Service. UNITED STATES GOVERNMENT MANUAL. Washington, D.C.: Government Printing Office, 1974-- . Annual.

> Official organization handbook of the government. Published as UNITED STATES GOVERNMENT ORGANIZATION MANUAL from 1935 to 1974. Includes sections on the agencies of the legislative, executive, and judicial branches; descriptions concerning the establishment, internal structure, authority, functions, and related matters for each major organ, department, or agency, as well as for the principal subsidiary units; materials on quasiofficial agencies and selected multilateral and bilateral international organizations; series of government structure charts; and brief descriptions of abolished and transferred agencies and governmental functions. Also contains a list of representative publications of departments and agencies of the government.

THE PRESIDENT

This section deals with basic documents of the executive, principally the president, and does not include analyses of, and materials about, these offices and agencies, which are provided in chapter 7. The official documents given below consist largely of compilations of, and guidance to, presidential messages and proclamations, executive orders, administrative regulations, reports, press releases and conferences, and, to assist the researcher, some commentary on presidential papers and libraries.

Presidential Inaugural Addresses, Messages, and Papers

Additional, unofficial collections of presidential papers are presented in chapter 23.

INAUGURAL ADDRESSES

INAUGURAL ADDRESSES OF THE PRESIDENTS OF THE UNITED STATES, FROM GEORGE WASHINGTON, 1789, TO RICHARD MILHOUS NIXON, 1973. Washington, D.C.: Government Printing Office, 1974. 283 p.

> An earlier edition published in 1961. Presumably will be updated from time to time. Contains the full texts of all inaugural addresses, without commentary.

STATE OF THE UNION MESSAGES

THE STATE OF THE UNION MESSAGES OF THE PRESIDENTS, 1790-1966.
Edited by Fred L. Israel. 2 vols. New York: Chelsea House, 1966. 3,264 p.

COLLECTED MESSAGES

A COMPILATION OF THE MESSAGES AND PAPERS OF THE PRESIDENTS,
1789-1897. 11 vols. Washington, D.C.: Government Printing Office, 1896-
99.

> Contains the texts of the annual and special messages of the presi-
> dent to Congress, inaugural addresses, executive orders, and presi-
> dential proclamations. Various privately sponsored editions of this
> compilation have been published. A version of this compilation,
> down to 1924, consisting of twenty volumes, is available on
> microfiche from the Brookhaven Press of Washington, D.C.

THE MESSAGES AND PAPERS OF JEFFERSON DAVIS AND THE CONFEDER-
ACY, 1861-1865. 2 vols. New York: Chelsea House, 1966.

> First compiled in 1900 by Congressman James D. Richardson. Con-
> tains the documents of Jefferson Davis and the Confederacy, in-
> cluding diplomatic correspondence.

PRESIDENTIAL MESSAGES AND STATE PAPERS. Compiled by Julius W. Muller. 10 vols. New York: Review of Reviews, 1917.

> Collection of the texts of presidential messages to Congress, pro-
> clamations, executive orders, and similar state papers. Selected,
> not complete.

PRESIDENT MONROE'S MESSAGE. Washington, D.C.: Government Printing
Office, 1974. 128 p.

> Portrays the events, people, and climate of the United States at
> the time of President Monroe's address to Congress on December 2,
> 1823. The story of the Monroe Doctrine's formulation, reception,
> and impact on world events is related through the lives of impor-
> tant statesmen from the United States and abroad.

PUBLIC PAPERS OF THE PRESIDENTS OF THE UNITED STATES. Washington,
D.C.: Government Printing Office, 1957-- .

> Begun with the public papers of President Harry S. Truman, and
> continues to date. Published on a chronological year basis for
> each incumbent president. May be more than a volume per year.
> Contain presidential messages, presidential statements, joint state-
> ments with leaders of foreign governments, speeches, remarks, press
> statements, and the like. Appendixes list White House releases
> from which final selections are made, proclamations and executive

orders (published in the FEDERAL REGISTER and the CODE OF
FEDERAL REGULATIONS, cited in the next subsection of this
chapter), giving their number and subject, and executive reports
required by Congress. The law governing the compilation of
this series authorizes the issuance of volumes also for selected
earlier years; such publication was commenced with four volumes
for the Hoover administration, 1929 to 1932/1933.

WEEKLY COMPILATION OF PRESIDENTIAL DOCUMENTS. Washington, D.C.:
National Archives and Records Service, General Services Administration, 1965-- .

Contains statements, messages, proclamations, executive orders,
and other presidential materials released by the White House as of
the end of each week.

Executive Orders and Administrative Regulations

CODE OF FEDERAL REGULATIONS. Washington, D.C.: Government Printing
Office, 1938-- . Irregular.

Contains the texts of presidential proclamations, executive orders,
administrative regulations and orders, and similar documents of
legal and administrative significance in force at the time of compilation. Materials organized in sections according to the titles
used in the UNITED STATES CODE, listed in a later section,
p. 543. Title 22 is concerned with the general field of foreign
relations.

CODIFICATION OF PRESIDENTIAL PROCLAMATIONS AND EXECUTIVE OR-
DERS. Washington, D.C.: Government Printing Office, 1979. 791 p.

Reference guide to presidential proclamations and executive orders
that have general applicability and continuing effect; covers period
of 20 January 1961-20 January 1977.

FEDERAL REGISTER. Washington, D.C.: Government Printing Office, 1936-- .
Daily except holidays. Annual cumulations. Monthly, quarterly, and annual
indexes.

Contains the texts of presidential proclamations, executive orders,
important administrative regulations, and similar documents. Since
June 1938, the texts of rules, regulations, and orders are arranged
according to the titles used in the UNITED STATES CODE.

LIST AND INDEX OF PRESIDENTIAL EXECUTIVE ORDERS, UNNUMBERED
SERIES. Edited by Clifford L. Lord. Newark, N.J.: New Jersey Historical
Records Survey, 1943. 389 p.

Concerned with unnumbered series of executive orders covering the
period from 1789 to 1940.

PRESIDENTIAL EXECUTIVE ORDERS, NUMBERED 1-8030, 1862-1938. Edited by Clifford L. Lord. 2 vols. New York: Books for Historical Records Survey, 1944. Distributed by Archives Publishing Co.

Volume 1 lists executive orders; index in volume 2.

Occasionally, specialized aspects of executive orders are given separate treatment, illustrated by the following:

U.S. Congress. Senate. Special Committee on National Emergencies and Delegated Emergency Powers. EXECUTIVE ORDERS IN TIMES OF WAR AND NATIONAL EMERGENCY: REPORT OF THE SPECIAL COMMITTEE ON NATIONAL EMERGENCIES AND DELEGATED EMERGENCY POWERS, UNITED STATES SENATE. Committee Print. 93d Cong., 2d sess. Washington, D.C.: Government Printing Office, 1974. 283 p. Bibliog.

Provides analysis, chronological listing of executive orders currently in effect, examples of executive orders issued pursuant to emergency powers statutes, executive decisions in time of emergency, executive directives in time of war or armed hostilities, and the like.

_____, SUMMARY OF EXECUTIVE ORDERS IN TIMES OF WAR AND NATIONAL EMERGENCY: A WORKING PAPER. 93d Cong., 2d sess. Washington, D.C.: Government Printing Office, 1974. 69 p. Bibliog.

Contains descriptive analysis, selected lists of presidential proclamations and executive orders, a brief history of the use of executive orders, and several appendices.

Presidential Reports

The president submits a good many periodic and special reports to the Congress and the nation, which are incorporated in other sections of this compilation. The following are merely illustrative of such materials:

ECONOMIC REPORT OF THE PRESIDENT. Washington, D.C.: Government Printing Office, 1947-- . Annual.

U.S. FOREIGN POLICY FOR THE 1970'S: A REPORT TO THE CONGRESS BY RICHARD NIXON, PRESIDENT OF THE UNITED STATES. 4 vols. Washington, D.C.: Government Printing Office, 1970-73.

Each volumes carries a subtitle. Issued for the years 1970 to 1973. Constitutes a descriptive account of U.S. foreign relations, generally arranged in parts concerned with selected important themes, and usually including an analysis of the machinery and process of policy making.

Press Releases and Conferences

THE JOHNSON PRESIDENTIAL PRESS CONFERENCES. 2 vols. New York: Coleman Enterprises, 1978. 1,089 p.

THE KENNEDY PRESIDENTIAL PRESS CONFERENCES. New York: Coleman Enterprises, 1978. 647 p.

THE NIXON PRESIDENTIAL PRESS CONFERENCES. New York: Coleman Enterprises, 1978. 426 p.

U.S. President. PRESS CONFERENCES. Washington, D.C.: Brookhaven Press, 1971.

> 35 mm. microfilm records of all press conferences of Woodrow Wilson, Calvin Coolidge, Herbert Hoover, Franklin Roosevelt, and Harry Truman, covering the period 1913-52. President Warren G. Harding did not hold any press conferences.

White House. "Press Releases." Washington, D.C.: White House. Irregular.

> No official titles, but generally the heading indicates that each is a release emanating from the White House and gives its date of issue. Provide the texts of presidential statements, addresses, communications, proclamations, and the like, concerning various subjects, including foreign policy and relations. Often contain substantial background information not available in other official and unofficial publications. Practice varies, but several hundred may be issued in a single year.

Commentary: Presidential Papers and Libraries

Berry, J. "No More Presidential Libraries." LIBRARY JOURNAL 99 (1 November 1974): 2787.

> Editorial against proliferation of presidential libraries.

Cole, Garold L. "Presidential Libraries." JOURNAL OF LIBRARIANSHIP 4 (April 1972): 115-29.

Cook, J. Frank. "'Private Papers' of Public Officials." AMERICAN ARCHIVIST 38 (July 1975): 299-324.

Drewry, Elizabeth B. "The Role of Presidential Libraries." MIDWEST QUARTERLY: A JOURNAL OF CONTEMPORARY THOUGHT 7 (October 1965): 53-65.

Horn, David E. "Who Owns Our History?" LIBRARY JOURNAL 100 (1 April 1975): 635-39.

Jones, H.G. "Presidential Libraries: Is There a Case for a National Presidential Library?" AMERICAN ARCHIVIST 38 (July 1975): 325-28.

Kirkendall, Richard S. "Presidential Libraries--One Researcher's Point of View." AMERICAN ARCHIVIST 25 (October 1962): 441-48.

Lewis, Finlay. "Presidential Papers: An Attempt to Own History." NATION, 19 October 1974, pp. 366-69.

Shelley, Fred. "Manuscripts in the Library of Congress: 1800-1900." AMERICAN ARCHIVIST 11 (January 1948): 3-19.

_____. "The Presidential Papers Program of the Library of Congress." AMERICAN ARCHIVIST 25 (October 1962): 429-34.

Vose, Clement E. "Presidential Papers as a Political Science Concern." P.S. 8 (Winter 1975): 8-18.

Weisberger, B.A. "The Paper Trust." AMERICAN HERITAGE 22 (April 1971): 38-41.

Additional information about, and guidance to, centers of presidential papers are provided by the following:

DIRECTORY OF SPECIAL LIBRARIES AND INFORMATION CENTERS. Edited by Margaret Labash Young and Harold Chester Young. 5th ed. 2 vols. Detroit: Gale Research Co., 1979.

> A guide to special libraries, research libraries, information centers, archives, and data centers maintained by government agencies, business, industry, educational institutions, the press, and other agencies. Entries arranged alphabetically. Reference made to the following presidential libraries and collections (given chronologically): Rutherford B. Hayes, Herbert Hoover, Franklin D. Roosevelt, Harry S. Truman, Dwight D. Eisenhower, John F. Kennedy, Lyndon B. Johnson.

Center for the Study of the Presidency--Library. New York, N.Y.

> Founded in 1965, the Center maintains a library of materials and biographical archives on the presidency and functions as a research clearinghouse. It also publishes periodicals and studies on the presidency.

U.S. Library of Congress. Manuscript Division. Washington, D.C.

Contains collections of presidential papers from Washington to Coolidge. Also publishes indexes to the papers of individual presidents, 1960--, which run from a few pages to multiple volumes.

U.S. National Archives. Washington, D.C.

The National Archives and Records Service administers a nation-wide complex that includes the National Archives Building in Washington, D.C., some fifteen federal records centers, and the individual presidential libraries which have been separately established, beginning with President Herbert Hoover. Issues printed general guides to the records of these separate libraries, entitled HISTORICAL MATERIALS IN THE ---------- LIBRARY, each prepared by the director of the particular library, at irregular intervals.

CONGRESS

This section provides guidance primarily to the general documentation of Congress and its chambers, committees, and members. Entries refer largely to official resources and, unless otherwise noted, are publications of Congress. A comprehensive listing of descriptive and analytical materials on Congress and its role in the conduct of foreign relations is given in chapter 8. Additional congressional publications on specific functional topics are included in other sections of this chapter--such as diplomatic and treaty documentation--and in other chapters where they are substantively most relevant.

Congressional Directories and Guides

OFFICIAL CONGRESSIONAL DIRECTORY. Washington, D.C.: Government Printing Office, 1887-- . Annual.

Formerly titled CONGRESSIONAL DIRECTORY (1809-86), contains biographies of members of Congress, a variety of statistical information about Congress, names of legislative officials, with titles and addresses of legislative, executive, and judicial agencies of the national government, the District of Columbia, and foreign diplomatic and consular establishments in the United States. Includes maps of congressional districts and various indexes. Intended as a handy reference volume for members of Congress and other officials.

Additional, unofficial directories and guides, produced by Congressional Quarterly and listed in chapter 8 include:

INSIDE CONGRESS. 2d ed. 1979. 194 p.

See p. 161.

MEMBERS OF CONGRESS SINCE 1789. 1977. 181 p.

See p. 161.

CONGRESSIONAL QUARTERLY'S GUIDE TO CONGRESS. 2d ed. 1976. 1000 p.

See p. 161.

Early Papers

AMERICAN STATE PAPERS: DOCUMENTS, LEGISLATIVE AND EXECUTIVE, OF THE CONGRESS OF THE UNITED STATES. 38 vols. Washington, D.C.: Gales and Seaton, 1832-61.

> Selected and edited under the authority of Congress. Each of the classes has its own set of volume numbers, and the final volume of each class contains an index. Also see citation for class I in subsection on "Basic Historical Collections" of diplomatic correspondence and documents in the section on the Department of State, pp. 552-53.

> Class I.   FOREIGN RELATIONS. 6 vols. 1789-1828.
> Class II.   INDIAN AFFAIRS. 2 vols. 1789-1827.
> Class III.   FINANCE. 5 vols. 1789-1828.
> Class IV.   COMMERCE AND NAVIGATION. 2 vols. 1789-1823.
> Class V.   MILITARY AFFAIRS. 7 vols. 1789-1838.
> Class VI.   NAVAL AFFAIRS. 4 vols. 1794-1836.
> Class VII.   POST OFFICE DEPARTMENT. 1 vol. 1790-1833.
> Class VIII.   PUBLIC LANDS. 8 vols. 1790-1837.
> Class IX.   CLAIMS. 1 vol. 1790-1823.
> Class X.   MISCELLANEOUS. 2 vols. -1789-1823.

STATE PAPERS AND PUBLICK DOCUMENTS OF THE UNITED STATES FROM THE ACCESSION OF GEORGE WASHINGTON TO THE PRESIDENCY, EXHIBITING A COMPLETE VIEW OF OUR FOREIGN RELATIONS SINCE THAT TIME. 2d ed. 10 vols. Boston: Wait and Sons, 1817.

> Covers the period from the time of Washington to 1815. Volume 10 contains confidential papers not published previously. General arrangement is chronological.

House Documents

The following are largely generic categories of documents, published since 1789. Selected specific documents and collections are listed elsewhere, where functionally appropriate.

House Documents. Washington, D.C.: Government Printing Office, 1789-- . Irregular.

Papers ordered to be printed by the House of Representatives that
are not published in HOUSE REPORTS or HOUSE HEARINGS.
Cover a wide variety of subjects, including many reports on various aspects of foreign relations, some of which are cited in specific functional sections of this compilation. Individual reports
identified by Congress, session, and publication number.

House Hearings. Washington, D.C.: Government Printing Office, 1789-- .
Irregular.

Identified by Congress, session, and, when there are multiple
volumes, hearings number. Contain transcripts of testimony given
before committees and subcommittees of the House of Representatives.

"House Journal." JOURNAL OF THE HOUSE OF REPRESENTATIVES OF THE
UNITED STATES. Washington, D.C.: Government Printing Office, 1789-- .
1 vol. per sess. of Congress. Index.

Account of the proceedings of the House of Representatives, including motions, legislative proposals, actions taken, and votes.
Does not include speeches or explanatory matter. Includes compilation of rulings made on points of order.

House Reports. Washington, D.C.: Government Printing Office, 1789-- .
Irregular.

Reports of House committees and subcommittees, dealing with proposed legislation, and containing findings on matters under investigation. At times, include testimony taken, but this is usually
published separately in House Hearings, cited above.

Senate Documents

The following are largely generic categories of documents, published since
1789. Selected specific documents and collections are listed elsewhere, where
functionally appropriate.

"Executive Journal of the Senate." JOURNAL OF THE EXECUTIVE PROCEED-
INGS OF THE SENATE OF THE UNITED STATES. Washington, D.C.: Government Printing Office, 1828-- . Irregular.

Printed some years after the event concerned. Present an account
of the proceedings of the closed executive sessions of the Senate.
Useful for revealing action taken on nominations, treaties, and
similar matters. When executive sessions are open sessions, proceedings and debates appear in the CONGRESSIONAL RECORD,
p. 541.

Senate Documents. Washington, D.C.: Government Printing Office, 1789-- . Irregular.

> For comment concerning nature, see House Documents, p. 537.

Senate Executive Documents. Washington, D.C.: Government Printing Office, 1789-- . Irregular.

> Papers printed by the Senate concerning its executive functions, especially in connection with its approval of nominations and treaties. Confidential and not published until released by order of the Senate.

Senate Executive Reports. Washington, D.C.: Government Printing Office, 1789-- . Irregular.

> Of specific interest, see reports of the Senate Committee on Foreign Relations. Printed on the order of the Senate.

Senate Hearings. Washington, D.C.: Government Printing Office, 1789-- . Irregular.

> For comment concerning nature, see House Hearings, p. 538.

"Senate Journal." JOURNAL OF THE SENATE OF THE UNITED STATES. Washington, D.C.: Government Printing Office, 1789-- . 1 vol. per session of Congress.

> For comment concerning nature, see "House Journal," p. 538.
> Does not include proceedings of the executive sessions of the Senate.

Senate Reports. Washington, D.C.: Government Printing Office, 1789-- . Irregular.

> For comment concerning nature, see House Reports, p. 538.

Additional Congressional Committee Documents

Aside from the general types of documents noted above and individual congressional committee publications cited elsewhere in the functional sections of this compilation, the following types of materials may be useful, especially those emanating from the House Committee on International Relations (formerly the Committee on Foreign Affairs) and the Senate Committee on Foreign Relations.

Committee Prints.

> Generally prepared by the staffs of committees. Usually constitute background briefs and studies prepared for committee use. Available to the public.

Joint Committee Reports, Staff Studies, and Similar Documents.

Similar in nature to the reports and similar documents prepared for and published by House and Senate committees, except that they are prepared for joint congressional committees or jointly by comparable functional committees of the two congressional chambers.

Legislative Calendars.

Contain cumulative records of bills and resolutions under consideration by individual committees, such as the Senate Committee on Foreign Relations. Also contain a chronology of legislative proposals, giving their status in a particular congressional session.

Additional categories of similar documentation produced for and by congressional committees include:

Authorization Reports.

Provides analysis concerning legislation and programs, including for the conduct of foreign relations, appropriations authorizations for the Department of State and such related agencies as the U.S. Information Agency, the Agency for International Development, the Arms Control and Disarmament Agency, and the Peace Corps. May contain section-by-section analysis of legislation and appropriations breakdowns.

Reports on Special Discussions and Conversations.

Concern meetings between individuals or groups of members of Congress and foreign dignitaries. Available to members of Congress.

The following bibliographies and indexes to congressional committee documents may be useful for additional guidance to research resources.

Field, Rochelle, ed. BIBLIOGRAPHY AND INDEXES OF U.S. CONGRESSIONAL COMMITTEE PRINTS: FROM THE SIXTY-FIRST CONGRESS (1911) THROUGH THE NINETY-FIRST CONGRESS, FIRST SESSION (1969), IN THE U.S. SENATE LIBRARY. Compiled by Gary Halverson, Laura J. Kaminsky, Vera Wadell, and Jody Cohen. 2 vols. Westport, Conn.: Greenwood, 1976.

_____. BIBLIOGRAPHY AND INDEXES OF U.S. CONGRESSIONAL COMMITTEE PRINTS: FROM THE SIXTY-FIFTH CONGRESS (1917) THROUGH THE NINETY-FIRST CONGRESS, FIRST SESSION (1969), NOT IN THE U.S. SENATE LIBRARY. Compiled by Laura J. Kaminsky, Gary Halverson, and Mark Woodbridge. Westport, Conn.: Greenwood, 1977. 257 p.

U.S. Congress. INDEX OF CONGRESSIONAL COMMITTEE HEARINGS PRIOR TO JANUARY 3, 1935, IN THE UNITED STATES SENATE LIBRARY. Washington, D.C.: Government Printing Office, 1935. 1,056 p.

> Concerns committee hearings that are not confidential. Arranged by subject, by Senate, by joint committees, and by bill numbers. Includes alphabetical index by functional subject.

Journals and Enactments

The debates of Congress have been published under the following titles. Included in these compilations of the texts of congressional debates are issues of foreign affairs, including Senate confirmation of appointments and approval of treaties.

ANNALS OF THE CONGRESS OF THE UNITED STATES, 1789-1824. 42 vols. Washington, D.C.: Gales and Seaton, 1834-56.

REGISTER OF DEBATES IN CONGRESS, 1824-1837. 14 vols. in 29. Washington, D.C.: Gales and Seaton, 1825-37.

THE CONGRESSIONAL GLOBE, 1833-1873. 46 vols. in 111. Washington, D.C.: John C. Rives, 1834-73.

CONGRESSIONAL RECORD. Washington, D.C.: Government Printing Office, 1873-- . Daily while Congress in session. Biweekly compilation. One corrected compilation/session.

> Contains a record of the debates and the public proceedings of the House of Representatives and the Senate. Legislative history of bills and resolutions, with an index, included in bound session volumes.

The following entries, concerning enactments of Congress, are arranged in accordance with the legislative process, and chronologically thereunder. The last item is unofficial.

DIGEST OF PUBLIC GENERAL BILLS AND RESOLUTIONS. Washington, D.C.: U.S. Library of Congress, 1936-- . Monthly while Congress in session.

> Brief accounts of public bills and resolutions introduced in Congress, giving a digest of their provisions, and indicating the status of bills acted upon and enacted. Does not give complete legislative histories, but deals only with introduction, committee reference, and final action. Arrangement by bill numbers.

PUBLIC LAWS (Slip Laws). Washington, D.C.: Government Printing Office, 18--? to date. Irregular.

The first printed form in which the laws of the United States appear, each law in a separate pamphlet or leaflet. Printed as
soon as possible after their approval by the president. Numbered
serially in the order in which they are approved.

UNITED STATES STATUTES AT LARGE. Washington, D.C.:   Government
Printing Office, 1875-- . Annual.

Published 1848-75 by Little, Brown. Contain the texts of public
laws, reorganization plans, constitutional amendments, private laws,
concurrent resolutions, and proclamations. Include lists of contents
and individual and subject indexes. One or more volumes published for each session of Congress.

Through 1951, volumes were published in parts, a portion of part
2 or part 3 being concerned with treaties and agreements. This
portion provided separate lists of treaties and international agreements and their full texts. Volume 64 (1950-51) was the last in
which the texts of treaties appeared; this volume also included a
cumulative list of all treaties and international agreements contained in the first 64 volumes. Since 1951, the texts of treaties
and international agreements have been published separately on
an annual basis by the Department of State, as noted later in the
section on "Lists of Treaties and Agreements," p. 576.

REVISED STATUTES. 1873. UNITED STATES STATUTES AT LARGE. Vol. 18,
part 1. Washington, D.C.: Government Printing Office, 1875.

A compilation of the permanent laws in force on December 1, 1873.
Enacted as an aggregate on June 22, 1874. Does not include the
texts of treaties and agreements, which are compiled in part 2 of
volume 18. Organized by subject in seventy-four "titles."

SUPPLEMENT TO THE REVISED STATUTES. 2 vols. Washington, D.C.: Government Printing Office, 1891, 1901.

Volume 1 on the period from 1874 to 1891, and volume 2 on
1892-1901. Provide condensed versions of the STATUTES AT
LARGE, chronologically reprinting the texts of general acts of
a permanent nature in order to keep the REVISED STATUTES current.

CODE OF LAWS OF THE UNITED STATES . . . OF A GENERAL AND PER-
MANENT CHARACTER IN FORCE DECEMBER 7, 1925. UNITED STATES STAT-
UTES AT LARGE. Vol. 44, part 1. Washington, D.C.: Government Printing
Office, 1926. 2,452 p.

Compilation of the texts of general and permanent laws in force
at the end of the 68th Congress. A cumulative supplement subsequently provided after each session of Congress. Material organized topically by "titles."

UNITED STATES CODE. Washington, D.C.: Government Printing Office, 1926-- . Irregular.

Provides an organized compilation of general and permanent laws of the United States in force at the time of publication of the up-dated version. Organized topically by "titles," the following of which are of most concern to the conduct of American foreign relations:

Title 8	Aliens and Nationality
Title 10	Armed Forces (formerly Army and Air Force)
Title 14	Coast Guard
Title 15	Commerce and Trade
Title 19	Customs Duties
Title 22	Foreign Relations and Intercourse
Title 34	Navy (now included in Title 10)
Title 48	Territories and Insular Possessions
Title 50	War and National Defense

Contains a short as well as a detailed table of contents, with a detailed index in the final volume. See the following entry.

UNITED STATES CODE ANNOTATED. St. Paul, Minn.: West, 1926-- . Irregular, with supplements.

Provides an organized compilation of general and permanent laws of the United States, together with annotations to decisions of federal and state courts, as well as uncodified laws and treaties. Organized according to the same titles and subdivisions as is the UNITED STATES CODE.

Selected Special Foreign Relations Publications

These sources are arranged as follows: annual compilations of legislation on foreign affairs, an analysis of executive reporting requirements contained in legislation, several compilations of studies and other documentation produced under congressional auspices which are arranged chronologically, and the comprehensive review of foreign and security relations of the Senate "Jackson Subcommittees."

FOREIGN RELATIONS LEGISLATION

LEGISLATION ON FOREIGN RELATIONS--WITH EXPLANATORY NOTES. Washington, D.C.: Government Printing Office, 1957-- . Annual.

Originally titled LEGISLATION ON FOREIGN RELATIONS--WITH EXPLANATORY NOTES and published annually in a single volume; changed to LEGISLATION ON FOREIGN RELATIONS THROUGH 19--, and published in 3 volumes. Volumes 1 and 2 contain legislation and related documents and are revised and republished annually; volume 3, which is revised and republished occasionally, contains treaties and related documents.

Prepared for the Senate Committee on Foreign Relations and the House Committee on International Relations. Compiled by the Department of State, the Library of Congress, and other agencies. Consists largely of the texts of legislation, resolutions, executive orders, and some basic treaties and agreements. Handy reference volume for members of Congress and other officials. Major parts of the volume on foreign assistance, agricultural commodities, the Peace Corps, the Department of State and the Foreign Service, information and educational and cultural exchange programs, the United Nations and other international organizations, financial institutions, war powers and collective security, energy and natural resources, arms control and disarmament, aviation and space, the seas and maritime affairs, tariff and trade, and similar matters. Summary, comprehensive table of contents, and index in each volume.

EXECUTIVE REPORTS TO CONGRESS

REQUIRED REPORTS TO CONGRESS IN THE FOREIGN AFFAIRS FIELD. 93d Cong., 1st sess. Washington, D.C.: Government Printing Office, 1973. 427 p.

Prepared by the Foreign Affairs Division of the Library of Congress for the House Committee on International Relations and the Senate Committee on Foreign Relations. Periodically updated and issued in revised form. Previously entitled REPORTING REQUIREMENTS IN LEGISLATION ON FOREIGN RELATIONS, 1970. 53 p.

By legal stipulation, Congress requires the executive and administrative agencies to file various periodic and special reports, which generally are published either by such agencies or by congressional committees. Congress has established more than one hundred such requirements, spread through more than fifty enactments. Of the regularized reports required, most must be submitted annually-- dealing, by way of illustration, with U.S. participation in the United Nations (cited later in this chapter, p. 589), contributions to international organizations, foreign assistance, cultural and educational exchange, aeronautics and space developments and policy, and the activities of such agencies as the Atomic Energy Commission, Arms Control and Disarmament Agency, Export-Import Bank, International Claims Commission, and the Peace Corps. A substantial number must be filed semiannually, and a few are issued quarterly. The largest number of reports are not required to be prepared at regular intervals or by specific dates; either the timing is discretionary or depends on the development of events which may or may not occur. There is considerable variation in the requirements as to who is to file the report and to whom it is to be addressed. This compilation includes a summary table of citations to provisions of law regarding reporting requirements and a compilation of the relevant textual provisions of law.

Supplemented by the following report.

IMPROVING THE REPORTING REQUIREMENT SYSTEM IN THE FOREIGN AF-
FAIRS FIELD. Washington, D.C.: Government Printing Office, 1974. 104 p.

Analysis of developments during 1973, with commentary on specific
functional areas, including units of the Department of State, foreign assistance and other aspects of foreign economic policy,
military assistance, national security, international organization
and cooperation, information and educational exchange programs,
and other matters. Includes responses on reporting requirements
transmitted by various agencies, including the Department of State,
and a model of a reporting requirement.

OTHER STUDIES AND COMPILATIONS

REVIEW OF THE UNITED NATIONS CHARTER. Washington, D.C.: Government Printing Office.

Consists of three sets of documents, prepared by and for the U.S.
Senate. Committee on Foreign Relations, as follows:

REPORT OF THE COMMITTEE ON FOREIGN RELATIONS. 81st
Cong., 2d sess., Report no. 2501, 1950.

A COLLECTION OF DOCUMENTS. 83d Cong., 2d Sess., 1954
895 p. Bibliog.

HEARINGS (13 Parts), 1954-55.

REPLIES FROM FEDERAL AGENCIES TO QUESTIONNAIRE SUBMITTED BY THE
SPECIAL SUBCOMMITTEE ON GOVERNMENT INFORMATION OF THE COM-
MITTEE ON GOVERNMENT OPERATIONS. Committee Print. 84th Cong.,
1st sess. Washington, D.C.: Government Printing Office, 1955. 552 p.

A compendium of statements on the public availability of documents and information, provided by some sixty government agencies,
including the Department of State, the National Security Council,
the Central Intelligence Agency, the U.S. Information Agency,
and others that are concerned with foreign as well as domestic
affairs.

CONTROL AND REDUCTION OF ARMAMENTS. Final Report of the U.S.
Senate, Committee on Foreign Relations, Subcommittee on Disarmament, Senate
Report no. 2501, 85th Cong., 2d sess. Washington, D.C.: Government Print-
ing Office, 1958. 663 p.

This contains an analysis with appendixes, together with an annex
consisting of previous reports and a second annex containing ten
staff reports.

U.S.-LATIN AMERICAN RELATIONS: COMPILATION OF STUDIES. Washington, D.C.: Government Printing Office, 1960. 828 p.

Seven studies on political developments, economic and commodity problems, Soviet influence in Latin America, the Organization of American States, and similar matters. Contains an index and a statistical appendix.

UNITED STATES FOREIGN POLICY: COMPILATION OF STUDIES. Washington, D.C.: Government Printing Office, 1961. 1473 p.

Consists of an introductory statement, fourteen studies prepared by different unofficial agencies and institutions, and a letter to retired Foreign Service Officers and their commentary. Includes a summary table of contents, individual study tables of contents, and a general index. Study no. 9, titled "The Formulation and Administration of United States Foreign Policy," prepared by the Brookings Institution, is especially pertinent. Other studies on major geographic areas, basic policy aims, operational matters, and ideology.

DOCUMENTS ON INTERNATIONAL ASPECTS OF THE EXPLORATION AND USE OF OUTER SPACE, 1954-1962. Senate Document no. 18, 88th Cong., 1st sess. Washington, D.C.: Government Printing Office, 1963. 407 p.

Contains nearly 200 documents covering a twelve-year period. Staff Report prepared for the U.S. Senate, Committee on Aeronautical and Space Sciences.

SURVEY OF THE ALLIANCE FOR PROGRESS: COMPILATION OF STUDIES AND HEARINGS. Senate Document no. 91-17, 91st Cong., 1st sess. Washington, D.C.: Government Printing Office, 1969. 865 p.

Consists of series of reports, staff studies, and hearings, dealing with economic, financial, political, and military issues.

INTERNATIONAL COOPERATION IN OUTER SPACE: A SYMPOSIUM. Senate Document no. 92-57, 92d Cong., 1st Sess. Washington, D.C.: Government Printing Office, 1971. 732 p.

Comprises some 40 papers, studies, and reports, organized in five parts dealing with the United States' and international space cooperation, the United Nations and outer space, intergovernmental international organizations concerned with space matters, the international scientific community and professional associations dealing with outer space, and U.S. foreign relations and the future of international space cooperation. Also includes six appendixes providing the texts of selected treaties and agreements. Prepared for the U.S. Senate, Committee on Aeronautical and Space Sciences.

INTER-AMERICAN RELATIONS: A COLLECTION OF DOCUMENTS, LEGISLATION, DESCRIPTIONS OF INTER-AMERICAN ORGANIZATIONS, AND OTHER MATERIAL PERTAINING TO INTER-AMERICAN AFFAIRS. Prepared by United States, Senate, Committee on Foreign Affairs, 92d Cong., 2d Sess. Washington, D.C.: Government Printing Office, 1972. 648 p.

Contains collection of reference materials dealing with inter-American affairs, including descriptive analysis, legislation, treaties, international organization resolutions, and similar materials, together with a list of treaties and other international agreements between the United States and Latin American countries.

FOREIGN POLICY CHOICES FOR THE 70S AND 80S. 94th Cong., 1st and 2d sess. 2 vols. Washington, D.C.: Government Printing Office, 1976. 730 p.

This is a survey, involving thirteen hearings conducted by the Senate Committee on Foreign Relations, in connection with the bicentennial, to probe the long-range foreign policy goals of the United States. Separate sessions and sections deal with popular perceptions of foreign policy, global resources, national goals and values, foreign policy values and goals, future United States foreign policy role, public opinion, the world environment, and worldwide survey of public attitudes.

JACKSON SUBCOMMITTEE REPORTS

The "Jackson Subcommittees" of the Senate Committee on Government Operations produced a comprehensive volume of materials during the period from 1959 to the early 1970s. These subcommittees, chaired by Senator Henry M. Jackson, launched, in 1959, as the Subcommittee on National Policy Machinery, were superseded by the Subcommittee on National Security Staffing and Operations in 1962, and the Subcommittee on National Security and International Operations in 1965. These alterations in title were reflected in changes in focus and resultant publications. The documentation produced by the subcommittees embraces a broad spectrum of materials, including hearings, staff studies, bibliographies, anthologies of essays and documents, statements, reports, and conclusions and recommendations. The materials produced in the first two stages were published individually and collectively, whereas those of the third stage were published only in individual form.

The emphasis or focus of the subcommittees progressed as follows: national security machinery and policy, 1959-62; the secretary and Department of State, diplomats and overseas missions, and relations between Washington and the field, as well as continuing interest in national security policy and machinery, 1963-64; and the Atlantic Alliance, planning-programming-budgeting (PPB), the National Security Council, and international negotiation, 1965-72.

A number of the publications produced by the subcommittees have been cited in other sections of this compilation, where they are functionally most relevant. The following merely lists the aggregate collections of the subcommittee's publications:

ORGANIZING FOR NATIONAL SECURITY. 3 vols. Washington, D.C.: Government Printing Office, 1961.

Volume 1 on hearings (1,338 p.), volume 2 on a collection of
studies and background materials (484 p.), and volume 3 on staff
reports and recommendations (100 p.).

ADMINISTRATION OF NATIONAL SECURITY. 88th Cong., 1st and 2d sess.
Washington, D.C.: Government Printing Office, 1963-64. 600 p.

Consists of staff reports and hearings. Additional separate publications constitute a bibliography, a compilation of selected papers,
and an analysis of the American ambassador and the problem of
coordination of functions abroad.

Some of the materials produced by the Jackson subcommittees were also published unofficially, including the following:

Jackson, Henry M., ed. THE ATLANTIC ALLIANCE. New York: Praeger,
1967. 309 p.

_____. THE NATIONAL SECURITY COUNCIL. New York: Praeger, 1965.
311 p.

_____. THE SECRETARY OF STATE AND THE AMBASSADOR. New York:
Praeger, 1964. 203 p.

Unofficial Publications

The following unofficial publications are useful guides to the current activities
of Congress:

CONGRESSIONAL INDEX. Chicago, New York, and Washington: Commerce
Clearing House, 1953-- . 1 vol. per sess. of Congress.

A loose-leaf compilation concerning legislation pending in Congress.
Lists and indexes all public bills. Reports on progress from the
introduction of legislation to final disposition. Sections identified
by marginal tabs. Separate sections concerned with a Senate
status table, a House status table, an index to enactments, voting
records of members, and the like. Separate section on treaties.

CONGRESSIONAL QUARTERLY WEEKLY REPORT. Washington, D.C.: Congressional Quarterly, 1950-- . Weekly.

Provides a handy, unofficial account of contemporary developments
in Congress. First published 4 times a year as the CONGRESSION-
AL QUARTERLY, 1945-47. Changed to a weekly in 1948, under
the title CONGRESSIONAL QUARTERLY LOG FOR EDITORS.
Changed to its present title in 1950.

CONGRESSIONAL ROLL CALL. Washington, D.C.: Congressional Quarterly. 1969-- . Annual.

Provides a chronology and analysis of all roll-call votes taken in the House of Representatives and the Senate for the year. Gives a complete record of how every member of Congress voted on every issue.

REVIEW: (#) SESSION OF THE CONGRESS AND INDEX OF AEI PUBLICATIONS. Washington, D.C.: American Enterprise Institute, 1970-- . Annual.

Summary of congressional activity, containing an overview which summarizes major legislation enacted and significant action not completed, vetoes, a digest of major laws (including those concerned with foreign affairs), a summary of action on the budget, and a number of appendixes, including a history of bills enacted into public law and a table of bills and corresponding public law numbers.

DEPARTMENT OF STATE

The following is a selected list of publications of the Department of State, arranged according to various categories. Other materials are provided in chapter 9 and in other sections and chapters of this compilation, where they are topically and functionally most pertinent.

For a description of the unpublished records of the Department of State, beginning in 1789, see PRELIMINARY INVENTORY OF THE GENERAL RECORDS OF THE DEPARTMENT OF STATE (RECORD GROUP 59), published by the National Archives in 1963. A complementary listing and finding aid covering the records of diplomatic and consular posts abroad is provided in Special List no. 9, LIST OF FOREIGN SERVICE POST RECORDS IN THE NATIONAL ARCHIVES (RECORDS GROUP 84), published by the National Archives in 1958. Other National Archives lists and inventories for the study of the conduct of American foreign affairs include:

LIST OF DOCUMENTS RELATING TO SPECIAL AGENTS OF THE DEPARTMENT OF STATE, 1789-1906. Compiled by Natalia Summers. Special List, no. 7. Washington, D.C.: Government Printing Office, 1951. 229 p.

LIST OF NATIONAL ARCHIVES MICROFILM PUBLICATIONS. Washington, D.C.: Government Printing Office, 1968. 108 p.

Especially the section on the Department of State, pp. 8-33.

RECORDS OF UNITED STATES PARTICIPATION IN INTERNATIONAL CONFERENCES, COMMISSIONS, AND EXPOSITIONS. Compiled by H. Stephen Helton. Preliminary Inventory, no. 76. Washington, D.C.: Government Printing Office, 1955. 161 p. Supplement, compiled by Marion M. Johnson and Mabel D. Brock, 1965. 22 p.

Official Publications and Resources

RECORDS RELATING TO INTERNATIONAL BOUNDARIES. Compiled by Daniel T. Goggin. Preliminary Inventory, no. 170. Washington, D.C.: Government Printing Office, 1968. 98 p.

A broad, descriptive listing of government resources accessible for investigation and research may be found in:

FOREIGN AFFAIRS RESEARCH: A DIRECTORY OF GOVERNMENTAL RE-SOURCES. Washington, D.C.: Office of External Research, U.S. Department of State, 1967. 83 p.

    Supersedes GOVERNMENT RESOURCES AVAILABLE FOR FOREIGN AFFAIRS RESEARCH, published in 1963 and revised in 1965.

General commentary on the availability of diplomatic archives throughout the world is provided in the following:

PUBLIC AVAILABILITY OF DIPLOMATIC ARCHIVES. Rev. ed. Washington, D.C.: Office of the Historian, U.S. Department of State, 1976. 18 p.

    An earlier version, bearing the same title, published in 1968. Foreign government diplomatic archive availability is summarized in the preceding chapter, p. 518.

Spaulding, E. Wilder. "The Publication of Diplomatic Papers of Other Governments." AMERICAN JOURNAL OF INTERNATIONAL LAW 41 (April 1947): 365-77.

New publications of the Department of State are listed in the weekly issues of the DEPARTMENT OF STATE BULLETIN, and an annual listing of available publications is provided in:

FOREIGN RELATIONS OF THE UNITED STATES--PRICE LIST 65. Washington, D.C.: Government Printing Office, Annual. Cumulative.

    Contains descriptions and prices of publications on international affairs issued by the Department of State, other related agencies, and Congress.

Unless otherwise noted, all entries in this section were produced by the Department of State.

Guides to Publications

MAJOR PUBLICATIONS OF THE DEPARTMENT OF STATE: AN ANNOTATED BIBLIOGRAPHY. Washington, D.C.: Government Printing Office, 1965-- . Irregular.

A pocket guide to current and selected earlier publications of the Department of State, arranged in various categories. Annotated and indicates whether specific publications are out of print.

A POCKET GUIDE TO FOREIGN POLICY INFORMATION MATERIALS AND SERVICES OF THE U.S. DEPARTMENT OF STATE. Washington, D.C.: Government Printing Office, 1968-- .

A pocket guide to current publications and services, including such matters as films, filmstrips, television news features, and the like, with annotations.

PUBLICATIONS OF THE DEPARTMENT OF STATE. 3 vols. Washington, D.C.: Government Printing Office, 1929-53, 1953-57, 1958-60. 207 p., 230 p., 116 p.

Covers the respective periods 1929-53, 1953-57, and 1958-60. A general catalog of publications, giving the title, Department of State publication number, series number, date of publication, number of pages, and price. Generally consists of several parts, including an alphabetical subject listing, a list of periodicals of the Department of State, and an index by series of publications. Subsequently, new publications listed in the weekly DEPARTMENT OF STATE BULLETIN.

PUBLICATIONS OF THE DEPARTMENT OF STATE. Washington, D.C.: Government Printing Office, 1938. 19 p.

Address by Cyril Wynne, Chief, Division of Research and Publications of the Department of State.

SELECTED PUBLICATIONS: DEPARTMENT OF STATE. Washington, D.C.: Government Printing Office, 1950?-- . Bimonthly.

A short listing of current Department of State publications, usually consisting of a single sheet printed on both sides.

SELECTED UNITED STATES GOVERNMENT PUBLICATIONS. Washington, D.C.: Government Printing Office, 1946-- . Bimonthly.

Contains descriptions of newly issued government publications on foreign relations as well as other subjects.

Chronologies

EVENTS IN UNITED STATES-CUBAN RELATIONS: A CHRONOLOGY, 1957-1963. Committee Print. 88th Cong., 1st sess. Washington, D.C.: Government Printing Office, 1963. 28 p.

Prepared by the Department of State for the Committee on Foreign Relations, United States Senate.

LANDMARKS IN FOREIGN AFFAIRS, 1945-1948: A CHRONOLOGY. Washington, D.C.: Government Printing Office, 1949. 28 p.

> A systematized listing of important events in the foreign relations of the United States, with dates.

LANDMARKS IN FOREIGN AFFAIRS, 1949-1950: A CHRONOLOGY. Washington, D.C.: Government Printing Office, 1952. 111 p.

> Similar to preceding entry.

A SELECT CHRONOLOGY AND BACKGROUND DOCUMENTS RELATING TO THE MIDDLE EAST. 94th Cong., 1st sess. Washington, D.C.: Government Printing Office, 1975. 313 p.

> Prepared for Committee on Foreign Relations, United States Senate. Earlier versions published, commencing in 1967, contain more detailed coverage of the earlier period.

Diplomatic Correspondence, Documents, and Papers

This section is concerned with basic and selected comprehensive compilations of diplomatic correspondence and papers, indexes to them, and commentaries respecting them. Unless otherwise noted, they are Department of State publications. Various ad hoc listings, compilations, and commentaries are provided in the subsection on "Other Selected Publications" and the separate subsections on "Geographic Area Materials" and listings of publications on specific functional topics, provided later in this chapter.

BASIC HISTORICAL COLLECTIONS

The first five entries are in chronological order; the rest are given alphabetically.

THE REVOLUTIONARY DIPLOMATIC CORRESPONDENCE OF THE UNITED STATES. Edited by Francis Wharton. 6 vols. Washington, D.C.: Government Printing Office, 1889.

THE DIPLOMATIC CORRESPONDENCE OF THE UNITED STATES OF AMERICA, FROM THE SIGNING OF THE DEFINITIVE TREATY OF PEACE, 10TH SEPTEMBER, 1783, TO THE ADOPTION OF THE CONSTITUTION, MARCH 4, 1789. 7 vols. Washington, D.C.: F.P. Blair under government contract, 1833-34. 3d ed. 3 vols. Published by J.C. Rives, 1855.

U.S. Congress. FOREIGN RELATIONS. In AMERICAN STATE PAPERS: DOCUMENTS, LEGISLATIVE AND EXECUTIVE, OF THE CONGRESS OF THE UNITED STATES, class I. 6 vols. Washington, D.C.: Gales and Seaton, 1832-61.

Covers 1789–1828. Documents included selected under the authority of Congress. Materials arranged chronologically and include
the texts of treaties, messages, diplomatic notes and other communications, and the like. Index and list of documents in each
volume.

_____. STATE PAPERS AND PUBLICK DOCUMENTS OF THE UNITED STATES
FROM THE ACCESSION OF GEORGE WASHINGTON TO THE PRESIDENCY,
EXHIBITING A COMPLETE VIEW OF OUR FOREIGN RELATIONS SINCE THAT
TIME. 2d ed. 10 vols. Boston: Wait and Sons, 1817.

This compilation covers the period from the time of Washington to
1815. Volume 10 contains confidential state papers not published
previously. General arrangement is chronological.

FOREIGN RELATIONS OF THE UNITED STATES. Washington, D.C.: Government Printing Office, 1862-- . Irregular.

Originally titled PAPERS RELATING TO FOREIGN AFFAIRS, which
was changed to PAPERS RELATING TO THE FOREIGN RELATIONS
OF THE UNITED STATES in 1870, to FOREIGN RELATIONS OF
THE UNITED STATES: DIPLOMATIC PAPERS in 1932, and to its
current abbreviated title following World War II. Initially, one
volume published for each year; since 1932, there have been five
or more volumes per year; no volume published for the year 1869.
At present, some 270 volumes in the series.

Contains the texts of diplomatic communications, exchanges of
notes, reports, and other official papers relating to the foreign
relations and diplomacy of the United States. Occasionally includes texts of treaties and agreements. Materials arranged by
country, grouped by geographic areas; selected functional fields
arranged separately in recent years, including national security
affairs, foreign economic policy, and the United Nations. Generally, each volume indexed separately.

Occasionally special appendices, supplements, and series published
as part of the overall series, dealing with a particular country,
territory, event, or negotiation, as follows:

1894. Appendix 2, AFFAIRS IN HAWAII. 1895.
1902. Appendix 1, WHALING AND SEALING CLAIMS
AGAINST RUSSIA. 1903.
1914. Supplement, THE WORLD WAR. 1928.
1915. Supplement, THE WORLD WAR. 1928.
1916. Supplement, THE WORLD WAR. 1929.
1917. Supplement 1, THE WORLD WAR. 1931.
1917. Supplement 2, THE WORLD WAR. 2 vols. 1932.
1918. Supplement 1, THE WORLD WAR. 2 vols. 1933.
1918. Supplement 2, THE WORLD WAR. 1933.
1918. RUSSIA. 3 vols. 1931–32.
1919. Russia. 1937.
THE LANSING PAPERS, 1914-1920. 2 vols. 1939.

PARIS PEACE CONFERENCE, 1919. 13 vols. 1942-47.
JAPAN, 1931-1941. 2 vols. 1943.
THE SOVIET UNION, 1933-1939. 1952.

Special volumes of documentation relating to World War II summit
conferences separately published, as follows (given chronologically
according to the dates of the conferences);

CONFERENCES AT WASHINGTON, 1941-1942, AND CASA-
BLANCA 1943. 1968.
CONFERENCES AT WASHINGTON AND QUEBEC 1943. 1970.
CONFERENCES AT CAIRO AND TEHRAN 1943. 1961.
THE CONFERENCE AT QUEBEC 1944. 1972.
THE CONFERENCES AT MALTA AND YALTA 1945. 1955.
CONFERENCE OF BERLIN (POTSDAM) 1945. 2 vols. 1960.

A COMPILATION OF THE MESSAGES AND PAPERS OF THE CONFEDERACY,
INCLUDING THE DIPLOMATIC CORRESPONDENCE, 1861-1865. Edited by
James D. Richardson. 2 vols. Nashville: United States Publishing Co., 1905.

Volume 1 on congressional messages and papers and biographical
sketches of certain leaders; volume 2 on diplomatic communications,
arranged chronologically, as well as index and additional biographical sketches.

DIPLOMATIC CORRESPONDENCE OF THE UNITED STATES: CANADIAN RE-
LATIONS, 1784-1860. 4 vols. Edited by William R. Manning. Washington,
D.C.: Carnegie Endowment for International Peace, 1940-43.

Provides diplomatic correspondence and contains some photocopies
of maps and of certain original papers.

DIPLOMATIC CORRESPONDENCE OF THE UNITED STATES: INTER-AMERICAN
AFFAIRS, 1831-1860. Edited by William R. Manning. 12 vols. Washington,
D.C.: Carnegie Endowment for International Peace, 1932-39.

Volumes on Argentina; Bolivia and Brazil; Central America, 1831-
50; Central America, 1851-60; Chile and Colombia; Dominican
Republic, Ecuador, and France; Great Britain; Mexico, 1831-48;
Mexico, 1848-60; Netherlands, Paraguay, and Peru; Spain; and
Texas and Venezuela.

DIPLOMATIC CORRESPONDENCE OF THE UNITED STATES CONCERNING THE
INDEPENDENCE OF LATIN-AMERICAN NATIONS. Edited by William R.
Manning. 3 vols. Washington, D.C.: Carnegie Endowment for International
Peace, 1925.

Covers the period from 1810 to 1830. Arranged by country. Some
documents excerpted.

Official Publications and Resources

INDEXES TO HISTORICAL COLLECTIONS

This section is chronologically arranged. A current, updated general index is in preparation by the Department of State.

INDEX TO UNITED STATES DOCUMENTS RELATING TO FOREIGN AFFAIRS, 1828-1861. Edited by Adelaide R. Hasse. 3 vols. Washington, D.C.: Carnegie Institution of Washington, 1914-21.

An index to published records, documents, papers, correspondence, legislation, and judicial decisions on international and diplomatic questions. Arranged by names of individuals and subjects.

GENERAL INDEX TO THE PUBLISHED VOLUMES OF THE DIPLOMATIC CORRESPONDENCE AND FOREIGN RELATIONS OF THE UNITED STATES, 1861-1899. Washington, D.C.: Government Printing Office, 1902. 945 p.

PAPERS RELATING TO THE FOREIGN RELATIONS OF THE UNITED STATES: GENERAL INDEX, 1900-1918. Washington, D.C.: Government Printing Office, 1941. 507 p.

CURRENT DOCUMENTATION

The following are presented in chronological order, based on the time period covered:

PEACE AND WAR: UNITED STATES FOREIGN POLICY, 1931-1941. Washington, D.C.: Government Printing Office, 1943. 874 p.

A shorter version, minus the texts of documents, published in 1942. Contains a descriptive statement of U.S. relations with the Axis powers to the time of the attack at Pearl Harbor, pages 1-151, with the remainder of the volume consisting of the texts of relevant documents. Includes such topics as: Japanese conquest of Manchuria, 1931-32; disarmament discussion, 1932-34; the Italian conquest of Ethiopia, 1935-36; the Japanese attack on China, 1937; the European crisis, 1938; the European war, 1939-41; relations with Japan, 1938-41; and the Pearl Harbor attack.

A DECADE OF AMERICAN FOREIGN POLICY: BASIC DOCUMENTS, 1941-49. Prepared by the Department of State. Senate Document, no. 123. 81st Cong., 1st sess. Washington, D.C.: Government Printing Office, 1950. 1381 p.

A compilation of 313 documents, including policy statements, addresses, treaties and agreements, statutes, constitutive acts of international organizations, communiques, and the like. Grouped chronologically within parts dealing with such subjects as wartime documents looking toward peace, conferences on the peace settlement, United Nations: basic organization, United Nations: spe-

cialized agencies, the inter-American system, defeated and occupied areas, other areas of special interest to the United States,
and current international issues. Includes table of contents and
summary index.

Wilcox, Francis O., and Kalijarvi, Thorsten V. RECENT AMERICAN FOR-
EIGN POLICY: BASIC DOCUMENTS, 1941-1951. New York: Appleton-
Century-Crofts, 1952. 927 p.

Largely a reprinting of the preceding item, with some updating.

IN QUEST OF PEACE AND SECURITY: SELECTED DOCUMENTS ON AMERI-
CAN FOREIGN POLICY, 1941-1951. Washington, D.C.: Government Printing Office, 1951. 120 p.

A handy collection of more than fifty basic documents, grouped as
World War II documents, documents relating to defeated and occupied areas (Germany and her allies, Japan, Austria, and Korea),
and documents relating to security against aggression.

AMERICAN FOREIGN POLICY, 1950-1955: BASIC DOCUMENTS. 2 vols.
Washington, D.C.: Government Printing Office, 1957.

Provides approximately 3,250 pages of documentation. Continues
the practice begun in A DECADE OF AMERICAN FOREIGN POLI-
CY, cited above, but is more comprehensive in its inclusion. Published shortly after the years to which it pertains, served as an
interim compilation prior to the publication of the volumes of the
FOREIGN RELATIONS series. Commenced a series identified in
the following entry. Includes a comprehensive index at the end
of the second volume.

AMERICAN FOREIGN POLICY: CURRENT DOCUMENTS, 1956-1967. 12 vols.
Washington, D.C.: Government Printing Office, 1959-69.

A series of annual compilations of documentation, continuing the
two-volume anthology cited in the preceding entry. Intended to
provide ready access to basic documentation at an early date.
Materials arranged in fourteen parts: overall policy, United Nations
and international law, seven sections on particular regions and
countries, disarmament and atomic energy, trade, foreign assistance,
educational and cultural exchange, and the Department of State.
Separate index in each annual volume.

COMMENTARY ON FOREIGN RELATIONS DOCUMENTATION

Cole, Wayne S. "Access to Government Documents: Current Developments,
United States and British Diplomatic Records." Paper presented at Annual
Meeting of the American Historical Association, December 1972, in New
Orleans. 14 p.

Franklin, William M. THE AVAILABILITY OF DEPARTMENT OF STATE REC-
ORDS. Washington, D.C.: Government Printing Office, 1973. 8 p. Reprinted from the DEPARTMENT OF STATE BULLETIN 68 (29 January 1973):
101-7.

_____. "The Future of the FOREIGN RELATIONS Series." In THE NA-
TIONAL ARCHIVES AND FOREIGN RELATIONS RESEARCH, edited by Milton
O[dell]. Gustafson, pp. 61-68. Athens: Ohio University Press, 1974.

Gustafson, Milton O[dell]. "State Department Records in the National Archives: A Profile." PROLOGUE 2 (Winter 1970): 175-80.

_____, ed. THE NATIONAL ARCHIVES AND FOREIGN RELATIONS RE-
SEARCH. Athens: Ohio University Press, 1974. 292 p.

Symposium of sixteen invitational papers on various aspects of the
subject, including general aspects of foreign relations documents,
domestic influences on foreign policy, diplomacy of war and peace,
and the major geographic areas.

Laise, Carol C. "Department Discusses Recent Steps to Improve Its Declassification Program." DEPARTMENT OF STATE BULLETIN 70 (17 June 1974):
663-69.

_____. "Department Gives Views on Proposed Amendments to Freedom of In-
formation Act." DEPARTMENT OF STATE BULLETIN 71 (26 August 1974):
313-20.

Leopold, Richard W. "The FOREIGN RELATIONS Series: A Centennial Esti-
mate." MISSISSIPPI VALLEY HISTORICAL REVIEW 49 (March 1963): 595-
612.

_____. "The FOREIGN RELATIONS Series Revisited: One Hundred Plus Ten."
JOURNAL OF AMERICAN HISTORY 59 (March 1973): 935-57.

McLaughlin, Andrew C. REPORT ON THE DIPLOMATIC ARCHIVES OF THE
DEPARTMENT OF STATE, 1789-1840. 2d ed. Washington, D.C.: Carnegie
Institution, 1906. 73 p.

Perkins, E.R. "FOREIGN RELATIONS OF THE UNITED STATES: Ninety-one
Years of American Foreign Policy." DEPARTMENT OF STATE BULLETIN 27
(22 December 1952): 1002-7.

Plischke, Elmer. "Research on the Administrative History of the Department of
State." In THE NATIONAL ARCHIVES AND FOREIGN RELATIONS RESEARCH,
edited by Milton O[dell]. Gustafson, pp. 73-102. Athens: Ohio University
Press, 1974.

_____. "Research on the Conduct of United States Foreign Relations." IN-
TERNATIONAL STUDIES QUARTERLY 15 (June 1971): 221-50.

Trask, David F., and Slany, William Z. "What Lies Ahead for the FOREIGN
RELATIONS Series?" THE SOCIETY FOR HISTORIANS OF AMERICAN FOR-
EIGN RELATIONS NEWSLETTER 9 (March 1978): 26-29.

Wilson, Robert R. "A Hundred Years of FOREIGN RELATIONS." AMERICAN
JOURNAL OF INTERNATIONAL LAW 55 (October 1961): 947-50.

Annual reports and commentary on the FOREIGN RELATIONS series, the Historical Office of the Department of State, and the Secretary of State's Advisory Committee on FOREIGN RELATIONS are generally published annually
in the AMERICAN HISTORICAL REVIEW, the AMERICAN JOURNAL OF INTER-
NATIONAL LAW, and the AMERICAN POLITICAL SCIENCE REVIEW (or PS).

International Law Compilations

The first six items are basic compilations, chronologically arranged, with the
sixth being an annual supplement to the first five. The last two items are
special compilations concerned with special topics. These are Department of
State publications.

Cadwalader, John L., ed. A DIGEST OF THE PUBLISHED OPINIONS OF
THE ATTORNEYS-GENERAL, AND OF THE LEADING DECISIONS OF THE
FEDERAL COURTS, WITH REFERENCE TO INTERNATIONAL LAW, TREATIES,
AND KINDRED SUBJECTS. Washington, D.C.: Government Printing Office,
1877. 290 p.

>	Topics arranged alphabetically.

Wharton, Francis, ed. DIGEST OF THE INTERNATIONAL LAW OF THE UNI-
TED STATES. 1886. Rev. ed. 3 vols. Washington, D.C.: Government
Printing Office, 1887.

>	In general, organization and content similar to Hackworth's com-
>	pilation, described below.

Moore, John Bassett, ed. A DIGEST OF INTERNATIONAL LAW. 8 vols.
Washington, D.C.: Government Printing Office, 1906.

>	Content and organization similar to Hackworth's compilation, de-
>	scribed below. This was a cumulative compilation, superseding
>	Wharton's DIGEST, cited above. General index in volume 8.

Hackworth, Green H., ed. DIGEST OF INTERNATIONAL LAW. 8 vols.
Washington, D.C.: Government Printing Office, 1940-44.

Extracts from diplomatic communications, departmental instructions
and rulings, treaties and agreements, a variety of archival materials, and editor's notes and comments. Concerned with diplomacy,
treaties, recognition, acquisition and loss of territory, national
jurisdiction, nationality, the high seas and territorial waters,
aliens, extradition, intervention, claims, modes of redress, war,
neutrality, and similar subjects. General index in volume 8.

Whiteman, Marjorie M., ed. DIGEST OF INTERNATIONAL LAW. 15 vols.
Washington, D.C.: Government Printing Office, 1963-73.

Continues where Hackworth's DIGEST, cited above, ends. Similar
coverage and organization, but more comprehensive than the earlier DIGESTS. General index in volume 15.

DIGEST OF UNITED STATES PRACTICE IN INTERNATIONAL LAW. Compiled
by the Office of the Legal Adviser of the Department of State. Washington,
D.C.: Government Printing Office, 1973-- . Annual.

This annual series, updating the earlier DIGESTS, consists of materials selected on the basis of importance in the development of
international law, its role in confirming international legal pre-
cedent, or for purposes of noting the record of significant areas of
international law.

Moore, John Bassett, ed. HISTORY AND DIGEST OF INTERNATIONAL ARBI-
TRATIONS TO WHICH THE UNITED STATES HAS BEEN A PARTY. 6 vols.
Washington, D.C.: Government Printing Office, 1898.

Certain of these volumes designated as congressional documents.
Covers the period from 1783 to the 1890s. In addition to the
texts of documents involved in the arbitrations, some volumes contain additional pertinent information. A detailed table of contents
for the series, a table of cases reported arranged alphabetically,
a table of cases cited, and a list of authorities in volume 1. The
texts of treaties relating to such arbitrations, arranged alphabetically, and a subject index for the first five volumes in volume 5.
Volume 6 on maps concerning the arbitrations included in the
series.

Whiteman, Marjorie M., ed. DAMAGES IN INTERNATIONAL LAW. 3 vols.
Washington, D.C.: Government Printing Office, 1937-43.

Volume 1 on the bases of damages including arrest, detention,
imprisonment, and expulsion, personal injury, and death cases.
Volume 2 on property, personal and real. Volume 3 on contracts
and concessions, indirect and other damages, rates of exchange,
and payment and distribution. Also provides an index of cases by
title referred to in the volumes, together with a general subject
index.

Diplomatic and Consular Missions and Officials

Unless otherwise noted, these are Department of State publications

THE BIOGRAPHIC REGISTER. Washington, D.C.: Government Printing Office, 1833-- . Irregular.

Originally titled REGISTER OF THE DEPARTMENT OF STATE, later changed to BIOGRAPHIC REGISTER OF THE DEPARTMENT OF STATE, and in the 1960s to its current title. In some years annual issues merely supplemented to bring the previous issue up to date. Provides an alphabetical compilation of the biographies of officials of the Department of State, the Foreign Service, and certain other agencies, such as the Agency for International Development, the Peace Corps, the U.S. Arms Control and Disarmament Agency, and the U.S. Information Agency. Occasionally contains additional pertinent information, including abbreviation symbols utilized by the Department of State, departmental and Foreign Service personnel classifications, honor awards recipients, chronological lists of presidents and secretaries of state, lists of the diplomatic agents of the United States, and the like. The 1874 edition, part 2, also presents an historical succession of American diplomatic incumbents in each country and of diplomatic representatives or agents to or from the United States during the century 1774 to 1874. The 1937 edition contains similar special information, including, in chapter 17, a complete list of U.S. diplomatic agents from revolutionary times to 1937. After 1974, issued only as classified editions with limited distribution.

DIPLOMATIC LIST. Washington, D.C.: Government Printing Office, 1893-- . Irregular. Quarterly.

Initially published under the title FOREIGN LEGATIONS IN THE UNITED STATES 1887-93. Constitutes a list of foreign diplomatic representatives in Washington, with their addresses. Arrangement alphabetical according to name of country, with individual names arranged on the basis of personal rank, also provides an order of precedence and a list of national holidays.

EMPLOYEES OF DIPLOMATIC MISSIONS. Washington, D.C.: Government Printing Office, 1948-- . Monthly, -- . Quarterly, -- .

From 1948 to 1952, titled LIST OF EMPLOYEES IN THE EMBASSIES AND LEGATIONS IN WASHINGTON NOT PRINTED IN THE DIPLOMATIC LIST, which was later changed to LIST OF EMPLOYEES OF DIPLOMATIC MISSIONS, and than to its current title. Gives the names and addresses of employees of foreign diplomatic representatives in Washington. Arranged alphabetically by country and alphabetically by name of individual thereunder.

FOREIGN CONSULAR OFFICES IN THE UNITED STATES. Washington, D.C.:
Government Printing Office, 1932-- . Irregular, 1932-40. Annual, 1941-- .

Contains a complete and official listing of foreign consular offices
in the United States, together with their jurisdictions and personnel. Arranged alphabetically by country, giving the location of
the consular establishment, the name and rank of consular officials,
their jurisdiction, and the date of recognition of the consular officials.

FOREIGN SERVICE LIST. Washington, D.C.: Government Printing Office,
1828-1975. Irregular. 3 per year, 1961-62; 4 per year, 1964; 3 per year,
1965-75.

Originally published as LIST OF MINISTERS, CONSULS, AND
OTHER DIPLOMATIC AGENTS OF THE UNITED STATES IN FOR-
EIGN COUNTRIES. After various changes in title, published
under its recent title from 1931-75. Contains a list of American
embassies, legations, and consulates abroad, arranged by country,
providing the names of American officers, their rank, salary, and
assignment. Includes members of the Foreign Service and such
other agencies as the Agency for International Development, the
Peace Corps, and the U.S. Information Agency. When published
quarterly, 1890-1953, the January Issue contained a description
of consular districts and presented a tariff of Foreign Service fees.
Also contained an alphabetical index of the names of all persons
included.

KEY OFFICERS OF FOREIGN SERVICE POSTS: GUIDE FOR BUSINESS REPRE
SENTATIVES. Washington, D.C.: Government Printing Office, 1962-- .
3 per yr.

Lists key U.S. officers at Foreign Service posts, including embassies, legations, and consular establishments. Supersedes the FOR-
EIGN SERVICE LIST, cited above.

PHOTOGRAPHIC REGISTER: THE AMERICAN FOREIGN SERVICE. Washington, D.C.: American Foreign Service Association, 1936. 172 p.

Supplement to the FOREIGN SERVICE JOURNAL 13 (November
1936). An unofficial publication depicting pictorially the officers
of the Foreign Service. Also provides a comprehensive collection
of photographs of American embassy, legation, and consulate buildings abroad.

UNITED STATES CHIEFS OF MISSION, 1778-1973. Compiled by Richardson
Dougall and Mary Patricia Chapman. Washington, D.C.: Government Printing Office, 1973. 239 p.

A tabular listing of principal American diplomatic representatives
abroad, arranged by country to which accredited. Also lists chiefs
of mission to international organizations and presidential appointees

in the Department of State and ambassadors at large. Contains an alphabetical index to all persons cited, and indicates which were career officers.

UNITED STATES CHIEFS OF MISSION, 1973-1974. Washington, D.C.: Government Printing Office, 1975. 52 p.

Supplements and updates the preceding entry.

Guidance to archival materials, produced by the National Archives as part of its records-description program, may be useful for comprehensive and comparative studies--illustrated by the following.

U.S. National Archives. LIST OF FOREIGN SERVICE POST RECORDS IN THE NATIONAL ARCHIVES. Compiled by Mark G. Eckhoff and Alexander P. Marro; revised by Mario Fenyo and John Highbarger. Washington, D.C.: National Archives, 1967. 35 p.

Citations are to records maintained by American diplomatic and consular missions abroad, arranged alphabetically by name of country, with indication of years covered, and quantity of records. Appendices provide a geographical list of consular posts and agencies, and official regulations governing the maintenance of Foreign Service post records.

Periodicals and Press Releases

Unless otherwise noted, these are Department of State publications.

CURRENT FOREIGN POLICY. Washington, D.C.: Government Printing Office, 1972-- . 2 per month.

Short pamphlets, generally three or more pages, on individual subjects, providing information about U.S. policy positions of current interest.

DEPARTMENT OF STATE BULLETIN. Washington, D.C.: Government Printing Office, 1939-- . Weekly. Semiannual index.

Supersede the DEPARTMENT OF STATE PRESS RELEASES and the TREATY INFORMATION BULLETIN, first published in 1929. Expanded format designed to provide the public and interested government agencies with information on developments in the field of foreign relations and on the work of the Department of State and the Foreign Service. Contains articles by public officials, addresses by the president, secretary of state, and other officials, news notes, current information on selected treaties and agreements, copies of important press releases, and similar materials. Includes semiannual listings of current Department of State publications.

DEPARTMENT OF STATE FIELD REPORTER. Washington, D.C.: Government Printing Office, 1952-54. Bimonthly.

> Contains information on developments in educational, scientific, cultural, technical, and other phases of international cooperation as an element of U.S. foreign relations.

DEPARTMENT OF STATE NEWSLETTER. Washington, D.C.: Government Printing Office, 1947-- . Monthly.

> An in-house journal of interest particularly to the personnel of the Department of State, the Foreign Service, and related agencies. Sections devoted to such matters as general interest; news events; vacancies, appointments, promotions, retirements, and resignations; unit and bureau affairs; and current publications on foreign relations.

FAR HORIZONS. Washington, D.C.: Government Printing Office, 1968-77. Quarterly.

> Newsletter of the National Security Council's Under Secretaries Committee, Subcommittee on Foreign Affairs Research (FAR). Designed to promote communication between the private research community and government agencies supporting foreign affairs research.

FOREIGN AFFAIRS RESEARCH PAPERS AVAILABLE. Washington, D.C.: Office of External Research, Department of State, 1964-- . Monthly.

> Provides information about papers (published and unpublished) collected from scholars, private research organizations, and government sources. Lists title, author or issuing agency, affiliation, length, sponsor, meeting at which presented (where applicable), and similar identifying information. Arrangement by major geographic areas, with separate sections on the United States and on worldwide subjects. Copies of papers cited acquired by the Foreign Affairs Research Documentation Center of the Department of State, which renders them available to government officials.

FOREIGN POLICY BRIEFS. Washington, D.C.: Government Printing Office, 1951-67. Biweekly.

> One-page summary accounts of major current events, based on official statements, reports, and documents, compiled as an aid to achieve wider understanding of foreign relations developments.

FOREIGN SERVICE JOURNAL. Washington, D.C.: American Foreign Service Association, 1924-- . Monthly.

> Not a government publication; the primary journal of the Foreign Service Association. Covers a wide variety of subjects of interest to the Foreign Service, and presents the personal views and posi-

tions of respective authors. Also contains items of news, book reviews, and similar materials.

GIST. Washington, D.C.: Bureau of Public Affairs, Department of State, 1969-- . Irregular.

One or two-page summary statements on selected subjects of current interest. One or more issued each month, and occasionally one will supersede an earlier issue on the same subject. A handy reference aid on U.S. foreign relations, primarily for government use.

INTERNATIONAL EDUCATIONAL AND CULTURAL EXCHANGE. Washington, D.C.: Government Printing Office, 1967-- . Quarterly.

Prepared by the U.S. Advisory Commission on International Educational and Cultural Affairs. Contains articles on various aspects of educational and cultural exchange, both private and public. Intended to serve as a forum for the expression of divergent views on pressing issues in the field.

ISSUES IN U.S. FOREIGN POLICY. Washington, D.C.: Government Printing Office, 1968-72. Irregular.

Series of educational pamphlets on contemporary foreign relations problems of public interest. Intended to identify problems rather than propose solutions. Accompanied by discussion guides.

"Press Releases." Washington, D.C.: Department of State, 1912-- . Irregular.

Issued in printed or processed form, at varying times, and under changing titles. Occasional press releases issued since about 1912, with the issuance of mimeographed releases beginning after World War I. From 1929 to 1939, printed "Department of State: Press Releases" issued weekly. At times, numbered sequentially through the calendar year, averaging two or three per day. Since 1939, the more important releases also printed in the DEPARTMENT OF STATE BULLETIN, cited above. In general, contain the texts of addresses and policy statements, communiques, diplomatic communications, and news items. Sometimes contain comprehensive analyses of particular issues or developments.

Country and Regional Information

Unless otherwise noted, these are Department of State publications.

AREA HANDBOOK: [Name of Country]. Prepared by the Department of the Army. Washington, D.C.: Government Printing Office, 1962-64-- . Irregular.

Each handbook on one foreign country's basic institutions: social (history, geography, ethnic groups, and religions); political (system of government, foreign relations); and economic (trade, agriculture, and economic structure). Each contains a bibliography for further reading and research.

BACKGROUND NOTES: [Name of Country or Territory]. Washington, D.C.: Government Printing Office, 1954-- . Irregular.

Individual brief, factual descriptions of the history, government, economy, geography, and foreign relations of more than 150 of the world's countries and other territorial entities.

GEOGRAPHIC BULLETINS. Washington, D.C.: Government Printing Office, 1963-- . Irregular.

Surveys relating to geographic data respecting various political entities of the world. Some on specific countries. Others of a more general nature, such as:

No. 1. PROFILES OF NEWLY INDEPENDENT STATES. 1967. 32 p.
No. 2. STATUS OF THE WORLD'S NATIONS. Rev. ed. 1978. 19 p. With map.
No. 3. SOVEREIGNTY OF THE SEA. 1969. 33 p.
No. 5. UNITED STATES AND OUTLYING AREAS. 1965. 15 p.
No. 8. COMMONWEALTH OF NATIONS. 1968. 44 p.

INTERNATIONAL BOUNDARY STUDIES (LAND). Washington, D.C.: Government Printing Office, 1963-64-- . Irregular.

Series of specific boundary papers.

LIMITS IN THE SEAS (MARITIME BOUNDARIES). Washington, D.C.: Government Printing Office. Irregular.

Series of studies relative to the geographic aspects of the law of the sea.

NATIONAL BASIC INTELLIGENCE FACTBOOK. Washington, D.C.: Government Printing Office, 1978-- . Annual.

CIA publication. Gives basic data on foreign countries, including information on each country's people, type of government, economy, transportation system, defense forces, and other basic factors.

A POCKET GUIDE TO [Name of Country]. Department of Defense. Washington, D.C.: Government Printing Office, 1953-- . Irregular.

Handy guidebooks, originally written for U.S. troops assigned to foreign countries. Provide a brief history of the country, culture, religions, holidays, and landmarks.

Other Selected Publications

Aside from the publications listed elsewhere in this compilation, the following illustrate ad hoc studies produced by the Department of State. Some of these bear the names of their authors or compilers, which are listed first.

Burke, Lee H. HOMES OF THE DEPARTMENT OF STATE, 1774-1976. Washington, D.C.: Government Printing Office, 1977. 57 p.

> History of the buildings occupied by the Department of State and its predecessors.

Franklin, William M. PROTECTION OF FOREIGN INTERESTS: A STUDY IN DIPLOMATIC AND CONSULAR PRACTICE. Washington, D.C.: Government Printing Office, 1947. 328 p.

> An historical survey and analysis of the protection practices of the United States, with special emphasis on the World War II experiences.

Saucerman, Sophia. INTERNATIONAL TRANSFERS OF TERRITORY IN EUROPE, WITH NAMES OF AFFECTED POLITICAL SUBDIVISIONS AS OF 1910-1914 AND THE PRESENT. Washington, D.C.: Government Printing Office, 1937. 244 p.

> Part 1 on countries existing in 1914 that lost territory; part 2 on countries existing in 1914 that acquired territory; part 3 on countries established subsequent to 1914; and part 4 on countries of the Balkan area. Under each part, countries arranged alphabetically. Includes an index and several maps.

Savage, Carlton, ed. POLICY OF THE UNITED STATES TOWARD MARITIME COMMERCE IN WAR, 1776-1918. 2 vols. Washington, D.C.: Government Printing Office, 1934, 1936.

> Volume 1 on the period 1776-1914, and volume 2 concerned with World War I. Includes pertinent documents in each volume with their titles listed separately in a table following the general table of contents. A detailed official account of the policy of the United States concerning its neutral rights and duties as they affect maritime commerce in time of war.

FOREIGN POLICY AND THE DEPARTMENT OF STATE. Washington, D.C.: Government Printing Office, 1976. 30 p.

> A summary description, with illustrations, of the Department of State's position on American foreign policy.

LISTS OF VISITS OF FOREIGN CHIEFS OF STATE AND HEADS OF GOVERNMENT TO THE UNITED STATES, 1789-- . Washington, D.C.: Government Printing Office, 1968-- . Annual.

Contain introductory statements and chronological lists of trips and visits, indicating the countries from which foreign dignitaries come to the United States, with dates and nature of the trips or visits.

LISTS OF VISITS OF PRESIDENTS OF THE UNITED STATES TO FOREIGN COUNTRIES, 1789-- . Washington, D.C.: Government Printing Office, 1968-- . Annual.

Contain introductory statements and chronological lists of trips and visits, indicating countries to which the president travelled, with dates and nature of the visits.

POSTWAR FOREIGN POLICY PREPARATION, 1939-1945. Prepared by Harley A. Notter, et al. Washington, D.C.: Government Printing Office, 1950. 726 p.

A narrative and documentary record of the structure and conduct of the preparation of U.S. post-World War II foreign policy by the Department of State.

THE PROBLEM OF RECOGNITION IN AMERICAN FOREIGN POLICY. Research Project, no. 174. Washington, D.C.: 1950. 94 p.

UNITED STATES FOREIGN POLICY: AN OVERVIEW, JANUARY 1976. Washington, D.C.: Government Printing Office, 1976. 48 p.

A short statement of broad foreign policy issues of national importance, with a conceptual basis from which current foreign policy proceeds. In recent years, updated periodically.

THE UNITED STATES PASSPORT--PAST, PRESENT, FUTURE. Prepared by U.S. Department of State, Passport Office. Washington, D.C.: Government Printing Office, 1976. 242 p.

A comprehensive historical study of the U.S. passport.

In-House Studies

Along with the many other individual publications of the Department of State, there are also a host of in-house studies and reports. Some of these are security classified or are otherwise limited to internal governmental use. Occasionally, they are not made publicly available because they are in preliminary form. Still others become available, but on a limited basis, furnished on the request of the researcher. Since World War II, the Office of the Historian (formerly the Historical Office) of the Department of State has produced hundreds of these studies and reports of two basic types: more fundamental and substantial "research projects" and less comprehensive, shorter "research memoranda." These are undertaken in response to specific needs and official requests from the White House, the Congress, senior departmental officers, or other gov-

ernment agencies. Several of these studies are included elsewhere in this compilation where they are functionally appropriate. For commentary on this research resource and the work of the Office of the Historian, see:

Costrell, Edwin M. "Using the Record of Yesterday's Events Today." DEPART-
MENT OF STATE NEWSLETTER, no. 185 (December 1976): 24-25.

The following illustrate examples of this type of official resource:

"Armed Actions Taken by the United States Without a Declaration of War,
1789-1967." August 1967. 34 p.

"Assaults on United States Diplomatic, Consular, and Information Installations
Abroad, 1900-1965." September 1965. 95 p.

"Chronology of Political Developments Affecting Berlin, 1945-1956." April
1956. 125 p.

"Office of the Counsellor of the Department of State." April 1961. 8 p.,
with supplements.

"The Problem of Recognition in American Foreign Policy." August 1950. 94 p.
Bibliog.

"The Protocol Function in United States Foreign Relations: Its Administration
and Development, 1776-1968." October 1968. 85 p.

"The Rank of Counsellor Historically in the Department of State, 1909-1961."
March 1961. 8 p.

"U.S. Policy Toward Latin America: Recognition and Non-Recognition of
Governments and Interruptions in Diplomatic Relations, 1933-1974--A Tabular
Summary." June 1975. 116 p.

OTHER DEPARTMENTS AND ADMINISTRATIVE AGENCIES

Other executive departments, especially the Commerce, Defense, Justice, and
Treasury Departments, and many administrative agencies and subsidiaries collectively produce a large quantity of documentation and official publications
concerned with major and tangential aspects of the conduct of American foreign
relations. These consist of such materials as historical archives, working papers,
registers and directories of personnel, periodic and occasional reports, descriptive and analytical surveys, periodicals and yearbooks, statistical compilations,
and special studies. Resources on historical and contemporary developments of
former and existing agencies are available to the researchers in differing forms

and at a variety of locations. The following represent the more relevant of such administrative agencies:

ACTION (amalgamating the Peace Corps and the Domestic Volunteer Service), 1971-- .

Agency for International Development, 1961-- . (See below for its predecessors.)

Central Intelligence Agency, 1947-- .

Civil Aeronautics Board, 1938-- .

Export-Import Bank, 1934-- .

Federal Communications Commission, 1934-- .

Federal Maritime Commission, 1961-- .

Federal Trade Commission, 1914-- .

Foreign Claims Settlement Commission, 1954-- .

Immigration and Naturalization Service, 1891-- .

International Communication Agency, 1978-- .

National Aeronautics and Space Administration, 1958-- .

National Archives and Records Service (General Services Administration), 1949-- .

National Historical Publications and Records Commission (formerly National Historical Publications Commission), 1934-- .

National Security Council, 1947-- .

Nuclear Regulatory Commission, 1974-- .

Office of Management and Budget (formerly Bureau of the Budget), 1921-- .

Office of Special Representative for Trade Negotiations, 1975-- .

Panama Canal Company (abolished by the Panama Canal Treaty of 1978), 1948-78.

U.S. Arms Control and Disarmament Agency, 1961-- .

U.S. Information Agency, 1953-1978 (Superseded by International Communication Agency).

U.S. International Trade Commission (formerly U.S. Tariff Commission), 1916-- .

Other agencies, of a more restricted scope, include bipartite boundary commissions (with Canada and Mexico) and joint defense commissions (with Brazil, Canada, and Mexico). Still others, of historical importance, which have been terminated or superseded, are illustrated by the following. For a complete list of former agencies, see appendix A of the current issue of the UNITED STATES GOVERNMENT MANUAL (cited in the first section of this chapter, p. 530), which also lists contemporary literature concerning individual agencies and their published periodic reports.

World War II Agencies:

Board of Economic Warfare, 1941-43.

Foreign Economic Administration, 1943-45.

Lend-Lease Administration, 1941-46.

Office of Alien Property Custodian, 1942-47; later also Office of Alien Property, 1961-66.

Office of Strategic Services, 1942-45.

Office of War Information, 1942-45.

War Food Administration, 1942-45.

War Shipping Administration, 1942-46.

Predecessors of the Agency for International Development (AID) (Chronological):

Economic Cooperation Administration, 1948-51.

Mutual Security Agency, 1951-53.

Foreign Operations Administration, 1953-55.

International Cooperation Administration, 1955-61.

Executive Office Planning and Mobilization (Chronological):

Office of Civil and Defense Mobilization, 1958-61.

Office of Emergency Planning, 1961-68.

Office of Emergency Preparedness, 1968-74 (functions transferred to Federal Energy Agency, 1974).

Others:

American-Mexican Claims Commission, 1942-47.

Atomic Energy Commission, 1946-74.

Committee for Reciprocity Information (for Trade Agreements), 1934-63.

Federal Aviation Agency, 1958-66.

Foreign Commerce Service, 1927-39.

Interagency Council on International Educational and Cultural Affairs, 1964-73.

International Claims Commission, 1950-54.

National Advisory Council on International Monetary and Financial Problems 1945-65.

National Aeronautics and Space Council, 1958–73.

Office of Agricultural War Relations, 1916–42 (functions transferred to War Food Administration).

Peace Corps, 1961–71 (superseded by ACTION).

President's Foreign Intelligence Advisory Board, 1969–77.

St. Lawrence Seaway Development Corporation, 1954–71 (functions transferred to Department of Transportation).

Current reference to the publications of these and other agencies may be found in the MONTHLY CATALOGUE OF UNITED STATES GOVERNMENT PUBLICA-TIONS, and its predecessors, referred to earlier in the section on General Bibliographical Guidance and Sources, p. 526. A general survey of selected compilations, periodic reports, and other materials of some of these departments and agencies is provided in the following:

Plischke, Elmer, ed. AMERICAN FOREIGN RELATIONS: A BIBLIOGRAPHY OF OFFICIAL SOURCES. College Park: Bureau of Governmental Research, University of Maryland, 1955. Reprint. New York: Johnson Reprint Corp., 1966. 71 p.

> Contains a comprehensive, annotated list of nearly two hundred collections and other items, as of the mid-1950s, including many periodic reports. Provides separate sections on the National Archives, registers and directories of personnel, and reports and periodicals of the military and other departments and agencies, as well as those concerned with dependent territories. Part 5, "Other Departments and Agencies," pp. 29–44.

In addition, the Department of State, other agencies of the government, and the Library of Congress also maintain working files and archives of documentation on international organizations in which the United States holds (or previously maintained) membership, or to which it is represented by observership missions. These international institutions embrace the United Nations and its specialized agencies, the International Court of Justice, the Organization of American States and other agencies constituting the inter-American system, the International Monetary Fund and International Bank and regional financial institutions, multipartite alliance and collective defense arrangements (such as the North Atlantic Treaty Organization, the Central or Mideast Treaty Organization, and the Southeast Asia Treaty Organization, which was terminated in 1977), commodity agencies, and many others.

TREATIES AND AGREEMENTS

Throughout its history, the United States has pursued a liberal practice of publishing the texts of and information concerning its treaties and international agreements. This section contains the principal documents and compilations relevant to the treaties and agreements published by Congress and the Department of State, general multinational treaty series (including those of the League of Nations and the United Nations) together with related indexes of research significance, and selected unofficial compilations of and commentaries on treaties and agreements, including several functional treaty lists.

Congress

Aside from the periodic publication of treaties and agreements in the UNITED STATES STATUTES AT LARGE, as indicated earlier, p. 542, Congress has also authorized their publication in the cumulative compilations listed in this section. Arrangement is chronological.

LAWS OF THE UNITED STATES. 10 vols. Philadelphia and Washington, D.C.: John Bioren and W. John Duane, vols. 1-5, and others, vols. 6-10, 1815-45.

> Known as the Bioren and Duane collection. Volume 1 on the texts of treaties with the Indians and with foreign powers, 1778-1814. General index to 1814 in volume 5. Supplemented by volumes 6-10, which provide the texts of treaties from 1815 to 1845. Total collection provides the texts of U.S. treaties from 1778 to 1845.

UNITED STATES STATUTES AT LARGE. Vols. 7 and 8. Boston: Charles C. Little and James Brown, 1848, 1846.

> Volume 7 on texts of treaties with the Indians from 1778 to 1845, and volume 8 on texts of treaties with foreign nations from 1778 to 1845.

TREATIES AND CONVENTIONS CONCLUDED BETWEEN THE UNITED STATES OF AMERICA AND OTHER POWERS SINCE JULY 4, 1776. Edited by J.C. Bancroft Davis. Washington, D.C.: Government Printing Office, 1871. 912 p.

> Also published in the REVISED STATUTES in 1875. Provides the texts of treaties and agreements from 1776 to 1871. Arranged alphabetically by country and chronologically thereunder. Supplemented by an appendix published in 1873, also edited by J.C. Bancroft Davis, and by a supplement published in 1876, edited by John C. Cadwalader. These were published to be bound with the basic compilation to provide a single volume covering the period from 1776 to 1876.

REVISED STATUTUES RELATING TO THE DISTRICT OF COLUMBIA, REVISED STATUTES RELATING TO POST ROADS, AND PUBLIC TREATIES OF THE UNITED STATES IN FORCE ON THE FIRST DAY OF DECEMBER, 1873. UNITED STATES STATUTES AT LARGE, vol. 18, part II. 3 subparts. Washington, D.C.: Government Printing Office, 1875.

> This contains the texts of treaties and agreements with foreign countries from 1776 to 1873. They are arranged alphabetically by country and chronologically thereunder.

TREATIES AND CONVENTIONS CONCLUDED BETWEEN THE UNITED STATES OF AMERICA AND OTHER POWERS SINCE JULY 4, 1776. Edited by John H. Haswell. Washington, D.C.: Government Printing Office, 1889. 1434 p.

> Covers the period from 1776 to 1887. Treaties and agreements arranged in three groups: bilateral treaties, arranged alphabetically by country and chronologically thereunder; multilateral treaties; and the most recent treaties, contained in a supplement.

COMPILATION OF TREATIES IN FORCE. Compiled by Henry L. Bryan. Washington, D.C.: Government Printing Office, 1899. 779 p.

> A chronological list of all treaties (except postal conventions) from 1778 to 1899 to which the United States subscribed. Provides the texts of certain treaties and agreements. Aside from treaty texts, also includes summary statements, pertinent protocols, Senate resolutions consenting to ratification, and references to the location of the treaty and agreement texts in other official publications.

TREATIES, CONVENTIONS, INTERNATIONAL ACTS, PROTOCOLS, AND AGREEMENTS BETWEEN THE UNITED STATES OF AMERICA AND OTHER POWERS. 4 vols. Washington, D.C.: Government Printing Office, 1910-38.

> Vols. 1 and 2, 1776-1909. Compiled by William M. Malloy. Senate Document, no. 357. 61st Cong., 2d sess., 1910.
>
> Vol. 3, 1910-23. Compiled by C.F. Redmond. Senate Document, no. 348. 67th Cong., 4th sess., 1923.
>
> Vol. 4, 1923-37. Compiled by Edward J. Trentwith. Senate Document, no. 134. 75th Cong., 3d sess., 1938.
>
> A single compilation in volumes 1 and 2, with supplements in volumes 3 and 4. Includes bilateral treaties and agreements, arranged alphabetically according to the names of the signatories, followed by multilateral instruments, arranged chronologically. Detailed tables of contents in individual volumes. Cumulative lists of treaties contained in the series in volumes 3 and 4. Appendixes in volume 3: (1) the texts of international instruments by virtue of which rights, indemnities, and reparations might be claimed by the United States, arranged alphabetically by name of signatories, (2) the texts of the World War I peace treaties and other agreements of the Paris Peace Conference signed by the United States. Complete list of all treaties in the order in which they were proclaimed, with citations to the STATUTES AT LARGE, in volume 4.

U.S. Congress. House of Representatives. Committee on Foreign Affairs. COLLECTIVE DEFENSE TREATIES. Committee Print. 91st Cong., 1st sess., 1969. Washington, D.C.: Government Printing Office, 1969. 514 p.

> Compilation of provisions of the collective defense treaties in which

the United States has agreed to the use of its military forces for
the mutual defense of the parties. Includes a chronology of developments.

In addition to the above publications, the Senate usually publishes documents,
including hearings, concerning individual treaties and agreements under consideration for approval for ratification. A number of Senate publications on
the general treaty process are given in chapter 17.

Department of State

Many of the compilations, indexes, and listings of treaties and agreements published in congressional documents were prepared by the Department of State.
Some early materials were also published by the Department of State, and,
since early in the twentieth century, and especially since World War II, these
have been published systematically by the Department--primarily in the TREA-
TIES AND OTHER INTERNATIONAL ACTS SERIES, TREATIES AND OTHER
INTERNATIONAL AGREEMENTS OF THE UNITED STATES OF AMERICA, and
UNITED STATES TREATIES AND OTHER INTERNATIONAL AGREEMENTS, listed
below. Jointly, these three compilations provide the texts of all treaties and
of all major executive agreements that have become effective for the United
States since 1776. Treaty and agreement compilations and other documentation
are grouped in three categories: compilations, series, and indexes, which
provide the texts of treaties and agreements; lists of treaties and agreements;
and publications providing information concerning them. Listings are generally
chronological and by related groupings. Most are Department of State publications.

COMPILATIONS, SERIES, AND INDEXES

Elliot, Jonathan, ed. DIPLOMATIC CODE OF THE UNITED STATES OF
AMERICA: EMBRACING A COLLECTION OF TREATIES AND CONVENTIONS
BETWEEN THE UNITED STATES AND FOREIGN POWERS, FROM THE YEAR
1778 to 1827. Washington, D.C.: By the editor, 1827. 668 p.

Includes the texts of treaties for the period from 1778 to 1827,
U.S. laws relating to privileges accorded foreign ministers in the
United States and American consuls abroad, the texts of acts and
proclamations regarding treaties, extracts from foreign treaties that
affected the United States, and references to cases decided by
U.S. federal and state courts involving questions related to American foreign relations.

_____. THE AMERICAN DIPLOMATIC CODE: EMBRACING A COLLECTION
OF TREATIES AND CONVENTIONS BETWEEN THE UNITED STATES AND FOR-
EIGN POWERS FROM 1778 TO 1834. 2 vols. Washington, D.C.: By the
editor, 1834.

A revised and updated edition of the preceding item. Also designed
to serve as a concise diplomatic manual.

Miller, David Hunter, comp. and ed. TREATIES AND OTHER INTERNATION-
AL ACTS OF THE UNITED STATES OF AMERICA. 8 vols. Washington, D.C.:
Government Printing Office, 1931-48.

> Volume 1 on a plan of the compilation, lists of treaties, various
> tables and other general information. Volumes 2 to 8 on the texts
> of treaties and agreements for the period from 1776 to 1863. In-
> cludes only treaties and international acts that have been effectu-
> ated. Does not include treaties with Indians and postal conven-
> tions. Arranged chronologically by names of countries. Useful
> background information also supplied.

Rockhill, W.W., ed. TREATIES AND CONVENTIONS WITH OR CONCERN-
ING CHINA AND KOREA, 1894-1904, TOGETHER WITH VARIOUS STATE
PAPERS AND DOCUMENTS AFFECTING FOREIGN INTERESTS. Washington,
D.C.: Government Printing Office, 1904. 555 p.

_____. TREATIES, CONVENTIONS, AGREEMENTS, ORDINANCES, ETC.,
RELATING TO CHINA AND KOREA (OCTOBER 1904-JANUARY 1908). Washington, D.C.: Government Printing Office, 1908. 320 p.

UNITED STATES TREATY SERIES. Washington, D.C.: Government Printing
Office, 1908-46. Irregular.

> Treaties numbered serially, beginning with number 489; these num-
> bers constitute the treaty file numbers in the Department of State
> archives. Prior to 1929, includes both treaties and agreements;
> after 1929, includes only treaties submitted to the Senate for ap-
> proval. Each treaty text published separately in pamphlet form,
> giving the text in the languages of the original instrument and the
> dates of signature, ratification, and proclamation. Not printed
> in a complete, bound collection.

EXECUTIVE AGREEMENT SERIES. Washington, D.C.: Government Printing
Office, 1929-46. Irregular.

> Agreements numbered serially from number 1 to number 506. Each
> agreement text published separately in pamphlet form, giving the
> text in the languages of the original instrument, the date of signa-
> ture, and the date of effectuation. Not printed in a complete,
> bound collection.

TREATIES AND OTHER INTERNATIONAL ACTS SERIES (TIAS). Washington,
D.C.: Government Printing Office, 1945-- . Irregular.

> Supersedes and combines the TREATY SERIES and EXECUTIVE
> AGREEMENT SERIES, cited above. Treaties and agreements num-
> bered serially, commencing with number 1501. Each text pub-
> lished separately in pamphlet form, giving the text in the languages
> of the original instrument and the dates of signature, ratification,
> proclamation, and implementation. These are not printed in a com-

plete, bound collection. Listed in the DEPARTMENT OF STATE
BULLETIN as they become applicable.

TREATIES AND OTHER INTERNATIONAL AGREEMENTS OF THE UNITED
STATES OF AMERICA, 1776-1949. 13 vols. Washington, D.C.: Government
Printing Office, 1968-76.

> Contains treaty and agreement texts to 1949. Supersedes the older
> publications of Malloy, Redmond, and Trentwith, listed in the pre-
> ceding section, p. 573. Cumulative compilation of treaties and
> agreements, which, together with the following entry, constitutes
> a comprehensive collection of U.S. treaties and agreements from
> 1776 to date. Volumes 1 to 4 on multilateral treaties and agree-
> ments, arranged chronologically by date of signature. Bilateral
> treaties and agreements, beginning with volume 5, grouped under
> the name of the country with whom they were concluded, arranged
> in alphabetical order.

UNITED STATES TREATIES AND OTHER INTERNATIONAL AGREEMENTS.
Washington, D.C.: Government Printing Office, 1950-- . Annual.

> A continuing series consisting of several volumes and parts each
> calendar year. Instruments numbered and arranged in the order in
> which they are published in the TREATIES AND OTHER INTER-
> NATIONAL ACTS SERIES, cited above, beginning with number
> 2010. Each treaty and agreement text published in the languages
> of the original instrument and accompanied by a list of pertinent
> dates. Index at the end of each volume. Prior to the publica-
> tion of this compilation, treaties and other international agreements
> were printed in UNITED STATES STATUTES AT LARGE; a complete
> list of treaties and agreements published to 1950 will be found in
> 64 Stat., pt. 3, noted above, p. 576, 577 and above.

NUMERICAL LIST OF THE TREATY SERIES, EXECUTIVE AGREEMENT SERIES,
AND TREATIES AND OTHER INTERNATIONAL ACTS SERIES. Department of
State Publication 3787. Washington, D.C.: Government Printing Office, 1950.
87 p.

> This is a reprint of appendix II of TREATY DEVELOPMENTS, June
> 1949. See citation below.

SUBJECT INDEX OF TREATY SERIES AND EXECUTIVE AGREEMENT SERIES,
JULY 1, 1931. Washington, D.C.: Government Printing Office, 1932. 214 p.

> Handy guide to treaties and executive agreements contained in the
> two Department of State series, cited above.

LISTS OF TREATIES AND AGREEMENTS

A LIST OF TREATIES AND OTHER INTERNATIONAL ACTS OF THE UNITED

STATES OF AMERICA IN FORCE ON DECEMBER 31, 1932. Washington, D.C.: Government Printing Office, 1933. 172 p.

> Issued as a supplement to the TREATY INFORMATION BULLETIN, no. 39 (December 1932). Treaties and other international acts arranged according to certain major groupings, and, within each subsection, grouped as multilateral and bilateral instruments, and chronologically thereunder. Identified by short title giving the place of signing and important dates. Also provides cross-references to other treaty compilations.

A LIST OF TREATIES AND OTHER INTERNATIONAL ACTS OF THE UNITED STATES OF AMERICA IN FORCE ON DECEMBER 31, 1941. Washington, D.C.: Government Printing Office, 1944. 275 p.

> Contents and coverage similar to those described in the preceding entry. Superseded by UNITED STATES TREATY DEVELOPMENTS, cited later, p. 579.

LIST OF TREATIES SUBMITTED TO THE SENATE, 1789-1934. Washington, D.C.: Government Printing Office, 1935. 138 p.

> Provides a list of treaties, without texts, giving pertinent dates, the countries concerned, the subject, the TREATY SERIES number, whether submitted to the Senate, disposition by the Senate, and similar information.

LIST OF TREATIES SUBMITTED TO THE SENATE, 1935-1944. Washington, D.C.: Government Printing Office, 1945. 20 p.

> Companion to the preceding entry. For a description of its contents, see the preceding item. Covers treaties number 929 to number 1048. Also provides a list of treaties pending in the Senate on December 31, 1944, and treaties awaiting further proceedings. Subsequently, this information incorporated in UNITED STATES TREATY DEVELOPMENTS, described in the following section, p. 579.

LIST OF TREATIES SUBMITTED TO THE SENATE, 1789-1931, WHICH HAVE NOT GONE INTO FORCE, OCTOBER 1, 1932. Washington, D.C.: Government Printing Office, 1932. 25 p.

> A chronological list of treaties that have not gone into effect. Does not include treaties with the Indians.

NUMERICAL LIST OF THE TREATIES SERIES, EXECUTIVE AGREEMENT SERIES, AND TREATIES AND OTHER INTERNATIONAL ACTS SERIES. Washington, D.C.: Government Printing Office, 1950. 87 p.

A list of U.S. treaties and agreements, from 1795 to the end of the 1940s, giving the identification number of each, the country or countries with whom negotiated, date of signature, subject, and citations. Reprinted from UNITED STATES TREATY DEVELOPMENTS through June 1949.

A TENTATIVE LIST OF TREATY COLLECTIONS. Washington, D.C.: Government Printing Office, 1919. 103 p.

Prepared for the Paris Peace Conference; initially a classified document, but subsequently made public. Constitutes a compilation of general collections of treaties of all countries. Deals with special groups of treaties resulting from international congresses and conferences, and with treaties of individual states, grouped into compilations of multilateral treaties and bilateral treaties.

TREATIES IN FORCE: A LIST OF TREATIES AND OTHER INTERNATIONAL AGREEMENTS OF THE UNITED STATES IN FORCE ON . . . . Washington, D.C.: Government Printing Office, 1956-- . Annual.

Earlier issues of a similar nature were published in 1932 and 1941, as noted above. Arranged in two parts, followed by an appendix. Part 1 on bilateral treaties and other agreements listed by country or other political entity, alphabetically arranged, and thereunder by functional subject headings, with postal arrangements for territorial possessions of a country at the end of the appropriate country listing. Part 2 on multilateral treaties, arranged by subject headings, together with a list of states which are parties to each agreement. A consolidated tabulation of documents affecting international copyright relations of the United States given in the appendix.

UNITED STATES DEPARTMENT OF STATE CATALOGUE OF TREATIES, 1814-1918. Washington, D.C.: Government Printing Office, 1919. 716 p. Bibliog. Reprint. New York: Oceana, 1964.

Prepared for the Paris Peace Conference; initially a classified document, but subsequently made public. Provides a chronological list of the treaties of all countries from 1814 to 1918, a selected list of treaties for the period from 1353 to 1814 with an index, a chronological list of general international agreements, a chronological list of general inter-American agreements, and a general index by Countries. Also indicates where texts of treaties may be found and the languages in which they are printed.

INFORMATION CONCERNING TREATIES

In addition to the following, contemporary information concerning the consummation, implementation, and status of treaties and agreements may be found in the current issues of the DEPARTMENT OF STATE BULLETIN.

TREATY DEVELOPMENTS, 1944. Washington, D.C.: Government Printing
Office, 1945. 36 p.

Provides data regarding signatures, ratification, adherences, re-
newals, terminations, withdrawals, and other developments which
occurred during 1944. Organized in three parts: treaties in
force on January 1, 1944, with developments in 1944; treaties
that entered into force in 1944; and pending treaties, with developments in 1944. Arranged by subject, with cross-references
to other publications.

TREATY INFORMATION BULLETIN. 5 vols. Washington, D.C.: Government
Printing Office, 1929-39.

Originally issued monthly, in pamphlet form. Since 1939, this
information incorporated into the DEPARTMENT OF STATE BULLE-
TIN. Materials presented under five headings: promotion of
peace, political, humanitarian, economic, and miscellaneous.
Descriptive and background materials given, together with important dates and information concerning changes and ratification.
Texts or extracts of texts supplied. Includes cross-references to
statutes, the TREATY SERIES, cited above, p. 575, and other publications. Each bulletin has its own index, with cumulative indexes
in volumes 3 and 5.

UNITED STATES TREATY DEVELOPMENTS. Washington, D.C.: Government
Printing Office, 1947-51. Var. pag.

A loose-leaf system, published as a volume in 1947, and kept up
to date by supplements and replacements. Constitutes a combina-
tion and extension of the following: A LIST OF TREATIES AND
OTHER INTERNATIONAL ACTS OF THE UNITED STATES OF
AMERICA IN FORCE ON DECEMBER 31, 1941; LIST OF TREATIES
SUBMITTED TO THE SENATE; and TREATY DEVELOPMENTS, 1944,
which are cited earlier, pp. 576, 577, and above. Presents pertinent
dates, names of signatories, references, supplementary and authorizing
legislation, executive action, and court opinions, but not the full
texts of treaties and agreements. Information arranged by date of
signature, with reference to the treaty or executive agreement
series number.

General Multinational Treaty Series and Indexes

The materials included in this section are concerned with multinational collections of, indexes to, and profiles of treaties and agreements. Four general
compilations are listed first, in chronological sequence--including a collection
of documents covering the period 1648 to 1918, a collection covering the
period from 1841 to date, the League of Nations series, and the United Nations
series--followed, in alphabetical order, by various indexes, lists, and commentaries on such treaties and agreements.

Perry, Clive, comp. CONSOLIDATED TREATY SERIES, 1648-1918. Vol. 1-- .
Dobbs Ferry, N.Y.: Oceana, 1969-- .

> Sponsored by the Council of Europe, the American Society of
> International Law, and the British Institute of International and
> Comparative Law. When completed, expected to consist of ap-
> proximately two hundred volumes. Provides the texts of treaties
> and agreements from 1648 to the time the League of Nations
> series commenced. Texts in the original languages, with a con-
> temporary translation into English or French, or the main provisions
> given in English, where this is deemed useful. Indicate the ori-
> ginal parties, when the treaty came into force, whether it con-
> tinues in effect, and how it may have been terminated or super-
> seded. Arranged chronologically, with years covered indicated in
> the title of each volume.

BRITISH AND FOREIGN STATE PAPERS. London: His Majesty's Stationery
Office, 1841-- . Annual.

> A collection of treaties and other state papers for various countries
> since 1812.

LEAGUE OF NATIONS TREATY SERIES. 205 vols. and 9 index vols. Geneva:
Secretariat of the League of Nations, 1920-44.

> Compilation of the treaties and agreements deposited with and re-
> gistered by the League of Nations, published in their original
> languages. Superseded by the UNITED NATIONS TREATY SERIES,
> cited next.

UNITED NATIONS TREATY SERIES. New York: Secretariat of the United
Nations, 1945-- . Indexed periodically.

> Compilation of treaties and agreements, similar to and succeeding
> the LEAGUE OF NATIONS TREATY SERIES, including the treaties
> and agreements deposited with and registered by the United Nations.

Grenville, John. MAJOR INTERNATIONAL TREATIES, 1914-1973. New York:
Stein and Day, 1974. 575 p.

> Short history and analysis of major treaties and agreements since
> the beginning of World War I, with the texts of the most important.

Harvard Law School Library. INDEX TO MULTILATERAL TREATIES: A CHRON-
OLOGICAL LIST OF MULTI PARTY INTERNATIONAL AGREEMENTS FROM
THE SIXTEENTH CENTURY TO 1963, WITH CITATIONS TO THEIR TEXT. Dobbs
Ferry, N.Y.: Oceana, 1965. 301 p.

Lay, S. Houston, ed. AIR AND AVIATION TREATIES OF THE WORLD. 10
vols. and loose-leaf binder index projected. Dobbs Ferry, N.Y.: Oceana, 1979-- .

Myers, Denys P. MANUAL OF COLLECTIONS OF TREATIES AND OF COL-
LECTIONS RELATING TO TREATIES. Cambridge, Mass.: Harvard University
Press, 1922. 685 p.

> Printed at the expense of the Richard Manning Hodges Fund. In-
> cludes sections on general collections, collections by countries,
> collections by subject matter, and international administration.
> An appendix on the publication of treaties.

Rohn, Peter H., ed. TREATY PROFILES. Santa Barbara, Calif.: A.B.C.-Clio
Press, 1976. 256 p.

> A quantitative analysis of the treaty-making behavior of the inter-
> national community, 1945-65. Each country and international or-
> ganization profiled in a standard format, showing its leading treaty
> partners, time trends, topical data, registration frequency, asym-
> metry patterns, and other factors. About one-third of the text on
> analysis of trends, and two-thirds on factual supportive data.

_____, ed. WORLD TREATY INDEX. 5 vols. Santa Barbara, Calif.:
A.B.C.-Clio Press, 1975.

> A comprehensive index to international treaties and agreements
> covering the period 1920 to 1970. Combines citations to approxi-
> mately twenty-three thousand international arrangements, covering
> the League and United Nations Treaty Series and some forty nation-
> al treaty collections in a single reference system. Also provides
> data on national, regional, and global trends and patterns.

United Nations. Legal Department. LAWS AND PRACTICES CONCERNING
THE CONCLUSION OF TREATIES, WITH A SELECT BIBLIOGRAPHY ON THE
LAW OF TREATIES. New York: United Nations, Legislative Series, 1953.
Bibliog.

Vambery, Joseph T., and Vambery, Rose V., eds. CUMULATIVE LIST OF
TREATIES AND INTERNATIONAL AGREEMENTS REGISTERED WITH THE UNITED
NATIONS, DECEMBER 1969-DECEMBER 1974. 2 vols. Dobbs Ferry, N.Y.:
Oceana, 1977.

> A comprehensive, manageable reference list of treaties and agree-
> ments registered with the United Nations.

Other Specialized and Unofficial Collections and Indexes

This section provides unofficial treaty materials on a variety of functional topics
and other selections, giving treaty texts and, in some cases, also commentary
and analysis concerning treaties and agreements.

American Bar Association. THE COMMERCIAL TREATY INDEX. 2d ed. Lexington, Mass.: Lexington Books, 1975.

American bilateral nontariff commercial treaties series, in country-by-country sequence.

Canada. Department of External Affairs. TREATIES AND AGREEMENTS AFFECTING CANADA IN FORCE BETWEEN HIS MAJESTY AND THE UNITED STATES OF AMERICA WITH SUBSIDIARY DOCUMENTS, 1814-1925. Ottawa, Canada: Acland, 1927. 578 p.

Carnegie Endowment for International Peace. TREATIES AND AGREEMENTS WITH AND CONCERNING CHINA, 1919-1929. Washington, D.C.: 1929. 282 p.

Davenport, Francis Gardiner, ed. EUROPEAN TREATIES BEARING ON THE HISTORY OF THE UNITED STATES AND ITS DEPENDENCIES. 4 vols. Washington, D.C.: Carnegie Endowment for International Peace, 1917-37.

Chronological arrangement covering the period from 1648 to 1815.

Deak, Francis, and Jessup, Philip C., eds. A COLLECTION OF NEUTRALITY LAWS, REGULATIONS AND TREATIES OF VARIOUS COUNTRIES. 2 vols. Washington, D.C.: Carnegie Endowment for International Peace, 1939.

Provides the texts of laws, regulations, and treaties and agreements given under the names of various countries, arranged alphabetically. Also provides a chronology of treaties concerned with neutrality, including the names of the parties.

Diamond, Walter H., and Diamond, Dorothy B., eds. INTERNATIONAL TAX TREATIES OF ALL NATIONS: A COLLECTION AND RETRIEVAL SOURCE. 10 vols. and loose-leaf index. Dobbs Ferry, N.Y.: Oceana, 1977.

A compilation of 950 treaties, originally published in the UNITED NATIONS TREATY SERIES (see citation on p. 580), arranged chronologically as issued by the United Nations, with individual editorial commentary and current status. Includes separate index volume, arranged alphabetically by country, providing guidance to the treaties.

Finley, M.I., and Adelson, Howard, eds. MAJOR PEACE TREATIES OF ANCIENT AND MEDIEVAL HISTORY, 1300 B.C.-1648. 3 vols. New York: Chelsea House, 1970.

Provides the texts of treaties, in English, from the Egyptian-Hittite Treaty to the Treaty of Westphalia. Continued by the compilation of Fred L. Israel, cited below.

Fischer, Peter, ed. CONCESSIONARY AGREEMENTS: A COLLECTION OF CONCESSIONARY AND RELATED AGREEMENTS BETWEEN STATES AND NATIONALS OF OTHER STATES. 16 vols. projected. Dobbs Ferry, N.Y.: Oceana, 1975-- . In progress.

Compilation of legal instruments between states and foreign nationals and corporations, covering the period from medieval papal grants to date. Annotated material arranged chronologically.

Gamble, John K., ed. INDEX TO MARINE TREATIES. Seattle: University of Washington Press, 1972. 438 p.

Habicht, Max, ed. POST-WAR TREATIES FOR THE PACIFIC SETTLEMENT OF INTERNATIONAL DISPUTES. Cambridge, Mass.: Harvard University Press, 1931. 1109 p.

Chronological arrangement for treaties covering the period 1918 to 1928. Includes chapters on the analysis of treaties, reservations contained in treaties, methods of investigating disputes and conciliation, and methods of arbitration and adjudication. Also includes, in appendixes, an alphabetical list of signatory states and the treaties to which they are parties and a list of commissions of investigation and conciliation (by country).

Hill, Charles E., ed. LEADING AMERICAN TREATIES. New York: Macmillan, 1931. 399 p.

Presents the historical setting and the chief provisions of fifteen leading American treaties to the end of the 1920s.

Hudson, Manley O., ed. INTERNATIONAL LEGISLATION: A COLLECTION OF MULTIPARTITE INTERNATIONAL INSTRUMENTS OF GENERAL INTEREST. 9 vols. Washington, D.C.: Carnegie Endowment for International Peace, 1931-50.

Provides the texts of treaties and conventions for the period 1919 to 1945. Chronological arrangement with a subject index appended.

Israel, Fred L., ed. MAJOR PEACE TREATIES OF MODERN HISTORY, 1648-1967. 4 vols. New York: McGraw-Hill, 1967.

A compilation of seventy-seven important peace treaties, from the Treaty of Westphalia to the time of publication. Chronological arrangement in ten sections, with each section prefaced with commentary. A companion to the compilation of M.I. Finley and Howard Adelson, cited above.

Johnston, Charles R., ed. LAW AND POLICY OF INTERGOVERNMENTAL PRIMARY COMMODITY AGREEMENTS. 2 loose-leaf vols. with supplements. Dobbs Ferry, N.Y.: Oceana, 1976-- .

Provides texts of commodity trade agreements concerning cocoa, coffee, copper, olive oil, petroleum, sugar, tin, wheat, and the like. Includes constitutive agreements, international agency rules, United Nations resolutions, and other documents, as well as analysis.

MacMurray, J.V.A. TREATIES AND AGREEMENTS WITH AND CONCERNING CHINA, 1894-1919. 2 vols. New York: Oxford University Press, 1921.

Manning, William R., ed. ARBITRATION TREATIES AMONG THE AMERICAN NATIONS TO THE CLOSE OF THE YEAR 1910. Washington, D.C.: Carnegie Endowment for International Peace, 1924. 472 p.

A compilation of arbitration treaties and arbitral clauses of other treaties signed and ratified among American states before the close of 1910. Chronological arrangement with a chronological table in each volume, giving the date of signature, the names of the signatory states, and the nature of the arbitration.

Oakes, Augustus, and Mowat, R.B., eds. THE GREAT EUROPEAN TREATIES OF THE NINETEENTH CENTURY. Oxford: Clarenden, 1918. 403 p.

Ruster, Bernd, ed. INTERNATIONAL PROTECTION OF THE ENVIRONMENT: TREATIES AND RELATED DOCUMENTS. 20 vols. projected. Dobbs Ferry, N.Y.: Oceana, 1975-- . In progress.

Contains bilateral and multilateral treaties, agreements, and resolutions dealing with the protection of the environment.

Scott, James Brown, ed. THE HAGUE CONVENTIONS AND DECLARATIONS OF 1899 AND 1907. 3d ed. 5 vols. New York: Oxford University Press, 1918.

Provides the texts of the conventions and other instruments negotiated at the Hague Conferences of 1899 and 1907, for the codification of the laws of war and neutrality.

_____. TREATIES FOR THE ADVANCEMENT OF PEACE. New York: Oxford University Press, 1920. 152 p.

Part 1 on the texts of treaties for the advancement of peace between the United States and other countries, arranged alphabetically according to country. Part 2 concerned with unperfected treaties.

Stockholm International Peace Research Institute. ARMS CONTROL: A SURVEY AND APPRAISAL OF MULTILATERAL AGREEMENTS. London: Taylor and Francis, 1978. 238 p.

Tomasevich, J. INTERNATIONAL AGREEMENTS ON CONSERVATION OF MARINE RESOURCES WITH SPECIAL REFERENCE TO THE NORTH PACIFIC. Stanford: California Food Research Institute, 1943. 297 p.

Inquiry into problems, aims, techniques, limitations, and achievements of representative commodity agreements, and conclusions concerning effective future use of such instruments in international cooperation following World War II.

TREATIES AND ALLIANCES OF THE WORLD: AN INTERNATIONAL SURVEY COVERING TREATIES IN FORCE AND COMMUNITIES OF STATES. New York: Scribner, 1968. 214 p.

U.S. Arms Control and Disarmament Agency. ARMS CONTROL AND DIS-ARMAMENT AGREEMENTS: TEXTS AND HISTORY OF NEGOTIATIONS. Washington, D.C.: Government Printing Office, 1977. 187 p.

> Contains an introduction and the texts of nineteen treaties and agreements, each prefaced with a descriptive introduction. Each agreement followed by a table of signatories, their dates of signature, and dates of deposit of ratification or accession.

Wallenstein, Gerd, ed. INTERNATIONAL TELECOMMUNICATION AGREE-MENTS. 3 loose-leaf vols. projected. Dobbs Ferry, N.Y.: Oceana, 1977-- . In progress.

> Gives the texts of treaties in force and an analysis of the substance of telecommunications treaties and agreements, with a description of the International Telecommunication Union system as a model for additional agreements in other fields.

Wiktor, Christian L., ed. UNPERFECTED TREATIES OF THE UNITED STATES OF AMERICA. 5 vols. projected. Dobbs Ferry, N.Y.: Oceana, 1976-- . In progress.

> Provides the texts of all treaties concluded by the United States since 1776 that, for whatever reason, did not go into force. Supplements the official compilations of texts of treaties and agreements listed above for the Department of State, pp. 575-76.

Individual Treaties and Agreements

The following is a selected list of separate official publications providing the texts of and commentary on individual and related groups of recent U.S. treaties and agreements. Congressional hearings and other documents are not included, but they may be consulted for additional information and analysis on such treaties and agreements. Arrangement is chronological, according to the dates of the treaties or agreements.

Robinson, Chalfont. HISTORY OF THE RECIPROCITY TREATY OF 1854 WITH CANADA. Washington, D.C.: Government Printing Office, 1911. 42 p.

Cushing, Caleb. THE TREATY OF WASHINGTON: ITS NEGOTIATION, EXECUTION, AND THE DISSENSIONS RELATING THERETO. New York: Harper, 1873. 280 p.

> Concerns treaty of 1871 with Great Britain providing for arbitration of the Civil War Alabama claims.

TREATY OF PEACE BETWEEN THE UNITED STATES AND SPAIN, SIGNED AT THE CITY OF PARIS, DECEMBER 10, 1898, WITH SENATE JOINT RESOLUTION NO. 240, FIFTY-FIFTH CONGRESS, THIRD SESSION, . . . AND THE VOTES UPON SAID TREATY AND JOINT RESOLUTION AND THE AMENDMENTS IN THE SENATE. Senate Document, no. 182. 57th Cong., 1st sess. Washington, D.C.: Government Printing Office, 1902. 16 p.

AMERICAN AND BRITISH CLAIMS ARBITRATION UNDER THE SPECIAL AGREEMENT CONCLUDED BETWEEN UNITED STATES AND GREAT BRITAIN, AUGUST 18, 1910; REPORT OF FRED K. NIELSEN, AGENT AND COUNSEL FOR THE UNITED STATES. Washington, D.C.: Government Printing Office, 1926. 638 p.

TREATY FOR THE RENUNCIATION OF WAR: TEXT OF THE TREATY, NOTES EXCHANGED, INSTRUMENTS OF RATIFICATION AND OF ADHERENCE, AND OTHER PAPERS. Washington, D.C.: Government Printing Office, 1933. 315 p.

Concerns the Pact of Paris (or Anti-War Treaty) of 1928.

GERMANY SURRENDERS UNCONDITIONALLY: FACSIMILES OF THE DOCUMENTS. Washington, D.C.: Government Printing Office, 1945. 41 p.

THE END OF THE WAR IN THE PACIFIC: SURRENDER DOCUMENTS IN FACSIMILE. Washington, D.C.: Government Printing Office, 1945. 24 p.

THE INTERNATIONAL COURT OF JUSTICE: SELECTED DOCUMENTS RELATING TO THE DRAFTING OF THE STATUTE. Washington, D.C.: Government Printing Office, 1946. 167 p.

Contains a comprehensive analysis of the negotiations involved in transmuting the Statute of the League's Permanent Court into the Statute of the United Nations' International Court of Justice. Focuses primarily on content and language change.

MAKING THE PEACE TREATIES, 1941-1947. Washington, D.C.: Government Printing Office, 1947. 150 p.

TREATIES OF PEACE WITH ITALY, BULGARIA, HUNGARY, ROUMANIA, AND FINLAND (ENGLISH VERSIONS). Washington, D.C.: Government Printing Office, 1947. 241 p.

THE SIGNING OF THE NORTH ATLANTIC TREATY. Washington, D.C.: Government Printing Office, 1949. 66 p. Photos.

Includes the treaty text, and statements made at the time of signing.

NORTH ATLANTIC TREATY: DOCUMENTS RELATING TO THE NORTH ATLANTIC TREATY. Washington, D.C.: Government Printing Office, 1949. 128 p.

LONDON AND PARIS AGREEMENTS, SEPTEMBER–OCTOBER 1954. Washington, D.C.: Government Printing Office, 1954. 128 p.

> Contains documents relating to NATO, the Brussels Treaty of 1948, and the termination of the occupation regime in the Federal Republic of Germany.

ARMISTICE IN KOREA: SELECTED STATEMENTS AND DOCUMENTS. Washington, D.C.: Government Printing Office, 1953. 29 p.

MILITARY ARMISTICE IN KOREA AND TEMPORARY SUPPLEMENTARY AGREEMENT: AGREEMENT SIGNED AT PANMUNJOM, KOREA, JULY 27, 1953. Washington, D.C.: Government Printing Office, 1953. 130 p.

THE AUSTRIAN STATE TREATY: AN ACCOUNT OF THE POSTWAR NEGOTIATIONS TOGETHER WITH THE TEXT OF THE TREATY AND RELATED DOCUMENTS. Washington, D.C.: Government Printing Office, 1957. 99 p.

INTERNATIONAL CONFERENCES AND ORGANIZATIONS

Whereas in earlier years, U.S. international conference participation was usually ad hoc and occasional, prior to World War II, this increased to a yearly average of approximately forty conferences, and by the late 1970s, the United States attended some eight hundred to one thousand conferences and sessions of international agencies each year. The official documentary materials on such a proliferation of conferences has become massive. For a time, the Department of State published printed reports on all major conferences. This peaked in the 1950s, and, since that time, such publications have been occasional.

It is official practice for U.S. delegations to international conferences to submit written reports to the Secretary of State when so instructed. Normally, an unclassified report is required for all conferences, and supplementary classified reports are also submitted when, in the judgment of the Department of State or the chairman of the American delegation, this is warranted. Generally, conference reports are in processed form, and copies of the unclassified reports are available on request. Reports contain the exact title of the conference, site of meeting and inclusive dates, background and agenda, lists of countries represented officially and by observers with the size of delegations, a list of the members of the U.S. delegation, organization of the conference, report on the work of conference committees, determinations and achievements of the gathering, and the delegation's conclusions.

The materials provided in this section include several general studies and compilations of information and documentation on international conferences and a selected list of individual printed conference reports. Information concerning other conferences may be obtained from the Office of International Conferences of the Department of State.

General Studies and Compilations

AMERICAN DELEGATIONS TO INTERNATIONAL CONFERENCES, CON-
GRESSES AND EXPOSITIONS AND AMERICAN REPRESENTATION ON INTER-
NATIONAL INSTITUTIONS AND COMMISSIONS, WITH RELEVANT DATA.
Washington, D.C.: Government Printing Office, 1933–42. Annual.

> Annual volumes on fiscal years 1931–32 through 1940–41. Super-
> seded by PARTICIPATION OF THE UNITED STATES GOVERNMENT
> IN INTERNATIONAL CONFERENCES, listed below.

INTERNATIONAL AGENCIES IN WHICH THE UNITED STATES PARTICIPATES.
Washington, D.C.: Government Printing Office, 1946. 322 p.

> Provides descriptive analyses concerning some fifty international
> agencies, grouped as general, agricultural, commercial and finan-
> cial, commodity, educational and cultural, political and legal,
> social and health, and transport and communications. Discussion
> on origin and development, membership, purposes and functions,
> structure, relations with other international organizations, finances,
> current status, and similar matters, supplemented with a selected
> bibliography for each agency. Includes lists of multilateral and
> bilateral agencies with which the United States was affiliated dur-
> ing the preceding ten years and a list of international organizations
> of which the United States was not a member. Superseded by the
> following entry.

INTERNATIONAL ORGANIZATIONS IN WHICH THE UNITED STATES PARTICI-
PATES, 1949. Washington, D.C.: Government Printing Office, 1950. 335 p.

> Provides descriptive analyses concerning some sixty-five international
> organizations. Arrangement and treatment similar to that described
> in the preceding entry. Two appendixes provided: one lists the
> international organizations in which the United States participated
> but which have been terminated or superseded or which became in-
> active after 1945, and the second is a chart indicating the member-
> ship of states in the components of the United Nations and its spe-
> cialized agencies.

PARTICIPATION OF THE UNITED STATES GOVERNMENT IN INTERNATIONAL
CONFERENCES. Washington, D.C.: Government Printing Office, 1947–62.
Annual.

> Annual volumes on fiscal years 1945–46 to 1959–60. Conferences
> and sessions of agencies of international organizations grouped into
> major functional categories, giving such information as the compo-
> sition of the American delegation, principal officers, participation
> by other countries, and a summary of the action taken. A summary
> volume, under the same title, pertaining to the World War II
> period, July 1941 to June 1945, was published separately; see De-
> partment of State Publication 2665, Conference Series 89.

REVIEW OF THE UNITED NATIONS CHARTER: A COLLECTION OF DOCU-
MENTS. Senate Document, no. 87. 83d Cong., 2d sess. Washington,
D.C.: Government Printing Office, 1954. 895 p.

> Consists of 186 documents by and about the United Nations,
> grouped into sections concerned with background, action by Con-
> gress, selected problem areas, such as national sovereignty and the
> United Nations, treaties and domestic law, membership and repre-
> sentation, development of the General Assembly, voting in the
> Security Council, collective security, and financing, as well as
> official attitudes toward charter review. Includes several appen-
> dixes, including a chronology of the development of the United
> Nations and a list of references to nonofficial sources.

SCHEDULE OF INTERNATIONAL CONFERENCES. Washington, D.C.: Office
of International Conferences, Department of State, 1963-- . Quarterly.

> A chronological listing of international conferences and sessions of
> agencies of international organizations which the United States in-
> tends to attend. Each quarterly issue covers a six month period,
> with conferences and sessions listed chronologically for each month,
> giving the name of the conference or agency, the place of meet-
> ing, and the possible dates of the session. Published largely for
> planning purposes.

UNITED STATES CONTRIBUTIONS TO INTERNATIONAL ORGANIZATIONS.
Washington, D.C.: Government Printing Office, 1953-- . Annual.

> Contains an introduction, a descriptive analysis of the contributions
> of states to individual international organizations--global, regional,
> and bipartite--with commentary on budgetary and financial deli-
> berations and action, supplemented with summary tables.

U.S. PARTICIPATION IN THE UN: REPORT BY THE PRESIDENT TO THE
CONGRESS FOR THE YEAR ----. Washington, D.C.: Government Printing
Office, 1945-- . Annual.

> Describes the work of the United Nations throughout the calendar
> year and the policy and position of the U.S. government in its
> various organs, specialized agencies, and subsidiary administrative
> units. Generally includes sections on political and security mat-
> ters, economic and social affairs, dependent territories, legal de-
> velopments, and budgetary and administrative problems. Includes
> in appendixes, key documents, a description of the various units
> of the United Nations, a brief statement on and members of U.S.
> missions, and, in earlier reports, also a selected list of United
> Nations documents and publications.

VOTES AT (number of session) LAST REGULAR SESSION OF THE GENERAL AS-
SEMBLY. Prepared by Bureau of International Organization Affairs, Department
of State. Washington, D.C.: Government Printing Office, 1946-- . Annual.

A list of roll-call votes of each session of the General Assembly
of the United Nations.

Individual Conference Reports

The following are reports on individual conferences and meetings, published by
the Department of State unless otherwise noted, largely since World War I.
Arrangement is chronological within each subsection.

GENERAL PEACE, CONSTITUTIVE, AND GLOBAL CONFERENCES

PROCEEDINGS AND DOCUMENTS OF THE UNITED NATIONS MONETARY
AND FINANCIAL CONFERENCE, BRETTON WOODS, NEW HAMPSHIRE,
JULY 1-22, 1944. 2 vols. Washington, D.C.: Government Printing Office,
1948.

PROCEEDINGS OF THE INTERNATIONAL CIVIL AVIATION CONFERENCE,
CHICAGO, ILLINOIS, NOVEMBER 1-DECEMBER 7, 1944. Washington, D.C.:
Government Printing Office, 1948-49.

THE UNITED NATIONS CONFERENCE ON INTERNATIONAL ORGANIZATION,
SAN FRANCISCO, CALIFORNIA, APRIL 25 TO JUNE 26, 1945: SELECTED
DOCUMENTS. Washington, D.C.: Government Printing Office, 1946. 992 p.

CHARTER OF THE UNITED NATIONS: REPORT TO THE PRESIDENT ON THE
RESULTS OF THE SAN FRANCISCO CONFERENCE, BY THE CHAIRMAN OF
THE UNITED STATES DELEGATION, THE SECRETARY OF STATE, JUNE 26,
1945. Washington, D.C.: GOVERNMENT PRINTING OFFICE, 1945. 226 p.

INTERNATIONAL HEALTH CONFERENCE, NEW YORK, N.Y., JUNE 19 TO
JULY 22, 1946: REPORT OF THE UNITED STATES DELEGATION, INCLUDING
THE FINAL ACT AND RELATED DOCUMENTS. Washington, D.C.: Govern-
ment Printing Office, 1947. 145 p.

MAKING THE PEACE TREATIES, 1941-1947. Washington, D.C.: Government
Printing Office, 1947. 150 p.

PARIS PEACE CONFERENCE, 1946: SELECTED DOCUMENTS. Compiled by
Velma H. Cassidy. Washington, D.C.: Government Printing Office, 1947.
1442 p.

INTERNATIONAL TELECOMMUNICATION CONFERENCES, ATLANTIC CITY,
NEW JERSEY, MAY-OCTOBER, 1947. Washington, D.C.: Government Printing Office, 1948. 192 p.

INTERNATIONAL CONFERENCE ON SAFETY OF LIFE AT SEA, APRIL 23-JUNE
10, 1948. Washington, D.C.: Government Printing Office, 1948. 201 p.

CONFERENCE FOR THE CONCLUSION AND SIGNATURE OF THE TREATY OF PEACE WITH JAPAN, SAN FRANCISCO, CALIFORNIA, SEPTEMBER 4-8, 1951: RECORD OF PROCEEDINGS. Washington, D.C.: Government Printing Office, 1951. 468 p.

THE CONFERENCE ON ANTARCTICA, WASHINGTON, OCTOBER 15-DECEMBER 1, 1959: CONFERENCE DOCUMENTS, THE ANTARCTIC TREATY, AND RELATED PAPERS. Washington, D.C.: Government Printing Office, 1960. 78 p.

UNITED NATIONS CONFERENCE ON DIPLOMATIC INTERCOURSE AND IMMUNITIES, VIENNA, AUSTRIA, MARCH 2-APRIL 14, 1961. Washington, D.C.: Government Printing Office, 1962. 65 p.

GENERAL AGREEMENT ON TARIFFS AND TRADE, ANALYSIS OF UNITED STATES NEGOTIATIONS, 1960-1961 TARIFF CONFERENCE, GENEVA, SWITZERLAND. 3 vols. Washington, D.C.: Government Printing Office, 1962.

SAFEGUARDING OUR WORLD ENVIRONMENT: THE U.N. CONFERENCE ON THE HUMAN ENVIRONMENT, STOCKHOLM, JUNE 1972. Washington, D.C.: Government Printing Office, 1972. 32 p.

STOCKHOLM AND BEYOND, REPORT OF SECRETARY OF STATE'S ADVISORY COMMITTEE ON THE 1972 UNITED NATIONS CONFERENCE ON THE HUMAN ENVIRONMENT. Washington, D.C.: Government Printing Office, 1972. 152 p.

INTER-AMERICAN CONFERENCES AND MEETINGS

INTER-AMERICAN CONFERENCES, 1826-1933: CHRONOLOGICAL AND CLASSIFIED LISTS. Washington, D.C.: Government Printing Office, 1933. 34 p.

REPORT OF THE DELEGATES OF THE UNITED STATES OF AMERICA TO THE SEVENTH INTERNATIONAL CONFERENCE OF AMERICAN STATES, MONTEVIDEO, URUGUAY, DECEMBER 3-26, 1933. Washington, D.C.: Government Printing Office, 1934. 346 p.

REPORT OF THE DELEGATION OF THE UNITED STATES OF AMERICA TO THE INTER-AMERICAN CONFERENCE FOR THE MAINTENANCE OF PEACE, BUENOS AIRES, ARGENTINA, December 1-23, 1936. Washington, D.C.: Government Printing Office, 1937. 280 p.

REPORT OF THE DELEGATION OF THE UNITED STATES OF AMERICA TO THE EIGHTH INTERNATIONAL CONFERENCE OF AMERICAN STATES, LIMA, PERU, DECEMBER 9-27, 1938. Washington, D.C.: Government Printing Office, 1941. 229 p.

CHACO PEACE CONFERENCE: REPORT OF DELEGATION OF UNITED STATES TO PEACE CONFERENCE HELD AT BUENOS AIRES, JULY 1, 1935–January 23, 1939. Washington, D.C.: Government Printing Office, 1940. 198 p.

REPORT OF THE DELEGATE OF THE UNITED STATES OF AMERICA TO THE MEETING OF THE FOREIGN MINISTERS OF THE AMERICAN REPUBLICS, HELD AT PANAMA, SEPTEMBER 23–OCTOBER 3, 1939. Washington, D.C.: Government Printing Office, 1940. 81 p.

SECOND MEETING OF THE MINISTERS OF FOREIGN AFFAIRS OF THE AMERI-CAN REPUBLICS, HABANA, JULY 21–30, 1940: REPORT OF THE SECRETARY OF STATE. Washington, D.C.: Government Printing Office, 1941. 108 p.

REPORT OF THE DELEGATION OF THE UNITED STATES OF AMERICA TO THE INTER-AMERICAN CONFERENCE ON PROBLEMS OF WAR AND PEACE, MEXICO CITY, MEXICO, FEBRUARY 21–MARCH 8, 1945. Washington, D.C.: Government Printing Office, 1946. 371 p.

INTER-AMERICAN CONFERENCE FOR THE MAINTENANCE OF CONTINENTAL PEACE AND SECURITY, QUITANDINHA, BRAZIL, AUGUST 15–SEPTEMBER 2, 1947. Washington, D.C.: Government Printing Office, 1948. 225 p.

NINTH INTERNATIONAL CONFERENCE OF AMERICAN STATES, BOGOTA, COLOMBIA, MARCH 30–MAY 2, 1948. Washington, D.C.: Government Printing Office, 1948. 317 p.

PROCEEDINGS OF THE INTER-AMERICAN CONFERENCE ON CONSERVATION OF RENEWABLE NATURAL RESOURCES, DENVER, COLORADO, SEPTEMBER 7–20, 1948. Washington, D.C.: Government Printing Office, 1949. 782 p.

FOURTH MEETING OF CONSULTATION OF MINISTERS OF FOREIGN AFFAIRS OF AMERICAN STATES, WASHINGTON, D.C., MARCH 26–APRIL 7, 1951: REPORT OF THE SECRETARY OF STATE. Washington, D.C.: Government Printing Office, 1953. 88 p.

TENTH INTER-AMERICAN CONFERENCE, CARACAS, VENEZUELA, MARCH 1–28, 1954. Washington, D.C.: Government Printing Office, 1955. 221 p.

ALIANZA PARA EL PROGRESO--THE RECORD OF PUNTA DEL ESTE. Washing-ton, D.C.: Pan American Union and United States, Agency for International Development, 1961. 40 p.

> Contains documents published following a Special Meeting of the Inter-American Economic and Social Council, held at the ministerial level at Punta del Este, Uruguay, August 5–17, 1961.

OTHER CONFERENCES AND MEETINGS

Also see materials cited in section on summit diplomacy in chapter 7, and FOREIGN RELATIONS volumes on World War II summit conferences listed above, p. 554.

CONFERENCE ON THE LIMITATION OF ARMAMENTS, WASHINGTON, NOVEMBER 12, 1921-FEBRUARY 6, 1922. Washington, D.C.: Government Printing Office, 1922. 1,757 p.

CONFERENCE ON THE LIMITATION OF ARMAMENT, SUBCOMMITTEES, WASHINGTON, NOVEMBER 12, 1921-FEBRUARY 6, 1922. Washington, D.C.: Government Printing Office, 1922. 747 p.

Companion to the preceding entry. Basic documentation in both.

PROCEEDINGS OF LONDON NAVAL CONFERENCE OF 1930, AND SUPPLE-MENTARY DOCUMENTS. Washington, D.C.: Government Printing Office, 1931. 306 p.

THE LONDON NAVAL CONFERENCE, 1935: REPORT OF THE DELEGATES OF THE UNITED STATES OF AMERICA, TEXT OF THE LONDON NAVAL TREATY OF 1936, AND OTHER DOCUMENTS. Washington, D.C.: Government Printing Office, 1936. 444 p.

CONFERENCE OF BRUSSELS, NOVEMBER 3-24, 1937, CONVENED IN VIRTUE OF ARTICLE 7 OF NINE-POWER TREATY OF WASHINGTON OF 1922. Washington, D.C.: Government Printing Office, 1938. 82 p.

THE BERLIN CRISIS: A REPORT ON THE MOSCOW DISCUSSIONS, 1948. Washington, D.C.: Government Printing Office, 1948. 61 p.

FOREIGN MINISTERS MEETING: BERLIN DISCUSSION, JANUARY 25-FEBRU-ARY 18, 1954. Washington, D.C.: Government Printing Office, 1954. 241 p.

THE KOREAN PROBLEM AT THE GENEVA CONFERENCE, APRIL 26-JUNE 15, 1954. Washington, D.C.: Government Printing Office, 1954. 193 p.

THE BANGKOK CONFERENCE OF THE MANILA PACT POWERS, FEBRUARY 23-25, 1955. Washington, D.C.: Government Printing Office, 1955. 46 p.

THE GENEVA CONFERENCE OF HEADS OF GOVERNMENT, JULY 18-23, 1955. Washington, D.C.: Government Printing Office, 1955. 88 p.

Contains documents relating to Germany, European security, dis-armament, and contacts between East and West.

THE GENEVA MEETING OF FOREIGN MINISTERS, OCTOBER 27-NOVEMBER

16, 1955. Washington, D.C.: Government Printing Office, 1955. 307 p.

A follow-up meeting to the heads of government conference, referred to in the preceding entry.

NORTH ATLANTIC TREATY ORGANIZATION MEETING OF HEADS OF GOVERNMENT, PARIS, DECEMBER 1957. Washington, D.C.: Government Printing Office, 1958. 117 p.

FOREIGN MINISTERS MEETING, MAY–AUGUST 1959, GENEVA. Washington, D.C.: Government Printing Office, 1959. 603 p.

BACKGROUND OF HEADS OF GOVERNMENT CONFERENCE, 1960: PRINCIPAL DOCUMENTS, 1955–1959, WITH NARRATIVE SUMMARY. Washington, D.C.: Government Printing Office, 1960. 478 p.

EVENTS INCIDENT TO THE SUMMIT CONFERENCE. Hearings. 86th Cong., 2d sess., May 27, June 1–2, 1960. Washington, D.C.: Government Printing Office, 1960. 302 p.

Contains statements by the secretary of state and other officials, a chronology of the U-2 incident, and background documents.

GENEVA CONFERENCE ON THE DISCONTINUANCE OF NUCLEAR WEAPON TESTS: HISTORY AND ANALYSIS OF NEGOTIATIONS. Washington, D.C.: Government Printing Office, 1961. 641 p.

Contains analysis and documents.

INTERNATIONAL NEGOTIATIONS ON ENDING NUCLEAR WEAPON TESTS, SEPTEMBER 1961–SEPTEMBER 1962. Washington, D.C.: Government Printing Office, for the United States Arms Control and Disarmament Agency, 1962. 333 p.

THE WASHINGTON SUMMIT: GENERAL SECRETARY BREZHNEV'S VISIT TO THE UNITED STATES, JUNE 18–25, 1973. Washington, D.C.: Government Printing Office, 1973. 63 p.

CONFERENCE ON SECURITY AND COOPERATION IN EUROPE: FINAL ACT, HELSINKI, 1975. Washington, D.C.: Government Printing Office, 1975. 27 p.

ECONOMIC, SOCIAL, CULTURAL, AND ENVIRONMENTAL AFFAIRS

The following are selected official publications concerning cultural, economic, environmental, and social affairs. Additional, largely unofficial materials on these matters are provided in several sections of chapter 17. Also of importance as resources are the periodic reports to Congress of the Agency for International Development and other relevant departments and administrative agencies.

COMMUNICATING FOR UNDERSTANDING. Washington, D.C.: Government Printing Office, 1947-- . Irregular.

Issued under various titles. Concerns the Department of State's international educational and cultural exchange program.

CULTURAL RELATIONS PROGRAMS OF THE DEPARTMENT OF STATE. Washington, D.C.: Government Printing Office, 1976-- . Irregular.

Two volumes have been published in this series, titled AMERICA'S CULTURAL EXPERIMENT IN CHINA, 1942-1949, 233 p. and INTER-AMERICAN BEGINNINGS OF U.S. CULTURAL DIPLOMACY, 1936-1948, 365 p.

FOR FREE MEN IN A FREE WORLD: A SURVEY OF HUMAN RIGHTS IN THE UNITED STATES. Washington, D.C.: Government Printing Office, 1969. 249 p.

Provides a commentary on each of the thirty articles of the Universal Declaration of Human Rights, with respect to the progress made in the United States.

HUMAN RIGHTS. Washington, D.C.: Government Printing Office, 1977. 29 p.

A collection of seven documents.

HUMAN RIGHTS: UNFOLDING OF THE AMERICAN TRADITION. Washington, D.C.: Government Printing Office, 1968. 127 p.

Includes excerpts from documents and statements that underlie the American tradition of human rights.

HUMAN RIGHTS CONDITIONS IN SELECTED COUNTRIES AND THE U.S. RESPONSE. Prepared by the Foreign Affairs and National Defense Division, Congressional Research Service, U.S. Library of Congress. Committee Print 95th Cong., 2d sess. Washington, D.C.: Government Printing Office, 1978. 372 p.

HUMAN RIGHTS IN THE INTERNATIONAL COMMUNITY AND IN U.S. FOREIGN POLICY, 1945-76. 95th Cong., 1st sess. Washington, D.C.: Government Printing Office, 1977. 58 p.

INTERNATIONAL EDUCATIONAL AND CULTURAL EXCHANGE: A HUMAN CONTRIBUTION TO THE STRUCTURE OF PEACE. Washington, D.C.: Government Printing Office, 1974. 44 p.

LANDMARKS IN THE HISTORY OF THE CULTURAL RELATIONS PROGRAM OF THE DEPARTMENT OF STATE, 1938 TO 1976. Compiled by J. Manuel Espinosa. Washington, D.C.: Government Printing Office, 1976. 26 p.

THE STATUS OF HUMAN RIGHTS IN SELECTED COUNTRIES AND THE U.S. RESPONSE. Prepared by the Foreign Affairs and National Defense Division, Congressional Research Service, U.S. Library of Congress. Committee print, 95th Cong., 1st sess. Washington, D.C.: Government Printing Office, 1977. 79 p.

TECHNOLOGY AND FOREIGN AFFAIRS. Washington, D.C.: Government Printing Office, 1976. 335 p.

> A report, prepared by T. Keith Glennan, to Deputy Secretary of State Charles W. Robinson. Focuses on the work of the Department's Bureau of Oceans and International Environmental and Scientific Affairs.

U.S. OVERSEAS LOANS AND GRANTS AND ASSISTANCE FROM INTERNATIONAL ORGANIZATIONS: OBLIGATIONS AND LOAN AUTHORIZATION. Washington, D.C.: Government Printing Office, 1964-- . Annual.

> A statistical report prepared by AID for the use of congressional committees primarily concerned with foreign aid. Presents dollar value of all U.S. economic and military assistance, tabulated by country and itemized by program and fiscal year, from July 1945 to the end of the current fiscal year.

For additional guidance to resources on documentation respecting human rights, consult:

CHECKLIST OF HUMAN RIGHTS DOCUMENTS. Austin: School of Law, University of Texas, 1976-- . Monthly.

> A bibliography produced by the Tarlton Law Library, providing listings of human rights documents and treaties concerned with human rights, arranged by countries and organizations.

ARMS CONTROL AND DISARMAMENT

Unless otherwise noted, the following materials have generally been produced by the Department of State through 1960, and thereafter by the U.S. Arms Control and Disarmament Agency.

ARMS CONTROL AND DISARMAMENT: A QUARTERLY BIBLIOGRAPHY WITH ABSTRACTS AND ANNOTATIONS. Washington, D.C.: Arms Control and Disarmament Bibliography Section, U.S. Library of Congress, 1964-73. Quarterly.

> Lists current literature in English, French, German, and Russian.

ARMS CONTROL AND DISARMAMENT AGREEMENTS: TEXTS AND HISTORY OF NEGOTIATIONS. Washington, D.C.: Government Printing Office, 1975. 159 p.

ARMS CONTROL REPORT. Washington, D.C.: Government Printing Office, 1976. 73 p.

DISARMAMENT AND SECURITY: A COLLECTION OF DOCUMENTS, 1919–1955. Washington, D.C.: Legislative Reference Service, U.S. Library of Congress, 1956. 1035 p.

> Issued by U.S. Congress, Senate, Foreign Relations Committee, 84th Cong., 2d sess. Committee Print.

DISARMAMENT IN OUTLINE: CHECK LISTS OF PRINCIPAL DEVELOPMENTS, 1945–1960. Washington, D.C.: Government Printing Office, 1960. 148 p.

DOCUMENTS ON DISARMAMENT, 1945–1959. 2 vols. Washington, D.C.: Government Printing Office, 1960.

> Prepared by the Department of State.

DOCUMENTS ON DISARMAMENT, 1960-- . Washington, D.C.: Government Printing Office, 1960-- . Annual.

> The volume for 1960 prepared by the Department of State, and subsequent volumes prepared by the U.S. Arms Control and Disarmament Agency.

INTERNATIONAL CONTROL OF ATOMIC ENERGY: GROWTH OF A POLICY. Washington, D.C.: Government Printing Office, 1946. 281 p.

INTERNATIONAL CONTROL OF ATOMIC ENERGY: POLICY AT THE CROSSROADS. Washington, D.C.: Government Printing Office, 1948. 251 p.

REVIEW OF INTERNATIONAL NEGOTIATIONS ON THE CESSATION OF NUCLEAR WEAPON TESTS, SEPTEMBER 1962-SEPTEMBER 1965. Washington, D.C.: Government Printing Office, 1966. 103 p.

U.S. ARMS CONTROL AND DISARMAMENT AGENCY ANNUAL REPORT TO THE CONGRESS. Washington, D.C.: Government Printing Office, 1962-- . Annual.

> Describes the activities of the Arms Control and Disarmament Agency for the preceding year.

WORLD MILITARY EXPENDITURES AND ARMS TRANSFERS. Washington, D.C.: Government Printing Office, 1966-- . Annual.

> Title varies. Recent issues have been cumulative for the ten years preceding publication.

Additional guidance to disarmament literature may be found in the following:

United Nations. Secretariat. DISARMAMENT: A SELECTED BIBLIOGRAPHY, 1962-1964. New York: United Nations, 1965. 95 p.

U.S. Department of the Army. DISARMAMENT: A BIBLIOGRAPHIC RECORD, 1916-1960. Prepared by the Office of Special Assistant to the Joint Chiefs of Staff for Disarmament Affairs. Washington, D.C.: Government Printing Office, 1960.

The following periodical may be of use for contemporary official information concerning arms control and disarmament:

U.S. ARMS CONTROL AND DISARMAMENT AGENCY. Washington, D.C.: U.S. Arms Control and Disarmament Agency, 1961-- . Irregular.

> A series of individual, unnumbered but dated statements issued by the Arms Control and Disarmament Agency. Short, usually four or more pages, either processed or printed, containing policy statements and analyses, speeches, releases, and the like.

GEOGRAPHIC AREA MATERIALS

The following are illustrations of the substantial quantity of materials produced by the Department of State and other government agencies concerned with particular geographic areas and foreign countries. Unless otherwise noted, they are the products of the Department of State. Arrangement is by general geographic area, and alphabetical thereunder.

American Republics

AMERICAN-MEXICAN CLAIMS COMMISSION: REPORT TO THE SECRETARY OF STATE. Washington, D.C.: Government Printing Office, 1948. 676 p.

BOUNDARIES OF THE LATIN AMERICAN REPUBLICS: AN ANNOTATED LIST OF DOCUMENTS, 1493-1943. Compiled by Alexander Marchant. Washington, D.C.: Government Printing Office, 1944. 386 p.

A CASE HISTORY OF COMMUNIST PENETRATION--GUATEMALA. Washington, D.C.: Government Printing Office, 1957. 73 p.

INTER-AMERICAN EFFORTS TO RELIEVE INTERNATIONAL TENSIONS IN THE WESTERN HEMISPHERE, 1959-1960. Washington, D.C.: Government Printing Office, 1962. 410 p.

MEMORANDUM ON THE MONROE DOCTRINE. Prepared by J. Reuben Clark. Washington, D.C.: Government Printing Office, 1930. 236 p.

An historic, basic policy paper on the Monroe Doctrine, redefining official U.S. policy.

OUR SOUTHERN PARTNERS: THE STORY OF INTER-AMERICAN COOPERATION. Washington, D.C.: Government Printing Office, 1962. 59 p.

PEACE, BUENOS AIRES, ARGENTINA, DECEMBER 1-23, 1936. Washington, D.C.: Government Printing Office, 1937. 280 p.

U.S. POLICY TOWARD LATIN AMERICA: RECOGNITION AND NON-RECOGNITION OF GOVERNMENTS AND INTERRUPTIONS IN DIPLOMATIC RELATIONS, 1933-1974. Washington, D.C.: Government Printing Office, 1975. 116 p.

Europe

AID TO GREECE AND TURKEY: A COLLECTION OF STATE PAPERS. Washington, D.C.: Government Printing Office, 1947. 83 p.

DOCUMENTS ON GERMAN UNITY. 4 vols. Frankfurt, Germany: Office of the U.S. High Commissioner for Germany (HICOG), 1951-53.

GERMANY, 1947-1949: THE STORY IN DOCUMENTS. Compiled by Velma H. Cassidy. Washington, D.C.: Government Printing Office, 1950. 631 p.

OCCUPATION OF GERMANY: POLICY AND PROGRESS. Washington, D.C.: Government Printing Office, 1947. 241 p.

SOVIET SUPPLY PROTOCOLS: WARTIME INTERNATIONAL AGREEMENTS. Washington, D.C.: Government Printing Office, 1947. 156 p.

TRIAL OF THE MAJOR WAR CRIMINALS BEFORE THE INTERNATIONAL MILITARY TRIBUNAL, NUREMBERG, 14 NOVEMBER 1945-1 OCTOBER 1946. 42 vols. Nuremberg, Germany: Secretariat of the Tribunal under the jurisdiction of the Allied Control Authority for Germany, 1947-49.

TRIAL OF WAR CRIMINALS BEFORE THE NUREMBERG MILITARY TRIBUNALS, UNDER CONTROL COUNCIL LAW NO. 10, NUREMBERG, OCTOBER 1946-APRIL 1949. 15 vols. Washington, D.C.: Office of the Judge Advocate General, Department of the Army, 1949-53.

U.S. Congress. Senate. Committee on Foreign Relations. DOCUMENTS ON GERMANY, 1944-1970. Prepared by the Historical Office of the Department of State. 92d Cong., 1st sess. Rev. ed. Washington, D.C.: Government Printing Office, 1971. 897 p.

U.S. Department of State. Office of United States Chief of Counsel for Prosecution of Axis Criminality. NAZI CONSPIRACY AND AGGRESSION. 8 vols. plus supplements. Washington, D.C.: Government Printing Office, 1946-48.

Special Studies on Germany (High Commission Period)

The Historical Division of the Office of the U.S. High Commissioner for Germany (HICOG), as an adjunct of the Historical Office of the Department of State, published a series of monographs on German affairs. These were published in Mehlem/Bad Godesberg, Germany, during the period 1951-53. These are listed, with tables of contents and with historical commentary on the project, in the following, which is one of the series:

Lee, Guy A. GUIDE TO STUDIES OF THE HISTORICAL DIVISION, OFFICE OF THE U.S. HIGH COMMISSIONER FOR GERMANY. 1953. 131 p.

The following list of these monographs is arranged according to major functional subjects:

ORGANIZATION

Gillen, J.F.J. THE EMPLOYMENT OF GERMAN NATIONALS BY THE OFFICE OF THE U.S. HIGH COMMISSIONER FOR GERMANY. 1952. 118 p.

Lee, Guy A. THE ESTABLISHMENT OF THE OFFICE OF THE U.S. HIGH COMMISSIONER FOR GERMANY. 1951. 92 p.

_____. FIELD ORGANIZATION OF THE OFFICE OF THE U.S. HIGH COMMISSIONER FOR GERMANY, 1949-1951. 1952. 138 p.

_____. "The Organization of the Office of the U.S. High Commissioner for Germany, 1949-1952, With Special Reference to Planning for Embassy Status." Mimeographed. 1953. 215 p.

_____, ed. DOCUMENTS ON FIELD ORGANIZATION OF THE OFFICE OF THE U.S. HIGH COMMISSIONER FOR GERMANY, 1949-1951. 1952. 70 p.

Plischke, Elmer. THE ALLIED HIGH COMMISSION FOR GERMANY. 1953. 215 p.

_____. HISTORY OF THE ALLIED HIGH COMMISSION FOR GERMANY: ITS ESTABLISHMENT, STRUCTURE, AND PROCEDURES. 1951. 122 p.

POLITICAL AFFAIRS

Gillen, J.F.J. STATE AND LOCAL GOVERNMENT IN WEST GERMANY, 1945-1953, WITH SPECIAL REFERENCE TO THE U.S. ZONE AND BREMEN. 1953. 131 p.

Plischke, Elmer. ALLIED HIGH COMMISSION RELATIONS WITH THE WEST GERMAN GOVERNMENT. 1952. 209 p.

_____. REVISION OF THE OCCUPATION STATUTE FOR GERMANY. 1952. 95 p.

_____. THE WEST GERMAN FEDERAL GOVERNMENT. 1952. 182 p.

ECONOMIC AFFAIRS

Baldy, Francis H. "Chronological Record: Reorganization of the West German Coal and Iron and Steel Industries Under Allied High Commission Law No. 27." Mimeographed. 1952. 260 p.

Brauer, Anna C. "The German Housing Program and U.S. Aid." Mimeographed. 1953. 292 p.

Gillen, J.F.J. "Deconcentration and Decartelization in West Germany, 1945-1953." Mimeographed. 1953. 126 p.

_____. LABOR PROBLEMS IN WEST GERMANY WITH SPECIAL REFERENCE TO THE POLICIES AND PROGRAMS OF THE OFFICE OF LABOR AFFAIRS OF THE OFFICE OF THE U.S. HIGH COMMISSIONER FOR GERMANY. 1952. 119 p.

Loehr, Rodney C. THE WEST GERMAN BANKING SYSTEM. 1952. 126 p.

Schmidt, Hubert G. FOOD AND AGRICULTURAL PROGRAMS IN WEST GERMANY, 1949-1951. 1952. 202 p.

_____. THE LIBERALIZATION OF WEST GERMAN FOREIGN TRADE, 1949-1951. 1952. 124 p.

_____. "Reorganization of the West German Coal and Iron and Steel Industries Under the Allied High Commission for Germany, 1949-1952." Mimeographed. 1952. 204 p.

_____, ed. "Documents on the Reorganization of the West German Coal and Iron and Steel Industries Under the Allied High Commission for Germany, 1949-1952." Mimeographed. 1952. 113 p.

PUBLIC AFFAIRS

Gillen, J.F.J. THE SPECIAL PROJECTS PROGRAM OF THE OFFICE OF THE U.S. HIGH COMMISSIONER FOR GERMANY. 1952. 76 p.

McClaskey, Beryl R. THE HISTORY OF THE U.S. POLICY AND PROGRAM IN THE FIELD OF RELIGIOUS AFFAIRS UNDER THE OFFICE OF THE U.S. HIGH COMMISSIONER FOR GERMANY. 1951. 107 p.

Pilgert, Henry P. COMMUNITY AND GROUP LIFE IN WEST GERMANY WITH SPECIAL REFERENCE TO THE POLICIES AND PROGRAMS OF THE OFFICE OF THE U.S. HIGH COMMISSIONER FOR GERMANY. 1952. 91 p.

_____. THE EXCHANGE OF PERSONS PROGRAM IN WESTERN GERMANY. 1951. 89 p.

_____. THE HISTORY OF THE DEVELOPMENT OF INFORMATION SERVICES THROUGH INFORMATION CENTERS AND DOCUMENTARY FILMS. 1951. 86 p.

_____. PRESS, RADIO AND FILM IN WEST GERMANY, 1945-1953. 1953. 123 p.

_____. THE WEST GERMAN EDUCATIONAL SYSTEM WITH SPECIAL REFERENCE TO THE POLICIES AND PROGRAMS OF THE OFFICE OF THE U.S. HIGH COMMISSIONER FOR GERMANY. 1953. 136 p.

_____. WOMEN IN WEST GERMANY WITH SPECIAL REFERENCE TO THE POLICIES AND PROGRAMS OF THE WOMEN'S AFFAIRS BRANCH, OFFICE OF PUBLIC AFFAIRS, OFFICE OF THE U.S. HIGH COMMISSIONER FOR GERMANY. 1952. 72 p.

BERLIN

Plischke, Elmer. BERLIN: DEVELOPMENT OF ITS GOVERNMENT AND AD-MINISTRATION. 1952. 257 p.

Plischke, Elmer, and Pilgert, Henry P. "U.S. Information Programs in Berlin." Mimeographed. 1953. 108 p.

Schmidt, Hubert G. ECONOMIC ASSISTANCE TO WEST BERLIN, 1949-1951. 1952. 135 p.

OTHERS

Korman, John G. "U.S. Denazification Policy in Germany, 1944-1950." Multilithed. 1952. 153 p.

McClaskey, Beryl R. THE FREE GERMAN YOUTH AND THE DEUTSCHLAND-TREFFEN: A CASE STUDY OF SOVIET TACTICS. 1951. 171 p.

Far East and Pacific

AGGRESSION FROM THE NORTH--THE RECORD OF NORTH VIET-NAM'S CAMPAIGN TO CONQUER SOUTH VIET-NAM. Washington, D.C.: Government Printing Office, 1965. 64 p.

Blakeslee, George Hubbard. THE FAR EASTERN COMMISSION: A STUDY IN INTERNATIONAL COOPERATION, 1945 TO 1952. Washington, D.C.: Government Printing Office, 1954. 240 p.

CHINESE COMMUNIST WORLD OUTLOOK: A HANDBOOK OF CHINESE COMMUNIST STATEMENTS: THE PUBLIC RECORD OF A MILITANT IDEOLOGY. Washington, D.C.: Government Printing Office, 1962. 139 p.

DOCUMENTATION ON THE VIET-NAM AGREEMENT. Washington, D.C.: Government Printing Office, 1973.' 36 p.

> Contains an address by President Nixon, a news conference of Henry Kissinger, and the text of the agreement and protocols.

A HISTORICAL SUMMARY OF UNITED STATES-KOREAN RELATIONS, WITH A CHRONOLOGY OF IMPORTANT DEVELOPMENTS, 1834-1962. Washington, D.C.: Government Printing Office, 1962. 138 p.

INTERNATIONAL MILITARY TRIBUNAL FOR THE FAR EAST [RECORD OF PROCEEDINGS]. Washington, D.C.: Department of State, n.d. 49,858 p.

> Sets available at the National Archives, the Library of Congress, and a few academic institutions. An index to the "Transcript of Proceedings" provided in Paul S. Dull and Michael Takaaki Umemura, THE TOKYO TRIALS: A FUNCTIONAL INDEX TO THE PROCEEDINGS OF THE INTERNATIONAL MILITARY TRIBUNAL FOR THE FAR EAST (Occasional Papers, no. 6. Ann Arbor: University of Michigan Press, 1957, 94 p.). A general guide to this compilation provided by Solis Horwitz, THE TOKYO TRIAL (No. 465. New York: Carnegie Endowment for International Peace, 1950, 112 p.).

KOREA, 1945 TO 1948. Washington, D.C.: Government Printing Office, 1950. 124 p.

JAPAN: FREE WORLD ALLY. Washington, D.C.: Government Printing Office, 1957. 55 p.

MANCHURIA: REPORT OF COMMISSION OF ENQUIRY APPOINTED BY LEAGUE OF NATIONS. Washington, D.C.: Government Printing Office, 1932. 148 p.

NORTH KOREA: A CASE STUDY IN THE TECHNIQUES OF TAKEOVER. Washington, D.C.: Government Printing Office, 1961. 121 p.

Report of a Department of State research mission sent to Korea in October 1950, to study conditions prior to June 1950.

OCCUPATION OF JAPAN: POLICY AND PROGRESS. Washington, D.C.: Government Printing Office, 1946. 173 p.

POLITICAL REORIENTATION OF JAPAN, SEPTEMBER 1945 TO SEPTEMBER 1948: REPORT OF GOVERNMENT SECTION, SUPREME COMMANDER FOR THE ALLIED POWERS. 2 vols. Washington, D.C.: Government Printing Office, 1949.

Contains reports and documents on the control of Japanese external affairs and on various aspects of government and political affairs.

THE RECORD ON KOREAN UNIFICATION, 1943-1960: NARRATIVE SUMMARY WITH PRINCIPAL DOCUMENTS. Washington, D.C.: Government Printing Office, 1960. 241 p.

THE REPUBLIC OF CHINA. Washington, D.C.: Government Printing Office, 1959. 63 p.

SOUTHEAST ASIA: BUILDING THE BASES. Washington, D.C.: Government Printing Office, 1975. 484 p.

Provides the history of the construction of American military bases in Southeast Asia during the Vietnam conflict.

A THREAT TO THE PEACE--NORTH VIET-NAM'S EFFORT TO CONQUER SOUTH VIET-NAM. 2 parts. Washington, D.C.: Government Printing Office, 1961. 53 p., 102 p.

TRUST TERRITORY OF THE PACIFIC ISLANDS, ----. Washington, D.C.: Government Printing Office, 1948-- . Annual.

Published by the Department of the Navy, 1948-1951; the Department of the interior, 1952-1953; and the Department of State since 1954.

U.S. Congress. Joint Committee on the Investigation of the Pearl Harbor Attack. PEARL HARBOR ATTACK. Hearings. 79th Cong., 1st sess. 39 Parts. Washington, D.C.: Government Printing Office, 1946.

U.S. Congress. Senate. Committee on Foreign Relations. BACKGROUND IN-
FORMATION RELATING TO SOUTHEAST ASIA AND VIETNAM. Rev. ed.
93d Cong., 2d sess. Washington, D.C.: Government Printing Office, 1974.
455 p.

Includes a summary of events in Southeast Asia (1948–73) and official documents on United States–Vietnam relations (1950–74).

UNITED STATES POLICY IN THE KOREAN CONFLICT, JULY 1950–FEBRUARY
1951. Washington, D.C.: Government Printing Office, 1951. 52 p.

UNITED STATES POLICY IN THE KOREAN CRISIS, 1950. Washington, D.C.:
Government Printing Office, 1950. 68 p.

UNITED STATES RELATIONS WITH CHINA, WITH SPECIAL REFERENCE TO
THE PERIOD 1944–1949. Washington, D.C.: Government Printing Office,
1949. 1054 p.

A special publication prepared by the Department of State and
submitted by the president to Congress. Consists of a record of
the five crucial years preceding the communist takeover in China,
pages 1–409, supplemented with a chronology of principal events
appearing at the front of the volume and the texts of some 186
documents, pages 413–1054.

Africa, Middle East, and South Asia

AFRICA AND THE UNITED STATES—IMAGES AND REALITIES: BACKGROUND
BOOK, 8TH NATIONAL CONFERENCE, U.S. NATIONAL COMMISSION FOR
UNESCO, BOSTON, OCTOBER 22–26, 1961. Washington, D.C.: Govern-
ment Printing Office, 1962. 212 p.

AFRICAN PROGRAMS OF U.S. ORGANIZATIONS. Washington, D.C.: Government Printing Office, 1965. 132 p.

A selective directory describing African programs of more than
seven hundred American nongovernmental organizations and institutions.

Howard, Harry N. THE DEVELOPMENT OF UNITED STATES POLICY IN THE
NEAR EAST, 1945–1951. Washington, D.C.: Government Printing Office,
1952. 15 p.

THE SUBCONTINENT OF SOUTH ASIA: AFGHANISTAN, CEYLON, INDIA,
NEPAL, PAKISTAN. Rev. ed. Washington, D.C.: Government Printing Office, 1962. 76 p.

THE SUEZ CANAL PROBLEM, JULY 26–SEPTEMBER 22, 1956. Washington,
D.C.: Government Printing Office, 1956. 370 p.

U.S. POLICY IN THE MIDDLE EAST: SELECTED DOCUMENTS, DECEMBER 1973-NOVEMBER 1974. Washington, D.C.: Government Printing Office, 1975. 35 p.

U.S. POLICY IN THE MIDDLE EAST: SELECTED DOCUMENTS, NOVEMBER 1974-FEBRUARY 1976. 1976. 126 p.

UNITED STATES POLICY IN THE MIDDLE EAST, SEPTEMBER 1956-MAY 1957: DOCUMENTS. Washington, D.C.: Government Printing Office, 1957. 425 p.

Other Areas

SPACE LAW: SELECTED BASIC DOCUMENTS. 94th Cong., 2d sess. Washington, D.C.: Government Printing Office, 1976. 464 p.

> Contains the texts of a series of treaties and agreements concerning outer space, commentary on various matters, the texts of U.S. space legislation and policy, and a list of previous staff reports concerning space activities. Also provides guidance to earlier congressional studies on the subject.

UNITED STATES POLICY AND INTERNATIONAL COOPERATION IN ANTARCTICA. Washington, D.C.: Government Printing Office, 1964. 56 p.

> A message of the president, September 2, 1964, transmitting a report prepared by the Historical Office of the Department of State. House Document, no. 358. 88th Congress, 2d session.

THE UNITED STATES AND THE THIRD WORLD--A DISCUSSION PAPER. Prepared by Ralph Stuart Smith. Washington, D.C.: Government Printing Office, 1976. 65 p.

SELECTED UNOFFICIAL COLLECTIONS OF OFFICIAL DOCUMENTS

This section is comprised largely of a selected list of unofficial compilations and collections of documents concerned with American government, history, and foreign relations. These supplement such materials listed elsewhere in this chapter (as in the section on treaties and agreements); single-volume anthologies, largely intended as textbooks, that are included in chapter 15; and other compilations incorporated elsewhere where they are functionally appropriate. In this section, series of compilations are listed first, followed by individual and ad hoc collections.

DOCUMENTS ON AMERICAN FOREIGN RELATIONS. Various compilers. Boston and later Princeton, N.J.: World Peace Foundation, 1939-51. New York: Harper for Council on Foreign Relations, 1952-- . Annual.

> Arrangement varies, but generally includes sections and subsections

devoted to various aspects of the conduct of foreign relations and to specific geographic areas. Includes such documents as official statements, reports, releases, addresses, legislation, diplomatic communications, treaties and agreements, and similar instruments.

DOCUMENTS ON INTERNATIONAL AFFAIRS. London: Royal Institute of International Affairs, 1933-- . Irregular. Annual, 1947-- .

Includes the texts of treaties and agreements, addresses, diplomatic communications, and similar instruments. Includes subject index.

THE DYNAMICS OF WORLD POWER: A DOCUMENTARY HISTORY OF U.S. FOREIGN POLICY, 1945-1973. Edited by Arthur M. Schlesinger, Jr. 5 vols. New York: Chelsea House, McGraw-Hill, 1973.

A collection of selected, significant documents, including verbatim communiques, letters, speeches, policy papers to and from the president, Congress, military and diplomatic officials, and their world-wide counterparts. Arranged according to major geographic areas and the United Nations.

HISTORIC DOCUMENTS OF ----. Washington, D.C.: Congressional Quarterly, 1972-- . Annual.

Anthology of basic documents on a broad range of topics, including foreign relations. Includes presidential statements, court decisions, commission reports, special studies, and speeches of national and international significance. Some excerpted.

U.S. FOREIGN POLICY DOCUMENTS. Edited by Nicholas O. Berry. 4 vols. Brunswick, Ohio: King's Court Communications, 1978.

A collection of official documents, principally of the executive branch of the government, including addresses, policy statements, memoranda, and treaties and agreements. Covers, in four volumes, the periods 1620-1876, 1877-1932, 1933-63, and 1963-77.

The following are essentially ad hoc compilations of official documents:

Challener, Richard D., ed. UNITED STATES MILITARY INTELLIGENCE, 1917-1927. 30 vols. New York: Garland, 1978.

Especially vols. 1-10, 16-26.

Commager, Henry Steele, ed. DOCUMENTS ON AMERICAN HISTORY. 5th ed. New York: Appleton-Century-Crofts, 1949.

A chronological compilation of fundamental sources to illustrate the course of American history, from the time of the discoveries to the date of publication. Consists of treaties, laws, speeches, court decisions, party platforms, and the like. Includes chronological table of contents and alphabetical subject index.

Etzold, Thomas H., and Gaddis, John Lewis, eds. CONTAINMENT: DOCU-
MENTS ON AMERICAN POLICY AND STRATEGY, 1945-1950. New York:
Columbia University Press, 1978. 512 p.

Hazard, Ebenezer. HISTORICAL COLLECTIONS: CONSISTING OF STATE
PAPERS, AND OTHER AUTHENTIC DOCUMENTS, INTENDED AS MATERIALS
FOR AN HISTORY OF THE UNITED STATES OF AMERICA. 2 vols. Philadel-
phia: T. Dobson for the author, 1792-94.

Keith, Arthur B., ed. SPEECHES AND DOCUMENTS ON INTERNATIONAL
AFFAIRS. 2 vols. New York: Millard, 1938.

> Volume 1 on such matters as the Fourteen Points, Versailles Treaty,
> Washington Conference, Balfour Note, Locarno Pacts, Kellogg-
> Briand Pact, Manchurian crisis, and German rearmament. Volume
> 2 on Austrian relations with Germany and Italy, the Franco-Soviet
> Pact, Italy and Abyssinia, the British Commonwealth, and the pre-
> servation of peace in the inter-World War period. Subject index
> in each volume.

Plischke, Elmer, ed. INTERNATIONAL RELATIONS: BASIC DOCUMENTS.
2d ed. Princeton, N.J.: Van Nostrand, 1962. 194 p.

> Contains 230 basic illustrative documents grouped into eleven chap-
> ters dealing with organization for the conduct of foreign relations;
> diplomatic and consular credentials and immunities; treaty making;
> international conferences; international organizations; the state,
> independence, and recognition; territorial expansion, the seas,
> and airspace; economic and social affairs; international law and
> the resolution of disputes; national security; and international con-
> flict and war. Includes treaties and agreements, reference tables,
> structure and flow charts, diplomatic communications, policy state-
> ments, exchanges of notes, and similar instruments. Illustrates pri-
> marily U.S. experience. Many documents reproduced in facsimile.
> Includes an index.

Snyder, Louis L. FIFTY MAJOR DOCUMENTS OF THE TWENTIETH CENTURY.
New York: Van Nostrand, 1955. 185 p.

> Documents arranged chronologically, including treaties and agree-
> ments, addresses, diplomatic communications, communiques, statutes,
> and the like. A handy pocket volume without index.

Woodrow Wilson Foundation. OFFICIAL DOCUMENTS: TEXTS OF SELECTED
DOCUMENTS ON U.S. FOREIGN POLICY, 1918-1952. New York: 1952.
76 p.

> Contains thirteen selected documents concerned largely with the
> period following World War II, including the Atlantic Charter,
> the United Nations Declaration, Yalta Communique, Potsdam Agree-

ment, Rio Treaty, North Atlantic Treaty, Mutual Defense Treaty with the Philippines, ANZUS Treaty, and the Japanese Security Treaty, together with the League of Nations Covenant and Wilson's Fourteen Points. A pocket-size pamphlet without index.

In addition to the items listed above, the researcher may find the documentary collections published by Documentary Publications, Salisbury, North Carolina, to be useful. More than three dozen individual collections have been produced, some of them consisting of more than a single volume. They are designed to provide selected, basic raw materials which are largely unavailable outside of U.S. archives. Also of value are the collections of documents published by University Publications of America, of Washington, D.C., illustrated by the following.

DOCUMENTS OF THE NATIONAL SECURITY COUNCIL, 1947-1977. 5 reels of microfilm. Washington, D.C.: University Publications of America, 1980.

Includes over five hundred reports and action papers.

O.S.S./STATE DEPARTMENT INTELLIGENCE AND RESEARCH REPORTS. 14 parts. Washington, D.C.: University Publications of America, 1976-79.

Contains over 3,000 reports, arranged by country or geographic area, such as World War II occupied territories, the Middle East, and Latin America. The documents were used as data and analyses for the formulation of foreign policy.

RECORDS OF THE JOINT CHIEFS OF STAFF, 1946-1953. 14 parts. Washington, D.C.: University Publications of America, 1980.

Parts deal with meetings of the Joint Chiefs of Staff, demarcation of strategic areas, military assistance, psychological and nonconventional warfare, industrial mobilization, geographic areas, and the like.

GUIDE FOR REQUESTING U.S. GOVERNMENT DOCUMENTS

A CITIZEN'S GUIDE ON HOW TO USE THE FREEDOM OF INFORMATION ACT AND THE PRIVACY ACT IN REQUESTING GOVERNMENT DOCUMENTS. Washington, D.C.: Government Printing Office, 1977. 59 p.

Part IV

MEMOIRS AND BIOGRAPHICAL LITERATURE

Aside from the historical, descriptive, analytical, theoretical, and assessory literature and other resources on the various aspects of the conduct of American foreign affairs--dealt with in parts I to III--a substantial quantity of biographical and memoir literature, written by and about those involved, affords a wealth of information on the diplomatic relations of the United States. These materials pertain to a broad spectrum of individuals, ranging from top-level policy makers and legislators in Washington to practitioners in remote capitals and consular posts and from the ranking members of the national bureaucracy, presidential special emissaries, and ambassadors to those serving on the staffs of embassies, consulates, and other missions, as well as members of their families. Even though, in both absolute and relative terms, those who publish their papers, journals, or memoirs represent but a fraction of potential, in the aggregate, their publications are quantitatively substantial and qualitatively varied. In addition, their literary contribution is uniquely useful in that they provide a perspective not available in other studies.

Except for the materials that deal with presidents, secretaries of state, and a small corps of other officials who are centrally involved, such resources are often overlooked or ignored by the researcher. In part, this is due to the fact that, except for some principals above the ambassadorial and assistant secretary levels, the production of such literature is largely ad hoc and occasional, depending on the motivation and ability of the individual potential author and the rewards he may expect.

In earlier times these published materials frequently constituted collections of letters, essays, and addresses, together with journals and diaries. Others consisted of autobiographies, memoirs, and reminiscences. In more recent years, the published collection of papers has become exceptional (except for presidents), and the quantity of genuine autobiographies and memoirs has declined. Far more attention, even of retired professional diplomats, has been devoted to policy commentary and analysis, chronicling of events in the foreign relationships of the United States, and assessment of the functioning and place of the United States in world affairs or the role and problems of the Department of State and, more particularly, the Foreign Service. Some memoirs and biographical reviews are scholarly and enlightening contributions, others are largely public relations accounts motivated by visions of literary immortality in the best seller lists, and still others are of the "I-was-there-when" type of recollections. Nevertheless, as a group, these materials provide a rich, diversified, and important resource for the study of American foreign relations.

Chapter 23

AUTOBIOGRAPHIES, BIOGRAPHIES, COMMENTARIES,
DIARIES, AND MEMOIRS

The materials provided in this chapter consist of selected autobiographies,
biographies, reminiscences, memoirs, descriptive and analytical commentaries,
papers, diaries, journals, and collections of letters, essays, and addresses by
and about American statesmen, ambassadors and ministers, consuls, professional
diplomats, members of their families, and other persons connected with U.S.
foreign relations. These materials do not pertain to presidents, members of
Congress, Cabinet members, or military officers--unless they served as diplomats in the field or as secretaries of state--nor do they pertain to the envoys
of other countries accredited to Washington or to foreign statesmen dealing
with the government of the United States and its emissaries. Nor does this
chapter provide reference to the unpublished papers of American diplomats.

Additional guidance may be found in a number of more limited and specialized
bibliographies. Of special historical significance is:

Bemis, Samuel Flagg, and Griffin, Grace Gardner, eds. GUIDE TO THE
DIPLOMATIC HISTORY OF THE UNITED STATES. Washington, D.C.: Government Printing Office, 1935. 979 p.

> Covers the period from the Revolution to 1921. Not strictly a
> bibliography, but a guide to put the user in touch with pertinent
> materials of various types. Bibliographical chapters topically and
> chronologically arranged in part 1. Part 2 on the sources of mate-
> rials, both U.S. and foreign. Indexes to collections of personal
> papers and to the authors cited in appendixes.

Extensive bibliographies of biographical and memoir literature on the secretaries
of state may be found in:

Bemis, Samuel Flagg, ed. THE AMERICAN SECRETARIES OF STATE AND
THEIR DIPLOMACY. 10 vols. New York: Knopf, 1927-29.

> Covers the secretaries of state from the Revolution to Secretary
> Charles Evans Hughes. Includes bibliographies, supplementing
> biographical commentary.

Ferrell, Robert H., ed. AMERICAN SECRETARIES OF STATE AND THEIR DIPLOMACY. New York: Cooper Square, 1963-- . Irregular.

> Supplements and continues the Bemis series listed in the preceding entry. Includes separate volumes, prepared by different authors, dealing with individual secretaries of state, beginning with Frank B. Kellogg, as listed earlier in chapter 9, p. 190.

Graebner, Norman A., ed. AN UNCERTAIN TRADITION: AMERICAN SECRE-TARIES OF STATE IN THE TWENTIETH CENTURY. New York: McGraw-Hill, 1961. 341 p. Bibliog.

> Consists of an introductory statement and separate chapters by in-dividual authors on fourteen secretaries of state, from John Hay to John Foster Dulles.

Comprehensive bibliographical listings of materials on statesmen (including presi-dents, presidential candidates, Cabinet members, members of Congress, and others concerned with foreign affairs) as well as diplomats and consuls, since 1900, are provided in:

Plischke, Elmer, ed. AMERICAN DIPLOMACY: A BIBLIOGRAPHY OF BIOG-RAPHIES, AUTOBIOGRAPHIES, AND COMMENTARIES. College Park: Bureau of Governmental Research, University of Maryland, 1957. 27 p.

_____ . "Bibliography on United States Diplomacy." In INSTRUCTION IN DIPLOMACY: THE LIBERAL ARTS APPROACH, edited by Smith Simpson, pp. 299-342. Monograph, no. 13. Philadelphia: American Academy of Political and Social Science, 1972.

Specific summary biographical data on members of the Department of State and the Foreign Service are included in the periodically published THE BIOGRAPHIC REGISTER of the Department of State, cited in chapter 22, p. 560.

An exhaustive compilation of the published works, primarily monographs, of those American diplomats and consuls who have served abroad since the 1770s, irrespective of rank or subject matter, is available in:

Boyce, Richard Fyfe, and Boyce, Katherine Randall, eds. AMERICAN FOREIGN SERVICE AUTHORS: A BIBLIOGRAPHY. Metuchen, N.J.: Scarecrow, 1973. 321 p.

> Illustrates the variety of literary production of American diplomats largely professional--and includes textbooks, plays, poetry, fiction, songs, and music, as well as memoirs and commentaries.

Analysis of this variety of writings, irrespective of subject matter, but restricted to ranking diplomats, principally chiefs of mission and officials of the Depart-ment of State down to the assistant secretaries, is summarized in:

Plischke, Elmer. "Diplomats as Authors." In his UNITED STATES DIPLOMATS AND THEIR MISSIONS: A PROFILE OF AMERICAN DIPLOMATIC EMISSARIES SINCE 1778, pp. 117-30. Washington, D.C.: American Enterprise Institute, 1975.

An official guide to biographical sources is provided by:

Kline, Jane, comp. BIOGRAPHICAL SOURCES FOR THE UNITED STATES. Washington, D.C.: U.S. Library of Congress, 1961. 58 p.

Substantive and functional commentaries on foreign policy and relations, written by diplomats and other practitioners, are incorporated in earlier chapters of this compilation. The listing that follows represents principally the biographical, memoir, and related literature of U.S. diplomats and consuls since the achievement of American indpendence. Only monographs and collections of letters and papers are included. Reference to journal and other essay literature, though substantial, is not provided. Brief annotations are supplied where they are deemed necessary to establish the identity or foreign relations significance of the author or the subject of individual entries and, occasionally, when information concerning the relevance of the volume may be helpful.

Acheson, Dean G. FRAGMENTS OF MY FLEECE. New York: Norton, 1971. 221 p.

Selected speeches, articles, and papers.

_____. MORNING AND NOON. Boston: Houghton Mifflin, 1965. 288 p.

Autobiography of youth and early career.

_____. THE PATTERN OF RESPONSIBILITY: FROM THE RECORD OF DEAN ACHESON. Edited by McGeorge Bundy. Boston: Houghton Mifflin, 1952. 309 p.

_____. POWER AND DIPLOMACY. Cambridge, Mass.: Harvard University Press, 1958. Reprint. New York: Atheneum, 1963. 137 p.

_____. PRESENT AT THE CREATION: MY YEARS IN THE STATE DEPARTMENT. New York: Norton, 1969. 798 p.

_____. SKETCHES FROM LIFE OF MEN I HAVE KNOWN. New York: Harper, 1961. 206 p.

Pen portraits of the author's contemporaries.

_____. STRENGTHENING THE FORCES OF FREEDOM: SELECTED SPEECHES AND STATEMENTS . . . FEBRUARY 1949-APRIL 1950. Washington, D.C.: Government Printing Office, 1950. 192 p.

_____. THIS VAST EXTERNAL REALM. New York: Norton, 1973. 298 p.

Collection of essays written after retirement as secretary of state.

Adams, Charles Francis. DIARY. Edited by Marc Friedlaender and L.H. Butterfield. 6 vols. Cambridge, Mass.: Belknap, 1964–74.

Adams, John. DIARY AND AUTOBIOGRAPHY. Edited by L.H. Butterfield. 4 vols. Cambridge, Mass.: Belknap, 1961.

_____. THE JOHN ADAMS PAPERS. Edited by Frank Donovan. New York: Dodd, Mead, 1965. 335 p.

_____. LETTERS FROM A DISTINGUISHED AMERICAN: TWELVE ESSAYS BY JOHN ADAMS ON AMERICAN FOREIGN POLICY, 1780. Washington, D.C.: Government Printing Office, 1978. 66 p.

Letters serialized in THE GENERAL ADVERTISER and the MORNING INTELLIGENCER of London and attributed to "A Distinguished American."

Adams, John Quincy. THE DIARY OF JOHN QUINCY ADAMS, 1794–1845: AMERICAN DIPLOMACY, AND POLITICAL, SOCIAL, AND INTELLECTUAL LIFE FROM WASHINGTON TO POLK. Edited by Allen Nevins. New York: Ungar, 1928. 586 p.

_____. MEMOIRS OF JOHN QUINCY ADAMS, COMPRISING PORTIONS OF HIS DIARY, 1795–1848. Edited by Charles Francis Adams. 12 vols. Philadelphia: Lippincott, 1874–77.

_____. WRITINGS OF JOHN QUINCY ADAMS. Edited by Worthington Chauncey Ford. 7 vols. New York: Macmillan, 1913–17.

Allen, Horace Newton. KOREA: FACT AND FANCY. Seoul, Korea: Press of Methodist Publishing House, 1904. 285 p.

By secretary of legation and later minister at Seoul, 1890–1905.

_____. THINGS KOREAN: A COLLECTION OF SKETCHES AND ANECDOTES, MISSIONARY AND DIPLOMATIC. New York: Revell, 1908. 256 p.

Allen, Katharine M. FOREIGN SERVICE DIARY. Washington, D.C.: Potomac, 1967. 285 p.

By wife of George V. Allen, Ambassador to Iran, Yugoslavia, India, and Greece.

Allison, John Murray. ADAMS AND JEFFERSON: THE STORY OF A FRIEND-SHIP. Norman: University of Oklahoma Press, 1966. 349 p.

> Served as assistant secretary of state and ambassador to Japan, Indonesia, and Czechoslovakia.

_____. AMBASSADOR FROM THE PRAIRIE--OR, ALLISON WONDERLAND. Boston: Houghton Mifflin, 1973. 452 p.

Anderson, Isabel Weld [Perkins]. PRESIDENTS AND PIES: LIFE IN WASHINGTON, 1897-1919. Boston: Houghton Mifflin, 1920. 290 p.

> By wife of Ambassador Larz Anderson.

Anderson, Larz. LARZ ANDERSON: LETTERS AND JOURNALS OF A DIPLOMAT. Edited by Isabel [Weld Perkins] Anderson. New York: Revell, 1940. 672 p.

Anderson, Richard Clough, Jr. THE DIARY AND JOURNAL OF RICHARD CLOUGH ANDERSON, JR., 1814-1826. Edited by Alfred Tischendorf and E. Taylor Parks. Durham, N.C.: Duke University Press, 1964. 342 p.

> Served as first diplomatic representative to Colombia, in 1820s.

Andrews, Christopher Columbus. RECOLLECTIONS, 1829-1922. Edited by Alice E. Andrews. Cleveland: Clark, 1928. 327 p.

> Served as minister to Sweden and Norway and consul general to Brazil. Edited by his daughter.

Angell, James Burrill. REMINISCENCES. New York: Longmans, Green, 1912. 258 p.

> Served as minister to China and Turkey.

_____. SELECTED ADDRESSES BY JAMES BURRILL ANGELL. New York: Longmans, Green, 1912. 285 p.

Armstrong, Hamilton Fish. THOSE DAYS. New York: Harper and Row, 1963. 151 p.

> Served in Department of State and as special assistant to the American ambassador in London.

_____, ed. FIFTY YEARS OF FOREIGN AFFAIRS. New York, Praeger, 1972. 501 p.

Arnold, Julean Herbert. CHINA THROUGH THE AMERICAN WINDOW. Shanghai: American Chamber of Commerce, 1932. 85 p.

Served in China, 1902-38, as consular officer and in overseas service of Department of Commerce.

Ashabranner, Brent K. A MOMENT IN HISTORY. New York: Doubleday, 1971. 392 p.

Served in Africa and Asia.

Attwood, William. THE REDS AND THE BLACKS: A PERSONAL ADVENTURE. New York: Harper and Row, 1967. 341 p.

Served as ambassador to Guinea and Kenya.

Bacon, Robert. FOR BETTER RELATIONS WITH OUR LATIN AMERICAN NEIGHBORS: A JOURNEY TO SOUTH AMERICA. Washington, D.C.: Carnegie Endowment for International Peace, 1915. 186 p.

Served as assistant secretary of state, secretary of state, and ambassador to France.

_____. ROBERT BACON: LIFE AND LETTERS. Edited by James Brown Scott. Garden City, N.Y.: Doubleday, Page, 1923. 459 p.

Baker, Ray Stannard. AMERICAN CHRONICLE: THE AUTOBIOGRAPHY OF RAY STANNARD BAKER. New York: Scribner, 1945. 531 p.

Served as special commissioner to Britain, France, and Italy, 1918, and at Paris Peace Conference, 1919.

Baldridge, Letitia. OF DIAMONDS AND DIPLOMATS. Boston: Houghton Mifflin, 1968. 337 p.

Autobiography of private secretary to wife of Ambassador David K. Bruce and secretary to Ambassador Clare Boothe Luce.

_____. ROMAN CANDLE. Boston: Houghton, Mifflin, 1956. 308 p.

Biography of Ambassador Clare Boothe Luce.

Ball, George W. DIPLOMACY FOR A CROWDED WORLD: AN AMERICAN FOREIGN POLICY. Boston: Little, Brown, 1976. 356 p.

Served as under secretary of state and U.S. representative to the United Nations.

_____. THE DISCIPLINE OF POWER: ESSENTIALS OF A MODERN WORLD STRUCTURE. Boston: Little, Brown, 1968. 363 p.

Barlow, Joel. LIFE AND LETTERS OF JOEL BARLOW, LL.D. Edited by Charles Burr Todd. New York: Burt Franklin, 1972. 306 p.

Served as consul at Algiers and minister to France.

Bax, Emily. MISS BAX OF THE EMBASSY. Boston: Houghton Mifflin, 1939. 310 p.

Served as secretary at the American Embassy in London, 1902-14.

Bayard, Richard Henry. BAYARD PAPERS. Washington, D.C.: American Historical Association, 1913.

Served as charge d'affaires in Belgium.

Beam, Jacob Dyneley. MULTIPLE EXPOSURE: AN AMERICAN AMBASSADOR'S UNIQUE PERSPECTIVE ON EAST-WEST ISSUES. New York: Norton, 1978. 317 p. Bibliog.

Served as ambassador to Poland, Czechoslovakia, and the USSR.

Beaulac, Willard L. CAREER AMBASSADOR. New York: Macmillan, 1951. 262 p.

Autobiography of twenty-seven years in the Foreign Service. Served as ambassador to several Latin American countries.

_____. CAREER DIPLOMAT: A CAREER IN THE FOREIGN SERVICE OF THE UNITED STATES. New York: Macmillan, 1964. 199 p.

_____. A DIPLOMAT LOOKS AT AID TO LATIN AMERICA. Carbondale, Ill.: Southern Illinois University Press, 1970. 148 p.

Beers, Burton F. VAIN ENDEAVOR: ROBERT LANSING'S ATTEMPTS TO END THE AMERICAN-JAPANESE RIVALRY. Durham, N.C.: Duke University Press, 1962. 207 p. Bibliog.

Belmont, August. LETTERS, SPEECHES AND ADDRESSES OF AUGUST BELMONT. New York: Privately printed, 1890. 236 p.

Served as minister to the Netherlands in the 1850s.

Benet, Stephen Vincent. SELECTED LETTERS. Edited by Charles A. Fenton. New Haven, Conn.: Yale University Press, 1960. 436 p.

Served as clerk of Embassy at Paris.

Benton, William. THE VOICE OF LATIN AMERICA. New York: Harper, 1961. 204 p. Bibliog.

Served as assistant secretary of state and as a delegate to international conferences.

Berding, Andrew H. DULLES ON DIPLOMACY. Princeton, N.J.: Van Nostrand, 1965. 184 p.

Served as assistant secretary of state.

Berle, Adolf A. LATIN AMERICA: DIPLOMACY AND REALITY. New York: Harper and Row, 1962. 144 p.

> Served as assistant secretary of state, ambassador to Brazil, and in other diplomatic capacities.

_____. NAVIGATING THE RAPIDS, 1918-1971: FROM THE PAPERS OF ADOLF A. BERLE. Edited by Beatrice Bishop Berle and Travis B. Jacobs. New York: Harcourt Brace Jovanovich, 1973. 859 p.

_____. NEW DIRECTIONS IN THE NEW WORLD. New York: Harper, 1940. 141 p.

_____. TIDES OF CRISIS: A PRIMER OF FOREIGN RELATIONS. New York: Reynal, 1957. 328 p.

Biddle, Cordelia Drexel. MY PHILADELPHIA FATHER: AS TOLD TO KYLE CRICHTON. Garden City, N.Y.: Doubleday, 1955. 256 p.

> About Joseph Drexel Biddle, who served in several diplomatic appointments.

Bigelow, John. RETROSPECTIONS OF AN ACTIVE LIFE. 5 vols. New York: Baker and Taylor, 1909-13.

> Served as consul general in Paris and minister to France.

Bingham, Jonathan Brewster. SHIRT-SLEEVE DIPLOMACY: POINT 4 IN ACTION. New York: Day, 1954. 303 p.

Bishop, Joseph Bucklin. JOHN HAY, SCHOLAR, STATESMAN: AN ADDRESS DELIVERED BEFORE THE ALUMNI ASSOCIATION OF BROWN UNIVERSITY, JUNE 19, 1906. Providence, R.I.: Standard, 1906. 29 p.

Bjerk, Roger Carl William. "Kennedy at the Court of St. James: The Diplomatic Career of Joseph P. Kennedy, 1938-1940." Ph.D. dissertation, Washington State University, 1971. 252 p.

Bland, Larry Irvin. "W. Averell Harriman: Businessman and Diplomat, 1891-1945." Ph.D. dissertation, University of Wisconsin, 1972. 532 p.

Blumenfeld, Ralph, et al. HENRY KISSINGER: THE PRIVATE AND PUBLIC STORY. Bergenfield, N.J.: New American Library, 1974. 326 p.

Bohlen, Charles E. THE TRANSFORMATION OF AMERICAN FOREIGN POLICY. New York: Norton, 1969. 130 p.

> Blaustein Lectures at Columbia University, 1969. By a career For-

eign Service officer who served in ranking diplomatic and Department of state posts, including ambassador to France, the Philippines, and the Soviet Union.

_____. WITNESS TO HISTORY, 1929-1969. New York: Norton, 1973. 562 p.

Bond, Beverly Waugh. THE MONROE MISSION TO FRANCE, 1794-1796. Baltimore: Johns Hopkins Press, 1907. 104 p.

Bonsal, Philip W. CUBA, CASTRO AND THE UNITED STATES. Pittsburgh: University of Pittsburgh Press, 1971. 318 p.

By a career diplomat who served as ambassador to Cuba.

Bonsal, Stephen. UNFINISHED BUSINESS: PARIS-VERSAILLES, 1919. Garden City, N.Y.: Doubleday, Doran, 1944. 313 p.

Served as charge d'affaires in Madrid, Peking, Tokyo, and Korea. Provides excerpts from his diary while President Wilson's confidential interpreter at the Paris Peace Conference at the end of World War I.

Bowen, Herbert Wolcott. RECOLLECTIONS, DIPLOMATIC AND UNDIPLO-MATIC. New York: Hitchcock, 1926. 320 p.

Served as minister to Iran and Venezuela.

Bowers, Claude G. CHILE THROUGH EMBASSY WINDOWS, 1939-1953. New York: Simon and Schuster, 1958. 375 p.

Served as ambassador to Spain and Chile.

_____. MY LIFE; THE MEMOIRS OF CLAUDE BOWERS. New York: Simon and Schuster, 1962. 346 p.

_____. MY MISSION TO SPAIN: WATCHING THE REHEARSAL FOR WORLD WAR II. New York: Simon and Schuster, 1954. 437 p.

Bowie, Robert R. SHAPING THE FUTURE: FOREIGN POLICY IN AN AGE OF TRANSITION. New York: Columbia University Press, 1964. 118 p.

Served as adviser to U.S. high commissioner to Germany after World War II and as director of Policy Planning Staff of Department of State.

Bowles, Chester. AFRICA'S CHALLENGE TO AMERICA. Berkeley and Los Angeles: University of California Press, 1956. Reprint. Westport, Conn.: Negro Universities Press, 1970. 134 p.

Served as ambassador to India, ambassador at large, and under secretary of state.

_____. AMBASSADOR'S REPORT. New York: Harper, 1954. 415 p.

_____. AMERICAN POLITICS IN A REVOLUTIONARY WORLD. Cambridge, Mass.: Harvard University Press, 1956. 131 p.

_____. IDEAS, PEOPLE, AND PEACE. New York: Harper, 1958. 151 p.

_____. THE MAKINGS OF A JUST SOCIETY: WHAT THE POSTWAR YEARS HAVE TAUGHT US ABOUT NATIONAL DEVELOPMENT. Delhi, India: University of Delhi, 1963. 120 p.

_____. THE NEW DIMENSIONS OF PEACE. New York: Harper, 1955. 391 p.

_____. PROMISES TO KEEP: MY YEARS IN PUBLIC LIFE, 1941-1969. New York: Harper and Row, 1971. 657 p.

_____. TOMORROW WITHOUT FEAR. New York: Simon and Schuster, 1946. 88 p.

_____. A VIEW FROM NEW DELHI: SELECTED SPEECHES AND WRITINGS, 1963-1969. New Haven, Conn.: Yale University Press, 1969. Bombay: Allied, 1969. 268 p.

Boyce, Richard Fyfe. THE DIPLOMAT'S WIFE. New York: Harper, 1956. 230 p.

By career Foreign Service officer.

Braden, Spruille. DIPLOMATS AND DEMAGOGUES: THE MEMOIRS OF SPRUILLE BRADEN. New Rochelle, N.Y.: Arlington House, 1971. 496 p.

Briggs, Ellis O. ANATOMY OF DIPLOMACY: THE ORIGIN AND EXECUTION OF AMERICAN FOREIGN POLICY. New York: McKay, 1968. 248 p.

By a career diplomat who served as ambassador to Dominican Republic, Uruguay, Czechoslovakia, Korea, Peru, Brazil, and Greece.

_____. FAREWELL TO FOGGY BOTTOM: THE RECOLLECTIONS OF A CAREER DIPLOMAT. New York: McKay, 1964. 306 p.

Brodie, Fawn M. THOMAS JEFFERSON: AN INTIMATE HISTORY. New York: Norton, 1974. 591 p. Bibliog.

Bryan, William Jennings. HEART TO HEART APPEALS. New York: Revell, 1917. 189 p.

Collection of speeches covering a quarter century.

_____. THE OLD WORLD AND ITS WAYS. St. Louis: Thompson, 1907. 574 p.

Describes a tour around the world and journeys through Europe.

_____. SPEECHES OF WILLIAM JENNINGS BRYAN, REVISED AND ARRANGED BY HIMSELF. 2 vols. New York: Funk and Wagnals, 1909.

Bryan, William Jennings, and Bryan, Mary Baird. THE MEMOIRS OF WILLIAM JENNINGS BRYAN. Philadelphia: Winston, 1925. 560 p.

Bryn-Jones, David. FRANK B. KELLOGG: A BIOGRAPHY. New York: Putnam, 1937. 308 p.

Buchanan, Wiley T., Jr. RED CARPET AT THE WHITE HOUSE. New York: Dutton, 1964. 256 p.

Served as chief of protocol.

Buchanan, William-Insco. THE CENTRAL AMERICAN PEACE CONFERENCE HELD AT WASHINGTON, D.C., 1907: REPORT OF MR. WILLIAM-INSCO BUCHANAN REPRESENTING THE UNITED STATES OF AMERICA. Washington, D.C.: Government Printing Office, 1908. 97 p.

Buhite, Russell D. NELSON T. JOHNSON AND AMERICAN POLICY TOWARD CHINA, 1925-1941. East Lansing: University of Michigan Press, 1968. 163 p.

About Nelson T. Johnson, a career Foreign Service officer.

_____. PATRICK J. HURLEY AND AMERICAN FOREIGN POLICY. Ithaca, N.Y.: Cornell University Press, 1973. 342 p. Bibliog.

About Hurley, who served as minister to New Zealand and ambassador to China.

Bullitt, Orville H., ed. FOR THE PRESIDENT: PERSONAL AND SECRET— CORRESPONDENCE BETWEEN FRANKLIN D. ROOSEVELT AND WILLIAM C. BULLITT. Boston: Houghton Mifflin, 1972. 655 p.

About William C. Bullitt, a career diplomat who served as ambassador to Moscow and Paris.

Bullitt, William Christian. THE GREAT GLOBE ITSELF: A PREFACE TO WORLD AFFAIRS. New York: Scribner, 1946. 310 p.

Bundy, McGeorge, ed. THE PATTERN OF RESPONSIBILITY. Boston: Houghton Mifflin, 1952. 309 p.

> Concerns the public record of Secretary of State Dean G. Acheson, from January 1949 to August 1951.

Bundy, William P., ed. TWO HUNDRED YEARS OF AMERICAN FOREIGN POLICY. New York: New York University Press, 1977. 251 p.

> Anthology of essays on historical foreign relations positions of the United States. Editor served as assistant secretary of state.

Burke, Bernard Vincent. "American Diplomats and Hitler's Rise to Power, 1930–1933: The Mission of Ambassador Sackett." Ph.D. dissertation, University of Washington, 1966. 381 p.

> About Sackett, who served as ambassador to Germany

Burns, Richard Dean. "Cordell Hull: A Study in Diplomacy, 1933–1941." Ph.D. dissertation, University of Illinois, 1960. 355 p.

Byrnes, James F. ALL IN ONE LIFETIME. New York: Harper, 1958. 432 p.

_____. SPEAKING FRANKLY. New York: Harper, 1947. 324 p.

Cabot, John Moors. TOWARD OUR COMMON AMERICAN DESTINY. Medford, Mass.: Fletcher School of Law and Diplomacy, 1955. 214 p.

> By a career diplomat, who served as assistant secretary of state for inter-American affairs.

Caldwell, John Cope, and Gayn, Mark. AMERICAN AGENT. New York: Holt, 1947. 220 p.

> Account of John Caldwell, American agent in China, 1943–44.

Campbell, Thomas Moody, Jr. "The Role of Edward R. Stettinius, Jr., in the Founding of the United Nations." Ph.D. dissertation, University of Virginia, 1964. 336 p.

Campbell, Thomas Moody, Jr., and Herring, George C., Jr., eds. THE DIARIES OF EDWARD R. STETTINIUS, JR., 1943-1946. New York: New Viewpoints, 1975. 544 p.

Cardozo, Michael H. DIPLOMATS IN INTERNATIONAL COOPERATION: STEPCHILDREN OF THE FOREIGN SERVICE. Ithaca, N.Y.: Cornell University Press, 1962. 142 p.

Carmona, Israel. "Anatomy of a Diplomatic Failure: A Study of the Tenure of Ambassador James Rockwell Sheffield in Mexico, 1924-1927." Ph.D. dissertation, University of Southern California, 1969. 278 p.

Cathcart, James Leander. THE DIPLOMATIC JOURNAL AND LETTER BOOK OF JAMES LEANDER CATHCART, 1788-1796. Worcester, Mass.: American Antiquarian Society, vol. 64, pp. 303-46.

> Served as consul to Tripoli and consul general at Algiers, Tunis, Madiera, and Cadiz.

Cerwin, Herbert. IN SEARCH OF SOMETHING: THE MEMOIRS OF A PUB-LIC RELATIONS MAN. Los Angeles: Sherbourne, 1966. 318 p.

> By a Foreign Service reserve officer.

Cheng, Peter Ping-Chii. "A Study of John Foster Dulles: Diplomatic Strategy in the Far East." Ph.D. dissertation, Southern Illinois University, 1964. 674 p.

Child, Maude Parker. THE SOCIAL SIDE OF DIPLOMATIC LIFE. Indianapolis: Bobbs-Merrill, 1926. 306 p.

> By the wife of Ambassador Richard Washburn Child. See also entries for Maude Parker, p. 656.

Child, Richard Washburn. A DIPLOMAT LOOKS AT EUROPE. New York: Duffield, 1925. 301 p.

> Served as ambassador to Italy.

[Childs, James Rives.] BEFORE THE CURTAIN FALLS. Indianapolis: Bobbs-Merrill, 1932. 333 p.

> Anonymous fictionalized memoir.

_____. FOREIGN SERVICE FAREWELL: MY YEARS IN THE NEAR EAST. Charlottesville: University of Virginia Press, 1969. 192 p.

Choate, Joseph Hodges. ARGUMENTS AND ADDRESSES OF JOSEPH HODGES CHOATE. Collected and edited by Frederick C. Hicks. St. Paul: West, 1926. 1189 p.

> Served as ambassador to Great Britain.

_____. LIFE OF JOSEPH HODGES CHOATE AS GATHERED CHIEFLY FROM HIS LETTERS. Edited by Edward Sandford Martin. 2 vols. New York: Scribner, 1927.

_____. THE TWO HAGUE PEACE CONFERENCES. Princeton, N.J.: Princeton University Press, 1913. 109 p.

Clarfield, Gerald H. TIMOTHY PICKERING AND AMERICAN DIPLOMACY, 1795-1800. Columbia: University of Missouri Press, 1969. 233 p. Bibliog.

Clay, Henry. THE LIFE AND SPEECHES OF THE HONORABLE HENRY CLAY. Edited by Daniel Mallory. 2 vols. Hartford, Conn.: Andrus, 1855.

_____. THE PAPERS OF HENRY CLAY. Edited by James F. Hopkins. 5 vols. Lexington: University of Kentucky Press, 1959-73.

_____. THE WORKS OF HENRY CLAY: COMPRISING HIS LIFE, CORRES-PONDENCE AND SPEECHES. Edited by Calvin Colton. 10 vols. New York: Putnam, 1904.

Cleaver, Charles G. "Frank B. Kellogg: Attitudes and Assumptions Influenc-ing His Foreign Policy Decisions." Ph.D. dissertation, University of Minnesota, 1956. 415 p.

Clements, Kendrick Alling. "William Jennings Bryan and Democratic Foreign Policy, 1896-1915." Ph.D. dissertation, University of California (Berkeley), 1970. 436 p.

Cleveland, Harlan. THE OBLIGATIONS OF POWER. New York: Harper and Row, 1966. 168 p.

    Served as assistant secretary of state and as permanent representa-tive to the Council of NATO.

Collier, William Miller. AT THE COURT OF HIS CATHOLIC MAJESTY. Chi-cago: McClurg, 1912. 330 p.

    Served as minister to Spain and later as ambassador to Chile.

Conant, James B. GERMANY AND FREEDOM: A PERSONAL APPRAISAL. Cambridge, Mass.: Harvard University Press, 1958. 117 p. Bibliog.

    Served as ambassador to Germany.

_____. MY SEVERAL LIVES: MEMOIRS OF A SOCIAL INVENTOR. New York: Harper and Row, 1970. 701 p. Bibliog.

Coolidge, Harold J., and Lord, Robert H. ARCHIBALD CARY COOLIDGE: LIFE AND LETTERS. New York: Houghton Mifflin, 1932. 368 p.

    A.C. Coolidge served at 1919 Paris Peace Conference.

Coolidge, John Gardner. RANDOM LETTERS FROM MANY COUNTRIES. Boston: Marshall Jones, 1924. 408 p.

    Served in several appointments abroad and in Department of State.

_____. A WAR DIARY IN PARIS, 1914–1917. Cambridge, Mass.: Riverside, 1931. 283 p.

Coolidge, Thomas Jefferson. THE AUTOBIOGRAPHY OF T. JEFFERSON COOLIDGE, 1831–1920. Boston: Houghton Mifflin, 1923. 311 p.

Served as minister to France.

Cooper, Chester L. THE LOST CRUSADE: AMERICA IN VIETNAM. New York: Dodd, Mead, 1970. 559 p. Bibliog.

Served with OSS in the China–Burma–India theater, on the U.S. delegations to the Geneva Conference on Indo-China, the 1954 conference in Manila which established SEATO, the 1961–62 Geneva Conference on Laos, and the 1966 summit conference in Manila of Vietnam war allies, and also from 1964 to 1967 on the White House staff.

Cortissoz, Royal. THE LIFE OF WHITELAW REID. 2 vols. New York: Scribner, 1921.

About Reid who served as ambassador to Great Britain, 1905–13.

Corwin, Thomas. LIFE AND SPEECHES OF THOMAS CORWIN: ORATOR, LAWYER, AND STATESMAN. Edited by Josiah Morrow. Cincinnati: Anderson, 1896. 477 p.

Served as minister to Mexico.

_____. SPEECHES OF THOMAS CORWIN, WITH A SKETCH OF HIS LIFE. Edited by Isaac Strohm. Dayton, Ohio: Comley, 1859. 518 p.

Cox, Samuel Sullivan. DIVERSIONS OF A DIPLOMAT IN TURKEY. New York: Webster, 1887. 685 p.

Craig, Gordon Alexander, and Gilbert, Felix, eds. THE DIPLOMATS, 1919–1939. 2 vols. Princeton, N.J.: Princeton University Press, 1953. 700 p.

Crane, Katherine. MR. CARR OF STATE: FORTY-SEVEN YEARS IN THE DEPARTMENT OF STATE. New York: St. Martin, 1960. 365 p.

Cresson, William Penn. FRANCIS DANA: A PURITAN DIPLOMAT AT THE COURT OF CATHERINE THE GREAT. New York: Mcveigh, Dial Press, 1930. 397 p.

Croly, Herbert D. WILLARD STRAIGHT. New York: Macmillan, 1924. 569 p.

About Willard Straight, a career Foreign Service officer who served in China and Korea.

Crowe, Philip Kingsland. DIVERSIONS OF A DIPLOMAT IN CEYLON. London: Macmillan, 1957. 318 p.

Served as ambassador to Ceylon, South Africa, and Norway.

Cudahy, John. THE ARMIES MARCH: A PERSONAL REPORT BY JOHN CUDAHY. New York: Scribner, 1941. 304 p.

Served in various diplomatic appointments, including ambassador to Poland, Ireland, and Belgium.

_____. THE CASE FOR THE KING OF THE BELGIANS. New York: n.p., 1940. 34 p.

Cummins, Lejeune. "The Origin and Development of Elihu Root's Latin American Diplomacy." Ph.D. dissertation, University of California (Berkeley), 1964. 325 p.

Current, Richard Nelson. SECRETARY STIMSON: A STUDY IN STATECRAFT. New Brunswick, N.J.: Rutgers University Press, 1954. 272 p.

Curti, Merle Eugene. BRYAN AND WORLD PEACE. Northampton, Mass.: Department of History, Smith College, 1931. 262 p.

Cushing, Caleb. THE CUSHING REPORTS. Edited with introduction by Margaret Diamond Benetz. Salisbury, N.C.: Documentary Publications, 1976. 161 p.

First diplomatic reports by American ambassador journeying through Egypt, Barbary States, India, and Ceylon, on route to China, in 1840s, with biographical introduction.

_____. OUTLINES OF THE LIFE AND PUBLIC SERVICES, CIVIL AND MILITARY, OF WILLIAM HENRY HARRISON OF OHIO. Boston: Weeks, Jordan, 1840. 71 p.

About Harrison, who served as minister to Colombia. By Cushing, who served as minister to Spain and held other diplomatic appointments.

Dallas, George Mifflin. DIARY OF GEORGE MIFFLIN DALLAS, UNITED STATES MINISTER TO RUSSIA, 1837-39. Edited by Susan Dallas. Philadelphia: Lippincott, 1892. 214 p.

Served as minister to Russia and the United Kingdom.

_____. A SERIES OF LETTERS FROM LONDON WRITTEN DURING THE YEARS 1856, '57, '58, '59, '60. Edited by Julia Dallas. 2 vols. Philadelphia: Lippincott, 1869.

Dallek, Robert. "Roosevelt's Ambassador: The Public Career of William E. Dodd." Ph.D. dissertation, Columbia University, 1964. 328 p.

>About Dodd, who served as ambassador to Germany.

Daniels, Jonathan. THE END OF INNOCENCE. Philadelphia: Lippincott, 1954. 351 p.

>Recollections of the son of Josephus Daniels, a Cabinet member during the Wilson administration and ambassador to Mexico.

Daniels, Josephus. SHIRT-SLEEVE DIPLOMAT. Chapel Hill: University of North Carolina Press, 1947. 547 p.

>Served as ambassador to Mexico.

_____. THE WILSON ERA: YEARS OF PEACE, 1910-1917. Chapel Hill: University of North Carolina Press, 1944. 615 p.

>Served as secretary of the navy during the Wilson administration.

_____. WILSON ERA: YEARS OF WAR AND AFTER, 1917-1923. Chapel Hill: University of North Carolina Press, 1946. 654 p.

Darlington, Charles Francis, and Darlington, Alice B. AFRICAN BETRAYAL. New York: McKay, 1968. 359 p.

>Served as ambassador to Gabon.

Darnell, Michael Russell. "Henry P. Fletcher and American Diplomacy, 1902-1929." Ph.D. dissertation, University of Colorado, 1972. 527 p.

>About Fletcher, who served as ambassador to Chile, Mexico, Belgium, and Italy, and as under secretary of state.

Davies, John Paton, Jr. FOREIGN AND OTHER AFFAIRS. New York: Norton, 1964. 219 p.

>By a career Foreign Service officer.

Davies, Joseph Edward. MISSION TO MOSCOW. New York: Simon and Schuster, 1941. 683 p.

>Served as ambassador to Soviet Union.

_____. OUR SOVIET ALLY IN WAR AND PEACE. New York: National Council of American-Soviet Friendship, 1944. 15 p.

Davis, Jack. "The Latin American Policy of Elihu Root." Ph.D. dissertation, University of Illinois, 1956. 235 p.

Davis, Nathaniel P. FEW DULL MOMENTS: A FOREIGN SERVICE CAREER. Philadelphia: Dunlap, 1967. 158 p.

Served as Foreign Service officer in various posts.

Davis, William Brownlee. EXPERIENCES AND OBSERVATIONS OF AN AMERICAN CONSULAR OFFICER DURING THE RECENT MEXICAN REVOLUTION. Chula Vista, Calif.: n.p., 1920. 248 p.

Held several vice consular posts.

Dawes, Charles Gates. ESSAYS AND SPEECHES. Boston: Houghton Mifflin, 1915. 427 p.

Served as vice president, ambassador to Great Britain, and in other posts.

_____. JOURNAL AS AMBASSADOR TO GREAT BIRTAIN. New York: Macmillan, 1939. 442 p.

_____. A JOURNAL OF REPARATIONS. London: Macmillan, 1939. 527 p.

_____. A JOURNAL OF THE GREAT WAR. 2 vols. Boston: Houghton Mifflin, 1921.

Concerns World War I.

Deane, John Russell. THE STRANGE ALLIANCE: THE STORY OF OUR EFFORTS AT WARTIME COOPERATION WITH RUSSIA. New York: Viking, 1947. 344 p.

Served as head of U.S. military mission to Moscow during World War II.

Deane, Silas. PARIS PAPERS: OR, MR. SILAS DEANE'S LATE INTERCEPTED LETTERS TO HIS BROTHERS, AND OTHER INTIMATE FRIENDS IN AMERICA. New York: Rivington, 1782. 141 p.

Served as secret agent and commissioner.

DeLeon, Edwin. THIRTY YEARS OF MY LIFE ON THREE CONTINENTS. 2 vols. London: Ward and Downey, 1890.

Served as diplomatic agent and consul.

Denby, Charles. CHINA AND HER PEOPLE: BEING THE OBSERVATIONS, REMINISCENCES AND CONCLUSIONS OF AN AMERICAN DIPLOMAT. 2 vols. Boston: Page, 1906.

Served as chief clerk of the Department of State and minister to China.

Dennett, Raymond, and Johnson, Joseph E., eds. NEGOTIATING WITH THE RUSSIANS. Boston: World Peace Foundation, 1951. 310 p.

    Symposium by ten Americans who negotiated with the Soviets, 1940–50.

Dennett, Tyler. AMERICANS IN EASTERN ASIA. New York: Barnes and Noble, 1941. 725 p. Bibliog.

_____. JOHN HAY: FROM POETRY TO POLITICS. New York: Dodd, Mead, 1933. 476 p.

Dennis, Alfred Lewis P. ADVENTURES IN AMERICAN DIPLOMACY, 1896–1906. New York: Dutton, 1928. 537 p.

Dickson, Peter. KISSINGER AND THE MEANING OF HISTORY. New York: Cambridge University Press, 1978. 288 p.

Dix, John Adams. MEMOIRS OF JOHN ADAMS DIX. Compiled by Morgan Dix. 2 vols. New York: Harper, 1883.

    Served as minister to France.

Dobney, Frederick J., ed. SELECTED PAPERS OF WILL CLAYTON. Baltimore: Johns Hopkins Press, 1971. 298 p.

    Clayton served as assistant and under secretary of state.

Dodd, Martha. MY YEARS IN GERMANY. London: Golancz, 1940. 319 p.

    By the daughter of U.S. ambassador to Germany.

_____. THROUGH EMBASSY EYES. New York: Harcourt, Brace, 1939. 382 p.

Dodd, William Edward. AMBASSADOR DODD'S DIARY, 1933–1938. Edited by William E. Dodd, Jr., and Martha Dodd. New York: Harcourt, Brace, 1941. 464 p.

Donovan, James Britt. STRANGERS ON A BRIDGE: THE CASE OF COLONEL ABEL. New York: Atheneum, 1964. 423 p.

    By man who negotiated with the Soviet government concerning the exchange of Soviet spy Rudolf Abel and U-2 pilot Francis Gary Powers.

Douglass, Frederick. A BLACK DIPLOMAT IN HAITI: THE DIPLOMATIC CORRESPONDENCE OF U.S. MINISTER FREDERICK DOUGLASS FROM HAITI, 1889–

1891. Edited and introduction by Norma Brown. 2 vols. Salisbury, N.C.: Documentary Publications, 1977.

———. FREDERICK DOUGLASS: SELECTIONS FROM HIS WRITINGS. Edited by Philip S. Foner. New York: International Publishers, 1964. 95 p.

Served as minister to Haiti.

———. THE LIFE AND WRITINGS OF FREDERICK DOUGLASS. Edited by Philip S. Foner. 4 vols. New York: International Publishers, 1950-55.

———. THE MIND AND HEART OF FREDERICK DOUGLASS: EXCERPTS FROM SPEECHES OF THE GREAT NEGRO ORATOR. Adapted by Barbara Ritchie. New York: Crowell, 1968. 201 p.

Downing, Marvin Lee. "Hugh R. Wilson and American Relations With the League of Nations, 1927-1937." Ph.D. dissertation, University of Oklahoma, 1970. 289 p.

About Wilson, who was a career diplomat.

Draper, William Franklin. RECOLLECTIONS OF A VARIED CAREER. Boston: Little, Brown, 1908. 411 p.

Served as ambassador to Italy.

Dufault, David Vawter. "Francis B. Sayre and the Commonwealth of the Philippines, 1936-1942." Ph.D. dissertation, University of Oregon, 1972. 517 p.

About Sayre, who served as assistant secretary of state and in various diplomatic capacities.

Dulles, Eleanor Lansing. JOHN FOSTER DULLES: THE LAST YEAR. New York: Harcourt, Brace, and World, 1963. 244 p.

Dulles, John Foster. A PEACE TREATY IN THE MAKING: JAPANESE PEACE CONFERENCE, SAN FRANCISCO, SEPTEMBER 4-8, 1951. Washington, D.C.: Government Printing Office, 1951. 55 p.

Dulles, Michael Guhin. JOHN FOSTER DULLES: A STATESMAN AND HIS TIMES. The Hague: Nijhoff, 1972. 432 p.

Dunham, Donald. ENVOY UNEXTRAORDINARY. New York: Day, 1944. Reprint. London: Hammond, Hammond, 1946. 166 p.

Served for brief period as Foreign Service officer.

_____. ZONE OF VIOLENCE: THE BRUTAL, SHOCKING STORY LIVED BY AN AMERICAN DIPLOMAT BEHIND THE RED CURTAIN. New York: Belmont, 1962. 188 p.

Eagles, Keith David. "Ambassador Joseph E. Davies and American-Soviet Relations, 1937-1941." Ph.D. dissertation, University of Washington, 1966. 376 p.

Egan, Maurice Francis. RECOLLECTIONS OF A HAPPY LIFE. New York: Doran, 1924. 374 p.

> Served as minister to Denmark.

Einstein, Lewis. A DIPLOMAT LOOKS BACK. Edited by Lawrence E. Gelfand. New Haven, Conn.: Yale University Press, 1968. 269 p. Bibliog.

> Served as minister to Costa Rica and Czechoslovakia; also served in half dozen other countries.

_____. INSIDE CONSTANTINOPLE: A DIPLOMATIST'S DIARY DURING THE DARDANELLES EXPEDITION, APRIL-SEPTEMBER 1915. New York: Dutton, 1918. 291 p.

Eisenhower, Milton. THE WINE IS BITTER: THE UNITED STATES AND LATIN AMERICA. New York: Doubleday, 1963. 342 p.

> Served as presidential special envoy on number of diplomatic missions to Latin America.

Ellis, Lewis Ethan. FRANK B. KELLOGG AND AMERICAN FOREIGN RELATIONS, 1925-1929. New Brunswick, N.J.: Rutgers University Press, 1961. 303 p. Bibliog.

Eppinga, Richard Jay. "Aristocrat, Nationalist, Diplomat· The Life and Career of Huntington Wilson." Ph.D. dissertation, Michigan State University, 1972. 373 p.

> About Wilson, who served as assistant secretary of state and as minister to Romania, Bulgaria, and Argentina.

Esherick, Joseph W., ed. LOST CHANCE IN CHINA: THE WORLD WAR II DESPATCHES OF JOHN S. SERVICE. New York: Random House, 1974. 409 p.

> About Service, who was Foreign Service officer serving in China and other Asian posts.

Farnsworth, Beatrice. WILLIAM C. BULLITT AND THE SOVIET UNION. Bloomington: Indiana University Press, 1967. 244 p.

> About Bullitt, a career diplomat who served as ambassador to Moscow and Paris.

Finer, Herman. DULLES OVER SUEZ: THE THEORY AND PRACTICE OF HIS DIPLOMACY. Chicago: Quadrangle, 1964. 583 p.

Concerns Secretary of State Dulles and the Suez crisis of 1956.

Finney, Charles G. THE OLD CHINA HANDS. Garden City, N.Y.: Doubleday, 1961. 258 p.

Fonzi, Gaeton. ANNENBERG: A BIOGRAPHY OF POWER. New York: Weybright and Talley, 1970. 246 p.

About Annenberg, who served as ambassador to Great Britain.

Foster, John Watson. A CENTURY OF AMERICAN DIPLOMACY. Boston: Houghton Mifflin, 1900. 497 p.

Served as secretary of state and in various diplomatic posts.

_____. DIPLOMATIC MEMOIRS. 2 vols. Boston: Houghton Mifflin, 1909.

_____. THE PRACTICE OF DIPLOMACY AS ILLUSTRATED IN THE FOREIGN RELATIONS OF THE UNITED STATES. Boston: Houghton Mifflin, 1906. 401 p.

Francis, David Rowland. RUSSIA FROM THE AMERICAN EMBASSY, APRIL, 1916-NOVEMBER, 1918. New York: Scribner, 1921. 361 p.

Furdell, William J. "Cordell Hull and the London Economic Conference of 1933." Ph.D. dissertation, Kent State University, 1970. 247 p.

Gade, John A. ALL MY BORN DAYS: EXPERIENCES OF A NAVAL INTELLIGENCE OFFICER IN EUROPE. New York: Scribner, 1942. 408 p.

Served in the Baltic states, Belgium, and Portugal.

Galbraith, John Kenneth. AMBASSADOR'S JOURNAL. Boston: Houghton Mifflin, 1969. 656 p.

Served as ambassador to India.

Gallatin, Abraham Alphonse Albert. ALBERT GALLATIN: AUTOBIOGRAPHY. Portland: Maine Historical Collections, vol. 6, 1859, pp. 93-105.

Served in several early diplomatic appointments and as minister to France and Great Britain, as well as secretary of the treasury.

_____. THE WRITINGS OF ALBERT GALLATIN. Edited by Henry Adams. 3 vols. New York: Antiquarian, 1960.

Gallatin, James. A GREAT PEACEMAKER. Edited by Count Gallatin. New York: Scribner, 1914. 314 p.

Served as secretary to Albert Gallatin.

Gallman, Waldemar John. IRAQ UNDER GENERAL NURI: MY RECOLLECTIONS OF NURI AL-SAID, 1954-58. Baltimore: Johns Hopkins Press, 1964. 241 p. Bibliog.

Served as Foreign Service officer.

Garwood, Ellen Clayton. WILL CLAYTON: A SHORT BIOGRAPHY. Austin: University of Texas Press, 1958. 164 p.

About Will Clayton who served as under secretary of state.

Gerard, James Watson. FACE TO FACE WITH KAISERISM. New York: Doran, 1918. 380 p.

Served as ambassador to Germany.

_____. MY FIRST EIGHTY-THREE YEARS IN AMERICA: THE MEMOIRS OF JAMES W. GERARD. Garden City, N.Y.: Doubleday, 1951. 372 p.

_____. MY FOUR YEARS IN GERMANY. New York: Doran, 1917. 448 p.

Geren, Paul Francis. BURMA DIARY. New York: Harper, 1943. 57 p.

Served as Foreign Service officer in various posts and as deputy director of the Peace Corps.

Gibson, Hugh S. A DIPLOMATIC DIARY. London and N.Y.: Hodder and Stoughton, 1917. 296 p.

By a career diplomat, who served as minister or ambassador to Poland, Switzerland, Belgium and Luxembourg, and Brazil.

_____. HUGH GIBSON, 1883-1954: EXTRACTS FROM HIS LETTERS AND ANECDOTES FROM HIS FRIENDS. Edited by Perrin C. Galpin. New York: Belgian-American Educational Foundation, 1956. 163 p.

_____. A JOURNAL FROM OUR LEGATION IN BELGIUM. Garden City, N.Y.: Doubleday, Page, 1917. 360 p.

_____. THE ROAD TO FOREIGN POLICY. Garden City, N.Y.: Doubleday, Doran, 1944. 252 p.

Gibson, Hugh S., and Vauclain, Samuel M. POLAND: HER PROBLEMS AND HER FUTURE. New York: American-Polish Chamber of Commerce and Industry, 1920. 22 p.

Gilbert, Jerry Don. "John Foster Dulles' Perceptions of the People's Republic of China: A Study of Belief Systems and Perception in the Analysis of Foreign Policy Decision-Making." Ph.D. dissertation, Texas Tech University, 1973. 258 p.

Glad, Betty. CHARLES EVANS HUGHES AND THE ILLUSIONS OF INNO-CENCE: A STUDY IN AMERICAN DIPLOMACY. Urbana: University of Illinois Press, 1966. 365 p.

Glad, Paul W., ed. WILLIAM JENNINGS BRYAN: A PROFILE. New York: Hill and Wang, 1968. 251 p. Bibliog.

Golan, Matti. THE SECRET CONVERSATIONS OF HENRY KISSINGER: STEP-BY-STEP DIPLOMACY IN THE MIDDLE EAST. New York: Quadrangle, 1976. 280 p.

Goodman, Allan E., ed. NEGOTIATING WHILE FIGHTING: THE DIARY OF ADMIRAL C. TURNER JOY AT THE KOREAN ARMISTICE CONFERENCE. Stanford, Calif.: Hoover Institution, 1978. 500 p.

Goold-Adams, Richard J.M. JOHN FOSTER DULLES: A REAPPRAISAL. New York: Appleton-Century-Crofts, 1962. 309 p.

Graff, Frank Warren. "The Strategy of Involvement: A Diplomatic Biography of Sumner Welles, 1933-1943." Ph.D. dissertation, University of Michigan, 1971. 467 p.

> About Welles, a Foreign Service officer, who served in various diplomatic posts and as under secretary of state.

Graubard, Stephen R. KISSINGER: PORTRAIT OF A MIND. New York: Norton, 1973. 288 p.

Greer, Virginia Leonard. "Charles Evans Hughes and Nicaragua, 1921-1925." Ph.D. dissertation, University of New Mexico, 1954. 203 p.

Grew, Joseph Clark. REPORT FROM TOKYO: A MESSAGE TO THE AMERI-CAN PEOPLE. New York: Simon and Schuster, 1942. 88 p.

_____. REPORT FROM TOKYO: A WARNING TO THE UNITED NATIONS. London: Hammond, Hammond, 1943. 103 p.

_____. TEN YEARS IN JAPAN. New York: Simon and Schuster, 1944. 554 p.

_____. TURBULENT ERA: A DIPLOMATIC RECORD OF FORTY YEARS, 1904-1945. Edited by Walter Johnson. 2 vols. Boston: Houghton Mifflin, 1952.

Griffis, Stanton. LYING IN STATE. Garden City, N.Y.: Doubleday, 1952. 315 p.

Served in several diplomatic appointments.

Griffiths, John Lewis. THE GREATER PATRIOTISM: PUBLIC ADDRESSES BY JOHN LEWIS GRIFFITHS, AMERICAN CONSUL GENERAL AT LONDON: DELIVERED IN ENGLAND AND AMERICA. With a memoir by Caroline Henderson Griffiths. New York: Lane, 1918. 230 p.

Served as consular officer in Liverpool and London.

Griscom, Lloyd Carpenter. DIPLOMATICALLY SPEAKING. Boston: Little, Brown, 1940. 476 p.

Served as minister to Persia and Turkey and as ambassador to Brazil and Italy.

Grollman, Catherine Anne. "Cordell Hull and His Concept of a World Organization." Ph.D. dissertation, University of North Carolina, 1965. 281 p.

Guggenheim, Harry F. THE UNITED STATES AND CUBA: A STUDY IN INTERNATIONAL RELATIONS. New York: Macmillan, 1934. 268 p.

By an industrialist who served in diplomatic capacity, particularly in negotiations on technical matters.

Guhin, Michael A. JOHN FOSTER DULLES: A STATESMAN AND HIS TIMES. New York: Columbia University Press, 1972. 404 p.

Gutierrez, Gilbert George. "Dean Rusk and Southeast Asia: An Operational Code Analysis." Ph.D. dissertation, University of California (Riverside), 1974.

Hagerman, Herbert James. LETTERS OF A YOUNG DIPLOMAT. Santa Fe, N.M.: Rydal, 1937. 191 p.

Served as secretary of Embassy in St. Petersburg.

Hale, Edward Everett. FRANKLIN IN FRANCE: FROM ORIGINAL DOCUMENTS, MOST OF WHICH ARE NOW PUBLISHED FOR THE FIRST TIME. 2 vols. Boston: Roberts, 1887-88.

Hale, Richard W., ed. LETTERS OF WARWICK GREENE, 1915-1928. Boston: Houghton Mifflin, 1931. 309 p.

About Green, who served as President Wilson's commissioner at Peace Conference on Baltic states.

Hanks, Richard Kay. "Hamilton Fish and American Isolationism, 1920-1944." Ph.D. dissertation, University of California (Riverside), 1971. 440 p.

About Fish, who served as secretary of state.

Hardy, Arthur Sherburne. THINGS REMEMBERED. Boston: Houghton Mifflin, 1923. 361 p.

Served in several diplomatic appointments, including minister to Persia, several Balkan countries, Switzerland, and Spain.

Harper, James William. "Hugh Lenox Scott: Soldier, Diplomat, 1876-1917." Ph.D. dissertation, University of Virginia, 1968. 268 p.

Harriman, Florence Jaffray. MISSION TO THE NORTH. Philadelphia: Lippincott, 1941. 331 p.

Served as minister to Norway.

Harriman, W. Averell. AMERICA AND RUSSIA IN A CHANGING WORLD: A HALF CENTURY OF PERSONAL OBSERVATION. New York: Doubleday, 1971. 328 p.

Served in various diplomatic capacities, including ambassador to Russia, under secretary of state, ambassador at large, and as presidential special emissary.

_____. PEACE WITH RUSSIA? New York: Simon and Schuster, 1959. 174 p.

Harriman, W. Averell, and Abel, Elie. SPECIAL ENVOY TO CHURCHILL AND STALIN, 1941-1946. New York: Random House, 1975. 595 p.

Harris, Townsend. THE COMPLETE JOURNAL OF TOWNSEND HARRIS, FIRST AMERICAN CONSUL GENERAL AND MINISTER TO JAPAN. New York: Doubleday, Doran, 1930. 616 p.

_____. SOME UNPUBLISHED LETTERS OF TOWNSEND HARRIS. Edited by Shio Sakanshi. New York: Japan Reference Library, 1941. 72 p.

Harrison, Thomas Skelton. THE HOMELY DIARY OF A DIPLOMAT IN THE EAST, 1897-1899. Boston: Houghton Mifflin, 1917. 364 p.

Served as consular official in Egypt.

Harrison, William Henry. REMARKS OF GENERAL HARRISON, LATE ENVOY TO THE REPUBLIC OF COLOMBIA, ON CERTAIN CHARGES MADE AGAINST HIM BY THAT GOVERNMENT. TO WHICH IS ADDED AN UNOFFICIAL LETTER FROM GENERAL HARRISON TO GENERAL BOLIVAR, ON THE AFFAIRS OF COLOMBIA: WITH NOTES, EXPLANATORY OF HIS VIEWS OF THE PRESENT STATE OF THAT COUNTRY. Washington, D.C.: Gales and Seaton, 1830. 69 p.

> Served as minister to Colombia.

Hatch, Alden. AMBASSADOR EXTRAORDINARY: CLARE BOOTHE LUCE. New York: Holt, 1956. 254 p.

> About Luce's service as ambassador to Italy.

Hawthorne, Nathaniel. OUR OLD HOME. 2 vols. Boston: Houghton Mifflin, 1883.

> Includes memoirs of consular service in Liverpool.

Hay, John Milton. ADDRESSES OF JOHN HAY. New York: Century, 1906. 353 p.

> Served in diplomatic capacity in Paris, Vienna, and Madrid, as ambassador to Great Britain, and as secretary of state.

_____. LETTERS OF JOHN HAY AND EXTRACTS FROM DIARY. Selected by Henry Adams and edited by Mrs. [Clara Louise Stone] Hay. 3 vols. Washington, D.C.: Gordian Press, 1908.

_____. THE LIFE AND LETTERS OF JOHN HAY. Edited by William Roscoe Thayer. 2 vols. Boston: Houghton Mifflin, 1915.

Hayes, Carlton J.H. WARTIME MISSION IN SPAIN, 1942-1945. New York: Macmillan, 1945. 313 p.

Heinrichs, Waldo H., Jr. AMERICAN AMBASSADOR: JOSEPH C. GREW AND THE DEVELOPMENT OF THE UNITED STATES DIPLOMATIC TRADITION. Boston: Little, Brown, 1966. 460 p.

Heller, Deane, and Heller, David. JOHN FOSTER DULLES: SOLDIER FOR PEACE. New York: Holt, Rinehart, and Winston, 1960. 328 p.

Hendrick, Burton J. THE LIFE AND LETTERS OF WALTER HINES PAGE. 3 vols. Garden City, N.Y.: Doubleday, 1922-25.

> About Page who served as ambassador to Great Britain during World War I.

Hibben, Paxton. THE PEERLESS LEADER. New York: Farrar and Rinehart, 1929. 446 p.

On William Jennings Bryan.

Hill, Leslie Brooks. "Charles Evans Hughes and United States Adherence to an International Court: A Rhetorical Analysis." Ph.D. dissertation, University of Illinois, 1968. 405 p.

Hilliard, Henry Washington. SPEECHES AND ADDRESSES, 1839-1854. New York: Harper, 1855. 497 p.

Served as charge d'affaires in Belgium and as minister to Brazil.

Hilton, Ralph. WORLDWIDE MISSION: THE STORY OF THE UNITED STATES FOREIGN SERVICE. New York: World, 1970. 256 p.

Served in the Department of State and as a Foreign Service reserve officer for two decades.

Hinton, Harold B. CORDELL HULL: A BIOGRAPHY. Garden City, N.Y.: Doubleday, Doran, 1942. 377 p.

Holsti, Ole Rudolf. "The Belief System and National Images: John Foster Dulles and the Soviet Union." Ph.D. dissertation, Stanford University, 1962. 286 p.

Hooker, Nancy H., ed. THE MOFFAT PAPERS: SELECTIONS FROM THE DIPLOMATIC JOURNALS OF JAY PIERREPONT MOFFAT, 1919-1943. Cambridge, Mass.: Harvard University Press, 1956. 408 p.

About Moffatt, a career Foreign Service officer who served in various posts abroad, in the Department of State, and as minister to Canada.

Hoopes, Townsend. THE DEVIL AND JOHN FOSTER DULLES: THE DIPLOMACY OF THE EISENHOWER ERA. Boston: Little, Brown, 1973. 562 p. Bibliog.

Horn, James John. "Diplomacy by Ultimatum: Ambassador Sheffield and Mexican-American Relations, 1924-1927." Ph.D. dissertation, State University of New York (Buffalo), 1969. 211 p.

Hornbeck, Stanley Kuhl. THE UNITED STATES AND THE FAR EAST. Boston: World Peace Foundation, 1942. 100 p.

By a long-time member of the Department of State.

Horstmann, G. Henry. CONSULAR REMINISCENCES. Philadelphia: Lippincott, 1886. 420 p.

Served as consul in Germany.

Horton, George. RECOLLECTIONS GRAVE AND GAY: THE STORY OF A
MEDITERRANEAN CONSUL. Indianapolis: Bobbs-Merrill, 1927. 331 p.

Horton, Rushmore G. THE LIFE AND PUBLIC SERVICES OF JAMES BUCHAN-
AN: LATE MINISTER TO ENGLAND AND FORMERLY MINISTER TO RUSSIA
. . . AND SECRETARY OF STATE, INCLUDING THE MOST IMPORTANT OF
HIS STATE PAPERS. New York: Derby and Jackson, 1856. 428 p.

Hostetter, John Harold. "John Foster Dulles and the French Defeat in Indochina." Ph.D. dissertation, Rutgers University, 1972. 196 p.

House, Edward Mandell, and Seymour, Charles, eds. WHAT REALLY HAP-
PENED AT PARIS: THE STORY OF THE PEACE CONFERENCE, 1918-1919,
BY AMERICAN DELEGATES. New York: Scribner, 1921. 528 p.

House, personal adviser to President Wilson, served as a member
of the president's conference delegation to draft World War I peace
treaties.

House, Lewis. "Edwin V. Morgan and Brazillian-American Diplomatic Relations, 1912-1933." Ph.D. dissertation, New York University, 1969. 160 p.

About Morgan, a career diplomat for over three decades, who
served as ambassador to Brazil.

Howe, M.A. DeWolfe. GEORGE VON LENGERKE MEYER. New York:
Dodd, Mead, 1919. 556 p.

About Meyer, who served as ambassador to Italy and Russia, in
addition to serving as postmaster general and secretary of the navy.

Howells, William Dean. LIFE AND LETTERS OF WILLIAM DEAN HOWELLS.
Edited by Mildred Howells. 2 vols. Garden City, N.Y.: Doubleday, Doran,
1928.

Served as consul in Venice.

_____. SELECTED EDITION OF WILLIAM DEAN HOWELLS. 32 vols. Bloom-
ington: University of Indiana Press, 1968.

_____. SELECTED WRITINGS OF WILLIAM DEAN HOWELLS. Edited by
Henry Steele Commager. New York: Random House, 1950. 946 p.

Hoyt, Jo Wasson. FOR THE LOVE OF MIKE. New York: Random House, 1966. 210 p.

> By wife of Foreign Service officer. On diplomatic and consular service.

Hubert, Mary Gabriel. "The Role of Nelson Trusler Johnson in Sino-American Diplomatic Relations, 1930-1935." Ph.D. dissertation, Catholic University of America, 1964. 305 p.

Hull, Cordell. THE MEMOIRS OF CORDELL HULL. 2 vols. New York: Macmillan, 1948.

Humphreys, David. THE MISCELLANEOUS WORKS OF DAVID HUMPHREYS. Gainesville, Fla.: Scholar's Facsimiles-Reprints, 1968. 394 p.

> Served as early secret agent in London, Lisbon, and Madrid, and as minister to Spain.

Huntington-Wilson, Francis M. MEMOIRS OF AN EX-DIPLOMAT. Boston: Humphries, 1945. 373 p.

> Served as charge d'affaires to Tokyo and as assistant and under secretary of state.

Huntley, Theodore A. THE LIFE OF JOHN W. DAVIS. New York: Duffield, 1924. 295 p.

> About Davis who served as ambassador to Great Britain.

Hurst, Carlton Bailey. THE ARMS ABOVE THE DOOR. New York: Dodd, Mead, 1932. 377 p.

> Experience of author in consular service.

Ingram, Alton Earl. "The Root Mission to Russia, 1917." Ph.D. dissertation, Louisiana State University, 1970. 332 p.

Irving, Washington. LETTERS FROM SUNNYSIDE AND SPAIN. Edited by Stanley T. Williams. New Haven, Conn.: Yale University Press, 1928. 80 p.

> Served in diplomatic missions to Madrid and London and as minister to Spain.

_____. SPANISH PAPERS. 2 vols. New York: Putnam, 1895.

_____. WASHINGTON IRVING DIARY, SPAIN, 1828-29. New York: Hispanic Society of America, 1926. 142 p.

Izard, Ralph. CORRESPONDENCE OF MR. RALPH IZARD OF SOUTH CARO-
LINA. Edited by Anne Izard Dess. New York: Francis and Co., 1844.
389 p.

> Served as early diplomatic agent in southern Europe.

Jablon, Howard. "Cordell Hull, the State Department, and the Foreign Policy
of the First Roosevelt Administration, 1933-1936." Ph.D. dissertation, Rutgers
University, 1967. 266 p.

Jay, John. THE CORRESPONDENCE AND PUBLIC PAPERS OF JOHN JAY.
Edited by Henry P. Johnston. 4 vols. New York: Putnam, 1890-93.

> Served as minister to Spain and secretary for foreign affairs.

_____. THE DIARY OF JOHN JAY DURING THE PEACE NEGOTIATIONS
OF 1782. New Haven, Conn.: Yale University Library, 1934. 17 p.

_____. THE LIFE OF JOHN JAY, WITH SELECTIONS FROM HIS CORRES-
PONDENCE AND MISCELLANEOUS PAPERS. Edited by William Jay. 2 vols.
New York: Harper, 1833.

Jefferson, Thomas. THE WRITINGS OF THOMAS JEFFERSON. Edited by Paul
L. Ford. 10 vols. New York: Putnam, 1892-1900.

> Served as minister to France and secretary of state.

_____. THE WRITINGS OF THOMAS JEFFERSON. Edited by Andrew J.
Lipscomb, editor in chief; Albert Ellery Bergh, managing editor. 20 vols. Washington, D.C.: Thomas Jefferson Memorial Association of the United States, 1905.

Jessup, Philip Caryl. THE BIRTH OF NATIONS. New York: Columbia University Press, 1974. 361 p.

> Incorporates and amplifies the Barnette Miller Lectures at Wellesley
> College, November 1971, and concerns the independence of such
> countries as Korea, Indonesia, Morocco, Tunis, Libya, and "Man-
> chukuo."

_____. ELIHU ROOT. 2 vols. New York: Dodd, Mead, 1938.

Johnson, Arthur M. WINTHROP W. ALDRICH: LAWYER, BANKER, DIPLO-
MAT. Cambridge, Mass.: Harvard University Press, 1968. 484 p.

> About Aldrich, who served as ambassador to Great Britain.

Johnson, Hallett. DIPLOMATIC MEMOIRS: SERIOUS AND FRIVOLOUS. New
York: Vantage, 1963. 207 p.

> Served as Foreign Service officer in various posts and as ambassador
> to Costa Rica.

Johnson, Robert Underwood. REMEMBERED YESTERDAYS. Boston: Little, Brown, 1923. 624 p.

Served as ambassador to Italy.

Johnson, Willis Fletcher. GEORGE HARVEY--"A PASSIONATE PATRIOT." Boston: Houghton Mifflin, 1929. 436 p.

About Harvey, who served as ambassador to Great Britain.

Joiner, Harry M. AMERICAN FOREIGN POLICY: THE KISSINGER ERA. Huntsville, Ala.: Strode, 1977. 308 p.

Jones, Henry Paschal. "John Foster Dulles and United States Involvement in Vietnam." Ph.D. dissertation, University of Oklahoma, 1972. 312 p.

Kalb, Marvin, and Kalb, Bernard. KISSINGER. Boston: Little, Brown, 1974. 577 p.

Kane, Nathaniel Stephen. "Charles Evans Hughes and Mexican-American Relations, 1921-1924." Ph.D. dissertation, University of Colorado, 1970. 321 p.

Kelly, Hank [Henry W.], and Kelly, Dot [Dorothy]. DANCING DIPLOMATS. Albuquerque: University of New Mexico Press, 1950. 254 p.

Foreign Service experiences in the Peruvian Amazon area.

Kennan, George F. AMERICAN DIPLOMACY: 1900-1950. Chicago: University of Chicago Press, 1951. 146 p.

Charles R. Walgreen Foundation lectures. By a career Foreign Service officer, who served as ambassador to the Soviet Union and Yugoslavia and in other posts.

_____. FROM PRAGUE AFTER MUNICH: DIPLOMATIC PAPERS, 1938-1940. Princeton, N.J.: Princeton University Press, 1968. 266 p.

_____. MEMOIRS, 1925-1950. Boston: Little, Brown, 1967. 583 p.

_____. MEMOIRS, 1950-1963. Boston: Little, Brown, 1972. 368 p.

Kerbey, Joseph Orton. AN AMERICAN CONSUL IN AMAZONIA. New York: Rudge, 1911. 370 p.

Served with Pan American Union and as consul in Brazil.

Kihl, Mary Rambo. "A Failure of Ambassadorial Diplomacy: The Case of Page and Spring Rice, 1914-1917." Ph.D. dissertation, Pennsylvania State University, 1968. 233 p.

Killian, James R., Jr. SPUTNIK, SCIENTISTS, AND EISENHOWER: A MEMOIR OF THE FIRST SPECIAL ASSISTANT TO THE PRESIDENT FOR SCIENCE AND TECHNOLOGY. Cambridge, Mass.: M.I.T. Press, 1977. 313 p. Bibliog.

King, Rufus. THE LIFE AND CORRESPONDENCE OF RUFUS KING. Edited by Charles R. King. 6 vols. New York: Putnam, 1894-1900.

Kirk, Lydia [Chapin]. POSTMARKED MOSCOW. New York: Scribner, 1952. 278 p.

By the wife of the ambassador to the Soviet Union.

Kissinger, Henry A. AMERICAN FOREIGN POLICY. 3d ed. New York: Norton, 1974. 304 p.

Expanded version of following item. Collection of essays and policy statements.

_____. AMERICAN FOREIGN POLICY: THREE ESSAYS. New York: Norton, 1969. 143 p.

_____. THE NECESSITY FOR CHOICE. New York: Harper, 1961. 370 p.

_____. NUCLEAR WEAPONS AND FOREIGN POLICY. New York: Harper, 1957. 455 p.

_____. THE TROUBLED PARTNERSHIP. New York: McGraw-Hill, 1965. 266 p.

Concerns Atlantic Alliance.

_____. THE WHITE HOUSE YEARS. Boston: Little Brown, 1979. 1,521 p.

Kist, Glenn Joseph. "The Role of Thomas C. Dawson in United States Latin American Diplomatic Relations, 1897-1912." Ph.D. dissertation, Loyola University of Chicago, 1971. 469 p.

About Dawson, who served as consul and as minister to Dominican Republic, Colombia, Panama, Nicaragua, and in Department of State.

Kitchens, Allen Hampton. "Ambassador Extraordinary: The Diplomatic Career of Joseph Hodges Choate." Ph.D. dissertation, George Washington University, 1971. 514 p.

About Choate, who served as ambassador to Great Britain and head of U.S. delegation to second Hague Conference, 1907.

Koerner, Gustav P. MEMOIRS OF GUSTAV KOERNER, 1809-1896. Edited by Thomas J. McCormac. 2 vols. Cedar Rapids, Iowa: Torch, 1909.

Served as minister to Spain.

Koskoff, David E. JOSEPH P. KENNEDY: A LIFE AND TIMES. Englewood Cliffs, N.J.: Prentice-Hall, 1974. 643 p.

About Kennedy, who served as ambassador to Great Britain.

Ladenburger, John F. "The Philosophy of International Politics of John Foster Dulles, 1919-1952." Ph.D. dissertation, University of Connecticut, 1969. 269 p.

Landau, David. KISSINGER: THE USES OF POWER. Boston: Houghton Mifflin, 1972. 250 p.

Lane, Arthur Bliss. I SAW FREEDOM BETRAYED. London: Regency, 1949. 217 p.

By a career diplomat, who served as ambassador to Poland. Reprint of following item.

_____. I SAW POLAND BETRAYED: AN AMERICAN AMBASSADOR REPORTS TO THE AMERICAN PEOPLE. Indianapolis: Bobbs-Merrill, 1948. 344 p.

Langer, Robert. SEIZURE OF TERRITORY: THE STIMSON DOCTRINE AND RELATED PRINCIPLES IN LEGAL THEORY AND DIPLOMATIC PRACTICE. Princeton, N.J.: Princeton University Press, 1947. 313 p. Bibliog.

Lansing, Robert. BIG FOUR AND OTHERS OF THE PEACE CONFERENCE. Boston: Houghton Mifflin, 1921. 213 p.

On World War I peace conference. By secretary of state under President Wilson and a member of his delegation to the peace conference.

_____. THE PEACE NEGOTIATIONS: A PERSONAL NARRATIVE. Boston: Houghton Mifflin, 1921. 328 p.

_____. WAR MEMOIRS OF ROBERT LANSING. Indianapolis: Bobbs-Merrill, 1935. 388 p.

Larkin, Thomas Oliver. THE LARKIN PAPERS: PERSONAL, BUSINESS, AND OFFICIAL CORRESPONDENCE OF THOMAS OLIVER LARKIN, MERCHANT AND U.S. CONSUL IN CALIFORNIA. Edited by George P. Hammons. 10 vols. Berkeley: University of California Press for Bancroft Library, 1951.

Served as consul and confidential agent.

Laurens, Henry. CORRESPONDENCE OF HENRY LAURENS OF SOUTH CARO-LINA. New York: Zenger Club, 1861. 240 p.

Served as minister to the Netherlands in 1779 and as colleague of Benjamin Franklin, John Adams, and John Jay for peace negotiations at close of Revolutionary War.

_____. "A Narrative of the Capture of Henry Laurens, of His Confinement in the Tower of London." SOUTH CAROLINA HISTORICAL SOCIETY COLLECTION 1 (1857): 18-68.

_____. THE PAPERS OF HENRY LAURENS. Edited by Philip M. Hamer and George C. Rogers. 4 vols. Columbia: University of South Carolina Press, 1972.

Laurens, John. A SUCCINCT MEMOIR OF THE LIFE AND PUBLIC SERVICE OF COLONEL JOHN LAURENS, AIDE-DE-CAMP TO GENERAL WASHINGTON AND SPECIAL ENVOY TO THE FRENCH COURT DURING THE WAR OF THE AMERICAN REVOLUTION. . .. Albany, N.Y.: Williamstadt, 1867. 250 p.

Served as secretary to legation in Paris and as special minister to France.

Lawrence, May Viola [Tingley]. A DIPLOMAT'S HELPMATE. San Francisco: Crocker, 1918. 50 p.

By the wife of the first minister to Korea.

Leach, Paul R. THAT MAN DAWES. Chicago: Reilly and Lee. 1930. 349 p.

About Dawes, who served as ambassador to Great Britain and in other capacities.

Leahy, William D. I WAS THERE: THE PERSONAL STORY OF THE CHIEF OF STAFF TO PRESIDENTS ROOSEVELT AND TRUMAN--BASED ON HIS NOTES AND DIARIES MADE AT THE TIME. New York: Whittlesey, 1950. 527 p.

Lee, William. LETTERS OF WILLIAM LEE, SHERIFF AND ALDERMAN OF LONDON: COMMERCIAL AGENT OF THE CONTINENTAL CONGRESS IN FRANCE, AND MINISTER TO THE COURTS OF VIENNA AND BERLIN, 1766-1783. Edited by Worthington Chauncey Ford. 3 vols. Brooklyn: Historical Printing Club, 1891.

Served as early commercial agent and as commissioner to Vienna, Berlin, and the Netherlands.

Lee, William. A YANKEE JEFFERSONIAN: SELECTIONS FROM THE DIARY AND LETTERS OF WILLIAM LEE OF MASSACHUSETTS WRITTEN FROM 1796-1840. Cambridge, Mass.: Belknap, 1958. 311 p.

Served as consul to Bordeaux and Paris.

Legare, Hugh Swinton. WRITINGS OF HUGH SWINTON LEGARE: LATE ATTORNEY GENERAL AND ACTING SECRETARY OF STATE OF THE UNITED STATES. Edited by Mary S. Legare. 2 vols. Charleston, S.C.: Burges and James, 1846.

Served as charge d'affaires to Belgium.

Leopold, Richard W. ELIHU ROOT AND THE CONSERVATIVE TRADITION. Boston: Little, Brown, 1954. 222 p.

Lester, Charles Edwards. MY CONSULSHIP. 2 vols. New York: Cornish, Lamport, 1853.

Served as consul general in Geneva.

Levine, Erwin L. THEODORE FRANCIS GREEN. 2 vols. Vol. 1: THE RHODE ISLAND YEARS, 1906-1936; Vol. 2: THE WASHINGTON YEARS, 1937-1960. Providence, R.I.: Brown University Press, 1963, 1971. 222 p., 179 p.

Lin, C.Y. KISSINGER'S DIPLOMACY. Brunswick, Ohio: King's Court, 1975.

Link, Arthur S. WILSON THE DIPLOMATIST: A LOOK AT HIS MAJOR FOREIGN POLICIES. New York: New Viewpoints, 1957. 184 p.

Lisagor, Peter, and Higgins, Marguerite. OVERTIME IN HEAVEN: ADVENTURES IN THE FOREIGN SERVICE. Garden City, N.Y.: Doubleday, 1964. 275 p.

Anecdotes of diplomatic life, stressing courage and resourcefulness.

Liska, George. BEYOND KISSINGER: WAYS OF CONSERVATIVE STATECRAFT. Baltimore: John Hopkins Press, 1975. 159 p.

Lockmiller, David A. ENOCH H. CROWDER: SOLDIER, LAWYER, STATESMAN. Columbia: University of Missouri Press, 1955. 286 p. Bibliog.

About Crowder, who served as ambassador to Cuba.

Lodge, Henry Cabot. THE STORM HAS MANY EYES: A PERSONAL NARRATIVE. New York: Norton, 1973. 272 p.

Served as ambassador to the United Nations, twice as ambassador to Vietnam, and as ambassador to Germany. Also participated in negotiating Vietnam settlement in Paris.

Lohbeck, Don. PATRICK J. HURLEY. Chicago: Regnery, 1956. 513 p.

About Hurley, who served as minister to New Zealand, special representative to the Soviet Union and various Near Eastern countries, and ambassador to China.

Lombard, H.C.C. WASHINGTON WALTZ: DIPLOMATIC PEOPLE AND POLICIES. New York: Knopf, 1941. 271 p.

Long, Breckinridge. THE WAR DIARY OF BRECKINRIDGE LONG. Edited by Fred L. Israel. Lincoln: University of Nebraska Press, 1966. 410 p.

Served as ambassador to Italy, assistant secretary of state, and delegate to Dumbarton Oaks meetings.

Long, John Cuthbert. BRYAN: THE GREAT COMMONER. New York: Appleton, 1928. 421 p.

Concerns William Jennings Bryan.

Loring, George Bailey. A YEAR IN PORTUGAL, 1889-1890. New York: Putnam, 1891. 313 p.

Served as minister to Portugal.

Loss, Richard Archibald John. "Secretary of State Dean Acheson: The Political Dimension." Ph.D. dissertation, Cornell University, 1971. 352 p.

Lowell, James Russell. LETTERS OF JAMES RUSSELL LOWELL. Edited by Charles Eliot Norton. 2 vols. New York: Harper, 1894.

Served as minister to Spain and to Great Britain.

_____. NEW LETTERS OF JAMES RUSSELL LOWELL. Edited by M.A. DeWolfe Howe. New York: Harper, 1932. 364 p.

McClintock, Robert. THE MEANING OF LIMITED WAR. Boston: Houghton Mifflin, 1967. 239 p.

Served as ambassador to Cambodia, Lebanon, and Venezuela.

McCloy, John J. THE CHALLENGE TO AMERICAN FOREIGN POLICY. Cambridge, Mass.: Harvard University Press, 1953. 81 p.

Godkin Lectures, Harvard University. Served as U.S. high commissioner to Germany and in other capacities.

McDonald, James Grover. MY MISSION IN ISRAEL, 1948-1951. New York: Simon and Schuster, 1951. 303 p.

Served as ambassador to Israel.

McLane, Robert Milligan. REMINISCENCES, 1827-1897. N.p., 1903. 165 p.

Madison, James. THE PAPERS OF JAMES MADISON. Edited by William Hutchinson and William M.E. Rachal (vols. 1-7) and by Robert Rutland and William M.E. Rachal (vols. 8-10). 10 vols. Chicago: University of Chicago Press, 1962-77.

Marsh, Caroline Crane. LIFE AND LETTERS OF GEORGE PERKINS MARSH. New York: Scribner, 1888. 479 p.

Martin, E.S. LIFE OF JOSEPH H. CHOATE. 2 vols. New York: Constable, 1920.

About Choate, who served as ambassador to Great Britain at the turn of the century.

Masingill, Eugene Frank. "The Diplomatic Career of Henry Lane Wilson in Latin America." Ph.D. dissertation, Louisiana State University, 1957. 266 p.

May, Joseph Turner. "John Foster Dulles and the European Defense Community." Ph.D. dissertation, Kent State University, 1969. 263 p.

Mazuzan, George Thaire. "Warren R. Austin: A Republican Internationalist and United States Foreign Policy." Ph.D. dissertation, Kent State University, 1969. 364 p.

Mecklin, John. MISSION IN TORMENT: AN INTIMATE ACCOUNT OF THE U.S. ROLE IN VIETNAM. Garden City, N.Y.: Doubleday, 1965. 318 p.

Served as Foreign Service reserve officer.

Megargee, Richard. "The Diplomacy of John Bassett Moore: Realism in American Foreign Policy." Ph.D. dissertation, Northwestern University, 1963. 424 p.

About Moore, who served as assistant secretary of state and counselor of the State Department.

Mende, Elsie [Porter]. AN AMERICAN SOLDIER AND DIPLOMAT, HORACE PORTER. New York: Stokes, 1927. 390 p.

About Porter, who served as ambassador to France.

Merchant, Livingston T., ed. NEIGHBORS TAKEN FOR GRANTED: CANADA AND THE UNITED STATES. New York: Praeger, 1966. 166 p.

Served as ambassador to Canada, held various posts in the Department of State, and was appointed to a number of other diplomatic posts.

Meriwether, Lee. AFTER THOUGHTS: A SEQUEL TO MY YESTERYEARS. Webster Groves, Mo.: International Mark Twain Society, 1945. 441 p.

> Served as special assistant to U.S. ambassador to France during World War I. Sequel to following item.

_____. MY YESTERYEARS: AN AUTOBIOGRAPHY OF LEE MERIWETHER. Webster Groves, Mo.: International Mark Twain Society, 1942. 440 p.

_____. THE WAR DIARY OF A DIPLOMAT. New York: Dodd, Mead, 1919. 303 p.

Mesta, Perle S., with Robert Cahn. PERLE--MY STORY. New York: Mc-Graw-Hill, 1960. 251 p.

> Served as minister to Luxembourg.

Meyer, Armin H. ASSIGNMENT--TOKYO: AN AMBASSADOR'S JOURNAL. Indianapolis: Bobbs-Merrill, 1974. 396 p.

> Served as ambassador to Lebanon, Iran, and Japan.

Miller, David Hunter. MY DIARY AT THE CONFERENCE OF PARIS (WITH DOCUMENTS). 21 vols. New York: Appeal, 1924.

> Served on the advisory staff to the presidential delegation at the World War I peace conference.

Miller, William Johnson. HENRY CABOT LODGE: A BIOGRAPHY. New York: Heineman, 1967. 449 p. Bibliog.

> Concerns Ambassador Lodge.

Millspaugh, Arthur Chester. AMERICANS IN PERSIA. Washington, D.C.: Brookings Institution, 1946. 293 p.

> Directed two American financial missions to Iran, 1922-27 and 1943-45.

Milner, Cooper. "The Public Life of Cordell Hull, 1907-1924." Ph.D. dissertation, Vanderbilt University, 1960. 486 p.

Mitchell, Eleanor Swann. POSTSCRIPT TO SEVEN HOMES. Francestown, N.H.: Jones, 1960. 217 p.

> See following item. By the wife of a Foreign Service officer.

_____. SEVEN HOMES HAD I: EXPERIENCES OF A FOREIGN SERVICE WIFE. New York: Exposition, 1955. 172 p.

Moffatt, Jay Pierrepont. THE MOFFAT PAPERS: SELECTIONS FROM THE
DIPLOMATIC JOURNALS OF JAY PIERREPONT MOFFAT, 1919-1943. Edited
by Nancy Harrison Hooker. Cambridge, Mass.: Harvard University Press,
1956. 408 p.

By a Foreign Service officer.

Monroe, James. AUTOBIOGRAPHY. Edited by Stuart Gerry Brown. Syracuse, N.Y.: Syracuse University Press, 1959. 236 p.

_____. THE MEMOIRS OF JAMES MONROE, ESQ., RELATING TO HIS
UNSETTLED CLAIMS UPON THE PEOPLE AND GOVERNMENT OF THE UNITED
STATES. Charlottesville, Va.: Gilmer, Davis, 1828. 60 p.

Concerns claims for reimbursement for his two diplomatic missions
to France.

_____. THE WRITINGS OF JAMES MONROE. Edited by Stanislaus Murray
Hamilton. 7 vols. New York: Putnam, 1898-1903.

Monti, Luigi [Samuel Sampleton]. ADVENTURES OF A CONSUL ABROAD.
Boston: Lee and Shepard, 1878. 270 p.

Served as consul at Palermo.

Moran, Benjamin. THE JOURNAL OF BENJAMIN MORAN. Edited by Sarah
Agnes Wallace and Frances Elma Gillespie. 2 vols. Chicago: University of
Chicago Press, 1949.

Served as secretary to legation in London and as minister to Portugal, 1853-75.

Morgenthau, Henry. ALL IN A LIFETIME. Garden City, N.Y.: Doubleday,
Page, 1922. 454 p.

Served as ambassador to Turkey.

_____. AMBASSADOR MORGENTHAU'S STORY. Garden City, N.Y.:
Doubleday, Page, 1918. 407 p.

_____. I WAS SENT TO ATHENS. Garden City, N.Y.: Doubleday, Doran,
1929. 327 p.

Served as chairman of the Greek Refugee Settlement Commission.

Morison, Elting E. TURMOIL AND TRADITION: A STUDY OF THE LIFE AND
TIMES OF HENRY L. STIMSON. Boston: Houghton Mifflin, 1960. 686 p.
Bibliog.

Morris, Gouverneur. THE DIARY AND LETTERS OF GOUVERNEUR MORRIS. Edited by Anne Cary Morris. 2 vols. New York: Scribner, 1888.

> Served as minister to France.

Morris, Ira Nelson. FROM AN AMERICAN LEGATION. New York: Knopf, 1923. 287 p.

> Served as commissioner to Italy and minister to Sweden.

_____. HERITAGE FROM MY FATHER. New York: Privately printed by Mrs. I.N. Morris, 1947. 263 p.

Morris, Roger. UNCERTAIN GREATNESS: HENRY KISSINGER AND AMERICAN FOREIGN POLICY. New York: Harper and Row, 1977. 312 p.

Morrison, DeLesseps S. LATIN AMERICAN MISSION: AN ADVENTURE IN HEMISPHERE DIPLOMACY. New York: Simon and Schuster, 1965. 288 p.

> Served as ambassador to the Organization of American States.

Morrow, Elizabeth Cutter. THE MEXICAN YEARS: LEAVES FROM THE DIARY OF ELIZABETH CUTTER MORROW. New York: Spiral, 1953. 272 p.

> By wife of Ambassador Dwight Morrow, appointed to Mexico.

Morrow, John H. FIRST AMERICAN AMBASSADOR TO GUINEA. New Brunswick, N.J.: Rutgers University Press, 1967. 291 p.

Mosley, Leonard. DULLES: A BIOGRAPHY OF ELEANOR, ALLEN, AND JOHN FOSTER DULLES AND THEIR FAMILY NETWORK. New York: Dial, 1978. 530 p.

Motley, John Lothrop. JOHN LATHROP MOTLEY. New York: American, 1939. 482 p.

> Served as minister to Austria and Great Britain.

_____. JOHN LATHROP MOTLEY AND HIS FAMILY: FURTHER LETTERS AND RECORDS. Edited by his daughter and Herbert St. John Mildmay. New York: Lane, 1910. 321 p.

_____. THE WRITINGS OF JOHN LATHROP MOTLEY. 17 vols. New York: Harper, 1900.

Mott, Thomas Bentley. MYRON T. HERRICK, FRIEND OF FRANCE. Garden City, N.Y.: Doubleday, Doran, 1929. 399 p.

> About Herrick, who served as ambassador to France prior to and after World War I.

_____. TWENTY YEARS AS MILITARY ATTACHE. New York: Oxford, 1937. 242 p.

Mulhollan, Paige Elliott. "Philander C. Knox and Dollar Diplomacy, 1909-1913." Ph.D. dissertation, University of Texas, 1966. 291 p.

Munro, Dana G. INTERVENTION AND DOLLAR DIPLOMACY IN THE CARIBBEAN, 1900-1921. Princeton, N.J.: Princeton University Press, 1964. 553 p.

Served as minister to Haiti.

_____. THE UNITED STATES AND THE CARIBBEAN AREA. Boston: World Peace Foundation, 1934. 322 p.

Murphy, Robert D. DIPLOMAT AMONG WARRIORS. Garden City, N.Y.: Doubleday, 1964. 470 p.

By career Foreign Service officer who served as ambassador to Belgium and Japan, assistant secretary of state, and under secretary of state.

Murray, William Vans. LETTERS OF WILLIAM VANS MURRAY TO JOHN QUINCY ADAMS. Edited by Worthington Chauncey Ford. In AMERICAN HISTORICAL ASSOCIATION ANNUAL REPORT FOR THE YEAR 1912, pp. 341-715. Washington, D.C.: American Historical Association, 1914.

Served as minister to the Netherlands and France.

_____. POLITICAL SKETCHES: INSCRIBED TO HIS EXCELLENCY JOHN ADAMS, MINISTER PLENIPOTENTIARY FROM THE UNITED STATES TO THE COURT OF GREAT BRITAIN BY A CITIZEN OF THE UNITED STATES. London: Dilly, 1787. 96 p.

Muth, Edwin A. "Elihu Root: His Role and Concepts Pertaining to United States Policies of Intervention." Ph.D. dissertation, Georgetown University, 1966. 196 p.

Navarrete, George. "The Latin American Policy of Charles Evans Hughes, 1921-1925." Ph.D. dissertation, University of California (Berkeley), 1964. 428 p.

Nevins, Allan. HENRY WHITE: THIRTY YEARS OF AMERICAN DIPLOMACY. New York: Harper, 1930. 518 p.

About White, a career diplomat who, among other appointments, served as ambassador to Italy.

Nicolson, Sir Harold. DWIGHT MORROW. New York: Harcourt, Brace, 1935. 409 p.

About Morrow, who served as ambassador to Mexico.

Norton, Nile Brown. "Frank R. McCoy and American Diplomacy, 1928-1932." Ph.D. dissertation, University of Denver, 1966. 372 p.

O'Brien, Francis W., ed. THE HOOVER-WILSON WARTIME CORRESPOND-ENCE, SEPTEMBER 24, 1914, TO NOVEMBER 11, 1918. Ames: Iowa State University Press, 1974. 297 p.

O'Shaughnessy, Edith Louise. DIPLOMATIC DAYS. New York: Harper, 1917. 337 p.

By wife of Nelson O'Shaughnessy, who served in diplomatic capacity in Denmark, Germany, Austria, and Mexico.

_____. A DIPLOMAT'S WIFE IN MEXICO. New York: Harper, 1916. 355 p.

_____. VIENNESE MEDLEY. New York: Huebsch, 1924. 295 p.

Pace, Antonio. BENJAMIN FRANKLIN AND ITALY. Philadelphia: American Philosophical Society, 1958. 450 p.

Paddock, Paul. CHINA DIARY: CRISIS DIPLOMACY IN DAIREN. Ames: Iowa State University Press, 1977. 285 p.

Served as consul in Dairen, Manchuria, in 1948, and was the last American diplomat in the Peoples Republic of China during the cold war.

Page, Thomas Nelson. ITALY AND THE WORLD WAR. New York: Scribner, 1920. 422 p.

Served as ambassador to Italy during World War I.

Page, Walter Hines. THE LIFE AND LETTERS OF WALTER HINES PAGE. Edited by Burton J. Hendrick. 3 vols. Garden City, N.Y.: Doubleday, Page, 1923-26.

Palmer, Frederick. AMERICA IN FRANCE. New York: Dodd, Mead, 1918. 479 p.

_____. BLISS, PEACEMAKER: THE LIFE AND LETTERS OF TASKER HOWARD BLISS. New York: Dodd, Mead, 1934. 477 p.

About General Bliss, who served on President Wilson's peace conference delegation at the close of World War I.

Paolino, Ernest N. THE FOUNDATIONS OF THE AMERICAN EMPIRE: WILLIAM HENRY SEWARD AND UNITED STATES FOREIGN POLICY. Ithaca, N.Y.: Cornell University Press, 1973. 235 p. Bibliog.

Parker [Child], Maude. IMPERSONATION OF A LADY. Boston: Houghton Mifflin, 1934. 270 p.

By wife of Richard Washburn Child, diplomatic careerist who served as ambassador to Italy. See also entry for Maude Parker Child, p. 625.

_____. SECRET ENVOY. Indianapolis: Bobbs-Merrill, 1930. 302 p.

Parker, Peter. THE JOURNAL OF PETER PARKER. London: Smith, Elder, 1838. 75 p.

Served in several diplomatic posts, including commissioner to China.

Parsons, Edward Budd. "Admiral Sims' Mission in Europe in 1917-1919 and Some Aspects of United States Naval and Foreign Wartime Policy." Ph.D. dissertation, State University of New York (Buffalo), 1971. 444 p.

Patterson, Jefferson. DIPLOMATIC DUTY AND DIVERSION. Cambridge, Mass.: Riverside, 1956. 481 p.

Consists of letters of career Foreign Service officer.

_____. DIPLOMATIC TERMINUS: AN EXPERIENCE IN URUGUAY. Cambridge, Mass.: *Riverside, 1962. 113 p.

Correspondence and reminiscences.

Peterson, Harold F. DIPLOMAT OF THE AMERICAS: A BIOGRAPHY OF WILLIAM I. BUCHANAN, 1852-1909. Albany, N.Y.: SUNY Press, 1976. 458 p.

Peterson, Merrill D., ed. THOMAS JEFFERSON: A PROFILE. New York: Hill and Wang, 1967. 262 p. Bibliog.

Petrov, Vladimir. A STUDY IN DIPLOMACY: THE STORY OF ARTHUR BLISS LANE. Chicago: Regnery, 1971. 302 p.

About Lane who was a career diplomat who served as minister and ambassador to several countries, including Colombia and Poland.

Phelps, Edward John. ORATIONS AND ESSAYS OF EDWARD JOHN PHELPS-- DIPLOMAT AND STATESMAN. Edited by J.G. McCullough, with a memoir by John W. Stewart. New York: Harper, 1901. 475 p.

Served as ambassador to England and as U.S. representative in Bering Sea Arbitration.

Phillips, William. VENTURES IN DIPLOMACY. Boston: Beacon, 1953. 477 p.

By a career officer who served in several ranking diplomatic appointments and as under secretary of state.

Poinsett, Joel Roberts. THE PRESENT POLITICAL STATE OF MEXICO: A PREVIOUSLY UNPUBLISHED CONFIDENTIAL REPORT ON THE POLITICAL CONDITION OF MEXICO IN 1822, PREPARED FOR THE U.S. SECRETARY OF STATE. Edited with introduction by L. Smith Lee. Salisbury, N.C.: Documentary Publications, 1976. 87 p.

First diplomatic report on independent Mexico by special agent who later became first U.S. minister to Mexico.

Powers, Richard James. "Kennan Against Himself: From Containment to Disengagement; A Decade of U.S. Foreign Policy Making as Focused on the Ideas and Concepts of George F. Kennan, 1947-1957." Ph.D. dissertation, Claremont College, 1967. 250 p.

Pusey, Merlo J. CHARLES EVANS HUGHES. 2 vols. New York: Macmillan, 1951.

Chapters 39-54 on Hughes as secretary of state.

Rankin, Karl Lott. AFTER SEEING CHINA. Taipei: n.p., 1962. 174 p.

Served as ambassador to China and Yugoslavia.

_____. CHINA ASSIGNMENT. Seattle: University of Washington Press, 1964. 343 p.

Reed, Joseph Verner. TO THE EMBASSY. New York: Duell, Sloan, and Pearce, 1963. 241 p.

Memoirs of U.S. embassy in Paris.

Reinsch, Paul Samuel. AN AMERICAN DIPLOMAT IN CHINA. Garden City, N.Y.: Doubleday, Page, 1922. 396 p.

Served as minister to China during World War I.

Reischauer, Edwin O. BEYOND VIETNAM: THE UNITED STATES AND ASIA. New York: Knopf, 1967. 242 p.

Served as ambassador to Japan.

_____. TOWARD A NEW FAR EASTERN POLICY. New York: Foreign Policy Association, 1950. 61 p.

_____. TOWARD THE 21ST CENTURY: EDUCATION FOR A CHANGING WORLD. New York: Knopf, 1973. 195 p.

_____. THE UNITED STATES AND JAPAN. 1950. Reprint. Cambridge, Mass.: Harvard University Press, 1965. 396 p. Bibliog.

_____. WANTED: AN ASIAN POLICY. New York: Knopf, 1955. 276 p.

Richardson, Norval. LIVING ABROAD: THE ADVENTURES OF AN AMERICAN FAMILY. New York: Lippincott, 1938. 320 p.

> By a Foreign Service officer who served in Cuba, Denmark, Italy, Chile, Portugal, and Japan.

_____. MY DIPLOMATIC EDUCATION. New York: Dodd, Mead, 1923. 337 p.

Rinden, Robert Watland, with Seymour I. Nadler. LIFE AND LOVE IN THE FOREIGN SERVICE. Washington, D.C.: Foreign Service Journal, 1969. 60 p.

> By a Foreign Service reserve officer. Spoof providing series of photographs with humorous captions.

Roosevelt, Franklin Delano, and Pope Pius XII. WARTIME CORRESPONDENCE BETWEEN PRESIDENT ROOSEVELT AND POPE PIUS XII. Introduction and explanatory notes by Myron C. Taylor. New York: Macmillan, 1947. 127 p.

> With explanation by Taylor, who served as the president's special representative to the Vatican.

Root, Elihu. ADDRESSES ON GOVERNMENT AND CITIZENSHIP. Edited by Robert Bacon and James Brown Scott. Cambridge, Mass.: Harvard University Press, 1916. 552 p.

> Served as secretary of state under President Theodore Roosevelt.

_____. ADDRESSES ON INTERNATIONAL SUBJECTS. Edited by Robert Bacon and James Brown Scott. Cambridge, Mass.: Harvard University Press, 1916. 463 p.

_____. MEN AND POLICIES: ADDRESSES BY ELIHU ROOT. Edited by Robert Bacon and James Brown Scott. Cambridge, Mass.: Harvard University Press, 1925. 511 p.

_____. THE MILITARY AND COLONIAL POLICY OF THE UNITED STATES: ADDRESSES AND REPORTS BY ELIHU ROOT. Edited by Robert Bacon and James Brown Scott. Cambridge, Mass.: Harvard University Press, 1916. 502 p.

_____. THE UNITED STATES AND WAR: THE MISSION TO RUSSIA, POLITICAL ADDRESSES BY ELIHU ROOT. Edited by Robert Bacon and James Brown Scott. Cambridge, Mass.: Harvard University Press, 1918. 362 p.

Rosenau, James N. THE NOMINATION OF CHARLES "CHIP" BOHLEN. New York: Holt, 1958. 16 p.

About Bohlen, who was a career diplomat who served in various posts, including ambassador to France, the Philippines, and the Soviet Union.

Rostow, Walt W. VIEW FROM THE SEVENTH FLOOR. New York: Harper and Row, 1964. 178 p.

Refers to the floor of the Department of State on which the secretary and his principal deputies have offices; except for the reception rooms, located on the eighth floor, it is the top floor of the department.

Rounds, Frank W. A WINDOW ON RED SQUARE. Boston: Houghton Mifflin, 1953. 304 p.

Served as attache in U.S. Embassy at Moscow.

Rush, Richard. NARRATIVE OF A RESIDENCE AT THE COURT OF LONDON. London: Bailey, 1833. 460 p.

Served as acting secretary of state and minister to Britain and France.

_____. OCCASIONAL PRODUCTIONS: POLITICAL, DIPLOMATIC, AND MISCELLANEOUS. Philadelphia: Lippincott, 1860. 535 p.

Russell, Beatrice. LIVING IN STATE. New York: McKay, 1959. 272 p.

Author's reminiscences as the wife of a Foreign Service officer.

Russell, William. BERLIN EMBASSY. New York: Dutton, 1941. 307 p.

Served as clerk in Berlin Embassy.

Sands, William Franklin. OUR JUNGLE DIPLOMACY. Chapel Hill: University of North Carolina Press, 1944. 250 p.

Served as minister to Guatemala.

_____. UNDIPLOMATIC MEMORIES. New York: Whittlesey, 1930. 238 p.

Sawyer, Charles. CONCERNS OF A CONSERVATIVE DEMOCRAT. Carbondale: Southern Illinois University Press, 1968. 399 p.

Served as ambassador to Belgium, minister to Luxenbourg, and secretary of commerce.

_____. DIARY OF CHARLES SAWYER, AMBASSADOR TO BELGIUM, 1944. n.p.: n.d.

_____. DIARY OF CHARLES SAWYER, AMBASSADOR TO BELGIUM, 1945. n.p.: n.d.

Sayre, Francis B. EXPERIMENTS IN INTERNATIONAL ADMINISTRATION. New York: Harper, 1919. 200 p.

> Served as assistant secretary of state and as high commissioner to Philippines before World War II. Also was first representative to the Trusteeship Council of the United Nations.

_____. GLAD ADVENTURE. New York: Macmillan, 1957. 356 p.

Schrier, William. GERRIT J. DIEKEMA, ORATOR: A RHETORICAL STUDY OF THE POLITICAL AND OCCASIONAL ADDRESSES OF GERRIT J. DIEKEMA. Grand Rapids, Mich.: Aerdmans, 1950. 269 p.

> About Diekema, who served as minister to the Netherlands.

Schultejann, Mary Annunciata. "Henry L. Stimson's Latin American Policy, 1929-1933." Ph.D. dissertation, Georgetown University, 1967. 316 p.

Schurz, Carl. AUTOBIOGRAPHY: AN ABRIDGEMENT IN ONE VOLUME BY WAYNE ANDREWS. New York: Scribner, 1961. 331 p.

> Among other positions, served as minister to Spain.

_____. THE INTIMATE LETTERS OF CARL SCHURZ, 1841-1869. Edited by Joseph Schafer. Madison: State Historical Society of Wisconsin, 1928. 491 p.

_____. THE REMINISCENCES OF CARL SCHURZ. 3 vols. New York: Mc-Clure, 1907-8.

_____. SPEECHES, CORRESPONDENCE, AND POLITICAL PAPERS OF CARL SCHURZ. Edited by Frederick Bancroft. 6 vols. New York: Putnam, 1913. Reprint. New York: Negro Universities Press, 1969.

Schuyler, Eugene. SELECTED ESSAYS: WITH A MEMOIR BY EVELYN SCHUYLER SCHAEFFER. New York: Scribner, 1901. 364 p.

> Served in various diplomatic posts, including minister to Rumania, Greece, and Egypt.

Scott, James Brown. AMERICAN ADDRESSES AT THE SECOND HAGUE PEACE CONFERENCE, DELIVERED BY JOSEPH H. CHOATE, GENERAL HORACE PORTER, JAMES BROWN SCOTT. Boston: Ginn, 1910. 217 p.

By Scott who served as solicitor (legal adviser) in the Department of State.

_____. ELIHU ROOT'S SERVICES TO INTERNATIONAL LAW. New York: Carnegie Endowment for International Peace, 1925. 54 p.

About Root, who served as secretary of state.

_____. ROBERT BACON: LIFE AND LETTERS. Garden City: Doubleday, Page, 1923. 459 p.

About Bacon, who served as assistant secretary and as secretary of state.

Sebald, William J. WITH MACARTHUR IN JAPAN. New York: Norton, 1965. 318 p.

By Foreign Service officer who served in Japan, as ambassador to Burma and Australia, and as assistant secretary of state.

Seward, Frederick William. REMINISCENCES OF A WAR-TIME STATESMAN AND DIPLOMAT, 1830-1915. New York: Putnam, 1916. 489 p.

Served as assistant secretary of state in the 1860s and 1870s.

Seward, George Frederick. THE UNITED STATES' CONSULATES IN CHINA: A LETTER WITH INCLOSURES OF THE CONSUL-GENERAL IN CHINA TO THE SECRETARY OF STATE. Washington, D.C.: Privately printed, 1867. 74 p.

Seymour, Charles. AMERICAN DIPLOMACY DURING THE WORLD WAR. Hamden, Conn.: Archon, 1964. 427 p. Bibliog.

By a major historian of Wilson's policy during World War I.

_____, ed. THE INTIMATE PAPERS OF COLONEL HOUSE. 4 vols. Boston: Houghton Mifflin, 1927-28.

About House, who served as President Wilson's personal adviser and diplomatic representative and as a member of the U.S. delegation to the World War I peace conference.

Sharp, William G. WAR MEMORIES. Edited by Warrington Dawson. London: Constable, 1931. 431 p.

Served as ambassador to France.

Shaw, Samuel. THE JOURNALS OF MAJOR SAMUEL SHAW, THE FIRST AMERICAN CONSUL AT CANTON. Taipei, Taiwan: Ch'eng-Wen, 1968. 360 p.

Sherrill, Charles Hitchcock. A YEAR'S EMBASSY TO MUSTAFA KEMAL. New York: Scirbner, 1934. 277 p.

Concerns U.S. mission in Turkey.

Sherwood, Robert Emmet. ROOSEVELT AND HOPKINS: AN INTIMATE HISTORY. Rev. ed. New York: Harper, 1950. 996 p.

About Harry Hopkins, Roosevelt's personal adviser and diplomatic representative.

Shotwell, James Thomas. AT THE PARIS PEACE CONFERENCE. New York: Macmillan, 1937. 444 p.

Shuster, W. Morgan. STRANGLING OF PERSIA. New York: Century, 1912. 423 p.

Personal narrative of European diplomacy and oriental intrigue by an American appointed as treasurer-general of Persia (Iran).

Simpson, Bertram L. INDISCREET LETTERS FROM PEKING. New York: Dodd, Mead, 1907. 447 p.

Skinner, Robert Peet. ABYSSINIA OF TODAY: AN ACCOUNT OF THE FIRST MISSION SENT BY THE AMERICAN GOVERNMENT TO THE COURT OF THE KING OF KINGS, 1903-1904. New York: Longmans, Green, 1906. 227 p.

_____. OUR MISSION TO ABYSSINIA: CONSUL GENERAL SKINNER'S REPORT. Washington, D.C.: Government Printing Office, 1904. 8 p.

Smith, Arthur D.H. MR. HOUSE OF TEXAS. New York: Funk and Wagnalls, 1940. 381 p.

About House, who served as personal adviser to and special diplomatic representative of President Wilson.

_____. THE REAL COLONEL HOUSE. New York: Doran, 1918. 306 p.

Smith, Earl E.T. THE FOURTH FLOOR: AN ACCOUNT OF THE CASTRO COMMUNIST REVOLUTION. New York: Random House, 1962. 242 p.

Refers to the assistant secretaries' floor of the Department of State, on which many operational decisions are made.

Smith, Michael John J. "Henry L. Stimson and the Philippines." Ph.D. dissertation, Indiana University, 1970. 266 p.

Smith, Walter Bedell. MY THREE YEARS IN MOSCOW. Philadelphia: Lippincott, 1950. 346 p.

Served as ambassador to Moscow.

Smith, William L.G. OBSERVATIONS ON CHINA AND THE CHINESE. New York: Carleton, 1863. 216 p.

Served as consul in Shanghai.

Smythe, David Mynders. AMERICAN VICE-CONSUL. Boston: Christopher, 1942. 207 p.

Spaulding, E. Wilder. AMBASSADORS ORDINARY AND EXTRAORDINARY. Washington, D.C.: Public Affairs, 1961. 302 p.

Served as historian, editor, and officer of the Department of State and the Foreign Service.

Stackman, Ralph Robert. "Lawrence A. Steinhardt: New Deal Diplomat, 1933-1945." Ph.D. dissertation, Michigan State University, 1967. 406 p.

Standley, William Harrison, and Ageton, Arthur A. ADMIRAL AMBASSADOR TO RUSSIA. Chicago: Regnery, 1955. 533 p.

Standley, who served as Ambassador to the Soviet Union for eighteen months during World War II.

Stanton, Edwin F. BRIEF AUTHORITY: EXCURSIONS OF A COMMON MAN IN AN UNCOMMON WORLD. New York: Harper, 1956. 290 p.

Author served as Foreign Service officer and as ambassador to Japan.

Starr, Daniel P. "Nelson Trusler Johnson: The United States and the Rise of Nationalist China, 1925-1937." Ph.D. dissertation, Rutgers University, 1967. 367 p.

Stettinius, Edward Reilly, Jr. ROOSEVELT AND THE RUSSIANS: THE YALTA CONFERENCE. Edited by Walter Johnson. Garden City, N.Y.: Doubleday, 1949. 367 p.

Served as secretary of state at the time of the Yalta Conference.

Stimson, Henry L. AMERICAN POLICY IN NICARAGUA. New York: Scribner, 1927. 129 p.

Served as secretary of state and secretary of war.

_____. THE FAR EASTERN CRISIS: RECOLLECTIONS AND OBSERVATIONS. New York: Harper, 1936. 293 p.

Stimson, Henry L., and Bundy, McGeorge. ON ACTIVE SERVICE IN PEACE AND WAR. New York: Harper, 1948. 698 p.

Stoessinger, John G. HENRY KISSINGER: THE ANGUISH OF POWER. New York: Norton, 1976. 234 p.

Stourzh, Gerald. BENJAMIN FRANKLIN AND AMERICAN FOREIGN POLICY. 2d ed. Chicago: University of Chicago Press, 1969. 335 p.

Straus, Oscar Solomon. UNDER FOUR ADMINISTRATIONS: FROM CLEVE-LAND TO TAFT. Boston: Houghton Mifflin, 1922. 456 p.

> Served as minister and as ambassador to Turkey.

Strobel, Edward Henry. MR. BLAINE AND HIS FOREIGN POLICY: AN EX-AMINATION OF HIS MOST IMPORTANT DISPATCHES WHILE SECRETARY OF STATE. Boston: Hall, 1884. 69 p.

Strong, Theron G. JOSEPH H. CHOATE--NEW ENGLANDER, NEW YORKER, LAWYER, AMBASSADOR. New York: Dodd, Mead, 1917. 390 p.

> About Choate, who served as ambassador to Great Britain.

Stuart, John Leighton. FIFTY YEARS IN CHINA: THE MEMOIRS OF JOHN LEIGHTON STUART, MISSIONARY AND AMBASSADOR. New York: Random House, 1954. 346 p.

Swerczek, Ronald Emil. "The Diplomatic Career of Hugh Gibson, 1908-1938." Ph.D. dissertation, University of Iowa, 1972. 391 p.

> About Gibson, a career diplomat who served in various and import-ant assignments.

Taylor, Maxwell D. RESPONSIBILITY AND RESPONSE. New York: Harper and Row, 1967. 84 p.

> Served as chairman of the Joint Chiefs of Staff, ambassador to Vietnam, and presidential adviser.

_____. THE UNCERTAIN TRUMPET. New York: Harper, 1960. 203 p.

Thayer, Charles Wheeler. BEARS IN THE CAVIAR. Philadelphia: Lippincott, 1951. 303 p.

> By a Foreign Service officer.

_____. DIPLOMAT. New York: Harper, 1959. 299 p.

_____. GUERILLA. New York: New American, 1963. 175 p.

Study of guerilla warfare as it relates to diplomacy.

Thayer, William Roscoe. JOHN HAY. 2 vols. Boston: Houghton Mifflin, 1915. Reprinted as THE LIFE AND LETTERS OF JOHN HAY. Boston: Houghton Mifflin, 1915 and 1929.

Thompson, Waddy. RECOLLECTIONS OF MEXICO. New York: Wiley and Putnam, 1846. 304 p.

Served as minister to Mexico.

Timmons, Bascom Nolly. PORTRAIT OF AN AMERICAN: CHARLES GATES DAWES. New York: Holt, 1953. 344 p.

About Dawes, who served as ambassador to Great Britain.

Traphagen, Jeanne Carol. "The Inter-American Diplomacy of Frank B. Kellogg." Ph.D. dissertation, University of Minnesota, 1956. 355 p.

Tuchman, Barbara W. STILWELL AND THE AMERICAN EXPERIENCE IN CHINA, 1911-1945. New York: Macmillan, 1970. 621 p. Bibliog.

Van Dusen, Henry P., ed. THE SPIRITUAL LEGACY OF JOHN FOSTER DULLES. Philadelphia: Westminster, 1960. 232 p.

Largely essays and addresses.

Vare, Daniele. THE LAUGHING DIPLOMAT. Garden City, N.Y.: Doubleday, Doran, 1938. 448 p.

Reminiscences of diplomatic career, containing humorous anecdotes of travels and meetings with statesmen, other diplomats, writers, musicians, and others.

Varg, Paul A. OPEN DOOR DIPLOMAT: THE LIFE OF W.W. ROCKHILL. Urbana: University of Illinois Press, 1952. 141 p. Bibliog.

About Rockhill, who served as assistant secretary of state, chief clerk in the department, and minister to Greece, Rumania, and Turkey.

Viereck, George Sylvester. THE STRANGEST FRIENDSHIP IN HISTORY: WOODROW WILSON AND COLONEL HOUSE. New York: Liveright, 1932. 375 p.

About House, who served as Wilson's personal adviser and special diplomatic representative.

Villard, Henry S. AFFAIRS AT STATE. New York: Crowell, 1965. 254 p.

By a career diplomat, who served as minister to Libya and ambassador to Senegal and Mauritania.

Wadsworth, James J. THE PRICE OF PEACE. New York: Praeger, 1962. 127 p.

Served in various high level administrative and diplomatic posts, including U.S. mission to the United Nations.

Wallace, Hugh Campbell. THE SPEECES OF THE HONORABLE AMERICAN AMBASSADOR TO FRANCE, 1919-1921. Paris: Plon Nourrit, 1921. 195 p.

Wallace, Lewis. LEW WALLACE: AN AUTOBIOGRAPHY. 2 vols. New York: Harper, 1906.

Served as minister to Turkey.

Washburne, Elihu Benjamin. RECOLLECTIONS OF A MINISTER TO FRANCE, 1869-1877. 2 vols. New York: Scribner, 1887.

_____. UNITED STATES EMBASSY, FRANCE. Washington, D.C.: Government Printing Office, 1878. 222 p.

Welles, Sumner. SEVEN DECISIONS THAT SHAPED HISTORY. New York: Harper, 1951. 236 p.

By a Foreign Service officer, who served in various diplomatic appointments, including under secretary of state.

_____. THE TIME FOR DECISION. New York: Harper, 1944. 431 p.

_____. WE NEED NOT FAIL. Boston: Houghton Mifflin, 1948. 143 p.

_____. WHERE ARE WE HEADING? New York: Harper, 1946. 397 p.

_____. WORLD OF THE FOUR FREEDOMS. New York: Columbia University Press, 1943. 121 p.

Weymouth, Lally, ed. THOMAS JEFFERSON: THE MAN . . . HIS WORLD . . . HIS INFLUENCE. London: Weidenfeld and Nicolson, 1973. 254 p.

Whalen, Richard J. THE FOUNDING FATHER. New York: New American, 1964. 541 p.

On Joseph P. Kennedy, ambassador to Great Britain and father of President John F. Kennedy.

Wheaton, Henry. SOME ACCOUNT OF THE LIFE, WRITINGS, AND SPEECHES OF WILLIAM PINKNEY. Philadelphia: Small, 1826. 616 p.

About Pinkney, who served as minister to Great Britain and Russia.

Wheeler, Post, and Rives, Hallie Erminie. DOME OF MANY-COLOURED GLASS. Garden City, N.Y.: Doubleday, 1955. 875 p.

By Wheeler, who served in several diplomatic appointments.

White, Andrew Dickson. THE AUTOBIOGRAPHY OF ANDREW DICKSON WHITE. 2 vols. New York: Century, 1905.

Served as minister to Russia and ambassador to Germany.

_____. THE FIRST HAGUE CONFERENCE. Boston: World Peace Foundation, 1912. 123 p.

Whitlock, Brand. BELGIUM: A PERSONAL NARRATIVE. 2 vols. New York: Appleton, 1919.

Served as minister and as ambassador to Belgium during and after World War I.

_____. THE LETTERS AND JOURNAL OF BRAND WHITLOCK. Edited by Allan Nevins. 2 vols. New York: Appleton-Century, 1936.

Whitney, Thomas Porter. RUSSIA IN MY LIFE. New York: Reynal, 1962. 307 p.

Served as attache in Russia.

Wikoff, Henry. THE ADVENTURES OF A ROVING DIPLOMATIST. New York: Petridge, 1857. 299 p.

Served as attache in London and as a British Foreign Office agent in France.

_____. A NEW YORKER IN THE FOREIGN OFFICE AND HIS ADVENTURES IN PARIS. London: Truebner, 1858. 299 p.

_____. THE REMINISCENCES OF AN IDLER. New York: Fords, Howard, and Hulbert, 1880. 596 p.

Williams, John Brown. THE NEW ZEALAND JOURNAL, 1842-1844, OF JOHN BROWN WILLIAMS OF SALEM, MASSACHUSETTS. Edited by Robert W. Kenny. Salem, Mass.: Peabody Museum of Salem, 1956. 120 p.

Williams, Joyce Ellen Grigsby. "Colonel House and Sir Edward Grey: A

Study in Anglo-American Diplomacy." Ph.D. dissertation, Indiana University, 1971. 235 p.

    About House, who served as President Wilson's personal diplomatic representative.

Williams, Samuel Wells. A JOURNAL OF THE PERRY EXPEDITION TO JAPAN (1853-1854). Edited by Frederick Wells Williams. Yokohama: Kelly and Walsh, 1910. 259 p.

    Journal of member of the Perry expedition.

Williams, Wayne C. WILLIAM JENNINGS BRYAN. New York: Revell, 1923. 127 p.

Williamson, John Gustavus Adolphus. CARACAS DIARY, 1835-1840. Edited by Jane Lucas de Grummond. Baton Rouge: Camelia, 1954. 444 p.

Willson, Beckles. AMERICA'S AMBASSADORS TO ENGLAND (1785-1929). New York: Stokes, 1929. 497 p.

_____. AMERICA'S AMBASSADORS TO FRANCE (1777-1927). New York: Stokes, 1928. 433 p.

Wilson, Francis Mairs Huntington. MEMOIRS OF AN EX-DIPLOMAT. Boston: Bruce Humphries, 1945. 373 p.

    Served as diplomatic officer in Tokyo and in the Department of State, concluding as assistant secretary.

Wilson, Henry Lane. DIPLOMATIC EPISODES IN MEXICO, BELGIUM, AND CHILE. Garden City, N.Y.: Doubleday, Page, 1927. 399 p.

Wilson, Hugh Robert. A CAREER DIPLOMAT: THE THIRD CHAPTER--THE THIRD REICH. Edited by Hugh R. Wilson, Jr. New York: Vantage, 1960. 112 p.

_____. DIPLOMACY AS A CAREER. Cambridge, Mass.: Riverside, 1941. 52 p.

_____. DIPLOMAT BETWEEN WARS. New York: Longmans, Green, 1941. 344 p.

_____. THE EDUCATION OF A DIPLOMAT. New York: Longmans, Green, 1938. 224 p.

Winant, John Gilbert. LETTER FROM GROSVENOR SQUARE: AN ACCOUNT OF A STEWARDSHIP. Boston: Houghton Mifflin, 1947. 278 p.

Served as ambassador to Great Britain during World War II; Grosvenor Square is the location of the American Embassy in London. Deals with pre-Pearl Harbor period.

_____. OUR GREATEST HARVEST: SELECTED SPEECHES. London: Hodder, 1950. 228 p.

Winfield, Louise. LIVING OVERSEAS. Washington, D.C.: Public Affairs, 1962. 237 p.

Wolf, Charles, Jr. INDONESIAN ASSIGNMENT. University: University of Alabama Press, 1952. 61 p.

Wood, Eric Fisher. THE NOTE-BOOK OF AN ATTACHE: SEVEN MONTHS IN THE WAR ZONE. New York: Century, 1915. 345 p.

Concerns World War I.

Woolery, William Kirk. THE RELATION OF THOMAS JEFFERSON TO AMERICAN FOREIGN POLICY, 1783-1793. Baltimore: Johns Hopkins Press, 1927.

Wright, C. Ben. "George F. Kennan, Scholar-Diplomat: 1926-1946." Ph.D. dissertation, University of Wisconsin, 1972. 512 p.

Wright, Esmond, ed. BENJAMIN FRANKLIN: A PROFILE. New York: Hill and Wang, 1970. 227 p.

Yost, Bartley. MEMOIRS OF A CONSUL. New York: Vantage, 1955. 186 p.

By a career officer who served in a number of foreign posts and in the Department of State.

Yost, Charles Woodruff. THE AGE OF TRIUMPH AND FRUSTRATION: MODERN DIALOGUES. New York: Speller, 1964. 244 p. Bibliog.

By a Foreign Service officer who served in various posts, including ambassador to Laos, Syria, Morocco, and the United Nations.

_____. THE INSECURITY OF NATIONS: INTERNATIONAL RELATIONS IN THE TWENTIETH CENTURY. New York: Praeger, 1968. 276 p. Bibliog.

Young, Andrew. ANDREW YOUNG AT THE UNITED NATIONS. Edited by Lee Clement. Salisbury, N.C.: Documentary Publications, 1978. 189 p.

Young, John Russell. MEN AND MEMORIES: PERSONAL REMINISCENCES. Edited by Mary D. Young. 2 vols. New York: Neeley, 1901.

Served as minister to China.

Zeiger, Henry A. THE REMARKABLE HENRY CABOT LODGE. New York: Popular Library, 1964. 144 p.

Concerns Ambassador Lodge, who served in Vietnam, at the United Nations, in the Paris peace talks (Vietnam), and as ambassador at large.

AUTHOR INDEX

In addition to authors, this index includes editors, compilers, and issuing agencies or institutions (when no author or editor is given). In addition, for the last chapter, diplomats, officials of the Department of State, and others involved in foreign relations--who are the subjects of biographies and other memoir materials--are also included. Generally, titles of rank and nobility (such as ambassador, consul general, admiral, general, Lord, and Sir) are omitted. Alphabetization is letter by letter. Numbers refer to page numbers.

A

Author Index

Author Index

Author Index

Author Index

Author Index

Author Index

Author Index

Author Index

Author Index

Author Index

Nash, Henry T. 138, 201, 255, 267, 330, 331
Nathan, James A. 23
Nathan, Richard P. 115
National Civil Service Reform League 226
Nau, Henry R. 413
Navarette, George 654
Neal, Harry Edward 213
Neblet, William H. 272
Needler, Martin C. 332, 338, 345
Neef, Marian G. 324
Neilson, Francis 27
Nelson, Donald Marr 407
Nelson, Joan M. 407
Nelson, Keith L. 432
Nelson, Michael 293
Nelson, Otto L. 226, 271
Nelson, Randall H. 393
Nerval, Richard 220
Neubauer, Deane E. 483
Neustadt, Richard E. 115, 128, 154
Nevins, Allan 136, 616, 654, 667
Newcombe, Alan 438
Newcombe, Hanna 438
Newcomer, James Roger 192
Nichols, Roy F. 48, 417
Nickerson, Hoffman 432
Nicolson, Harold 11, 14, 69, 257, 369, 655
Nieburg, Harold L. 481
Nielson, Waldemar A. 272
Niemela, Pirkko 486
Niezing, Johan 438
Nigro, Felix A. 176
Nihart, Brook 245
Nimmo, Dan 486
Niskanen, William A., Jr. 293
Nitze, Paul H. 149, 279
Nixon, Richard M. 221, 246, 247, 450
Noble, George Bernard 190
Nobleman, Eli E. 128
Nogee, Joseph L. 36
North, Robert C. 315, 450
Northedge, F.S. 432, 450
Northrup, Robert M. 183
Norton, Charles Eliot 649
Norton, Henry K. 33, 205

Norton, Hugh Stanton 297
Norton, Nile Brown 655
Nossiter, Bernard D. 654
Nostrand, Howard Lee 48, 413
Notter, Harley A. 567
Nourse, Edwin G. 297
Nuechterline, Donald D. 292
Numelin, Ragnar J. 12, 29

O

Oakes, Augustus 584
O'Brien, Francis W. 142, 655
O'Brien, William V. 432
O'Connor, James P. 301
O'Connor, John F. 443
O'Connor, Raymond Gish 39, 281
O'Davoren, William 39
Odell, Talbot 132
Odier, Pierre Gabriel 59
O'Donnell, Charles P. 69
Offutt, Milton 420
O'Flaherty, J. Daniel 6
Ogburn, Charles, Jr. 346
Ogdon, Montell 57
Ogene, Francis C. 362
Ogul, Morris S. 154, 180, 308
O'Leary, Michael Kent 407, 477, 478, 482
Oleszek, Walter J. 162, 163
Olin, Spencer C., Jr. 432
Oliver, Covey T. 393
Oliver, James Knowles 25, 348
Olson, William C. 23
Olton, Roy 13
Olverson, John B. 274
Opie, Redvers 400, 432
Oppenheim, Felix E. 305
Oppenheimer, Bruce I. 162
Oppenheimer, Martin 264, 438
Organization for Economic Coopera- tion and Development 413
Organski, A.F.K. 22
Ornstein, Norman J. 362
Osborne, John 74, 205, 221
Osgood, Robert E. 432
O'Shaughnessy, Edith Louise 52, 655
Oster, Jon F. 151
Ostgaard, Einar 357

Author Index

Author Index

Author Index

Author Index

Author Index

Author Index

Author Index

Author Index